URBAN PLANNING

and

MUNICIPAL PUBLIC POLICY

URBAN PLANNING
and
MUNICIPAL
PUBLIC POLICY

by

DONALD H. WEBSTER

Professor of Political Science
Chairman of the Graduate Curriculum in Urban Planning
and
Director of the Bureau of Governmental Research and Services
University of Washington

HARPER & BROTHERS, PUBLISHERS
New York

Library of Congress catalog card number: 58-5111

CONTENTS

Contents

PART II
SUBJECT MATTER OF PLANNING

PART III
THE MEANS OF PLAN IMPLEMENTATION

Subdivision Requirements and Public Policy Considerations

The Development of Public Policy in Subdivision Control

General Requirements Relating to Standards

Requirements for Construction and Installation of Improvements

The Administration of Subdivision Regulations

Administrative Supervision

Procedure for Securing Approval for Plat Recording

Enforcement of the Subdivision Regulations

PART IV
THE FUTURE OF PLANNING

PREFACE

The unprecedented developments which have taken place within our cities and metropolitan areas during the past several years have served to emphasize the vital necessity for intelligent planning of our urban communities. Unfortunately, urban planning has not reached its full potential as a force in furthering public policies. In part, this is due to the fact that the scope and nature of planning as a function of local government have not been clearly defined.

This book has been written in an endeavor to fill a gap in the planning literature by relating the subject matter of planning to the structure, functions, and processes of local government and to the legal powers and devices available for carrying plans into effect. The basic premise is that effective planning is not possible unless the planner is well grounded in the fundamental concepts of our system of government and unless the policy making officials are well informed on the scope and nature of planning and sympathetic to its purposes and uses. The approach is through a critical analysis of public policies with which planning is concerned.

Certain materials in the text pertaining to the subject matter of planning may appear elementary to the experienced professional planner. They are included in order to complete the picture of the scope and nature of the planning function for those without extensive professional experience. Certain other materials pertaining to services and programs usually considered as falling only within the peripheral interest of the planner have been included because of their interrelation with subject matter commonly associated with planning and in order to provide a background for understanding the organization, powers, processes, and overall policy objectives of local government.

The term "urban planning" as used in this publication applies to planning for the entire urban community, irrespective of whether the

area lies within, or without, the corporate limits of a given municipality. However, the framework of local government for planning is
considered herein principally with reference to municipal corporations.
This approach has been used primarily for two reasons. The first is
that urban planning, for the most part, is carried out by municipalities. The second is that to differentiate among the practices and organizations for planning of every type of governmental unit would
produce more confusion than clarification. Basically, the responsibilities are the same. The differences lie largely in the scope of activities
and nature of functions performed.

In preparing this manuscript, I am deeply indebted to many of my
associates in the Bureau of Governmental Research and Services of
the University of Washington. In particular, I should like to acknowl-
edge the helpful criticisms and suggestions received from Ernest H.
Campbell, Associate Director, Joshua H. Vogel, Planning and Public
Works Consultant, and Floyd M. Jennings, Planning Consultant. I
am also very much indebted to Mrs. Isabel Linville, who has typed
the manuscript and provided material aid in verifying many citations.
Also acknowledged is the assistance of Miss Ruth Jeffries, Political
Science Librarian, who has made available numerous source materials
used in the publication.

DONALD H. WEBSTER

Seattle, Washington
February 1, 1958

Part I

GOVERNMENTAL FRAMEWORK OF PLANNING

CHAPTER 1

Planning Within the Framework
of American Government

PLANNING AS A BASIS FOR GOVERNMENT ACTION

Planning is neither a new nor a novel responsibility of local government. Cities from time immemorial have engaged in planning as the basis for intelligent governmental action. Many examples of city planning in Europe and Asia can be traced back for more than 5000 years. Evidences of planning are to be found in America in all our major colonial cities. In fact, none of our large urban communities could have developed and prospered without the benefit of planning. Nevertheless, it has been only within recent years that planning has become established as a distinct process within the framework of government, carried out by an agency created for that purpose, and administered by a staff specially trained in the techniques essential to the performance of the task. This concept of planning in the United States has evolved through various stages of public and private responsibility including planning by contract, planning by civic improvement clubs, planning by the independent planning commission, and planning through an integrated planning department.

Today, most civic-minded business and professional men and public officials have come to realize that proper planning under the guidance of a public agency offers the urban community the most logical means of solving the numerous problems resulting from the growth of population, the expansion of industry, and the changes growing out of our technological and scientific developments. They have become aware that economic benefits of intelligent planning are reflected in lower tax rates, stability of investments, and better business opportunities, and that social benefits are attained through the development of better cultural opportunities, convenience of living, and the amenities of home and community life. They are also coming to recognize that planning offers some hope for the rebuilding of deteriorated areas.

THE PLANNING FUNCTION OF LOCAL GOVERNMENT

The increasing extent to which local governmental officials are relying upon planning agencies for guidance in making public policy decisions emphasizes the need for understanding the urban planning[1] function in its appropriate relationship to our democratic society, our constitutional system, our governmental structure, and the many powers and processes of local government.

The Nature of Planning. Planning is a process of government which looks to the future for the purpose of influencing the well-being of the people. Planning should encourage the study of the community in the light of modern technology and current economic and social trends. It should seek to protect the good features of the community and to improve those which are substandard. Planning is essentially a process of understanding human needs and of influencing and shaping future public policy to serve those needs most effectively. However, because past policies have failed to protect our resources and have neglected our social standards, many of the efforts of planning must be directed toward restoring equilibrium, satisfying current wants, and providing for the needs which such policies have engendered. Thus, in its operations, planning involves both organized foresight and corrective hindsight. As a process, it is concerned with research, with prophecy, and with value judgments.

The primary emphasis of urban planning is on the physical development of the community. In the broad sense, planning is concerned with the orderly relation of all functions which government performs directly or through regulation. Physical planning and program planning cannot be completely separated. In almost every instance physical planning has a close relationship to the policies and objectives of some functional program or service.

[1] Urban planning is distinguished from city planning in that it is concerned with the urban community and not limited necessarily to the corporate boundaries of the municipality.

The purpose of planning is to provide the information and expert advice necessary to insure that priority will be given to projects in the order of their importance and that all governmental functions will be carried on in the best possible relationship to each other. It is not the function of planning to assert general jurisdiction over the day-to-day activities of the operational departments. Therefore, only those aspects of each departmental operation which are essential to carrying out a well-coördinated program for community development and community living are appropriately the subject matter of planning. Those activities which are not closely related to this purpose are not within the scope of planning.

For example, in dealing with the matter of traffic, the planning agency may justifiably give consideration to such matters as the width of streets, the designation of one-way couplets, and the location of thoroughfares, not only because they may provide a means of relieving traffic congestion, but also because streets have important functions in providing access, light, and air and have an important bearing on other phases of economic and social development. On the other hand, the enforcement of speed laws, the erection of traffic signs, and the assignment of policemen to traffic duty are normally outside the scope of general planning. Likewise, the planning agency may be very much interested in such matters as the location of water mains and the size of sewer lines since it has a direct responsibility in forecasting population growth and directing land use. Normally, however, it will find little reason to become concerned with the actual construction of the facilities, the collection of charges for supplying services, or the routine duties connected with the operation of the systems.

Planning and the Formulation of Public Policy.   Public policy consists of the means, methods, and principles that the government chooses for the attainment of desired ends. Public policy in a democratic form of government develops through an expression of the popular will. To a considerable degree, the popular will, as ascertained by public officials, is determined as a result of pressures. Pressures come from many conflicting interests and must be weighed in the light of community values with which public policy is concerned. Oftentimes these values are highly subjective. Planning attempts to introduce a degree of objectivity into this realm of subjective judgments.

From the standpoint of practical politics, public policies, no matter how sound, cannot be successfully carried out over a long period of time in the face of strong public opposition. Sometimes opposition to sound policies as determined by public officials does arise. The reason may lie in the organized activities of strong special interest groups or simply from a lack of understanding on the part of the public. Where such a situation exists, the public officials having responsibility for choosing between two or more courses of action must decide whether to succumb to the opposition or exercise their own judgment for what they consider to be the best interests of the community. The fact that there is need for making a decision under such circumstances usually indicates a lack of planning effectiveness in the community, at least in so far as public understanding and public support are concerned.

The failure of the public to support certain policies for community betterment is often due to the fact that the planning officials have failed to take the public into their confidence in the development of plans on which policy decisions are based. Unless the public has been kept informed during the period when policy is being formulated, it is seldom possible to create a favorable climate of public opinion sufficient to overcome pressures and combat opposition at the time the policy decision is to be made.

Experience clearly demonstrates that if planning procedures are to be effective in creating acceptance of policy decisions, they need to be developed through human interaction, understanding, and participative support. The success of the program requires that more attention be paid to people than to the mechanics of planning. This idea is very well expressed in a recent issue of the *Newsletter* of the American Society of Planning Officials as follows: "Too often planning has had a bad name because it lost sight of human beings it was supposed to benefit. The plan for social betterment was conceived by experts, "sold" to reluctant citizens, and carried into action by paid employees. But planning has a different meaning and outcome when people take precedence over blueprints." [2]

Goals and Objectives of Planning. The overall objective of any urban planning program should be to direct the development of the community in an intelligent and orderly manner according to a preconceived plan. Planning should work for a well-balanced and integrated community. The goal should be the best community that can be attained.[3] Unfortunately, in most of our cities, planning is largely

[2] "Planning People," *ASPO Newsletter*, Vol. 18, No. 2, February, 1952.
[3] *Planning Goals* (San Jose, Calif.: Santa Clara Planning Commission, 1952), Monograph No. 2.

a corrective and preventive process. Planning agencies very rarely have the opportunity to plan a community from its inception. Planning has usually begun after much of the physical layout has been set and after the pattern of land use has been affected by uncontrolled developments. Thus, the accomplishments through planning may be greatly circumscribed as a result of costly mistakes of the past.

Planning must be realistic. It must not be misguided by the unfounded hopes and ambitions of citizens of a community for great industrial or commercial expansion or by their desires for public facilities or programs which are clearly not attainable within the resources and capabilities of the community. The fact that plans must be realistic does not mean, however, that planning should not be imaginative and farsighted. Effectiveness of urban planning requires vision. Imaginative schemes, through modification and refinement, may frequently develop into practical proposals.

The objectives of urban planning are both economic and social. The community plan should seek to influence the location of people, commerce, and industry in a way to promote the best living and working conditions and to contribute to the efficient operation and management of business activities. The dollars-and-cents objectives are realized through stabilized land uses and a sound economic base and equitable tax policy. The human values are achieved through planned community development which results in improved health conditions, expanded facilities for play and recreation, the removal of blight, and increased opportunities for personal comforts and enjoyment.

In establishing goals for community development, the planner must always keep in mind the fundamental values in individual liberty and property rights sought to be preserved by our constitutional system. Planning is not intended to fit each individual into an appropriate place in a planned society, but rather to provide an orderly environment that will insure the greatest possible freedom for all. One of the difficulties of planning in a free society is that of resolving the question of what things should be accomplished, regulated, or controlled by government and what should be left for private enterprise or individual determination.

PLANNING IN A DEMOCRATIC SOCIETY

Today in America, conscious planning is a part of the political and civic life of almost every progressive and forward-looking community.

Nevertheless, many persons throughout the United States tend to regard planning as undemocratic in principle and not a legitimate and respectable responsibility of government.

Planning and Governmental Authority. To some persons the word "planning" is a red flag that signifies government regimentation. In the minds of these people planning in government is associated with the idea of a planned economy. Governmental planning suggests to them such vague concepts as authoritarian control, totalitarianism, dictatorship, and government by the expert as distinguished from the absence of planning which they associate with such other vague concepts as capitalism, private enterprise, liberty, free competition, and *laissez faire*. Such persons seem to associate planning with totalitarian governments, but for some reason feel that the idea of planning is not compatible with democratic processes in a free society.

To a considerable extent, opposition to planning based upon this distinction results from a misconception of the planning function. The fundamental error is the belief that planning by government gives government additional control over the lives, liberties, and properties of the individual. The fact is that planning as a separate governmental function adds nothing whatsoever to the powers of government. The regulation of individuals and their property rights results from policy decisions formulated and executed by those who exercise the political power.[4] Planning, properly conceived, serves only as an arm to these political representatives to aid them in gathering, evaluating, and interpreting essential data to serve as a basis for making intelligent policy decisions. Under this concept, the planning function is compatible with the policy making responsibilities of either democratic or nondemocratic societies. Many services and functions which must be carried on by governments are much the same regardless of form or philosophy. The major differences arise in the aims, objectives, and processes. These differences, nevertheless, have important implications in planning.

Democracy and the Democratic Process. To understand the function of planning in the democratic process, it is first necessary to determine what is embraced in the word "democracy." No definition of democracy is entirely adequate. To some persons it represents a form of government and to others a way of social life.[5] The meaning

---

[4] For a discussion of constitutional aspects of specific planning objectives see: Norman Williams, Jr., "Planning Law and Democratic Living," *Law and Contemporary Problems*, School of Law, Duke University, Vol. 20, No. 2, pp. 317–350, Spring, 1955.

[5] Hillman M. Bishop and Samuel Hendel, *Basic Issues of American Democracy*—A

of the word democracy has been a subject on which the political philosophers have filled many volumes. Included in the concept may be the character of the electorate, the relationship between government and the people, or the absence of privileges based upon economic differences, birth, race, or creed.

The word democracy, as it came down from the Greek philosophers, denotes a form of government in which the ruling power of the state is vested in members of the community as a whole as distinguished from a particular class or classes.[6] In this sense democracy means the rule of the masses or the majority as distinguished from the rule of classes.

The modern concept of democracy in America is, however, concerned with far more than simply majority rule. It is concerned both with the substance of law and with the processes of government. American democracy as it has developed embodies the idea of both individual liberty and equality before the law. This concept of democracy is based in part upon our system of law as distinguished from personal government. During the nineteenth century the ideals of government which came to be generally accepted included the idea of freedom of opinion, equality before the courts, and free economic enterprise.[7] There is some doubt whether all these ideals would be generally accepted today as the essence of democratic government, and even where they are accepted, there is a wide divergence of opinion as to the best means and methods for their realization.

Perhaps the so-called democratic society can best be characterized in distinguishing it from the nondemocratic society. Authoritarian governments, although differing both in form and ideology, have in common the glorification of the state in which the interests and life of the individual are subjected. The emphasis of government is upon duties of the citizens to obey and not upon rights or liberties. The individual has no rights against government which can be enforced in the courts.[8]

Democracies are distinguished from authoritarian governments, not only by the rule that protects individual liberty, but also by the proc-

---

Book of Readings (New York: Appleton-Century-Crofts, Inc., 1948), p. 16. Quoting from Harold J. Laski.

[6] James Bryce, Modern Democracies (New York: The Macmillan Company, 1921), p. 20.

[7] Francis W. Coker, Democracy, Liberty and Property—Readings in the American Political Tradition (New York: The Macmillan Company, 1942), p. 11.

[8] J. A. Corry, Elements of Democratic Government (New York: Oxford University Press, 1947), p. 475.

esses by which democratic governments function. In a democratic society there is the opportunity of government by public opinion. Decisions are arrived at after discussion which permits all causes and all parties to be heard, including minorities as well as majorities. Free education, which provides outlets for discovery and expression, are vital in the process. Among the most important of the characteristics is the freedom to discuss political issues, with the right to differ concerning them, and to resolve these differences by resort to the ballot box rather than to force.

POLITICAL CONCEPTS INFLUENCING PLANNING PROCEDURES AND PUBLIC POLICIES

In every free society there is a wide divergence of opinion as to the part government should play in controlling individual behavior and in directing the physical, economic, and social development of the community. The prevailing philosophy establishes the guideposts and sets the limits within which plans may be made and carried out. Local government is concerned primarily with the tasks of supplying essential services, regulating persons and property in the interest of public health and safety, and providing for the general welfare. Individual views as to what specific services and functions government should provide and what means should be used to provide them differ according to each individual's philosophy on the general purpose of government.

CONFLICTING PHILOSOPHIES ON THE PURPOSE OF GOVERNMENT

Prevailing views on the purpose of government have varied with the times, with the conditions which prevail in a community, and with the background of the inhabitants. The extremes of opinion are represented by the views of the conservative and present-day liberal.[9] The doctrine of the conservative leans in the direction of *laissez faire* individualism. The liberal philosophy favors the use of governmental authority to improve society through reforms.

The conflict between the philosophy of the conservative and the present-day liberal is the same that has confronted our policy makers from the time our Constitution was adopted. It involves the basic and fundamental question of what affairs government ought to direct

[9] The philosophy of the present-day liberal is in some respects quite the opposite of that of the orthodox liberal.

and control and what it ought to leave, with as little interference as possible, to individual or private action. The conservative philosophy is based upon the doctrine of *laissez faire* which holds that the state should interfere as little as possible with the working of the economic affairs as determined by individuals. Under this theory, individuals would be encouraged to create the greatest possible wealth for themselves, which in turn would tend to create the greatest possible wealth for society. The doctrine of *laissez faire* holds that state interference in economic matters decreases the wealth of society since economic activities are diverted from natural channels into nonproductive channels.[10]

Essentially, the doctrine of the modern liberal is the doctrine of the welfare state and is essentially collectivistic. The theory is benevolent and its primary concern is public welfare. The conservative, on the other hand, takes the view that benevolent government cannot exist except through the denial of inalienable rights, that unlimited government eventually leads to tyranny, and that the appropriate role of government is that of referee or umpire.

Economic and Cultural Laissez Faire. The idea of *laissez faire*, which is associated with liberty and individualism, is concerned with two aspects, economic and cultural. *Laissez faire* on the economic side is characterized by noninterference of government in business and industry. *Laissez faire* on the cultural side is concerned with freedom to inquire, to learn to write, and to express ideas.[11] Although both of these aspects are closely associated in time and development and have their emphasis upon nonintervention, the same person may not always be an advocate of both economic and cultural *laissez faire*. Frequently an individual who may be an ardent believer in freedom of speech may at the same time strongly support extensive governmental controls over certain types of business activities. Another individual who may enthusiastically favor a hands-off policy of government with respect to business may think it entirely proper for government to employ any methods it chooses in an effort to discover and stamp out subversive activities. This distinction is important in view of the tendency to identify as the same democracy, liberty, and capitalism.

Doctrine of Liberalism. The liberal doctrine disagrees with the

[10] Joseph S. Roucek, George B. DeHuszar, and Associates, *Introduction to Political Science* (New York: Thomas Y. Crowell Company, 1950), p. 104.

[11] Charles A. Beard, *Public Policy and the General Welfare* (New York: Farrar & Rinehart, Inc., 1941), p. 101.

doctrine of *laissez faire* on the ground that it is inadequate to meet the needs of modern society and is actually a device for exploitation.[12] The doctrine of the liberal thus opposes the doctrine of limited government and free enterprise. This theory advocates that the state should take positive action to promote the general welfare, even though this may involve intervention in economic life. Government according to this doctrine is a necessary good rather than a necessary evil. The purpose of government is not merely to prevent lawlessness and disorder, but it is to provide strong and active measures to guide its citizens and develop the environment in which they live.

The liberal advocates a fair distribution of the necessities of life. He believes in public ownership of many utilities, but he would not abolish the system of private property. He favors humanitarian government and would utilize governmental powers to eliminate economic inequalities resulting from unrestrained competition. Those who hold to this philosophy disagree with the conservative that competition will provide a proper balance between services and prices, keep interest at reasonable rates, stimulate production, and promote the general good. They contend instead that profit taking leads to exploitation, monopolies, exhaustion of natural resources, and destruction of competition. Their view is that such matters as social security, wages and hours, working conditions, old age pensions, health and employment insurance, housing, and medical care are all proper subjects for purposes of governmental regulation.[13]

Umpire or Service Role. Although much has been said and written about the protection of property from government intervention, the practice of government in America has never been one of economic *laissez faire*. Nevertheless, certain governmental policies and court decisions pertaining to the powers of government have been influenced by this philosophy. Since the turn of the century, the role of government has very definitely shifted in the direction of providing a positive and creative force in the life and development of the community.[14] The distinction between the umpire state and the service state is that the umpire state assumes no initiative but serves as a restraining force when various interests threaten to disturb the stability of the existing order, whereas the service state undertakes to fulfill the needs of the community whatever they may be. The only

---

[12] Roucek, *op. cit.*, p. 105.
[13] Roucek, *op. cit.*, p. 107.
[14] Marshall E. Dimock, *Modern Politics and Administration* (New York: American Book Company, 1937), p. 8.

legitimate functions of the umpire state are to protect its citizens both from within and without and to act as umpire in order to minimize and guide conflicts of interest. The legitimate functions of the service state, on the other hand, are as broad as the group interests of the community. In addition to protection and the umpiring of conflicts, government has important responsibilities in planning, providing direct services, and giving guidance and direction in many aspects of the community's economic and social life.

During the period from about 1868 to 1933, in the United States, there was a great deal of support for the theory that rights of property guaranteed by the Constitution of the United States were in substance the same rights claimed for property under the doctrine of economic *laissez faire*. Under this theory government had no power either to interfere with the ownership of property or the way in which the owners saw fit to use their property and income therefrom. Those who supported this theory insisted that the responsibility of government was to preserve order for the owners of property, but that government should not intervene in the use of that property to promote the public welfare or to provide social benefits.[15]

With the advent of the "New Deal" under the leadership of President Franklin D. Roosevelt, governmental policies were oriented more in the direction of the service state. Government at all levels assumed a major responsibility for both the economic and social welfare of the people. While the pace in this direction has been slowed under the administration of President Dwight D. Eisenhower, it has not been reversed. A new concept, that of "welfare capitalism," has been suggested by certain Republican leaders to describe the role that business should play to head off the rapid drift to the welfare state.[16] Under this concept business would assume new and greater responsibilities in attaining the aims and aspirations of the people in the promotion of peace, in the development of free institutions, and in the securing of higher standards of living. This theory does not advocate, however, that government should surrender any of its coercive powers.

Public or Private Enterprise. How far and in what fields government should supply services or control and regulate private action involves both questions of political philosophy and of public policy. Certainly, today, our communities are faced with a situation involving

---

[15] Beard, *op. cit.*, p. 119.
[16] Alpheus Thomas Mason, *Security Through Freedom* (Ithaca, N.Y.; Cornell University Press, 1955), pp. 148–181.

fluid population, expanding economy, changing concepts of social values, desires for higher standards of living, and a greater degree of specialization in labor and industries. All these factors produce complex problems of living together. They increase the problems of housing, police protection, fire protection, transportation, traffic, recreation, and the supplying of numerous and sundry services which are demanded by the people. Most of these services and functions cannot be provided by private enterprise.

Municipal ownership of water, gas, light and power utilities is now found throughout the United States, and many other types of facilities formerly thought of as being outside the scope of governmental operations have been taken over as public responsibilities. The gradual transition of many activities from private to public enterprises has made it difficult to draw a distinction between the so-called proprietary activities and the traditional services of government. Although the trend is toward more and more public ownership and control, strong voices still point to the lurking dangers in this move toward increasing socialism. One danger is the possible loss of incentives, individual initiative, ambition, and personal responsibility. Another is that when a government becomes the owner and operator of an enterprise, it becomes a partisan and may not be able to preserve its impartiality as umpire and protector of its citizens.[17]

Planning According to the Political Aims. Without attempting to resolve the course which government should follow between the two extremes of *laissez faire* and the collectivist theory of the welfare state, it seems clear that government today can no longer leave completely to the individual the development and the exploitation of all the physical, economic, and human resources of our communities. The consequences of such a practice are too serious to contemplate. Fortunately, local government is not required to choose between the extremes of either point of view.

Planners must plan in accordance with the philosophy of the governments they serve. In the final analysis our philosophy is determined by what we expect of government. Governmental planning in general is subordinate to the political aims. It has the derived purpose of providing ways and means for the realization of power policies. Actually, terms such as "conservative" and "liberal," "capitalistic" and "socialistic" societies, and "umpire" or "welfare" states are mean-

---

[17] Herbert C. Mayer, "Individualism vs. Collectivism," *The County Officer*, Vol. 17, No. 9, pp. 259–264, September, 1952.

ingless as descriptive of our governmental operations since these terms are not absolute but relative. It is not difficult to point to policies of government which can be identified with all these vague terms.

Planning in the United States must be built primarily upon a capitalistic system, even though certain of the aims and objectives of public policy may be described as socialistic. Socialistic planning tends to disregard private ownership. Planning in America is, however, concerned with protecting and preserving private property interests. However, these interests must be weighed in the balance with social objectives which may, for their promotion and protection, require the exercise of rigid controls over property.[18]

Regardless of their political views, few people today will contend that government should act merely as a traffic cop to punish those who encroach upon the property rights and liberties of others. It is self-evident that if a governmental unit is to carry out effectively any plans for a well-ordered community, some degree of compulsion or restraint must be asserted over some individuals with respect to their persons and property. With the complexity of modern living, government is forced to provide a positive program for the orderly development of all community resources in an effort to achieve the greatest good for the greatest number. To do this effectively, government must proceed according to some plan. Planning in this sense does not necessitate deciding questions of public policy, regulating lives and businesses, or enforcing laws. These methods of control by governments exist whether government operates with a plan or without a plan.

CONSTITUTIONALISM

The legal sanctions by which planning is made effective rest upon governmental authority. Since governmental authority in the United States must be exercised within the limits of our federal and state constitutions, it is important that planners understand the fundamental principles embraced in the concept of American constitutionalism. The Constitution of the United States, together with the laws made pursuant thereto, and all treaties made or to be made under the authority of the United States, are the supreme law of the land, and the judges of every state are bound thereby notwithstanding any provisions in the constitution or laws of any state to the contrary.[19]

---

[18] See Williams, op. cit., pp. 317–350, for a discussion of legal considerations in accomplishing the economic and social objectives of planning.

[19] Art. VI.

Nature of Our Constitutional System. The basic concept of American constitutionalism is limited government. It embodies the idea of the rule of law that government shall not be permitted to do whatever its officials please.[20] Although the Federal Constitution makes no reference to municipal corporations or other units of local government, the provisions of the Federal Constitution are binding upon them since their powers come from the states and the states can confer no greater powers than they themselves possess. Each state in the Union also has its own constitution which is the supreme law of that jurisdiction. Powers of local units of government in a particular state must, therefore, be exercised in accordance with the provisions of the constitution of that state as well as within the limits of the Federal Constitution.

A constitution in the broad sense includes much more than the formal written document commonly referred to as the Constitution. In the broad sense it consists not only of the written document but also of the numerous court decisions which have construed its meaning and the customs and usages which have developed under its operation. The primary functions of a constitution are (1) to determine the general organization and structure of government, (2) to define the powers of government, and (3) to indicate the limits upon the exercise of those powers.[21] In the case of the Federal Constitution there is also the important function of distributing powers between the central government and the states and of defining the dividing line between them.

Since the written document which is generally referred to as the constitution is only the core of the Constitution, an understanding of the American constitutional system can be gained only through a study of the customs and practices which have modified and expanded the meaning of the written document, the statutes which have been enacted to elaborate the governmental structure, and the court decisions which have interpreted and applied the provisions of the written Constitution. This is true whether consideration is being given to the Federal Constitution or to constitutions of the several states.

Many of the features of both federal and state constitutions are the product of historical precedent and the political philosophy of

[20] Leslie Lipson, *The Great Issues of Politics* (Englewood Cliffs, N.J.: Prentice-Hall, Inc., 1954), p. 236.
[21] John Mabry Mathews, *The American Constitutional System* (New York: McGraw-Hill Book Company, Inc., 1940), p. 7.

the generation in which they were written. Others have developed as a part of an evolutionary process by which the constitutions, through interpretation and custom, have been adapted to changing economic, social, and political conditions. Among those features which have had a profound influence upon the character of our government are the theory of federalism, the principle of separation of powers, the doctrine of judicial review, and the concept of limited government.

Federalism. The federal principle which distributes the powers of government between the national government and the states is not of great practical importance in the matter of urban planning except as it may relate to the respective areas of control which may be exercised by the states and the national government. When the Constitution of the United States was adopted in 1787, the emphasis was upon the reserved or residual power in the states. The first ten amendments, ratified in 1791, were designed to strengthen this theory and to secure the protection of individual liberties against encroachment of the central government. During the long period of our constitutional evolution there has been a constant shift of power from state governments to the central government until today it may be strongly urged that we no longer function as a federal form of government.[22] In the evolutionary process the national powers have been greatly broadened through judicial interpretation and although the principle has not been repudiated by the courts, national responsibilities have been extended to encompass almost the whole field of government. Nevertheless, national powers have not been exercised to the fullest extent legally possible due to the factors of popular will and a sense of self-restraint on the part of the national government.[23]

Separation of Powers and Checks and Balances. The constitutional doctrines of separation of powers and checks and balances have significance for planning to the extent that they influence the placement and functioning of the planning agency in the governmental structure and the exercise of rule making powers which may be sought to be conferred upon the agency. The application of these doctrines may also have a bearing upon the administrative machinery and procedures employed for plan execution.

At the time the Constitution of the United States was adopted,

---

[22] William H. Riker, *Democracy in the United States* (New York: The Macmillan Company, 1953), p. 319.

[23] *Ibid.*, p. 326.

the principle of separation of powers was regarded by the leading political theorists as an essential part of constitutional government as a means of protection against autocratic and tyrannical authority. Democracy was conceded to have its own capacity for tyranny through the suppression of individual liberty by the majority. Separation of powers sought to prevent this by the device of dividing the powers of government among constitutionally established branches and placing limitations upon their exercise. The principle of separation of powers as conceived at the time of the drafting of the Federal Constitution divided the powers of the national government among three branches—the legislative, the executive, and the judicial. The legislative powers were given to Congress, the executive powers to the President, and the judicial powers to the courts. The same plan of distribution has been adopted by the constitutions of all the states.

The principle of separation of powers has come to be recognized not only as a fundamental principle of governmental organization but also as a rule of constitutional law. In applying the principle as a rule of law, courts have frequently invalidated legislative acts which sought to confer broad rule making powers upon the executive branch or other agencies as being unconstitutional delegations of legislative power and have denied legislative bodies the power to control the appointment and removal of certain executive officials.

As a further means of preventing the accumulation of the powers of government in the same hands, the Federal Constitution and the several state constitutions have also adopted a system of checks and balances. Actually the system of checks and balances constitutes an exception to the principle of separation of powers since it intermingles rather than compartmentalizes the powers according to legislative, executive, and judicial classifications. Examples of the system of checks and balances are the powers given to the President and state governors to participate in legislation through the power of veto and to participate in judicial matters by granting pardons and other acts of clemency to persons convicted of crimes. Further illustrations are the power given to Congress to impeach, try, and remove the President, and similar power given to most state legislatures to impeach the governor and certain other elective officers.

The purpose of this system is to prevent hasty and ill-considered action through the necessity of compromise and review. Admitting the fact that this purpose is achieved, it must be recognized that the system also often prevents or delays the passage of desirable legislation. The system of separation of powers and checks and balances has sometimes been referred to as one of the central paradoxes of American institutions. The paradox results from trying to operate by democratic methods under a constitutional system designed to impede the process.[24]

The principle of separation of powers has not been utilized by municipal corporations and other units of local government to the same extent that it has been by the federal government and the states. To a degree, the principle is followed in the mayor-council plan of municipal government, but is not in other plans of organization. In fact, the manager-council plan represents a definite movement away from the separation of legislative and executive functions and in the direction of the parliamentary type found in many other countries.[25] This plan is based on the theory that the basic functions of government are two in number rather than three. The two are politics and administration.[26]

Checks and balances are really appropriate only under the concept that that government is best which governs least. The increased demands for services being placed on municipal governments has made this concept somewhat out of date. Today, when most municipalities must assume responsibilities for so much of the general economic and political well-being of the people, operation under a system of separation of powers and checks and balances has proved too cumbersome. Furthermore, the improvement of the political processes has come to provide much more effective protection against tyranny than that provided by these mechanisms. Under more responsive forms of municipal government, it is also possible to develop more positive functional programs.

Doctrine of Judicial Review. One of the most important features of both the Federal Constitution and the state constitutions in relation to the development of the law of planning is the power exercised by the courts to declare laws unconstitutional.[27] This power has come to be known as the doctrine of judicial review. Strangely enough, this fundamental power was not expressly conferred upon the courts by the Federal Constitution but has been derived by implication from the provision of the Federal Constitution that declares

[24] Riker, op. cit., p. 161.
[25] Dimock, op. cit., p. 170.
[26] J. Roland Pennock, Administration and the Rule of Law (New York: Farrar & Rinehart, Inc., 1941), p. 14.
[27] See Marbury v. Madison, 1 Cranch 137, 2 L.Ed. 60 (1803).

that the judicial power of the United States should extend to all cases in law and equity arising under the Constitution.[28] However, there had been several instances prior to the holding of the Constitutional Convention of 1787 in which state courts had invalidated state legislation found to be in conflict with state constitutions.[29]

The power of judicial review has been exercised by both state and federal courts from the lowest to the highest tribunal. The power may be exercised by the federal courts to declare either a federal or state law invalid if it conflicts with the Federal Constitution. The power may be exercised by state courts to invalidate state laws which are in conflict with either the state or Federal Constitution and may declare federal laws unconstitutional if they conflict with the Federal Constitution.[30] The doctrine is also exercised in refusing to give effect to statutes which the court finds are in excess of the constitutional power of the legislature to enact. Although courts are bound to give effect to both statutes and the Constitution, the Constitution is the superior law and must prevail in cases of conflict.

The doctrine of judicial review has been one of the most controversial features of the American constitutional system. Opponents have contended that it results in judicial supremacy rather than in establishing the courts as one of the equal and coördinate branches of government under the system of separation of powers. The justification has seemed to arise out of the need for having some authority whose decision is final. In authoritarian forms of government finality of decision rests with the executive authority. In Great Britain, final authority rests with Parliament and there is no constitutional appeal to the courts. The American doctrine of judicial review, which places the responsibility for final decision in the courts, came about primarily as a result of the concepts of the written constitution peculiar to this country.

Power and the Concept of Limited Government.   Under a constitutional system such as we have in the United States, the extent to which compulsion and restraint may be legally asserted by government raises questions of fundamental law as well as questions of public policy. Constitutional government is concerned with both power and liberty. Public policies of government are effectuated by governmental power. Any government which cannot enforce its laws and preserve the order necessary to carry out decided policy will soon

[28] Art. III, Sect. 2, Cl. 1.
[29] Mathews, *op. cit.*, p. 221.
[30] *Ibid.*

cease to be a government. Power is the essence of government and the central concept of politics. Included within the elements of power are the relationships of individuals and groups to society, the control of human behavior and some degree of consent or coercion in accomplishing the aims and objectives of government. Powers of government are asserted and exercised in many ways. Among the most important of the specific powers are those of taxation, appropriation, eminent domain, and the police power. These specific powers represent means and methods by which government is enabled to carry out its policies and maintain order within society.

The powers of government are not unlimited. In the United States, governmental authority must be exercised within the limits of our federal and our state constitutions. In this country, perhaps to a greater degree than in any other, we have sought to stabilize and regularize political life by means of written constitutions. The goal of constitutionalism has been to establish a system of limited government which places restraints upon those governing as well as upon the governed. Restraints upon government may be on behalf of personal liberty or with respect to methods of procedure.

Constitutionalism is opposed to arbitrary government and to the unrestrained will of rulers. It seeks to create a government of laws as distinguished from a government of men. Under our constitutional system, those who exercise the powers of government must do so within the limits set by the Constitution which is superior to the ordinary law of the jurisdiction. Even the political will of the majority cannot be carried out if that will is not consistent with the principles contained in the Federal Constitution and the constitution of the state. Our constitutional government was created with the basic philosophy of providing a system of superior law which would confer upon government those powers essential to the functioning of government, but, at the same time, preserve to the individual those fundamental rights of life, liberty, and property which, under an autocratic or totalitarian form of government, are completely at the mercy of the state.

In theory, constitutional law, as distinguished from statute law, is concerned with fundamental principles which must be observed by governments as well as by individuals. The application of these principles to changing conditions is not always clear. The constitutional limits upon governmental authority and governmental action are matters that are continuously before the courts for construction and determination. The extent of governmental powers and constitutional limitations is of vital concern to carrying out public policy. In certain instances the execution of public policy may require taking property from private ownership for public use. Other circumstances may justify the exercise of governmental authority to restrict the way in which one may develop his property or to compel him to change the use which he is making of it. In other instances governmental authority may define the manner in which one may operate his business, determine the place where his business may be located, or prohibit the business altogether. As has already been pointed out, the extent to which such authority may be exercised under our constitutional system is not unlimited even though it be done with the approval of the majority.

Constitutional Limitations on Local Government Action.   The Constitution of the United States includes a number of specific limitations upon the powers of states which apply equally to subordinate units of local government. From the standpoint of plan implementation, the most important of these are the provisions which prohibit the states from impairing the obligation of contracts,[31] abridging the privileges and immunities of citizens of the United States, depriving any person of life, liberty, or property without due process of law, and denying any person within its jurisdiction the equal protection of the laws.[32] Of these, the due process clause and the equal protection of laws clause of the Fourteenth Amendment are most frequently invoked in contesting the legality of state and local governmental action.

The due process clause has been construed by the courts more than any other provision of the Constitution in defining the limits of state and local powers. It has been held to afford protection against oppressive, capricious, and arbitrary action of government in general and to enable the courts to pass judgment upon the reasonableness of the specific application of local laws and regulations. Although the language of the due process clause is somewhat vague, it has been interpreted by the courts to protect substantive rights of liberty and property as well as procedural rights. Through it the courts have attempted to apply the general principles of justice by preventing the unrestrained and unreasonable exercise of governmental authority.[33]

[31] Art. I. Sec. 10.
[32] Fourteenth Amendment, Sec. 1.
[33] The guarantee of due process is considered more fully in Chap. 4 in connection with the limitations on the police power and eminent domain.

The equal protection clause has been construed to prevent arbitrary discriminations against persons or classes of persons. This clause does not prohibit government from classifying persons for the purpose of applying different regulations where the classification is reasonable in relation to the objectives of the regulation. The clause is held to guarantee equal rights to persons under like circumstances, but does not require government to apply uniform rules to all persons if not similarly situated. The equal protection clause has been invoked frequently to protect persons from discrimination by government based upon race or color. The clause provides protection not only against unreasonable legislation, but also against the exercise of administrative action in a manner resulting in discrimination, even though the law under which the officials operated was fair on its face.[34]

In addition to these specific limitations set forth in the Constitution, there are other restrictions upon states and local units of government that are implied from the grant of powers to the national government or from the nature of the Constitution itself. States and local governments, for example, may not enact legislation or take any other governmental action, the effect of which would place an undue burden upon interstate or foreign commerce. This is because of the power given to the national government to regulate commerce among the several states and with foreign countries. Furthermore, states and local governments may not interfere in any way with the legitimate operations of the national government which is supreme within the realm of affairs delegated to it by the Constitution.

Not only must local laws and regulations not conflict with the Federal Constitution and national laws and treaties, but they must conform to the provisions of the state constitution and the state statutes and common law of the jurisdiction. Many provisions are to be found in state constitutions which duplicate those of the Fourteenth Amendment of the Federal Constitution designed to protect freedom of speech, freedom of the press, security against unreasonable searches and seizures, the taking of private property for public use without just compensation, and depriving persons of life, liberty, or property without due process of law.

Most state constitutions also contain many other restrictions on the powers of local government. Some of those most commonly found establish specific limitations upon taxing powers and indebtedness,

[34] *Yick Wo v. Hopkins*, 118 U.S. 356, 30 L.Ed 220 (1886).

the granting of franchises, the annexation of territory, forms of governmental organization, and other matters as to which general powers have been conferred. Other restrictions upon local authority arise simply from the fact that state legislatures have failed to enact enabling statutes conferring powers upon subordinate units of government.

It is within this legal framework and with full realization of the values which our constitutional system seeks to preserve that the planner must find the solution to the demands for developing a better community in which to live.

CHAPTER 2

Government at the Local Level

THE UNITS OF LOCAL GOVERNMENT

The appropriate place of planning in an urban society cannot be determined without a fairly accurate understanding of the functions, legal nature, and structural organization of local government. For the most part, urban planning is conducted by cities. However, since many functions of government in the urban community are provided by units of government other than municipalities, urban planning must take into account the functional responsibilities of these other governmental units as well.

It is not the purpose of this chapter to present a comprehensive picture of the governmental structure or the functions of all the various units of local government. The aim is merely to identify the general characteristics of the principal units, to indicate some of the major problems of governing the urban community, and to suggest certain possible solutions for the government of metropolitan areas.

Many of the difficulties encountered in achieving effective planning in urban areas stem from the multiplicity of governmental units and the lack of adequate governmental machinery to integrate their functions. The tabulation by the United States Bureau of the Census shows the total number of governmental units in the United States in 1952 to be 116,743.[1] This is a reduction in number from the total of 155,116 shown in the 1942 Census Bureau Report. This reduction is accounted for principally by the consolidation of school districts

[1] United States Department of Commerce, Bureau of the Census, *Governments in the United States in 1952*, State and Local Government Special Studies No. 31 (Washington, D.C.: U.S. Government Printing Office, 1953), pp. 1–2.

and the elimination of townships. However, the number of special districts increased during this period by 48 percent and the number of municipalities by 3.4 percent.[2] A high percentage of the governmental units are to be found in metropolitan areas. The Census Report of 1942 [3] listed five metropolitan areas each having over 500 units of government, the New York-Northeastern, New Jersey-Connecticut area included 1039 units of government; the Chicago area, 821; the Pittsburgh area, 613; the St. Louis area, 535; and the Philadelphia area, 522. The average number of units of government per metropolitan district was in excess of 110.

A unit of government has been defined as an organized entity possessing the following attributes: "a resident population occupying a defined area that has a legally authorized organization and governing body, a separate legal identity, the power to provide certain public or governmental services, and a substantial degree of autonomy including legal and actual power to raise at least a part of its own revenue." [4] Thus to constitute a unit of government there must be an organized entity which has governmental character for the purpose of managing its own affairs and which has a substantial degree of autonomy from other units of government.[5] This definition would exclude geographical areas such as congressional districts, legislative districts, and judicial districts which are created for election purposes but which have no responsibility for governmental operation.

The Federal Constitution makes no reference to local government, leaving the legal nature, organization, powers, and jurisdiction to be determined by the several states. State legislatures, subject to the provisions of state constitutions, have complete authority to create, dissolve, or otherwise control the existence, powers, and functions of all its political subdivisions.[6]

Local units of government have developed in part in response to the demands of individual communities for a local agency to supply local public services and in part out of the needs of the particular states for local agencies to carry out certain state policies. It is natural,

---

[2] *Ibid.*

[3] United States Department of Commerce, Bureau of the Census, *Governmental Units in the United States in 1942* (Washington, D.C.: U.S. Government Printing Office, 1953), pp. 1–2.

[4] William Anderson and Edward W. Weidner, *American City Government* (New York: Henry Holt and Company, Inc., 1950), p. 172.

[5] United States Department of Commerce, Bureau of the Census, *Local Government Structure in the United States* (Washington, D.C.: U.S. Government Printing Office, 1954), p. 1.

[6] The grant of powers is of course subject to limitations upon the powers of the state since a state can grant no power that it does not possess.

therefore, that wide differences exist in their characteristics not only among the different states, but also within a single state. Nevertheless, by avoiding detailed consideration of these innumerable variations, it is possible to classify most local governmental units, for purposes of description, according to their general purpose, legal nature, and functions performed.

MUNICIPAL GOVERNMENT

In comparison with the government of rural areas, the political organization needed for urban communities is very complex. Nearly every aspect of urban life involves complicated relationships of social and economic interests. With the concentration of industrial and commercial activities in areas of high population density, local government has had to assume a correspondingly greater responsibility in providing services, in regulating individual conduct, and in promoting and directing the most advantageous pattern of community development.

Characteristics of the Urban Community. People living in rural areas are able to do many things for themselves or through group action which in urban areas must be performed for them by government. Many rural dwellers may safely and adequately supply their needs for water from individual wells and secure a fair measure of fire protection through informal or voluntary organizations. In urban communities these requirements cannot be met on an individual or group basis and become the responsibility of local government. Furthermore, inhabitants of densely populated communities require many public services which are not required at all in rural areas such as garbage disposal, traffic control, and street cleaning. Other governmental responsibilities which exist in rural communities, such as law enforcement, promotion of public health, and highway construction and maintenance become much more complex in urban communities.[7] Urban living requires a high degree of organization of business, institutions, and government. The complexity of human relationships of people who live in close proximity necessitates the adoption of many rules and regulations to govern their behavior and to promote the highest and most orderly development of their interests and community well-being.[8]

[7] The major functions of municipal government, particularly as they relate to planning, are considered in Chaps. 4 and 5.

[8] For a discussion of the human relationships in city life, see Wilbur C. Hallenbeck, *American Urban Communities* (New York: Harper & Brothers, 1951), p. 35.

There is no sharp dividing line that distinguishes the urban community from the rural community. In general, urban areas are associated with built-up centers of population, concentrations of homes, industry and commerce, and places of streets and buildings rather than farms and fields.[9] Urbanization is largely a product of the industrial revolution. It is characterized by the dominance of cities over the major aspects of our social, economic, and political life. More than half of the people of the United States live in cities and approximately two-thirds live in urban territory.

In order to understand the problems of urban government it is necessary to draw a distinction between the city as a corporation and the urban community. Each municipal corporation has political boundaries which frequently do not coincide with the entire urban community of which it is the center. With the present trend toward suburban living and industrial decentralization, it is indeed rare that the boundaries of the political unit and the socioeconomic city do coincide. This lack of identity presents serious difficulty in planning the development of the urban community since the essential powers and organization for effective plan implementation are, for the most part, restricted to the area within the boundary limits of the municipalities.

Legal Nature of Municipal Corporations.   The unit of local government which has proved to be best suited for meeting the needs of the urban community has been the municipal corporation. The term "municipal corporation" is used to cover the many incorporated urban places known as cities, boroughs, villages, and towns. The distinction between cities and these other municipal corporations is primarily one of population. The term "city" is normally used to refer to the larger municipal corporations and implies a more highly developed trade and industrial center than do the terms "village," "borough," and "town." [10] Although state statutes frequently grant different powers and provide different plans of organization for municipal corporations of different classes, their legal nature and general purposes are essentially the same.

An understanding of the principal elements of the corporate form of organization is essential to the comprehension of the many legal relationships of municipal government and its functional responsibilities. A corporation is essentially a legal device by which the law

[9] Anderson and Weidner, op. cit., p. 14.
[10] The term "town" as used to apply to the small incorporated municipality is to be distinguished from the "New England town."

attributes a single legal personality to a group of individuals. As a result of the act of incorporation, property may be acquired, held, and disposed of in the name of the corporation. A corporation may sue and be sued in its own name without involving its members individually. Corporate debts are satisfied from the assets of the corporation rather than from those of the individual members who compose it. One of the major characteristics of a corporation is immortality. Its life is perpetual and neither the death of any of its members nor changes of membership affect its legal existence.

Corporations are either public or private. A municipal corporation is one form of public corporation. The feature of a municipal corporation most important in distinguishing it from other public corporations is the power and right of local self-government.[11] The principal elements which are necessary to constitute a municipal corporation are: (1) a legal creation or incorporation pursuant to the state constitution or state statute, and frequently, but not always, evidenced by a charter containing the corporate powers, (2) a corporate name by which it is known and under which all corporate acts are done, (3) inhabitants in whom are vested the political and corporate powers which are carried out through duly constituted officers, and (4) a place or prescribed territory within which the corporate functions are exercised.[12]

Municipal corporations differ from private corporations in a number of respects. A brief reference to the major differences helps to point up the legal characteristics of municipal corporations.[13] Private corporations are formed primarily for the purpose of pursuing objectives in the special interests of the corporate members as distinguished from the interest of the general public. Frequently, the interest of profit making is dominant in private corporations, but this is not always true as private corporations are also formed for religious, charitable, scientific, and other nonprofit motives. The type of service rendered does not necessarily distinguish between private and municipal corporations. For example, in some communities, certain local services such as transportation, power and light, and water may be supplied by private corporations and in others by mu-

[11] See p. 39 for a discussion of the distinguishing characteristics of municipal corporations and quasi-municipal corporations.

[12] Eugene McQuillin, The Law of Municipal Corporations, 3d ed. (Chicago: Callaghan & Company, 1949), Vol. 1, Sec. 2.07, pp. 451–456.

[13] For the most part these same differences apply as between private corporations and all public corporations.

nicipal corporations.[14] The most important feature distinguishing the municipal corporation from private corporations is that it is created to function as a governmental agency and that the state and the public have an exclusive interest in it.[15]

Although both municipal and private corporations are incorporated under authority of the state, municipal corporations are subject to more extensive controls than are private corporations. Charters of private corporations are held to be contractual resulting from the voluntary acceptance by the corporation of the terms of the charter or incorporating act. Once the corporation is formed, the state may not alter or withdraw the terms of the grant except to the extent that the right to do so was reserved at the time of incorporation. This rule is based upon the provision contained in Article I, Section 10 of the Federal Constitution forbidding states to enact laws impairing the obligation of contract.[16] The contract clause of the Federal Constitution does not, however, prohibit a state from abolishing a municipal corporation or altering the terms of its charter at will since municipal corporations are held to be created by law and not by contract. This is true even though state statutes may make their creation dependent upon the voluntary initiation and approval of the inhabitants of the area incorporated. Incorporation confers no vested rights upon municipal corporations which may be asserted against the state since they are creatures of the state to carry out state policies as well as to perform local functions.

Another important distinction between municipal corporations and private corporations is the basis of membership in the corporation. For the most part, membership in private corporations is determined by the ownership of stock or some other evidence of voluntary association. Membership in a municipal corporation is determined by residence within the corporate boundaries. Membership of persons living within the incorporated area is an involuntary matter, except as one is free to change his place of residence. As long as a person remains within the corporate boundaries, he is subject to the jurisdiction of the municipality with all the responsibilities and benefits which this entails.

Powers of Municipal Corporations. Municipal corporations may

---

[14] Such services when supplied by private corporations are usually held to be affected with a public interest and subject to extensive public regulation and control.

[15] Ernest B. Schulz, *American City Government, Its Machinery and Processes* (New York: Stackpole and Heck, Inc., 1949), p. 48.

[16] *Dartmouth College v. Woodward*, 4 Wheaton 518, 4 L.Ed. 629 (1819).

exercise only those powers which have been delegated to them by the state. Municipalities have no inherent right of self-government and may not act, no matter how urgent the matter may be, unless there has been a grant of legal authority from the state to do so. Powers may be granted by express terms or by implication. The primary sources from which the powers are derived are the constitutions of the state, state statutes, the municipal charter, and the rules of common law and equity. Implied powers are inferred from the express grants and from the objectives and purposes for which the municipality was created. In general, courts, in construing the powers of municipal corporations, have adopted a rule of strict construction under which doubts concerning grants of authority are resolved against the municipality. According to the much-quoted rule of municipal powers as stated by Judge Dillon, a municipal corporation possesses the following powers and no others: (1) those granted in express words, (2) those necessarily or fairly implied in or incident to the powers expressly granted, (3) those essential to the accomplishment of the declared objects and purposes of the corporation—not simply convenient but indispensable.[17]

Municipal powers are sometimes conferred by general or blanket grants of authority and sometimes by an enumeration of specific powers. The blanket grant of authority gives cities somewhat greater freedom since they may deal with many local matters without the necessity of having to obtain specific enabling legislation. The vagueness of blanket grants may, however, necessitate numerous court decisions before the meaning and intent become clear, thereby resulting in an enumeration through litigation. The grant of powers through specific statutory enumeration makes it possible for the legislature to exercise more direct control over municipal functions. It also tends to reduce the doubts concerning the scope of the power of the municipalities and consequently avoids much of the litigation resulting from the uncertainty of blanket grants. On the other hand, the practice of specific enumeration forces municipalities to have to obtain enabling legislation before they may undertake any new function, no matter how badly needed. This may frequently involve heavy community costs in terms of delay and inconvenience. The most practical plan appears to be a compromise in which the blanket grant is combined with certain enumerated powers.

[17] J. F. Dillon, *Commentaries on the Law of Municipal Corporations*, 5th ed. (Boston: Little, Brown & Company, 1911), Vol. 1, Sec. 237.

A number of states, in an effort to work out a more satisfactory relationship between the state and its municipalities, have adopted constitutional provisions establishing powers of municipal home rule. Quite commonly these provisions apply only to cities over a certain population. Under home rule powers, municipalities are enabled to frame, adopt, and amend their own charters and to exercise considerable freedom from state control in the management of their local affairs. The idea of home rule is based upon the principle that government should be kept as close to the people as possible and that the inhabitants of each community should be permitted to control those affairs which are of local concern. While this principle is one that meets with general acceptance, there has been no end of practical difficulties in trying to define what are strictly local affairs as distinguished from matters of state concern.

If cities are to function as agents of the state as well as corporations to provide for local needs, they obviously cannot be set up as completely independent governments within the state. However, the unsatisfactory experience of cities with state interference in local affairs, together with the difficulties they have encountered in securing enabling legislation necessary to solve urgent local governmental problems, furnishes ample evidence of the need for devising a workable plan of constitutional home rule.

Powers which are granted to municipal corporations cannot be transferred to private individuals or agencies or to other public agencies. Courts have also held that where statutes or charters designate particular officials as responsible for exercising certain powers, this responsibility cannot be delegated to others. The reason for this rule arises out of the need for keeping responsibility where it has been placed by law. Sometimes, however, powers are conferred upon the municipality without reference to any officer or official. Since the council is held to have the residual powers of the city, it is responsible for all powers not assigned to any other persons.

The courts recognize an exception to the rule against delegating municipal powers in the case of ministerial functions. Ministerial functions are those which involve little or no discretion and are undertaken to effectuate predetermined objectives. The city council may not, for example, delegate the matter of determining whether a particular public improvement should be undertaken since this involves the exercise of judgment and discretion. The actual construction, however, is a ministerial function which may be delegated.

Ministerial powers may include such matters as the selection of ways and means, the determination of questions of fact, and the exercise of judgment in the method to be used in carrying out policy decisions.

Powers of municipal corporations are classified in many ways. One of the most significant classifications is that which distinguishes between powers as governmental and corporate. Governmental powers are sometimes referred to as public, and corporate powers are often designated as proprietary or private. This distinction between governmental and corporate powers is of importance in several branches of the law and particularly in determining questions of municipal liability in tort. The distinction is not always clear and has been a source of confusion not only to laymen, but to judges and lawyers as well. In general, governmental functions are those which municipal corporations perform as agents of the state to carry out matters of concern to the state as a whole such as police protection, fire protection, and public health. Corporate functions are those which are undertaken to provide for the peculiar needs and serve the special interests of inhabitants of the municipality. Courts are almost unanimous in classifying as corporate such functions as the operation of transit systems, water supply systems, light and power facilities, and other utilities. There are many functions, however, which courts have not classified uniformly. Among these are such activities as the ownership and operation of swimming pools, garbage disposal, parks, playgrounds and golf courses, and the construction and maintenance of streets, sidewalks, sewers, and other types of public improvements.

Municipal Liability. In performing the various municipal functions, municipalities, acting through their officers, employees, or agents frequently inflict injuries upon individuals or damages to property. In some instances these injuries are the consequences of necessary governmental action performed in a proper manner. In others, they result from failure to act, from negligence in the performance of an act, from intentional trespass, or from the creation and maintenance of a nuisance. Such injuries fall into the class of private wrongs, known in law as torts, for which municipalities may, under certain circumstances, be liable in damages. They are to be distinguished from criminal acts which are wrongs against the public.[18]

The rules governing municipal liability in tort have developed primarily from the common law. The state has the power, however, to limit or extend the liability of municipalities by statute or by con-

[18] The same act may sometimes constitute both a tort and a crime.

stitutional provision. Since municipal corporations can act only through officers, employees, or agents, liability for tort is based upon the rule of "respondeat superior" which makes the employer liable in damages for the wrongful acts of his employees or agents who are acting within the scope of their authority.

One of the fundamental principles of our legal system is that a state may not be sued without its consent. The basis for the principle is that there is no legal right against the authority that makes the law on which the right depends.[19] Since municipalities are said to function in a dual capacity, the immunity of the state from liability for tort has been held to apply to municipal corporations when performing governmental functions as agents of the state, but in the performance of functions which are corporate in nature the immunity of the state does not apply. Thus, the liability of the municipality to respond in damages for wrongful acts of employees and agents is made to depend upon the character of the function which is being performed. For example, a person who may be injured by the negligent operation of a fire truck may not be able to recover damages from the city for his injuries,[20] whereas the city would be required to respond in damages if the injury resulted from negligence in the operation of a vehicle of the water department.

The distinction between governmental and corporate functions has no application to municipal liability on contracts. If the contractual agreement falls within the scope of its legal powers, a municipality is liable to the same degree as a private corporation. However, a municipality does not guarantee its authority to contract, and there may be no recovery against it if the contract entered into is *ultra vires*, that is, outside of the scope of its corporate power. Contracts which fall within the powers of the city may sometimes be invalid because of some defect of procedure such as failure properly to call for bids or to have the contract signed or countersigned by the proper officers. Some courts are inclined to treat such contracts as quasi contracts and allow recovery on a *quantum meruit* basis.[21]

Forms of Municipal Government. The structural machinery by which the powers of municipal government are exercised is an im-

[19] *Kawananakoa v. Polyblank*, 205 U.S. 349, 51 L.Ed. 834 (1907). Frequently it has been said that the rule is based upon the old maxim that the king can do no wrong.

[20] The individual employee may be liable for the consequences of his wrongful acts, but frequently he is not financially responsible.

[21] Charles M. Kneier, *City Government in the United States* (New York: Harper & Brothers, 1947), p. 235.

portant factor in encouraging active voter participation, attracting capable personnel into government service, and establishing clear-cut lines of authority which fix responsibility for policy decision and administration essential to good government. Although government policies must be shaped and administered by individuals, the form and structure of government furnish the machinery within which they carry out their work. No matter how good the workmen, they cannot do their best with poor tools.

More experimentation with forms of government has been carried on by municipal governments than at any other level. Some municipalities have utilized the principle of separation of legislative and executive powers with various shades of weak or strong executives. Others have combined legislative and executive responsibilities in the same governing body. Still others have sought to separate governmental responsibilities on the basis of policy making and administration.

Forms of municipal government are usually classified under three types: the mayor-council plan, the commission plan, and the council-manager plan. The classification of forms of government under these three plans tends to create an oversimplification of the matter of structural organization, and in some instances may be misleading as there are so many hybrid plans and many variations within each type. Nevertheless, there are some significant features of each plan that distinguish one from the other. Although each form of government has its strong supporters, it is not possible to establish conclusively that one form is the best for every city. Much depends upon its adaptability to local needs and conditions, the size of the municipality, its historical background, and current problems.

The mayor-council form of government is usually classified as either the weak mayor-council plan or the strong mayor-council plan. Both types are identified by an elected council which is presumed to exercise the legislative functions, and by the elective mayor who is presumed to exercise the executive functions. Checks and balances in varying degrees are employed under both types. The chief characteristic of the weak mayor-council plan is the weakness of the mayor as a chief executive. Under this plan there are usually few appointments which he can make that do not require the confirmation of the council, and frequently the executive responsibility is shared with a number of other elected administrative department heads or semiautonomous boards or commissions over whom he has no effective control. With administration thus diffused, the mayor is, nevertheless, held publicly responsible for the administration of municipal affairs although he does not possess adequate authority to fulfill this responsibility.

The strong-mayor plan makes the mayor the dominant figure in municipal government, not only in administrative matters, but also in policy making as well. He is the political leader of the city as well as the chief executive. The strong-mayor plan tends to fix administrative responsibility in a single individual, the mayor, and vests in him important powers of appointment and removal of department heads and makes him responsible for preparing the budget for council consideration. The mayor, under this plan, is given important powers over legislation through the exercise of the veto which can usually be overridden only by extraordinary majority of the council. Except for the application of the system of checks and balances, the strong-mayor plan makes a separation of powers according to legislative and executive responsibility.

The commission form of government, which originated about 1901, broke away from the traditional doctrine of separation of powers by placing both legislative and executive powers in a small commission of from three to nine members, five being the most common number. The commissioners collectively comprise the legislative branch and individually are responsible for administration. As a legislative body, the commission formulates municipal policy, and as individuals they serve as heads of the administrative departments to carry out the policy.

Usually one of the members of the commission is selected to serve as mayor. Under some plans he is elected to this position by the voters and in others he is chosen by the commission. The mayor functions as titular head of the city and presides at meetings of the commission. He does not have power of veto over matters of legislation and his powers of appointment are usually no greater than those of other members. The chief weakness of the plan has been the lack of a responsible executive necessary to unify administrative action and fix administrative responsibility. The commission plan, which was widely adopted during the early part of this century, has declined very much in popularity in recent years.

The form of government which has been most generally advocated by political scientists during the past quarter century is the council-manager plan. Under this plan a small council is elected at large. One of its members, selected as mayor, is the ceremonial head of the

municipality and presides at council meetings. The chief characteristic of the council-manager plan is the differentiation made between
the policy making function and the administrative function. This is
a concept entirely different from the separation of legislative and
executive powers found in the mayor-council plan. Under the council-
manager form, the city council which formulates the policy is elected
by the voters, but the manager who carries out the policy is appointed by the council and is responsible to it. The manager may be
dismissed by the council at any time. The manager is chosen for his
professional administrative ability and is free to carry out policies
without interference from the council as to his methods or the appointment of his subordinates.[22] Although the plan seeks to separate
politics and administration, this does not mean that the manager has
no voice in policy matters or the council no voice in administration.
Practical operation of the plan necessitates a close working relationship between the manager and the council to whom he is responsible.
In many matters the manager must provide leadership in recommending and shaping public policy. Once policy decisions are made,
however, it becomes the duty of the manager to carry out the policies
to the best of his ability irrespective of his personal views concerning
them.

The chief argument in support of the manager plan is that it enables the municipality to select the chief administrator on the basis
of his ability as an administrator rather than because of his skill as a
politician. The plan concentrates administrative authority in the
hands of a single individual and makes it possible for him to coördinate the various activities of all departments. He has the responsibility of preparing the budget for council approval and of providing
the council with information and expert advice on matters necessary
for intelligent policy decision including planning the development
of the community.

Although the role of planning is the same for municipalities regardless of the form of government, the position of the planning agency
in the organizational structure may vary considerably according to
the form of government. In some instances this has a bearing upon
the nature of the planning agency itself and also upon the relation-

[22] *Forms of City Government* (Austin, Tex.: Institute of Public Affairs, University
of Texas, 1954), p. 17. Appointments may be required to be made subject to established civil service rules.

ships of the planning agency with the policy making branch and the administrative departments.[23]

COUNTY GOVERNMENT

The most universal of all units of local government is the county. County government in some form is to be found in every state, and as a general rule every part of the state falls within the area of some county.[24] There are some exceptions to this. Altogether, there are 47 areas in the United States which have been consolidated in whole or in part with city governments or have no county government. In the case of Denver and San Francisco, county and municipal functions have been consolidated into city-county governments. In certain other cases, such as St. Louis, Baltimore, and a number of Virginia cities, the municipalities are legally separated from the county and the county functions are performed by the municipality. Land areas in Rhode Island designated as counties are not actually organized as local governments but serve primarily as judicial districts.[25] There are four unorganized counties in South Dakota. Other areas that do not fall within some county are the District of Columbia and Yellowstone Park, located in Idaho, Montana, and Wyoming.[26]

Size and Characteristics.   Counties vary to such a degree in area and population that it can hardly be said that there is a typical county. Populations range from that of Alpine County, California, and Loving County, Texas, each with about 300 inhabitants, to that of Cook County, Illinois, which has a population of about 4,000,000.[27] In the matter of area, almost as striking contrasts exist. Counties range in size from that of Arlington County, Virginia, with an area of 25 square miles to that of San Bernardino, California, with 20,175 square miles.[28] As a rule counties tend to be larger in the Western and Mountain states with sparse populations, but great variations exist within the individual states, both in the East and in the West. Of the 3050 counties in the United States approximately 2400 are

[23] See pp. 87–91.

[24] In Louisiana the primary subdivision of the state is called the parish, but the functions are practically the same as they are in counties in other states.

[25] Clyde F. Snider, *American State and Local Government* (New York: Appleton-Century-Crofts, Inc., 1950), p. 291.

[26] Paul W. Wager (ed.), *County Government Across the Nation* (Chapel Hill: University of North Carolina Press, 1950), p. 8.

[27] Lane W. Lancaster, *Government in Rural America* (New York: D. Van Nostrand Company, Inc., 1952), p. 47.

[28] *Ibid.*, p. 48.

distinctly rural areas. The remaining counties are predominantly urban in character, containing one or more important incorporated municipalities or relatively large unincorporated areas which are urban in character. The degree of urbanization has a very definite bearing upon the functions counties may be called upon to perform, and, consequently, has an important relationship to planning.

Legal Nature. In distinguishing between the legal natures of counties and cities, courts have frequently referred to counties as quasi-municipal corporations, and cities as municipal corporations. The difference rests in the main upon the primary purpose for which each is created. Municipal corporations usually come into existence at the behest of the voters who live within their jurisdictions. They are created primarily for the purpose of satisfying local needs, promoting local interests, and contributing to the convenience of the inhabitants of a particular locality.[29] Although municipal corporations serve to carry out certain policies of the state, they are designed primarily to fulfill the needs of local inhabitants. Quasi-municipal corporations, on the other hand, are created primarily to carry out state purposes and, therefore, possess relatively fewer corporate powers to satisfy local needs. The distinction between municipal corporations and quasi-municipal corporations should not be exaggerated, however, because both municipal corporations and quasi-municipal corporations are creatures of the state, and both derive their powers and duties from the state legislature subject to provisions of the state constitutions. Since counties are created primarily to serve the interests of the state, in most jurisdictions they are clothed with the immunities of the state against legal action based on tort liability. There are some exceptions.

County Functions. Although counties have always been considered as units of local government, they exist primarily as administrative subdivisions of the state for the purpose of administering state policy decided by the state legislature. County government was devised at a time when it was believed that decentralized administration of state functions was convenient and desirable. For the most part, counties have little discretion in the selection of the functions they are required to perform or the organization by which they will be carried out. The fact, however, that county officials are chosen by local election and are responsible to the local electorate provides a

---

[29] Schulz, op. cit., p. 50.

degree of local discretion in the choice of means to be employed in carrying out policy which may often have the effect of modifying policy itself. This is illustrated by the variations that occur in establishing valuations of real and personal property for tax levies, and in the maintenance of roads and standards of public health services.

The traditional county functions include law enforcement through the sheriff, maintenance of local jails and detention institutions, poor relief and aid to the blind and other unfortunates, public health services for the inhabitants in unincorporated areas, the administration of elections, judicial administration, and the recording of deeds, marriage licenses, certain vital statistics, and other records. In addition to the numerous functions required to be performed by state law, there are increasing numbers of county functions that are authorized by enabling legislation but are optional to the individual counties. In recent years the functions of counties, in some jurisdictions, have been somewhat broadened to include responsibility for providing certain services of a corporate or proprietary nature such as are usually associated with municipalities. To a considerable extent the newer functions have developed in response to the demands of the unincorporated urban communities.

Among some of the newer county functions which have been assumed in response to local demands are those concerned with the operation and administration of airports, hospitals, libraries, parks and recreational facilities, and public housing. Some counties which are more highly urbanized have also undertaken to provide such services as sewerage and garbage disposal, fire protection, water supply and other utilities, and some have engaged in rather extensive activities in the fields of planning, zoning, subdivision control, and building regulation. In these matters, counties function very much in the same capacity as municipal corporations. For the most part, however, they continue to serve primarily as creatures of the state for carrying out state policy and supplying the local governmental needs of rural areas.

Structural Organization. With a few exceptions, the structural organization of county government has remained in substantially the same form since county government was first established in this country. The organization is so complicated and varies to such a degree throughout the country that brief generalizations describing its features fail to present an accurate picture. In general, the powers and duties of counties are divided among numerous elective and appointive officers, boards, and commissions. Although the functions of county government are primarily administrative, only a very few reorganized counties have any kind of integrated administrative structure. Each elective official in the typical county is virtually a little government unto himself, independent of all other elective county officials and responsible only to the electorate. Coördination of related activities under such structure is extremely difficult.[30]

The most important single body of county officials is the "county board," which is known by various titles in different jurisdictions, including the "board of county commissioners," the "board of supervisors," the "county court," the "police jury," and the "board of freeholders."[31] County boards vary in size from one member to more than 50 members. Wayne County, Michigan, has 84 members. Half of the counties have three members or less. The duties of the county board are more administrative and judicial than legislative. As a rule the county board acts by resolution rather than by ordinance although the granting of certain ordinance powers to county boards has increased. The county boards usually are given power to levy taxes, appropriate money, and issue bonds. County boards are usually responsible also for managing county property, awarding contracts, passing upon claims and bills, and making certain appointments to carry out the administrative tasks with which the board is charged. While county boards are commonly granted supervisory powers over county affairs, they have in fact little authority over other elective officials except through their control over the budget and other fiscal matters.

In addition to the county board, most counties have a long list of other officials, most of whom are elected by direct vote. Among those most commonly found are the sheriff, prosecuting attorney, clerk of the court, coroner, county judge, justices of the peace, auditor, clerk, treasurer, assessor, registrar of deeds, superintendent of schools, engineer or surveyor, constables, health officer, and others. As new responsibilities have been given to counties, there has been a tendency to further diffuse administrative responsibility by placing the new function under special boards or commissions with autonomous or semiautonomous status. Illustrations of such boards and commissions are those created to administer libraries, public health, public

[30] Snider, op. cit., p. 304.
[31] Wager, op. cit., pp. 10–11. (Twenty-seven different titles are in use in the United States).

welfare, hospitals, parks and recreation activities, personnel, airports, planning, and zoning. The multiplication of these agencies seems to be explained in large part by the lack of confidence of the legislature in the existing county structure. However, the result has been to add further to the disjointed organization and increase the difficulties of coördinating administration.[32] Under these conditions it is obvious why planning has not made greater progress at the county level.

OTHER UNITS OF LOCAL GOVERNMENT

In most sections of the United States the responsibility for providing local government is shared by the county and municipalities with other local units. Among the most important of these are the New England towns, townships, school districts, and special districts. Some of these continue to exist today largely because of their historical origin and because of the public resistance to change. Others have been instituted primarily because of the unsatisfactory areas for administration provided by the established units or because of the inadequacy of powers of existing units to cope with the demands imposed upon present-day governments.

The New England Town.   In the New England states, the county is relatively unimportant as a local government institution. Most of the functions performed by counties in other parts of the country are performed by towns in New England. Many variations are to be found both with respect to powers and organization, but the general characteristics are quite similar. Towns serve as areas for local law enforcement and the administration of petty justice and also for the assessment and collection of property taxes not only for the town but also for the use of the county and the state. Town government is concerned primarily with the administration of highways, public health, poor relief, and schools. In some instances, especially in the more densely populated areas, towns are empowered by statute to provide fire protection, water supply, sewage disposal, and many other services commonly supplied in other sections of the country by cities and villages.[33] In fact, many of the New England towns are incorporated and others occupy a legal position quite analogous to that of municipal corporations. Even where municipalities exist within a town, services such as schools and fire protection are often supplied on a town-wide basis.

[32] *Ibid.*, p. 14.
[33] *Ibid.*, p. 46.

Historically the New England town had a religious background. Its boundaries were made more or less coextensive with the parish in order to provide a political unit for the religious congregation. The town began as a rather compact settlement which had its center around the town hall, the church, and the stockade and included the fields surrounding the villages.[34] As the need for protection grew less, the town came to encompass a number of communities, and its boundaries were established by dividing the state into political-geographical areas. Except for a small area in northern Maine and a few incorporated cities, the entire area of the New England states is served by town government.

One of the principal features of New England town government is the annual town meeting. Originally the town meeting represented one of the best examples of pure democracy. All persons eligible to vote assembled at these meetings, heard reports, engaged in debate, adopted ordinances, voted appropriations, and elected officers. Special town meetings were also called as needed. Most of the important questions of public policy were resolved at these open meetings. The administration required by these decisions was carried out through a number of elective officials including a board of selectmen, clerk, tax collector, assessors, justices of the peace, constables, and other officers, boards, and commissions.

Although many of the features of the town meeting have been preserved, the complexity of governmental problems, along with the great increase of population, has necessitated some modifications of the plan. In some of the more populous areas it has been necessary to abandon the open town meeting and substitute a limited or representative type of assembly. Delegates to the limited meeting are usually chosen by districts. Since the town, like other units of government, is a creature of the state legislature, most of the major organizational changes have come about through changes in state laws.

In the matter of administration there have been many modifications also. The increased responsibilities placed upon town government in recent years have led to a more integrated type of administrative structure. At the end of 1951, the town-manager plan had been adopted by 126 New England towns.[35] Under this plan the policy making functions are still exercised through the town meeting, but administrative responsibilities are integrated under the town manager.

[34] Lancaster, op. cit., p. 35.
[35] Ibid., p. 44.

In many towns, however, the original town meeting and administrative organization have not been greatly modified.

Townships. Outside New England there developed in 16 states an area of local government called the township.[36] In some of the eastern states, including New York, New Jersey, and Pennsylvania, the township developed rather spontaneously very much as did the New England town. Its boundaries were frequently irregular following the pattern of settlement, and its area corresponded in size to that of the New England town. These townships are to be distinguished from the so-called congressional townships of the western states which were laid out by federal surveyors while the land was still a part of the public domain.

In laying out the western townships some attention was given to the natural features of the land, but for the most part they were geographical areas each six miles square. This arbitrary means of establishing boundaries was used in part for identifying the territory surveyed, but also to provide ready-made political subdivisions for local government in this sparsely settled area.[37] Local government was not established in all these townships, but where it was, the boundaries of the congressional and the civil township usually coincided. However, in some states where the population was sparse, two or more congressional townships were sometimes combined to form one civil township.

Because of differences in origin, settlement, and local conditions, township government varies greatly from state to state and even within a single state. Sometimes township government is established in certain counties but not all. In the state of Washington, for example, township government has been organized in only two of the 39 counties and in these only on a partial basis. In some states townships are separate and distinct from municipalities, whereas in others they may overlie both cities and villages. In other jurisdictions they may overlie villages but not cities.

In many states, the statutory powers and the plan of governmental organization very closely resemble those of the New England town, but in no section of the country does the township have the vitality which the town has retained in New England. This is due in a large

[36] Illinois, Indiana, Iowa, Kansas, Michigan, Minnesota, Missouri, Nebraska, New Jersey, New York, North Dakota, Ohio, Pennsylvania, South Dakota, Washington, and Wisconsin. They are called towns in Minnesota, New York, and Wisconsin.

[37] Lancaster, *op. cit.*, p. 62.

part to the fact that the artificial boundaries did not coincide with the social groupings or regional interests. Township government in most of the states is gradually declining in importance. In many states most of the township functions have now been transferred to the counties, and for all practical purposes the township has ceased to exist except as a legal description. The retention of the township as a political entity under these conditions seems to be supported largely out of sentiment, vested interests, or because of a few minor local functions which they still perform. Frequently the local function is only to provide a unit of representation for electing members to the county board or to a tax equalization board.

The most important function of the rural township is that of maintaining country roads. This responsibility accounts for about 40 percent of the operating expenditures and more than half of the capital outlays of all the townships. School operations account for the next largest item.[38] In a few jurisdictions townships still have some responsibilities in property assessment, law enforcement, public health, and election administration. In some of the more densely populated areas, particularly in Michigan, New Jersey, and Pennsylvania, the township continues to function as an important unit of local government. Certain townships function very much on the order of municipal corporations, and in addition to the usual township functions, they may operate hospitals, libraries, parks, sanitation facilities, and provide fire protection, police protection, water supply, and many other services normally required by an urban community.

As functions of townships vary from state to state, so does the governmental structure. Half of the 16 states that authorize township government provide by statute for township meetings modeled after the New England town.[39] In a few states the township meeting still functions in a limited way. Usually, township government is managed by one or more elected trustees or supervisors. In some states, as is the case in Indiana, the voters elect the principal administrative officer, the "trustee," and also an advisory board of three. Terms of each are four years. The duties of the board are concerned primarily with fiscal affairs. It adopts the budget, authorizes borrowing of

[38] United States Bureau of the Census, *Finances of Townships and New England Towns, 1942* (Washington, D.C.: U.S. Government Printing Office, 1944). In Indiana, North Dakota, and South Dakota, the township rather than the school district is the unit for financing and administering the elementary schools.

[39] Illinois, Michigan, Minnesota, Nebraska, North Dakota, South Dakota, Washington, and Wisconsin.

money, determines tax rates and levies, and approves contracts. Other elective officials include the justice of the peace and constable.[40]

In Kansas the elective township offices are those of trustee, clerk, treasurer, two justices of the peace, and two constables. The trustee, clerk, and treasurer constitute the township board. The board also sits as the township audit board, in which capacity it exercises general supervision and management of the township finances. In counties which do not operate under the county unit road system and where the care of roads is under the township, the board also functions as the township board of highway commissioners.[41]

In Pennsylvania, the general control of township affairs is vested in three supervisors who are popularly elected. Other elected officials include an assessor, a tax collector, three auditors, two justices of the peace, and one or more constables. The board of supervisors appoints a township secretary and a treasurer.[42] In Michigan the governing body is a township board of five members with the supervisor as chairman. The supervisor, in addition to his township duties, represents his township on the county board of supervisors.[43]

Special Districts and Local Authorities. The growing demand for specialized services which are not provided in a given locality by the established units of government has led to the creation of numerous special-purpose districts and local authorities. For the most part, these districts and authorities are single-purpose in character as distinguished from multifunctional units of general government such as counties, cities, and towns. They are usually classified as quasi-municipal corporations. Single-purpose districts have been created to fulfill a wide variety of local needs relating to such matters as fire protection, water supply, sewage disposal, drainage, flood control, airports, cemeteries, irrigation, sanitation, weed control, parks, and many others. The functions, powers, and organizational structure are provided by state statute.

The number of special-purpose districts has multiplied greatly during the past 20 years, particularly in the unincorporated urban areas. It has been estimated that in the state of California more than 4000 special-purpose districts have been organized under 100 separate laws to provide more than 30 special functions.[44] About the same number

[40] Wager, op. cit., p. 273.
[41] James W. Drury, *Township Government in Kansas* (Lawrence, Kansas: University of Kansas Publications, 1954), Governmental Research Series No. 10, p. 21.
[42] Wager, op. cit., p. 203.
[43] *Ibid.*, p. 260.
[44] Stanley Scott and John C. Bollens, *Special Districts in California Local Govern-*

of special functions are carried on by single-purpose districts in the state of Washington.[45]

The special authority serves much the same purpose as the special district. Local authorities have been created as special public corporations for the ownership and operation of ports, airports, hospitals, sanitation facilities, and various types of utilities. Quite frequently authorities which originated as single-purpose units have developed into multifunctional units, but none to the extent to place them in the category of units of general government.[46]

There have been many reasons why special districts have been so extensively utilized. For the most part their creation can be traced to one or more of the following: (1) The political boundaries of municipalities or other existing units of government in the urbanized area do not correspond with the area in which the particular service is needed or desired; (2) Incorporation or annexation may be unnecessary or uneconomical because there is not a need or demand for general municipal services in the particular area at the time the special district is organized; (3) The solution to the particular problem of government by any other means at the particular time is impractical or not politically feasible; (4) Independence of the desired service from the general units of government is regarded as a means of insuring local control and keeping the function free from politics; and (5) The use of the special district may be a means of escaping certain tax or debt limitations which would be applicable if the functions were provided by existing governmental units.[47]

As a general rule, special-purpose districts and authorities are administrative rather than legislative in character, acting by resolution rather than by ordinance. Most districts are headed by a board or commission composed of from three to five members, although some boards are larger. There is no common pattern in the composition of boards or in the manner in which they are selected. Quite commonly the boards are elected, but in some instances they are appointed, in whole or in part, or are ex officio.[48] Where boards are

ment (Berkeley, Calif.: Bureau of Public Administration, University of California, 1949).

[45] Governmental Units in the State of Washington (Seattle: Bureau of Governmental Research and Services, University of Washington, 1956), mimeo tabulation.

[46] For a detailed study of the nature of public authorities, their development, organization, financing, and the legal considerations and problems in their use, see Council of State Governments, Public Authorities in the States, A Report of the Governors' Conference (Chicago: 1953).

[47] John C. Bollens, "When Services Get Too Big," National Municipal Review, Vol. 38, No. 10, pp. 498–503, November, 1949.

[48] Snider, op. cit., p. 364.

appointed, the appointing authority may be the mayor of the city, the county board, the court, the governor of the state, or some other local or state official. Quite commonly the board appoints a director or chief administrator to supervise the work of the district.

The multiplication of single-purpose special districts, with overlapping boundaries, has produced a very complex and confused pattern of local government in many areas. In some places the special district has come to be regarded as an evil rather than a solution to a problem of governmental organization. This subject is specially considered in the following section on metropolitan problems.

The School District. In a sense the school district falls under the classification of single-purpose special districts. However, the school district differs from most other special districts in that it serves as the basic unit of the state for providing financial support and administrative supervision of the elementary and secondary schools.[49] Although organized to carry out state policy through a system of decentralized administration, school districts are, nevertheless, independent local governmental units. The autonomous school district is a unique American institution organized outside of the structure of the units of general government.

Within recent years, there has been a very marked reduction in the number of school districts. The reports of the United States Bureau of the Census show a total of 67,346 organized school districts in 1952 as against 108,579 such districts in 1942. This has come about largely through the abolition of one-room school districts and through consolidation and reorganization programs carried out pursuant to state laws.

Outside of incorporated municipalities, the boundaries of school districts are seldom coterminous with those of any other unit of local government. School districts operating within municipalities commonly have boundaries which coincide with those of the city. However, the boundaries of municipal school districts often include some area that is not within the corporate limits of the city.

School district affairs are universally supervised by a board of school directors. As a rule, this board is popularly elected, although in some of the larger cities the members are appointed by the mayor with confirmation by the council. In most jurisdictions the board of directors exercises wide authority over school affairs in the district.

---

[49] The school district is used in 26 states. In the other states, 9 utilize the township, and 12, the county as the basic unit. In Delaware the state serves as the unit.

It manages the school properties, levies the taxes for school support, purchases supplies and equipment, arranges transportation for pupils, and hires the teachers and employees.

Today in many of the states, much greater supervision is being exercised by state authorities over school administration and operations. State laws have vested in the state superintendent of public instruction or state boards of education authority to certify eligibility of teachers and standardize courses of study. Most of the states have also found it necessary to provide greater financial support both for supplementing local revenues and for equalizing educational opportunities in poorer districts.

With respect to urban planning, the functions of the school district and authority of the school administration have important implications. Even though the school system is operated as a unit of government legally independent from that of the city, no comprehensive plan can be complete without taking into account the educational needs and requirements and the aims and objectives of educational policy.

THE PROBLEMS OF METROPOLITAN GOVERNMENT

The governmental structure in highly urbanized areas cannot be fully appreciated from a mere description of the legal nature and characteristics of each unit of government performing functions within the area. In order to understand the problem of governing the metropolitan community, it is necessary to examine the functioning of the various units of government in relation to one another. It is the purpose of the following discussion to point out some of the most important of these relationships, to indicate some of the principal problems of metropolitan government, and to evaluate certain proposed solutions to the problems.

Today, millions of residents in the United States live in densely populated suburbs near every large city but not legally a part of it. These suburban areas are, by economic and social ties, components of a single urban community with essentially the same needs for public services and governmental controls as the areas lying within the city boundaries. Whatever developments take place within either area vitally affect the other. The government of metropolitan communities has been a matter of concern to students of municipal organization for more than a half century. Although much data have been gathered and many studies have been published with reference to such communities, very little has been accomplished toward making them function as integrated political units.[50]

Any program for promoting the orderly development of the central city, the nearby municipalities, or the unincorporated urban fringe must be based upon comprehensive planning which takes into account the needs and interests of the entire urban area. Even then, good planning may be defeated because of the difficulties encountered in effectuating the plan. In most instances governmental authority in the unincorporated metropolitan areas is exercised by a number of autonomous or semiautonomous governments, none of which has jurisdiction coinciding with the urbanized area and most of which have legal authority only to provide services for a single purpose. Thus, in addition to the problems normally faced by municipal corporations in carrying plans into effect, plan implementation in the urban fringe is further complicated by the problems of unsatisfactory political boundaries, inadequate governmental authority, and lack of means for coördinating action among the established units of government. While the problems discussed herein are normally accentuated in the large metropolitan areas, they are found in varying degrees even in most of the smaller urban communities.

CHARACTERISTICS OF METROPOLITAN AND URBAN COMMUNITIES

Except by definition, there is no clear line for determining when a particular area becomes a metropolis. One of its chief characteristics is high density of population. However, a metropolitan area has many other recognizable characteristics including the predominantly urban features of congestion, industrialization, mobile population, and a substantial degree of unity in its economic and social life. Quite commonly, but not always, the metropolitan area consists of one relatively large and dominant city and a number of nearby smaller satellite cities and unincorporated suburbs.[51] The metropolitan area may also

[50] For a very comprehensive study, see *The Government of Metropolitan Miami* (Chicago: Public Administration Service, 1954). See also *Report and Recommendations for the Eighty-Eighth Session of the General Assembly, State of Indiana,* Submitted by the Metropolitan Area Study Commission of Marion County (Indianapolis: November 1, 1952). See also *Metropolitan Seattle—The Shape We're In!* (Seattle: The Municipal League of Seattle and King County, 1955). See also *Government in the Metropolitan Seattle Area* (Seattle: Bureau of Governmental Research and Services, University of Washington, 1956), Report No. 133.

[51] United States Department of Commerce, Bureau of the Census, *The Growth of Metropolitan Districts in the United States: 1900–1940* (Washington, D.C.: U.S. Government Printing Office, 1947), p. 3.

include some adjacent rural and semirural areas which are tied socially and economically to the central city or its satellites.

Metropolitan and Urban Areas Defined. The Bureau of the Census has established a rather complicated formula which it uses to define what it calls a "standard metropolitan area." This area is defined in connection with each city of 50,000 or more population in 1950. Where two cities of 50,000 or more are located within 20 miles of each other, they are ordinarily classified within the same standard metropolitan area. The classification used by the Bureau of the Census embraces the county in which the city is located and may include contiguous counties if they qualify according to certain criteria concerned with (1) density of population and the character of the county as a place of work for nonagricultural workers, and (2) the social and economic integration with the central city.[52] Under this formula, the 1950 census designated 168 standard metropolitan areas containing a population of 83,929,863—or approximately 56 percent of all of the people of the United States.[53]

There are many urbanized areas other than those included within the "standard metropolitan areas." The Census Bureau definition of urban areas is also arbitrary. In general, the boundaries follow recognized physical features such as roads and streams, but not necessarily the boundaries of counties or other political units. According to the classifications used for the 1950 census of population, approximately two-thirds of the population of the United States live in urban areas. The urban population total was 96,467,686 as compared to the rural population of 54,229,675.

The Bureau of the Census distinguishes between urban and rural areas by defining urban territory to comprise (1) places of 2500 inhabitants or more incorporated as cities, boroughs, and villages, (2) the densely settled urban fringe, incorporated or unincorporated, around cities of 50,000 or more, (3) unincorporated places of 2500 inhabitants or more outside of any urban fringe, and (4) towns of 2500 inhabitants or more except in New England, New York, and Wisconsin where "towns" are simply minor civil divisions of counties. All other territory is considered to be rural.[54] For determining the

[52] United States Department of Commerce, Bureau of the Census *U.S. Census of Population* (Washington, D.C.: U.S. Government Printing Office, 1950), Vol. 1, Summary.

[53] As of January 1, 1957, there were 174 standard metropolitan areas.

[54] *Ibid.* See also International City Managers' Association, *The Municipal Year Book, 1954* (Chicago: 1954), p. 21.

area to be included in the urban fringe, the 1950 census included
(a) incorporated places of 2500 or more as determined by the 1940
census or subsequent censuses conducted prior to 1950, (b) incorporated places with fewer than 2500 inhabitants containing an area
with a concentration of 100 dwelling units or more with a density in
this concentration of 500 units or more per square mile, (c) unincorporated territory with at least 500 dwelling units per square mile,
(d) territory devoted to commercial, industrial, transportational, recreational, and other purposes functionally related to the central city,
(e) outlying noncontiguous areas, incorporated or unincorporated
having the required dwelling unit density located within one and
one-half miles of the central contiguous urban area measured along
the shortest connecting highway, and (f) other outlying areas within
one-half mile of noncontiguous areas which are within one and one-
half miles of the central contiguous area and which meet the minimum residential density rule. This population density established for
urban areas represents approximately 2000 persons per square mile,
and normally is the minimum found associated with a closely spaced
street pattern.[55]

Although the Bureau of the Census definitions of metropolitan
and urban areas are helpful for classifying population data and identifying urban characteristics, they may not always represent the most
appropriate areas for establishing metropolitan government. Boundaries for governmental units designed to perform functions on a
metropolitan basis will of necessity have to be determined with reference to a number of factors including (1) population density, (2)
social and economic integration, (3) service needs and demands, (4)
legal considerations, (5) political feasibility, and (6) effects upon the
economic base of the region.

The Chaos of Areas: Causes and Consequences. The history of
almost every metropolitan community has been that the governmental
machinery in the urban fringe has developed piecemeal to meet each
service demand as it arises without serious thought as to how the
organization relates to other local service needs or to the governmental structure of the community as a whole. To a considerable
degree, the explanation for the piecemeal approach can be found in
the motivations for suburban living. There are many reasons for the

[55] For a discussion of changes in metropolitan and urban definitions made for the
1950 census, see Housing and Home Finance Agency, *Population Growth in Standard
Metropolitan Areas 1900–1950 with an Explanatory Analysis of Urbanized Areas* (Washington, D.C.: U.S. Government Printing Office, 1953).

migration of residents to the suburbs. In some cases the motivation is economic. Often, home owners, businessmen, and industrialists locate in territory outside of the corporate limits in order to obtain real estate at lower costs or to secure the advantages of lower property assessments and lower tax rates. In some instances they are moved by a desire to get away from the restrictions of building regulations, zoning, and other forms of municipal government control. In other cases the reason is to find more desirable residential conditions including light, air, cleanliness, outdoor life, and less congestion.

As the suburban areas become more densely populated, there arises the demand for governmental services and regulations which are normally supplied by municipal corporations. However, since the suburban dweller moved to the suburbs to get out of the city, he is naturally reluctant to have the political authority of the city from which he migrated extended to embrace his new residence. Consequently, the tendency has been to turn to some other means of supplying the governmental services he needs. One of the devices most frequently employed is the single-purpose district. This is commonly used for supplying water, fire protection, drainage, sewage disposal, weed abatement, public health, and numerous other demands. Since such districts are ad hoc authorities for providing a particular service to a particular section of a larger urban area, there is rarely any correspondence in the boundaries of one district with that of others.

In many of our metropolitan communities, the number of units of government with overlapping boundaries has multiplied to such a point that there is created a virtual chaos of areas. Sometimes the boundaries of special districts may be the same as the city or county, but more commonly they embrace a smaller or larger area. While in general the boundaries of the county include more territory than the principal city, there are many cases where a city may cover more area than the county. In fact, a city may include the area of several counties. Sometimes the boundaries of a city and a county may be identical, as in the case where there has been a county-city consolidation. Quite frequently, the boundaries of a municipal school district are identical with those of a city, but very often the boundaries of the school district are larger. Generally speaking, the boundaries of one district are rarely established with reference to others. History shows that boundaries once established are very difficult to change.

Government under these conditions is carried out by a bewildering jumble of authorities.[56] Such a system of governmental organization produces many disastrous consequences. It causes confusion to the voter because of numerous elections, usually with long ballots. The opportunity for real popular control is lessened and the rule of the entrenched politician is favored. Problems of administration and finance are greatly complicated because of problems of legal jurisdiction and lack of coördinating governmental machinery. Whereas the total cost of governmental services tends to increase with the multiplicity of jurisdictions, the efficiency of services tends to decrease due to the lower quality of personnel, duplication but inadequacy of proper equipment, lack of understanding of proper techniques, and the costly duplication of procedures. The overall result is that suburban residents soon find, not only that their governmental structure is extremely complex, but also that in order to secure the services they need, their property assessments and tax rates become higher than those within the city limits.

The Need for More Effective Metropolitan Government. The problem of areas has significance in the performance of almost every governmental function. As a general proposition, each unit of local government has responsibility for the welfare of only those inhabitants who dwell within its respective boundaries. Legal jurisdiction is normally coextensive with the boundary limits. However, programs for the development of highways, airports, transit systems, and many other improvements and facilities are of concern for the whole metropolitan region. Furthermore, the pollution of streams, the spread of fire, the creation of nuisances from obnoxious odors, smoke, and noise, the blighting effects of uncontrolled land use, the movement of people, and the need for utility services do not respect political boundaries. To cope with such problems there is a need to devise some kind of governmental machinery which will be more effective for formulating and executing public policies on a metropolitan area level. Divided responsibility among the numerous governmental units has failed to produce a workable scheme for securing the facilities and services which government is required to provide.[57]

The difficulties encountered because of the profusion of authori-

[56] An excellent discussion of the problem of metropolitan areas and the record of solutions is contained in a recent publication by the Council of State Governments. See John C. Bollens, *The States and the Metropolitan Problem* (Chicago: The Council of State Governments, 1956).

[57] Philadelphia Housing Association, Citizens' Council on City Planning, *Organization for Metropolitan Planning* (Philadelphia: October, 1949), p. 2.

ties and the confusion of boundaries have led students of government and administration to suggest various plans for achieving greater governmental responsibility and more efficient management of governmental affairs in metropolitan areas. Most of these proposals have met with certain drawbacks and none has as yet had universal acceptance. Finding an acceptable solution which will provide the necessary authority over the entire metropolitan area, and, at the same time, preserve the interests of local autonomy for each identifiable area is one of the most immediate and pressing problems of local government today.

Solutions to the Problem of Metropolitan Government

An examination of population statistics gives no hope that the urban-rural fringe problem will grow less serious in the near future. Between 1940 and 1950 the population of the suburban areas increased 35 percent, while at the same time the population of the central cities increased only 13 percent. The overall national rate was 14.5 percent. Thus, the suburban growth was almost two and one-half times the national rate, while the central city grew at a rate below the national average. Many of the suburban residents earn their living and maintain their recreational and cultural ties in the central city. This situation has added to the financial burdens of the full-time residents of the central city, since the increased costs of government attributable to this mobile population are not shared by the part-time suburban residents.

Taxation. The impact of the suburbs upon the central city is manifested in a number of ways. Among the most obvious of these is the increased traffic congestion creating demands for new streets and highways, additional parking facilities, and improved means of traffic control. Supplying these needs entails heavy expenditures. At the same time, the financial position of the central city is weakened because of the fact that with the flight to the suburbs, real property in certain districts tends to deteriorate.[58] Where the deterioration has a blighting effect, the city not only suffers a tax loss but also may incur future costs of redevelopment.

[58] Suburban migration may also result in a shift of control of city politics and thereby have an important effect on municipal policies due to the fact that suburban living quite commonly has its strongest appeal to persons in the higher economic groups. See Doris D. Reed and Thomas H. Reed, *The Cincinnati Area Must Solve Its Metropolitan Problems* (Cincinnati: Stephen H. Wilder Foundation, Public Affairs Division, 1953), pp. 8–9.

Many students of municipal government are of the opinion that the so-called "daylight citizens" should carry part of the financial burdens which they help to create. Because of the fact that the political boundaries generally limit the taxing jurisdiction of the city, no system of taxation has been devised which seems to be entirely satisfactory for this purpose. Municipal retail sales taxes do not always achieve the desired result and frequently tend to encourage shopping centers to locate outside the city boundaries. One type of tax that has frequently been urged and which has been used with some success is an income tax on payrolls which is levied upon residents and nonresidents whose earnings are allocable to the central city.[59] The justification for such a tax is that it is levied for the privilege given to nonresidents as well as residents of the opportunity of earning a living within the city. Such a tax is found in at least four states: Pennsylvania, Ohio, Kentucky, and Missouri.[60] It seems apparent, however, that the solution to the urban fringe problem is not to be found in any device which sets the central city and the suburban area in opposition to each other. The only sound approach is one which will lead to a harmonious working relationship through a proper integration of all functional responsibilities of government for the area as a whole.

Annexation. It is generally conceded that the municipal corporation has proved to be the most satisfactory type of political organization for providing local government services in urbanized areas. On first thought, it would seem, therefore, that the simplest and most logical means of eliminating the profusion of governments and the confusion of boundaries would be simply to extend the legal boundaries of the city to include all the outlying urbanized territory. By such action the powers of the municipality would become operative to perform all necessary municipal functions throughout the entire metropolitan area.

Although many annexations are constantly taking place, unfortunately this device has not proved to be a practical solution to the metropolitan problem.[61] The lag between the expansion of territorial boundaries and the growth of population could be illustrated by the experience of virtually every large city. For example, between 1920

[59] Robert A. Sigafoos, "Municipal Finance and Metropolitan Areas," *Public Management*, Vol. 35, p. 127, June, 1953. A tax on nonresidents only would seem to be unconstitutional on grounds of discrimination.

[60] *Ibid.*

[61] *The Municipal Year Book, 1954*, op. cit., pp. 41-49.

and 1950, the population of the Seattle metropolitan district increased from 347,955 to 660,098 or 90 percent, while at the same time the population of the city of Seattle increased from 315,312 to 467,591 or 48 percent. During this same 30-year period, Seattle's area increased by only 2.45 square miles or 3.4 percent.[62] In 1953 Seattle annexed 15.29 square miles, which was the second largest annexation in the United States during that year. The largest annexation was by Tampa, Florida, which added 46 square miles. Only two other cities, Midland, Michigan, and El Paso, Texas, annexed more than 10 square miles during 1953.[63] In 1955 Kansas City annexed 48 square miles, El Paso 27 square miles, Palm Springs 15 square miles, and Corpus Christi 14 square miles. For the most part, however, annexations have been small or nonexistent.

The history of annexation has been one of sporadic, piecemeal extensions, resulting in annexations which were premature in some cases and too late for effective planning in others. Very rarely have they been carried out as a part of a comprehensive plan for the whole metropolitan community. Annexation efforts face many obstacles, ranging from militant opposition to complacent indifference. The greatest resistance to annexation has come from the fringe areas, particularly the wealthier suburbs.[64] Poorer districts which have been unable to provide the normal municipal services by other means are more likely to favor annexation. Many efforts toward annexation are defeated simply because the benefits are not properly explained. In any event, the residents of the fringe areas are usually in control of the decision since, in most jurisdictions, their approval is necessary to effect the merger.

From the point of view of the central city, a number of perplexing legal and policy matters are involved in the issues of annexation. The uneven distribution of population raises questions as to whether a plan for annexation should include only the built-up area or whether it should also include areas which will be developed in the near future. If the city fails to include the undeveloped area, many problems may arise from uncontrolled land use which will present serious difficulties when the territory eventually comes into the city. On the other hand, if the territory is annexed prematurely, the city may become involved in many financial difficulties in attempting to supply the

[62] Seattle City Planning Commission, *Growth by Annexations, City of Seattle 1869–1953* (Seattle: June 1, 1953), current planning research, No. 11, mimeo, 6 pp., p. 2.
[63] *The Municipal Year Book, 1954, op. cit.,* pp. 41–42.
[64] Schulz, *op. cit.,* p. 188.

service demands to the people in the sparsely settled area. It is a well-known fact that initially the annexation of purely residential areas constitutes a liability to the city since the cost of servicing these areas is considerably greater than the immediate yield the city receives from taxes or other income. This is not true, however, in the case of annexation that includes substantial business and industrial property.

Where the central city is surrounded by a number of small incorporated suburbs, the problem of annexation is more complicated. In some instances where this situation exists, the central city has "jumped across" or gone around the incorporated suburbs in taking in new territory. Generally speaking, legislatures have been very reluctant to establish procedures which would let one incorporated municipality annex another incorporated area. The procedure by which two municipal corporations may be joined is known as consolidation. In deference to the spirit of local self-government, the process of consolidation is usually more complicated.

There are also many complicated problems involved in annexing areas which include school districts and certain special districts. Many of these districts have established bonded indebtedness or have incurred other long-term obligations. Some of them own considerable property and equipment. Under such conditions, the question must be resolved as to whether these obligations should be liquidated and the property owners in the annexed area be placed under the same tax base as other taxpayers of the city, or whether special obligations should be carried by property in the area annexed. Sometimes the reverse situation presents a problem. The city annexing the area may have outstanding obligations for capital improvements incurred many years prior to annexation. The question then arises as to whether or not the residents in the newly acquired area should assume a proportionate share of all the obligations of the central city. Obviously, tax administration becomes much simpler if all residents can be placed on the same tax base.

In most states the annexation must be initiated by petition of a certain percentage of the voters in the territory proposed to be annexed and approved by the voters in the territory at general or special elections. Quite commonly, the consent of the city is given by the favorable action of its legislative body. However, the rules of procedure vary considerably from state to state.

In an effort to facilitate timely action, the legislature of the state of Tennessee took steps during the 1955 session to liberalize the procedure for annexation by permitting municipal boundaries to be extended by ordinance as well as by referendum.[65] This statute is aimed at accomplishing annexations at times most advantageous to the city and the entire urban community.[66] An interesting companion measure passed at the same session is designed to act as a brake upon the formation of small satellite municipalities near the boundaries of an existing incorporated city. The law establishes generally a minimum population of 200 as a requisite for incorporation, but incorporations within three miles of an existing incorporated city or town require a minimum of 500 inhabitants.[67]

One of the most unique and successful procedures for annexation is that of the state of Virginia. In Virginia, annexation is entirely a matter of judicial procedure in which the central city sues for the additional territory it desires to acquire. The determination is thus made according to the logic and proof which are introduced in the court. No election is held at any stage of the proceedings. Final decision is a judicial determination to be made in accordance with certain criteria provided by statute. If by these criteria the court finds that annexation is in the best interest of all concerned, it will approve the annexation and establish the boundary lines. This procedure would seem to offer more hopes for solving the problem of metropolitan government by annexation than the procedures of most other states.[68]

Extraterritoriality. Although the general rule is that cities may exercise jurisdiction only within their territorial boundaries, most states have granted municipalities extraterritorial powers for certain specified purposes. For the most part, these powers are conferred to enable the city (1) to acquire property and construct facilities outside its territorial boundaries, such as water reservoirs, sewage disposal plants, and parks, in order to provide services to the inhabitants of the city, (2) to provide services such as water supply, fire protection, and sanitary services to inhabitants in the adjacent unincorporated areas, and (3) to regulate individual conduct and property uses in

[65] Chap. 113, Public Acts of 1955, State of Tennessee.

[66] Joe B. Whitlow, Jr., Annexation Made Easier," *The Tennessee Planner,* Tennessee State Planning Commission, Vol. XV, No. 5, April, 1955.

[67] Chap. 295, Public Acts of 1955, State of Tennessee.

[68] For a current discussion of the procedures and problems involved under the Virginia system of annexation, see Chester W. Bain, "Terms and Conditions of Annexation Under the 1952 Statute," *Virginia Law Review,* Vol. 41, No. 8, pp. 1129–1158, December, 1955. See also Chester W. Bain, "Annexation: Virginia's Not-So-Judicial System," *Public Administration Review,* Vol. XV, No. 4, pp. 251–261, Autumn, 1955.

the adjacent unincorporated area in the interest of promoting the public health, safety, morals, and general welfare of both the city and the outlying area.

There are many cases where it becomes necessary for a city to go outside its corporate boundaries in order to provide adequate services for its own inhabitants. It is quite common for states to enact enabling legislation authorizing cities to acquire property beyond their corporate limits and construct water supply reservoirs, pipe lines, parks, bridges, ferry docks, and other facilities to enable them to serve their own inhabitants. Such powers must be conferred by the state as cities have no inherent extraterritorial powers. However, where extraterritorial powers to construct public works are granted, the power of eminent domain to carry out the grant is usually inferred.[69] Powers such as these are essentially for the benefit of the city and may be of little significance in solving the governmental problems of the entire metropolitan area.

In a number of metropolitan communities where integrated government has not been achieved, central cities have extended water mains, sewer lines, fire protection, garbage collection, library, and other facilities to provide municipal services to the suburban dweller. Usually this is done under contract with individuals or special districts. Such services are usually furnished at higher service charges than are paid by the city resident, but often at a substantially lower cost than the suburbanite would pay if he were subject to all taxes of the city. Such arrangements have worked out quite satisfactorily with respect to services for which a specific charge is made. For those which are normally financed out of general taxes, such as fire protection, there are legal and practical difficulties involved.

The extension of municipal services is often opposed on the ground that it is only a partial solution to the problem of metropolitan government and frequently tends to delay a more satisfactory solution, to the detriment of all concerned. Suburban dwellers who receive most of the municipal services without incorporation are not likely to be enthusiastic about annexation or some other solution.[70] Unreasonable delay in working out an integrated metropolitan government is likely to spell future economic waste and lower amenities of

---

[69] Russell W. Maddox, "Cities Step Over the Line," *National Municipal Review*, Vol. XLIV, No. 2, p. 82, February, 1955.

[70] Victor C. Hobday, "Should Cities Provide Services to Suburbs or Extend City Limits," *Tennessee Government*, Vol. IX, No. 3, p. 1, November–December, 1950.

living in terms of poorly planned streets, improperly located parks and playgrounds, and unregulated property uses.

Extraterritorial extensions of the police power are principally of two kinds: (1) regulations which are imposed upon persons outside the city limits as a condition to the exercise of some business activity or privilege within the city, and (2) regulations which are not imposed with respect to exercising any privilege within the city. The first type of regulation presents fewer legal complications since, in a strict sense, it is not an extraterritorial regulation. It is commonly employed with respect to inspecting dairies, slaughterhouses, bakeries, and various food processing plants whose owners propose to sell their products within the city.

As a general rule, extraterritorial grants of police power are strictly construed against the municipality. The Constitution of the State of Washington, for example, authorizes any county, city, town, or township to enforce, within its limits, all such local police, sanitary, and other regulations as are not in conflict with general laws.[71] In construing this provision the Supreme Court of Washington in the case of *Brown v. Cle Elum*,[72] invalidated a statute enacted by the legislature authorizing cities to enact penal ordinances operative beyond their territorial limits for the protection of their water supply. The court held that the words "within its limits" acted as a restriction upon the legislature to grant extraterritorial police power to cities.

Extraterritorial police power has been granted by different states for a number of purposes. Baltimore, for example, was given power by the state legislature to prevent the introduction of contagious or infectious diseases within 3 miles on land or 15 miles on water. Chicago has authority to establish regulations with respect to noxious trades within 1 mile of the city boundaries. The state of Indiana has authorized the cities to adopt measures to protect watercourses for 10 miles beyond their boundaries in the interest of preventing streams from becoming polluted. They also have been given jurisdiction 4 miles beyond their borders for the purpose of locating certain industries, preventing the depositing of garbage or other waste materials, abating nuisances, regulating the location of cemeteries, establishing quarantine regulations, and preventing vice and immorality.[73]

[71] Article XI, Section 11, *Constitution of the State of Washington*.
[72] 145 Wash. 588, 590, 261 Pac. 112 (1927). See also Ernest H. Campbell and Sidney Coleman, *Licensing by Washington Cities* (Seattle: Bureau of Governmental Research and Services, University of Washington, December, 1951), Report No. 117, p. 40.
[73] Kneier, *op. cit.*, p. 365.

Cities have frequently been given authority to establish regulations controlling subdivisions outside their territorial boundaries. This type of control has been of considerable value in preventing developments of a type which might constitute a financial burden to the city upon annexation or result in building which is not in harmony with the comprehensive plan. In a few jurisdictions, cities have been granted extraterritorial zoning powers to prevent the development of inharmonious land uses in their urban fringe areas. Omaha, Nebraska, for example, may zone for a distance of 3 miles beyond its corporate limits. Some cities have been given zoning authority extending for as much as 5 miles beyond their boundaries. To date, however, extraterritorial zoning has had only limited application.[74]

One of the major difficulties encountered in solving metropolitan problems by extraterritorial jurisdiction comes from the fact that people in the central city are usually not willing to have their tax money spent for purposes outside the boundaries of the city. Since cities do not usually have any means of levying taxes against persons residing in the suburbs, the matter of finance often defeats solutions by this means even though practical and constitutional. On the other hand, persons living in the suburban area usually do not look with favor upon controls being exercised over them by the central city because of the fact that they have no voice in determining policies or methods of administration. Extraterritorial powers are usually regarded by them as undemocratic in principle. Opposition on this ground seems likely to limit their use.

Special Districts. As has previously been indicated, the single-purpose special district has been utilized extensively in a number of states as a means of meeting the governmental problems of metropolitan areas. Such districts are perhaps the least understood of all units of local government. Between 1940 and 1950 the number of special districts in the United States increased by 48 percent. The total number in existence in 1952 as tabulated by the Bureau of the Census was 12,319. Of this total, one-half are found in six states: Illinois 1546, California 1390, New York 968, Missouri 886, Kansas 724, and Washington 644.[75]

Special districts are generally of two types: (1) the quasi-municipal

[74] See pp. 370–373.
[75] United States Department of Commerce, Bureau of the Census, *Governments in the United States in 1952*, op. cit., p. 4. These districts are in addition to school districts which are in a sense also single-purpose special districts.

district, and (2) the metropolitan district.[76] The quasi-municipal type is usually smaller in size and organized to provide a single service for a particular segment of the unincorporated area. The metropolitan district is usually larger and is sometimes organized for multiple purposes. Examples of the metropolitan district are the Metropolitan Water District of Southern California, the Sanitary District of Chicago, the Massachusetts Metropolitan Transit District, and the Seattle Port District.

Special districts were first utilized to carry out functions which existing units of government were not well suited to provide, for example, the drainage of swampy lands.[77] Today the special district has come to be used to provide almost every conceivable type of public service including those related to fire protection, water supply, lighting, utility sewer operation, hospitals, airports, weed control, ferry operation, mosquito abatement, public health, libraries, parks, police protection, roads, and many others. The profusion of special districts in some areas has become so great that students of government regard it, not as a possible solution to a governmental problem, but an evil in itself for which a cure must be found.[78]

Although the special district has proved to be quite effective in performing certain specific functions, it has failed as a device for unified metropolitan government largely because of the extreme difficulty of integrating the numerous functions performed by these autonomous authorities. While a fairly good case may be made for the creation of a special district as a temporary means of meeting urgent needs of a metropolitan community pending the development of more effective metropolitan government, the fact is that once established their existence tends to become permanent. Job holders and others with vested interests in their continuance are almost certain to oppose their abolition. Residents of the area, because of inertia or persuaded by arguments that the special district provides the most democratic means of local self-government, are likely to resist any changes in the system in the direction of more integrated metropolitan government.

Reforms in County Government. Among the proposals which have been made for solving the metropolitan problem is that of giv-

[76] Special districts are referred to by other names such as single-purpose districts, ad hoc authorities, and special authorities.

[77] Kirk H. Porter, "A Plague of Special Districts," *National Municipal Review*, Vol. 22, No. 11, pp. 544–547, 574, November, 1933.

[78] Kneier, *op. cit.*, p. 364.

ing the county powers to perform services of a municipal nature in unincorporated urban areas.[79] While this proposal might afford a solution in counties which are predominantly urban in character, a number of problems are presented if the county has wide variations in population density and an absence of social and economic integration. If these diversities exist, uniform services cannot be provided efficiently and economically throughout the county.

Even with respect to counties where uniformity of function does not constitute a serious problem, little progress has been made in conferring corporate powers on the county. This is perhaps due largely to the traditional concept of the county as a political subdivision of the state for carrying out state governmental policy rather than as a municipal corporation for providing local services. Many persons believe that those activities which are municipal in character should be performed by municipal governments and oppose transferring municipal functions to counties. Today, however, there are some changes taking place with respect to the role of the county. In a number of jurisdictions, counties are now enabled to adopt charters of their own choosing and in some they are vested with other attributes of corporate status.

In 1953, the legislature of the state of California enacted a statute which specifically recognizes the duty of counties as instrumentalities of state government to furnish extended governmental services to densely populated unincorporated areas.[80] The legislature justified its action by citing the unprecedented growth of population in such areas and in the belief that the residents should have made available to them reasonable alternative methods of securing governmental services. The establishment of a county service area may be instituted by the Board of Supervisors on their own initiative or upon petition signed by 10 percent of the registered voters in the territory proposed to be included. A county service area may be established to provide one or more services including police protection, structural fire protection, parks and recreation, and any other governmental services counties are authorized by law to perform. The act provides that taxes

[79] For a well-considered plan for the integration of county and municipal functions, see *Plan of Improvement for the Governments of Atlanta and Fulton County, Georgia,* Report and Recommendations of the Local Government Commission of Fulton County (Atlanta, Georgia: January, 1950). This plan went into effect in 1952.

[80] Chap. 858, Laws of California, 1953. Chap. 2.2, Part 2 of Division 2 of Title 3 of the Government Code.

shall be levied within such areas in an amount sufficient to pay for the extended services.

The slowness of counties to respond to the needs for local services is also due to the unsatisfactory organization of county government and the lack of confidence that voters seem to have in the efficiency of county administration. For the most part, county government is highly decentralized with administrative responsibility divided among an elective board and numerous elected officers. While such a system may be suitable to the needs of a simple agricultural economy, it is not adequate to cope with the complex problems of a metropolitan community.[81] Consequently, many persons feel that reorganization of county government along modern municipal lines is a condition precedent to any statutory authorization conferring powers upon counties as a means of achieving metropolitan integration.[82]

Even if the objections suggested are overcome, there is the further obstacle of boundaries. Since county boundaries have been established arbitrarily, it is a rare instance if they ever coincide with the metropolitan area. Change of county boundaries is usually a difficult process. In the event that the metropolitan area lies in two or more counties, there exists a difficult problem of integrating services and coördinating policies. Even where the entire metropolitan area is within a single county, some machinery must be developed to insure integration between the corporate county and the municipalities and other units of government comprising the metropolitan area.

One of the plans frequently suggested for achieving integrated county-municipal government is that of city-county consolidation. The purpose of this plan is to reduce the number of units of government and avoid the duplication of functions. Where city and county are consolidated, the city-county then performs all the responsibilities of a county and a city within the areas consolidated. Within the area of consolidation this plan offers some very distinct advantages. However, a consolidated city and county must also operate within legal boundaries, and eventually many fringe area problems tend to develop as they do around the boundaries of any municipality. When such a development occurs, the obstacles to effectuating territorial expansion are usually greater than with cities generally. The procedure of extending county boundaries in most jurisdictions is much more

[81] Edward W. Weidner, *The American County: Patchwork of Boards* (New York: National Municipal League, 1946), pp. 15–21.

[82] Thomas H. Reed, "Hope for Suburbanitis," *National Municipal Review*, Vol. 39, No. 11, pp. 542–553, December, 1950.

complicated than is the procedure for annexation of territory to a municipality.

Another type of problem is involved if the area consolidated includes a considerable amount of territory which is rural in character. In such instances it is not practical to attempt to provide uniform services throughout the corporate limits. If citizens located in different parts of the city-county are given differential treatment, it generally follows that differential tax rates should apply.[83] Unless authorized by the constitution, this may give rise to legal as well as policy questions. The city and parish of Baton Rouge appears to have made considerable progress in resolving this problem by providing for the classification of areas within the city-parish as urban, industrial, and rural.[84] Incorporated areas are permitted to continue their corporate status and even annex adjacent territory. Differential tax rates are provided in rural and commercial areas in recognition of the difference in obligations assumed by the corporation for carrying out municipal services in each of these areas.

In some instances, city-county consolidation has constituted a separation of that part of the county which is regarded as identified with the interests of the city with which it is consolidated. This is the case with the city-counties of Baltimore, San Francisco, St. Louis, Denver, and a few others. The State of Virginia is unique among the states in providing that all first-class cities (over 10,000 population) are at the same time counties.[85] The Virginia statutes establish procedures by which a city may annex territory from an adjoining county.

Metropolitan State Agencies.   In a few metropolitan areas, state agencies have been used with considerable success for performing functions on a metropolitan basis. Among these are the Metropolitan District Commission, Boston, Massachusetts, and the Port of New York Authority.[86] Boston was the first city in the United States to become the center of a metropolitan area. By the middle of the nineteenth century a number of problems had arisen which seemed to necessitate joint action by local units of government. The need for coördinated action centered primarily around the problems of drain-

[83] For one of the most recent and interesting proposals involving this principle, see *Plan of Metropolitan Government for Nashville and Davidson County* (Nashville: Nashville and Davidson County Planning Commissions, October, 1956).

[84] Sec. 1.08, Baton Rouge, Louisiana Charter, City and Parish Consolidation, 1947.

[85] Raymond B. Pinchbeck, "City-County Separation in Virginia," *National Municipal Review*, Vol. 29, No. 7, pp. 467–472, July, 1940.

[86] The operation of the Port of New York Authority is discussed in connection with interstate compacts.

age, sewage disposal, water pollution, parks and recreation, and the supply of water. As early as 1868 special boards and commissions were established to study these problems.[87] As a result of a constitutional amendment adopted in 1918, a general administrative reorganization took place under which the Metropolitan District Commission was created to take over the powers, duties, and responsibilities of the Metropolitan Parks and Water Districts and the Metropolitan Sewage Commission. The jurisdiction of the Commission covers an area of 472 square miles embracing an aggregate of 43 cities and towns, including Boston. The Commission is administered by a commissioner and four associate commissioners, all of whom must be residents of the district at the time of their appointment and one of whom must be a resident of Boston.

The general work of the Commission is carried out through four divisions, including park engineer, park maintenance division, water division, and sewage division. Each division is administered by a director who also serves as Chief Engineer of the Division. The work of each division is concerned with construction, operation, and maintenance. The expenses of the Commission are paid initially by the state. These are then assessed back to the various municipalities making up the district for which the expenses were incurred. The proportion of the cost to be paid by each municipality is determined by the Commission, under a formula prescribed by law.

Judged by results, the Metropolitan District Commission has served as a useful device in solving a number of metropolitan problems. Its work is reflected in the fine park system and the solution of the critical sewage and water problems. The principal criticism which has been directed at this type of solution is that, being a state-created agency, it is removed from local control. Those who have analyzed the situation seem to be of the opinion that the withdrawal of such functions from the political control of local government was inevitable in working out a solution to the problem that confronted the Boston Metropolitan Area. Nevertheless, the matter of local control is an important factor in establishing any system of metropolitan government, and failure to give proper recognition to it is likely to defeat any proposals for a unified area approach in most communities.

Federated Metropolitan Government. A plan which appears to

[87] Sanford S. Farness, *Organizations for Metropolitan Planning*, Citizens' Council on City Planning and the Philadelphia Housing Association (Philadelphia: October, 1949), p. 23.

offer the most hopeful means of securing political integration within metropolitan areas and at the same time preserving the identity and local autonomy of the constituent local units of government is municipal federalism. The federal plan is a compromise solution to the problem of unified governmental control over the entire metropolitan area. Like all compromises, it has its advantages and disadvantages. Under the federal plan, certain powers of the cities and other local units are transferred to a metropolitan corporation which is authorized by law to carry out governmental functions of a regional character. Other powers continue to be exercised by each of the local units of government. The boundaries of the metropolitan corporation normally would be coextensive with the metropolitan community and should be easily altered to conform to changes in population and character of the area.

One of the earlier applications of the federal principle is in the government of London where the functional responsibilities are divided among the administrative county of London and 27 Metropolitan Boroughs.[88] In the United States, an approach to the federal plan is found in New York where each of the boroughs exercises certain responsibilities with respect to the maintenance of streets, sewers, and certain other facilities and the administration of the building code. Actually, however, the New York system is more in the nature of an administrative district plan than a federal plan, since policy decisions are formulated by the city government with decentralization limited to administrative matters.[89]

The most recent adoption and perhaps best example of a federated metropolitan government is that of Toronto, Canada. The Toronto plan which became effective on January 1, 1954, is a federation of 13 cities and is known as the "Municipality of Metropolitan Toronto." It serves a community of 1,250,000 persons.[90] The Metropolitan Council, which administers the metropolitan government, consists of 12 representatives of the city of Toronto and 12 suburban representatives. Area-wide functions, such as assessment, transit, and planning are entrusted to the metropolitan municipality. Metropolitan

---

[88] J. H. Warren, *The English Local Government System* (London: Allen and Unwin, Ltd., 1946), Appendix A.

[89] Schulz, *op. cit.*, p. 198.

[90] Winston W. Crouch, "Metropolitan Government in Toronto," *Public Administration Review*, Vol. 14, No. 2, pp. 85–95, Spring, 1954.

The Municipal Year Book, 1954, op. cit., pp. 37–38.

Frederick G. Gardiner, *The Municipality of Metropolitan Toronto—A New Answer to Metropolitan Area Problems*, an address to the American Bar Association Convention (Boston: August 25, 1953).

roads and arterial highways are financed on the basis of 50 percent by the metropolitan government and 50 percent by the Province of Ontario. As of January 1, 1954, the Metropolitan Corporation acquired from the local municipalities all the assets which are to be used by the Metropolitan Corporation for metropolitan services. No compensation is paid to the municipalities other than the assumption by the Metropolitan Corporation of the outstanding debenture debts in respect of such assets.

With respect to certain functions, such as water supply and sewage disposal, there is a division of authority between the existing incorporated cities and the metropolitan government. With respect to water, for example, the metropolitan corporation became the owner of all pumping stations, treatment facilities, reservoirs, and trunk mains used to supply water in the 13 municipalities. Under the new federal plan, the metropolitan government distributes water to the municipalities at wholesale through meters at their borders. Each city then handles the retail sale and distribution within its corporate limits. By a similar arrangement the Metropolitan Corporation owns the sewage treatment plants and sewer trunk mains and accepts the sewage from each of the 13 municipalities for treatment and disposal. Local sewage collection systems and collection charges are under the control of each municipality. Local water distribution, sewage collection systems, local public works, police and fire protection, unemployment relief, local planning, streets that are not included in a metropolitan network, general administration, and administration of certain grants-in-aid from the Ontario government are left to the constituent cities. The County of York still provides certain services such as those concerned with roads and law enforcement in certain areas of the county.[91]

While the federal plan has attracted a great deal of interest, it has received little practical application. In the minds of some persons it appears to be too complicated. In many respects it fails to satisfy the proponents of unified metropolitan government, while at the same time it antagonizes others who strongly support the idea of local determination and control. On the other hand, it is argued by the

[91] Compare the federated plan for metropolitan Miami, Florida. See *The Government of Metropolitan Miami* (Chicago: Public Administration Service, 1954). Under this plan government of Dade County would be abolished and county functions assumed by the proposed metropolitan government. A constitutional amendment, approved at the 1956 general election, permits Dade County to adopt a home rule charter to effectuate this plan. Compare also enabling legislation of State of Washington, Ch. 213, Laws of Washington, 1957.

supporters of municipal federation that the federal idea carries with it the merits of centralization along with the advantages of decentralization. Although it is certain that the plan will not satisfy the wishes of those who favor complete integration, it well deserves study and consideration as a feasible compromise of conflicting sectional and jurisdictional interests.

Under the federal principle each major unit of government would simply become a component part of a larger federated city and would have representation on the federal legislative body which would set policies in affairs of metropolitan interest. Each local unit would continue to have its own separate government and would retain authority over local affairs. One of the chief difficulties is to find a feasible plan of representation and a satisfactory method of selecting the governing body. If each unit of government is granted representation on the basis of population, the legislative body is almost certain to be unwieldy.

Another major difficulty in applying the federal principle is to determine what functions should remain under control of the component units and what should be vested in the metropolitan government. In resolving this question many compromises may have to be made in order to satisfy the various component units of the federation. Unless adequate powers are conferred upon the metropolitan government, the federal principle would have little value as a solution to the metropolitan problem.[92] Reluctance of localities to surrender any powers they now possess to accomplish this objective would seem to constitute a serious obstacle.

Voluntary Intergovernmental Coöperation. For certain purposes, government in metropolitan areas may be integrated through voluntary coöperative arrangements of two or more units of government. Coöperative action assumes a variety of forms and may be based upon informal understandings or upon formal agreements.[93] A number of states have enacted enabling legislation specifically authorizing coöperative undertakings. The state of Wisconsin, for example, authorizes any city, village, town, county, or school district to enter into agreements with any other unit of government for the joint or coöperative exercise of any power or duty required or authorized by statute and may provide a plan for prorating any expenditure involved. This

---

[92] Kneier, op. cit., p. 361.

[93] For recommendations as to state enabling legislation, see Council of State Governments, *Suggested State Legislation, Program for 1956* (Chicago: Council of State Governments, October, 1955), pp. 24–30.

statute would appear to be sufficiently broad to permit two or more municipalities to do jointly virtually anything which they are empowered to do separately.[94] In addition to this general statute, specific authority for coöperative action has been granted in a number of fields including airports, fire protection, hospitals, health, libraries, parks and recreation, personnel, building construction, sewerage service, street construction, harbor development, and others. A very similar grant of powers is found in Minnesota under the "Joint Powers Act." [95]

Studies which have been made recently indicate that the interjurisdictional agreement is a device more extensively used than is generally supposed. In Wisconsin, nearly all cities and villages maintaining paid or volunteer fire departments either provide outside fire service to neighboring towns or have formal or informal reciprocal fire protection arrangements with nearby municipalities.[96] A survey of the Philadelphia metropolitan area revealed that 44 percent of the municipalities on the Pennsylvania side and 31 percent on the New Jersey side are parties to road pacts, and almost one-fifth of the municipalities are parties to pacts concerned with sewage disposal.[97] In the Los Angeles metropolitan area wherein 45 incorporated cities operate in close proximity with each other, coöperative arrangements are largely responsible for maintaining harmonious relations in many fields of activity.[98]

Intergovernmental coöperation is usually characterized by one of the following types of action, (1) joint enterprise, (2) furnishing services by one unit of government to others, (3) mutual aid, or (4) parallel action. Joint enterprise has often been quite successful in providing public services such as milk inspection, meat inspection, and other types of health and sanitary functions,[99] and in matters such as the centralized purchasing of supplies and materials. For this purpose two or more units of government enter into an agreement to

[94] "Joint Municipal Services," *The Municipality*, Vol. 50, No. 5, p. 93, May, 1955.
[95] "Intermunicipal Coöperation in Minnesota," *Information Service*, League of Minnesota Municipalities, February, 1953, 13 pp., mimeo.
[96] *The Municipality*, loc. cit.
[97] Jeptha J. Carrell, "Learning to Work Together," *National Municipal Review*, Vol. XLIII, No. 10, p. 526, November, 1954.
[98] Winston W. Crouch, *Metropolitan Los Angeles, A Study in Integration*, XV Intergovernmental Relations (Los Angeles: The Haynes Foundation, 1954), p. 107.
[99] See for example Joseph A. Hearst, *Milk Inspection and Milk Standards in King County* (Seattle: Bureau of Governmental Research and Services, University of Washington, October, 1947), Report No. 77.

employ a qualified individual or create a department to perform the necessary duties involved.

The rendering of services by one unit of government for other units of government is fairly common in supplying water, police services, tax collection, inspection services, or the disposal of sewage and refuse. Mutual aid which is based upon the principle of exchange of services has perhaps been used most extensively for providing reciprocal aid in fire fighting. The principle has many other possible applications for dealing with emergencies such as civil defense, floods, earthquakes, epidemics, and other disasters.[100]

Parallel action is quite commonly undertaken as a result of informal understandings rather than formal agreements. By enacting uniform regulations pertaining to such matters as zoning, building construction, and subdivisions, and by frequent conferences with respect to administrative policies, cities and counties may accomplish a great deal in the direction of promoting the most appropriate land use and preventing the development of substandard buildings and improper subdivisions which eventually might result in high costs of local government and low tax returns.[101]

Although voluntary coöperative action of one type or another offers numerous possibilities for integrating municipal functions in metropolitan areas, it is extremely unlikely that all governmental functions can be coördinated by such efforts. Even though there may be the desire on the part of all public agencies to coöperate, the problems of metropolitan areas appear to be too numerous and too complex to be solved effectively solely on a voluntary basis. Intergovernmental coöperation certainly should not be overlooked as a means of eliminating duplications of functions and in meeting specific problems pending the adoption of a more satisfactory solution.

Interstate Compacts. Metropolitan communities that lie within the boundaries of two or more states are faced with added legal and practical difficulties of integrating governmental functions. The 1950 census report disclosed that 23 of the standard metropolitan areas extend over state boundaries and an additional 28 border on state boundaries. Many municipalities located on or near the state border

---

[100] Assembly of the State of California, *Preliminary Report of the Assembly Interim Committee on Municipal and County Government Covering Fringe Area Problems in the County of Los Angeles*, January 17, 1953, p. 59.

[101] Assembly of the State of California, *Final Report of the Assembly Interim Committee on Municipal and County Government Covering Fringe Area Problems in the State of California*, March 27, 1953, p. 12.

have discovered to their dismay that the control of air and water pollution, the supplying of water, the disposal of sewage, and the construction of bridges and tunnels as well as the carrying out of numerous other local responsibilities have far-reaching interstate implications.[102] To some degree it has been possible for such municipalities to solve certain of these problems by voluntary coöperation.[103] Such arrangements, however, amount to only a piecemeal attack on the problem of functional integration. Any comprehensive approach requires the establishment of an agency clothed with authority to perform functions throughout the interstate metropolitan area. The creation of such an agency would necessitate agreement by each of the states concerned and the consent of Congress under the compact clause of the Federal Constitution.[104] Thus far the interstate compact has had rather limited use in creating agencies for metropolitan government. Among the most important of such agencies are the Port of New York Authority, the Water Front Commission of the Port of New York, and the Bi-State Development Agency of the Missouri-Illinois Metropolitan District.[105]

The Port of New York Authority was created in 1921 as the result of a series of problems which had grown out of differences between the states of New York and New Jersey over matters of boundaries and legal jurisdiction. The activities with which the Port Authority is concerned are primarily those which fall within the purview of all three levels of government: federal, state, and local. Among these are airport planning and water front and transportation development which must be coördinated with the Civil Aeronautics Administration, the Interstate Commerce Commission, and the Army Engineers. The planning and development of bridges and tunnels must be carried out in close coöperation with the highway departments of both states and with the municipalities located within the district.[106]

By terms of the compact and implementing statutes, the Port of New York Authority as the joint agency of the states of New York and New Jersey has the duty to coöperate with the municipalities of

102 Daniel R. Grant, "The Government of Interstate Metropolitan Areas," *The Western Political Quarterly*, Vol. VIII, No. 1, pp. 90–107, March, 1955.

103 Betty Tableman, *Governmental Organization of Metropolitan Areas* (Ann Arbor: University of Michigan Press, 1951), p. 39.

104 *Constitution of the United States of America*, Article I, Section 10.

105 There are other agencies created by compact which are concerned with metropolitan problems. These include the Delaware River Port Authority, the Delaware River Toll Bridge Commission, and the Philadelphia Port Authority. See *The Book of the States, 1954–1955* (Chicago: The Council of State Governments, 1954), pp. 16–39.

106 Farness, *op. cit.*, p. 18.

the Port District in the development of their land, sea, and air terminal facilities. The Authority functions under a board of directors made up of 12 commissioners appointed for six-year overlapping terms. The governors of each state appoint six commissioners respectively. Generally speaking, the board is free from direction or control by the states. However, the governors may exercise a veto over the action of any of the commissioners from their respective states. The Port of New York is not a taxing unit of government. It is a self-supporting agency financing itself through operating revenues. Revenue bonds issued for the purpose of constructing public improvements are retired from the revenue-producing projects. The revenue bonds are not backed by the states or their political subdivisions. The primary purpose of the Port of New York Authority is to operate interstate facilities and undertake promotional work relating to the development of the Port. It does not have regulatory powers.

In 1953 the states of New York and New Jersey, with the consent of Congress, entered into another compact creating a "Water Front Commission" having rather comprehensive regulatory powers over a number of phases of industry and labor management with the port district whose boundaries are identical with those of the Port of New York Authority. This commission was given power to finance its operations by imposing taxes upon employers in the regulated industries. This is the first instance of taxing powers being conferred upon an agency by interstate compact.[107] This method of financing may be utilized by the commission until such time as the legislatures of the respective states provide other means for its support. While the creation of the Water Front Commission was no doubt a practical expedient for providing certain police power controls which the Port of New York Authority was not empowered to provide, the adding of an independent layer of government for this purpose would seem, in principle, to be a step away from unified administration.

The Bi-State Development Agency of the Missouri-Illinois Metropolitan District was established by compact, signed by the State of Illinois and the State of Missouri in 1949, and ratified by Congress in 1950. The compact creates the "Missouri-Illinois Metropolitan District" and provides that it shall include the city of St. Louis, the counties of St. Louis, St. Charles, and Jefferson in Missouri, and the counties of Madison, St. Clair, and Monroe in Illinois. Within this district, the Bi-State Development Agency has both operational and

---

[107] *The Book of the States, 1954–1955*, op. cit., pp. 16–17.

advisory functions. With respect to the first, it is empowered to construct, maintain, and operate bridges, tunnels, airports, and terminal facilities. With respect to its advisory function, it is charged with the duty of making plans to be submitted to the communities within the district for streets, highways, parking areas, terminals, water supply, sewage and drainage facilities, recreational facilities, land use matters, and other matters in which joint action of the various communities is beneficial.[108] The Agency has no taxing powers and is specifically prohibited from taking any action which will affect the finances of any city, town, county, school district, or other governmental subdivisions. The Agency may charge and collect fees for the use of facilities owned and operated by it and may issue bonds upon the security of the revenues to be derived from its facilities and properties. It may also receive for its lawful activities contributions of moneys appropriated by municipalities, counties, state or other political subdivisions or agencies, or by the federal government or any federal agency.

The Agency is administered by a board of ten commissioners, five appointed by the governor of each state for five-year terms. The commissioners serve without pay. The Agency has taken steps to acquire ownership of existing Mississippi River bridges and has undertaken a number of comprehensive surveys relating to sewers, highways, public health, and harbor development.[109]

Perhaps one reason why the compact has not been used more extensively as a device for the integration of governmental functions in interstate metropolitan communities is the difficulty of securing ratification. Major questions of policy must be ironed out by the respective legislatures. This procedure is often tedious and long drawn out. State legislatures are reluctant to confer broad powers upon semiautonomous agencies over which they do not have final control. In addition, there is the task of securing the consent of Congress. Furthermore, the financing of the activities of an interstate agency and the enforcement of its policies often present serious difficulties. Thus, any solution by compact is likely to be slow, cumbersome, and uncertain both in negotiation and in operation. Nevertheless, the compact offers about the only feasible means of establishing metropolitan government over areas which lie within the geographical jurisdiction

---

[108] See Metropolitan Plan Association, *Guide Book 1954, Metropolitan St. Louis Area Development* (St. Louis: December, 1953), for recommended activities and proposals based on appraisals of metropolitan needs for improvement.

[109] *The Book of the States, 1954–1955, op. cit.,* pp. 34–35.

of more than one state and with respect to matters outside the scope of federal authority. For this reason, metropolitan communities which are harassed by the legal limitations of state boundaries may well give more serious attention to the practical use of the interstate compact.

General Considerations.   Basically the problem of government in metropolitan areas is one of providing adequate governmental machinery for performing on a metropolitan basis those functions which are area wide in scope and of leaving to the incorporated municipalities, the counties, and other major units of government, jurisdiction over those functions which can appropriately be carried out on a localized basis. Which of the various approaches may be most appropriate in a given community will depend upon their political acceptance and legal feasibility as well as the nature and extent of the governmental problems. The annexation or consolidation of all territory into one municipality offers the most completely unified plan for both policy making and administration. It seems quite certain, however, that this solution is not generally acceptable, at least by the majority of suburban residents. Perhaps, for most communities, some type of federal plan will represent the highest degree of unification that can be achieved through voluntary acceptance of all inhabitants of the area.

Convincing as the case for integration appears to be, the road to its accomplishment is beset by innumerable obstacles. Some of these are legal, others are political. Perhaps the political hurdles are actually more serious since they usually are the factors that prevent solutions to the legal problems. In order to achieve reforms, proponents of integration must overcome the fears of centralization, forcible annexation, and domination by the central city. Opponents of integration are often able to employ effectively such symbols as "local self-government," "home rule," the "little red schoolhouse," "dictatorship," and the "corrupt city." [110] The use of such symbols is often much more effective upon the voter than any factual or statistical arguments that the proponents can make to prove that integration would be more economical and efficient or result in a more orderly plan of community development.

---

[110] Victor Jones, "Politics of Integration in Metropolitan Areas," *Annals of the American Academy of Political and Social Science*, Vol. 207, pp. 161–167, January, 1940.

CHAPTER 3

The Planning Agency and
Planning Administration

THE PLANNING AGENCY IN THE ADMINISTRATIVE STRUCTURE

The functions of local government are performed by many separate offices, departments, and agencies. In order to achieve efficient and harmonious government, it is necessary to establish a system of organization which places each agency in its appropriate relationship to all others and which provides for a proper distribution of powers and duties among them.

THE LEGAL BASIS OF PLANNING

Planning, like other functions of local government, must be exercised within the legal framework of constitutions, statutes, charters, ordinances, resolutions, rules, and regulations. Since, in legal theory, units of local government are creatures of the state, all authority to engage in local planning activities is derived from state statutes or grants of home rule powers by the state constitution.

Enabling Legislation. In most states, the basic authority for municipalities to engage in planning is provided through planning enabling legislation. This legislation varies in considerable detail from state to state. Usually the enabling legislation is permissive in character rather than mandatory which means that action by the local legislative body is necessary to enable the municipality to engage in planning activities. Generally, the planning enabling legislation contains provisions relating to (1) organization of the planning agency,

(2) the powers and duties of the planning agency, and (3) procedures for exercising the powers and duties. In addition to the basic planning enabling statute, there are other legislative acts which must be considered as part of the legal framework for planning. These include the legislation relating to zoning, subdivision control, and platting, urban redevelopment and urban renewal, mapped streets, and many other substantive matters without which planning would be ineffective.[1]

Among the several states, there is little agreement as to what part of the planning legislation should be detailed in state legislation and what should be left to local ordinance and to administrative regulation. Certain advantages are to be found in each practice depending somewhat on the attitude of the courts in the particular jurisdiction toward planning. If the courts are inclined to construe municipal powers strictly, detailed state legislation may be desirable. However, if a more liberal attitude is taken by the courts, enabling legislation written in more general terms will permit municipalities a degree of flexibility that will enable them to work out their planning organization and solve their planning problems in a manner best suited to the local needs of each community.

Planning legislation in the United States has been influenced considerably by a number of model planning acts. In 1922 a committee for the United States Department of Commerce prepared a Standard State Zoning Enabling Act and in 1927 another committee for the Department prepared a Standard City Planning Enabling Act. The Zoning Enabling Act was revised in 1926 and the City Planning Enabling Act was revised in 1928. The revisions made some changes with respect to organization, but among the most significant differences was a recognition that the scope of planning embraced not only the physical aspects of the community but also was concerned with economic and social betterment. Other influential model acts are contained in the book, *Model Laws for Planning Cities, Counties and States*.[2] These model acts include a municipal planning enabling act, a municipal subdivisions regulation act, a municipal mapped-streets act, and a municipal zoning enabling act.

The advisability of adopting so-called model acts in totality is doubtful because of the fact that legal terminology as well as general

---

[1] Court decisions on the constitutionality of planning controls are considered in subsequent chapters.

[2] Edward M. Bassett, Frank B. Williams, Alfred Bettman, and Robert Whitten, *Model Laws for Planning Cities, Counties and States*, Harvard City Planning Studies, Vol. VII (Cambridge: Harvard University Press, 1935).

laws and conditions vary so greatly from state to state. Nevertheless, any state or locality contemplating the enactment of planning legislation can profitably study these model acts for ideas which will be helpful in developing organizational structure, procedures, practices, and phraseology. Likewise, much value can be found in a study of the practices and experiences of other states which have made notable progress in the field of local planning. Each state must, however, enact that legislation which best suits the needs of its local communities, which conforms to the requirements of the state constitution, and which is consistent with general policies of the state legislature.

Local Planning Legislation.   Under most enabling statutes, local legislative action is necessary to create the local planning agency and to put planning into operation. While the local legislative body is usually given authority to supplement the provisions of the enabling statute by local ordinances, it may not enact any legislation which is inconsistent with the state act. Certain cities in some jurisdictions are empowered to implement and supplement state enabling statutes by municipal charter. As a general rule, however, it is not considered advisable to include detailed provisions of planning legislation in the municipal charter since it tends to make the law too inflexible. Frequently it is desirable to make changes in organization, procedures, grants of powers, and in the substantive content of the law. In most jurisdictions, charter changes cannot be made without approval by the voters. This process is slow and cumbersome and frequently involved in political controversy. Although the inclusion of detailed provisions in the charter may tend to make planning legislation more secure, this value seems to be outweighed by the value of flexibility. Charter provisions should establish the position of the planning agency in the organizational framework and indicate its general powers but leave the details to be provided by ordinance.

Under some state laws and municipal charters, the city council is permitted to delegate to the planning agency or to some administrative officer the power to fill in details of the planning law by the adoption of rules and regulations. In some instances these amount to the making of policy decisions. Rules and regulations adopted pursuant to delegated authority may have the force and effect of law. One of the most common illustrations of the delegated powers is that which gives the local planning agency authority to adopt subdivision regulations without the necessity of securing the approval of the municipal legislative body.

The granting to the planning commission powers to make binding decisions in matters of public policy raises a number of important questions of functional responsibility. Responsibility for enacting municipal legislation is normally the function of the city council. The adoption of the comprehensive plan without the necessity of approval of the city council may be justified on the ground that this is only a step in plan making and does not establish legal relationships until it or some element of it becomes official.[3] A different situation arises with respect to the adoption of subdivision regulations since their adoption constitutes a legislative act establishing important legal relationships. Inasmuch as the content of such regulations falls within the realm of major policy decision, adoption is logically a responsibility of the legislative body rather than the planning agency. However, there are some rather persuasive arguments for vesting authority in the planning agency to adopt subdivision and platting regulations because of the intimate relationships of such regulations to the comprehensive plan.[4]

While the planning agency certainly should participate in the drafting of all planning legislation, including those ordinances and regulations required to effectuate the plans, its role should normally be one of recommendation rather than final action. Final action involves policy decision which should be the responsibility of the politically chosen legislative branch. Neither does it appear to be good practice to provide that no amendments to the planning ordinance, including ordinances implementing planning or adoption of any official plan, shall become effective except with the concurrence of the planning agency. The planning agency in the long run can be more effective by functioning in an advisory role than it can be in functioning as a quasi-legislative body.

Federal Aids to Planning. Considerable impetus was given to local planning by the National Housing Act of 1954,[5] which authorizes grants of federal funds to facilitate and stimulate planning in small municipalities and in metropolitan and regional areas. Section 701 of the Act provides as follows:

To facilitate urban planning for smaller communities lacking adequate

[3] See pp. 131 and 266 for the significance of plan adoption.
[4] See pp. 444–445 for a discussion of this point.
[5] 68 Stat. 640 (1954), 40 U.S.C.A. 461 (Supp. 1954).

planning resources, the Administrator is authorized to make planning grants to State planning agencies for the provision of planning assistance (including surveys, land use studies, urban renewal plans, technical services and other planning work, but excluding plans for specific public works) to cities and other municipalities having a population of less than 25,000 according to the latest decennial census. The Administrator is further authorized to make planning grants for similar planning work in metropolitan and regional areas to official State, metropolitan, or regional planning agencies empowered under State or local laws to perform such planning. Any grant made under this section shall not exceed 50 per centum of the estimated cost of the work for which the grant is made and shall be subject to terms and conditions prescribed by the Administrator to carry out this section.

One of the main objectives back of this legislation is to encourage communities to develop comprehensive plans which will help to further the national policy of combating slums and urban blight. Federal assistance for these purposes is authorized to those communities which "face up to the problems of urban decay and undertake long-range programs directed to its prevention." [6]

Eligibility for planning grants is not limited to planning activities leading to urban renewal programs. Eligible planning activities include such matters as the proper location and character of public works, public improvement programs and capital budgets, location and effects of government installations or major industries, and the formulation of zoning and subdivision regulations and other land-use controls.[7] Metropolitan planning assistance is aimed at developing coördinated planning of an entire area including both the area outside and within the central city or cities but not with developments within a particular city which are of purely local interest.

Grants for planning assistance to small municipalities can be paid only to official state planning agencies. These grants must be made within the framework of the state and local laws and all urban planning contracts and all planning work performed under the grant must be authorized by state and local laws. Grants for metropolitan or regional planning may be received by an official state, metropolitan, or regional planning agency empowered under state or local laws to

---

[6] Recommendations made by the President in his message to the Congress on January 25, 1954, submitting his legislative program for meeting the housing needs.

[7] For a list of planning activities eligible for federal grants to small municipalities, see Housing and Home Finance Agency, A Guide to Urban Planning Assistance Grants (Washington, D.C.: February, 1955), pp. 1–9·1–10.

For eligible activities in metropolitan areas, see ibid., pp. 2–11·2–12.

perform such planning. The federal grant may not exceed 50 percent of the estimated cost of the work for which the grant is made and is subject to regulations prescribed by the Administrator of the Housing and Home Finance Agency. Federal grants are not intended to replace state funds but rather to encourage increased state participation.[8]

PLANNING AS AN ADMINISTRATIVE FUNCTION

Although almost every important progressive city has established a planning agency of one type or another, the acceptance of planning is by no means universal. Furthermore, the creation of a planning agency in a community, even where adequate legal powers are granted to it, is no guarantee that the community will have effective planning. Planning effectiveness also depends upon the character of the administrative organization, the quality of the planning personnel, the amount of financial support, and the degree of understanding of the objectives of planning by the legislative branch, the chief executive, the department heads, and the public.

Principles of Organization. Once planning becomes accepted as a function of local government, the agency created to carry it out must be fitted into the structural organization.[9] The operation of government is concerned with two basic functions—politics and administration. Politics relates to the matter of formulating public policies, and administration relates to those activities concerned with the effectuation or fulfillment of public policies. The legislative branch of government is concerned primarily with politics or the formulation of public policies, whereas the executive branch is concerned principally with administration or the fulfillment of public policies. In a sense the judicial branch also participates in the administrative process through the adjudication of legal controversies and the enforcement of laws. The organization of the various agencies of government for carrying out their basic responsibilities is an important element in the governmental process.

Although few persons will deny the importance of administrative organization, there is no unanimous agreement as to any one best type of structure. However, professional administrators and students of government tend to agree upon certain broad concepts and prin-

---

[8] *Ibid.*, p. 1–6 and 2–9.

[9] Although the terms "local planning" and "urban planning" are used throughout this book to indicate a scope of planning not necessarily confined to city planning, the place of the planning agency in the administrative structure is considered primarily with respect to municipal government.

ciples. One of these is that all administration should be integrated under a single head responsible to the voters directly or to them indirectly through the popularly elected legislative body. Under this concept, the plan of structural organization is represented as a triangle with lines of authority and responsibility running directly from the chief executive or chief administrative officer at the triangle's apex to department heads, and through them and the heads of bureaus and other departmental subdivisions to the employees lowest in the employment scale who represent the base of the triangle.[10] This plan, which is based upon the principle of hierarchy, has the values of simplicity, directness, responsiveness, and fixed responsibility under the chief executive.

In spite of these values of the integrated structure, there are, nevertheless, many persons who are much concerned with the possible dangers of a strong executive and prefer a type of administrative structure which will tend to curb executive authority through the device of dividing the administrative powers among a number of agencies not directly responsible to the chief executive. Under certain forms of government, in which the structure is nonintegrated, some of the administrative functions are given to administrative officials who are elected by the people and in other cases are vested in boards or commissions which are appointed but which are quite independent of the chief executive. This plan of organization is represented by the weak mayor-council and commission forms of government and by the governmental structure found in most counties. In avoiding the dangers believed to be inherent in a strong executive, the nonintegrated type of organization so divides administrative authority that fixed responsibility is virtually impossible, and coördination of administration can be achieved only by coöperation which may frequently be difficult.

Those students of government who support the integrated type of administrative organization usually favor single-headed departments over boards and commissions for management functions. The chief advantages of the single-headed department is that responsibility of management is clearly established. Coördination under the chief executive is thereby more easily achieved. The arguments for the single-headed department are particularly persuasive for functions which require quick decisions and quick action such as are involved

[10] John M. Pfiffner, *Municipal Administration* (New York: The Ronald Press Company, 1940), p. 20.

in the operation of police, fire, and public health. Where, however, the work of the department is essentially quasi-legislative or quasi-judicial in nature, a rather strong case can be made for a multiheaded department. Rules and regulations and decisions based upon hearings, when made by a board or commission, are often more readily accepted by the public.

For performing certain functions, particularly those concerned with cultural activities such as libraries, parks, and recreation, there may be some advantage in having the management under a lay board or commission.[11] Particularly is this true when the function is new and has not had general public acceptance. Under these circumstances, high purposed and enthusiastic lay boards may be able to accomplish more than can be done under a department headed by a director.[12] There can be no doubt as to the value of lay participation in the operation of many governmental functions. However, this value can usually be realized under departmental organization by enlisting citizen participation through advisory boards or special citizens' councils.

Efficient governmental operation requires that departments be organized on the basis of major functions. Those functions which are closely related should be grouped together in one department. Efforts should be made to avoid bringing together in a single department miscellaneous groups of relatively unrelated activities. Obviously, the concept of unifunctional organization must be given a practical application since the classification of functions too narrowly will result in a multiplicity of small departments making coördination of administration difficult. If functional classification is carried to the other extreme, it could reduce the number of departments to such a degree as to make functional organization meaningless. Under any division of responsibility according to function, many fields of activity will overlap or impinge upon the others. To avoid unnecessary confusion and duplication of effort, the functions of each department and agency and their dividing lines of authority need to be clearly defined.

Administrative functions are frequently distinguished on the basis of their major objectives under classifications designated as line, staff, and auxiliary. The so-called line functions are those which are oper-

[11] Boards and commissions may be of various types. They may be full-time administrative boards or commissions, ex officio boards or commissions, or part-time lay boards and commissions. There are relative advantages and disadvantages of each type.

[12] The same argument is not necessarily valid for heading a department by a full-time administrative board or by a board composed of ex officio members.

ational and which are performed for the direct benefit of the public such as providing water, collecting garbage, providing fire and police protection, constructing and maintaining streets, and operating various utilities. Staff functions are not concerned directly with the operation of units which render services to the public but rather with investigation, study, research, and planning designed to assist the chief executive and operational departments in rendering their services. Although staff officers do not command, they do provide information and advice and make recommendations for the purpose of aiding in both formulating and executing public policies. Auxiliary functions are those which are of a secondary nature in that they render services to the government itself and not directly to the public. Such services eventually benefit the public in that they provide the necessary "housekeeping" functions essential to achieving the primary objectives. Auxiliary services include such activities as the keeping of accounts, the purchasing of supplies and materials, the maintenance and management of physical property, and the selection and placement of personnel. Some agencies may perform activities which combine different kinds of functions. For example, the central personnel agency may perform a staff function when advising on matters of personnel policy and an auxiliary function when actually engaged in personnel administration.[13]

Planning as a Staff Responsibility. The role of the planning agency in the administrative process must not be confused with that of the politician or the administrator. This does not mean that the planning function must be insulated from them. In fact, the value of planning depends largely on how closely the planning agency works with those agencies of government concerned with policy making and administration. To the extent that the planning agency performs a staff function it has neither power of policy decision nor policy execution except as to matters which fall within the operations of the planning agency itself.[14] As a staff agency its function is to observe and study problems of government and administration which relate to the physical development of the community, to develop plans and proposals for their solution, and to make recommendations, but not to act. The planning agency has a responsibility to advise but not to

[13] W. Brooke Graves, *Public Administration in a Democratic Society* (Boston: D. C. Heath and Company, 1950), p. 44.

[14] The planning agency does have direct responsibility for making the land-use plan and is commonly given responsibility for administration of the subdivision ordinance and certain other matters.

propagandize either the governmental agencies or the public. It is neither a civic body acting as a watchdog over administration nor a public body exercising powers of veto. For the best success in planning it must enjoy the complete confidence of the executive and the legislative body and work in harmony with both.

One of the greatest values to be derived from planning is from its role of coördinating departmental planning. The gathering of information for the purpose of devising plans and making policy recommendations brings the planning agency in close touch with all operating departments. It must be clear, however, that the establishment of a central planning agency is not intended to eliminate the necessity of the operating departments to plan. The function of the planning agency is to take an overall view of the plans of the various departments and to attempt to integrate them into a comprehensive plan.[15]

In evaluating the departmental proposals, the planning agency must consider not only what is proposed to be done but also how it is proposed to be accomplished. Overall planning involves considerations of purpose, policy, procedure, progress, and program in each major operation and a determination of how these can best be consolidated and fitted into the aims and objectives of the comprehensive plan. In studying departmental operations and proposals with the objective of coördinating planning, it is essential that the planning agency avoid going too far into the technical details of departmental operation. It is not the function of the central planning agency to supplant the activities of the various departments, but rather to supplement their work and to promote closer coördination among the plans which they prepare.[16] This does not mean that the planning agency should undertake no plans on its own initiative. It merely emphasizes the importance of the role of the planning agency in coördinating administrative activities.

The role of the planning agency in coördinating departmental planning does not carry with it powers to issue orders or directives to operational departments. To grant it such powers would be unfortunate and would destroy much of its value as a staff agency. The issuance of orders is a responsibility of line management and should be exercised by the responsible administrative officials. Nevertheless, the

[15] Robert Averill Walker, *The Planning Function in Urban Government* (Chicago: University of Chicago Press, 1950), p. 174.
[16] National Resources Board, "Report—December 1, 1934" (Washington, D.C.: U.S. Government Printing Office, 1934), p. 85.

planning agency may be very influential in directing departmental operations through recommending policies and procedures.

Legislators, administrators, and planners frequently fail to observe the importance of distinguishing between line and staff operations. In certain instances planners have been inclined to seek administrative authority and legislative bodies or executives have been disposed to delegate line responsibilities to an active or vigorous planning agency. If this is done, a distortion of functions is very apt to result, and the planning agency may lose some of its effectiveness. Neither should the planning agency be loaded down with heavy duties relating to appeals and other matters of adjudication which detract or divert it from its primary responsibility of comprehensive planning.

The Planning Agency and Administrative Organization.   The concept of planning as a separate and distinct function of local government, carried out by a governmental agency organized for that purpose, is of relatively recent origin. The idea first received nationwide attention at the National Planning Conference held in Washington, D.C. in 1909. Since that time, planning organization as well as the substance of planning has progressed in evolutionary stages from that of civic improvement clubs, civic planning committees, and the independent planning commissions toward the status of an official planning department fully integrated in the administrative structure of government. For the most part, planning organization today is in an intermediate stage where the planning program is being carried out by an official agency headed by a lay citizens' commission, occupying a semiautonomous position, and functioning somewhat at arms length from the operating departments. However, this situation appears to be in a state of transition. Within the past few years a number of our large cities have moved in the direction of integrating their planning agencies in the administrative structure. One of the more recent steps taken in this direction was by the city of Chicago which enacted an ordinance, effective January 1, 1957, reconstituting its planning agency as a full-fledged executive department. The planning commission will be continued but only as an advisory board to the new city planning department.[17]

Since planning is concerned both with policy determination and policy execution, it is obvious that the proper location of the planning

[17] *Planning and Civic Comment* (Commentaries) December, 1956, pp. 25–26. Other major cities which have planning departments include San Francisco, Los Angeles, Denver, and Phoenix.

agency in the structural organization is of important significance. Although at the present stage of planning development, it cannot be clearly demonstrated that one type or organization is best suited for all communities, it seems clear that most cities have not given adequate consideration to the proper placement of the planning agency in the administrative structure.

Historically, the concept of planning by a separate agency originated as a civic activity. During the early part of the twentieth century a number of civic-minded persons began to turn their attention to problems of slum clearance and the improvement of social and cultural conditions in the community. Among the early developments, from the organizational standpoint, were the civic improvement associations which were largely concerned with the improvement of slum conditions and the development of parks and civic art. These efforts were often promoted by philanthropic and public-spirited citizens. Their success depended largely upon the leadership and financing of a few individuals. A subsequent development was that of the city planning committees which largely supplanted the work of the civic improvement groups. These committees which were also civic, as distinguished from governmental, were led and financed by business and professional men interested in protecting and increasing property values in their communities through street improvements, zoning, and other programs. The work of some of the more successful committees was carried on with the aid and assistance of a paid technical staff.

The achievements of these committees, in developing community plans to cope with the accelerated urban growth and all the accompanying problems, led to the establishment of official city planning commissions which now have generally replaced the voluntary citizen committees. Although the exact number of official planning agencies in existence is not known, it has been estimated that the total is approximately 1000.[18] This estimate probably includes many planning commissions that are comparatively inactive. The International City Managers' Association lists 795 cities of over 10,000 population with planning agencies in 1953.[19] The typical official planning agency is headed by an unpaid citizen board or commission and is semiautonomous in the organizational structure. Commonly, the individual

[18] Walker, op. cit., p. 133. In 1940 the American Society of Planning Officials estimated the number at 1600.

[19] The Municipal Year Book, 1954 (Chicago: The International City Managers' Association, 1954), p. 294.

members of the commission are appointed by the mayor for staggered terms which overlap and which are longer than the term of the mayor who makes the appointment. In some cases the appointment must be confirmed by the council. In a few jurisdictions members of the planning commission are elected by the voters.

Two reasons for the development of the semiautonomous planning commission have been suggested. One reason is the historical origin of planning from the work of citizen organizations. In this respect the planning function is not unlike that of many existing municipal functions which originally were set up under independent boards, but which by the evolutionary process have now been assimilated into the administrative hierarchy of local government. The second reason, which is closely related to the historical background, is that many sponsors of the planning movement have believed that public officials are frequently not sympathetic to the purposes of planning and, therefore, in order to make the planning program secure from political change, they have thought it necessary to give the planning agency an independent legal status with freedom from executive control.

Today there are many planners as well as students of administration who strongly urge that the idea of autonomy be abandoned and that the planning agency be integrated within the administrative structure. This would mean the elimination of the lay board or commission and the placement of the planning function under a department headed by a full-time director responsible to the office of the chief executive. The appointment of a director of planning does not in itself constitute integration within the administration. Lines of responsibility determine the matter.

The strongest case for integrating planning into the administrative hierarchy is based upon the idea that planning is comprehensive in scope and that plans can be carried into execution only by official sanction. Effective planning is possible, therefore, only if the planning agency has the complete confidence, interest, and respect of those who decide and execute policy. As a staff arm of the chief executive, planning becomes an integral part of the administrative process rather than an activity functioning somewhat at arm's length from it. This theory of organization rests upon the principle that since responsibility for policy decisions resides with the elective officials, who are accountable to the voters, so must responsibility for proper planning rest with those same officials in so far as planning serves as a basis for policy determination.

The argument is sometimes made that placing planning under the direction of an independent commission protects it from political control and domination by the executive. Admitting the possibility of political control, it must be recognized that the political branches of the government are directly responsible to the people for both policy determination and administration. This includes responsibility for public planning activities. Since planning is carried out only through political action, it is unrealistic to try to think of it as unrelated to politics. By this test, the values of harmony and a unified approach to the solution of community problems, resulting from integrating the planning process into the administrative structure, would seem to outweigh the doubtful value of insulating it from the influence of politics by the device of placing it under an independent commission which is outside the administrative hierarchy. Plans, no matter how good they may be, which do not have the support of the political branches of government are of no value to the community since they are ineffectual for lack of implementation.[20]

The case for the integrated planning department is particularly strong under forms of government based upon the principle of administrative integration, such as exists under the council-manager and strong mayor-council forms of municipal government. The case is not so strong under nonintegrated plans such as the commission and weak mayor-council plans. Under the nonintegrated plans of organization, neither the mayor nor any other single official has adequate authority to control and coördinate administrative activities either through the powers of appointment and removal or by the issuance of orders and directives. Coördination under such plans is achieved largely by coöperation rather than through centralized administrative authority. Under such conditions, it appears that the semiautonomous planning commission may function as effectively as a planning department responsible to the mayor. Integration of administration is not possible in any event inasmuch as the form of government, itself, is based upon the principle of nonintegration.

The arguments for the elimination of the lay commission in favor of an integrated planning department do not mean that citizen participation in planning is unimportant. Under the integrated plan of organization, lay boards or committees should still be used but in an advisory rather than in a directive capacity. The advice and sugges-

---

[20] See Charles S. Ascher, "City Planning, Administration and Politics," *Land Economics*, Vol. XXX, Number 4, pp. 320–328, November, 1954.

tions of intelligent lay members are invaluable to the planning staff in the development of the comprehensive plan. Citizen participation is also of great value in interpreting decisions to the public and in helping to inform the public on the meaning and importance of special features of the plan and planning activities.

The place of the planning agency in the council-manager plan of municipal government warrants some special consideration. Planning originated in part out of the need for a qualified agency with a professionally trained staff to undertake studies, ascertain facts, and develop plans of a specialized or technical nature to aid the nonprofessional mayor and the council in reaching sound decisions of public policy. With the advent of the council-manager plan, the administrative duties of the elected mayor greatly decreased in scope and importance. The chief administrative officer under this plan is the manager who is a professionally trained administrator. Quite frequently, he has the technical knowledge and resources to conduct his own studies and ascertain his own facts for the purpose of making recommendations on policy matters and for coördinating departmental plans. Planning agencies have under these circumstances sometimes found their work areas preëmpted by the manager and his staff.[21]

This situation emphasizes the importance of having the role of the planning agency and its position in the administrative structure carefully defined. Under the council-manager plan of municipal government, the manager assumes responsibility for the work of all operating departments, boards, and commissions, and is directly answerable to the council on all matters of administration. Because of this dominant position of the manager in administrative matters and his liaison with the municipal legislative body, serious problems may arise if the planning agency is in a position to give advice directly to the city council, independently of the manager. The adoption of the manager plan does not in any way lessen the need for the planner,[22] but it does necessitate that the planning agency be organized to function within the theory and framework of this plan of government.

The Role of the Planning Consultant.   Comprehensive planning,

---

[21] William I. Goodman, "The Planner's Relationship with the City Manager," *Journal of the American Institute of Planners*, Vol. XIX, No. 3, p. 147, Summer, 1953.

[22] "Both management and planning must have competent, well-rounded knowledge of many fields as they apply to municipal affairs. Each complements the other and each is dependent upon the other for success." Roger V. Pearce, "City Management and City Planning," *Texas Municipalities*, Vol. XLIII, No. 10, October, 1956, p. 308.

to be effective, must be conducted on a continuous basis. For this reason, it seems essential that it be carried out by an official planning agency created for that purpose. Nevertheless, there is a great deal of public planning which is undertaken by private planning consultants under contract with public agencies. Although the private consultant cannot fulfill all the planning needs of most major communities, there are many areas of service for the professionally trained and qualified planning consultant. Many small communities which have a need for planning studies find that they have neither the volume of work nor the financial resources to employ a full-time qualified staff. Under these circumstances, their requirements for technical help may often be supplied by engaging, for a short period of time, a trained planning consultant. Even large communities, with competent planning staffs, may find occasions for utilizing the specialized services of private consultants in connection with the development of plans for specific projects. When a planning consultant is used for this purpose, he should be engaged by the planning director and work under his direction. He should not be employed as a "detective" or "watchdog" and should not exercise overall supervision over the planning staff.

Reports to the International City Managers' Association indicate that 184 cities of over 10,000 population expended money for planning consulting services during the year 1953. The reports seem to indicate that although 54 cities of over 50,000 population spent money for consulting services, the larger cities tend to rely more upon permanent staffs. In the cities with populations between 10,000 and 20,000 only 9 percent had full-time employees, whereas 20 percent in this class expended money for consulting services. In cities of over 50,000, 68 percent had one or more full-time employees and 27 percent of the cities in this classification expended money for consulting services. It thus appears that at some stage of population growth, cities seem to decide that planning can be carried out more economically by a full-time planning staff than by consultants.[23]

With the growing consciousness of planning as a profession of its own, there has been an increased interest on the part of many persons trained in the principles and techniques of planning to establish themselves in private consulting work. There can be no doubt but that these consultants have contributed much to the cause of urban planning. It seems quite certain that planning interest in certain com-

[23] *The Municipal Year Book, 1954, op. cit*, p. 295.

munities has been aroused by the fact that a few citizens promoting planning have brought in a consultant whose work has convinced the people of the community of the value of planning.[24]

Some evidence of the maturing of the planning consultant as a separate and distinct professional group is to be found in the statement on "Professional Consultants' Services and Fees" approved by the American Institute of Planners on April 25, 1952, and the "Code of Professional Conduct" adopted by the Institute on January 10, 1948. These statements are aimed at promoting the professional welfare of the professional planner by suggesting standards to be observed in the performance of services, in making financial arrangements, and in calculating fees.[25]

The statement of the Institute on the subject of Professional Consultants' Services and Fees recognizes that proper competition is healthy and sometimes is required under municipal procedures. It suggests that a client about to select a planning consultant and to establish his fee should:

1. Determine the general scope of the planning program to be undertaken.
2. Review the qualifications and experience of prospective consultants with relation to the proposed planning program.
3. Hold conferences with each prospective consultant and have him submit his ideas as to the program he would suggest to meet the planning problem and have him also make a statement of the fee or other basis of payment as well as an estimate of the total probable cost.
4. Explore the differences between the programs submitted on the basis of value and cost, bearing in mind the relative value of the particular experience and capabilities of the planning consultants under consideration who would actually be working on the program.

There are a number of considerations which should be borne in mind by any community contemplating planning exclusively through the use of private consultants. Private planning consultants are in business for private gain and are, therefore, interested in promoting and selling their services.[26] Quite commonly, this results in the sell-

[24] Walker, op. cit., p. 207.

[25] See special report, Committee on Professional Services, American Institute of Planners, "Professional Consultants' Services and Fees," approved April 25, 1952. Also Committee on Code of Ethics, American Institute of Planners, "Code of Professional Conduct," adopted January 10, 1948.

[26] The contract planning consultant is not to be confused with the planning consultant employed in certain states by research bureaus, state agencies, or associations of cities to aid municipalities in developing and carrying out their planning programs. For example, see Chap. 54, Laws of Washington, 1945.

ing of a "package plan" which may tend to be regarded by both officials and the public as the end in itself. They may develop the feeling that "the job is now done since we now have a plan." Since the consultant is not usually employed on a full-time basis, the common practice of operation is for him to undertake his study, prepare his report, make his recommendations, collect his fee, and then move on to the performance of another contract. Too often the private planning consultant has failed to impress upon the community the importance of making planning a continuous function, or if he has, the community is unable to retain him on a year-around basis.[27]

Effective planning cannot be achieved by a "one shot" application. Plans must be kept up to date to meet new developments, new ideas, and changed conditions. Where planning is performed only by the private consultant, its level of interest may fail to continue on an even keel. For example, a great deal of enthusiasm may occur and considerable money may be spent at the time the planning consultant is engaged and while the plans are being developed. However, after the report is filed, there may be a tendency for the people of the community to relax in an atmosphere of complacency without full appreciation of the fact that no real value comes from the planning unless it is implemented through proper legislation, administrative action, and public information. The work of the planning consultant cannot substitute for that of an active, well-staffed, and well-organized planning agency. Without an active planning agency to follow through, by keeping current plans before the politically responsible officials, planning is apt to fall by the wayside as public officials are unlikely to be guided for any extended period of time by the process of continuously referring to a ready-made plan.

INTERNAL AND EXTERNAL RELATIONSHIPS

No matter how well the planning agency is organized or how competent the technical staff, the planning program cannot be completely successful unless satisfactory relationships are established and maintained with the operating departments, other units of government, and with the public. Successful planning depends to a considerable extent upon teamwork.

Interdepartmental Relationships. Obviously, there is bound to be some overlapping in the planning activities of the operational

---

[27] Where, however, a "service contract" is employed to supplant or supplement the old type of "plan contract," some of these criticisms are minimized.

departments and those of the planning agency. Nevertheless, there should be no fundamental conflicts if the chief executive, the legislative body, the department heads, and the planning agency understand their respective responsibilities and function accordingly. The planning agency, better than any single department, is in a position to take an overall view of the community needs. It should not attempt to assume political leadership or to gauge the political feasibility of particular proposals. This is the responsibility of the politician or the elected official. Neither is it the responsibility of the planning agency to attempt to influence the means and methods by which operating departments carry out their programs unless these procedures affect the comprehensive plan.

The degree of planning effectiveness is dependent very much upon the working relationships established between the director and the staff members of the planning agency, and department heads and subordinates. The extent to which these relationships need to be formalized depends upon the size of the city and a number of other factors. There is no substitute for confidence and mutual understanding. In the larger jurisdictions, relationships with the various departments may be maintained through periodic conferences and the exchange of brief statements of plans and contemplated programs.

Planning can be successful only when it has demonstrated its usefulness to operating departments. In the final analysis, the planning agency must obtain most of the information which it needs for developing comprehensive plans from the departments which it serves and which must enforce the policies of government. Its function is to develop the framework for departmental plans and furnish information to departments to enable them to avoid conflicts with the operational plans of other departments. For example, the planning agency which is working closely with all operating departments is in a position to give immediate advice as to whether the proposed erection of a high tension line may interfere with an approach to a proposed airfield or whether the proposed development of a park conforms to the plans for a public housing project. The multiplicity of possible conflicts such as these illustrates the necessity for a single agency which possesses the necessary factual information to guide policy making officials in developing a unified governmental program.

In order to maintain a necessary position of impartiality, the planning agency must avoid becoming involved in jurisdictional fights, or in furthering the ambitions of individuals, or in the building up of departmental empires. Its function is to help develop the departmental programs which are consistent with the comprehensive plan. It should seek to eliminate conflicts and duplication, stimulate community interest, and provide technical assistance. At the same time, the planning agency must be flexible in its approach so that it can work toward proper adjustments of policy to meet the practical requirements of administration.[28]

There are no set guides to the maintenance of good interdepartmental relations. Much depends upon the personality of the director and the department heads. Work through coöperation is always better than through directives. The planning agency should avoid propagandizing administrative departments or attempting to influence policies by developing pressures through citizens' organizations. The planning director and staff should be in a position to offer counsel and advice, but credit for governmental programs and policies should go to the chief executive or department head.

Intergovernmental Relationships. Comprehensive planning for the urban community requires that each municipality, county, school district, and other units of government functioning in the area take into account the plans of each other. Functional programs carried out by one unit of local government, without regard to the programs of the others, are almost certain to result in haphazard community development. Unless school districts plan the location of their buildings in a municipality with regard to the proposed land use program of the municipality, great waste of money and public inconvenience may result. Also, insurmountable traffic problems will arise unless the street program of the city and the highway program of the county are harmoniously developed. Numerous public services such as recreation, public health, drainage, water supply, and control of nuisances can be carried out effectively only if satisfactory intergovernmental planning relations are established among the various units of local government concerned with these responsibilities.

Sound urban planning is also dependent upon the coördination of state and federal projects and programs with the plans of the urban community. The construction of a state highway through an urban community or the location of a United States military establishment

---

[28] "The planning agency, however, can analyze alternative policies. It can help determine what benefits can be achieved as against what costs will be incurred by different specific policies." Martin Meyerson, "Building the Middle-Range Bridge of Comprehensive Planning," *Journal of the American Institute of Planners*, Vol. XXII, No. 2, Spring, 1956, p. 61.

in a city has a definite impact upon the community. Governmental programs which involve such matters as the development of natural resources, the control of pollution, the administration of public health, or the awarding of large defense contracts to local plants, vitally affect the local planning picture. Planning is also affected by general state legislation and administrative action. Every state has in effect numerous statutes which, although not enacted with urban planning in mind, nevertheless affect or circumscribe planning by the municipality. Many activities in which cities are permitted to engage are subject to state regulations and fiscal controls. Urban planners, therefore, need to be familiar with pertinent state legislation and must keep in close touch with the rules of state commissions or departments which exercise regulatory control over private and public enterprises and the financing of local improvement projects.

Federal agencies may also exercise control over urban plans. For example, under its authority to control and regulate interstate commerce and prevent obstructions to navigation, the federal government may exert considerable influence over local plans which contemplate harbor developments or the erection of structures over, or upon, navigable waters. Another type of federal control over planning is through congressional legislation in aid of public housing, urban renewal, municipal airports, streets, public health, and many other functions. These statutes providing financial grants are usually conditional upon compliance with certain requirements laid down by federal act or by the rules and regulations of the agency administering the program in connection with which the grant is made.

Relations with the Public. Planning in the democratic process is a citizen responsibility as well as an official one. At what time and in what manner the general public should be brought into the process are matters on which no definite rules can be laid down. The direct relationships which the planning agency should establish with the public vary with the position of the planning agency in the administrative structure, the attitude of the general public toward planning, practical politics, and other factors peculiar to the particular community.

Under our system of representative government, public policy over the long period is formulated in accordance with public opinion. Frequently, the continuance of an elective official in office is due to how well and consistently he gauges public sentiment and whether he acts in accordance with it. Two theories of representative government have long been debated. One holds that elective officials are mere servants of the people whose duty it is to carry out the wishes of the people whether or not the elected representatives believe them to be wise. The opposing theory is that public officials are elected because of their leadership, qualifications, and special fitness for office, and that it is their responsibility, after proper study and deliberation, to make their decisions on questions of public policy in accordance with their judgment of what is best in the public interest. Obviously, strict adherence to the first theory deprives the public of the value of expertness and professionalism which is of importance in weighing the consequences of political action on many complex public questions. On the other hand, complete adherence to the latter theory may frequently lead to political suicide. Practical politics and sound administration dictate a course somewhere between the two. Public officials are frequently faced with the choice of bowing to the popular will and adopting a policy which, in their expert judgment, appears to be unsound or following what they believe to be a wiser course of action but which does not at the time seem to have popular support.

Since the planning program is one which vitally concerns the daily life of many people, it is especially necessary that the planning agency be in close touch with community thinking. Leadership from the planning agency is necessary, but successful planning must be by the community and not for it. The text book of the International City Managers' Association on local planning administration suggests three important points which are necessary if the planning agency wishes to enlist the coöperation and interest of citizens as a whole:[29]

First, people are most likely to be interested in matters they understand. It is important, therefore, that they understand the objectives and methods of planning and understand the basic and essential character of long-range planning in the solution of problems of community development. Second, people are most ready to take action in matters in which they feel a sense of personal participation and responsibility. To the maximum extent possible, citizens should be brought into the process of making plans and making planning decisions. Third, many people in a city are interested in different special aspects of its development. These interests can be used as important spark plugs if individuals can be made to see the interrelationships between their special interests and the comprehensive plan for the development of the community.

[29] *Local Planning Administration* (Chicago: The International City Managers' Association, 1948), p. 57.

Effective planning requires not merely a public awareness and understanding of the planning process but also actual citizen participation. Citizen participation makes planning more acceptable, and placing it in a democratic framework prevents it from being dominated by the technician. Proper liaison between the planning agency and the public can be maintained in a number of other ways.[30] Among these are the establishment of special citizens' advisory committees. Their function is twofold: to provide the planning agency with invaluable advice and information and to help keep the general public informed of the planning program.[31] It is important, however, that when such committees are created, their responsibilities and relationship to the planning agency be clear-cut.[32]

The planning agency may find that the greatest benefits from public participation can be derived from working closely with various community civic organizations. These groups are important agencies both for providing citizen education and fostering interest for desirable planning legislation. In some other instances the most valuable help may come from special citizens' committees organized for the purpose of aiding in the development of specific projects. However, there is real value in establishing some permanence in citizens' organizations in order to insure continuity in the program of civic education. The International City Managers' Association reports that 44 cities of over 10,000 population follow the practice of having an unofficial citizens' planning committee operating in conjunction with the official planning agency for greater citizen participation and public relations.[33] Recognition and identification with a program in which there is a

[30] For an outline and concise discussion of steps necessary to develop public interest and participation in public affairs, see William B. Baker, *et al., Taking Action in the Community* (Chicago: Adult Education Association of the U.S.A., 1955), pamphlet, 48 pp. Some cities may find it advisable to set up a public relations program to handle all matters of public information. If this is done, the public relations of the planning agency must be fitted into the whole program.

[31] In Riverside, California, seven citizen advisory committees have been created to make recommendations for the capital improvement program with respect to civic centers, utilities, parking and transportation, public health and safety, public works, airports, parks, trees, and recreation. Three members of the city council and two members of the planning commission work with each committee. Oren L. King, "Citizens Help to Prepare Long-Range Program," *Public Management*, Vol. XXXVI, No. 6, p. 131, June, 1954.

[32] Charles McKinley, "Some Principles of Organization," *Public Administration Review*, Vol. XII, No. 3, pp. 164–165, Summer, 1952.

[33] *The Municipal Year Book, 1954, op. cit.,* p. 293.

feeling of accomplishment are of great importance in providing continuous support.[34]

The planning agency at various stages of the planning process may find it necessary and advisable to utilize many devices for disseminating public information and ascertaining public sentiment. These may include meetings, hearings, debates, and the conduct of polls and surveys. The planning agency, at times, will need to utilize all the media of information in the community, including the press, radio, and television. Seldom does one single approach reach all of the public.[35] Oftentimes, considerable aid can be obtained from enlisting the help of the public schools and by interesting the student body in specific projects of planning.

While the planning agency must assume leadership in developing public interest and crystallizing public opinion with respect to approved planning proposals, it is most important that it does not attempt to assume political leadership or resort to methods which might be classified as propaganda. There is a very fine line of distinction between the dissemination of public information and the dissemination of propaganda. Selling is part of a professional's job, but the planner who takes his program to the public should be certain that he can support his recommendations by factual data and sound public policy.

Professional planners must not become impatient with the slow process involved in bringing the community along with the thinking of the planning experts. This slowness is a penalty of our democratic process. In the long run, planning progresses much further when it is based upon public understanding and acceptance. Planning in a democratic society must be built from the bottom upward and not be imposed from the top down.

The principal aim of direct public participation in the planning process from the earliest stages is to develop a community feeling of responsibility for the plan. Among many citizens the feeling still prevails that planning is simply one more interference with the freedom of the individual. Active citizen participation tends to dispel this idea and to create a public consciousness that planning can be carried on democratically with the actual result of enlarging the scope of individual freedom. If public support is to be secured, the public must

[34] *Civic Education in Planning*, American Institute of Planning, Subcommittee on Civic Education, October, 1951.

[35] W. J. Connelly, "Creating Good Public Relations for Your Borough Government," *New Jersey Municipalities*, Vol. XXXI, No. 4, p. 27, April, 1954.

have an awareness and understanding of the purposes and objectives of planning, recognize the need for planning in a given community, and have confidence in the necessity for certain governmental controls adopted to carry the plan into effect.

Prudent consultation with segments of the public interested in a specific project has two important results. In the first place, it creates good will for the planning agency, and in the second place, it frequently results in a more useful or workable plan or program. It also may contribute to greater public support for the completed project.[36] In carrying out a public relations program in planning, the planner is to be cautioned that he should undertake no public programs which are not approved by the mayor and city council, since these officials are the responsible political officials who must answer to the voters.

Public relations are also of utmost importance in day-to-day contacts in the administration of planning legislation. Frequently, the attitude of a citizen toward planning may be influenced more by the manner in which the laws are carried out than by the effect of the law itself. It is not always possible to send an applicant or protestant away from a hearing or conference happy. Sometimes, however, his dissatisfaction results from the manner in which he has been treated or because he does not understand the reasons why the action has been taken. An effort should always be made to explain the reason for the official action and the principles which lie behind it. It is most important that rulings and interpretations be based upon the law and upon sound planning principles, and be applied without political favoritism. Nothing will destroy public confidence in the planning agency more quickly than the making of decisions based on political considerations.[37] Political decisions should be left to the elected officials.

THE ORGANIZATION OF THE PLANNING AGENCY

It is obvious that the realization of the aims and objectives of urban planning depend to a high degree upon the caliber and competence of the personnel of the planning agency, the size of the technical staff, and the amount of the budget allotted for planning operations. Intelligent and well-trained professional employees working under able

[36] Charles E. Doel, "Public Participation in Planning for Better Living," *Parks and Recreation Magazine*, Vol. 37, No. 6, p. 1, June, 1954.

[37] Arthur H. Adams, "The Planning Commissioner—His Qualifications and Conduct," *Western City*, p. 54, June, 1952.

leadership are basic to good planning. No amount of energy, enthusiasm, or interest in the community can substitute for qualified personnel possessing an understanding of the philosophy of public planning and a working knowledge of the operations and responsibilities of government. However, qualified personnel can achieve their best results only if the planning agency is well organized and properly financed.

The Planning Commission

Although 92 percent of all cities of over 10,000 population carry on some kind of planning, there is little uniformity in the organization of municipal planning agencies. The prevailing form is the independent or semiautonomous commission. The weaknesses of this type of organization, from the standpoint of integration in the administrative structure, have already been considered. Since, however, it appears that most planning agencies at the local level, for some years to come, will be directed by boards or commissions, special attention should be given to their membership, qualifications, and functions.

Composition, Selection, and Competence. The composition and size of planning commissions and the terms of office of commission members are commonly specified in the state enabling statutes. Planning commissions in almost all jurisdictions are composed of private citizens or of private citizens and certain ex officio members. Citizen members are usually appointed by the mayor, although in some jurisdictions the power of appointment is vested in the city council or commission, in the city manager, or in the commissioner of public works. Where appointment is by the mayor, confirmation of the city council is sometimes required. In a few cities members of the commission are elected. To preserve the independent status of the commission, statutes commonly provide that members may be removed only for cause, such as for inefficiency, neglect of duty, or malfeasance in office. Under such statutory provisions, the mayor or other official who is given power of removal must file a statement of his reasons.

Wide variations are also to be found in the size of planning commissions and the terms of office of the members. The number of lay citizen members ranges from 2 to 35.[38] Most of the commissions consist of memberships of from three to nine. The median membership is six.[39] Terms of office vary from one to seven years. Staggered or

[38] *The Municipal Year Book, 1954, op. cit.,* p. 294.
[39] *Ibid.*

overlapping terms are commonly provided in order that all the memberships do not become vacant in the same year.[40] As a general rule commission members serve without compensation, although in some jurisdictions they are reimbursed for authorized travel or other necessary expenses.

In a great many jurisdictions, certain officials such as the mayor, city engineer, commissioner of public works, director of parks and recreation, or others serve as ex officio members along with the lay citizen members. In a few instances the entire commission consists of ex officio members. The primary reason for including ex officio members is to enable the planning commission to secure closer coordination with the various governmental departments or agencies and to maintain necessary contact with those public officials most directly concerned with the planning function. However, the liaison value of this practice is open to serious doubt. Most of the ex officio members have full-time interests in administering their own departments and seldom are in a position to develop an overall view in their thinking on planning problems.[41] Frequently their work is so heavy that they do not find the time to attend meetings of the planning commission. Furthermore, it is not practical to represent every department or agency concerned with the planning function on the planning commission. Consequently, those activities such as public works, which are usually most heavily represented, are likely to give planning an undue orientation in that direction.

The placement of planning under the direction of the semiautonomous commission has been justified upon the grounds that: (1) it keeps planning above politics since the commission is not absorbed into the administrative structure under the dominance of the mayor, (2) an unpaid lay citizens' commission, not subject to removal by the mayor except for cause, will take a long-range view of current planning proposals, and (3) the citizen commission can effectively interpret the work of the technical staff to the public and to the public officials.

It has frequently been assumed that by removing the planning commission from direct political control of the mayor or council that the action taken by the commission will tend to be more objective and nonpartisan. There is grave doubt, however, whether experience bears out this assumption. Robert A. Walker, who has given a great

---

[40] Austin F. Macdonald, *American City Government and Administration* (New York: Thomas Y. Crowell Company, 1951), p. 463.
[41] Walker, *op. cit.*, p. 162.

deal of study to this question, concludes that the "claim that planning commissions are more objective than elected public officials must be rejected." [42] Planning commissions, as a rule, have not been as representative of voter interests as are city councils. Commission members have been drawn heavily from realtors, business executives, lawyers, engineers, and architects but rarely from groups identified with labor, welfare, or education. The preponderance of membership from executive and ownership groups would seem to explain why planning in most communities has been confined to the physical aspects of the community and why so little attention has been given by planning commissions to public health, relief, slum clearance, taxation, and other social and economic problems.

It is also doubtful whether the unpaid lay citizen commission has any special competence to insure that a long-range view will be taken of planning problems. Long-range planning must be predicated upon a thorough understanding of the very complicated and ever-changing field of municipal activities as well as upon a comprehension of the purposes, objectives, and ramifications of planning. Most planning commissioners are very busy men who find it virtually impossible to spare the time necessary to acquaint themselves with the essential information to enable them to give intelligent guidance to the planning program. [43] For the most part, therefore, the professional staff and the elected officials are in a better position to see the long-range planning implications of proposed policies, projects, and programs.

The justification of the lay commission as an interpreter and supporter of the work of the professional staff appears to have somewhat more merit than the other two grounds. Planning commission members usually represent stable and influential groups within the community. Their statements often carry much weight in securing public support for planning proposals. Although the greatest part of the public relations programs is usually carried on by the professional staff rather than members of the commission, there frequently arise situations in public hearings or in the handling of controversial issues in which the lay commission can provide the professional planner much needed moral support. [44] Frequently, the planning commission may be of real service in interpreting planning to the mayor, city

[42] Walker, op. cit., p. 155.

[43] There are, of course, many notable exceptions.

[44] American Society of Planning Officials, Planning, 1952, Proceedings of the Annual National Planning Conference held in Boston, Massachusetts, October 5–9, 1952 (Chicago: 1952), p. 197.

council, and other public officials. In particular, the influence of commission members may be of great importance in securing appropriations for the planning program. As a general rule, however, it seems that the planning commission is more useful as an interpreter of planning to the public than it is to the public officials. The narrow concepts of planning held by many planning commissions have often been responsible for the failure of the elected officials to appreciate the possibilities of comprehensive planning. Generally speaking, public officials are inclined to place more reliance upon the opinions of the professional planning staff than upon those of the lay commission members.

In spite of the admitted weaknesses of the part-time, semiautonomous commission, there are, nevertheless, many authorities who feel that the planning commission is the backbone of modern city planning. This view is supported on the grounds that the planning commission represents a cross section of community interests, serves as a sounding board or trial balloon for new ideas, acts as a buffer between the technicians and the public, and relieves the city council of many details. Planning commissions may also be instrumental in securing community participation, promoting public interest in planning, and by virtue of their status in the community are able to get planning effectuated.[45] The degree to which these results are achieved in actual practice depends very much upon the qualifications of the members of the commission.

Qualifications of Members. The weighting of planning commissions with realtors, architects, engineers, lawyers, and business executives has resulted in part from a feeling that technical knowledge or professional training constitutes the most desirable qualifications for membership on a planning commission. Realtors have been selected because of the occupation of planning agencies with land use controls; engineers and architects, because of the emphasis which planning has given to design and public works projects; lawyers, because of the great amount of attention given to legal problems of zoning and subdivision control and the establishment of procedures for hearings and appeals. Actually, however, the technical or professional competence of commission members is not of major importance, at least in the large cities, since almost all technical matters are handled by the professional staff. Far more valuable assets of planning com-

---

[45] Herman D. Ruth, "Expert Testimony of Mr. Arbuthnot," *Journal of the American Institute of Planners,* Vol. 20, p. 37, Winter, 1954.

mission members are leadership, intelligence, integrity, sound judgment, civic-mindedness, unselfishness, and a sincere desire to contribute to the public welfare of the community.

The Chamber of Commerce of the United States has set forth a number of guideposts for the creation of planning commissions.[46] Among the suggestions for the composition of a planning commission are the following:

1. A relatively small membership (from five to nine).
2. Citizens of recognized standing in the community.
3. A sincere, objective, and forward-looking interest in the municipality as a whole.
4. Freedom from partisan politics.

The report proceeds to point out that successful planning requires that a commission be a real working partnership and not merely a debating society.

It is very difficult to specify requirements which can be given practical application in all cases. One school of thought holds that it is desirable to have on the planning commission, people who have a great deal of time, such as retired business or professional men. Others suggest that various types of skills and professional attainments be represented, such as those of the engineer, the architect, the lawyer, the trained welfare worker, and the realtor. Most persons who have given thought to the subject generally agree that the commission members should not have special allegiance to any geographical area or to any political or partisan group, but should be able to forget area or sectional interests and think of the welfare of the community as a whole.[47] On this point the following statement of qualifications suggested by Mr. Arthur H. Adams should meet with general approval.[48]

A member of a planning commission should be a person of mature years, preferably a property owner, possess a reputation for honesty, integrity and good judgment in the community; be so situated that he can afford to give all of the time necessary for a full performance of his duties on the commission, and, further, that he be willing to do so; he should be able to exercise tact and diplomacy on all occasions; he should be sufficiently well educated to be able to readily understand fairly complicated

[46] Chamber of Commerce of the United States, *City Planning and Urban Development* (Washington, D.C.: 1952), pp. 13–17.
[47] American Society of Planning Officials, *op. cit.*, p. 199.
[48] Arthur H. Adams, *op. cit.*, p. 54.

problems involving property, and to express himself understandably to persons having dealings with the commission.

The ideal commissioner is a "civic-minded" person who really wishes to perform a service for his community. He *should not* be a person who will allow his leanings toward capital, labor or politics or prejudices on account of race or religion to influence his decisions. In other words, he must respect the rights of all citizens. Failing in this he is certainly subject to the charge that he has been false to the trust imposed in him.

Powers, Duties, and Procedures.   Although the responsibilities and duties of the planning commissions vary with each jurisdiction, most commissions are commonly given authority to:

1. Develop a comprehensive plan.
2. Prepare platting regulations.
3. Review and act on all subdivision plans and other proposed land use developments.
4. Prepare a zoning ordinance.
5. Review and make recommendations on all amendments to the comprehensive zoning ordinance, including the drafting of revisions.
6. Review all special exceptions permitted under zoning which involve major land uses.[49]
7. Develop the comprehensive plan for urban redevelopment or urban renewal.[50]
8. Prepare or review the long-range capital improvement program.
9. Prepare mapped street plans and the official map.
10. Undertake such surveys and studies and prepare such reports as may be required to carry out the planning program.

In addition to the specific powers and duties relating to the subject matter of planning, the planning commission normally has many other powers and duties which it derives from statutory direction, authorization, or implication. Among these are the selection of personnel, approval of the work program of the staff, and the establishment of operational policies and procedures.

In some jurisdictions, enabling statutes have gone a long way in granting planning commissions broad powers independent of the legislative and executive branches. One practice followed in a number of cities is that of granting to planning commissions a qualified veto over city council action, if, after the adoption of the comprehensive

[49] It is common practice to vest the granting of special exceptions in the Board of Adjustment. See, however, p. 431.

[50] Project plans are usually developed by the renewal agency, although this is sometimes made the function of the planning agency.

plan, the planning commission disapproves of specific public improvements.[51] Sometimes the veto extends also to changes of zone classifications and other matters. Where the veto is exercised, the recommendations of the planning commission can usually be overridden only by two-thirds or three-fourths majority vote of the council. While such provisions are designed to protect the comprehensive plan from harmful action by a legislative body unsympathetic to planning, the practice is open to serious question. By giving the planning commission powers of policy decision, it takes the planning agency out of its advisory role, often placing it in antagonism with the city council. This may seriously endanger the good relations between the council and the planning commission. If the planning commission is to be divorced from current political controversies, veto powers over the council should not be granted. An anomalous situation is created where the semiautonomous commission which is neither responsible to the council, the administration, nor the electorate, is given powers of policy decision, the exercise of which may embarrass the responsible elected officials. A much sounder policy over the long run would seem to be to rely upon the force of public opinion to secure the adoption of planning recommendations. However, a requirement that the council shall not act on certain matters until after the recommendation of the planning commission is obtained, or other action of the commission has been taken, is not open to the same objection as long as the power of decision is not made subject to planning commission approval.

Planning commissions are usually accorded rather broad powers in establishing rules of procedure and internal organization. Among the first steps that must be taken by the commission to perfect its organization and to establish its operating policies are the election of a chairman and other officers, the creation of committees and the designation of committee members, the fixing of the time, place, and frequency of meetings, the handling of minutes and reporting at meetings, the drafting of resolutions, the release of publicity, and the establishment of working relations with staff, department heads, and outside agencies. The creation of subcommittees and the designation of subcommittee members are of great importance in the conduct of the planning program. The work of the commission can be greatly

---

[51] This practice was influenced by the provision of the "Standard City Enabling Act" prepared in 1928 by the Advisory Committee on City Planning and Zoning of the United States Department of Commerce.

expedited if its tasks are well divided through the use of standing committees which can give detailed attention to special phases of planning. As a matter of general policy, however, all matters of major importance should be considered by the entire commission. One of the chief values of the commission organization is that of obtaining the considered judgment of all members.

THE PLANNING STAFF

Successful planning in any city of appreciable size cannot be carried on by the commission alone. The key to planning effectiveness is the technically trained staff. Planning commission members, even though they possess the technical qualifications for planning, cannot devote the time necessary to conducting surveys, undertaking research, and gathering information required for developing plans and making recommendations for intelligent policy decisions. Essential data for effective planning can usually be assembled only by a qualified planning staff employed independently of other departments. Actually, however, a very small percentage of the municipalities which have established planning agencies have provided themselves with adequate planning staffs. Planning data, gathered by the International City Managers' Association from 858 cities reporting, indicate that 795 have official planning agencies, but only 233 have one or more full-time employees and 139 of these are in the group of 193 cities of over 50,000 population.[52]

Size, Composition, and Internal Organization.   The size and composition of the planning staff, of necessity, must depend upon many factors including the size of the city, the stage of the planning activities, the community interest in planning, the number of special projects under way at a given time, and many local conditions. In a small city, the planning work may frequently be done by one person, whereas in a large community, a staff of persons with many specializations may be required. There is such a great variation in the planning organization of cities, even among those of comparable size, that it is not possible to state what should be considered a typical planning staff.

The Municipal Year Book of 1954 [53] shows that among the cities of over 500,000 population, Chicago had 24 full-time employees; Detroit, 46; Los Angeles, 70; New York, 124; Boston, 8; Cleveland,

[52] *The Municipal Year Book, 1954, op. cit.,* p. 295.
[53] *Ibid.,* pp. 296–300.

33; Minneapolis, 10; Washington, D.C., 18; and Pittsburgh, 43. Among the cities within the population bracket of 250,000 to 500,000, the report shows that Kansas City, Missouri, had 25 full-time employees; Newark, N.J., 2; Omaha, 6; St. Paul, 5; San Antonio, 13; San Diego, 23; and Seattle, 20. Similar variations are found in the numbers of employees in all other population brackets. Approximately one-third of the cities with populations from 50,000 to 100,000 reported no full-time planning employees. About one-sixth of the cities in this group employed four or more. San Jose, California, reported nine full-time planning employees, and Richmond, California, reported eight. Less than one-fourth of the cities in the population bracket of 25,000 to 50,000 population had any full-time employees. None of these employed more than four persons and more than half of them employed only one. Obviously the above figures tell very little as to the effectiveness of planning since they neither indicate the stage of the planning program nor the extent to which planning activities are carried on through consultants or by arrangements with operating departments or through work of citizens' committees.

The city planning data contained in the Municipal Year Book of 1954 also indicate little uniformity in the staff direction in the various planning agencies or in the manner of selecting the planning director. Of the 795 cities having planning agencies, a total of 204 cities reported having a full-time director. Of these, 84 are cities of over 100,000 population. In 77 of the 204 cities, the planning director is selected by the planning commission; in 67 cities, by the city manager; in 18 cities, by the city council; and in 22 cities, by the mayor. Twenty cities did not report the manner of selection. An additional 178 cities reported that other city officials served as the planning director along with their other duties. In 48 of these cities, the city engineer served as planning director; the city manager, in 36; the chairman of the planning commission, in 24; the mayor, in 11; the building inspector, in 13 cities; and the director of public works, in 8 cities. Various other officials, including secretaries to the planning commission, city clerks, and administrative assistants to the city manager served as planning director in 38 cities.

From the statistics shown above, it is apparent that a very high percentage of planning agencies in the United States are functioning without the benefit of a full-time staff. In many cases, the planning function is represented by little more than the planning name, and often members of the planning commission have shown little interest in planning beyond the drafting of a zoning ordinance.[54] In other jurisdictions where no permanent staff is employed, rather extensive work in planning is carried on either by the members of the planning commission themselves, or by contract planning, the employment of consultants, or by the services of personnel of operating departments.

While recognizing that the size and composition of the planning staff must vary with the peculiar needs of each individual city, the International City Managers' Association, in its publication "Local Planning Administration," suggests that "every city of 50,000 population or more should have a permanent staff consisting, as a minimum, of an experienced city planner, at least one draftsman, and one stenographer." [55] For a city of 500,000, the Association suggests a permanent staff of from 15 to 20 persons headed by a director with at least ten years of experience. In a city of this size the professional staff should include persons with specialized training in engineering, architecture, and the social sciences (particularly political science, sociology, and economics), as well as six to ten draftsmen and clerks, and one or two stenographers. For the conducting of special surveys and investigations, a larger number of temporary employees may be required for taking census, checking traffic, and gathering other information.

Many small communities with budgets too limited to employ a full-time planner can frequently find some other solution to fulfilling their needs for professional services. Often this can be done by engaging a qualified planning consultant on a contract basis. For certain purposes, the local planning commission may find that valuable help can be obtained from the state university or interested state agencies. Another possibility for some communities is to work out an arrangement with other communities whereby they pool their resources to employ a joint planning staff whose time would be shared among them.[56] This approach also has the value of facilitating a regional outlook upon local problems.[57] Sometimes it may be found that public funds can be supplemented by private contributions of local industry

[54] Walker, op. cit., p. 219.
[55] Local Planning Administration, op. cit., p. 45.
[56] Chamber of Commerce of the United States, City Planning and Urban Development, op. cit., p. 18.
[57] Russell Van Nest Black, "Staffing Small Town Planning Commissions," Planning 1952, Proceedings of the Annual National Planning Conference Held in Boston, Massachusetts, October 5–9, 1952 (Chicago: American Society of Planning Officials, 1952), p. 143.

and civic-minded citizens. Usually such organizations as the local Chamber of Commerce, service organizations, civic clubs, the school board, and other interested public and private organizations can be of help in raising funds for such purposes.

The internal organization of the planning agency is governed by the size of the staff and the emphasis given to special aspects of planning. In the small staff, little or no formal organization is required. In those agencies having a large number of employees it is necessary to organize the work program under divisions within the agency and to assign personnel to these divisions according to their qualifications and specializations. These divisions will of necessity vary with the planning activities of the particular agency. Possible subdivisions may include all or some of the following: (1) Division of the Comprehensive Plan, (2) Division of Land Use, (3) Division of Streets and Highways, (4) Division of Mapping and Zoning, (5) Division of Research and Statistics, (6) Division of Capital Budget and Program, and (7) Division of Platting and Subdivision. One of the most important considerations to bear in mind in setting up the internal organization of the planning agency is to insure that a proper division is made between the long-term planning activities and those activities which are concerned with the immediate and routine administration of the planning program. This distinction is necessary to prevent the pressure of day-to-day tasks from diverting the time and attention of the staff from important long-range planning projects.[58]

Staff Participation in Plan Making. Full participation of staff members in the development of the planning program contributes both to general staff interest and to individual initiative. Joint participation in the study and analysis of the various features of the community and in the presentation of the results causes the specialized work of the staff members to become more meaningful when the planning stage is reached. The reconnaissance survey and the interpretation of basic data offer the best possible opportunities for creating staff teamwork.

In staffs where a high degree of specialization exists, consultation before decisions are made utilizes the individual training and varying points of view of staff members and helps to insure that all aspects of the problem essential to good planning have been considered. Although such practices may be time consuming, the time is well justified in morale factors, in relating each staff member's part in the

[58] *Local Planning Administration*, op. cit., p. 47.

planning process to the whole, in the educational value for staff members of limited training, and in the values of a unified approach by all personnel.

Qualifications and Training. The background, training, and experience essential to qualify one as a competent professional planner are not very well standardized. Planning is an emerging profession. It has not as yet achieved the recognition and acceptance of professional status that is accorded to the fields of engineering, architecture, law, and many others. One of the reasons for this is its immaturity. Perhaps of more significance is the difficulty in defining the scope of the profession and the field of knowledge which the practitioner must master in order to qualify.

The fact that planning is now being carried on in many cities by persons who are not well qualified has undoubtedly had an adverse effect upon the prestige of the profession as well as the cause of city planning. Actually, many cities, particularly those of under 100,000 population which have planning staffs, have set up little or no standards or requirements for education and experience. In its survey on planning personnel conducted in 1949, the Subcommittee on Personnel Classification and Standards of the American Institute of Planners found that in many cases where job descriptions had been set up, the credentials of the present incumbent were given as prerequisite for the job. In some cases a civil engineer's license was required as a prerequisite.[59]

Until quite recently, city planning was thought of primarily as an engineering blueprint called the master plan which represented the planner's ideas of how the streets, parks, transportation systems, public buildings, and other physical facilities should be located and designed in proper relationship to each other. This master-plan blueprint was generally looked upon as the end product of planning to be repeated perhaps once a decade.[60] Planning no longer proceeds under this concept. It is today regarded by the profession as a continuous function, comprehensive in scope, aimed at the unified development of the community, taking into account all the physical, social, economic, and fiscal elements collateral thereto.[61]

[59] American Institute of Planners, *Findings of the 1949 National Survey on Planning Personnel*, Preliminary Recommendations on Improved Personnel Practice, Subcommittee on Personnel Classification and Standards (Cambridge, Mass.: 1950), p. 14.

[60] Howard K. Menhinick, "The Training of City Planners," *Proceedings, American Society of Engineers*, Vol. 80, Separate No. 423, p. 423–1—423–2, March, 1954.

[61] American Institute of Planners, *Code of Professional Conduct*, adopted as a Policy Statement by the Institute, January 10, 1948.

The fact that planning in the past has been concerned largely with public improvements and design has resulted in most planners' being drawn from the fields of engineering and architecture. Today, since the concept of planning has come to embrace such subjects as housing, slum clearance, land use, urban redevelopment and renewal, financial planning, public works programming, and related matters, the participation and collaboration of persons trained in the disciplines of sociology, economics, geography, political science, and law are essential. Planning requires the services of both generalists and specialists.

Generalists are needed to carry out the important coördinating responsibilities which help to insure that each project and program fits properly into the total picture. Such persons must have executive and leadership ability to qualify them to direct the planning operations and to work successfully with the elected public officials, the heads of the operating departments, and with the public. Training and experience in public administration and a thorough grounding in the legal nature, structure, functioning, and politics of local government are vital to the performance of the coördinating function. The specialists, on the other hand, with their more specialized training in various disciplines are essential to the development of the many technical aspects of the planning program and the effectuation of the plan. It is they who conduct the research, make the analyses, draft the plans, and prepare and assemble the important data required for making policy recommendations. The generalists and the specialists must function as a team. Both are necessary to effective planning and both are part of the group comprising the planning profession, although each may have a very different background of education and experience.

Today, a number of colleges and universities are offering graduate professional degrees in urban planning, city planning, or regional planning. Although differing in many respects, these graduate programs all recognize the importance of providing a broad background of training from the disciplines of political science, economics, geography, sociology, engineering, and architecture. The usual approach is to build the curriculum around a number of core planning courses concerned with such subjects as the theory of urban planning, urban planning and government, graphic presentation, site planning, planning legislation, social statistics, traffic and transportation, urban renewal, planning methods and techniques, and practical problems designed to develop and test the application of planning principles. To these are added a number of related courses from the contributing disciplines.[62] Most of the institutions also require that the student acquire some practical experience through an internship program and the preparation of a thesis on a specific planning project. Through experience with this type of training there is coming to be recognized a body of knowledge and skills, the mastery of which constitutes the qualifications of the professional planner.[63]

The importance of a broad general background for planning education is pointed out in the somewhat facetious comment contained in a recent issue of the *Journal of the American Institute of Planners*: [64]

A planner with a civil engineering background tends to emphasize drainage, sewer and water extensions, street-widening, elimination of grade crossings and streetcar track removal; a planner with an architectural background tends to emphasize civic centers, monumental buildings, harmonious exteriors and quality of design; a planner with a landscape architectural background emphasizes scenic parks, recreation, site planning, tree planting and scenic vistas; a planner with a background in geography tends to emphasize topography, climate, weather, water resources, soil condition and land forms; a planner with a background in sociology tends to emphasize family and communal relationships, social interaction, physical influences on group and individual behavior and the psychological effects of planned as against unplanned environment; the planner with a background in public administration tends to emphasize the management function of the chief executive, capital budget programming, smoother relations with the planning commission and the city council, chain of command and interdepartmental relationships; the planner with the background in law tends to . . .

Personnel Classifications and Job Descriptions.   The immaturity

[62] For a comparison of the graduate planning courses offered by institutions of higher learning, see Frederick J. Adams, *Urban Planning Education in the United States* (Cincinnati, Ohio: The Alfred Bettman Foundation, 1954). For an excellent discussion of the background and current needs in planning education, see Harvey S. Perloff, "Education for Planners: Past, Present and Future," Journal of the American Institute of Planners, Vol. XXII, No. 4, Fall 1956, pp. 186–217.

[63] Among the many colleges and universities that are now offering professional training in urban or regional planning are the following: University of California, University of Chicago, Columbia University, Cornell University, University of Florida, Georgia Institute of Technology, Illinois Institute of Technology, University of Illinois, Iowa State College, University of Kansas, Massachusetts Institute of Technology, Michigan State College, University of Michigan, University of North Carolina, University of Oklahoma, University of Pennsylvania, Rutgers University, University of Southern California, University of Texas, University of Washington, University of Wisconsin, Yale University.

[64] Herman D. Ruth, *op. cit.*, p. 36.

of planning as a profession is indicated to some extent by the great lack of standardization of titles of staff personnel. An examination of the reports of planning commissions will reveal that different jurisdictions use various and sundry titles for employees performing similar tasks. Furthermore, the same titles used in different jurisdictions do not indicate, necessarily, that the person holding that title is performing comparable duties or that he is performing at the same level of responsibility. Among the titles commonly employed by planning agencies are Director, Secretary, Executive Secretary, Planning Engineer, Assistant Engineer, Senior Planner, City Planner, Junior Planner, Administrative Assistant, Draftsman, Stenographer, Manager, Clerk, Investigator, and Planner of various grades.[65]

The values of developing appropriate and standardized nomenclature are obvious. Not only is the professional status enhanced, but also it makes it possible to devise a more systematic scheme for handling of personnel, including the assignment of duties. Moreover, it aids in the establishment of more equitable pay scales, and in facilitating the matter of transfers and promotions. Sometimes the use of an inappropriate title may have an influence upon the selection of personnel and the assignment of duties. The use of the term "planning engineer" has frequently been criticized on the ground that it stresses the engineering aspects of planning and, where used, has given planning a bias in that direction.

In recent years, a number of efforts have been made to encourage the adoption of uniform titles and job descriptions for professional planning personnel. In 1949, the American Institute of Planners, through its Subcommittee on Personnel Classification and Standards, undertook an extensive survey of professional city and regional planning positions for the purpose of gathering current and comparable information on salaries and staffs in order to evaluate current personnel practices and to make recommendations for improved standards.[66]

As a result of this survey, and the recommendation of its subcom-

---

[65] At the time the Subcommittee on Personal Classification and Standards of the American Institute of Planners made its survey on planning personnel in 1949, the United States Civil Service Commission did not recognize city and regional planning as a profession and, consequently, jobs of that nature were classified under allied professions such as "engineer," "landscape architect," "economic analyst," "business economist," "industrial specialist," etc. Subsequently, the Commission decided to recognize the city and regional planning profession and has set up a classification system covering it.

[66] American Institute of Planners, op. cit., p. 9.

mittee, the American Institute of Planners, in April, 1950, approved the following classification system for the planning profession:

Level	Descriptive Category of Questionnaire	Preferred Descriptive Category	Suitable Job Titles	General Nature of Responsibility
1	Newcomer	JUNIOR	Junior Planner Assistant Planner	Performance of assigned technical work of limited scope under careful supervision.
2	Full-Fledged	SENIOR	Associate Planner Planner Senior Planner	Performance of assigned technical work of an advanced nature demanding independent judgment and initiative under little or no supervision and often requiring supervision of the work of assistants.
3	Division Chief	PRINCIPAL	Principal Planner Head Planner Chief Planner Division Chief Assistant Director	Complete, consistent direction of a specific broad field of planning activity involving supervision of a considerable technical staff.
4	Director	DIRECTOR	Planning Director Executive Director	Complete charge of work of planning staff and of representing the planning office before government officials and the public.

In recommending the above classification system, the report of the Institute recognizes that actual job descriptions at any level may naturally vary to a considerable degree among planning areas of various sizes in which planning problems may differ. It is suggested, however, that such a system will facilitate the comparison of personnel data in planning areas of the same size group and also make it possible to develop a uniform system of job titles for all size groups based on these generalized types of responsibility. Suitable education and experience should be required for each professional planning job. The amount of the experience for each particular job should be established in progressive stages varying with the level of the job responsibility. Weight should be given to the nature of the experience as well as to the length of experience. Requirements should be kept reasonably flexible in order to attract competent persons of varied professional experience.

The Subcommittee on Personnel Classification and Standards of the American Institute of Planners included in its *Findings of the 1949 National Survey on Planning Personnel* a number of representative job descriptions of various professional levels selected from cities of varying sizes. As illustrative of the job description for the position of "Director of Planning" in an area with a population of 100,000 to 500,000, the report included an example from Long Beach, California, which was as follows: [67]

DUTIES: Plans, organizes and directs the activities or professional, technical, administrative and clerical personnel engaged in the compilation, analysis and interpretation of data affecting community planning; acts as staff adviser to the Planning Commission, City Council and other city officials on problems related to municipal planning, confers with civic groups and participates in planning conferences; supervises the administration of the zoning, subdivision and setback ordinances; prepares and administers the Master Plan within the policies of the Planning Commission; organizes and conducts planning studies; formulates and recommends programs for the physical development of the city and its environments; selects and trains staff personnel; prepares and administers the departmental budget; writes comprehensive reports; speaks to public gatherings.

QUALIFICATIONS: 4 years in an accredited college or university with major in city or community planning; architecture, engineering, landscape architecture, or public administration. Administrative experience in addition to the minimum experience requirement may be substituted for education, year for year. 5 years of professional experience in planning, architecture, engineering, landscape architecture, or public administration, 3 years of which shall have been in an administrative position in either city, county, or regional planning.

The United States Civil Service Commission in a recent announcement of an examination for City Planner (Grades GS-7 to GS-15) to fill positions in Washington, D.C., and nearby areas prepared a small folder setting forth a rather detailed description of the work and the requirements of education and experience to be met by the applicants. The folder describes the work of city planners as follows: [68]

City planners administer, advise on, supervise, or perform professional work in the development of comprehensive plans, programs, and regulations for the orderly physical growth and renewal of cities, towns, metropolitan areas, and other population centers, with the objective of promoting their economic, social, and general welfare. Within statutory limits and in close coöperation with local authorities they collect, analyze, evaluate, and present facts, trends, and proposals, and develop integrated plans and

[67] *Ibid.*, pp. 18–19.
[68] Announcement No. 410 Issued: June 29, 1954. X-118 Modified. United States Civil Service Commission, Washington 25, D.C., p. 2.

recommendations for future growth and renewal. The work includes, among other items, consideration of population and income trends, construction costs, public finances, intergovernmental relationships, and existing and future needs for land use, public utilities, community facilities, housing, circulation, and transportation.

The quality and difficulty of the duties to be performed and the degree of responsibility to be assumed vary with the grade level, becoming progressively greater with each successively higher grade.

The general requirements for education and experience are specified as follows: [69]

A. Successful completion of a full 4-year or longer curriculum leading to a bachelor's degree in an accredited college or university, with major study in city or regional planning, architecture, landscape architecture, or civil engineering; or successful completion of a full 4-year or longer curriculum leading to a bachelor's degree in an accredited college or university, which has included at least 36 semester hours of courses in any combination of at least 2 of the following subjects or fields: city or regional planning, architecture, landscape architecture, civil engineering, urban geography, housing, public administration, economics, urban sociology.

B. Four years of successful and progressive technical experience which must show that the applicant has acquired an understanding of the fundamental principles, skills, and techniques underlying a professional knowlelge of city planning comparable to that which would have been acquired through the successful completion of a full 4-year curriculum as described under "A" above, and that the applicant possesses the ability to apply them in the professional practice of city planning. The content of the experience will be evaluated on the basis of its comparability to a full 4-year professional curriculum, both in the extent and quality of work done. This evaluation will take into consideration the type and variety of experience, the basic knowledges used and needed, and the applicability of the work to the courses in a normal professional curriculum of study in these fields.

The successful completion of college work in nonaccredited institutions will be accepted on the same basis as indicated immediately above, provided that such institutions give instruction of definitely collegiate level and that the State university of the State in which the institution is located accepts the courses and gives advanced credit for them. (In those States where there is no State university, the evaluation and acceptance of college credit as made by the State department of education will be accepted.)

[69] *Ibid.*, pp. 2–4.

In addition to meeting the basic requirements listed above, applicants must show experience as provided below:

This experience must have been of a broad and comprehensive nature gained on the staff of a public planning board, commission, agency, etc., or private planning organization, and must have been concerned with comprehensive city planning as distinct from "limited" aspects of planning functions, i.e., economics, architectural, engineering, and population studies (applicants may substitute such limited experience on a restricted basis— see below). For each higher grade level the experience must clearly show progression in responsibility assumed, complexity, difficulty and scope of assignments, importance of decisions made, consultative and advisory duties, public relations, and administrative and technical abilities.

For grade GS-7, one year of successful professional experience in city or regional planning is specified. More extensive and responsible experience is required for each of the higher grades. The top grade, GS-15, specifies the following requirements: [70]

For GS-15: Four years of broad and progressive planning experience, including at least 1 year of extremely important and completely responsible experience in one of the branches of planning equivalent in grade level to that required of GS-14 planners. This experience must have demonstrated a comprehensive knowledge of planning principles and their application, ability of the highest order in the organization, direction, and coördination of planning activities of major importance and magnitude, and administrative leadership of outstanding character. For eligibility in this grade the applicant's attainments as a planner must have been such as to have given him wide recognition by the city planning profession.

The announcement points out that the required amount of experience will not in itself be accepted as proof of qualification for a position. The applicant's ability to perform all the duties of the position must be established through his record of experience and training. Length of experience beyond the required minimum is not considered as important as demonstrated success in fulfilling duties of a responsible nature. Where experience in planning is limited to one phase of planning, such as economic, engineering, architectural, or some social phase, such experience is accepted as qualifying on the basis of one year of such experience for six months of the required general comprehensive experience up to a maximum of two years of credit for any grade level. This limited experience may not, however, be used to meet the required one year of experience at the level of

[70] Ibid., p. 5.

the next grade below, for any of the grades above grade GS-7. The United States Civil Service requirements also permit limited substitution of graduate study in an accredited college or university for comprehensive experience up to a maximum of two years of such experience. Completion of the requirements of the master's degree may be substituted for one year of experience, and completion of all the requirements for a doctor's degree may be substituted for two years of the required experience.

Voluntary Assistance. In every large community the bulk of the planning work must be carried out by the staff of professional employees. There are, however, many tasks involved in the planning process which may often be assumed by the help of voluntary workers. Particularly is this true with respect to planning projects which involve the gathering of population data, taking of traffic counts, and the collection of various types of information on a community-wide basis. The effective use of voluntary workers requires a great deal of organization and staff preparation, but for many purposes may serve as a means of augmenting the professional staff to a degree which otherwise would not be possible within the city's budget limitations. Small communities may at times find it necessary to rely almost exclusively upon voluntary help. Although persons undertaking these tasks must be selected with care, obviously the requirements discussed above as essential qualifications for professional planners are not applicable to such workers. It should also be kept in mind that the use of voluntary assistants often provides an excellent means of promoting public understanding and acceptance of the planning program.

THE PLANNING BUDGET

Planning, like every other municipal function, costs money. On the other hand, many communities are beginning to awaken to the fact that failure to plan may result in costs which are many times higher than those required to support a well-staffed planning agency. Costs of nonplanning are reflected not only in material wastes but also in social values. More and more, planning is being looked upon as a money saving device by means of which community resources, both material and human, are properly developed and preserved. This, in part, explains the fact that planning budgets and planning staffs have greatly expanded during the past few years.

Recent Trends. Between 1936 and 1948, the annual expenditures for city planning rose from $1,636,700 to $4,140,300.[71] Since 1942 planning expenditures have increased at an even greater rate. In 1947, 186 cities reported annual expenditure of over $1000 for planning.[72] In 1951, 256 cities spent more than $1000 [73] and in 1953, 379 cities reported spending more than $1000 a year for planning.[74] More than five times as many cities spent over $10,000 a year for planning in the decade ending 1951 than was the case in the decade previously. According to the Municipal Year Book, only two cities in the United States, New York and Chicago, appropriated over $100,000 for planning in the year 1941.[75] In 1953, 17 cities appropriated amounts of over $100,000 for planning and five others appropriated $90,000 or more for this purpose.[76] In the same year New York spent $447,400; Philadelphia spent $423,500; and Los Angeles spent $396,700.

When planning expenditures are reduced to a per capita basis, the increase in the planning budgets becomes more apparent. Los Angeles, which spent 4.9 cents per capita for planning in 1941, increased its planning budget to 17.7 cents in 1951. Detroit spent 2.2 cents for planning in 1941 and 11.3 cents in 1951. Milwaukee increased its planning budget in the same period from 4.3 cents per capita to 19.4 cents and San Francisco, which provided 5.4 cents per capita in 1941, reported expenditures of 21 cents in 1951.[77] Part of the increased expenditures is attributable to the general rise in prices, but a considerable portion is due to the problems resulting from population growth and the pressures for more adequate zoning, subdivision control, urban redevelopment, and a general interest in better community planning.[78] In the six-year period, from 1946 through 1951, a total of 362 cities of over 10,000 population revised their zoning ordinances, and 258 cities either adopted or revised their subdivision control ordinances during this same period.[79]

Optimum Size.   The size of the planning budget, like the size of

[71] Walker, op. cit., p. 355.

[72] The Municipal Year Book, 1948 (Chicago: The International City Managers' Association, 1948), p. 247.

[73] The Municipal Year Book, 1952 (Chicago: The International City Managers' Association, 1952), p. 275.

[74] The Municipal Year Book, 1954, op. cit., p. 294.

[75] The Municipal Year Book, 1942 (Chicago: The International City Managers' Association, 1942), pp. 369–378.

[76] The Municipal Year Book, 1954, op. cit., pp. 296–300.

[77] Dennis O'Harrow, "Why This Interest in City Planning?" Public Management, Vol. XXXIV, No. 5, p. 98, May, 1952.

[78] Ibid., p. 99.

[79] Ibid., pp. 99–100.

the planning staff, varies with many factors. Each jurisdiction has its own special problems which make it necessary to provide a budget tailor-made to satisfy local needs. Among the variable factors which affect the budget requirements are such matters as the complexity of planning problems, geographical size and special features, the degree to which basic planning studies are completed, and the assignment of staff to responsibilities of a nonplanning nature. Any figures suggested for cities in any population bracket or on a per capita basis can be nothing more than a rule-of-thumb guide.

The report of the International City Managers' Association on Local Planning Administration suggests than an adequate planning staff for cities of from 50,000 to 100,000 population would require not less than 15 cents per capita and in smaller communities the cost would run 25 cents or even more.[80] As a very general standard, the Subcommittee on Personnel Classification and Standards of the American Institute of Planners suggests that a normal operating budget might vary between 15 cents per capita in communities with populations of over a million to about one dollar per capita in very small communities.[81] The Report states that about $7500 is the minimum budget for a small community employing a full-time professional planner. A budget of this size would permit the employment of only one professional planner and very limited secretarial and drafting assistance.

A study of per capita planning expenditures based upon 1951 budgets, indicated that 27 cities with populations of over 25,000 spent 20 cents or more per capita. Of these, 12 were in California and most had experienced rather rapid population growth, with its consequent municipal problems. San Mateo, for example, which had an increase in population of 114 percent between 1940 and 1950, spent 50.4 cents per capita for planning in 1951. Burbank, which increased 128 percent in population during this period, spent 49.3 cents per capita. Phoenix, Arizona, which had a population increase of 61.4 percent during the same ten-year period, spent 36 cents per capita for planning. The highest per capita planning expenditure reported for 1951 was $1.10 for El Paso, Texas, although the population increase for El Paso, between 1940 and 1950, was only 34.4 percent.[82]

[80] *Local Planning Administration, op. cit.,* p. 45.

[81] American Institute of Planners, *Findings of the 1949 National Survey on Planning Personnel,* Preliminary Recommendations on Improved Personnel Practice, Subcommittee on Personnel Classification and Standards (Cambridge, Mass.: 1950), p. 16.

[82] O'Harrow, *op. cit.,* p. 99.

Budget figures and per capita statistics such as these have certain value for making a comparative evaluation of planning activities in different communities, but they do not tell the whole story of planning effectiveness. In some of the smaller communities, a relatively good job of planning is done on a strictly voluntary basis. In others, a great deal of planning is carried on through the work of municipal employees paid by the operating departments. In still other jurisdictions, the planning agency is assigned responsibilities with respect to the administration of the zoning ordinance and other planning regulations which, in some jurisdictions, is assumed by administrative departments. Any true comparison of planning effectiveness would need to take into account all these factors as well as the special demands of the local planning program.

THE PLANNING PROGRAM AND PLANNING PROCEDURE

Each new planning agency is initially faced with making a determination of how to proceed to develop an adequate planning program. The most important part of such a program is the preparation of the comprehensive plan. To accomplish this successfully, both the planning commission and the planning staff should have a thorough understanding of the nature of the comprehensive plan, the elements included in it, the procedures by which it is developed, and the methods by which it is put into effect. Since the primary purpose of planning is to provide a basis for making intelligent policy decisions, the comprehensive plan must be based upon knowledge of the physical, economic, social, and political structure of the community and accepted goals for community development. Plan making must be preceded by a study and analysis of all the important facts, trends, and forces that influence the growth and character of the community.

The planning program normally is developed in three stages. The first stage is a reconnaissance survey which involves the gathering of essential data necessary to provide (a) a picture of what the community is like, and (b) trends and potentialities in community development. The second stage is that of plan making based upon an analysis and interpretation of the data assembled through the reconnaissance survey. The third stage is that of plan implementation which involves the utilization of those measures and devices which have been developed to carry the plans into effect.[83] In this third

[83] Harvey S. Perloff suggests a finer breakdown of the steps in the planning procedure

stage the planning responsibility is shifted largely from the planning agency to the legislative body and to the administrative officials who make the policy decisions and carry them into execution.[84] Nevertheless, the planning agency has a major role in this process. It has responsibility for the preparation of the zoning ordinance and amendments, for reviewing subdivision plats, for recommending the capital budget, and for many other programs and procedures to be instituted to make planning effective.

ASSEMBLY OF DATA FOR THE PLANNING STUDY

The planning agency is a research and fact-finding arm of municipal government. This does not mean that all data gathered must be the product of its own original research. In fact the success of the planning agency in assembling planning data may depend upon how well it utilizes the various public and private sources of information available to the community. Chambers of commerce, privately financed research organizations, civic groups, and many federal, state, and local agencies usually have much factual information and statistical data that are in usable form and available to the planning agency. To the extent that these data are complete and reliable, their use will avoid unnecessary duplication of research and save considerable money.

Planners must always keep before them the considerations of "for whom" and "for what purpose" the plans are being developed. The "power structure" of the community is very important in determining the orientation which must be given to the planning program since it is this structure that gives direction to public policies.[85]

Every forward-looking community would like to be able to make reasonable predictions as to the probable size, character, and composition of its population and its industrial and commercial potential as a basis for policies and programs designed to further its physical, social, and economic well-being. The success of the planning program is governed to a high degree by how accurately predictions are made. There are no crystal balls for planning. Community estimates must be made from a study of the historical background of the community, present conditions, current trends, and political forces as revealed

as follows: (1) Diagnosis, (2) Prognosis, (3) Policy and Programming, (4) Execution, and (5) Checking Results. Harvey S. Perloff, "Knowledge Needed for Comprehensive Planning," *Needed Urban and Metropolitan Research* (Oxford, Ohio: Scripps Foundation, Miami University, 1953), p. 5.

[84] See Part III, Plan Implementation.

[85] The power structure of a community consists of those forces and interests that dominate or control political action.

by such data as are found available or which can be assembled by the planner.

The data which any planning agency should assemble in order to inaugurate its planning program vary with the problems faced by the particular community and the immediate objectives of the planning program. In most communities there is neither the time nor the necessity for undertaking a grand survey for the purpose of gathering all types of data which conceivably may be useful as the planning program progresses. For the most part, the gathering of data is closely integrated in the analytical process of plan preparation and often is not identifiable as a separate activity. Nevertheless, the planner, at the outset, should undertake to familiarize himself with sources of information from which essential data can be secured and assembled as needed.

The International City Managers' Association suggests the following as the kind of data which should be readily available to the planner.[86]

1. *Physical:* (a) Regional geographic relationships, (b) topography, (c) geology, (d) meteorology and floods, (e) natural resources, (f) land use, (g) street, transit, and transportation facilities and their use, (h) public buildings, (i) civic art, architectural design, general appearance.
2. *Social:* (a) Population—growth, distribution, composition, characteristics, and trends, (b) health—births, deaths, infant mortality, diseases, (c) housing and rents, (d) education—public, parochial, private, (e) recreation—public and commercial, (f) dependency, relief, social services, (g) crime and delinquency.
3. *Economic:* (a) Manufactures, wholesale and retail trade, service industries, etc., (b) occupations and incomes, (c) employment and unemployment, (d) building costs, (e) transportation and transit costs, (f) water, power, fuel, waste disposal—availability and costs, (g) taxation, (h) migration and shifts of industry, business and population, (i) building construction and demolition, (j) trade area and markets.
4. *Financial:* (a) Assessed valuation of property subject to taxation, (b) tax levies and tax rates, (c) revenues from taxation and other sources, (d) operating expenditures, (e) debt charges and capital expenditures, (f) bond obligations and maturities.
5. *Legal:* (a) City charter or statutes pertaining to local government, (b) planning and related laws—state statutes and local ordinances, (c) laws concerning property conveyance, (d) laws governing municipal fiscal

---

[86] *Local Planning Administration, op. cit.,* p. 60.

operations, (e) laws concerning land acquisition and sale by city, (f) laws governing the financing of public improvements.

Since the purpose of assembling factual information is to facilitate the development of the comprehensive plan, it is obvious that the gathering of facts should not be an end in itself. In order to avoid becoming lost in a maze of miscellaneous data and statistics, the planning agency should concentrate on securing first that information which is most essential and most significant to the development of the plans. Almost every planning agency will find it necessary to acquire data concerning land use, real property values and potential uses, family composition, family income, population, traffic, land values, and tax delinquencies. Background information basic to the planning study can usually be obtained through a brief reconnaissance survey designed to provide (1) an overall view of the physical setting of the community including both natural and man-made features, (2) an appraisal of how the community makes its living, (3) an evaluation of the character and quality of living, and (4) a listing of the local sources for planning.[87]

PREPARATION AND ADOPTION OF COMPREHENSIVE PLAN

The second stage of the planning program is that of plan making. At this stage, the planning process enters the realm of public policy. The comprehensive plan developed from the assembly and analysis of basic data furnishes the basis for recommendations to the executive and legislative authorities to guide them in deciding upon alternative courses of public action.

Nature and Scope of the Plan. The broad objective of comprehensive planning is to relate, balance, and harmonize the physical, social, and economic features of the community in order to produce the greatest satisfaction out of community living. The function of the planning agency is to provide the coördinating machinery to insure that this objective is carried out. The comprehensive plan, which is often referred to as the "master plan," is a requisite tool in this process.

Essentially, the comprehensive plan is an outline for long-term community development which provides the planning agency with information from which it can judge and evaluate community

[87] For a detailed outline of steps in planning procedure, see *Action for Better Cities, A Guide for Community Planning*, Public Administration Service No. 86 (Chicago: 1943).

demands and requirements in making its recommendations to the executive authority and city council. It "embodies information, judgments, and objectives collected and formulated by experts to serve as both a guiding and predictive force." [88] The comprehensive plan is not necessarily a single map or document. It may consist of maps, reports, lists of proposed public improvements and various other forms of plan presentation. It is ever-changing and never complete.

The scope and content of the comprehensive plan has expanded with the development of the concept of comprehensive planning. The pamphlet entitled "Standard City Planning Enabling Act," issued by the United States Department of Commerce in 1928,[89] placed emphasis upon the master plan as a means of combining and coordinating the objectives and plans for all phases of the physical aspects of the city. Edward M. Bassett, in his book entitled *The Master Plan*,[90] published in 1938, advanced the thinking on the purpose and use of the plan in pointing out that the plan is never complete and in urging the importance of keeping the master plan separate from the official map in order that it remain dynamic and capable of quick alteration by the planning commission. This study emphasized the point of view that the master plan should be regarded and used as a working tool of the planning agency only.

A master plan should be a design for the coördination of the elements of the community plan. It should be kept inside the four walls of the planning commission, not a secret document but one capable of being readily changed, the last and best work of the commission.[91]

Mr. Bassett limited the scope of the master plan to seven elements:

1. Streets, which include pedestrian and vehicular bridges and tunnels.
2. Parks, including parkways.
3. Sites for public buildings.
4. Public buildings.
5. Public reservations.
6. Zoning districts.
7. Routes for public utilities and pierheads and bulkhead lines.

[88] Charles M. Haar, "In Accordance with a Comprehensive Plan," *Harvard Law Review*, Vol. 68, No. 7, 1955, p. 1155.

[89] United States Department of Commerce, Advisory Committee on City Planning and Zoning, *A Standard City Planning Enabling Act* (Washington, D.C.: U.S. Government Printing Office, 1928).

[90] Edward M. Bassett, *The Master Plan* (New York: Russell Sage Foundation, 1938), p. 62.

[91] *Ibid.*, p. 142.

Since 1938, the scope of the comprehensive plan has been further expanded. Today, the concept of the comprehensive plan not only reflects the planned physical developments but also indicates the proposed public programs for social and economic betterment.[92] This idea is being carried into the comprehensive plans of most of the cities which today are progressive in their planning outlook. The Los Angeles plan, for example, starts with the premise that the city is "a method of living—a mechanism or device for getting satisfactions out of life. The city, too, must have an objective—which may include comfort, beauty, happiness, or distinction in some field of joint endeavor." [93]

Professor Charles M. Haar, who has made a detailed analysis of the planning laws of the various states, points out that the comprehensive plan as represented by the typical enabling act has six broad types of uses: [94] "(1) a source of information; (2) a program of correction; (3) an estimate of the future; (4) an indicator of goals; (5) a technique for coördination; and (6) a device for stimulating public interest and responsibility." He recognizes that the comprehensive plan also has an important function in furnishing a guide to appropriate procedures and measures to be adopted for plan effectuation. However, this purpose can be served only if the plan is developed in accordance with the foregoing types of uses.

One of the weaknesses of planning has been the failure to recognize that the comprehensive plan should provide the basis for zoning, subdivision control, the circulation pattern, public improvement projects, and other means of plan implementation. In many jurisdictions such programs have been undertaken with little or no reference to the comprehensive plan. The bridging of this gap between plan making and plan implementation through the appropriate use of the comprehensive plan is one of the most important requisites of effective planning.[95]

[92] For a discussion of the historical development, see Charles M. Haar, "The Content of the General Plan: A Glance at History," *Journal of the American Institute of Planners*, Vol. 21, No. 2–3, pp. 66–70, Spring-Summer, 1955.

[93] Wilbur C. Hallenbeck, *American Urban Communities* (New York: Harper & Brothers, 1951), p. 552, quoting from George W. Robbins and L. D. Tilton (eds.), Los Angeles: Preface to a Master Plan (Los Angeles: Pacific Southwest Academy, 1941), Publication No. 19.

[94] Charles M. Haar, "The Master Plan: An Impermanent Constitution," *Law and Contemporary Problems*, Vol. 20, No. 3, pp. 353–418, Summer, 1955.

[95] To accomplish this, Professor Haar suggests the idea of giving the comprehensive plan the legal status of an "impermanent constitution" binding upon the legislative body in enacting implementing ordinances (*ibid.*). See, however, p. 132.

In preparing the comprehensive plan, the aim should be to include all the important community features in proper relationship to each other. Among these should be: (1) the location and character of proposed land uses, showing the areas to be designated for residential, business, commercial, and industrial purposes, (2) the location and character of proposed open spaces for recreation and cultural life such as parks, playgrounds, zoos, arboretums, and golf courses, (3) the avenues and means of travel, including streets and highways, transit systems, transportation facilities, railroads and terminals, airports, and waterways and facilities, (4) the location and character of public buildings such as city halls, auditoriums, schools, fire stations, and post offices, (5) the routes, location, design, and ownership of utility systems, including water supply, sewage disposal, gas distribution, and light and power, (6) specific programs and projects which may or may not be closely related to the other elements. Programs and projects would include slum clearance, urban renewal, elimination of traffic hazards, control of excessive land subdivision, relief of traffic congestion, improvement of transit facilities, the long-range public improvements program, and others. Since the comprehensive plan attempts to forecast the community development for a period of 20 to 30 years, it is necessary to think of the plan primarily in terms of long-range planning.

Presentation, Publication, and Adoption. Many methods are used for presenting the comprehensive plan. Map presentation is perhaps the most important of all methods. However, all the elements of the plan do not lend themselves to mapping. Some matters are subject to presentation only by text material in the form of reports. Others can best be presented by charts, graphs, or tabulations. For the purpose of arousing public interest, certain data may well be presented in the form of charts, statistics, or graphs which stimulate the imagination. All presentation should be accurate and convincing. Facts dramatically presented tend to appeal to pride and emotions. Although the comprehensive plan is primarily the tool of the planning agency, it also serves to provide both city officials and citizens with an understandable picture of the proposals and recommendations for urban development and, therefore, should be worded in language familiar to the lay citizen rather than in the technical vocabulary of the professional planner.

Some differences of opinion exist as to whether the comprehensive plan should be published and distributed. Most of those who oppose publication do so on the ground that publication implies completion. Since the plan is under constant change and revision, any published plan will soon be out of date and may be misleading as to current planning recommendations. It is urged, on the other hand, that public understanding and acceptance of planning is so vital to its success that the values of public information leading to advice and criticism greatly outweigh the disadvantages of publication. If the plan is published, care must be taken to inform the public that the publication represents only the best thinking of the planning agency as of a given time. Furthermore, the planning agency must keep in mind that publication does not represent any completed task. Planning will not be accomplished by distributing the plan to interested citizens, groups, and organizations, or by transmitting it to the mayor and city council. The continuing task of the planning staff in helping to formulate public policy remains.

The disadvantages of adopting the comprehensive plan by ordinance have already been indicated. Such action freezes it to the extent of requiring legislative action to change it. The legislative body may, nevertheless, recognize the plan for purposes of reference and for giving effect to certain of its elements without officially adopting it. A clear distinction should be made between the adoption of the comprehensive plan by the planning agency and the adoption of the official map by the legislative body. The comprehensive plan provides the pattern and guidelines for community development as represented by the best judgment of the planning agency as of a given time. Its adoption by the planning agency should not carry any legal binding effect.[96] The adoption of the official map, on the other hand, is a legislative act which gives legal sanction to specific elements of the plan by establishing certain controls over land use.

The enabling statutes of a number of states provide that whenever the planning commission shall have adopted the master plan, or any part thereof, no street, park, public building or structure, major utility, or other specified public facilities may be constructed or authorized until the location, character, and extent of these proposed developments have been submitted to the planning board for approval. Such reference is provided for in order to secure the advice of the planning agency before making a policy decision. A common

[96] "Long-range comprehensive plans commonly reveal a desired state of affairs. They rarely specify the detailed courses of action needed to achieve that desired state." Martin Meyerson, "Building the Middle-Range Bridge of Comprehensive Planning," *Journal of the American Institute of Planners*, Vol. XXII, No. 2, p. 62, Spring, 1956.

provision is to require the planning agency to report to the governing body in writing and in case of disapproval to give the reasons therefor. Some states give the municipal planning commission a suspensive veto by providing that the governing body can overrule its disapproval only by a recorded vote of not less than two-thirds of the entire membership. Under most of these statutes, failure of the planning commission to act on matters referred to it within a stipulated period of time, usually 30 to 45 days, is deemed to constitute approval.[97]

There is a sharp difference of opinion as to whether granting the planning agency the power of a suspensive veto is sound practice. Few persons would question the importance of taking every reasonable step to insure that proposed public projects be developed in conformity with the comprehensive plan. However, responsibility for final decision in matters of location, character, and extent of projects rests upon the elected legislative body. In the long run, good planning will probably be furthered more by keeping the planning agency free from the possibilities of conflict inherent in sharing the legislative function and by relying upon the confidence placed in its judgment and the persuasiveness of its advice.

IMPLEMENTATION OF THE PLAN

The third stage in the planning program is that of putting the plans into execution. The best of plans has public value only when made effective through the adoption of appropriate legislation and the day-to-day application of appropriate administrative procedures. The preparation and selling of plans involve the formulation of policy. The implementation of the plans involves policy decision and policy execution.

The methods by which plans are put into effect are the tools of plan accomplishment. They may be either negative controls or positive action. In some instances the plan must be carried out by the acts of private individuals. This occurs when individuals engage in business activities, erect buildings, or make other uses of their land in conformity with the planning laws. Such laws are usually restrictive in character and control the physical development of the community by placing limitations upon the use one may make of his

[97] For a digest of the principal provisions of the planning laws of the various states, see Housing and Home Finance Agency, *Comparative Digest of the Principal Provisions of State Planning Laws Relating to Housing, Slum Clearance and Urban Redevelopment* (Washington, D.C.: U.S. Government Printing Office, 1952).

property. In other instances, the plan is put into effect by direct action of government agencies as when the municipality constructs a public building or undertakes a slum clearance program. Most of the restrictive controls are supported by the "police power," which is an inherent power of the state to regulate individuals in their personal conduct and the use of their property in the interest of public health, safety, morals, and the general welfare. Plan implementation, through direct action of government, rests principally on the powers of eminent domain, taxation, and appropriation.

The devices by which the comprehensive plan is carried out are to be found in ordinances enacted by the local legislative body and the administrative rules and regulations adopted in conformity therewith. The most common methods of control are through the official map, the zoning ordinance, land subdivision regulations, and acts providing for capital improvements.[98] Somewhat less closely related to the day-to-day work of planning, but often as important to the accomplishment of the objectives of the comprehensive plan, are the legislative acts pertaining to such matters as public housing, urban renewal, off-street parking, the establishment of setback lines, and the control of traffic hazards. Not usually regarded as planning legislation but often of importance to the planner are the provisions of building codes, sanitary codes, fire prevention acts, and other safety measures. Since the public policy aspects of each of these major devices of implementation will be dealt with in detail at a later stage, they are considered here only for identification of purpose.

[98] These devices will be considered in more detail in subsequent chapters.

Part II

SUBJECT MATTER OF PLANNING

CHAPTER 4

Physical Planning and Community Development

Under the modern concept, the scope of urban planning is almost as broad as the field of municipal activities. Nevertheless, planning agencies in most of our cities continue to center their attention upon the physical aspects of the community. Physical planning is concerned with the general pattern of land use, the character and location of public buildings and structures, the design of streets, the location and development of transit and transportation systems, and all other physical facilities which are necessary or desirable to promote the economic betterment, comfort, convenience, and the general welfare. Obviously, physical planning cannot be separated from the program objectives of government. The physical plan is not a goal in itself. Rather, it supplies the pattern within which community life is carried on.

Since planning has its emphasis on the future, the planner must continuously be seeking an answer to the question of "what kind of a community should we build for tomorrow?" Unfortunately, most planners, faced with the necessity of finding solutions to immediate and pressing governmental problems, do not have the time to devote serious study to the long-range implications of many current policies. Consequently, policies relating to such matters as traffic, the location and design of streets, and the character of public buildings and facilities tend to be shaped for meeting short-range demands rather than toward developing a type of community that might eliminate or minimize many of the recurring problems. Decisions with respect to whether a street should be widened, whether off-street parking facilities should be provided, whether mass transportation facilities should be expanded, and whether certain blighted areas should be redeveloped need to be preceded by a determination of such questions as whether business should continue to be centered in the downtown business district or decentralized in neighborhood and outlying community shopping centers and business districts.[1]

For the most part, cities have not faced up to the decision of what kind of community is best for them. It is the responsibility of the planning agency to take the lead in providing the data which will make an informed determination of this question possible. The following discussion is not intended to suggest the plan of development that any given community should follow, but merely to indicate some of the major considerations that should be kept in mind in developing the physical plan and in establishing policies relating to it. In this chapter the emphasis is upon the space requirements of the community which should be understood by policy making officials. In the following chapter, the emphasis is upon services and programs which provide a background for many public policy decisions with which planning is concerned.

ENVIRONMENTAL OBJECTIVES OF PHYSICAL PLANNING

The pattern of uncontrolled growth which has taken place in most urban communities has not always resulted in the most appropriate land use and frequently has not provided the best environment in which to live or earn a living. The average citizen, however, is seldom aware that anything is wrong with the urban pattern of his community. He may feel that traffic does not move as it should or that there should be fewer slums or that more automobile parking is needed, but he is not likely to have any great awareness of the degree to which poor physical planning or the failure to plan may have affected his economy of time, his economic success, and his personal convenience and living enjoyment.[2]

[1] It is of interest to compare the approach which is being taken in Great Britain under the "New Towns Act of 1946" and "Town Development Act of 1952." The underlying policies and plans are outlined in Lloyd Rodwin, *The British New Towns Policy* (Cambridge: Harvard University Press, 1956).

[2] Louis Justement, *New Cities for Old, City Building in Terms of Space, Time and Money* (New York: McGraw-Hill Book Company, Inc., 1946), p. 5.

SOCIAL AND ECONOMIC FACTORS

Few features of the community have more direct bearing upon the general welfare of its inhabitants than the physical setting. Whenever a building is erected, an industry is located, a street is extended, or a utility line is laid, the physical setting is altered and fixed. The type of building, the kind of industry, the width of the street, and the location of the utility lines are matters of public concern. Since they affect the economic welfare and amenities of living, they are appropriately the subject matter for planning.

The physical plan of the community should seek to create the most appropriate utilization of space and the most efficient arrangement of services in order to insure the greatest economy practicable in time and movement, the preservation of property values and assets, and a full realization of the advantages and benefits of urban life.[3] Among the features of the physical plan which are most important in achieving these objectives are the pattern of private land use, the design of the street system, and the location and character of public buildings, open spaces, public facilities, and the location of transportation routes and utility lines.

Physical planning is concerned with the physical uses to which mankind diverts the surface of the earth and the space requirements for those uses. Its goal should be to utilize and develop the physical resources, to protect and enhance the economic well-being of the individual and the community as a whole, and to provide conditions of living which are conducive to smoothness and pleasantness in social relations and business activities. The physical plan should seek to bring together those uses which are compatible and complementary and to separate those which are incompatible or inharmonious. The physical plan should also try to relate those uses, both private and public, which will encourage an orderly commercial and industrial development and which will at the same time provide a safe, healthful, and pleasant environment for living.

THE AMENITIES OF PHYSICAL ENVIRONMENT

Within recent years, physical planning has tended to lay increased emphasis upon the environmental objectives of convenience, comfort, and pleasantness. These objectives are embraced within the concept of "amenities"—a word which has recently found its way into the

[3] *Action for Cities, A Guide for Community Planning* (Chicago: Public Administration Service, 1943), Publication No. 86, p. 52.

vocabulary of planners.[4] Many examples can be cited in which amenity considerations have been reflected in physical planning. The compact and efficient arrangement of shops in modern shopping centers is aimed at the convenience of the shopper. The comfort and privacy of individuals is recognized in the limitations of height and bulk, the spacing of buildings for light and air, and planned location of windows in one building with reference to others. The pleasing architectural design of public buildings is intended to add to the aesthetic enjoyment of persons living in the community.

For the most part, amenity considerations have been secondary objectives to policies directed toward the promotion of public health, safety, morals, and the general welfare. Gradually, however, they are coming to furnish the primary basis for certain major public policy decisions. Today, there is a great deal of uncertainty as to how far the courts will go in sustaining public policies which have as their sole objectives the promotion of individual comfort, pleasantness of surroundings, and aesthetic beauty. Some of the recent decisions seem to indicate a judicial willingness to recognize these as legitimate responsibilities of government.[5]

Physical planning to promote the amenities of environment should be aimed both at eliminating annoyances and at developing positive programs to increase living enjoyment. Unfortunately, the industrial age, which has created great economic wealth and which has been responsible for the growth of large urban communities, has not always produced the most pleasant and healthful environment in which to live. In certain of our cities, where atmosphere and topography combine to produce excessive conditions of "smog," the location and control of industry in the interest of reducing the amount of air pollution has become a matter of major concern. This is a problem to which few cities have as yet given adequate attention.

Another hazard of industrial life which seriously impairs the comfort and well-being of individuals is that of noise and vibration. A number of studies have shown that excessive noise contributes not only to general annoyance, but also to nervousness, irritability, fatigue, inefficiency, distraction, and sometimes illness.[6]

[4] Gerald Breese, ed., *An Approach to Urban Planning* (Princeton: Princeton University Press, 1953), p. 39.

[5] See for example *Berman v. Parker*, 348 U.S. 26, 75 S. Ct. 98 (1954), in which the Supreme Court of the United States declared that "It is within the power of the legislature to determine that the community should be beautiful as well as healthy, spacious as well as clean, well balanced as well as carefully patrolled."

[6] Edwin Rothman, "Philadelphia Bureau Asks City to Quiet Down," *GRA Reporter*, Vol. 6, No. 3, p. 34, Third Quarter, 1954.

To date, few cities have been able to solve the problems of noise and air pollution solely through industrial site planning. As a general rule, attention is not given to these annoyances until after they have become public nuisances in established areas.[7] At this stage the only remedy is through abatement proceedings or through expensive relocation or redevelopment programs.

Living enjoyment is also very much affected by the pleasing appearance of physical surroundings. For the most part, this factor of living enjoyment can be made an objective in public policies without detracting from utilitarian purposes. Most municipalities which are planning-minded are conscious of the value of promoting aesthetic values. The problems arise in devising a program which is both legally sound and politically acceptable.[8]

The limits of public policy in accomplishing aesthetic objectives are still to be defined by the courts.[9] Assuming for the moment that the legal obstacles are surmounted, there are difficulties on the practical side in establishing standards of aesthetic values and providing governmental machinery for enforcing these standards without undue regimentation and loss of individuality. Aesthetic considerations are relative. As our social standards change and our sensibilities become more refined, our ideas as to what is pleasing also change. What formerly was an acceptable design may at a later time come to offend our aesthetic tastes. Likewise, some advanced design which we do not now approve may in the future come to satisfy our desires. In this process it is of importance that rights of property are not sacrificed to the pleasure of ultra-aesthetic tastes.

PLANNING THE PATTERN OF URBAN LAND USE

For the most part, land use planning is based upon a classification of land uses, which seeks to bring together those uses which are compatible, and separate those which are not. It has as its primary objective the promotion of the most appropriate utilization of the land. The degree to which this objective is achieved is governed by the soundness of many public policy decisions. It is the purpose in the

[7] See the following chapter for a discussion of nuisance control and abatement.

[8] Christopher Tunnard, Sydney Williams, and Ralph S. Ellifrit, "Urban Aesthetics," *Planning 1953*, Proceedings of the National Planning Conference, Detroit, Michigan, October 11–15, 1953 (Chicago: American Society of Planning Officials, 1953), pp. 48–64.

[9] See *State ex rel. Carter v. Harper*, 182 Wis. 148, 196 N.W. 451 (1923) and compare with the language used in *Berman v. Parker*, 348 U.S. 26, 75 S.Ct. 98 (1954).

following discussion to point up some of the major problems, practices, and considerations involved in land-use planning which merit the attention of policy making officials as well as professional planners.

Land uses may be classified under various categories. One basis of classification is the following: (1) areas such as large reservations preserved in more or less their natural state for watersheds, protection of wild life, and for recreational purposes; (2) areas related to the productivity of the soil including uses for farming, grazing, timber, and horticulture; (3) areas used for industrial and extractive activities including mining, quarrying, manufacturing, and the processing of raw materials; (4) areas for living and carrying on domestic activities of daily life, including residential areas, shopping areas, schools, institutions, and urban recreation; and (5) areas comprised of a network of relatively narrow strips separating and yet joining all others used for communications, including streets, highways, transit and transportation systems, and lines for various kinds of utilities.[10] Some of these classifications are concerned with private land uses; some, with public uses; and some, with both. In almost every community there is also to be found a considerable amount of vacant land. In many cities vacant land accounts for more than 40 percent of the city's area.[11]

For purposes of urban planning, the significant private land uses are included in the following classifications:

1. Residential.
2. Community facilities, including schools, churches, and hospitals.
3. Local shopping centers.
4. General commercial areas, as the central business and services district.
5. Commercial amusement areas.
6. Heavy commercial areas, including automotive services, laundries, and dry cleaning businesses.
7. Garden factory areas, consisting of attractive landscaped one-story buildings.
8. General manufacturing, including plants having a limited amount of noise and nuisance.

[10] Master Plan of Land Use, Inventory and Classification (Los Angeles: The Regional Planning Commission, County of Los Angeles, 1941), p. 14.

[11] See Harland Bartholomew, Land Uses in American Cities (Cambridge, Mass.: Harvard University Press, 1955), pp. 73 and 97.

Specific uses of land indicated as percentages of total land use are sometimes based upon averages and sometimes upon special circumstances. They are included in the text to give an idea of relationship but are not suggested as norms or standards for any locality.

9. Heavy industry, which normally requires large sites on water or rail transportation facilities and which often involves a substantial nuisance to residential or other uses.[12]

Effective land-use planning must take into account all land uses, private and public. As the principal private property land uses in most urbanized areas are for residential, business, and industrial purposes, it is with these major classifications that zoning regulations are primarily concerned. Some lands devoted to truck farms and other agricultural uses are found in almost every urban community. Normally these do not represent a very substantial part of the urban land area and tend gradually to disappear as land becomes necessary for more intensive land use. The major public land uses are for streets, public utilities and public facilities, public buildings and institutions, and recreation. There are also some rather important minor public and semipublic uses.

RESIDENTIAL LAND USE

The proportion of land used for residential purposes is greater than that for any other use, private or public, although the proportion for streets is almost as great. In the average city, about 40 percent of the developed area is in residential use, of which about 80 percent is devoted to single-family dwellings.[13]

Character and Location of Residential Areas.   In assessing the needs of the community for residential land use, the planner must take into account the demands for both high-density and low-density residence areas. To a large degree, the area to be assigned to these respective uses is to be determined by the occupational character of the community, the population trends and forecasts, family income prospects, and the living habits and patterns of the inhabitants. These factors also have an important bearing in determining the percentage of high-cost and low-cost residences, the percentages of single-family and multiple-family dwellings, and the kind and amount of public, as well as private, housing. In meeting the demands for high-density uses, it is important that the standards for single-residence areas always be preserved. Where pressures of population become so great

[12] Norman Williams, Jr., "Land Use and Zoning," *An Approach to Urban Planning,* ed. Gerald Breese and Dorothy Whiteman (Princeton: Princeton University Press, 1953), pp. 40–42. There are other classes of land use which are commonly accepted by planners.

[13] *Local Planning Administration* (Chicago: The International City Managers' Association, 1948), p. 198.

as to make it seem necessary to convert low-density property to higher-density uses, it is usually preferable to permit the development of high-type multiple dwellings in an area rather than to reduce the yard spaces about single dwellings, resulting in crowding on small sites.

As a rule, municipalities find it advantageous to encourage the location of residential areas in places of favorable topography. In the selection of such areas, consideration should be given to their proximity to lakes and streams. Location selection must also take into account the proximity of shopping centers and recreational and cultural areas. An effort should be made to avoid the preëmption of land which might be better adapted to other purposes. On the other hand, pressures must be resisted which would alter the character of established residential areas by permitting rezoning for commercial or industrial uses because the property may be considered more valuable for such purposes.

The Neighborhood Concept.   A current trend in residential planning has been to define residential areas in relation to the neighborhood unit.[14] In most communities of any size neighborhood characteristics have tended to develop rather spontaneously around a number of outlying shopping centers. Nevertheless, there are a few examples of publicly planned neighborhood units. The neighborhood unit idea, which has been urged by planners in recent years, has as its purpose the development of clearly identifiable natural neighborhoods which would be built around such focal points as the school and community recreational areas. Frequently, such neighborhood units are set off by such natural barriers as traffic arteries, railroads, water, or open spaces. Dividing lines, however, are not always clear and one neighborhood often fades into another. One aim attributed to the concept is the development of neighborhood units of homogeneous groups having similarity of income, racial characteristics, and general interests. Some objections, however, have been raised on this score on the grounds of attempted social stratification and racial discrimination.[15]

---

[14] The "neighborhood" normally includes from 1000 to 2500 families on a land area of varying size. It is characterized by "a rather solid pattern of homes, linked by quiet streets, and centered about an elementary school, a meeting place (community hall) where men gather to discuss their common problems, a park where leisure hours may be whiled away." The "community" is "composed of two or more neighborhoods joined for common commercial service and common special service purposes." *Studies for a Comprehensive Plan*, Bellevue Report (Seattle: King County Planning Commission, December, 1952), p. 17.

[15] For a discussion involving homogeneous v. heterogeneous neighborhoods, see Nor-

As a rule, the neighborhood unit would provide housing for that population for which one elementary school is required. Sites for schools, a community hall, and recreational areas should be suitably grouped about a central point. Included within the neighborhood unit concept are one or more shopping districts which normally are laid out on the circumference of the unit, preferably at traffic junctions, and adjacent to similar districts of adjoining neighborhoods.[16] It is important in the planning of such areas that adequate attention be given to the street system. Each street should be proportioned to its probable traffic load and the system as a whole should be designed to facilitate traffic circulation within the unit, but to discourage its use for through traffic. Streets carrying heavy traffic become barriers to the cross movement of people as significantly as major physical obstacles.[17]

Since today much of the residential area is developed by subdividers, public control over neighborhood unit planning is effectuated principally through subdivision regulations, and although such regulations do not provide a positive means for developing neighborhood units, they are quite adequate in most instances since responsible subdividers are coming to realize that good neighborhood environment has values that can be measured in dollars and cents.

COMMERCIAL LAND USE

Unplanned business districts have tended to develop certain common patterns because of rental costs. Offices and financial institutions are usually found at the heart of the business district where rents are highest. Located in the next highest rent areas are the retail stores, with the theater districts to be found on the outskirts. Wholesale districts are usually found in the lower rent areas. In the average city, business districts occupy about 2 to 5 percent of the developed portions of the city. From the number of business failures and building vacancies, it would appear that more land is given to store frontage than the population can support. Nevertheless, municipalities are commonly faced with pressure for zoning additional areas for business purposes because of the property owners' belief that business property

man Williams, Jr., "Planning Law and Democratic Living," *Law and Contemporary Problems*, Vol. 20, No. 2, p. 325, Spring, 1955.

[16] Clarence Perry, *Housing for the Machine Age* (New York: Russell Sage Foundation, 1939), pp. 49–77.

[17] Wilbur C. Hallenbeck, *American Urban Communities* (New York: Harper & Brothers, 1951), p. 163.

commands higher values.[18] However, the problem of formulating sound commercial land-use policy is not one of precising the amount of land needed for this purpose since the total commercial needs represent, in any event, a small proportion of the whole urban area.[19] The important considerations are proper location and design and flexibility of space areas.

Central Versus Decentralized Shopping. Intelligent planning of our commercial areas cannot be carried out until we resolve the fundamental and basic question of whether public policies ought to be directed toward concentrating business in the downtown central business district or toward decentralizing more business activities to neighborhood or other outlying areas. In recent years, most large communities have been experiencing shifts in the location of business. For the most part, however, this has not been directed by comprehensive land-use planning, but rather from the inability of municipalities to solve the problems of traffic congestion and automobile parking. Some of our larger cities have made efforts to hold business to the core area, but, by and large, these efforts have not been very successful.[20] The most common approach has been to try to relieve traffic congestion through street widening, off-street parking, new arteries, and rapid transit. In many instances, however, this is found to be a vicious circle, since the effect of these measures has been merely to encourage more traffic, and thus increase the congestion and add to the difficulties of parking.

The movement of population to suburbs, followed by a shift of business from the core area, has resulted in the growth of many unplanned neighborhood shopping districts. However, the unplanned neighborhood shopping district has not always provided a satisfactory solution to the overall problem. Frequently, these shopping districts have grown up as shoestring developments along the main artery with the consequence of depreciated values in nearby property. This is a matter of serious concern which must be carefully watched.

Whenever the trend toward the shifting of business is evident, the community should take positive steps to influence the decentralization of businesses that do not need to be centralized in the core area. Re-

---

[18] Actual experience has shown that competition for lease of space may result in lower rents.

[19] *Master Plan of Land Use, Inventory and Classification, op. cit.,* p. 39.

[20] Does the fate of cities hang on parking or has the focal point of business in the downtown center become obsolete due to economic and technological changes of the last quarter century? Highway Research Board, *What Parking Means to Business* (Washington, D.C.: Automotive Safety Foundations, 1955), p. 3.

tail stores which deal primarily in "convenience goods" as distinguished from "shopping goods" may actually be located more advantageously in outlying districts. Shopping goods normally include articles identified by higher price and those with respect to which selectivity, style, and brand names are important. Shopping goods usually bring more income and are logically located in higher cost areas. Convenience goods which include such items as groceries, drugs, and magazines may more profitably be supplied in neighborhood areas where land is less costly.[21] In addition to retail stores supplying convenience goods, there are a number of other businesses such as warehouses, storage facilities, funeral parlors, and used-car lots which may also appropriately be located in neighborhood districts.[22]

The Planned Shopping Center. One of the most promising ideas for planned business decentralization is the planned shopping center. The concept of the planned shopping center differs materially from the conventional shopping district developed by individual proprietors in that the shopping center, planned with the automobile in mind, is designed as an integrated unit based upon studies of needs and economic conditions and potentials. Although experience with this type of planning has for the most part been limited to the past three decades, the pattern for successful shopping centers is becoming increasingly clear.[23] Obviously, financial success of such ventures is dependent upon the market. In order to attract customers, the shopping center must be well located with respect to service areas and readily accessible by automobile. No development should be undertaken unless based upon (1) a comprehensive economic survey and analysis, (2) an exhaustive traffic engineering study, and (3) a survey and analysis of the market potentials.[24]

The large outlying shopping center poses serious problems for the planner. The impact which these developments have upon traffic, population density, utility extensions, police and fire protection, and the general character of the surrounding area places them in a special category for planning and land-use control. Few comprehensive land-

[21] *Shopper Bottleneck*, A Report on the Chamber of Commerce Parking Clinic, Stockton, Calif., March 31, 1953 (Washington, D.C.: Chamber of Commerce of the United States, 1953), pp. 28–29.

[22] There is not universal agreement on this point of view. It is entirely possible that, in the future, attitude studies may be utilized by planners to a large extent for making determinations on alternate locations.

[23] Ross McKeever, *Shopping Centers, Planning Principles and Tested Policies* (Washington, D.C.: Urban Land Institute, July, 1953), Technical Bulletin, No. 20.

[24] "Planned Shopping Centers," *New Jersey Municipalities*, Vol. XXXI, No. 3, p. 11, March, 1954.

use plans have been drafted with the shopping center in mind. The general land-use classifications of the typical zoning ordinance are not always well designed for this specialized type of development. Because of the uncertainty as to the future interests of private capital, it is normally not feasible to attempt to zone precise site locations. For these reasons it may be found preferable to treat the large shopping center as a unique type of commercial enterprise affected with a public interest and authorize its location by special permit under regulations which will insure harmonious development of the project and the surrounding area.

If shopping centers are to avoid the mistakes that are now plaguing the downtown central business districts, careful attention must be given to design. Convenient off-street parking and a compact arrangement of shops within the center are essential to customer satisfaction. Where night shopping is contemplated, special attention should be given to efficient night lighting, policing, supervision of traffic and parking, and other matters which require practices different from those of predominantly day-time shopping.[25] Compatibility in land uses is also important. As a general rule, a combination of stores and residences is undesirable. Such a combination tends to create parking problems and makes for poor residential environment, particularly for children. However, the location of apartment houses as part of such areas may be consistent with the planned use of the district.

Shopping centers are of three general classifications: the small neighborhood shopping center, the larger community shopping center, and the regional shopping center. All three have in common off-street parking facilities and integrated architectural design. The neighborhood center is planned primarily to supply convenience goods. Its nucleus is the food market, the drug store, the cleaning establishment, and stores supplying daily needs. The community shopping center, which is designed to serve a larger population than the neighborhood, will normally include, in addition to the stores supplying convenience goods, barber shops and beauty parlors, a hardware store, a liquor store, and frequently stores handling a limited variety of "shopping goods" such as furniture and appliances. The regional shopping center is designed to serve a still larger population. It is normally located in densely populated areas and is readily accessible from traffic arteries. Frequently, it will draw customers from

[25] See Frank Emery Cox, "What Makes a Shopping Center Successful," reprint from *Architect and Engineer*, July and August, 1954, issues, pp. 19–20.

as far out as 20 or 30 minutes driving time. The planned regional shopping center will include one or more department stores in addition to the convenience and specialty shops found in the other shopping centers and will often offer a wide variety of merchandise generally supplied only in the downtown shopping district.

In some cases, the very size of the shopping center presents special problems. Some studies have indicated, for example, that shoppers do not want to walk more than 300 feet from where they park their cars.[26] If this factor is recognized, large shopping centers may find it necessary to establish shuttle busses or some conveyor system or include in the center a multilevel parking garage.

The Preservation of Older Districts. It is important that planners do not become so preoccupied with the development of new shopping centers that they fail to give adequate attention to the older business districts.[27] In most cities, the central business districts and the older business subcenters continue to supply the bulk of the needs of the urban population. Nevertheless, many of the older shopping districts have become casualties of the automobile age and the accompanying shifts of population and industry. The loss of business to the newer shopping centers has produced a current rate of deterioration which has become a matter of grave public concern in many of the urban communities throughout the country. The economic loss is felt not only by business men and property owners in these declining districts, but also is reflected in lower tax returns and higher proportionate costs of public services.

There is no denial that the current attention being given by land developers, merchants, and investors to the location and design of new integrated shopping centers is well justified. However, there is equal justification, in many of the same communities, for a vigorous and well-thought-out program of conservation, rehabilitation, and rebuilding of the older business districts to prevent them from becoming ghost shopping centers. Such programs are needed not only to protect and encourage private investment and municipal revenues, but also in order to preserve the integrity of adjacent residential

[26] Homer Hoyt, "Market Surveys for Shopping Centers," *Regional Shopping Centers Planning Symposium* (Chicago: American Institute of Planners, Chicago Region Chapter, June, 1952), p. 15. See also Highway Research Board, *op. cit.*, p. 31, which suggests that shoppers in larger cities are not willing to walk more than 600 feet from the place where they park, and that suburban shopping centers try to provide parking within 400 feet.

[27] See Victor Gruen, "Dynamic Planning for Retail Areas," *Harvard Business Review,* Vol. 32, No. 6, p. 53, November-December, 1954.

neighborhoods. Careful studies which have been made of this problem recognize that conservation and rehabilitation programs should be formulated and instituted only after there have been basic analyses of all relevant factors. These should include: (1) the planning analysis, for determining the economic necessity for preservation and the physical possibilities of redesign with relationship to traffic, transit, adjacent land use, and other planning elements; (2) the market analysis, for determining space requirements and the protection of the future economic structure of the district; and (3) the architectural analysis, for determining the possibilities of achieving physical unity and an attractive and pleasant environment.[28] Often, however, the real stumbling blocks are found not in making these determinations, but in the problems related to financing, legal technicalities, promotion, and politics.

In weighing questions of policy with respect to the advisability of instituting conservation and rehabilitation programs as against the encouragement of new shopping centers, it should be borne in mind that existing districts enjoy "proved" locations and established customers. The new center, on the other hand, involves a certain amount of gamble based upon future growth of the tributary area and other factors affecting shopping habits. While the new center must normally rely upon the automobile for bringing it customers, the older district is accessible by public transportation as well as the automobile. Nevertheless, these obvious advantages of the older districts are insufficient to compete with the new centers unless a positive conservation and rehabilitation program can be carried out which will eliminate the existing congestion and obsolescence and provide shopping conditions which are convenient and pleasant and which invite a festive atmosphere.[29]

INDUSTRIAL LAND USE

Since industrial payrolls form the economic foundation for virtually every large city, planning for industrial sites is a matter of vital importance. In certain relatively small specialized municipalities, economic progress is possible up to a certain point without dependence

[28] Richard Lawrence Nelson and Frederick T. Aschman, *Conservation and Rehabilitation of Major Shopping Districts* (Washington: D.C.: Urban Land Institute, 1954), Technical Bulletin No. 22, pp. 10–24.

[29] Howard T. Fisher, "The Development of Planned Shopping Centers," *Regional Shopping Centers Planning Symposium* (Chicago: American Institute of Planners, Chicago Region Chapter, June, 1952), p. 27.

upon major industry. Examples of this are communities which serve as health resorts or small trade centers in agricultural areas. For most urban communities, however, it has been found that, as a general rule, there must be one average basic industry, or its equivalent (as agriculture, mining, or tourist trade), for each 1000 inhabitants.[30] Plans designed for the promotion of the economic welfare need to take into account many factors which go to make up the economic base of the community.[31] Industrial development is one of the most important of these factors. However, if a well-balanced, diversified economy is to be achieved, industrial planning must be properly related to all other factors.

Area and Location Requirements. In planning for industrial area requirements, account must be taken not only of major industries, but also of minor or auxiliary industries, such as laundries, bakeries, and refrigerator plants which follow rather than precede population growth. These auxiliary industries in the aggregate require almost half as much land as the basic industry.[32] On the average, approximately 10 to 15 percent of the total developed area of a city is devoted to industrial uses.[33]

Few elements of the comprehensive plan have more direct bearing upon the economic well-being and amenities of living in the community than the selection of desirable locations for industrial districts. Policy considerations require that the heavy industries, particularly those plants which emit loud and raucous noises or produce objectionable fumes and odors, must be located in outlying areas, preferably on the leeward side to prevailing winds. Lighter industry, which is less obnoxious to living and working enjoyment, may be located nearer the urban center. Another factor which must be considered in the location of industrial districts is the cost of land. Generally speaking, industry should not have to compete for sites with commercial and residential uses. Most industrial enterprises cannot afford

[30] *Master Plan of Land Use, Inventory and Classification, op. cit.,* p. 41.
  Some estimates indicate that an industry employing 150 men provides direct support for 600 persons and indirect and direct support for 1000 to 1650 people. The predictive value of such estimates is shown in a recent study of the Dallas area. See Tom Lee McKnight, *Manufacturing in Dallas, A Study of Effects* (Austin: Bureau of Business Research, University of Texas, 1956), pp. 80–85.
[31] The opportunities and means for guiding and promoting the economy of the community are analyzed in a series of articles entitled "Mechanics of the Urban Economic Base" by Richard B. Andrews in *Land Economics* from May, 1953, to February, 1956.
[32] A basic industry is considered to be one which provides an economic basis for sustaining the population.
[33] *Local Planning Administration, op. cit.,* p. 212.

to pay as high a price for land as commercial businesses. For this reason, it has frequently been profitable for industries to utilize low-lying and filled-in lands which are accessible to railroad facilities and truck routes. It should be noted, however, that there is some current thought that consideration should be given to locating industry on the higher lands in order to help alleviate the conditions of smog which prevail in some areas. Obviously the benefits to be derived from such location must be weighed against the problems encountered in transportation and the demands for such lands for residential use, particularly if view property is involved.

The location of industries, which employ large numbers of workers, should be related to the location of residential areas. In determining this relationship, a number of factors must be taken into account. Among these are pleasantness of outlying home environment, amount of travel time involved, effect upon traffic congestion, availability for emergency calls, opportunities for health and recreational activities, and proximity to schools and various service facilities.

Land selected for industrial development should be fairly level and should be chosen with a view to possible industrial expansion. Area selection should take into account the size of area, soil and topography, load-bearing characteristics, the availability of utilities, means and methods of waste disposal, and access to the area by highway and railroad.[34] While industrial sites must be accessible to highways, the minor street system must be developed in a manner which will avoid the flow of traffic into the area but will facilitate the necessary circulation of traffic for industrial purposes.

Factors in Site Selection. The choice of an industrial site by industry involves the consideration of many factors. Among these are the availability of raw materials, transportation, location of markets, climate, water supply, electric power, labor supply, wage rates, existing industries, the physical site, services available, the tax structure, regulatory laws, and special inducements offered by the community. In some instances, one factor is of such importance that it overrides all others, as in the case of the production of aluminum which is dependent upon an adequate supply of electric energy. In most industries, however, the choice of location is not usually so limited by a single factor.[35]

[34] Gerald Breese, *Industrial Site Selection, Burlington County, N. J.—A Case Study of Existing and Potential Industrial Location* (Princeton, N. J.: The Bureau of Urban Research, Princeton University, 1954), p. 2. See also pp. 100–115 for an extensive bibliography on the many facets of industrial location.

[35] *Ibid.*, p. 30.

The primary economic requirements of industry, which are raw materials, markets, transportation, and labor, can often be met to a substantially equal degree in a number of different communities. Secondary values then become determining factors in industrial location. These include the general character of the community and the services which it offers, both governmental and private. Actually, some industries may be inclined to give preference to well-managed cities over others which would appear to offer superior economic advantages.[36] Often, the events which occur in a community affect the success of a business as much as the activities of the business itself.

Industries, in the selection of a plant location, look for intangible items as well as tangible ones. Employees are interested in a community having a good environment in which to bring up children. They want a place that is healthful and safe, and that has a good moral record. They are interested in adequate recreation facilities, schools, churches, suitable housing, and good shopping centers. Adequate labor supply and satisfactory labor relations often depend upon these factors. Louis B. Lundborg, Vice-President of the Bank of America, points out the interest of industry in local government services as follows:

There is not a business—not a profession—in any community in America that does not share directly in dollars-and-cents profit or loss from the improvement or the deterioration in (1) the physical condition of the city's physical plant; (2) the quality of service rendered by the city and other governmental agencies; (3) the quality of service rendered by civic and social agencies; and (4) the availability of community resources and facilities to improve the physical, mental, and moral health of the populace.[37]

The principal services and conditions which industry looks for from a community include, but are not limited to, the following:[38]

1. The selection and protection of suitable well-planned sites.
2. Availability of adequate utilities including water, electricity, gas, sewerage, and waste disposal.

[36] *Local Government Serevices and Industrial Development in the Southeast* (University, Ala.: Bureau of Public Administration, University of Alabama, 1952), pp. 3–4.
[37] Louis B. Lundborg, *Public Relations in the Local Community* (New York: Harper & Brothers, 1950), p. 15.
[38] Summary based on analysis of state surveys as outlined in: *Local Government Services and Industrial Development in the Southeast, op. cit.,* pp. 15–25. For a comprehensive but concise discussion of this subject, see Jerome P. Pickard, "Industry Location Factors," *Journal of the City Planning Division,* Proceedings of the American Society of Civil Engineers, Vol. 82, No. CP1, pp. 886 1-886-15, February, 1956.

3. Adequate provision for transportation including, water, rail, truck, air, and local transit.
4. Opportunities for employee training through the availability of libraries, trade schools, and evening college or university extension courses.
5. Maintenance of good schools and adequate school facilities.
6. An effective public health program including good hospital and medical facilities.
7. Adequate public recreational facilities and recreational programs including parks, playgrounds, swimming pools, golf courses, and nearness to hunting and fishing preserves.
8. Availability of comfortable modern housing.
9. An equitable and stable tax system and evidence of sound financial policies.
10. Efficient and effective governmental management.
11. Favorable living conditions taking into account comfort, convenience, physical attractiveness, and community attitudes.

Organized Industrial Districts.   In recent years a number of cities have taken a positive approach to the planning and development of controlled industrial land use through the creation of organized industrial districts. The Office of Technical Services of the United States Department of Commerce defines an organized industrial district as follows: "An 'organized' or 'planned' industrial district is a tract of land which is subdivided and developed according to a comprehensive plan for the use of a community of industries, with streets, rail lead tracts, and utilities installed before sites are sold to prospective occupants." [39]

The idea of the organized industrial district is to develop a planned industrial subdivision. As in the case of other types of subdivisions, the advantages to the community are in insuring that the future urban growth will provide a more aesthetic, orderly, and efficient pattern of land use. The utilization of such districts makes it possible for the community to give better direction to industrial location and to facilitate the industrial dispersion policy for providing greater security

[39] Theodore K. Pasma, United States Department of Commerce, *Organized Industrial Districts, A Tool for Community Development* (Washington, D.C.: U.S. Government Printing Office, June, 1954), p. 1. Among the districts which qualify under this definition are: Central Manufacturing District and Clearing Industrial District, Chicago; Fairfax Industrial District, Kansas City, Kansas; Airlawn and Trinity Industrial Districts, Dallas; Central Manufacturing District and Los Angeles Airport Industrial Tract, Los Angeles; Peachtree Industrial Boulevard District, Atlanta; Roosevelt Field and Bergen County Industrial Terminal in the New York area; and the Industrial Addition to Wichita.

against enemy attacks. Furthermore, the cost of extending utility and other municipal services is much less than it is for providing such services to widely scattered fringe area developments.

The advantages to industry are numerous. The owner of an industry who selects a site in an organized industrial district can be assured that needed facilities will be available when the plant moves in and that he will not be faced with antagonism and difficulties from the owners of abutting property. Furthermore, he will be adequately protected in his land use through established zoning control, private covenants, architectural controls, and proper design and landscaping. Through well-planned industrial subdivisions, many of the annoyances and handicaps of traffic congestion, inadequate parking facilities, cramped sites, and lack of loading facilities can be overcome. Investments are usually much better protected because of the efforts to bring together only compatible businesses.[40] Opportunities for improved employee satisfaction are increased through well-planned employee cafeterias and recreation facilities.

Industrial Promotion Programs. Planning, with respect to industry, is not limited to matters of site location and area and service requirements. During the past few years, urban planning has become increasingly concerned with programs aimed at attracting industry to the area. In many communities, civic groups have been organized for this purpose. While the organizational pattern varies, such groups are usually composed of merchants, industrialists, and community-minded businessmen and civic leaders. Sometimes the programs are carried out by profit or nonprofit corporations. Their principal objective, and sometimes sole objective, is getting new industry to locate in the city. Sometimes they may also serve to prevent an established firm from moving.[41] In some municipalities, the industrial development program has been undertaken as a governmental responsibility.

These programs, whether under public or private auspices, are of necessity very directly related to municipal policies pertaining to land use, public schools, libraries, recreation, transportation, public utilities, and virtually every other major type of public facility and program.

[40] For a detailed discussion of the policy considerations and procedures for developing an organized industrial district, see Theodore K. Pasma, op. cit. See also Victor Roterus, "Planned Industrial Districts," Journal of the City Planning Division, Proceedings of the American Society of Civil Engineers, Vol. 82, No. CP1, pp. 879–1-879–4, February, 1956.

[41] State of New York, Report of the Joint Legislative Committee on Commerce and Economic Development (Albany, N.Y.: Williams Press, Inc., 1954), Legislative Document No. 28, pp. 39–46.

Generally speaking, industrial promotion has been supported by business interests that would stand to gain from community growth, such as retailers, railroad companies, and real estate promotors. City officials have been interested from the standpoint of securing a broader tax base. On the other hand, opposition, both open and covert, sometimes occurs from existing firms who fear competition in the labor market or in the marketing of their products. City officials, as well as taxpayers, sometimes oppose industrial development programs because of the costs to the community for the extension of sewers and water mains, the construction of new streets, schools, and housing, and providing other facilities and services.

Financial Inducements for Industrial Location. A number of states have enacted legislation intended to authorize municipalities to promote industrial growth by using public funds to finance the acquisition of land for industrial use or the building and equipment of new plants or both.[42] Several states authorize the granting of special tax concessions to new industry.[43] The inducement of a new plant, the payment of low rents, and the prospect of eventual ownership at nominal value after bonds are retired often have a very strong appeal to an industry looking for a site. Approximately one-third of the states authorize preferential tax treatment by the state, by local government, or by both. Tax concessions are provided in various forms. Some states permit the exemption of new industries from property taxes, with certain exclusions, for a period of years. Others provide that assessments shall be made at a lower rate than on other property. Some states provide for special tax exemptions as of inventories, goods-in-process, and raw materials. On the other hand, several states specifically forbid tax discrimination. For example, under the Colorado and New York Constitutions, the state legislature may not grant any person, firm, or corporation any exemption from taxation. In Virginia, local units of government are prohibited by law from making any tax concessions to industry or to offer any special inducements to industry which are financed by local government.[44]

[42] Seven states: Alabama, Illinois, Kentucky, Louisiana, Mississippi, Nebraska, and Tennessee, have passed general legislation permitting local units of government to issue bonds to finance the constructing and equipping of plants for industry. See State of New York, op. cit., pp. 31–35.

[43] Among the states authorizing some form of preferential tax treatment by state or local government, or both, are Alabama, Arizona, Arkansas, Delaware, Florida, Georgia, Kentucky, Louisiana, Maryland, Massachusetts, Mississippi, Ohio, Oklahoma, South Carolina, Rhode Island, and Vermont. State of New York, op. cit., pp. 35–37.

[44] State of New York, op. cit., p. 37.

Another approach to the matter of industrial promotion has been the use of public funds for purposes of advertising the advantages of a particular community. At least two states, Kansas and Michigan, authorize certain municipalities to levy taxes for the purpose of creating a fund to be used to induce industries to locate therein. In Kansas, cities under 40,000 may levy a tax for this purpose, not to exceed one-half mill. Municipalities in Michigan may levy a special tax of four mills for the purpose of advertising, exploiting, and making known the industrial, commercial, educational, or recreational advantages of the city.

Unless specifically authorized by the state constitution, the use of special subsidies and tax concessions as inducements to private industry to locate in a given community may be open to serious question on grounds of constitutionality. Most state constitutions require that municipal funds be raised for "public purposes." Even though it may be conceded that a new business will result in some benefit to the community, this fact does not place the expenditure of public funds for this purpose in the same category as the expenditure of public funds for a slum clearance project, or for a water system, sewage disposal plant, or other utility which is essential to the welfare of the people as a whole. In the states where the issuance of bonds for industrial purposes has been upheld by the courts, the courts have usually relied upon the avowed objectives of eliminating unemployment, balancing the economy, and raising living standards.[45]

Aside from the constitutional aspects, there are serious doubts as to the wisdom of such subsidies and special tax concessions from the standpoint of sound public policy. It must be recognized that industrial promotion programs are often fostered by citizens whose primary interest is economic and selfish. Such persons expect to benefit directly or indirectly from industrial growth. Frequently, such growth is in the interest of the community as a whole, although in certain cases it may not be. Communities should, therefore, check very carefully all factors before offering subsidies or special tax concessions as inducements to industrial location. In the first place, such a policy may at times have the effect of attracting businesses of an unstable nature. Some industries lured by such inducements may choose their site location largely because of this advantage and overlook the shortcomings of the par-

[45] *Albritton v. Winona*, 181 Miss. 75, 118, 178 So. 799, appeal dismissed, 303 U.S. 627 (1938).
Newberry v. Andalusia, 257 Ala. 49, 57 So. (2d) 629 (1952).
Faulconer v. Danville, 313 Ky. 468, 232 S.W. (2d) 80 (1950).

ticular locality with respect to many basic requirements. Secondly, subsidies and tax concessions obviously are reflected in increased costs of government which must fall upon the residents and established businesses. This is a difficult position to justify from the standpoint of tax equity. Furthermore, communities which make concessions to one industry may find themselves obligated to extend concessions to others once the area has become associated with that particular industrial operation, thus multiplying the inequities of tax treatment.

There can be no question that if the right type of industry is brought to a community, it helps to create jobs, to keep young people at home, to strengthen the economy, increase the tax base, raise the standard of living, and make for a better balance of the economy. It must be recognized, on the other hand, that other communities may engage in the same competition which in the end may result in no gain for any particular community, but may bring undesirable industries to some and lead to the adoption of unsound financial practices.

Certainly, any decision which involves inducements for industrial location must be made with caution. The bringing in of new industries may not always be an unmixed blessing. From the standpoint of the community welfare, the building of a well-balanced community is of much greater importance than the size of the industrial development. If, for example, industrial expansion should create serious dislocations in the labor market; put a strain upon the school system, transportation system, or utility services; or produce problems of air pollution, law enforcement, or fire protection, the disadvantages of new industry might greatly exceed the benefits. The possibility of such disruptions in the life of the community should be fully explored. A community embarking upon a promotional program should give careful study to the kind of industry which it feels is best suited for the locality.

A community should ask such questions as:

1. Is the industry stable, in that the market for its product does not fluctuate greatly with the business cycle?
2. Is the business of a seasonal character, resulting in seasonal unemployment?
3. Is it likely that any workers will be brought in to meet the labor demands and, if so, what kind of people will they be; and how will this affect the original character of the community?
4. What evidence is there to give assurance that the business will be successful and maintain a continuity of operations?

5. Is the local supply of raw materials adequate to supply the industrial needs for an extended period of time?
6. What would be the effect upon the community if the industry should fail?
7. Will it add revenues directly or indirectly, compensating the community for the required expansion of public services?
8. If public revenues are not increased, can the community afford to provide the additional facilities and services required by the location of a new industry?
9. Is the new industry likely to create nuisances through pollution of streams or air or through the creation of loud and raucous noises?
10. Is the community in the position to make adequate provisions for transportation, labor, power, water supply, and other requirements which will be demanded as a result of industrial growth?

These, and many other questions should be carefully pondered and resolved before embarking upon any program which contemplates the use of public funds and attracting industry to the community. It is entirely possible that a community may oversell its advantages and make commitments which in the end will result in injury to business and to the community in general.[46]

Public and Semipublic Land Uses

In every urban community there are large areas of land that are reserved for "public and semipublic" uses. These uses are primarily concerned with providing services to the community as a whole or to some segment of the community. Included in this category are lands used for such purposes as streets, transportation routes and facilities, utilities, public buildings, schools, institutions, buffer zones, and parks and playgrounds. Public policies with respect to most of these land uses cannot be separated from the service responsibilities to which they relate. Therefore, certain aspects of this category of land use are considered in the following chapter in connection with the comprehensive planning of public services. Since, however, the land requirements for providing the multiplicity of community services represent a very substantial proportion of the total land area, the nature and extent of these uses are noted under this topical heading to help complete the picture of the land-use pattern.

[46] George B. Hurff, "What Kind of Industry Does Your Community Want?" *Municipal Government Problems of Interest to Florida* (Public Administration Clearing Service of the University of Florida, 1950), Studies in Public Administration, No. 4, pp. 15–22.

Streets, Utilities, and Public Services.   Probably no land use in the community is of greater importance to the community development than that which is devoted to streets and to providing utility and other public services. No city could survive and prosper without adequate means of communication, transportation, and distribution of water, power, and fuel, and the disposal of wastes. A considerable amount of land area within the community must, therefore, be devoted to highway uses, railway uses, airports, reservoirs, pumping plants, power plants, transmission lines, sewage disposal plants, broadcasting stations, and the routes, rights of way, and related facilities that are essential to providing such services.[47] Some of these uses require very substantial areas of land. Others require relatively little. Some utilize the surface or subsurface of the streets, and others must have separate rights of way and specific land areas.

Of these land uses, the streets are of primary importance. To a high degree the location and design of the streets determine the location and direction of the community developments. The streets serve to provide light and air for homes, stores, and other buildings as well as access, circulation, and fire safety. Furthermore, the streets determine the size and shape of the blocks and sometimes become the playground for children. Over the surface of the streets is carried both foot and vehicular traffic, including the operation of streetcars and buses. Along the streets are erected poles on which wires are strung for providing telephone and electric utility services. In the subsurface of the streets are laid mains and the pipes for carrying water, gas, and sewage, as well as conduits for wires, cables, and other utilities. In the average city the land area devoted to streets is second only to that for residential use. The proportion of total urban land area used for street purposes normally represents from one-fourth to one-third of the total area, exclusive of land which is vacant.[48]

In addition to the surface and subsurface area of the streets used by utilities, there is also considerable land area which must be devoted to facilities necessary to provide these utility services such as pumping plants, power substations, sewage disposal plants, garbage

[47] Streets and the transportation system are specially considered in this chapter under the heading, "Planning the System of Transportation." Water supply and the disposal of wastes are considered in the following chapter.

[48] Harland Bartholomew shows the average street use to be 28.10 percent of the developed area in central cities and 27.61 percent in urban areas. Bartholomew, op. cit., pp. 63, 112.

See also: Master Plan of Land Use, op. cit., p. 49.

disposal plants, broadcasting stations, telephone and telegraph exchanges, and many others. In the average city, the land which is used exclusively for such utility facilities represents only about ½ of 1 percent of the total land use. Unlike land used for residential, commercial, and industrial purposes, lands for providing communication, transportation, and utility services cannot be set aside in certain designated areas but must be located with reference to the needs of supplying service to the community.

For the most part, land used for streets and providing utility services is publicly owned. There is, however, considerable land owned by private companies which is devoted to providing services of a public or semipublic character. Railways and airlines provide good examples of such services. Quite commonly, land area used for railway purposes is classified as industrial use. In the average city, railway purposes require less than 5 percent of the total developed land area.[49] It seems unlikely that this ratio will increase. On the other hand, an increasing amount of land is being required for airports and air transportation facilities. Land required for air transportation is almost entirely for terminals, as distinguished from railways, which require rights of way for lines. The amount of space for air terminals, however, is somewhat larger than the corresponding area for rail terminal facilities.

A number of utilities using wires often require land not only for plant facilities but also for transmission lines. Sometimes the area used for this purpose is owned outright by the utility or by the public, and sometimes the utility has only a right of way over the land. In land-use surveys, lands serving transmission requirements are frequently classified as vacant, agricultural, or are assigned to various minor uses. To the extent that they are devoted exclusively to carrying transmission lines, they are more appropriately classified as lands used for supplying utility services.

Since wire utilities are usually located within rights of way of streets or along easements at the rear lines of lots, it is important that their placement be carefully coördinated with the street plan. Whether or not they should be located along the front or rear lot lines depends upon such factors as the topography, the depth of the lot, and the height and location of structures in the area. The wires for electric power, telephone, telegraph, fire alarms, police call systems, and others may be located overhead or in underground conduits. The

49 Bartholomew, op. cit., p. 58.

comprehensive plan should give special consideration to the feasibility of placing wires underground. Overhead wires are not only unsightly but also frequently interfere with trees and create fire hazards. However, the installation of wire utilities underground often involves extremely high costs, particularly if the installation is made after streets have been paved. Some cities are, nevertheless, finding it practical to solve the problem through the programming of public improvements under plans whereby a certain amount of wiring will be placed in underground conduits each year. In the case of new subdivisions, it is often possible to require underground installations as a condition of plat approval. Where placement of wires underground is not economically feasible, the use of one set of poles for two or more utility lines may serve a dual purpose of achieving substantial savings in investment costs and also of reducing the unattractiveness of the street.

As in the case of transmission lines, the assignment of certain utility plants and facilities to planned site locations is limited by the requirements for meeting service demands. Usually, however, they can be fitted into the planned land use without any serious handicap to the service. Under normal circumstances power generating plants should be restricted to industrial areas. Truck or repair facilities should be required to be located in either commercial or industrial districts. On the other hand, there are certain facilities such as telephone exchanges which cannot always be restricted to specific districts since they need to be located in the service area. Consequently, telephone exchange facilities are commonly permitted in residential districts. For the same reason, it is usually necessary to allow electric substations and transformers in residential districts. An accepted practice is to grant such uses on the basis of special permits issued on approval of the planning agency.[50] This enables the city to prevent the construction of a facility which is not in harmony with the surrounding area.

In addition to the types of public utilities already considered, some jurisdictions must plan for gas systems and central heating systems. With respect to these utilities, physical planning is concerned primarily with the proper location of lines and facilities and the protection of public safety. Gas mains are usually located in planting strips near the curbs or under the sidewalks. However, in some areas it may be found desirable to utilize alleys or rear lots. This has the

[50] *Local Planning Administration, op. cit.,* p. 128.

advantage of being able to serve two rows of houses rather than one. Since gas is highly inflammable, it is most essential that adequate regulations be established to insure safety both in the manner of distribution and the installation of facilities. Central heating is a utility in only a few cities. The problems from the viewpoint of the planner arise largely because of high pressures and high temperatures. Thus, it is important to make certain that the mains are properly placed with respect to other underground utilities such as water and gas lines, cables, and conduits. Steam lines must be accessible, well insulated, and properly supported.

Public Buildings and Institutional Uses. In every community of any size are to be found a number of public and semipublic buildings and facilities which are necessary to the conduct of government and the furnishing of public services of an institutional character such as those concerned with government, education, culture, health, religion, and charitable and social activities. Buildings and facilities needed for such purposes include city halls, fire stations, courthouses, post offices, schools, libraries, orphanages, hospitals, clinics, churches, auditoriums, community centers, museums, art galleries, and many others. Some of these are constructed, owned, and operated by government; some, by semipublic agencies; and some are privately constructed, owned, and operated. The amount of land in the average city devoted to such building and institutional uses ranges from 4 to 20 percent of the developed urban area.[51] About two-thirds of the area included under this classification is normally devoted to school uses.

The fact that government exercises direct control over the location and character of its public buildings places upon municipal authorities special responsibilities to locate and design municipal buildings in such a way as to promote the goals and objectives of the comprehensive plan. Frequently, this control provides the city with an unusual opportunity not only to satisfy functional and utilitarian demands, but also to enhance the civic beauty and build up civic pride.

All public buildings within municipalities are not, however, constructed, owned, and operated by the municipality. In many of our cities are also located public buildings of the federal government, the state, county, and school districts. Federal buildings may include post offices, courthouses, custom houses, hospitals, and office build-

---

[51] High percentages for such uses are frequently found in a small town which is a college or university center or governmental seat. See Bartholomew, op. cit., p. 68.

ings. Public buildings of the state may include office buildings, hospitals, prisons, armories, and correctional institutions. In some cities there are also to be found various county buildings such as courthouses, office buildings, jails, hospitals, and clinics. Virtually every municipality of any size will have one or many school buildings which are controlled by the municipal school district, the county, or the state. Municipal corporations are without legal authority to control the location and character of federal or state buildings and structures and have no authority to determine the location and character of county and special district buildings unless authorized by state law.[52] Sometimes this situation presents serious obstacles to coördinated municipal planning. However, municipalities will usually find that most of the goals and objectives of the comprehensive plan can be accomplished through the coöperative efforts of the responsible authorities concerned with the particular programs.

The location and character of public buildings must be governed to a large extent by the general purpose which they serve. Public buildings fall into two general classes: (1) Those which may be regarded as central type buildings intended to serve the entire community and, (2) those which are primarily neighborhood type buildings intended to serve sections of the community. This distinction is of special significance in determining location. It is normally not a function of the planning agency to make determinations of the size and the number of public buildings. This is a function of the service agencies. The planning agency does, however, have a very definite responsibility in assisting in securing appropriate locations and in working out the best possible design to fit into the planned land-use pattern. Public buildings should be so located as not to disrupt or interfere with business district functions or create unnecessary traffic congestion. Under some circumstances they may be located in a way to form a buffer or transition attraction between land uses and to focalize the city as an entity.

Public buildings of the central type may be grouped together or distributed in appropriate locations on sites not related to each other.

[52] The Attorney General of the State of Washington has ruled that municipalities may require school districts to comply with municipal building ordinances and building codes, provided they are reasonable, in view of Article XI, Section 11 of the State Constitution which provides that "any county, city, town or township, may make and enforce within its limits all such local police, sanitary and other regulations as are not in conflict with general laws." Opinion of Smith Troy, Attorney General, to Donald H. Webster, March 22, 1950.

In some communities there may be very definite advantages in favor of the civic center type of design. The civic center plan offers conveniences to the public who have dealings with several different public agencies as well as for the public officials who must work in close relationship with each other.[53] Certain communities may find that a civic center can be a factor in arresting blight over a particular area, in enhancing aesthetic values, or in affording greater opportunities for developing civic and cultural interest. However, the civic center idea may not always be feasible. In a given municipality there may be definite advantages in distributing public buildings within the central area in order that functional responsibilities will be better served. In reaching a decision as to which plan is better in a particular city, attention should be given to topographical factors, the current stage of building development, transit and traffic conditions, parking problems, and the general characteristics of the community.

Buildings of the neighborhood type include such buildings as fire stations, branch libraries, school buildings, community centers, and others which are designed for serving the special needs of a district. In selecting the site of such buildings, consideration should be given not only to present needs, but also to the anticipated needs resulting from the changing neighborhood, probable changes in the street system, and other developments which may affect the character of the service area. In the case of fire stations, for example, it is especially important to select general locations with regard to present and future building developments and specific sites where the street design is such as to provide ready access to all parts of the areas served.

The location and character of school buildings deserve special attention because they are normally the most numerous of all public buildings and because, quite commonly, the schools are not operated by the municipality but by school districts. This lack of integrated control makes it imperative that there be a high degree of coördination between the city planning agency and the authorities of the school system who are planning the location, size, and character of the school buildings. Schools should be located at points where there will be the least disturbance from noise, dust, odors, and vibration. The planning agency, through its gathering of basic data, will have information on population trends and proposed land use which are essential to intelligent school location. Furthermore, the planning of

[53] *Local Planning Administration, op. cit.,* p. 180.

school locations should be coördinated with plans for developing transit systems, traffic arteries, and parks and playgrounds.

The proper location of public buildings depends in part upon an orderly program of site acquisition. This program should be considered from a long-range point of view. In growing communities it is highly desirable to acquire and reserve sites in anticipation of future needs.[54] Otherwise, the city may be faced later with extremely high costs of condemnation. Even in established areas there is sometimes need for a long-range site acquisition program where relocation or expansion is contemplated. The requirements for public buildings are matters to be borne in mind in approving plats for subdivisions and in working out housing and urban redevelopment programs.

The planning of semipublic and private institutional land use involves many of the same considerations involved in land-use planning for public buildings. Hospitals, clinics, orphanages, churches, private schools, and many other institutions are an essential part of our community life and must be conveniently located with respect to their functional purpose and the area to be served. Nevertheless, it must be recognized that, to a degree, some of these institutions may have disturbing effects upon certain types of neighborhoods. Consequently, the depressing effects of hospitals, the noises of school children, the practicing of church choirs, and the congestion of traffic and parking which such institutions produce are factors which must be taken into account in the planning of institutional site locations. Land-use policy with respect to such institutional uses should seek to encourage the location and type of buildings which will best serve the community needs and at the same time minimize the detrimental effects. Municipalities do not have the same degree of control over such institutions as they do over public buildings. Institutional land-use policies are carried out largely under the police power. The most effective controls are established through zoning regulations, building codes, and by the use of special permits to insure that the particular building plan complies with reasonable requirements for off-street parking, height, lot size, and general appearance.

Recreational Areas and Public Open Spaces. Areas classified as recreational embrace a wide variety of uses including parks, play-

[54] Some municipalities have found it advantageous to create a department of real estate having among its functions that of acquiring, managing, and disposing of public buildings and certain other real properties. The need for such departments may be accentuated in communities that have extensive housing projects and urban redevelopment programs.

grounds, community centers, outdoor theaters, camp sites, beaches, golf courses, tennis courts, gymnasiums, arboretums, zoological gardens, scenic and historical sites, pleasure resorts, and open spaces of various kinds. Recreational lands include not only publicly owned areas, but also privately owned areas which are open to public or semipublic use.

The amount of land devoted to recreational uses and public open spaces varies greatly in different communities and, in fact, among different sections of the same community. The space required for recreational purposes depends very much upon the physical layout of the community as well as upon the interests, age groups, and the social and economic characteristics of its inhabitants. The National Park Service has suggested that for each city there should be one acre of accessible park or recreational space for each one hundred persons. It has also been suggested that out of the total area of each city, approximately 10 percent should be devoted to public recreation.[55] Land-use surveys indicate that few cities meet these recommended minimum standards. In a study of the land use in 44 incorporated cities in the Los Angeles area it was found that 5.8 percent of the gross urban used land was assigned to recreational uses. This represented approximately 4.60 acres per 1000 persons.[56] Although reports of the National Park Service show that the cities rated in the top quarter in each population classification under 1,000,000 more than meet this standard,[57] the situation probably is not as favorable as the figures would seem to indicate since, in many of these cities, a very high percentage of the land included in the calculation consists of large parks, reservations, and forest parks as distinguished from neighborhood recreational areas.

Location and types of use are often of greater significance than the total amount of acreage devoted to recreational purposes. Recreational facilities must be planned for all age groups and must be situated at locations that are reasonably accessible. The matter of accessibility varies greatly with the type of recreation facility. For example, facilities designed for small children need to be located conveniently, while convenience is not such an important factor in the location of camp sites and picnic areas.

[55] Local Planning Administration, op. cit., p. 165.
[56] Master Plan of Land Use, op. cit., p. 56. According to Bartholomew, about 7 percent of the developed area in the average city is devoted to parks and playgrounds. See Bartholomew, op. cit., p. 65.
[57] United States Department of the Interior, National Park Service, Municipal and County Parks in the United States, 1940, p. 2.

Recreational site planning demands that careful attention be given to the location of present and future residential districts, present population composition, population trends, probable population distribution and density, the location of present and future schools, the major street plan, and such other factors as have an important bearing on present and future recreational needs. In the selection of sites, an effort should be made to utilize, in so far as practical, areas which may be undesirable or uneconomical for other purposes. For example, steep hillsides, deep ravines, rocky promontories, and areas bordering on lakes and winding streams as well as low lying areas which are difficult to drain are often suitable for park purposes, but are not particularly satisfactory for other uses. However, such areas should not be selected for recreational use unless they are suitably located and reasonably accessible. Likewise, communities should guard against accepting grants of land for recreational purposes which may entail a wasteful expenditure of funds for development, maintenance, and operation.

Miscellaneous Land Uses. In every urban community there are a number of minor land uses which are not appropriately included in the major categories which have been discussed. Among these are such miscellaneous uses as those devoted to cemeteries, veterinarians' hospitals, and historical landmarks and monuments. The area devoted to these miscellaneous land uses seldom exceeds 2 percent of the total net urban used area. For convenience of classification, certain of these uses are often placed under one major category or another. Some of them, however, present problems of classification. Veterinarians' hospitals, for example, are sometimes placed under institutional, commercial, or industrial land uses. Cemeteries are frequently classified with utility or institutional uses. Historical landmarks and monuments may be classified with recreational uses.

Land areas for these minor urban land uses should be selected according to community needs for the particular function to be performed and with regard to their effect upon adjoining land uses. Certain of these uses such as cemeteries, for example, present special problems. While frequently cemeteries have been permitted to locate in residential districts, many communities have found that their presence there has a depressing effect upon the people in the area. On the other hand, it is sometimes shocking to the sensibilities of many persons to bury their relatives in business or industrial districts.[58] Con-

---

[58] Edward M. Bassett, *Zoning* (New York: Russell Sage Foundation, 1940), p. 217.

sequently, many municipalities, in recent years, have sought to promote the location of new cemeteries outside their corporate boundaries.[59] These same considerations are involved with respect to land used for crematories, except that crematories do not ordinarily require the amount of acreage necessary for cemetery use. The policy of requiring cemeteries and crematories to locate outside the city deserves more study before receiving general acceptance. Some cities have discovered that eventually the areas in which cemeteries become located are annexed, and they are then back within the corporate boundaries of the city but without reference to any planned land use.

PLANNING THE SYSTEM OF TRANSPORTATION

No single factor has had a greater impact upon the character of our cities than have our modes and routes of transportation. Mass transportation, which originated about 1830 with the horse-drawn omnibus, followed by the suburban railway in the 1850's, the cable car in the 1880's and the 1890's, and the elevated railway, electric streetcar, and the subway in the early 1900's, resulted in much greater mobility of city people and made possible the concentration of large industries in urban centers. Accessibility to the routes and terminals of these transportation systems has determined to a large degree the central points of most of our large urban communities. However, the development of the automobile and its extensive use for private transportation are greatly altering this pattern of urban growth.[60] Great areas of suburban land, formerly remote from the urban center, have been opened by automotive transportation not only for residential use, but also for the location of certain factories and business establishments.

While the increased use of the automobile has tended to free the citizen from dependence upon schedules and routes of the common carrier, it has, at the same time, produced a condition of traffic congestion which no large city has as yet successfully solved. Perhaps new developments in air travel, such as increased use of helicopters or other types of machines, may again alter the pattern of urban growth and relieve some of the congestion on the streets. This possibility must not be excluded in planning for transportation of people

[59] See Chap. 8, Zoning, p. 418.
[60] For a detailed study of the relationship between land use and traffic, see Robert B. Mitchell and Chester Rapkin, *Urban Traffic, A Function of Land Use* (New York: Columbia University Press, 1954).

and commodities in the city of the future. The successful use of helicopters for mail and passenger service between airports and central cities is already beyond the mere experimental stage. However, the current problems of transportation faced by municipalities are those arising from the increased dependence upon the automobile.

The location and character of the transportation system affect the physical plan in many ways. They not only determine the general direction of urban growth, but also are frequently a deciding factor in the location of commercial and industrial establishments and the place where a worker chooses his residence. However, the transportation system cannot be planned solely with reference to physical aspects. The pattern of streets and the location of the routes and terminals of transit and transportation systems must be established with a view to the convenience and facility with which persons and commodities are to be moved to, from, and within, the community. The overall transportation plan must be worked out with reference to many factors including travel habits, daily travel time, required schedules, available modes of transportation, traffic congestion, parking problems, profitableness of operations, public costs, and many other matters.[61]

It is essential that the overall system of transportation be developed in proper relationship to the overall plan of land use. The land use plan sets the pattern for the origin, destination, and volume of traffic. The plan of circulation facilitates the movement of persons and commodities which makes land utilization according to plan possible. Together, these plans provide the basic framework for much of the detailed planning represented by other elements of the comprehensive plan. Planning of specific projects is almost certain to be piecemeal unless developed within this framework. The following discussion of specific facilities and modes of transportation should be viewed in the light of this comprehensive approach.

THE STREET SYSTEM AND THE MOVEMENT OF TRAFFIC

If we recognize the subways and the elevated as parts of the street system, almost all urban traffic is carried by the streets. City streets were originally planned to serve three principal purposes: (1) to move traffic from one part of the city to another, (2) to provide

[61] Harmer E. Davis, "Some Observations on the Urban Transportation Problem," *Proceedings of the American Society of Civil Engineers,* City Planning Division, Vol. 81, Paper No. 769, pp. 769-4-769-6, August, 1955.

access, light, and air to abutting properties, and (3) to provide places for parking vehicles. Before the development of mechanized transportation, the volume of street traffic was slight and did not present a major municipal problem. A great deal of the travel within the city for conducting business was by foot, but as mechanized travel developed, cities spread out and traffic congestion increased. The automobile has simply intensified the problem which began with the advent of mass transportation.

The Private Automobile or Mass Transportation. With the increasing problem of traffic congestion in all of our major urban centers, cities must face up to the fundamental question of whether to plan for the movement of persons by the private automobile or by mass transportation. Today, in spite of the increasing traffic problem, parking difficulties, and the high cost of automobile travel, approximately half of the persons moving about within our urban communities insist on traveling by automobile. In the year 1940, a total of 32,450,000 vehicles was registered. By 1952, registrations had increased to more than 54 million. It has been estimated that by 1975 there will be in use 85 million motor vehicles.[62] There can be no question that the automobile and the truck which operate on relatively flexible highway routes provide a convenience of transportation which mass transportation systems cannot supply. This value must be weighed against the many statistical advantages favoring the development of mass transportation.

In every major city, engineers have been striving to increase the flow of automobile traffic by means of street widening, grade separation, freeways, traffic control, and other measures. In most cases, the inevitable result is merely to lure more automobiles into the traffic arteries and create new problems of traffic congestion and difficulties of parking in the central business areas. Consequently, many planners who have been giving careful study to the problem of traffic congestion believe that the transportation problem cannot be solved until city officials and the public are convinced of the necessity of developing and relying primarily on mass transportation. Traffic studies show that each automobile carries on the average of 1.7 passengers, whereas the number of persons carried by a streetcar averages 78 passengers or 43 times as many people as are carried in one automobile

[62] Donald C. Hyde, "Moving People in Urban Areas," *Planning 1953*, Proceedings of the Annual National Planning Conference, Detroit, Mich., October 11–15, 1953 (Chicago: American Society of Planning Officials, 1953), p. 68.

although the streetcar occupies only three times the amount of space of an automobile. A bus, on the average, carries 45 passengers or approximately 25 times the number of persons carried by an automobile, but occupies only about twice the space of an automobile.[63] Furthermore, streetcars and buses do not create a parking problem since they continue in service and do not require space for parking. A further argument advanced favoring reliance upon mass transportation is the matter of economy. It has been pointed out that, nationally, we are spending 46 billion dollars a year to move one-half of our people by automobile, whereas the other half is moved by common carrier at a cost of about 6 billion dollars.[64] Such comparative figures do not take into account the economic costs of providing street and off-street parking space for the persons who travel to and from the central business districts by automobile.

Although the foregoing statistics on space occupancy would seem strongly to favor concentration on mass transportation, it should not be assumed that street carrying capacity will be increased correspondingly by placing buses in operation on streets which are also used by private automobiles. Since buses must make frequent stops for loading and unloading passengers, the effective street width for passenger cars is substantially reduced because of the fact that automobiles tend to move primarily in the inside lanes to avoid being delayed at the stops. It has been estimated that buses moving in each direction reduce the effective street width for passenger automobiles by at least 12 feet.[65] This fact, however, is not a valid argument against the encouragement of mass transportation, but it is a matter to take into account in planning street use and street capacity.

Before any solution can be found to the transportation problem, cities must come to grips with the fundamental problem of what type of city they wish to develop. How vital is it to concentrate business in the central business district, and how important is it to plan cities

[63] William C. McBrien, "Moving People in Urban Areas," *Planning 1953*, Proceedings of the Annual National Planning Conference, Detroit, Michigan, October 11–15, 1953 (Chicago: American Society of Planning Officials, 1953), p. 67. According to current traffic counts reported by *Urban Land*, Vol. 13, No. 11, December, 1954, the average number of persons in automobiles is about 1.5. Modern transit vehicles seat as many persons as now ride in 30 to 35 automobiles. It requires 20 times as much space to move people by automobile as by public transit.

[64] E. L. Tennyson, "Moving People in Urban Areas," *Planning 1953*, Proceedings of the Annual National Planning Conference, Detroit, Michigan, October 11–15, 1953 (Chicago: American Society of Planning Officials, 1953), p. 78.

[65] United States Department of Commerce, *Highway Capacity Manual* (Washington, D.C.: U.S. Government Printing Office, 1950), p. 83.

so that persons who wish to travel by private automobile may do so? If the decision is made in favor of concentrating business in the central business district, reliance upon the automobile to move people to and fro rapidly and safely presents insurmountable problems, unless we are willing to expend huge sums of money in rebuilding our downtown areas, reconstructing our arteries for traffic, and providing adequate terminal parking facilities.[66] If, on the other hand, concentration of business in the central business district is determined to be of less importance, the opportunities to plan for transportation by automobile are immeasurably increased. It must be recognized, however, that even though traffic conditions make it possible for a high percentage of people to travel by private automobile, public transit is essential to the life of every large community. Another factor to bear in mind is that, in a great many communities, mass transportation systems are unable to operate today without the aid of subsidy. Consequently the encouragement of transportation by private automobile further adds to the financial plight of the transit system and the city's total economy.

Street Planning. Even though large municipalities may be successful in encouraging a greater use of public transportation, and even though the trend toward business decentralization continues, there seems little to indicate that the problem of traffic congestion will be greatly relieved. City planners and city engineers must continue to seek better means and facilities to insure that traffic moves swiftly and safely between all terminal points.

One of the most important elements in the solution of this problem is the design of the street system, which not only provides a means of access to and from the community, but determines the ease and safety with which people move from one part of the city to another. The street design, however, is not concerned exclusively with the movement of traffic. The street plan determines the size of the blocks which affects the types of buildings, pedestrian traffic, parking, and many other matters. Street planning, in furthering the movement of persons and commodities, is concerned principally with such matters as traffic flow, street sites, signals, safety zones, stoplights, one-way streets, street parking, off-street parking, truck and passenger segregation, street loading and unloading, routing for bypasses, and the

---

[66] For a discussion of the relationship of parking to the "downtown-suburban" conflict, see Highway Research Board, *What Parking Means to Business* (Washington, D.C.: Automotive Safety Foundation, 1955), p. 27.

establishment of grades. Closely related is the matter of traffic education and traffic enforcement.

Public policies with respect to street improvements designed to improve traffic conditions and the convenience and safety of travel must continuously balance the estimated costs of such improvements against such intangible and uncertain factors as loss of time and circulation between terminal points, costs to motorists through wear on motors, brakes, and other automotive equipment, gasoline consumption, and the definite but uncertain costs of accidents and deaths. The costs of accidents and deaths on our highways today are equal to the casualties of a war. Much can be done to reduce these costs through proper design of our street and highway system. The report of the President's Advisory Committee on a National Highway Program has pointed out the fact that the death rate on high-type, heavily traveled arteries of modern design, including controlled access, is only from one-fourth to one-half as much as it is on less adequate highways.[67] The report also points out that the average motorist today is paying considerably more for insurance to protect himself against accident costs than he pays the state in fuel taxes and license fees which furnish almost the entire support for the streets and highways over which he operates.

Street Classification and Design.   The modern concept of street planning requires that streets be specialized in function and designed in accordance with their function. In those cities which have developed without the benefit of good planning, the pattern of the street layout is difficult to change. The common pattern is that almost every street intersection carries through traffic in four directions. Streets in residential areas commonly are designed to carry trucking and heavy traffic which produce noise and congestion and create safety hazards, particularly in school and playground areas. For the most part, these streets which are too narrow for the traffic alone, in addition may have to serve as a means of access for nearby properties, provide parking space, and sometimes serve as rights of way for car lines.[68] Nevertheless, many existing streets can be converted to specialized use, and when any new streets are constructed, they can be

---

[67] The President's Advisory Committee on a National Highway Program, *A Ten Year National Highway Program, A Report to the President* (Washington, D.C.: U.S. Government Printing Office, January, 1955), pp. 11–12.

[68] Harold M. Mayer, "Moving People and Goods in Tomorrow's Cities," *The Annals of the American Academy of Political and Social Science,* Vol. 242, p. 122, November, 1945.

designed more nearly to permit each class of traffic to use a special type of street. For example, fast moving through traffic should not be delayed by curb parking, truck deliveries, or bus loading. Streets intended for private local access should not be congested by fast moving traffic. Each municipality should work out a master plan of highways, including a sound classification of streets according to their type of service, to insure the maximum of community benefits. The street classification plan should be worked out from the results of periodic traffic surveys and other data which furnish a basis for understanding the trends in population growth, the distribution of traffic, and the probable future traffic loads.

The street system of a municipality is made up of major streets and minor streets. Major streets include freeways, expressways, parkways, boulevards, major arteries, and other traffic arteries designed for the primary purpose of carrying traffic from one part of the city to another. Minor streets include all the streets whose primary purpose is to furnish access, light, and air to abutting property, and to serve as channels for utilities. Major streets frequently may have as a secondary function the same functions as minor streets. Minor streets may carry a certain amount of through traffic, but this should be discouraged. Lack of functional differentiation of streets tends to intensify the congestion of traffic and to increase accidents.

The design of major streets is an important factor in the movement of traffic. Major streets are usually laid out according to a gridiron or checkerboard plan, a radial-circumferential plan, or a combination of the two. In laying out the street pattern, the topography is probably the most important functional consideration. In areas which are relatively level and are not affected by natural barriers, the gridiron or checkerboard pattern offers a number of advantages. In the first place, it is easy to lay out, easy to describe, readily understood, and easy to number. It has the disadvantage of making diagonal crossings indirect and sometimes inconvenient. Furthermore, it offers some difficulties in differentiating between major and minor streets. From the aesthetic standpoint, the gridiron pattern often appears to be monotonous.[69]

Certain communities have found the adoption of a radial pattern using circumferential or diagonal crossings to be more satisfactory. Such a pattern adapts itself better to topography which may be irregular and makes it easier to establish functional routes. These radial

[69] *Local Planning Administration, op. cit.,* pp. 94–95.

highways are intersected at convenient distances by connecting highways. Diagonal crossings are usually added to secondary focal points. The radial type of design is developed through the extension of radial highways extending from the center or near the center of the city. The circumference or intersecting highway can also be used to bypass the center of the city and thus help to decrease traffic congestion in the central business area.[70] Many cities which have objected to bypass highways are finding that the city actually benefits through increase of local business and increase of property values.[71] The radial-circumferential type of design makes it easier to differentiate between major and minor streets than in the case of the checkerboard pattern. The chief objection to this type of street pattern is that it is more difficult to lay out. Furthermore, it sometimes creates subdivision problems because it results in irregularly shaped parcels of land. In some instances it tends to complicate the problems of utility installation.

Whichever street pattern or combination of street patterns is utilized, the street plan must give consideration to the functional distinction between major and minor thoroughfares. The proper classification of streets necessitates a knowledge of land use and proposed land use before classifications are made and before new streets are laid out. The distinction between major and minor streets is important for a number of reasons. Major streets carrying large volumes of traffic may frequently have injurious effects on abutting property and nearby property. Whether a street is a major or a minor one will regulate to a considerable extent the width of the street, the need for grade separations, whether there should be center or separation strips, and traffic controls.

Since it is desirable that minor streets discourage through traffic, it is sometimes desirable that they be laid out on a curved basis rather than straight. Also, much steeper grades are permitted for minor streets than in the case of major thoroughfares. In certain instances it may be found that dead-end streets or cul-de-sacs are desirable. A most important consideration to bear in mind, however, is that the layout of the minor streets should not be such as to interfere with the access of fire-fighting equipment.

Among the other important considerations to be taken into account in the design of the street system are the type and location of street

---

[70] For a discussion of the need for and the advantages and disadvantages of bypasses, see *How Bypasses Affect Business* (Washington, D.C.: Chamber of Commerce of the United States, 1956).

[71] *California Highways and Public Works*, Vol. 30, No. 7, 8, July and August, 1951.

intersections. The type and nature of the street intersection have an important bearing on the flow of traffic. It is also at intersections that most accidents occur. Whether a particular street should be a through street or a stop street must be considered from the standpoint of traffic movement and from the standpoint of safety. The matter of traffic view obstructions also enters into the plan of the street system. It is essential that there be adequate vision clearance at all intersections. This is best controlled through corner structure setbacks in residential districts, diagonal cutoffs in business districts, and plantings control.[72]

In many of the highly congested urban areas, cities are today looking to the use of freeways as a means of moving much of the long-distance, fast moving traffic. Usually special enabling legislation is required to permit the city to acquire, construct, or maintain freeways. Abutting property owners do not have any rights of access, light, or air as in the case of ordinary streets and highways. Quite frequently passenger car and truck traffic are accommodated in separate lanes. Cross streets are carried over or under, and the freeway is accessible at designated points by cloverleaf intersections and frequently by separation of grades. Access to the freeway is limited, usually to intervals of one mile. Since lanes for cars going in the opposite direction are separated by landscape strips or concrete barriers, head-on collisions are not possible. Turnouts for cars having mechanical difficulties are usually provided in order that the stream of traffic will not be blocked.[73]

Increasing Street Capacity.   Since in most communities the majority of streets were not planned to carry the present traffic flow, planners and street engineers are constantly struggling with the problems of how a street capacity may be increased and traffic flow facilitated. One of the most common solutions to the relief of traffic congestion has been that of street widening. This sometimes presents serious difficulties since it may require the tearing down of expensive buildings or the narrowing of sidewalks. The narrowing of sidewalks has its limitations in areas where pedestrian traffic is heavy. Experience in many communities with street widening has been that it has only led to a vicious circle, since the result has been to increase the volume of traffic without any reduction of congestion.

---

[72] Joshua H. Vogel and Ernest H. Campbell, *Municipal Regulation of Traffic View Obstructions* (Seattle: Bureau of Governmental Research and Services, University of Washington, February, 1953), Report No. 122, pp. 6–10.
[73] Mayer, *loc. cit.*

In recent years there have been a number of proposals for arcading sidewalks, which would mean moving them back until they come beneath the upper stories of abutting buildings.[74] Under these proposals, the outer supports of the abutting building would be supported at the curb by a row of pillars. The arcading of sidewalks involves expensive construction, but in most cases would be much less costly than condemning the entire building. At the present time, arcading for most cities would appear to be in a speculative stage. According to *Architectural Forum*, however, arcading is more feasible than most laymen realize and affords many advantages in addition to increasing the flow of traffic.[75] Not only does arcading add a lane for vehicular traffic by permitting space ordinarily occupied by sidewalks to be used for street purposes, but it provides sidewalks free of rain, snow, and intense sunshine. By removing sun glare and reflections, store window displays can be made more attractive. In this atmosphere pedestrians are more inclined to saunter and to stop to look at the displays. The transition from the outside to the inside is facilitated and shops along the arcade benefit.

Other proposals for increasing street capacity have been the building of double-deck streets. Such projects have been undertaken in a few cities such as Chicago and New York. This type of construction is extremely costly and appears to be feasible only where the pressure of traffic congestion seems to offer no other solution. Other devices which tend to facilitate the flow of traffic have been the differentiation of through traffic by bypass routes and construction of grade separations at cross streets to eliminate the congestion resulting from slowdown at street intersections. Some cities may find it possible to step up the day-to-day efficiency of their streets by comparatively simple and inexpensive techniques. Among these are (1) more efficient traffic routing, including the use of one-way streets, truck, and transit routes, (2) a better system of traffic regulation, including controls of parking, loading, turning controls, speed limits, and the installation of well-planned signs, signals, and other traffic control devices, and (3) making minor physical improvements through channelization and the redesign of intersections.[76]

[74] Austin F. Macdonald, *American City Government and Administration* (New York: Thomas Y. Crowell Company, 1949), p. 479.

[75] "The Arcade Makes a Comeback," *Architectural Forum*, Vol. 102, No. 1, pp. 93–97, January, 1955.

[76] The United States Chamber of Commerce, *How to Get the Most Out of Our Streets* (Washington, D.C.: 1954).

Street Lighting, Street Naming, and House Numbering.   In their efforts to facilitate the flow of traffic, many cities have failed to develop adequate systems of street lighting and of street numbering. Just as streets should be classified for functional use, so should they be classified for the purpose of meeting lighting requirements. It cannot be assumed that the functional classification will serve for the purposes of street lighting. Some streets, for example, those in certain commercial or industrial districts, may be extremely busy during the business hours and have almost no traffic at night. Lighting of such streets should be carried out primarily with a view to prevent crime. Other streets, such as those in the theater district, which have a heavy nighttime use in proportion to their daytime use, must be lighted in accordance with this usage. The adequacy of lighting on major thoroughfares is of extreme importance because of the fact that these streets carry high-speed through traffic and because a substantial proportion of the users may not be familiar with them. Special attention needs to be given to lighting the intersections where thoroughfares merge with streets to the central business district. This is important to facilitate the free flow of traffic and to safeguard against accidents. Every street has its own special lighting needs which must be worked out with reference to its use, width, paving, the planting of trees, and the character of the abutting property. The proper planning of street lighting is a highly scientific and specialized responsibility. The design and installation of the lighting system should be undertaken only after a careful survey and analysis of the needs by competent technicians.[77]

Persons who are unfamiliar with a city, or a locality within a city, encounter great difficulties in finding their way around unless the city has a good system of street naming and has adequate street signs properly placed. Many cities have not always appreciated the fact that a poor system of street naming contributes to traffic congestion as well as to delay and inconvenience of motorists and pedestrians. In adopting street names, care should be exercised to avoid, in so far as possible, the duplicating of names for different streets, avenues, and places, or of using names which, because of their similarity of spelling or pronunciation, may result in confusion. Cities have used many methods of street naming which are entirely satisfactory. These

---

[77] See Joshua H. Vogel and Ernest H. Campbell, *Planting, Maintenance, and Removal of Trees from Streets* (Seattle: Bureau of Governmental Research and Services, University of Washington, June, 1950), Report No. 111, pp. 45–60.

have included streets named after presidents, writers, colleges or universities, prominent local persons, and many others. Some cities rely largely upon numerical systems of naming, with distinctions between streets and avenues. Others combine the two, using numbers for streets running in one direction and names for streets running in another.

The important thing is to have a system which is not difficult to understand and which facilitates circulation. It goes without saying that any good system of street naming requires that the street signs be legible, of good design, and properly placed so that they can be readily seen by motorists without causing undue traffic delays. Along with the system of street naming, it is essential that there be worked out a sound and logical system of house numbering. Neat looking and properly located house numbers not only add to the appearance of the property, but also afford positive identification in case of police calls, fire emergencies, or civil defense. A good system of house numbering also facilitates store deliveries, mail service, and the gathering of data for city directories.[78] In cities laid out on the checkerboard plan, the problem of house numbering is quite simple, inasmuch as two central intersecting streets may be taken as base streets with house numbers running in each direction from these. In cities which use the radial-circumferential plan or in which the street pattern is irregular, the house numbering system becomes somewhat more complex. In such cases the system should be worked out after consultation with post office officials and the officers of the police and fire departments.

Off-Street Parking and Loading Facilities. One of the most serious obstacles to the free flow of traffic is the use of street space for parking and for loading and unloading. The fact is, however, that unless adequate parking and loading and unloading facilities are available at terminal points, streets cannot fulfill their primary purpose of moving persons and commodities to their destinations. With the constantly increasing pressure for more street capacity to handle the increasing volume of traffic, some solution must be found to the parking problem other than curb parking. The evolutionary process of dealing with the parking problem has followed a common pattern in a great many cities. In the first stage, angle parking gave way to parallel parking. In the next stage, limited-time parking replaced

[78] *News Bulletin* (Chicago: Public Administration Clearing House, Release No. 4, January 20, 1955).

unlimited-time parking. Next, the use of parking meters eliminated the privilage of free parking. Then, in the more congested streets, parking was prohibited altogether, or at least during the hours of peak traffic. This, in turn, has led to parking on side streets, some of which were in residential areas. This practice has raised objections because of the added danger to children, the blocking of driveways, and increased noise and inconvenience.

Statistics make it clear that curb parking in the highly congested areas is not feasible. Curb parking in the average city block reduces the street carrying capacity by approximately 45 percent. It requires a 68-foot street, which permits curb parking, to carry the same volume of traffic that can be carried by a 40-foot street without curb parking. The elimination of curb parking has long been resisted by merchants who fear such action injures their trade. Studies which have been made of the parking problem seem to indicate that the businessman has tended to overestimate the value of retaining curb parking. If the amount of curb space normally devoted to driveways, hydrants, and loading zones, which usually amounts to about 30 percent of the total, is disregarded, the curb in front of a 60-foot store will accommodate three parked cars. Surveys have shown that actually only about one-third of the available curb parking spaces are used by shoppers, and also that curb parkers spend only about one-fourth of the amount that is spent by persons using off-street parking facilities.[79] Even on an estimate that a store may gross between $10,000 and $50,000 per year from each parking space, it is apparent that this volume alone will not support a business of a 60-foot frontage located on one of the main streets.

At the present time, more and more cities tend to look upon off-street parking as the only solution to the problem. Whether or not the parking problem can be adequately solved by means of off-street parking facilities has not as yet been fully demonstrated.[80] It seems quite certain that no large city will be able to provide, in its central business district, sufficient parking space to accommodate every person who would prefer to drive his car in preference to using mass transportation. It has been estimated that in order to provide the amount of parking space to accommodate every automobile driver, the equivalent of two blocks in area of parking space would be needed

[79] F. D. Kuckuck, "Municipal Parking," The Municipality, Vol. 149, No. 1, pp. 7–8, January, 1954.

[80] Cleveland City Planning Commission, How Cleveland Merchants Can Secure Off-street Parking by the Benefit-Assessment Method, April, 1954, pp. 3–4.

for each block of business.[81] The well-planned suburban shopping center attempts to provide approximately 4 square feet of parking area for 1 square foot of store area. It seems unlikely that our large cities can hope to reach a ratio greater than 1 square foot of parking to 8 square feet of store space. Medium-sized cities can probably provide not more than a ratio of 1 to 4 or 1 to 2. Small cities may be able to provide a considerably larger percentage for parking. The necessity of solving the parking problem in the small cities is especially acute because of their normal lack of efficient mass transportation facilities and their higher daily and seasonal variation in the parking demand.[82] Any attempts to provide off-street parking in the large cities for all who wish to drive their cars would seem to be met with almost insuperable obstacles. Very little, if any, vacant land may be found in appropriate locations. Consequently, it would be necessary to convert some other use to parking. It has been estimated that to park all cars of persons who would prefer to drive to downtown Boston, for example, would necessitate tearing down about one-third of the downtown buildings and converting the space to parking facilities.[83]

Before any satisfactory solution is found to the parking problem, the issue of the relative responsibility of the city and that of private enterprise in solving the problem must be resolved. The cost of acquiring and developing off-street parking facilities is costly and frequently the return from such operations would be lower than that from the existing use. In some instances outdated building codes have prevented the erection of modern-type mechanical garages. These factors have been a major stumbling block to business in solving the problem.[84] On the other hand, when it is proposed that municipalities step in to provide the facilities, strong opposition is raised on the ground that government is in competition with private enterprise engaged in the parking business. As matters now stand, it seems that the only feasible solution in many jurisdictions must be one in which municipal governments coöperate with private business in an effort

[81] Kuckuck, op. cit.

[82] John H. Miller, *Parking Problems of Small Cities* (Albany: Municipal Police Chiefs Information and Training Extension Service of the New York State Conference of Mayors, New York State Association of Chiefs of Police, and the Municipal Training Institute of the State of New York, January, 1954), 6 pp., mimeo.

[83] "Urban Traffic Forum," *Architectural Forum*, Vol. 98, No. 2, p. 117, February, 1953.

[84] For an up-to-date study of the legal aspects, methods of finance, and practical solutions to the problem of off-street parking, see *A Survey of Municipal Off-Street Parking with Emphasis upon California Laws and Practices* (City of Los Angeles: City Administrative Officer, December, 1955).

to work out a satisfactory solution. The use of governmental powers has the advantage of making the assembly of land possible through powers of eminent domain which private business does not possess.[85] Also, by appropriate public controls, the municipality can insure that parking facilities once established will not be eliminated at some future time when they are vitally needed. With respect to financing under a coöperative plan, business, which stands to benefit, should assume the major burden of the costs.[86] The municipality, however, can justify a reasonable contribution in the interest of facilitating the movement of traffic.

One of the special facets of the parking problem which must be dealt with separately is that of loading and unloading commodities. A number of large cities have reduced this interference with traffic by restricting loading and unloading operations to off-peak traffic hours, particularly to night and early morning. Such limitations are not practical, however, in all cities and for all purposes. Wherever possible, loading and unloading should be accomplished in alleys and off-street entrances. If curb loading and unloading cannot be avoided, the location of zones for this purpose should be selected with care and such operations carefully supervised. One of the trends which offers one of the best solutions is the provision for trucking facilities on the inside of commercial and industrial establishments. Some department stores in large cities have found it feasible to bring trucks directly to the shipping departments on upper floors of the building either by elevators or by spiral ramps.[87] Such practices, where economically feasible, offer excellent opportunities to remove one of the most serious obstacles to the free flow of traffic.

If congestion continues to increase in the central business districts, it may be necessary to transform radically the design of our buildings and alter the pattern of our pedestrian and vehicular traffic. One of the most far-reaching plans that has been suggested is to take over the ground floor area of an entire district and convert it to space for parking and loading. Pedestrian passageways would be provided on the second-story level where the entrances and display frontage would be located. The streets would be left entirely free for the movement of vehicles.[88] Although such ideas at this time appear to be impractical, they nevertheless provide much food for thought.

[85] In some states special enabling legislation may be needed for this purpose.
[86] Cleveland City Planning Commission, op. cit.
[87] Mayer, loc. cit.
[88] Urban Land, Vol. 13, No. 6, p. 2, June, 1954.

In seeking the solution to the parking problem and the special facet of loading and unloading, the planning agency assumes a major role. The planning agency has a responsibility both to guide the location and character of private facilities and to recommend, if local conditions warrant, plans for municipally owned parking facilities or for facilities developed through the coöperative efforts of municipal government and private business. The planning agency should be prepared to evaluate the feasibility of proposed solutions and to determine whether a proposed project will further the planned physical development of the community or become a barrier to it. In the planning of parking facilities, attention should be given to the matter of aesthetics. Opportunities to eliminate existing eyesores by converting unsightly uses to parking are sometimes possibilities. However, without good planning, parking lots themselves may become eyesores.[89] The opportunities of avoiding this condition by appropriate landscaping have not been fully explored.

URBAN TRANSIT AND TRANSPORTATION SYSTEMS

As large cities continue to struggle with traffic congestion and off-street parking, it becomes increasingly clear that no solution can be found to the overall problem of moving persons and commodities except through the coördinated planning of all transportation facilities, including all forms of public conveyance.[90] As obvious as this statement seems to be, it is nevertheless true that most cities in recent years through their concentration on traffic problems have failed to give adequate attention to the development of convenient, comfortable, efficient, and economical means of public conveyance.[91] The result has been that equipment has become obsolete and service has deteriorated. The consequence has been loss of patronage and financial difficulties of operation.

Ever since World War II, mass transportation has been losing passengers to the private automobile. In 1954 transit lines carried 12,386,000,000 passengers. This was down 10.9 percent from the num-

[89] Local Planning Administration, op. cit., p. 112.

[90] A distinction is frequently made between transit systems and transportation systems. "Transit systems" include buses, streetcars, elevated railways, and subways. Elevated railways and subways, and frequently suburban steam and electric suburban railways are classified as "rapid transit" systems. Railroads, intercity bus and truck lines, and water and air transport are included under "transportation systems." Local Planning Administration, op. cit., p. 132.

[91] For a comprehensive discussion of the problems and needs of and solutions for public transportation, see Crowded Streets—A Symposium on Public Transportation (Washington, D.C.: Urban Land Institute, June, 1955), Technical Bulletin No. 26.

ber carried in 1953. The traffic in 1953 showed a drop of 8.2 percent from 1952.[92] In 1952 mass transportation systems carried 4 percent less passengers than in 1951, and in 1951 they carried 7 percent less than in 1950. The city of Seattle, whose population is approximately one-half million, reported that in 1954 its transit system carried 5,000,000 fewer paying passengers than it did in 1953. This represented a loss of 8.04 percent from the figure of 1953. Seattle transit system patronage at the present time is less than half of what it was during World War II.[93] Nevertheless, more than 60 percent of the persons traveling to downtown areas in cities with populations of over 100,000 rely upon mass transportation facilities. Of those cities within the 100,000 to 500,000 population bracket, about 40 percent of the travel is by mass transportation. The proportion using mass transit tends to increase with the size of the city. For all cities over one-half million, the percentage using mass transportation is 63 percent and in the very large cities, like New York and Philadelphia, the figure is approximately 80 percent.[94] Some form of public transportation is needed in virtually every city having a population of 10,000 or more. The demand for mass transportation depends upon many factors, such as the size and kind of city, the number of persons employed, the location of their residences with respect to the places of employment, the location of shopping centers with respect to residential areas, and the distances of homes from schools and recreational centers.

Factors in Determining the Type and Location of Transit Facilities. The choice of the type of transit system in most cities resolves itself to one of streetcars, motor buses, and trackless trolley buses. In certain of our densely populated urban areas, the need for rapid transit and the pressures to relieve streets of traffic congestion may cause the cities to turn to the elevated railway or the subway. Today, only four cities in the United States—New York, Chicago, Boston, and Philadelphia—have utilized the elevated and the subway to provide rapid transit. The city of Toronto, Canada, is just completing a subway which will become part of the metropolitan transit system.[95] In other

[92] *American Municipal News* (Chicago: American Municipal Association, March, 1955, p. 1.

[93] The Seattle *Times*, January 6, 1955, p. 2.

[94] "Urban Traffic Forum," *Architectural Forum*, Vol. 98, No. 2, p. 114, February, 1953.

[95] Frederick G. Gardiner, *The Municipality of Metropolitan Toronto—A New Answer to the Metropolitan Problem*, an address to the American Bar Association Convention, Boston, Mass., August 25, 1953.

cities, suburban rapid-transit commuting service is provided by steam or electric trains on private rights of way. From the standpoint of service, the elevated and the subway provide the most efficient means of transportation of any of the transit facilities. The chief obstacle to the subway is its large cost of construction, which makes its use feasible only in the largest cities and on the most heavily traveled routes.[96] Experience would seem to indicate that cities cannot support rapid-transit subways until their population approaches one million people.[97] Although elevated transit can be constructed at much less cost than the subway, it has certain other disadvantages which have caused its use to be curtailed in New York, Boston, and Philadelphia and have discouraged its adoption as a means of rapid transit in other cities.[98] Elevated structures tend to darken the streets, frequently drip grease and oil, and their supporting structures often interfere with street traffic. Objections are also raised against the elevated because their unsightly appearance and the noise which they produce are likely to depreciate property in the nearby vicinity.[99]

From the time mass transportation facilities first developed until the middle 1920's, the electric street railway was by far the most important method of urban transit. During the 1920's the motor bus and also the trackless trolley began to come into general use and since then have gradually tended to supplant the streetcar except in certain of the larger cities. Each type of facility has certain specialized advantages and disadvantages. The chief advantage of the streetcar is its suitability for highly congested areas, since it occupies the smallest number of square feet of street space per passenger of any of the modes of conveyance. Generally speaking, the streetcar has relatively low upkeep costs. However, the construction and maintenance costs of trackage place it at a disadvantage with bus and trolley operation. Although considerable improvements have been made in streetcars,

[96] Some thought has been given to the construction of a high-speed subway consisting of four tunnels traversing mid-Manhattan and extending westward into the Hackensack meadows of New Jersey and eastward to Sunnyside Yards on Long Island. The proposed train would travel at speeds up to 150 miles per hour. The estimated cost of construction would be about 900 million dollars. *Urban Land*, Vol. 13, No. 6, p. 2, June, 1954.

[97] *Local Planning Administration*, op. cit., p. 137.

[98] Harold M. Mayer, "Moving People and Goods in Tomorrow's Cities," *The Annals of the American Academy of Political and Social Science*, Vol. 242, p. 119, November, 1945.

[99] Experimentation with the monorail and other types of more modern equipment and structures may eventually overcome many of these objections.

for the most part they are noisier and have less comfortable riding qualities than buses or trolleys.

One of the chief advantages that motor buses have over streetcars is the flexibility of routing, since they are not required to follow fixed rails or definite routes. Since motor buses are small-unit carriers and do not require heavy outlays of capital costs for rights of way and power transmission lines, they can more economically serve areas with low population density than can streetcars or even trackless trolleys. Trackless trolleys have many of the advantages of motor buses in that they do not require large expenditures for track construction and maintenance, and assuming the availability of low-cost electric power, have the economy of small-unit operation. Although confined to fixed routes, the trackless trolley has a high degree of flexibility in traffic which rail transportation does not have. For economical operation, the trackless trolley normally requires a traffic density somewhat higher than that necessary for the operation of the motor bus. Among the important values of the motor bus in any integrated transit system, is its use as a feeder from areas of low population density and for providing connections between points where service is essential but traffic is light.[100]

Since the primary purpose of the transit system is to move people efficiently, the planning agency is vitally concerned with the routing of the transit vehicles to and through the city. The planning of transit system routes must be closely interrelated with street planning and other elements of the physical plan. Failure to develop long-range comprehensive plans may result in lost opportunities to solve transportation problems economically and efficiently. The uncertainties involved in the belated move on the part of the Seattle Transit Commission to have set aside the center strip of the planned freeway running north-south through the city for rapid-transit operations point up the importance of coördinating highway and transit planning.[101] Failure of large urban communities to develop a policy on rapid transit renders impossible any program of comprehensive planning aimed at the solution of the transportation problem. It is also essential in facilitating the flow of traffic that local transit planning and street planning be coördinated. Streets used for surface transit routes should be carefully selected. Normally, transit lines should

[100] *Local Planning Administration, op. cit.,* p. 136.
[101] "Transit Board Caught with Plans Down," *The Argus,* Vol. 62, No. 3, January 15, 1955 (Seattle, Wash.).

be confined to major streets. An effort should be made to lay out routes so that no persons in the areas served need to walk more than one-fourth mile or for more than about five minutes.[102]

It is important that great care be given to the routing of transit lines through the central business district. A number of schemes have been utilized with varying advantages and disadvantages. One plan sometimes referred to as the terminal system, routes transit lines through the outskirts of the business district. The advantage of this plan is that it keeps the central business area free from the congestion of transit vehicles. On the other hand, it may not adequately provide for central business district service. Another system, known as the loop service plan, brings the buses or streetcars directly into the central business district and returns them to the outskirts by the same route after making a loop through the central district. The main objection to this plan is that it adds to the congestion of the downtown area. A third plan which is sometimes used is the turnback service. Under this plan the transit vehicles pass through the central business district, then turn around and return. Under still other plans, the transit vehicle will continue on to the outskirts of another part of the city before returning. Obviously, the type of routing plan which fits the needs of one city may not be well suited to those of another. To the extent possible, it seems desirable to work out a routing plan which facilitates through service from one side of the city to another and which produces the least congestion in the central business district, but at the same time provides the essential service both to and within the central business area.

Community plans have frequently failed to lay sufficient stress upon the transportation system as a factor in determining the direction of population growth. Few people are willing to spend more than one hour in commuting to and from work. More are willing to spend not more than 30 to 40 minutes. The character of the transit facilities, the efficiency and cost of service, and the location of routes have an important influence upon the places where persons take up residence. These factors are of especial significance in the development of new districts since it may be possible to plan the transit system in a way to guide population growth rather than to follow it. The transit system also has an important bearing on the location of business and industry. Conceivably, convenience and efficiency of transportation may turn out to be the determining factors in resolving

---

[102] *Local Planning Administration, op. cit.,* p. 139.

the question of whether planning efforts should be aimed at concentrating business activities in the central area or toward greater commercial and industrial decentralization.

Railroad Facilities and Operations.   Since cities are not self-sufficient, their very existence as well as their ability to supply human wants are dependent upon various systems of transportation. Among the most necessary of these is the railroad. Railway transportation has played an important role both in the location and development of most of our large cities. Consequently, many aspects of railroad transportation, including the character of terminal facilities and many phases of railroad operations, are matters of great concern to the planner.

Since railway rights of way and easements, for the most part, were established prior to the time of planning consciousness, the planner should be aware of the problems and difficulties of putting into effect plans for communities which may require the rerouting of railway lines or major changes in the location of facilities. The features of most of our older cities are permanently affected by early decisions with respect to the granting of railroad rights of way and the locating of railway terminals. Many factory warehouses, wharves, and other establishments have developed in relation to them. This relationship in most cases is very difficult to change, even though from a planning point of view it may not represent the best land utilization. There are many ways, however, in which comprehensive urban planning may contribute to improved railroad transportation services. Among the most important of these are through plans aimed at more efficient terminal arrangements, the development of direct highway approaches to terminal facilities, the establishment of satisfactory transit connections, and the coördination of rail, water, and air transportation.

The city planner has an interest in the logical arrangement of railroad terminal facilities because of its bearing upon the efficiency and economy of transportation service, and also because an efficient arrangement aids the city in its plan to develop the most appropriate pattern of land use.[103] Rail terminals of different lines serving the community, if located far apart, necessitate transfers through the city which are time consuming, inconvenient, and costly. This applies

[103] Harold M. Mayer, "Emerging Developments in Intercity Transportation," *The Annals of the American Academy of Political and Social Science*, Vol. 242, p. 57, November, 1945.

to both passenger and freight transportation. It has been estimated that about one-half of the transportation costs are costs of terminal operation and that about two-thirds of the delays in the transportation of freight by rail result from delays at the terminals.[104] These heavy costs and delays are attributable to a substantial degree to the improper location or arrangement of terminals and the duplication of terminal facilities.

As highway and air transportation have developed and come into competition with railways, both passenger and freight transportation have become more specialized. Each kind of carrier tends to concentrate on that type of service for which it seems best suited. Highway transport has today taken over much of the short-distance transportation and a considerable part of the crosshauling within the cities. With railroads concentrating on medium and long-distance freight hauling, it has become feasible in many instances to move freight classification yards outside of the highly congested urban areas to land of lower value. Changes in modes of transportation have, in many instances, rendered large areas in central parts of the city obsolete both as to layout and location.[105] Such areas might be more appropriately utilized for low-cost housing, commercial development, or some other purpose. In some instances, the problems of land assembly to achieve these results may be of such difficulty that the planned rearrangement of land use can be carried out only through a program of urban redevelopment.

Every urban community which is served by railway is faced with the very difficult problems created by grade crossings of railroads and highways. The economic loss from traffic delays and accidents at these intersections is enormous. Railway highway crossings at grade also contribute to inefficient railroad operation and to public inconvenience. Since these hazards and inconveniences can be completely eliminated only where the thoroughfares and railway lines cross at different levels, the obvious solution is the separation of grades of streets and railways at the intersections. It must be recognized, however, that this is not possible in all instances because of the high cost involved. Nevertheless, each community should make grade separation an important consideration in the development of its street plan. For most cities, any large-scale program of grade separation should be

[104] *Local Planning Administration,* op. cit., p. 146.
[105] The successful use of belt lines in the Chicago area for the through movement of both freight and passengers is a good example.

undertaken as part of a long-range improvement program. Under such a program, the first steps should be to attempt to establish priorities for grade-crossing separation on the basis of relative hazards to safety and economic losses due to delay of traffic and rail transportation. In making this determination, it is necessary to take into account the volume of rail and highway traffic at particular intersections and also the physical conditions which surround the crossing, including such matters as visibility, street approach, and the angle of street-track intersection.

In cases where it is not feasible to establish grade separation, the community plan should look toward the redesign of the street system or railway system in order to reduce the number of crossings as much as possible. The improvement of traffic and transportation can be greatly facilitated by various measures aimed at removing obstructions to visibility, improving street grades or alignments, or by utilizing better protective devices and safety methods.

Water Transportation.   Cities located upon navigable bodies of water have many opportunities and responsibilities for planning that other cities do not have. Planning with respect to water facilities must take into account not only their use for transportation purposes, but also must consider their best utilization for industrial, commercial, and recreational purposes. Transportation by water is the most economical form of freight transportation for all communities in which the element of time is not an important factor. Many of our great cities owe their growth and prosperity to the advantages of water transportation and the availability of good harbor and shipping facilities. Certain types of industries have been attracted to communities where low-cost water transportation is accessible, and particularly to those communities where conditions favor the economical interchange of water-borne traffic with rail, highway, and air transportation. Planning for the development of water facilities must, therefore, be integrated with planning of other transportation facilities.[106] This necessitates that port facilities be readily accessible to all types of carriers.

If water transportation is to be facilitated, it is essential that port development be coördinated with water-front industrial development.

[106] For an elaboration of this point, see Roger H. Gilman, "Transportation Planning: The Port—A Focal Point," *Journal of the City Planning Division,* Proceedings of the American Society of Civil Engineers, Vol. 82, No. CP1, pp. 893-1-893-8, February, 1956.

Although the planner has a general concern with the character of port facilities, the matter of their design is normally a technical problem which is a primary responsibility of the port engineer. The planner does have a major responsibility, however, in developing policies that will promote the most efficient use of the water frontage of the urban community. The community plan must be aimed at trying to provide a proper balance for all demands for the use of water facilities, including commercial, industrial, recreational, and other purposes. Planning agencies should keep under review the changing requirements for dockage and other facilities which may result from the use of larger ships, from the location of new industries, or from changes in the mode of shipping which industry may utilize. In some instances, careful planning may make it possible to discontinue the operation of certain obsolete facilities, or those which are infrequently used, and convert the space which they occupy to more modern and efficient means of moving passengers and freight or to some other more appropriate land use. As in the case of railway terminals, the proper location and arrangement of port-passenger and port-freight terminals is one of the most important factors in the efficiency and economy of water transportation.

Air Transportation. The impact of air transportation is today being felt by almost every city, large or small. Air transportation for moving passengers, mail, and certain types of freight has become a most important link in our transportation system. Urban planning is concerned with many aspects of air transportation, but particularly with the location and development of airports and the coördination of air transportation with other means of transport. In recent years, the location and development of airports have influenced the pattern of growth of many communities as have the developments of railways and highways.[107]

The problems of airport planning vary to the extent to which the airports of a particular city may be a part of the national or international airway system, a feeder line, or a port designed merely to serve small private land planes, seaplanes, or recreational needs. While airport planning must be related to present and future local requirements, it may also be guided by standards and requirements laid down by the Civil Aeronautics Administration and by the State Aeronautics Commission. The location and development of airports in-

[107] *Airport Planning* (United States Department of Commerce, Civil Aeronautics Administration, July, 1952), p. 3.

volve a consideration of many complex factors. Whether or not the airport which is planned today meets the needs of air transportation of the future depends upon how accurately we may be able to estimate the type of aircraft that will be used in the future and the extent to which air travel will supplant travel by train, passenger automobile, or highway transport, and such factors as the growth of urban population, the direction of population growth, and the degree of urban decentralization. It is obvious that if communities which are growing rapidly can gauge their future airport needs at an early stage and acquire the necessary sites before the land-use pattern is established, the community will be able to develop a more rational plan for airport location and also avoid heavy acquisition costs in the future.

The basic consideration with respect to airport location and development is to serve the functional requirements of air transportation by promoting safe and efficient operation. At the same time, every effort should be made to insure that the airport transportation facilities are properly related to other means of transportation and to the most appropriate land utilization. Among the most essential considerations in the matter of site selection, from the standpoint of air transportation, are the physical features of the area. In so far as practical, it is desirable to have airports located in the vicinity of streams, railways, and major highways which can be readily seen from the air. Sites should be avoided where there is danger of obstruction from hills, mountains, or high structures which are likely to interfere with the air-traffic pattern.[108] Care should be exercised also to avoid site location in areas of smoke and fog. With the increasing use of high-speed planes, airport locations which can provide long runways and runway extensions have come to be an essential requirement. In the report of the President's Airport Commission, submitted by General Doolittle, it was recommended that in the case of new airports, cleared extensions should be provided at the end of each runway one-half mile in length and 1000 feet wide. This recommendation was made as a result of plotting the locations of 31 commercial and military crashes on the ground near airports during the six-year period.[109]

[108] See Paul Tillett and Myron Weiner, *The Closing of Newark Airport* (University, Ala.: University of Alabama Press, 1955), I.C.P. Case Series, No. 27.

[109] C. B. Friday, "Air Traffic Control in Congested Areas," *Municipal Problems 1952* (The Forty-third Annual Proceedings of the Conference of Mayors and Other Municipal Officials of the State of New York, Lake Placid, June 11, 12, and 13), pp. 105–107.

Other factors which are assuming greater importance in the planning for airports are those of noise and vibration. The use of turbine-powered aircraft has already begun to present serious problems of airfield location to many communities, inasmuch as only a few industries such as those which themselves produce loud noise can endure these airfields as neighbors. As yet, no satisfactory sound barriers have been found to provide a shield from the noise of these fast jet planes. Trees for this purpose seem to be virtually useless.[110] Unless the problem is solved through technological developments, planners will be obliged to revise much of their thinking on land-use planning.

In the interest of safety, as well as in the interest of developing harmonious land use in the surrounding area, cities are finding it necessary to enact airport zoning ordinances to control the height or prevent the erection of buildings, water towers, broadcasting towers, factory chimneys, high-tension wires and other structures that would interfere with the approaches to the airfield. One of the chief obstacles to airport zoning by municipalities has been the fact that most of the municipal airports are situated outside the corporate limits of the city. Since normally cities may exercise their police power authority only within the corporate boundaries, effective airport zoning has not always been possible.[111] This problem is being solved in more and more cities through the enactment of enabling legislation granting extraterritorial powers, or through airport zoning regulations worked out with counties or other local units of government.

Since the great value of air transportation lies in the speed with which it moves passengers and freight to their destinations, a large part of its efficiency depends upon the rapidity with which persons are moved to and from the airport. To a considerable extent, therefore, the future of air transportation is a ground problem as well as a problem of flight. This necessitates a careful selection of routes on the ground and a careful design of the street system in order to facilitate rapid movement to and from the airport.[112] The value of air transport to the community must, of necessity, be weighed against the cost of expenditures on street improvements which are necessary to provide ready access to the airport. Obviously, the use to which

[110] "Planners Puzzled Over Jets," *The American City*, Vol. 69, No. 10, p. 96, October, 1954.

[111] *Municipalities and Airport Zoning* (Chicago: The American Municipal Association, February, 1941), Report No. 145, p. 6.

[112] Carl Feiss, "Air Transportation," *Planning for Postwar Municipal Services*, An Analysis of Problems and Trends with Suggestions for Developing Local Policies (Chicago: The International City Managers' Association, 1945), pp. 61–63.

the airport is put has a bearing upon the importance of direct high-way access. If, for example, the airport serves primarily as a fueling station rather than a terminal point, the emphasis upon high-speed highways to serve the airport is less urgent. Although proximity to rail transportation and rapid-transit facilities are valuable, these are perhaps not as important as good direct highway service to and from the central part of the city.

A number of cities today are giving increased attention to the possibilities of helicopter service to provide transportation between the airport and the central business district. The city of Cleveland now has helicopter taxi service between Westside Airport and Lake Front Airport. Helicopter service is also in operation between Los Angeles International Airport and downtown Long Beach and between Miami Beach and West Palm Beach. Permits have been granted by the Civil Aeronautics Board or are pending for the operation of helicopter service in or within the vicinity of a number of other major cities, including New York, Chicago, Philadelphia, Pittsburgh, Fort Worth, Houston, Kansas City, Indianapolis, Minneapolis, and St. Paul.[113] If such service proves to be satisfactory, it may help to relieve the burden of constructing high-speed highways and make possible the location of airports at suitable locations more remote from the central city.

Helicopters seem likely to play a much greater role in the future in supplying air service between cities within 40 or 175 miles of each other. Since the speed of the helicopter is not likely to exceed 150 or 200 miles per hour, it is improbable that it will be able to compete with the faster fixed-wing aircraft for distances in excess of 175 to 200 miles.[114] The advantage of the helicopter is its ability to take off and land vertically, to stop in mid-air, and to fly in any direction. A number of cities today are recognizing the importance of this flexibility and are giving consideration to the development of heli-copter landing areas in downtown parts of the city. The city of Denver, Colorado, has requested the federal government to construct a heliport on the top of the proposed new post office annex. In the city of Dallas, a new hotel which is being built will provide for a 48- by 80-foot paved landing site for helicopters. Experience such as that of Trenton, New Jersey, seems to demonstrate the value of heliports located in the business district which may be reached from

[113] *News Bulletin* (Chicago: Public Administration Clearing House, Release No. 1 for January 17, 1955), p. 1.
[114] *Transportation by Helicopter 1955–1975* (New York: The Port of New York Authority, Aviation Department, 1952), p. 5.

the main hotels and most parts of the business district in a few minutes walk.[115]

As runways are not required, it is possible to provide helicopter landings in small open spaces, on docks, and on flat roofs of buildings braced for the purpose. Contrary to misconceptions, however, helicopters cannot land on any roof top. Landing platforms need to be carefully reënforced and should be provided with suitable guardrails and other protective devices. As in the case of planning for airports, the matter of site location of heliports is also of importance.[116] While structures such as smokestacks, flagpoles, towers, and chimneys are less of a menace to helicopters landing than to conventional airplanes, they are, nevertheless, factors to be considered in the location of heliports.[117] The protection of the neighborhood which may be depreciated from the noise which may be produced must also be taken into account.

The possibilities of the use of helicopters have not as yet been fully explored. The extent to which they are utilized in the future, both as a means of transporting passengers and freight from centers of population to air line terminals and for intercity travel, depends to a large degree upon government policy toward this means of conveyance. In the regulation of flight procedures for helicopters and the establishment of heliports, it seems essential that government policy should recognize the unique capabilities of the helicopter and develop rules in accordance with these capabilities. To simply apply to it the regulations applicable to fixed-wing aircraft would defeat the development of its potentialities.

Transportation by Conveyor Belt. Quite recently considerable attention has been given to the use of the conveyor belt as a specialized means of transportation. This device seems to offer some unusual possibilities for facilitating the movement of traffic in highly congested areas. For a number of years, belt conveyors have been used to transport bulk commodities. Commodities have been efficiently

[115] *Jersey Plans for a Better State* (Division of Planning and Development, New Jersey Department of Conservation and Economic Development, November, 1954), p. 6.

[116] *Heliport Location and Design* (New York: The Port of New York Authority, May, 1955).

[117] For a concise but rather comprehensive discussion of the status of helicopter transport and heliport location and design, see Robert Horonjeff and Howard S. Lapin, *Planning for Urban Heliports* (Berkeley, Calif.: The Institute of Transportation and Traffic Engineering, University of California, June, 1954), Research Report No. 19, 16 pp.

and effectively moved by this means of conveyance for distances up to 6 miles. The conveyor-belt principle has also been applied as a means of vertical transportation in the construction of escalators. A recent and successful installation in Jersey City indicates the conveyor belt may have other important uses as a means of moving persons.

What is believed to be the first moving sidewalk was installed in Jersey City, New Jersey, in the underground passage connecting the Erie Railroad terminal with a station of the Hudson and Manhattan transit system.[118] The present length of this sidewalk is 227 feet, of which 137 is at a 10 percent upgrade. The width of the belt is 66 inches which will accommodate three persons abreast. The belt will carry 10,800 persons per hour. It is driven at the rate of 120 feet per minute by a 20-horsepower motor. The motor can be reversed in order that the movement of the belt may conform to the direction of greatest pedestrian traffic. A similar speedwalk has been installed at Sam Houston Coliseum in Houston, Texas, to carry persons from a parking area across a bayou into the auditorium. This belt will move about 15,000 persons an hour.

The success of these experiments indicates possibilities of much more extensive use in moving pedestrian traffic in downtown business districts, within large shopping centers, airports, parking lots, and other places. Obviously, each belt has certain practical maximum lengths. At the present time this seems to be slightly in excess of 1050 feet. However, successive lengths of belt can be readily installed where distances require longer belts to serve the transportation needs.

In the city of New York, plans are being made for a much more complicated use of the conveyor belt than that which is in effect in Jersey City. The New York Transit Authority recently approved a contract to install 130 ten-passenger cars in a conveyor belt train for the purpose of providing shuttle service between Grand Central Station and Forty-Second Street.[119] Under the proposed plan the cars would cruise by the stations at a speed of a mile and a half an hour, which practical experience has shown would make possible easy boarding even by those who are infirm. By using a device of accelerating rollers, the speed of the cars upon reaching the tunnel would increase to 15 miles per hour. Then as the car approaches the next loading platform decelerating rollers would slow up the speed to one and one-half miles per hour to match the speed of the second moving

[118] "Conveyor Belts for Pedestrians," Urban Land, Vol. 13, No. 6, p. 1, June, 1954.
[119] New York World Telegram and Sun, November 5, 1954.

sidewalk serving the unloading platform. The cars, after passing the loading platform, are to be moved around by means of a turntable and then make the return trip in the opposite direction in a similar manner. The cars which operate bumper to bumper at the terminals are spaced approximately 75 feet apart as their speed is increased through the tunnel. It is estimated that the total capacity of this new system will be about 18,000 passengers per hour, which is almost 50 percent above the present hourly peak period.[120]

[120] Urban Land, op. cit., p. 3.

CHAPTER 5

The Comprehensive Planning of Municipal Services and Programs

In the preceding chapter, consideration was given to those public policies and municipal operations most closely related to space requirements and space utilization. It is the purpose of this chapter to direct attention to the service functions and program responsibilities of municipal government which are not so directly tied to the physical plan but which nevertheless have important comprehensive plan implications.

Some of the specific services and programs which are considered in this chapter are commonly regarded as having only peripheral interest to the planner. Actually, however, the objectives of physical planning and the objectives of the various operational functions of government are so interrelated that one may not be fully achieved without reference to the other. Together they make up the environmental pattern of urban living.

Elected policy making officials who do not understand the nature and purpose of planning proposals cannot be expected to carry them into effect. Neither can the planner conduct intelligent planning unless he has an appreciation of the functions, policies, and processes of the operational departments of government. It requires little demonstration to show how the supply or quality of water may have a bearing on plat approval, how fire protection methods may influence the design of streets, how police department operations may affect the planning and location of public buildings, or how the public health practices may be related to urban renewal programs. Unfortunately, however, too much planning is done by planners who pay inadequate attention to the programs and objectives of the operational departments.

The material in this chapter is included for the purpose of calling attention to some of the more important services and programs of local government with which the planner should be familiar if proper coördination is to be achieved between physical planning and program objectives. For the most part, these services and programs are concerned with supplying utility and sanitation needs, protecting life and property, and promoting the social welfare.

PUBLIC UTILITY AND SANITATION SERVICES

The term "public utilities" is somewhat ambiguous. According to legal definition, a public utility is a business affected with a public interest.[1] Although almost every business is to some degree affected with a public interest, certain activities such as the furnishing of water, electricity, transportation, and various other services have been held to be so essential to the life of the community as to justify special public control. Public control over such services has also been justified because of the fact that they are natural monopolies and, therefore, competition cannot be relied upon to secure adequate services at reasonable rates. Public control over utilities may be achieved by governmental regulation or by government ownership. One of the devices commonly used by municipalities for regulating services and rates is the franchise which gives a private company the right to occupy the streets in return for an agreement to furnish service of specified standard and rate of charge. Today, however, public control over rates is more generally achieved through regulation by state agencies. Private public utilities operating under such regulatory controls are recognized as legalized and regulated monopolies. Where regulation has failed to provide the standard of service which the inhabitants desire, cities have frequently turned to municipal ownership and operation. As a general rule, if service is adequate, rates are reasonable and public relations are satisfactory, pressures for public ownership and operation have usually not been strong.

Included under the classification of public utilities are facilities

[1] *New York Ice Company v. Liebmann*, 235 U.S. 262, 76 L.Ed. 747 (1932).

and operations for supplying water, light and power, natural and artificial gas, telegraph and telephone, transit, and transportation services. Quite frequently, the disposal of sewage and the disposal of garbage and refuse and other wastes are treated as public utilities. Sometimes wharves, docks, public markets, and airports are found in this classification. The designation of such services as public utilities is not of particular significance except for identifying the general characteristics of the type of service and the nature of the public controls which are commonly applied in the public interest. Some of these utilities, namely, transit and transportation, airports, and utilities using wires were considered in the preceding chapter because of the extent to which planning is concerned with their space requirements. The supplying of water and the disposal of wastes are also important elements in the physical plan, but because of the fact that utility policies and practices have such an important influence upon the rate and direction of urban growth and the pattern of urban development, they are separately considered in this chapter.

WATER SUPPLY

The development of an adequate water supply system is one of the most vital necessities of every community. Water supply has been an important factor in the location of cities, in the development of industries, and in the prosperity of particular regions. Water is required for sustaining life, safeguarding health, promoting sanitation, cooling air, providing fire protection, maintaining civic beauty through sprinkling lawns and open spaces, and supplying the needs of industry, commerce, and agriculture. So essential is water to the well-being of the community that most cities in the United States own and operate their own water systems, even though most of the other utilities are privately owned.

Adequacy. Although water usage varies greatly from city to city, the average daily consumption usually runs from 100 to 200 gallons per person. The amount of water required by any community is determined by the domestic, commercial, and industrial demands and by the requirements for public uses such as for fire fighting, street cleaning, fountains, swimming pools, parks, and maintaining lake levels. Normally, the consumption of water for domestic use in kitchens, bathrooms, and for drinking purposes, does not exceed 60 gallons per day per person. In some of the poorer districts it may be as low as ten gallons. Cities in which such industries as textiles, power plants, and paper manufacturing are located will have a very high industrial usage. High commercial usage will be found in cities which serve as terminals for railroads or for ships. In some cities air cooling devices in stores, office buildings, and theaters may account for as much as 20 percent of the total water consumption.[2] In estimating the quantity of water needed for any city there must be added to the anticipated uses an amount for loss through leakage and waste. In the average city this loss runs from 15 to 25 percent of the total amount of water delivered into the system. Some cities have found that through careful operation, the loss through waste and leakage can be materially reduced.[3] To a considerable extent, the amount of water wasted is related to the pressure that is carried in the mains. Since high pressures mean more leaks, experience indicates that in general it is desirable to maintain the lowest pressures compatible with satisfactory service.

The adequacy of a city water supply is concerned with quality as well as quantity. Water, to be of good quality, must be free from contamination and should measure up to accepted standards of taste, clearness, and softness. Only a very small percentage of the water that goes through the system is used for drinking purposes or in the preparation of food. Nevertheless, the whole supply must be safeguarded against contamination since, for most cities, there is no practical way of separating the water to be used for human consumption from that to be used for other purposes. Good water must not only be free from bacterial contamination but also should have a pleasant taste and be free from odor and color. Turbid water and water with an unpleasant odor may not be harmful to health, but is likely to be unpalatable and otherwise offensive. Very often colored water will damage the products of certain plants such as laundries. Water which contains an excessive amount of calcium and magnesium carbonates and sulphates is usually unsuitable for various industrial uses. Hard water leaves scale in pipes and boilers, destroys the effectiveness of soap, and often causes damage to cooking utensils. Although of less importance than other considerations of quality, it is an advantage to have water which is cool during the hot summer weather.

Storage and Treatment.   In order to provide their inhabitants with an adequate supply of water of good quality, cities must procure

[2] Harold Zink, *Government of Cities in the United States* (New York: The Macmillan Company, 1948), p. 445.

[3] *Local Planning Administration* (Chicago: The International City Managers' Association, 1948), p. 121.

sources of sufficient quantity and must develop methods and facilities for storing, protecting, purifying and distributing it. Various systems for impounding waters are utilized, depending upon the quantity of water required, the source of the supply, the topography of the area of supply and distribution, and the seasonal variations of supply and demand. Where waters are stored in open reservoirs, special consideration must be given to the problem of sanitary protection. If proper controls are established, and the water is treated prior to distribution, it is often possible to utilize both the catchment area and the impounding reservoir for certain recreational purposes, such as camping, boating, skating, fishing and even bathing.[4] Such uses cannot be tolerated if there is any possibility of pollution.[5] Almost every city is required to treat water to some degree. The character and extent of the treatment that is necessary vary with the quality of the water. Treatment may consist of filtration, aeration, chlorination, and the adding of chemicals to remove minerals or discoloration or to improve the taste. In most states periodic analyses of the water are required by the state health agency to insure that standards of purity will be met.

System Facilities. Since the system for the distribution of water represents an essential element in the comprehensive plan, it is important that the planning agency participate in planning the location and the reservation of sites for pumping plants, tanks, standpipes, reservoirs, mains, and all other system facilities. Where the needs of the system require the location of reservoirs and standpipes in residential areas, proper design and landscaping will help to prevent them from detracting from the civic beauty. Particular emphasis should be placed upon the coördination of water system planning and street planning since for the most part the network of water pipes is laid in the subsurface of the streets. The depth of the lines should be sufficient to give protection against freezing and impact. The size of the mains and the capacity of other facilities should be determined with regard to the area of service, density of population, and the probable future growth of the community.

Water pressure in the mains should be established according to the present and anticipated demands. It need not be the same for all districts. Difficulties usually arise when pressures are under 20 pounds

[4] Local Planning Administration, op. cit., p. 122.

[5] For an excellent discussion of practices necessary to achieve satisfactory water quality control see Mary McWilliams, Seattle Water Department History 1854–1954 (Seattle: Dogwood Press, 1955), pp. 135–150.

or over 70 pounds per square inch. Residential districts may not require pressures in excess of 30 pounds to the square inch. Downtown sections will require substantially higher pressures, perhaps up to 50 pounds or more. In order to insure adequate fire protection of the tall buildings, some of the larger cities have installed special high-pressure water systems carrying pressures up to 300 pounds per square inch.[6] Low pressures necessitate that more storage be available for pumping equipment in case of fire.

Nonresident Service.   During the past 25 years, virtually every city located within a highly urbanized area has been faced with demands to supply water to consumers outside its corporate limits. At times these demands have been opposed by members of the city council on the theory that supplying city conveniences to people outside the city would retard the growth of the city to the detriment of the citizens within the city.[7] However, the pressures from suburban residents have been sufficiently great to overcome this argument in most urban communities where the cities have legal authority to furnish water to nonresident users.[8] A variety of practices and combination of practices are to be found in the distribution of water to users located outside the corporate limits. In some instances the city may wholesale water to a district or public or private corporation which handles the retail distribution to its consumers; in some instances the city distributes the water directly to consumers; in other cases the city may sell the water at wholesale to a water district but contract to handle the reading of meters and the collection of accounts. The city of Seattle, for example, is currently furnishing water to 16 water districts and one municipal corporation in the Seattle metropolitan area and is also selling directly to individual consumers in adjacent areas.

The extent to which a particular jurisdiction may supply water and render services outside its jurisdiction is usually covered by state law or state constitutional provisions. In some states, as in the State of Washington, municipalities are permitted to sell surplus water. The State of New York recently amended its constitution to empower the legislature to authorize cities and certain other units of government to supply water, in excess of their own needs, to other public cor-

---

[6] Zink, op. cit., p. 450.

[7] McWilliams, op. cit., p. 224.

[8] As to the authority of the city to furnish water outside the city and for other legal requirements of administering water systems, see Ernest H. Campbell, *Legal Problems and Responsibilities in Administering Water Systems* (Seattle: Association of Washington Cities and Bureau of Governmental Research and Services, University of Washington, January 15, 1954), Information Bulletin No. 162.

porations or improvement districts and to contract indebtedness for that purpose. The amendment also empowers the legislature to authorize two or more public corporations or improvement districts to contract joint indebtedness for such a purpose.[9] It is not always clear under such provisions as to what constitutes surplus or excess water. Neither is it clear as to whether an extraterritorial service once undertaken can be discontinued if the city council should determine that it no longer has a surplus. Moreover, even if it were resolved that outside service could be discontinued, difficulties would be encountered if services were cut off to one outlying area and continued to others.

With the growing reliance of suburban residents upon the central city for their supply of water, it seems obvious that metropolitan communities should think in terms of a unified system with respect to both supply and distribution. The advantages are numerous, particularly in situations where several communities must draw upon the same source of supply, or where supplying water through a number of independent systems means costly duplication of facilities and frequently increased costs of financing. Furthermore, each growing municipality, in planning its supply and distribution system, must also bear in mind that many of the outlying areas may eventually be annexed, and by the proper design of the distribution system in adjacent unincorporated areas, future problems may be minimized.

Water System Finance. For most municipalities, the water system represents one of its largest capital investments. However, except under extraordinary conditions, the financing of the water supply system does not present serious problems. The principal reason is that the water system is a self-supporting enterprise, and in fact may often contribute to the city's general revenue either through furnishing water without cost for city operations or by turning over a percentage of profits to the city treasury. Furthermore, it has been the general experience that the construction of municipal waterworks has been fairly free from graft and corruption as compared to certain other types of public works.[10]

The common practice is to finance the original waterworks construction by the sale of general obligation bonds, backed by the general credit of the municipality or revenue bonds which are guaranteed

[9] Joseph J. Kelly, "Financial Developments—Sewers, Water and Workmen's Compensation," *Municipal Problems—1955*, (The Forty-Sixth Annual Proceedings of the Conference of Mayors and Other Municipal Officials of the State of New York, Buffalo, June 15, 16, and 17, 1955), p. 93.

[10] William Bennett Munro, *Municipal Administration* (New York: The Macmillan Company, 1935), p. 580.

solely by the revenues of the water system. Sometimes a combination of both types of securities may be used.[11] General obligation bonds issued for waterworks construction are frequently retired from the income from water operations. However, the fact that they are secured by the general credit of the municipality may provide a surer market at lower interest rates. The choice of securities to be used may often be governed by the general credit of the city and the city's current bonded indebtedness. The costs of later extensions and installations are usually financed out of current water revenues or from revenues derived from the sale of local improvement district bonds to be retired by assessments against the district to be benefited.

The principal factors governing consumer charges for water are: (1) costs of operation, (2) debt service, (3) reserves for anticipated costs of extensions and replacements, and (4) profits, if any, to be contributed to the general revenues of the city. The question of whether rates for water service should be fixed on a cost basis or on a basis to return an operating profit to the city is likely to be a matter of controversy.[12] Since one of the principal arguments for the ownership and operation of municipal utilities has been to eliminate the profit feature and provide services at lower rates, city officials are likely to encounter strong opposition if they look to water utility income as a major source of general revenues. Obviously, rates cannot be calculated on an exact cost basis, but it seems that in most communities the most acceptable policy is one where rates are based upon the first three factors indicated above. Some cities have sought to obtain general revenues by imposing a utilities tax or by making a charge against the operation equivalent to the taxes or fees which would normally be assessed against a similar utility if privately owned and operated. Actually, the result is the same as far as the consumer is concerned since the tax or charge becomes a part of the operating costs and is reflected in the rate structure to the same degree as a calculated profit.[13] Where water service is rendered to nonresident consumers, the general rule is that rates need not be the same as those charged to consumers residing within the corporate boundaries. It is

[11] See Chap. 7 for a discussion of the conditions governing the type of security to be issued.

[12] See *Modern Water Rates*, a booklet which reproduces a series of articles on water rates that was published in *The American City* in 1954 and 1955 (New York: The American City Magazine).

[13] The extent to which a municipality is permitted to operate its utilities at a profit or to secure revenues from them in the form of a tax is governed in some jurisdictions by state law.

common practice to charge nonresident consumers higher rates than residents to cover the additional expense of providing extended services and to compensate for costs of original construction borne solely by the taxpayers within the municipality.[14]

THE SEWERAGE SYSTEM AND SEWAGE DISPOSAL

One of the most important consequences of urban growth is the need for providing adequate sewers and efficient means of sewage treatment and effluent disposal. The system used for disposing of liquid wastes is called the sewerage system. The material carried in the sewerage system is sewage. Sewage is one of the most dangerous waste products of any community. Whereas, in sparsely settled areas sewage may be disposed of satisfactorily by the use of septic tanks, in densely populated areas expensive sewer installations become essential. An adequate supply of water is necessary to efficient operation.

Problems and Practices. Frequently, municipalities may find it very difficult to construct sewerage systems in certain areas because of the topography, the terrain, or drainage conditions. Where these conditions present serious obstacles, wise land-use planning should encourage the development of such areas for parks or recreational purposes, rather than for residential, commercial, or industrial uses. The layout of sewerage systems and the type of sewage disposal is governed largely by drainage conditions, since normally sewerage systems are not under pump pressure but are operated by gravity flow. Consequently, the planning of the sewerage system should be on a regional basis, taking into account the natural drainage areas. Since these areas do not always coincide with political boundaries, problems of governmental authority and organization are frequently involved.

The problem of sewage disposal has increased with the size of the modern city. Although the volume varies greatly from city to city, the average flow usually ranges from 100 gallons to 200 gallons per person per day. In cities which have a heavy industrial use, the average per capita flow is considerably higher. Whenever the city undertakes to establish a system of sewers, it is important that adequate provisions be made to take care of the demands that may be expected from the direction and growth of the city's population. Sewers, once constructed, can be supplemented only with great cost and public inconvenience. Failure to construct a system which meets the needs of

[14] For the legality of differential rates, see *Faxe v. the City of Grandview*, 48 Wn. (2d) 342, 294 P. (2d) 402 (1956).

the community may not only result in expensive alterations but also may possibly subject cities to liability for damages which may accrue therefrom.[15] While the sewer system should be planned in anticipation of the demands for many years in advance, it is obviously uneconomical to design sewers and sewer facilities much larger than are likely to be required in the foreseeable future.

Until quite recent years, the general plan for disposing of sewage was simply to empty it into rivers or other bodies of water. Thus, while the practice may have moved the wastes from the city itself, it frequently polluted the waters and created serious problems for other communities. As a consequence, many beaches have been contaminated and rendered unsatisfactory for recreation. Fish have been killed and serious illnesses and epidemics have resulted. In many instances state health departments or pollution control commissions have had to step in to help clear up serious conditions of pollution. Studies have shown that once large bodies of water are polluted, their original purity cannot be restored. The health problem created by discharging raw sewage has become so serious that many cities have found it necessary, either by their own decision or upon order by state agencies, to construct expensive sewage disposal plants.

Types of Systems. Sewerage systems are designed to carry off storm waters, to prevent erosion, and dispose of domestic, industrial, and commercial wastes. The type and capacity of the system must depend upon a number of considerations, including (1) present population and anticipated growth, (2) the character of the industries, (3) the amount of rainfall and the seasonal variations, (4) the topography, and (5) the nature of the drainage areas. Sewerage systems are generally of two types, the separate and the combined. Each system has its advantages and disadvantages. In the separate system, surface waters are collected and carried in one set of mains (storm water sewers), while domestic sewage is collected and carried away in an independent set of mains (sanitary sewers). In the combined system, the entire volume of surface waters and domestic wastes is carried in the same set of mains. Although the earlier practice in American cities tended to favor the combined system, at the present

---

[15] There is a split of judicial authority as to whether a city may be held liable for damages caused by the construction of a sewer of insufficient capacity to accommodate future needs. See Ernest H. Campbell, *Legal Aspects of Sewerage and Sewage Disposal* (Seattle: Association of Washington Cities and Bureau of Governmental Research and Services, University of Washington, December 20, 1953), Information Bulletin No. 160, p. 3.

time cities faced with the necessity of installing treatment plants and pumping equipment are finding it economical and essential to have a separated system. Otherwise all storm waters must be run through the sewage treatment plant requiring a capacity so large that costs oftentimes become prohibitive. A flood of storm water into the system also has a delaying effect on the bacteriological action.

While sanitary sewers are designed primarily to carry off domestic household wastes from bathroom, kitchen, and laundry, industrial wastes are usually carried by the sanitary system since frequently these wastes also need to be treated for bacteria. The principal determining factor as to whether a city uses a separate or sanitary system is the factor of cost. For the most part, storm sewers are simply a development of the communities natural drainage system. The major costs involved are the construction of large trunk sewers. The high cost of sanitary sewer systems is usually the construction of the treatment plant.

Treatment Plants. Various types of sewage treatment are employed, including simple screening, sedimentation, chemical treatment, activated sludge treatment, intermittent filtration, trickling and sprinkling filter systems, broad irrigation, and sewage disinfection.[16] The choice and design of the most satisfactory treatment plant presents a complex sanitary problem involving chemistry, bacteriology, and biology as well as engineering. No single type of disposal plant can be said to be best for all cities. The type of sewage disposal plant depends upon a number of factors including the quantity of the sewage, the nature of the sewage, and the location of other cities or settlements of people with respect to the body of water into which the sewage is discharged. A system which may be adequate in one community may be entirely inadequate for another. The selection of the type of disposal plant should be made by a municipality only after careful study of the local situation by a competent sanitary engineer. With respect to the matter of site selection, care should normally be taken to avoid locations in or near residential districts or in commercial areas. It is, however, possible under some circumstances to design and operate treatment plants which will not be offensive, aesthetically or otherwise. Sometimes there is no practical location other than the residential or business district. A number of cities which have had this problem have worked out plans which are com-

16 Munro, op. cit., pp. 305–310.

pletely harmonious with the area. Nevertheless, most people have a prejudice against their location near their homes or business.

Sewer Financing. The construction of sewer systems involves heavy capital outlays. Therefore, the financing of the sewerage system becomes a matter of concern to the planner as a part of the long-range capital-improvement program. Generally the initial costs of construction are financed through the issuance of general obligation bonds, revenue bonds, or special tax assessments levied against the area benefited, or by a combination of these methods. Quite frequently, the cost of constructing the main trunk sewers and treatment plant is carried by the city at large, whereas the cost of constructing the laterals is paid for by the property owners in the area serviced.[17] Bonds issued for the original construction are usually retired by direct tax levies, local improvement assessments, or from sewer rental and connection charges. Sewer rental charges are commonly used to cover the cost of operation and maintenance of the sewers and the disposal plant as well as the debt service on bonds issued for the original construction. Various systems of rental charges are employed including: (1) charges based upon a flat rate schedule with each dwelling paying a certain amount per year, (2) charges based upon the number of fixtures, as for example, so much for each bathtub, lavatory, and toilet, (3) charges based upon the nature of the sewage discharged as determined by certain tests or standards, or (4) charges based upon the amount of water used.[18]

An increasing number of cities have adopted the practice of combining sewer-service charges and water-department charges, thus basing the charge for sewer service upon the water billing.[19] There is some justification for this practice in that sewage flow has a relationship to the amount of water consumed. Furthermore, it simplifies the collections since the sewer charge and water charge can be handled in one billing. It also enables the city to enforce the payment of sewer-service charges by the device of cutting off the water supply if bills become delinquent. The practice of establishing sewer-service charges as a percentage of the water bill has been subject to some

[17] For a pratical discussion of sewer project financing, see Emil C. Jensen and Joshua H. Vogel, *Sewage Collection and Treatment Works in the State of Washington* (Seattle: Bureau of Governmental Research and Services, University of Washington, February, 1949), Report No. 86, also Supplement No. 1, April, 1954.

[18] Jensen and Vogel, Supplement No. 1, *op. cit.*, pp. 27–37.

[19] For a tabulation and classification of rates, methods of billing, and systems of financing sewers, see Colorado Municipal League, *Water and Sewer Services in Colorado* (Boulder, Col.: December 15, 1954).

criticism because of the fact that it does not afford any means of collecting charges from vacant lots not served with water although the value of such lots may nevertheless have been substantially increased as a result of the construction of the sewerage system.[20] Thus, the burden is placed upon the older and more developed areas, some of which may have already paid for their own sewers through ad valorem taxes or special assessments. This burden is somewhat equalized through the use of differential connection charges which favor the person who connects early. In cases where the combined billing of water charges and sewer charges is deemed advantageous, it is important that a clear distinction be maintained between the two. Water rates are generally established on a service-at-cost basis. Any misrepresentation or concealment of the true charge for water may be detrimental to good public relations.

COLLECTION AND DISPOSAL OF WASTES OTHER THAN SEWAGE

In addition to sewage, every community is faced with the necessity of disposing of large quantities of solid wastes including garbage, rubbish, ashes, street cleanings, trimmings from trees and hedges, dead animals, and all sorts of refuse resulting from trade, industry, and building operations. In rural communities self-disposal of wastes is normally the rule; but in areas of high population density, the responsibility for waste collection and disposal becomes that of government. Although the collection and disposal of many types of wastes are necessitated in the interest of health protection, public sanitation is not solely a health enterprise. Many types of refuse such as ashes, wooden crates, and broken concrete, even though allowed to accumulate, do not present a health menace. Nevertheless, their collection and disposal is a matter of municipal concern in the interest of public convenience, orderliness, and aesthetics. An adequate system for the collection and disposal of wastes has among its goals the protection of public health, the reduction of fire hazards, the reduction of stream pollution, the conservation of land and materials and the improvement of community appearance, and general livability.[21]

Garbage Collection. Of the various types of wastes, garbage is particularly related to the health of communities. Unless promptly collected and properly disposed of, it may become a breeding place

[20] John W. Cunningham, "Relationship of Water and Sewage Works," *Journal of the American Water Works Association*, Vol. 43, No. 11, pp. 937–940, November, 1951.

[21] *Municipal Administration* (Supplement contributed by Associated Institutes of Government of Pennsylvania Universities, April, 1953).

and source of food for insects, vermin, and rodents, and thus result in the spread of disease and epidemics. The garbage collection and disposal system begins with the city ordinance which needs to be drafted properly and properly enforced. To be effective, public controls should be established beginning with the initial step of collection and carried through the system of disposal.

In most of the large American cities today the collection of garbage is a municipal function, although in a few communities collection is carried out under private contract.[22] Irrespective of whether collection service is a public or a private responsibility, public policy should seek to further the following practices: (1) collection should be as quiet as possible in order not to produce unnecessary noise and disturbance, (2) collection methods, including the design of wagons and trucks, should be such as to prevent offensive odors from saturating the neighborhood, (3) collection should be carried out neatly and efficiently so that portions are not strewn all over the neighborhood, and (4) collection should be sufficiently frequent to prevent accumulations from being dangerous to health and offensive to the senses.

Methods of financing garbage collection systems vary greatly in different communities. Some cities have found it preferable to finance the collection through general taxes, thus providing "free" garbage collection service. Others have established collection service on a charge basis. In order that the public be adequately protected, most jurisdictions have found it advisable to make collection compulsory. However, a few communities, which have undertaken to supply garbage service on a charge basis, have found it necessary initially to place the collection on a voluntary basis in order to help sell the idea.[23] Where rates are charged for garbage collection, a number of methods have been employed. Generally, the basic charges are established: (1) by volume or number of cans collected at each pickup, or (2) by a flat rate. Frequently, cities include additional factors which increase this basic charge. Among these are (1) the classification of business, (2) the distance of carry, (3) the number of weekly collections, (4)

---

[22] For sample ordinances illustrating the different systems, see Joshua H. Vogel, *Garbage Collection in Washington Cities* (Seattle: Bureau of Governmental Research and Services, University of Washington, May, 1948), Report No. 88.

[23] *Garbage Collection and Disposal Methods and Practices in Washington Cities* (Seattle: Association of Washington Cities, University of Washington, February 5, 1954), Information Bulletin No. 163.

flights of stairs, (5) time required to make the collection, and (6) the kind of garbage collected.[24]

Garbage Disposal. The protection of public health requires not only a suitable garbage collection system but also a proper system of garbage disposal. Among the disposal methods commonly used are (1) the open dump, (2) the sanitary fill, (3) hog feeding, (4) composting, (5) reduction, (6) incineration, and (7) garbage grinding. Although the open dump may be satisfactorily used for disposal of various types of rubbish, for most communities it is an unsatisfactory means for disposing of garbage because it creates disagreeable odors and may attract insects, rodents, and vermin. Frequently, burning of garbage is practiced in open dumps. While this tends to reduce the menace to health, it may be obnoxious to nearby dwellings because of offensive odors and smoke. Furthermore, it may create a fire hazard. To avoid some of these results, a number of cities utilize the sanitary fill. Since under this system the incoming garbage is covered with earth at the end of each day, danger to health, disagreeable odors, and fire hazards are minimized. This method also permits garbage and refuse to be combined and stored in a single container and both combustibles and noncombustibles can be disposed of together. The sanitary fill may not be feasible in cities which have severe winters or which do not have landlocked ravines, swamps, or other land areas that are well suited for this type of disposal. Locations which drain into lakes or streams should not be used.

Hog feeding, although still a commonly used method of garbage disposal, has been abandoned in many communities in recent years because of illnesses and epidemics which have been attributed to feeding raw garbage to swine. A number of other cities which are continuing the practice have been required by law or ordinance to cook the garbage before it is fed. While hog feeding enables the city to realize some financial return from garbage disposal operations, this is offset to a degree because of the necessity of segregating garbage and because of the amount of care which must be exercised in locating and supervising hog farms in order to prevent them from becoming public nuisances.

Composting is a method which has been practised in a number of countries, but has not been used to any great extent in the United States. Its value is that the garbage is converted into useful agricultural humus or fertilizer and offers a disposal method which is

[24] *Ibid.*, p. 10.

sanitary and free of odors and nuisances. Its disadvantage is that it requires a segregation of metal, ceramics, and other noncumbustible materials, and also the grinding and treatment of combustible materials. While the process is costly, it is possible to recover a considerable amount of the expense through the sale of the finished compost.

Many of the larger cities are finding it increasingly necessary to rely on garbage disposal plants. Plants are of two general types: reduction and incineration. Through the reduction process, grease and fats are frequently extracted and the remainder may be used for fertilizer. Where the cooking process is used, unpleasant odors often result which makes the design of plant and the selection of site location of great importance.[25] The objectionable aspects of the reduction process have caused a number of cities to abandon it after a few years' use. If it is necessary to locate the plant a long way off, the cost of hauling the garbage is increased. Furthermore, the profits realized from reduction plants have generally proved to be small. Consequently, cities which have found disposal plants essential have tended to turn toward incineration.[26] Although incineration does not return any profit, it does provide a sanitary method and also avoids most of the nuisance features of the reduction process.

One of the most recent methods of disposing of food wastes is the home garbage grinder. This method is both clean and sanitary and results in food wastes being ground up and disposed of through the sewer system. However, the use of home grinders is not extensive and as of the present time it appears that they do not offer any hope of eliminating garbage collection and other means of garbage disposal. Refuse which is the greatest bulk must still be collected. Nevertheless, some public efforts are currently being directed toward promoting complete neighborhood conversion to on-the-site waste disposal. In Detroit, for example, the mayor has appointed a Committee on Food Waste Disposers to help the city obtain a more sanitary method of disposing of household wastes. This committee has initiated a campaign to promote the use of household disposal units by organizing a Sales Clinic for the 90 plumbing contractors operating in the city for the purpose of conducting a sales campaign to encourage conversion on an area basis.[27]

[25] Zink, op. cit., pp. 439–440.
[26] Munro, op. cit., p. 293.
[27] See Carl H. Walker, "Detroit's Plan for a Garbage Free City," *News Letter*, Public Works Engineers, Vol. 22, No. 8, p. 1, February, 1956.

Ashes and Rubbish. The collection and disposal of ashes and rubbish presents a somewhat different problem from that involved in the collection and disposal of garbage. Almost every conceivable system of rubbish collection is found to be employed by local communities. Some municipalities assume no responsibility whatsoever for the collection of ashes and rubbish. Some small cities simply provide dumps where rubbish may be piled. Other cities assume responsibility for collecting certain types of rubbish such as combustible matter but place the responsibility upon individuals or industrial plants to dispose of other types. Certain cities require a separation of garbage, rubbish, and any other types of refuse whereas others require none. Some cities sort or permit the rubbish to be sorted in order that metal, rubber, rags, paper, wood, and other salable items may be reclaimed. The salvaging of salable articles may be undertaken by the city or a permit for salvage may be granted to private individuals. Sometimes junk men pay an annual fee for the privilege of salvaging. Under some systems, the city assumes responsibility for collecting rubbish as a municipal function. In other instances, the city contracts with a private company or private individuals to render the service according to some agreed standard.[28]

Standards of Adequacy. It is not possible to indicate any standards of adequacy that are applicable to all cities for a satisfactory system of collection and disposal of garbage and refuse. Many factors must be taken into account including the number and kind of people, the density of population, the topography, climate, soil conditions, and the relationship to other communities. A resort city such as Miami Beach, Florida, whose cleanliness and civic beauty may be an important factor in attracting tourist trade, may find it desirable to place added emphasis upon keeping streets cleared of debris, spraying garbage receptacles to prevent the breeding of flies and other insects, and collecting tree trimmings on a year-around basis.[29] There are, however, certain points that should be borne in mind in planning any kind of collection and disposal system. The system should be one which (1) creates a minimum of annoyance to the inhabitants, (2) does not encourage the breeding of flies and rodents, (3) does not pollute the air as a result of the burning of refuse or garbage, (4) does not pollute streams or watersheds, (5) does not create a nuisance to

[28] Marguerite J. Fisher and Donald G. Bishop, *Municipal and Other Local Governments* (Englewood Cliffs, N. J.: Prentice-Hall, Inc., 1950), p. 546.
[29] C. E. Wright, "Refuse Collection Problems in a Resort City," *Public Works*, Vol. 86, No. 2, pp. 71–72, February, 1955.

the general public, (6) is properly related to the topography of the area, and (7) is consistent with the planned land use of the surrounding area and neighboring communities. In most states the disposal of garbage and other refuse is regulated to some degree by state law. Consequently, the state acts and judicial decisions should be carefully checked by municipal authorities before planning a system of waste collection and disposal.

PROTECTIVE FUNCTIONS

No functions of municipal government are more basic to an orderly society than those concerned with the protection of life, liberty, and property and the safeguarding of health, safety, and morals. For the most part, these functions are the responsibility of the police departments, the fire departments, the health departments, the law departments, and the courts. However, the fact that many other departments and agencies share in the protective functions of the community emphasizes the need for program coördination.

LAW ENFORCEMENT AND POLICE ADMINISTRATION

The concentration of large population groups in urban communities has greatly increased the needs for law enforcement and has multiplied the responsibilities placed upon police departments. Although the police department is generally thought of as a law enforcement agency, it has many other functions, including the prevention of crime, the repression of crime, the apprehension of law violators, the recovery of property, the location of missing persons, and the regulation of many kinds of noncriminal conduct. Among the most important regulatory matters are those involved in traffic control and the inspection of certain types of structures, businesses, and activities to insure compliance with established standards of sanitation and safety. In some cities police departments are also required to perform many other duties which are related only very indirectly to their major responsibilities, as for example, the licensing of pawnbrokers, poolrooms, dance halls, street venders, and the providing of temporary lodging for homeless persons and emergency relief for the destitute.[30]

Costs and Causes of Crime. The cost of crime in the United

---

[30] In a number of smaller cities police and fire departments have been combined in a public safety department. For a discussion of this type of organization, see Charles S. James, *Police and Fire Integration in the Small City* (Chicago: Public Administration Service, June, 1955).

States has been estimated to be in excess of ten billions of dollars per year.[31] Actually it is not possible to make an accurate determination of crime costs since it cannot be predicted what savings would be made if no crimes were committed and if no precautions were necessary to protect against future crimes. The cost of crime to a community is reflected in terms of loss or injury to lives and property and in the many indirect costs arising from law enforcement activities, the idleness and unproductiveness of the criminal population, the added costs of insurance, and the necessity for burglar alarms, armored car service, and numerous other types of protective devices.

The causes of crime vary with different communities and with different conditions within a community. The likelihood that a child will follow a life of crime is substantially reduced if he is brought up in a purely residential community and in a favorable home environment. On the other hand, the chances that a child will resort to crime are greatly increased when he is reared in a slum area or under conditions where he is subjected constantly to family conflicts, maladjustments in school, evil companions, and an environment where there is a great deal of disease, filth, or neglect. Furthermore, racial differences have been a factor in the rate of crime in many communities.

Until relatively recent times police departments paid little attention to the matter of crime prevention. Their attention was focused largely on the detection and investigation of crimes. In the modern police department today more and more officers have been assigned to crime prevention work. Crime prevention divisions of the police department are giving careful study to economic and social factors as they relate to the causes of crime and juvenile delinquency. Efforts are being made to establish closer relationships with social service and recreational agencies with the aim of developing a more wholesome city environment with facilities for indoor and outdoor activities in which the children may live and play.

Traffic Supervision. One of the major responsibilities of police departments today is that of traffic supervision. Police traffic divisions are charged not only with enforcing traffic regulations, but also with facilitating the flow of traffic. Traffic supervision, however, is not solely the responsibility of the police department. Municipal and state agencies that have authority to revoke or suspend drivers'

[31] E. H. Sutherland, *Principles of Criminology* (Philadelphia: J. B. Lippincott Company, 1934), p. 21.

licenses or take other action with respect to traffic matters participate in traffic supervision. The traffic engineer also has an important role in traffic supervision. Police departments, however, do have certain primary responsibilities, including (1) the investigation of traffic accidents, (2) the direction of traffic, and (3) the enforcement of traffic laws.

Investigation is aimed principally at determining the causes of accidents and fixing the guilt or responsibility if violations are involved. In connection with the traffic accident investigation, police officers are called upon to perform such related services as placing lights to warn approaching vehicles, giving first aid, summoning medical assistance, taking such precautions as are necessary to prevent fires and theft of goods, and rerouting traffic where necessary. Traffic direction is concerned with the matter of facilitating traffic during periods of congestion or emergencies and in answering inquiries with respect to routes, direction, and local regulations, and doing such other things as are necessary to expedite the flow of traffic. Traffic law enforcement has as its objectives the prevention of accidents and the adoption of measures which will serve as a deterrent to violators and potential violators.[32] Normally the deterrent effect is achieved through the imposition of penalties. However, the quality of a good enforcement program is not to be measured by the number of arrests, citations, and warnings but rather upon the degree of public acceptance and coöperation.

Coördination with Other Programs. The activities of the police department of every modern city must be coördinated with the work of numerous other agencies both within the municipality and in other units of government. Among the most important of the agencies concerned with law enforcement are the county sheriff, the county coroner, the prosecuting attorney, the state attorney general, the probation and parole agency of the state, the grand jury, the courts, and various federal agencies such as the Federal Bureau of Investigation, the Alcohol Tax Unit, the Bureau of Narcotics, the Secret Service, and the United States Post Office Department. Virtually every major municipal service and program has some relationship to some function of the police department. Street planning, for example, must be coördinated with traffic control. The location of police stations should be established with reference to civic neighborhoods. Programs

[32] *Municipal Police Administration* (Chicago: The International City Managers' Association, 1954), pp. 339–370.

of slum clearance are often justified because of the high rate and costs of crime and juvenile delinquency in the slum areas and the difficult problems of crime prevention. The design of streets, bridges, and underpasses, and the type of lighting which is used often are factors which tend to encourage or discourage the commission of crime. Also very closely related to the program of crime prevention is the development of adequate parks and recreational facilities and programs. The development of community centers and recreational athletic programs is one of the principal means of combating the problem of juvenile delinquency.

Police personnel are called upon to aid various agencies in the developing and carrying out of particular programs which are the major responsibilities of other agencies.[33] One of the heavy demands upon the police department is that of providing personnel to protect school children against traffic accidents and in aiding the schools in developing public education programs and safety training aimed at accident prevention and safe driving habits. Police personnel, in making their rounds, are often in a position to discover and report defects which may have developed in paving, utility lines, and other facilities and to notify the proper departments. Adequate fire fighting and fire prevention is facilitated by the work of the police in providing for special traffic rights to facilitate the movement of fire fighting equipment, in providing police personnel to handle the crowds that gather at fires, and to make investigations as to the cause of fire when arson is suspected.

Planning of Facilities. In order to have good police administration, it is essential that police departments be provided with modern equipment and with adequate housing facilities. Most law enforcement officers have frequently found that police stations are constructed without sufficient consultation with persons conversant with the requirements requisite to good police administration. Consequently, serious mistakes have been made with respect to size, location, or arrangement, thereby impairing the efficiency and effectiveness of law enforcement and the administration of justice. Recent studies of plans and specifications indicate that there are such variations in the needs of cities of comparable size that police stations and jails should not be designed and constructed without a careful study of the problems of the particular community.[34]

[33] *Ibid.*, pp. 55–61.
[34] Joshua H. Vogel, *Police Stations, Planning, and Specifications* (Seattle: Bureau of

Studies of police stations and jail facilities indicate that inadequate attention has been given to proper planning. Often police stations and jails are not allocated sufficient space or are located in attics, basements, and other unsuitable places. This not only is detrimental to the efficiency of the operation but also gives the impression that the law enforcement program is secondary to other functions. Among the features that are frequently not adequately considered in the planning of police stations are the facilities for off-street parking, space for expansion, light and air on all sides, separate entrances, separate heating and ventilation for jail quarters and other parts of the building, lighting and mechanical controls, loading space accessible to jails, and setbacks to prevent contacts between prisoners and outside persons.[35]

FIRE PREVENTION AND PROTECTION

The municipal fire department is concerned principally with two major objectives—the prevention of fires and fire fighting. Once a fire occurs, the immediate aims are to prevent loss of life and property damage, to control the fire in its place of origin, and, if possible, to extinguish it. In spite of improved methods of fire fighting and programs developed in the interest of fire prevention, thousands of lives and millions of dollars are lost each year as a result of fires.

Costs and Causes of Fires. It has been estimated that the annual fire loss in the United States is upwards of one-half billion dollars.[36] The annual loss of life from fire is approximately 10,000 persons with an additional 20,000 persons seriously injured. The costs of fires cannot be measured in terms of lives and property damage alone. In addition, there must be added the annual costs of fire departments paid by taxes, the cost of fire insurance, and the protective devices and precautionary measures taken by individuals and corporations. In 1953, the municipal expenditures for operating fire departments in cities of over 10,000 population averaged $6.66 per capita. In general, the per capita costs tend to rise with the size of the cities. Cities with populations between 10,000 and 25,000 in 1953 showed an average

Governmental Research and Services, University of Washington, August, 1954), Report No. 128.

[35] *Ibid.*, p. 3.

[36] *Municipal Fire Administration* (Chicago: The International City Managers' Association, 1950), pp. 3–4.

per capita cost of $4.62, whereas cities with populations of 500,000 showed a per capita cost of $7.25.[37]

According to the National Board of Fire Underwriters, approximately 25 percent of all fire losses in the United States are strictly preventable.[38] The preventable causes include defective chimneys, gas, hot ashes, lighted matches, open lights, petroleum, sparks on the roof, and stoves and furnaces. Another third of the fires are attributable to unknown causes. A high proportion of these are undoubtedly caused by smouldering cigarette butts, matches used to light cigarettes, sparks from machinery, spontaneous combustion, and many other causes which, if known, would be classed as preventable. Some of the most serious fires in our cities have resulted from the construction of buildings of nonfireproof materials. Since wood has been plentiful in the United States, it has often been utilized for construction in preference to other materials. Even buildings of which the exterior has been constructed of brick and stone have presented serious fire hazards because of the combustible materials used in floors, partitions, and other parts of the interior.

The amount of fire losses in any given city has a very important bearing upon the fire insurance rates in that city. For the purpose of determining fire insurance rates, cities are classified according to a number of different factors. The classification which is generally used throughout the United States by rating engineers is a grading schedule developed by the National Board of Fire Underwriters. This schedule which was devised in 1916 has been modified and revised periodically. The classification of cities is determined by a number of deficiency points based upon a total of 5000 which are distributed over nine major items including water supply, fire department, fire alarms, police, building laws, hazards, structural conditions, climatic conditions, and divergence in grading of water supply and fire department. The city in which fire protection is considered the best is the one that receives the lowest number of deficiency points. On the basis of this system, each city is placed in one of ten classifications according to the number of deficiency points charged against its fire defense.[39] The greatest number of deficiency points in these various items are water supply, with 1700, and fire department, with 1500.

[37] *Municipal Year Book, 1954* (Chicago: International City Managers' Association, 1954), p. 388.
[38] Zink, op. cit., p. 523.
[39] *The Municipal Year Book, 1954*, op. cit., pp. 389–390.

The deficiency points for structural conditions are next with a possible 700 deficiency points.

The Fire Prevention Program. A successful program of fire prevention is based upon four cardinal principles: (1) proper building construction, (2) the inspection and removal of hazardous conditions, (3) a campaign of education and publicity, and (4) a program of rigid investigation and prosecution of incendiaries.[40] Although in recent years fire prevention has been receiving a great deal more attention than formerly, fire departments nevertheless concentrate the greater part of their attention upon fire fighting. Fire prevention has concerned itself quite largely with routine inspections by personnel of fire departments and, through conducting educational campaigns, encouraging property owners to reduce the fire hazards on their property.[41] Routine fire inspections have as their principal objectives (1) the locating and correcting of fire hazards such as the accumulations of rubbish, unsafe wiring, and violations of state and local safety codes, and (2) familiarizing fire department personnel with building layouts and structural hazards. Educational campaigns are often conducted through the newspapers, radio publicity, and the schools. Such programs are aimed both at eliminating fire hazards and acquainting the public with techniques of fire prevention. Fire prevention is also concerned with the apprehension and punishment of persons guilty of arson and setting other incendiary fires. Incendiary fires, which include any fire maliciously kindled, constitute a considerable percentage of the total losses in any community. While it is not possible to ascertain the exact percentage of such fires, incendiary losses have been estimated as accounting for between 10 and 40 percent of the total losses.[42] The prevention of incendiary fires requires a close working relationship between the fire department and the police department. This program is frequently conducted by a team consisting of a police detective and a fire department officer who may give full or part time to these investigations.

Perhaps the most basic step in the fire prevention program of every city, large or small, is the adoption and enforcement of a modern and sound building code. The building code should establish ample fire limits surrounding business districts and should include prohibitions

[40] Charles M. Kneier, *Illustrative Materials in Municipal Government and Administration* (New York: Harper & Brothers, 1939), p. 539.

[41] E. B. Teschan, "Elimination of Fire Hazards in Residences," *The Municipality*, Vol. 50, No. 3, p. 52, March, 1955.

[42] *Municipal Fire Administration, op. cit.*, p. 526.

against frame construction within those limits. The code should also establish adequate specifications regulating the height and areas, stair and elevator wells and other vertical shafts, protection of exposed windows, minimum wall thicknesses, construction of chimneys and other heating appliances, improved types of modern construction, installation of adequate private fire apparatus such as standpipes and sprinkler systems, fire escapes, type, quality, and workmanship of building materials, type of roofing, and other matters in the interest of making structures fireproof or fire resistant.[43] Related ordinances which have as their major objective the prevention of fire are those regulating the installation and maintenance of electric wiring for light, power, and appliances and the storage and use of inflammable liquids, chemicals, explosives, and various types of combustible materials. A number of model ordinances relating to these subjects are recommended by the National Board of Fire Underwriters.[44]

Building codes and construction codes are of little use unless properly drafted and rigidly enforced. Inspectors employed for this purpose must be technically trained and personally honest. In the larger cities, a separate department may be needed for this purpose. Since inspections may be necessary in connection with matters of plumbing, types of construction, electrical equipment, elevators, heating plants, and public health regulations, municipalities should give careful consideration to the possibilities of consolidating a number of the inspection services required for enforcement of various kinds of construction codes. Such inspections should also be closely coördinated with the enforcement of the zoning ordinance.

A number of cities in the United States, following a practice that has been quite commonly used in European countries, have provided by ordinance for individual liability for the cost of unnecessary fires. Under such laws, any fires which result from negligence or noncompliance with orders of fire prevention authorities make the offenders liable for the value of the services rendered by the fire department, and, under some ordinances, also for damages caused to persons and property by the fire. Under a provision in the charter of the city of New York, this liability extends to personal injury or loss of life of any employee of the fire department, and under a Cleveland, Ohio,

[43] See Theodore Irving Coe, *Fire Safety in Commercial and Industrial Space* (AIA File No. R9, reprinted by the American Institute of Architects, January–February 1954, for The International Association of Fire Chiefs).

[44] For a current comprehensive code, see *National Building Code* (San Francisco: National Board of Fire Underwriters, 1955).

ordinance, liability has been held to extend to tenants who may suffer loss because the owner of the building is negligent in permitting fire hazards to exist.[45] Although ordinances imposing liability for fire losses have been adopted by only a relatively small number of cities, the use of such ordinances might well be studied by communities in connection with their programs to reduce the loss of lives and property due to carelessness and failure to comply with fire prevention regulations. It seems reasonable that persons whose negligence or violations resulted in the unnecessary use of the fire department should have to pay for the costs.

Fire Alarm Systems.   Since fire departments are dependent upon notification before sending out vehicles to fight fires, the use of an appropriate fire alarm system is imperative. Approximately 60 percent of all cities with populations over 5000 utilize fire alarm box systems. These systems usually have street boxes from which alarms are sent to the central headquarters of the fire department. When the switch is pulled at the box, the closed circuit is broken and the location of the box is identified at headquarters. From there, signals are sent to all stations either automatically or by operator informing them which apparatus is to respond. The most satisfactory systems employ telephone alarms as a supplement to the fire alarm boxes.[46] Most individuals are inclined to use the telephone rather than pull the switch on the corner fire alarm box. The reliance upon telephones alone has some possible disadvantages. Excited persons often give garbled or inaccurate statements as to the location of the fire. Telephones may be out of order in individual cases or there may be a general failure of the system during an emergency. In many business areas doors may be locked at night and telephones are not readily accessible.

In smaller cities where the installation of fire alarm boxes is not feasible, a number of plans have been worked out to meet local needs. In many of the smaller communities, having volunteer fire departments, no person is on duty on a continuous basis. A satisfactory solution is sometimes found by arranging to have telephone calls placed with a hospital, mortuary, rest home, or business establishment which is open on a 24-hour basis. The person on duty sounds the siren and calls the fire department, staying on the line until the first fireman arrives to take the necessary information. Some small

[45] Kneier, op. cit., pp. 542–549.

[46] Some cities have recently adopted improved fire-police telephone alarm systems for both police and fire emergencies. See *Public Management*, Vol. XXXVII, No. 2, p. 40, February, 1955.

communities have found a satisfactory system through the installation of a short-wave radio transmitter in the city hall with short-wave receivers in each volunteer fireman's home.[47] A system of multiple phones which ring in each volunteer fireman's home when the designated number is dialed has also proved satisfactory in some communities. The first one answering sounds the siren. Others coming on the line can talk to each other.

Station Location. Much of the efficiency of fire fighting depends upon the selection of good site locations for fire stations. Every city before authorizing the construction of a fire station should give careful consideration to such matters as the area to be served, the character of the district to be served, the street pattern, traffic congestion, relation to places of assembly, topography, adequacy of space for movement and care of equipment, disturbance to residential areas, and the existence of conditions which might interfere with the movement of fire trucks and other equipment. It is often helpful in planning the site location for the fire department, in collaboration with the planning agency, to make up a check list of requirements against which various proposed locations may be viewed.[48]

One of the primary requisites is that the immediate vicinity of a fire station should be free from land uses which make it difficult or dangerous for quick take-off of fire equipment. When fire equipment first begins to move, there is little time for warning pedestrians and vehicles in the adjacent area to get out of the way. After the fire vehicles are moving, the sirens can usually be heard in time to clear the way. Fire station equipment should move out from the station onto a street which is not an artery. However, automobile parking should not be permitted near the station. The street on which the fire equipment moves out should lead naturally across the city making a fire truck lane connecting with arteries and streets going in any other direction to the area of the fire. Fire stations should be removed from places of assembly such as auditoriums, churches, theaters, funeral parlors, schools, libraries, bus depots, and armories. Likewise stations should not be located near places where large numbers of

---

[47] George D. Smith, "Sounding Fire Alarms in Smaller Cities and Villages," *Michigan Municipal Review*, Vol. XXVII, No. 3, p. 43, March, 1954. See also *Fire Alarms in Small Cities* (Seattle: Association of Washington Cities in Coöperation with the Bureau of Governmental Research and Services, University of Washington, August 15, 1953), Information Bulletin No. 159.

[48] The fire station should not be combined with any other building, e.g., the city jail, unless it is clearly determined that the use for each purpose will not interfere with the use for the other.

pedestrians are likely to congregate or where many motor vehicles may be assembled or moved. Fire truck lanes should not pass hospitals and places of assembly if it is possible to avoid doing so.

Fire stations in the central district normally should be located away from the retail business district and toward the warehouse and industrial district where the noise and disturbance from take-off present the least problem. Where stations need to be located in a residential district, the take-off should be on a side street so that equipment does not move out in the face of the residences. The street on which the station is located should be wide enough to allow the equipment to turn easily. Hillside locations should be avoided if possible. Sites should be level and free from poles, trees, and other obstructions. There should be ample space for drill, hose drying facilities, and care of equipment.[49] The location of the station should be in close proximity to the area in which the most fires are likely to occur. This does not always mean that they need to be in the center of the area to be served, but they should not be on the outskirts. Location should take into account the age of buildings and the type of construction found in a given area and the importance of providing ample protection to extensive industries and warehouses. Where a river or railroad bisects an area to be served, the station should be located, if possible, on the side where there is the greatest fire hazard. In any event, it is essential that there be adequate crossings so that the use of the river and movement or stoppage of trains cannot cut off quick fire-fighting service.

SAFETY PROGRAMS

Safety is not limited to providing protection from criminals and fires. Every year thousands of persons are killed or seriously injured and many others suffer great financial loss from property destroyed or damaged as a result of what we call accidents. Many of the direct costs are apparent such as loss of earning power, medical expenses, and the damage to equipment. However, there are indirect costs that are not so evident. In fact, careful studies indicate that indirect costs average in the ratio of about four dollars for each dollar of direct costs. Among the important indirect costs are:

1. Loss of time by fellow employees who stop work to render aid, or out of sympathy, or for other reasons.

[49] For a symposium of ideas, plans, and sketches of fire stations, see The Circul-Air Corporation, *Fire Station Design* (Milwaukee: 1951).

2. Time of executives in assisting injured employees, investigating the cause of accident, preparing reports, and training new employees.
3. Loss of production due to upset, diverted interest, and other effects.
4. Loss of production due to stoppage of machines, damaged machines, or spoiled product.
5. Lessened effectiveness of injured employees after return to work.
6. Loss of business because of failure to fill orders on time.
7. Legal expenses in cases which are contested at law.[50]

Accidents occur from innumerable causes. Some may be due to physical defects of premises such as cracked sidewalks, broken steps, or improper lighting. Some may be the result of faulty equipment or inadequate protective devices in places of employment. Some may be caused from poor housekeeping practices such as the accumulation of rubbish or debris or the failure to put away tools or other articles. Others may simply be the result of carelessness such as jaywalking, or failure to observe the ordinary rules of safety.

The Responsibility of Government. Quite obviously, the responsibility for personal safety is not that of government alone. However, government does have a responsibility to keep its buildings, streets, sidewalks, and other property in a safe condition. It also has a direct responsibility for the safety of employees, patients, inmates, and students under the jurisdiction of government.[51] More and more governments are recognizing and assuming a greater role as guardians of the security of the people by maintaining many services and programs aimed at the prevention of accidents. Government has a responsibility to conduct its operations in such a way as to prevent injury to persons and property. Even where functions performed are classified under the rules of common law as "governmental" with respect to which the municipality is not liable in tort, there is, nevertheless, a moral obligation to take every reasonable step to insure to the public the highest standards of safety.

State and local governments, in recent years, have been recognizing a responsibility in the prevention of accidents from causes not related to governmental operations. Most of the steps and measures that are necessary to eliminate the causes of accidents must be taken

[50] United States Department of Labor, Bureau of Labor Standards, "Accident Costs," *Safety Subjects*, U.S. Government Printing Office, Washington, D.C., Bulletin No. 67 (revised), 1953, Chap. 4, p. 33.
[51] Daniel P. Webster, "Safety—Afterthought or Forethought," *Municipal Problems* (New York: Proceedings of the Forty-Fifth Annual Meeting of the Conference of Mayors and Other Municipal Officials of the State of New York, June 16, 17, and 18, 1954), pp. 124–129.

by individuals and employers. Agencies of government should, however, coöperate in safety programs and in many instances should take the lead in developing safety programs. The responsibility for preventing accidents cannot be that of any single functional department. Normally, the lead should come from the mayor or the city manager.

Organizing the Program.   Safety programs should not be developed as one-shot affairs. Success necessitates that they be based upon both short- and long-range objectives. The safety program must be well organized, utilizing the leadership of both governmental and private agencies. Efforts should be made to determine the major causes of accidents and to define the respective responsibilities of government, individuals, and employers in carrying out a safety program. Attention should be given to detecting and correcting the physical hazards. This should be followed by periodic inspections. As a part of the safety program, efforts should be made to study the cause, cost, and other related matters with a view to helping prevent recurrences. The program should develop and disseminate safety information, utilizing all the media available for bringing safety information to the attention of the public. Although accident prevention and safety information must be carried on continuously, it may frequently be helpful to provide for safety contests, competition, and merit awards in order to stimulate participation.

Obviously, the best of programs will not eliminate all accidents. However, through well-worked-out and properly administered safety programs, the accident rate can be materially reduced and communities may be much better prepared to meet emergencies which may arise from floods, fires, earthquakes, and other catastrophes. In working out community safety programs, a great deal of assistance can be obtained from the National Safety Council, the local safety council, local industries, casualty and insurance companies, and the United States Department of Labor.[52]

PUBLIC HEALTH PROTECTION

Public health is concerned with "the art and science of preventing disease, prolonging life and promoting physical and mental efficiency

[52] The United States Department of Labor has issued a number of valuable bulletins and reports on safety standards and safety programs which may be obtained from the U.S. Government Printing Office, Washington, D.C. Among them are: Guide to Community Safety Programs (1955); Accident Causes and Cause Coding (1955); Safety Subjects (1953); Proceedings of the President's Conference on Occupational Safety (May 1954); Reports of the Committee on Programs and Services, The President's Conference on Industrial Safety, 1949–1950, Bulletin No. 137.

through organized community effort." [53] No responsibility of government is more important to the happiness of the people and the welfare of the community. Actually, there is no clear-cut division between the work carried on by public health authorities and that carried out through the private practice of medicine. Primarily, the tasks of public health authorities are to improve the community sanitation, and reduce sickness and mortality from causes which affect a large segment of the population. However, public health departments do provide medical, dental, and nursing services to large numbers of individuals who are too poor to pay for private medical care. While public health agencies were originally concerned largely with environmental sanitation, today emphasis is equally upon prevention of illness and the furthering of good health practices. In many cases illness results in poverty and dependency which ultimately place the burden upon government. A well-organized health department pays off by raising health standards, lowering death rates, and reducing the financial load upon government.

Nature and Objectives of the Program. The public health program in the larger cities usually embraces all or most of the following matters: vital statistics, sanitation, control of communicable diseases, laboratory service, maternal and infant welfare, public health education, public nursing, and health research. The collection, tabulation, analysis, and interpretation of information concerning births, sickness, and deaths are important to the private physician as well as for purposes of planning public health activities. Sanitation responsibilities include the safeguarding of the water supply, not only for drinking but for cleansing and for recreational use as well. One of the major sanitation responsibilities is that of supervising the production and distribution of milk to insure its freshness and cleanliness. Milk inspection presents municipalities with a number of difficult problems due to the fact that the farms, and frequently the processing plants, are outside the city limits. Quite often the same supplier furnishes milk and milk products to a number of different cities. Unless regulations are standardized and their administration coördinated or carried out under some kind of joint program, a heavy burden may be placed upon the supplier by having to follow the requirements established by a number of different inspectors.[54] Most of the

[53] Fisher and Bishop, op. cit., p. 409.
[54] See *Milk Inspection and Milk Standards in King County* (Seattle: Bureau of Governmental Research and Services, University of Washington, October, 1947), Report No. 77. Also Ernest Howard Campbell, *Meat and Restaurant Inspection* (Seattle:

larger cities today also have sanitary codes which regulate the conditions under which meat and many other types of foods may be sold. Many cities also require health examinations for food handlers to protect against the transmission of communicable diseases.[55]

The control of communicable diseases is one of the most common and important of all the activities of the health department. By quarantine and other methods, health departments are able to check the spread of diseases. Among the measures commonly employed in providing this protection are: (1) registration of the disease, (2) identification of the disease, (3) isolation and supervision of the patient, (4) quarantine of exposed persons, (5) immunization of exposed persons, (6) investigation of sources and modes of infection, (7) release of patient from control, and (8) renovation of premises and sterilization of bedding and clothing.

One of the important services essential to effective health work is the laboratory service. A well-organized laboratory enables practicing physicians as well as public health officials to make quick, convenient, and reliable diagnoses of excreta, secretions, and tissues for the purpose of determining the nature and causes of diseases. Laboratory service is also essential for the analysis of food, drink, and drug specimens and for checking the purity of water and milk specimens. A more recent type of service is the analysis of smoke specimens and the testing of evidences of industrial poisoning.

Health programs for mothers and children usually include both prenatal and postnatal care. Through work of visiting nurses, instruction is given for the care of both the mother and the infant. Clinics are frequently made available for those unable to afford private medical and nursing service. Close coöperation between health authorities and school authorities is important in developing a program of school hygiene which should include periodic examinations, protection from unnecessary exposure, and the teaching of the fundamentals of nutrition. Working closely with the school health program is the public nurse service. To a greater extent than with any other public health activity, the public nurse comes in intimate contact with the people of the community, particularly with those of the lower income groups. The services of the public nurse are, therefore, important not only

---

Bureau of Government Research and Services, University of Washington, January, 1947), Report No. 70.

[55] Charles M. Kneier, *Illustrative Materials in Municipal Government and Administration* (New York: Harper and Brothers, 1939), p. 483.

in providing nursing care, but also because, through her activities, the department gathers accurate health statistics, makes possible the early diagnosis and treatment of disease, and secures information which is helpful in developing and improving health facilities.

Many of the accomplishments of promoting good public health come about not from the enforcement of laws and regulations, but from successful programs and campaigns of health education. Through the use of pamphlets, posters, charts, lectures, newspapers, radio, and television, attention can be directed to the importance of good health care and health practices. Health campaigns must be planned and worked out in the light of habits, beliefs, and traditions in the community. Frequently the problem of overcoming inertia, practices, and prejudices is a slow process. In the long run, however, the time spent on a well-planned campaign will pay big dividends in improving the health standards and health conditions of the community. As a further means of achieving progress in community health, it is imperative that there be constantly carried on a program of health research. A successful research program depends upon the availability of qualified personnel, modern equipment, and adequate finances. It is essential also that all the public and private agencies concerned directly and indirectly with the problems of public health coöperate with each other.

The Public Hospital. Closely related to the public health program is the public hospital. Quite commonly public hospitals are set up under the management of separate hospital boards and operated independently of the health department.[56] For the most part hospitals are owned and operated by churches, fraternal organizations, or by charitable or nonprofit corporations. In recent years an increasing number of hospitals have been constructed, owned, and operated by municipalities or other units of local government. To a considerable extent this development has been encouraged by the availability of grants from the Federal Government under the United States Hospital Survey and Construction Act of 1946.[57] The trend toward government hospitals seems likely to continue as long as privately owned hospitals are overcrowded. In general, public hospitals have been developed in order to augment private hospitals rather than replace them.

[56] Arthur W. Bromage, *Introduction to Municipal Government and Administration* (New York: Appleton-Century-Crofts, Inc., 1950), p. 607.
[57] Wade S. Smith, "Federal Aid Hospital Program Gets Under Way," *National Municipal Review*, Vol. XXXVI, p. 654, December, 1947.

One of the major purposes of the public hospital program has been to provide hospital care for those who cannot afford to pay the costs of private hospital service. However, public hospital care is not limited to charity cases. The fact that the emphasis is on care for persons in the lower income groups indicates that site location should be selected with a view to the convenience of such persons. In addition to providing hospitals for general service, many specialized hospitals have been established to care for spastic cases, the blind and deaf, mental ailments, tuberculosis, and certain contagious diseases or to provide care for certain groups of persons such as veterans.

Welfare Services. There are a number of aspects to the public welfare that are tied closely to the public health and hospital programs. Poverty, marital discord, loss of support, forsaken old folks, orphaned or abandoned children are related to the public health, public safety, and public morals as much as are disease, sanitation, slum conditions, and crime. Many of the welfare programs involve institutional care in hospitals, sanitariums, homes for dependent adults, orphanages, foster homes, correctional institutions, schools for the blind, and homes and institutions for the handicapped. Illness, poverty, dependency, and old age frequently go hand in hand. These services and institutions must be accounted for in the comprehensive urban plan even though for the most part the responsibility for welfare administration is centralized in the county under state supervision. In a great many instances both the health agency and the welfare agency are dealing with the same groups of people. Efficiency and economy of administration necessitate close coöperation between the two services.

CONTROL AND ABATEMENT OF NUISANCES

Virtually every urban community is faced with the problem of nuisances which arise within or near the corporate limits of the municipality. The control and abatement of nuisances present continuing problems and responsibilities to municipalities and to other units of local government. Nuisances are offensive actions or uses of property which may develop from a wide variety of causes. In certain cases they may be deliberately conceived, while in other cases they arise from conduct not intended to create a nuisance. Nuisances, in some cases, result from the inconsiderate exercise of personal rights and, in others, from the inconsiderate or inappropriate use of property. Public opinion as to what constitutes offensive actions or uses of property sufficient to create a nuisance has undergone progressive development in recent years. The existence of a nuisance in a given instance may depend very largely upon the character of the neighborhood. A machine shop, for example, which is a natural and legitimate part of an industrial area, may become a public nuisance when located in a residential area. It has frequently been observed that "A nuisance may merely be a right thing in a wrong place."

Classifications of Nuisances. In the broad sense, the term "nuisance" embraces anything that results in an invasion of one's legal rights. It arises from either an unreasonable, unwarrantable, or unlawful act or by reason of failure to act which results in material annoyance, inconvenience, discomfort, or damage to another or to the public. Certain acts, things, omissions, or uses of property have been declared by common law or statutes to be nuisances *per se* and as such are not permissible or excusable under any circumstances. Other acts, omissions, or property uses may be held not to be nuisances *per se* but become nuisances *in fact* when conducted in certain districts. For example, a plant for the manufacture of fireworks might be declared to be a nuisance *per se*, whereas a dance hall or amusement resort might be declared to be a nuisance if conducted in an exclusive residential district.

Nuisances are also classified as public nuisances and private nuisances. A public nuisance, in general, includes unlawful acts of omission, commission, or conditions which injuriously affect the health, safety, or morals of the public or occasion some substantial inconvenience, annoyance, or injury to the public. For example, the pollution of a navigable stream, the jeopardizing of public health by pollution of air, or the emission of loud and raucous noises may constitute a public nuisance. Sometimes an obstruction in a street or a dangerous condition in a public building may constitute a public nuisance. An individual who suffers damage from a public nuisance may maintain an action to have it abated only if he suffers some special damage from it. Merely suffering injury that is common to the general public is not sufficient.[58]

Private nuisances are those nuisances which violate only private rights, and occasion damage to just one or a few persons. Such nuisances are sometimes defined by statute to include every nuisance which is not embraced in the statutory definition of "public nui-

[58] *State ex rel. Sohlman v. Oldham,* 156 Wash. 484, 287 Pac. 680 (1930).

sance." [59] Such nuisances may give rise to an action for damages to the injured person. It should be recognized also that municipalities themselves may create, permit, or maintain nuisances as a result of nonfeasance or misfeasance of their officers or agents which will render the municipality liable for damages. Municipal liability may arise from such action even though the nuisance is not caused from the negligence of municipal officials and even though the municipality is engaged in the discharge of a governmental function in connection with the nuisance.[60]

Methods of Control or Abatement. There are a number of methods which are available to municipalities for the control or abatement of nuisances. Many types of public nuisances have been declared by statute to constitute crimes against public health, safety, and morals, and persons maintaining such nuisances are subject to criminal penalties. Such nuisances may include the operation of places of gambling, selling intoxicating liquor without a license, operating houses of prostitution, the pollution of water supply, the maintenance of fire hazards, and the erection of signs or obstructions on highways which may constitute hazards to traffic.

In a great number of instances nuisances may be eliminated through voluntary abatement. In other instances it is necessary to eliminate nuisances either through the process of summary abatement or through judicial procedure. Coöperation of the public should be the goal in seeking the abatement of nuisances. Cities should negotiate with property owners for the voluntary abatement of nuisances whenever possible. It is generally desirable to avoid litigation, and toward the accomplishment of that end it may be advisable, on occasions, to grant extensions of time to accomplish voluntary abatement. Particularly is this true in dealing with such problems as the elimination of noise and smoke. The crystallization of public opinion is often extremely helpful in carrying out a program of this kind.

Whenever it is necessary to use some legal remedy to abate a public nuisance, the municipal authorities must decide whether to proceed by summary abatement or by judicial proceedings. Summary abatement is employed when the condition is of such emergency nature that time does not permit the use of the judicial procedure. Quite

[59] Ernest Howard Campbell, et al., *Nuisances, Their Control and Abatement in the State of Washington* (Seattle: Bureau of Governmental Research and Services in coöperation with the Association of Washington Cities, July, 1949), Report 99, p. 4.

[60] For a discussion of municipal liability for nuisance, see *Kilbourn v. Seattle*, 43 Wn. (2d) 373, 261 P. (2d) 407 (1953).

commonly the conditions which justify the use of summary abatement are specified by ordinance. Under summary abatement procedure the appropriate administrative officials remove the conditions constituting the nuisance without first resorting to judicial proceedings. If, for example, city authorities find that certain buildings or telephone poles, by reason of their condition, constitute a fire or health hazard or menace to public safety, they may proceed to eliminate the condition without first securing authorization from the courts. When this procedure is used, it is advisable for the protection of the city that prior to the abatement of the nuisance, evidence in the form of photographs and other data be assembled to support its findings that an emergency exists sufficient to justify the summary abatement action. If the action should be challenged in court and the city could not justify the abatement, the city might be liable for damages sustained to the owner by reason of the destruction or removal of the building or condition.

When an emergency does not exist, which necessitates the immediate abatement by summary method, it is generally advisable to abate the nuisance by judicial procedure. Under this method, an ordinance is first enacted declaring the building or condition to be a fire or health hazard and a nuisance and directing its abatement by the owner within a specific time. Such ordinances usually require that an action be brought in court to abate the nuisance in the event the owner fails to comply with the ordinance. Under this procedure the court, prior to the abatement, determines whether or not the building or condition is a nuisance in fact and should be abated. If the court determines that there is a nuisance that should be abated, it directs the abatement pursuant to the order of the court. Although this procedure is longer, the abatement pursuant to court order protects the municipality against any claim for damages.

Air Pollution. Among the major nuisances which plague most of our large urban communities are conditions of smoke and other causes of air pollution. The smoke nuisance has long been a matter of grave concern to industrial communities [61] where pollution from smoke has been recognized as a menace to the health of the individual, lowering his vitality, increasing the death rate, and causing untold loss and injury to property.[62] Although many cities have enacted

[61] 4 *American City*, 210 (May, 1911).
[62] See Clarence A. Mills, *Air Pollution and Community Health* (Boston: The Christopher Publishing House, 1954) for a case study of the effects of air pollution in selected communities.

smoke-control ordinances, the problem of air pollution from smoke, exhausts, and gas from industrial operation is currently presenting one of the most difficult of all nuisance problems.[63] Lauren B. Hitchcock, president of the Southern California Air Pollution Foundation, Los Angeles, declared that "Scholars list air pollution among the four principal threats to the future of our cities, sufficient in combination to spell their doom. Congestion, noise, and the high cost of living are the others." [64] In a number of jurisdictions extensive research is being conducted in an effort to work out some means of eliminating causes of air pollution. In the State of Washington, the Washington State Health Council has recently approved a resolution of the Air Pollution Committee which calls for a state-wide study of air pollution problems to be directed by the State Pollution Control Commission. This study contemplates the investigation of toxicity of ozone as a possible irritation component of smoke.[65]

The problem of air pollution control looks to the abatement not only of smoke but also of conditions which produce soot, noxious acids, fumes, oxides, gases, vapors, and various chemical or industrial dusts that cause atmospheric contamination in amounts detrimental to the public welfare.[66] Air pollution control is also concerned with conditions which produce offensive odors, which, even though not affecting conditions of health, may adversely affect the amenities of living. One of the difficulties of dealing with the problem of air pollution is that no single method has ever been devised for eliminating the various types of pollutants such as gas dust and odors. Each problem has to be studied in the light of the causes, the atmospheric conditions, and other conditions in the community.[67] Obviously, the

[63] Eugene Odbert, "Municipal Control of Air Pollution," The Municipality, Vol. 50, No. 3, p. 51, March, 1955.

[64] The Seattle Times, December 30, 1954, p. 27.

[65] Occupational Health Newsletter, Vol. 3, No. 12, December, 1954, The Environmental Research Laboratory, School of Medicine, University of Washington.

[66] Campbell, et al., op. cit., p. 36. See also Harold W. Kennedy and Andrew O. Porter, "Air Pollution: Its Control and Abatement," Vanderbilt Law Review, Vol. 8, No. 4, pp. 854–857, June, 1955.

[67] For an excellent study of the causes of air pollution, methods of abatement, and means of control, see The Bureau of Public Administration, University of California, Air Pollution Control (Sacramento, Calif.: Assembly of the State of California, Assembly Interim Committee Reports, Vol. 13, No. 3, January, 1955). New York's Department of Air Pollution Control recently issued new air pollution regulations requiring, among other things, that gasoline buses be equipped with fume-reducing devices and that bus drivers not idle motors for more than three minutes while standing a bus at a route terminal. "New York City Issues New Air Pollution Regulations," The American City, Vol. 71, No. 3, p. 231, March, 1956.

problem cannot be solved by abating all the industrial operations, automobiles, and the many activities that contribute to the general condition. This would work economic chaos. The answer must be found through scientific and technological devices.[68]

Noise. Another nuisance condition that is difficult to control is that of noise. As in the case of air pollution, city noises and annoyances are by no means a new phenomenon. For many years steps have been undertaken to abate noise, but the problem has never been adequately solved. Generally speaking, annoyance caused by sound can be associated with: (1) the apparent loudness of the sound, (2) the particular frequency components present in the sound, (3) the prevailing background sound level, (4) the duration of the sound, (5) the length of time between occurrences of the sound, and (6) individual psychological factors which cannot be evaluated, such as degree of familiarity with the sound.[69] It has been definitely established that there is a close correlation between physical and mental well-being and quiet. Excessive noise may impair one's hearing and cause fatigue. Among the most annoying of the noise disturbances are those which interfere with sleep. Principal among these are the noises that result from sudden horns, exhausts, drills, vibrations, whistles, shouting, singing, and the playing of musical instruments.

Many cities have achieved a partial solution to the problem through enacting antinoise legislation. An ordinance enacted in Philadelphia, for example, lists nine prohibited noises and noise sources:[70]

1. Unusual sound devices, such as sirens, on ordinary motor vehicles.
2. Unnecessary auto horn-blowing.
3. Muffler cutouts and defective auto mufflers.
4. Improperly loaded vehicles.
5. Defective vehicles.
6. Careless handling of ash, trash, and garbage cans.
7. Horn-blowing, bell-ringing, and the like by peddlers.
8. Use of sound trucks and other broadcasting devices for advertising purposes.
9. Construction work between 6 P.M. and 6 A.M. (Eastern Standard Time), except by special permit.

[68] For practical suggestions for developing an air pollution control program, see Richard D. Schaffer, "Initiating a Program for Municipal Air Pollution Control," *Ohio Cities and Villages*, July, 1956, Vol. 4, No. 7, p. 164.

[69] Campbell, et al., op. cit., p. 28.

[70] Edwin Rothman, "Philadelphia Bureau Asks City to Quiet Down," *GRA Reporter*, Vol. 6, No. 3, p. 34, Third Quarter, 1954. See also Arthur Saltzstein, "Excessive Motor Vehicle Noises," *The Municipality*, Vol. 50, No. 3, p. 50, March, 1955.

A recent experience in Paris, France, provides some evidence that the reduction of noise contributes to the safety of inhabitants as well as to the amenities of environment. In the summer of 1954, the Paris police issued an edict which required Parisian motorists to rely on gears and brakes rather than on their horns. The result was that the accident rate dropped perceptibly, and according to a quotation from a recent issue of *France Actuelle* a fortnightly report on France written for Americans:

Almost overnight, Paris has changed from one of the noisiest to one of the quietest cities in the world. People cannot believe their ears. The 24-hour cacophony of horn-bleats and unmuffled racing motors is now reduced to a soothing hum as the city and its traffic quietly go about their business.

In September, 1953, there were 2607 auto accidents in Paris.

In September this year, with about 100,000 more cars on the streets, there were only 1712 accidents.[71]

While antinoise ordinances may help to reduce the noise menace under certain conditions, there are obviously limitations upon the extent to which governmental regulations may restrict sound in the interest of noise control.[72] Some especially difficult problems have arisen with respect to efforts to regulate the use of sound trucks for noncommercial purposes. The constitutional question which is usually raised in this connection is that of interference with freedom of speech.[73]

Radio and Television Interference. A different type of noise problem which is a matter of municipal concern is that which produces interference to radio and television transmission. Some of the interference may be due to other licensed transmitters operating on the same or near the same channel or wave length. This is called co-channel interference and cannot be entirely eliminated. A second type of interference is due to equipment which emits radio frequency energy for noncommunication purposes such as medical diathermy machines, electrically powered appliances and equipment, lighting and ignition systems, and various other types of electrical devices.

[71] New York *World-Telegram and Sun*, Friday, November 5, 1954, p. 17.

[72] In order to frame laws properly for the control of noise, it is necessary to have an understanding of the relationships existing among intensity, loudness, and annoyance. See Donald P. Loye, "The Legal Aspects of Noise Control," *Noise Control*, Vol. 2, No. 4, pp. 56–60, July, 1956.

[73] See *Saia v. New York*, 334 U.S. 558, 68 S.Ct. 1148, 92 L.Ed. 1087 (1948) and *Kovacs v. Cooper*, 336 U.S. 77, 69 S.Ct. 448 (1949). Campbell et al., *op. cit.*, p. 30.

Such interference is a matter of municipal concern because it constitutes a source of annoyance and is objectionable as constituting a nuisance in a degree similar to that of smoke annoyance, offensive odors, and loud noises.

Interference with radio and television communication is of public concern in another respect because of the fact that interruption of reception may disturb the efficient operation of vital safety service during periods of emergencies. While to some extent the problem of interference with reception is a matter for regulation by the Federal Communications Commission, municipalities also have a responsibility to prohibit, through ordinance, such interferences as may be controlled on a local level and which do not conflict with any federal legislation or regulations in this field.[74]

THE PROMOTION OF SOCIAL WELFARE

In a broad sense, the social welfare functions of government embrace all those services and responsibilities concerned with the educational, cultural, and recreational life, the general living conditions, and the various individual and group relationships of the inhabitants of the community. Quite commonly the term "social welfare" is used to refer to programs of public assistance or relief. These programs are not specifically dealt with in this chapter because of the extent to which they have become responsibilities of the states and the national government rather than of the municipalities and other local units of government.

It is not possible to distinguish clearly those functions designed to further social objectives from those aimed at promoting the physical development, economic welfare, or the protection of life and property. Any classification of specific services or programs must, of necessity, be somewhat arbitrary and can be supported only on the basis of major emphasis. For example, many functions classified as protective functions, such as crime prevention and the control of communicable diseases, have broad social objectives. On the other hand, certain policies underlying the educational, recreational, and housing programs are developed with the objective of promoting a better land use and of providing greater public safety and economic well-being.

[74] Charles S. Rhyne, *Municipal Regulations, Taxation and Use of Radio and Television* (Washington, D.C.: National Institute of Municipal Law Officers, Report No. 143, 1955), pp. 1–18.

General planning must be undertaken with an awareness of all these program objectives and in an effort to weld them together in a properly balanced overall program of community development.

The recognition that government has a responsibility for the social welfare is of relatively recent origin. The fact that government has been slow to undertake programs for the social betterment has been due in part to our general philosophy of the purpose of government and in part to the fact that social needs are somewhat more difficult to establish than are physical and economic needs. However, environmental conditions created by urbanization have more and more tended to focus attention upon our social problems with the result that today local governments have assumed many of the responsibilities for social betterment that were formerly considered the responsibilities of individuals, churches, and private organizations.

EDUCATIONAL AND CULTURAL PROGRAMS

During the pioneering era, the attention of the American people was occupied largely with the exploitation of natural resources, the building of industries, and the problems of settlement. Few functions of government were concerned with policies aimed at fostering culture and the arts. The past three quarters of a century, however, has witnessed a growing, widespread interest for public support of schools, libraries, museums, zoological gardens, aquariums, music, art galleries, arboretums, historical sites and exhibits, and many other institutions and activities for promoting the educational and cultural life of the community. To a considerable degree, the promotion of these interests has been aided and encouraged by the philanthropy of persons who have devoted substantial amounts of the fortunes they accumulated during the course of our industrial expansion to the establishment and endowment of many of these public and semipublic institutions.

Public Education.   Until about a century ago, free public education was generally regarded as a form of charity. Gradually there has developed the idea that education not only should be free, but also that it should be compulsory. Even so, not all education is provided through governmental service. A very substantial part of our common schools system, in both elementary and higher education, is supplied by parochial and private institutions. Although a different type of governmental responsibility exists with respect to private and parochial schools, nevertheless, their programs are a matter of concern to the state and their place in relation to the overall education program must be recognized in the development of the comprehensive plan.

The justifications advanced for public education have usually been on three grounds: cultural, economic, and civic. The cultural objectives are aimed at enabling the person to acquire information he will need to lead a full life in the society to which he belongs. The economic objectives are concerned with one's preparation to make a living. The civic objectives are related to developing a degree of understanding of the political, economic, and social problems in order that each individual may be prepared to participate in their solution.

The necessity for coördinating educational policies with the many services and programs of municipal government is obvious. In more than half of the states this must be accomplished by coöperative means because of the fact that public school education is administered by special school districts which are not integrated with the municipal government. During the earlier periods of our national development, the school district served a very useful purpose and continues to do so in many areas outside the incorporated municipalities. The justification for the independent school district within municipal corporations has also been vigorously supported on the grounds that schools are thus kept free from local politics. A further argument that has been advanced by school authorities is that schools are likely to receive greater financial support for educational purposes if their administration is conducted by an independent school district. While some of these arguments may have had merit in the past, it is questionable whether they have much validity today in view of the high quality of municipal government and the public concern with high standards of education.

Many students of government have urged a merger of school and city administration on the grounds that city government would have a more alert interest in education and that integration would provide a single focus for community efforts in all types of services such as police, fire, public works, public health and welfare, recreation, and education.[75] It is argued that under an integrated system services regularly provided by municipalities could be better utilized and that costly duplications could be avoided. Among the services which might be better utilized would be the city's centralized purchasing, its civil service for nonteaching personnel, and its engineering services for buildings and repairs. An integrated system should develop a better

[75] Bromage, *op. cit.*, p. 642.

coördination of tax programs, bond issues, and budgeting. Certain advantages would seem possible also in supplying water, light, and other utilities.

In spite of these rather persuasive arguments, there appears to be little evidence that complete integration is likely to be achieved in the near future. The coördination of education with other municipal functions must depend, therefore, upon the prevailing system of coöperation of school and municipal authorities. In many communities the relationships have been very satisfactory. Coöperative relationships have been particularly successful in the fields of public health, recreation, and library service. In the field of health this coöperation is most essential in the control of contagious diseases, particularly in programs in which immunization of children is deemed necessary. It has also been valuable in programs of health education and physical education. In the field of recreation, many school authorities and municipal recreation authorities are devising joint programs for the development and use of parks and school recreation facilities, and for a common system of indoor and outdoor playgrounds open the year around under a single corps of instructors. Many coöperative arrangements have also been worked out between the library and school authorities with respect to the use of books, rooms, and other facilities. In some jurisdictions it has also been found possible for schools to overcome some of the disadvantages of a nonintegrated system by contracting with municipalities for personnel services and by making arrangements with cities for centralized purchasing.

One aspect of school administration which is of special importance in planning is the matter of selection of sites for school buildings. Usually this is a responsibility of the school board. However, in some states, cities are given authority to approve or reject the sites selected by the school board. It should be apparent that in those jurisdictions in which municipalities are not granted any control over school site selection, a high degree of coördination between school authorities and municipal planning agencies is most essential. Although school boards may be most competent to evaluate possible sites from the standpoint of their current educational and administrative requirements, they cannot always make a wise choice without knowledge of the planned land use and other information which will indicate the probable future direction of population growth and population density. Intelligent school site selection also requires an understanding of the street plan, utility plan, transportation plan, and recreational plan.

Public Libraries. Support for public libraries has been a struggle against public indifference and political opposition. Although today the responsibility of public library service has become generally recognized, appropriations in most jurisdictions for library purposes have been inadequate, and in many jurisdictions the geographical areas for the purpose of library administration have not been satisfactory. The type of administration and control of public libraries varies widely throughout the country. The public library is operated in some jurisdictions as an agency of city government. In others, it is established as a school district library, and in still others, it is administered by a special library district. There are frequently combinations of these systems within the same state. In those jurisdictions in which public libraries are administered by separate districts or school districts, the districts are usually empowered to impose a separate tax for library purposes outside of the school levies or the municipal levies. While frequently the school district library is limited to the use of school children, quite commonly it serves secondarily to provide library service to the public.

In most municipalities the public library is a branch of the municipal government. The actual supervision of the library program is usually under a librarian who is responsible to a board. As a general rule, the members of the board are appointed by the mayor or the council or by the council on recommendation of the mayor. Although many students of government are, on principle, opposed to departments headed by lay boards or commissions, the management of public libraries has not presented many difficult administrative problems. Library boards have served to interpret the interests of the public to the librarian and in some jurisdictions have been very successful in securing more adequate appropriations from the city council than might have been the case had the function not been placed under the supervision of a board.

The American Library Association recognizes that the service of libraries centers about five basic objectives: education, information, research, aesthetic appreciation, and recreation.[76] Since libraries play an important role in both educational and recreational functions of

[76] Reginald R. Isaacs, "Educational, Cultural, and Recreational Service," *The Annals of the American Academy of Political and Social Science*, Vol. 242, p. 133, November, 1945.

government, their proper site location is important from the standpoint of planning. Convenience is one of the primary considerations. The central library should be located within a block or two of the main business district and should be convenient to main traffic arteries and transportation facilities. There should also be adequate off-street parking facilities near by. Branch libraries should normally be located within a mile or a mile and a half of the majority of the people whom the branch library is intended to serve. In newly developed areas and in other areas where population is not sufficiently dense to justify a branch library, the bookmobile may be a satisfactory means of providing valuable library service. Extended library services should be related to the characteristics of the area and the interests of the inhabitants. Therefore, it is necessary that the objectives of the service be clearly defined.

The problem of regional library service is one which must be considered in the planning of metropolitan or unincorporated urban areas. Inasmuch as city libraries have more and more tended to become the core of library service for regions that include the fringe urban areas and also certain rural areas, there is need to consider whether or not the city is the logical geographical area for library support and administration. In many jurisdictions library service is provided not only by municipalities but also by counties. In some others, regional library service is established either by separate library districts or through the joint action of two or more counties or other units of government. The necessity of establishing adequate library service on a wider geographic basis may have the ultimate effect of furthering the trend toward county and regional libraries and diminishing to some extent the importance of municipal libraries, at least in the smaller cities.

Museums and Zoological Gardens. The administration of museums and zoological gardens and certain other public and semipublic cultural institutions is usually not an integral part of the city government. Museums, and quite commonly zoological gardens, also occupy somewhat of a hybrid position in the legal structure of the municipality.[77] These institutions are oftentimes operated by museum or zoological societies or by semipublic or nonprofit corporations. Sometimes, however, they are administered as responsibilities of the department of parks and recreation. The financial support for

[77] John M. Pfiffner, *Municipal Administration* (New York: The Ronald Press Company, 1940), pp. 559–567.

museums is usually from endowments, membership fees, gifts, and taxation. Where these institutions are privately owned and operated as nonprofit or charitable organizations, frequently some form of government subsidy is provided in the form of tax exemptions or in furnishing certain services by the park or public works departments of the municipality.

In order that museums may play an increasing role in the educational program, the newer museums have attempted to create more popular interest in their service. This has often been accomplished through holding certain classes in the museums and by taking exhibits of masterpieces and objects of historical interest to the schools and to other places of assembly in outlying communities. The fact that one of the primary objectives of the museum is to uncover and present to the world rare and unique items having peculiar educational values does not necessitate the use of antiquated methods of exhibition. Close coöperation between the museum and school authorities is important to secure the greatest value from the museum collections. Methods of creating popular interest can usually be developed without sacrificing the scientific, scholarly, or artistic values of the museum items.

Zoological gardens also have an important educational value in acquainting both children and adults with animal life other than pets and domestic animals with which they may be familiar. Zoological gardens may require rather substantial areas of land. Often, areas not well suited for residential or business purposes because of topography or rock formations may be ideal for this use. However, convenience and accessibility are factors in site location and must be taken into account along with the physical characteristics and acquisition and maintenance costs. The revenue for operating zoological gardens is derived from a variety of sources including donations, admission charges, concession fees, and general taxes. Some cities, as for example, San Diego, California, have justified certain appropriations for zoos on the ground that the zoo has a direct benefit for the health department, coroner, and other officers who are able to make use of the zoological hospital and laboratory.[78]

Historical Sites. Some communities possess rich cultural values which are peculiar to the area. These arise largely from historical associations with battlegrounds, homes of famous persons, or places where notable events took place. Many of these communities in which

[78] Pfiffner, op. cit., p. 563.

such places are found have felt justified in expending public funds for the commemoration, preservation, and restoration of these places. Here, as in the case of many other cultural interests, the responsibilities of government as distinguished from those of historical societies or other private organizations, are not always clearly separated.[79] In some instances the state and also the United States Government have been interested in preserving certain historic places. For example, in 1948 Congress appropriated money to aid Philadelphia and the state of Pennsylvania in preserving Independence Hall and surrounding historic sites and buildings.[80] Three major reasons for safeguarding historical areas are suggested: (1) new business in the form of tourist trade is encouraged, (2) lessons of history are kept alive providing a link with the past, and (3) areas are saved from declining into slums.[81]

Churches.   Among the most important cultural influences in the community are the churches. However, the American tradition of religious freedom and separation of church and state removes them from government support and general governmental control. Nevertheless, churches are not to be excluded from consideration in developing public policies to promote cultural and other social objectives underlying the comprehensive plan. The planning agency can play a very important role in the encouragement of religious interests through efforts to facilitate the best possible site area and location. In determining site location, consideration needs to be given not only to the convenience of the congregation, but also to protection of the public from undue traffic congestion created by church activities, and to the preservation of land-use objectives. In densely populated areas, the parking problem may sometimes be solved by selecting sites near shopping centers where arrangements can be worked out for the use of commercial parking areas for evening or Sunday gatherings. The importance of religion in our cultural life is recognized by government in other ways. For example, many jurisdictions exempt churches and certain religious activities from general taxation. Such exemptions,

[79] Eighteenth-century Williamsburg was restored solely from the personal gifts of Mr. John D. Rockefeller, Jr., *Colonial Williamsburg*, Report by the President for the Year 1954, p. 6.

[80] For a brief account of activities of cities to preserve, protect, and reconstruct historical areas, see Public Administration Clearing House *News Bulletin*, Release No. 1, March 14, 1955.

[81] Public Administration Clearing House *News Bulletin*, Release No. 2, March 15, 1955.

if granted, cannot be applied to discriminate against or to favor any religious group.

Communities are tending more and more to recognize the fact that the church and planners have much to offer each other in achieving their respective goals.[82] The goal of the church is to guide the people of the community toward a better way of life. The goal of planning is to guide the growth of the community to provide the best possible environment for living that life. The two goals are interrelated.

The basic purpose of the church is the worship of God. The planner, however, also sees the church as a factor in the stabilization of land values, the increase in neighborhood solidarity and the fostering of community pride. He sees the church as a focal point for family activities and interests; religious education of children, filling a need not supplied by public schools; and finally, as a means toward the reduction of juvenile delinquency, crime, divorce, loose morals, and—on the positive side—the nurturing of the desire to do right.[83]

A difficult problem that most communities face in planning for churches is that of getting the right kind of church, of the right size, at the right location, without permiting an unduly large number of little churches scattered throughout the same general area. One of the most promising solutions to this problem is through comity or interdenominational coördination.[84] This approach often makes it possible to provide for the religious needs of smaller congregations and at the same time promote a more efficient plan of land use. Cooperative arrangements for the use of facilities is best worked out through an association of church people of the interested denominations. The encouragement of this approach enables the planner to avoid being charged with favoring one denomination over another in approving or revising a subdivision or land-use plan.

THE RECREATION PROGRAM

During the time when our economy was primarily agricultural, there was ample outdoor space for recreational purposes and recreation was not regarded as a function of government. In rural surroundings most

[82] John H. Shope, "The Need for Church Planning," *Journal of the American Institute of Planners*, Vol. XX, No. 3, pp. 122–125, Summer, 1954.

[83] William H. Claire, "The Church in the City Plan," *Journal of the American Institute of Planners*, Vol. XX, No. 4, p. 174, Fall, 1954.

[84] For a general discussion of the relationships between the church and the planning agency, see Robert C. Hoover and Everett L. Perry, *Church and City Planning* (New York: National Council of the Churches of Christ in the USA, 1955), Survey Guide 2.

persons were sufficiently near woods, streams, and open spaces to afford them ample opportunities to satisfy their outdoor recreational interests. Recreation was looked upon as a private responsibility. Today, however, in every large urban community, recreation has come to be recognized as one of the very essential governmental functions. The early idea that private initiative could be counted on to provide for the recreational needs of the people has been discarded.

Many factors have contributed to this change in public attitude. With the growth of our urban society, most of the opportunities for wholesome outdoor private recreation have been lost. Open spaces gave way to compact and crowded living quarters, noisy and dirty industrial sections, and congested streets. Thus, city life has destroyed many of the natural attractions of the more rural society. It has reduced the number of trees, flowers, and open spaces, and eliminated many of the former opportunities for hunting, fishing, and outdoor sports, and in their place, for the young people, it has often substituted street play, alley fights, vandalism, gang organizations, and other conditions which have resulted in a high rate of juvenile delinquency.

Another factor that has greatly influenced the need for public recreation is the increased amount of leisure time of both adults and children. For most employees, the working week has been reduced to not more than 40 hours. Child labor legislation has, to a considerable degree, prolonged the leisure of children to the ages of 16 or 18 years. Furthermore, the increased use of mechanical equipment and labor-saving devices in the home has materially lessened the hours of home work for both parents and children.

Purposes of Recreation.   One of the most fundamental characteristics of recreation in all its forms is that it is an activity in which the individual engages because of his own desires and free will and not because of compulsion. In planning for public recreation, it must be borne in mind that an activity which is recreation to one individual may be an actual chore for another. It therefore becomes essential that every public recreation program include a wide range of individual choices. Since the number of choices is almost infinite, there are many policy decisions to be made in selecting those facilities and programs which best suit the needs of a particular community. The general purpose of recreation thus becomes of significance. Although many theoretical explanations have been given of the reasons for recreation, there is, even today, no general agreement as to what the main objectives should be.

Under one theory, the function of recreation is to enable people to refresh themselves by engaging in activities which they are not required to undertake after they have exhausted their energies through labor. While this theory may explain the need for recreation for some, it does not for others. For example, it does not explain why children who have not exhausted their energy will begin the day with a round of play. Another explanation is that recreation is needed to release surplus energy. This theory, which is directly opposed to the recuperation theory, does not account for athletes or children engaging in recreational sports long after their surplus energy has been exhausted. Other theories which have been used to support the recreational program are based upon the individual's needs for education and self-expression.[85]

Whether or not the justification for public recreation is to be found in any or all of these explanations is perhaps unimportant. The fact is that public recreation is no longer considered as a frill but rather is accepted as an important function of local government that has a direct relationship to many other community values including the betterment of physical and mental health, the development of individual character, the prevention of crime, the enhancement of community solidarity, the building and sustaining of morale, and the promotion of community safety.

Recreation authorities have also strongly urged that recreation programs pay dollars and cents dividends as well as intangible returns.[86] Each year every large urban community pays many thousand dollars in taxes to care for the delinquents, the criminals, and the persons broken in mind and body who are a product of our complex urban society. In addition, there are enormous individual costs in terms of loss of life and illness. Business and industry also must bear the costs of diminished working efficiency resulting from frayed nerves and loss of working time from illness. To the extent that these costs are reduced by a sound program of public recreation, the community enjoys a true economic saving which should be weighed in establishing the recreation budget. A further matter that each municipality should consider is the fact that today industrial location is very strongly influenced by the recreational environment of the community. The attraction of a high-type labor force is sometimes gov-

[85] *Local Planning Administration, op. cit.,* p. 162.
[86] *Municipal Recreation Administration* (Chicago: The International City Managers' Association, 1948), pp. 9–16.

erned as much by availability of good parks, beaches, and recreation facilities as the impressiveness of large factory buildings.

Municipal Responsibility. Recognizing these facts, the question may still be raised as to whether or not municipal government is the most effective agency for providing public recreation facilities and services.[87] The International City Managers' Association has suggested several reasons why the task should be that of the municipality.[88] Among these are the following:

1. Municipal recreation affords a large percentage of the people their only opportunity for forms of wholesome recreation.
2. It is only through the use of governmental powers that adequate lands can be acquired.
3. Municipal recreation is democratic and inclusive in that it provides equal recreation opportunities for all regardless of their social, economic, racial, or religious background.
4. Municipal recreation is inexpensive in comparison with amounts spent for private forms of recreation or those furnished by commercial agencies.
5. The municipal government gives a higher degree of permanency to recreation than normally is provided by private agencies.
6. The job has become too large for any private agency. Reliance upon private agencies would deprive many individuals of the cultural values of group activities.
7. The municipality cannot afford not to provide recreation because of the demonstrated savings to the community in terms of lives, health, and safety.

In order to help fulfill the social needs for recreation, municipal governments have been finding it necessary to give increasing attention to both the acquisition of a wide variety of recreation facilities and to the administration of numerous different types of public recreation programs. Recreation differs from many of the other public services in that most individuals are inclined to think of it largely in terms of their own interests. Thus, the public responsibility for recreation is not as clearly identified as is the case with certain other public services such as health, police protection, and fire protection. Until recent years the obligation of the municipality for recreation

---

[87] See Ernest H. Campbell and Henry D. Ambers, *Washington Statutes Relating to Parks and Recreation with Annotations* (Seattle: Bureau of Governmental Research and Services, University of Washington, July, 1954), Report No. 127, for a compilation of state statutes and identification of the agencies having recreation responsibilities.

[88] Municipal Recreation Administration, *op. cit.*, pp. 31–33.

was met principally through providing parks and open spaces where people could get away from the congestion and enjoy the natural surroundings. Although the importance of parks has not been minimized or decreased, there has been a growing demand upon city governments to establish other types of facilities and also to provide for and conduct active recreational programs, including organized and supervised play.

The facilities and activities which have come to be included in the public recreation programs are extremely numerous. Progressive cities today attempt to meet the needs of both children and adults through providing not only parks but also various types of playgrounds, athletic fields, tennis courts, field houses, golf courses, skating rinks, bathing beaches, swimming pools, picnic and camp sites, community houses, buildings or structures for public concerts, and innumerable other types of facilities. In addition, many cities through organized programs seek to inspire interest in such things as dancing, playing of games, debating, drama, group singing, sewing, knitting, hobbies, and arts and crafts. In developing programs and recreation standards, municipalities may receive invaluable help from the National Recreation Association [89] and many other organizations interested in the field of recreation. However, each city must gear its recreational program to the general characteristics of the community, the age group in each neighborhood, and the major interests of the inhabitants.

Program Requisites. Although each recreation program must be tailored to the individual and social needs of the community, there are certain criteria that have been suggested as having such universal appeal that they are applicable to every community regardless of size or type.[90] Every recreation program should, among other things, be sufficiently broad and well distributed to provide equality of opportunity for all persons and to serve the needs of all age groups of both sexes. It should recognize the special needs of the handicapped, the dependent, and the aged. The program should seek to encourage recreation of family groups, but at the same time be sufficiently diversified to offer a wide range of individual choices in all activities. Activities need to be arranged to accommodate persons who have

[89] National Recreation Association, *Standards for Municipal Recreation Areas* (New York: National Recreation Association, 1948) and National Recreation Association, *Standards for Neighborhood Recreational Areas and Facilities* (New York: National Recreation Association, 1943).

[90] *Ibid.*, pp. 59–62.

different periods of free time, such as those who work at night or at odd hours or go to school. The recreation program should include activities requiring varying degrees of skill, aptitudes, and capacities, and those which are of a progressive nature in order to provide incentives to advance to higher achievement.

Activities should also be included which will stimulate self-leadership, thereby assisting individuals and groups to find their own recreational interests. The program should encourage recreational interests which will persist at the adult level. To every extent possible, the program should be given a democratic basis by allowing people an opportunity to participate and share in its planning and control. Good citizenship should be fostered through stressing team play and cooperation. A successful program needs to take into account the different tastes of individuals and develop recreational opportunities within the financial means of all the people. The program must be flexible and readily adaptable to the changing conditions and needs of the community.

Accessibility of Facilities. The extent to which recreational facilities are used by the public is governed to a high degree by the accessibility of the facility to the group of people it is designed to serve. Most public open spaces for recreation fall under the following major classifications: (1) neighborhood playgrounds and playfields, (2) parks, and (3) reservations for specialized activities. Neighborhood playgrounds and playfields should be designed with the age group characteristics of the neighborhood as a principal consideration. Convenience of location is a very important factor with this type of facility. Normally, children will not walk more than a half mile to use playgrounds. Most children using them live within one-fourth mile. Play lots for tiny tots must be within a few blocks of the service area.

Parks, which are used largely by adults and family groups as well as by children, may serve a very wide area or an entire city. Accessibility to parks is important, but convenience does not play such an important part as it does with respect to playgrounds and playfields. In the selection of areas for parks, consideration should be given, as far as possible, to utilizing sites which may be undesirable or uneconomical for other purposes. For example, steep, rocky or wooded areas may be suitable for park purposes, but not particularly satisfactory for other uses. Quite often areas of this type are offered to the community as a gift. Although gifts are an important means of acquisition, grants should not be accepted if the use of the land for parks would entail wasteful expenditures for development and maintenance, or if the location would not be suitable for the purpose specified in the grant. Moreover, gifts should be avoided if restrictive conditions in the grant might prevent the city from developing the area according to its most appropriate use as determined by the comprehensive plan.

With respect to reservations for many specialized activities, convenience is a much less important factor. Camp sites and picnic areas, for example, may frequently be established at some distance outside the city limits, assuming state enabling legislation exists. Likewise, convenient access is not an important factor in locating facilities for certain spectator sports, as a football stadium, since persons interested in attending football games seem willing to travel unusually long distances.

Financing the Program. The means of financing public recreational programs varies with the jurisdiction and with the type of recreational activity. Although fees are quite commonly charged for the use of certain facilities, for the most part recreational programs carried out by a municipal agency are financed out of appropriations from the general fund. This means that the public officials in charge of recreation facilities and programs must justify their budget estimates in the same manner as other departments. Adequate appropriations for recreation cannot be anticipated unless the purposes and the objectives of the public recreation program are clearly defined and represent to the public and the legislative body sound public policy. In a few jurisdictions, recreation has been supported by a special millage tax. This has been urged and accepted on the grounds that it permits more rapid development of recreation which has often had to wage an uphill battle in securing recognition alongside the more established public services.[91] There are, however, certain disadvantages to financing recreation by means of the special tax, inasmuch as it may, at a given time, be defeated and thereby jeopardize the entire program.

One of the major policies of a sound public recreation program should be to make the facilities available at the lowest possible costs so that persons of low income are not excluded. There has long been a practice in many communities of supporting certain recreational activities in whole or in part by charging fees. Usually the charging of fees has been restricted to facilities such as golf courses, camps,

[91] Bromage, op. cit., p. 637.

and boat facilities which, as a rule, require a rather heavy capital investment. The relation between use and fees charged is well demonstrated in the experience with golf course operations where raising or lowering the fee has correspondingly affected the amount of play.[92]

The question of whether a particular activity should pay its way wholly or in part by fees is not a matter which can be easily resolved. The charging of fees for golf, for the rental of horses, or for boats may tend to restrict these activities to persons of higher income groups. There is some question whether or not such a practice is in the public interest. It has sometimes been felt that recreation service for children under the age of 14 should be free. For this reason, municipal swimming pools, even though involving a rather heavy capital investment, are often free to children or service is provided at a nominal charge. Whether or not a charge is justified for a particular activity is a policy matter which should be carefully weighed by each community with reference to the overall objectives of the recreational program and the restrictive effect which a charge would have upon the use of the facility.

Administration of the Program. Throughout the United States there is a marked lack of uniformity in the administrative organization for recreation. In some jurisdictions, recreation is administered by a park department; in others it is administered by a school board; and in some it is administered by a recreation agency or department. Certain advantages and disadvantages may be urged with respect to each type of administration. One of the principal advantages of having the recreation program under the park department is that, as a general rule, recreational facilities such as playgrounds, swimming pools, and golf courses are controlled and maintained by the park department. Having the recreation program under the park department makes it easier to coördinate the park management and the general recreation program. Difficulties have sometimes been encountered in that the recreational program has been subordinated to the physical maintenance of the park system.

Among the advantages of having recreational activities administered by the school board is the fact that the school board controls many buildings and grounds which are important in the recreational program, and employs trained personnel regularly engaged in the physical education of the children in which recreational activities are extremely important. Since the schools, however, are accustomed to

---

[92] *Municipal Recreation Administration,* op. cit., p. 220.

thinking in terms of children, they are not always well suited to develop and administer recreational programs for adults. Consequently there may arise conflicts of program interests. In addition, the schools usually are not in a position to administer recreation programs on a year round basis. Certain types of recreational facilities such as golf courses, swimming pools, and picnic grounds are normally outside the interests of the school boards.

The independent recreation agency or department has certain advantages in that it is in the best position to focus public attention on recreation. By having recreation as a single purpose, its attention is not diffused with the operation of schools or the maintenance of parks. In a great many instances, the independent recreation agency will be able to utilize the facilities of the schools and the park department and other branches of local government, and, at the same time, develop certain aspects of its program through facilities of its own. Whether or not the advantages lie in the single recreation agency or in a combined recreation department may vary somewhat with the size of the city. In the larger cities there would seem to be greater justification for a separation of the park department from the department of recreation.[93]

Private and Semipublic Recreational Programs.   Even though local governments, during the last few decades, have assumed a major responsibility for providing for recreational needs, nevertheless, a great part of recreation is provided by individuals for themselves and through many semipublic and private agencies. Extensive recreational programs which supplement those of governmental authorities are carried on by the Young Men's Christian Association, the Young Women's Christian Association, the Boy and Girl Scouts, the Camp Fire Girls, the Catholic Youth Organization, the Young Men's Hebrew Association, and the Young Women's Hebrew Association. Many types of recreational programs for the benefit of employees are provided by industrial plants, department stores, and other business and commercial institutions. Churches within recent years have been giving more and more attention to recreational activities and programs. Almost every community also has a variety of clubs including golf clubs, tennis clubs, social clubs, theater clubs, glee clubs, orchestral societies, garden clubs, bird clubs, camera clubs, painting clubs, craft clubs, study clubs, and many others.

Also playing a part in the community recreational life are the vari-

[93] Fisher and Bishop, op. cit., pp. 472–475.

ous commercial agencies with which recreation is a business. These represent a wide variety of interests including travel agencies, vacation resorts, hotels, theaters, radio and television stations, motion pictures, night clubs, dance halls, amusement parks, bowling alleys, and various sports events. The mere enumeration of this great variety of recreational activities emphasizes the necessity for coöperative planning. Obviously, government should not assume all the responsibility for recreation. Its basic policy, however, should be to assure reasonable recreational opportunities for all. Consequently, the public recreation program must be developed with reference to the existing private and semipublic recreational programs and with reference to the economic status and interests of the inhabitants of the community. Some communities have found it advantageous to develop advisory councils to help coördinate the various recreational programs conducted by the various agencies.

THE HOUSING PROGRAM

Today, most Americans are quite conscious of the relationship between adequate housing and the social and economic welfare. Houses provide places of shelter, places of privacy, and places for the protection of personal property. It is within the home that most of the family relationships and functions are centered. The family dwelling is the housekeeping unit. It supplies the space and facilities for sleep and relaxation, the preparation of meals, maintenance of personal cleanliness, the care of clothing, the rearing of children, and much of the recreational and social life. Studies of family life and social conditions have made it increasingly clear that poor and inadequate housing is the basic cause of many family difficulties and has created serious problems for the community as a whole. Few people any longer will argue that housing is purely a matter of private concern. Its intimate connection with health, sanitation, crime, safety, and the development of an environment which fosters good citizenship has focused attention upon housing as a public responsibility of national importance. How far that responsibility goes is a policy question that has not as yet been fully resolved.

Inadequacy.   The inadequacy of housing has been concerned with both quantity and quality. The problem of quantity is inherent in the conditions produced by our growing population. Generally speaking, people need dwelling places before they can afford the costs of ownership or rental. Consequently, construction has tended to lag behind need. However, the problem is not simply one of constructing additional units. Many houses now being used are of substandard construction, lacking in essential facilities, or are in such a state of deterioration that they are not suitable for dwelling purposes. Inadequacy of quality arises largely from the fact that technological developments have rendered many of the older houses unsatisfactory for dwellings.[94] The prolonged use of such houses for dwellings results in part from the normal lag in construction of new units, in part from the reluctance of owners to regard outworn houses as expendable, and in part from the fact that many persons of low income, living in substandard houses, would not be able to pay the costs of purchase or rent of adequate housing if available. The combination of these factors has tended to increase slum areas faster than they can be eliminated. It has been estimated that one-third of the people in the United States live in substandard houses and that one-tenth live in houses, the conditions of which constitute a menace to their health and morals.[95]

The determination of what is substandard housing is not subject to precise measurement by any criteria which have universal acceptance. There are, however, certain factors on which there is rather general agreement and which may serve as a guide for making policy decisions with respect to developing programs for slum clearance, rehabilitation, health regulations, and the compulsory repair or closing of substandard buildings. These concern the availability of bathtub or shower, private toilets, inside cold running water, heating and cooking facilities, area of living and sleeping rooms, window space, and conditions of repair as they may affect health and safety.[96]

Local Housing Legislation. Local legislation with respect to housing has been of two general types: regulatory and promotional. Regulatory legislation involves the exercise of the police power for controlling such matters as the type of construction or the use of property, and in providing protection to the purchaser or tenant. Such legislation embraces a wide variety of subjects including zoning ordinances, building codes, wiring and plumbing codes, rent ceilings, and regulation pertaining to many matters such as home finance, foreclosures, and evictions. Although the regulation of housing matters

[94] Wilbur C. Hallenbeck, *American Urban Communities* (New York: Harper & Brothers, 1951), p. 377.

[95] Fisher and Bishop, *op. cit.*, p. 486.

[96] Coleman Woodbury (ed.), *Urban Redevelopment Problems and Practices* (Chicago: University of Chicago Press, 1953), pp. 5–54.

is of great importance, it does not, of course, produce adequate housing. Housing must be affirmatively provided. To the extent that it is not provided by private initiative, government, in the public interest, must assume a promotional role. To a high degree, this means emphasis upon housing for the low income groups and concentration on the related problems of eliminating slums. The slum problem cannot be solved by clearance and redevelopment of areas unless at the same time houses are provided for the slum dweller at rental rates or purchase prices he can afford to pay.[97]

The slum problem involves both economic and social considerations. The solution must be sought with both aspects in mind. The expenditure of public funds to promote higher standards of housing needs to be weighed against the social values to be gained from adequate housing for all groups. The decision as to the income level at which public assistance should be given, what minimum standards should be established, and what type of assistance should be provided present difficult questions for policy decisions. There are no simple answers to them. The harmful effects that living in a small, dirty, and unhealthy dwelling has upon a particular family is a matter of public concern, but major public policies for the most part have been formulated on the basis of the effect such living has upon the health, morals, and safety of the public in general and with regard to the economic burden which local government must carry if it fails to take appropriate action.

Federal Aids. The slowness of municipalities to recognize their responsibilities in promoting good housing, particularly in the face of problems created by the economic depression of the 1930's, led Congress to embark upon a legislative program aimed at fostering home construction and home ownership, and in aiding and encouraging local units of government to take steps to alleviate the housing shortage. The participation of the Federal Government in housing began in 1933 with the establishment of the Federal Housing Administration system of insuring home mortgages and the Home Loan Bank system of buying mortgages from building-and-loan associations, insuring their deposits, and buying their stock.

The most important step toward promoting municipal activity in the public housing field resulted from the Housing Act of 1937 which created the United States Housing Authority whose general purpose

[97] Hugh R. Pomeroy, "Urban Housing," *Planning for Postwar Municipal Services* (Chicago: The International City Managers' Association, 1945), p. 28.

is "to assist communities to remedy unsafe and unsanitary housing conditions and the acute shortage of decent, safe, and sanitary dwellings for families of low income, and to alleviate present and recurring unemployment." The authority was given a capital stock of $1,000,000 and was authorized to borrow up to $800,000,000 for making loans and subsidies to local housing agencies, which, under the state enabling legislation, are empowered to undertake the construction and management of the housing projects. Under most state laws, the local housing authority is governed by a board of commissioners appointed by the mayor or other elected officials. Usually there are five members appointed for specific terms, one of whom is designated as chairman. In order that they may carry out the purposes for which they were created, local housing authorities are authorized to exercise the right of eminent domain in acquiring land, to make contracts, to incur financial obligations, and to exercise certain other essential powers.

The loans made by the United States Housing Authority are required to be paid back in not more than 60 years. The subsidies represent a gift by the Federal Government to make up the difference between the rents paid by tenants of the project and the actual costs of operation. This rent subsidy is intended to make it possible for families of low income to have decent, safe, and sanitary housing which they otherwise could not afford. In order to be eligible for the subsidy, the municipality must clear out as many slum dwellings as the number of units in the housing project and must contribute to the project either in cash or in tax exemption an amount equal to 20 percent of that granted by the United States Housing Authority. Tenant eligibility under the United States Housing Authority program is limited to families who do not have a net income exceeding five times the rental of the dwelling unit. While tenancy is restricted to persons of low income, the public housing program is not a relief program and relief clients are not eligible.

Slum Clearance. In 1949 Congress broadened the federal housing legislation to extend financial assistance to local agencies for the purpose of eliminating slums and blighted areas through programs of urban redevelopment. At the same time, Congress also officially recognized the importance of comprehensive planning to the housing program. As a prerequisite to the granting of financial aid, the Housing Act of 1949 requires that a determination be made by the local governing body that the redevelopment plan conform to the general plan for the development of the locality as a whole. Such a general plan must be in existence on or before the date the redevelopment plan is approved by the governing body of the locality and must prescribe the local objectives as to land uses and the improvement of traffic, public transportation, public utilities, recreational and community facilities, and other public improvements.

In 1953, President Eisenhower appointed a special committee to study the government housing policies and make recommendations to develop a new and revitalized housing program. In its comprehensive report transmitted to the President under the date of December 14, 1953, the Committee emphasized that "no single recommendation of the Committee could be considered an adequate solution in itself—the program must be closely integrated, comprehensive, and meet the twin objectives of satisfying the demand of the American people for good homes and the maintenance of a sound and growing economy." [98] To accomplish these aims, the Committee recommended action in five areas: "First, a vigorous attack on slums and a broad effort to prevent the spread of slums; second, the effective maintenance and utilization of existing houses; third, a steady increase in the volume of building of new houses; fourth, special assistance for families of low income; fifth, reorganization of the Housing Agency itself for greater efficiency and economy." [99]

The Committee pointed out that a major goal of our housing program is to wipe out slums and to check the spread of blight. A piecemeal attack will not solve the problem as occasional thrusts at slum pockets will simply push the slums into other sections. The slum problem can be solved only by attacking the whole problem of urban decay, a problem that emphasizes the necessity of greater attention to comprehensive planning. In the opinion of the Committee, programs for slum prevention, for rehabilitation of existing houses and neighborhoods, and for demolition of worn-out structures and areas must advance along a broad unified front in order to accomplish the renewal of our cities and towns.

Urban Renewal. Following the major recommendations of this Committee, the President in his message to Congress on January 25, 1954, submitted his program for meeting the housing needs of the

[98] The President's Advisory Committee on Government Housing Policies and Programs, *Recommendations on Government Housing Policies and Programs*—A Report of the President's Advisory Committee on Government Housing Policies and Programs (Washington, D.C.: U.S. Government Printing Office, December, 1953), p. 1.
[99] *Ibid.*, p. 1.

nation. These proposals as approved by Congress are embodied in the Housing Act of 1954.[100] This act broadens the basis of financial assistance for programs to eliminate blight by providing aid not only for slum clearance and urban redevelopment, but also for measures concerned with code enforcement, rehabilitation, and neighborhood conservation. This broader approach to the elimination of slums and blighting factors has been termed "urban renewal." [101] The concept of urban renewal as embraced in the Report of the President's Advisory Committee on Government Housing Policies and Programs seeks to find the solution in terms of comprehensive planning:

We must improve the conditions of life in all urban residential areas through rebuilding those parts which can no longer serve their inhabitants usefully, through improvement, rehabilitation, and adequate maintenance of structures with a remaining useful life, through protection of all homes from adverse influences, through rearrangement of streets as necessary to reroute through traffic away from residences, through opening up spaces for parks, recreation grounds, and schools, through provision of needed common services and facilities and through community organization to build morale and instill a resurgence of pride and confidence.

We must undertake good municipal housekeeping in all areas of our cities, controlling nuisances, development and occupancy, maintaining order and cleanliness and rendering adequate common services as well as services to families and individuals suffering from problems of health, dependency or maladjustment.

We must rehabilitate the financial soundness of municipal governments and make necessary readjustments in the incidence of taxation which may distort desirable community development.

Remembering that the health and soundness of a community is reflected partly in its suitability to serve the life of its people, and partly in its immanent power to replace worn-out cells, and to maintain and adapt itself to changing requirements, we should strive to create those circumstances and relationships within our cities so that they will have this constructive vitality.[102]

---

[100] Approved August 2, 1954 (P.L. 560, 83d Congress).

[101] The subject of urban redevelopment and urban renewal is more fully considered in Chap. 10.

[102] The President's Advisory Committee on Government Housing Policies and Programs, op. cit., p. 133.

Part III

THE MEANS OF PLAN IMPLEMENTATION

CHAPTER 6

Plan Implementation

TRANSFORMING PLANS INTO PUBLIC POLICY

Community development along orderly lines presupposes a comprehensive plan showing all the physical features existing and proposed in their appropriate relationship to each other, taking into account population trends, present and anticipated service and program responsibilities, political and legal necessities, and the financial resources of the community. However, the making of the comprehensive plan is not an end in itself. Until implemented by governmental or citizen action, the plan has little value. As a plan, it represents at a given time the best judgment of the planning agency as to the proper course of action to be followed. In this stage it remains flexible and is not binding, either on government or individual. A different situation arises when the plan or any element of it is officially adopted as a policy decision.

Public policy decisions are carried into effect by various methods utilizing numerous legal and procedural devices. Some of these require the direct action of government. Others are dependent upon the action taken by individuals under the compulsion of government. In other instances public policies are effectuated through voluntary, coöperative, and noncoercive action. Often, a combination of several methods or devices is needed to achieve the policy objectives of a particular program.

PUTTING PLANS INTO OPERATION

As a general proposition, plans are transformed into public policy by legislative enactment or by some administrative action taken pursuant to law. Planners have used the term "plan implementation" to designate this stage of the planning process.[1] For the most part, municipal public policy is promulgated by ordinance duly enacted by the municipal legislative authority.[2] However, plan implementation includes all the official steps taken by government to carry the plans into operation whether performed by the legislative, executive, or judicial branches.[3]

Significance of Official Sanction. When the legislative body or appropriate administrative agency places the stamp of approval upon the plan or some element of the plan, it converts the ideas, thoughts, and recommendations of the planning agency into official governmental policy. Such action frequently creates new and important legal relationships and gives a degree of finality to planning by establishing certain rights, liabilities, and obligations. For example, it is one thing for the planning agency to set forth proposals for the location of new streets, parks, and public buildings, but it is a different thing from the standpoint of legal effect for the legislative body to adopt an "official map" on which precise street lines are laid out, the effect of which, under law, may be to deny owners of the land on which the street lines fall the right to erect buildings or structures within the boundaries thereof. It is one thing, also, to work up maps and plans for the purpose of guiding the most appropriate land use in a community, but a substantially different thing, from the standpoint of legal relationships, for the legislative body to adopt a zoning ordinance which prescribes a use for one piece of land which is different from that which may be made of an adjoining piece of land. In a similar way, the establishment of specific requirements by platting and subdivision regulations gives legal effect to plans which otherwise would remain unofficial and unexecuted. These new legal relationships created by plan adoption necessitate that government set up

[1] Other terms are "plan execution" and "plan effectuation."

[2] "The enactment of an ordinance ordinarily involves the following steps and proceedings: its reduction into a written form with more or less standard parts; its passage by the municipal legislative body, and action upon it by the mayor or other chief municipal magistrate; possible passage over his veto in the event he disapproves it; or its adoption through exercise of the initiative or referendum; and steps and proceedings relating to its attesting, recording, publication and custody, calculated to make and keep it an authenticated public document that establishes the legislative determination of the municipal corporation." Eugene McQuillin, *The Law of Municipal Corporations* (Chicago: Callaghan & Company, 1949), (3d ed.) Vol. 5, Sec. 16.01, p. 159.

[3] In a sense it also includes the acts of private individuals undertaken in compliance with decided public policy.

administrative machinery and institute administrative practices in order to insure that the policies decided upon will be carried into effect. The principal legal devices and administrative practices which planners have found most successful for carrying plans into operation are the subjects discussed in this and the succeeding chapters.

Timing of Plan Implementation. The significance of legislative action giving legal effect to the comprehensive plan or some element of it makes the timing of such action a matter of considerable consequence. If, for example, the official map or the zoning ordinance is adopted prematurely for a given area, it may freeze upon that part of the community a character which, in the light of unforeseen developments or more mature judgment, will appear unwise. On the other hand, the failure to take official action on some element of the plan in proper time may result in unplanned development of an area, which will create difficulties and make it costly when elements of the comprehensive plan are implemented at a future time. Therefore, the optimum timing for official action effectuating any element of the plan is a matter of considerable importance.

POWERS OF GOVERNMENT FOR PLAN IMPLEMENTATION

The primary basis of plan implementation is governmental authority. Governmental authority is exercised through a number of important, long-established powers, including the financial powers of taxation, appropriation, and borrowing, the power of eminent domain, the police power, the licensing power, and the penal power. These powers are possessed by governments whether they engage in conscious planning or not. Although planning as such adds nothing to the substantive powers of government, it may, nevertheless, afford the occasion for the exercise of certain powers and may determine whether or not these powers are exercised wisely or unwisely. The planner cannot develop an intelligent approach to the solution of planning problems without an understanding of the nature of these powers and the legal limitations that restrict their use. The major powers of importance in plan implementation are briefly considered in this section for the purpose of identifying their distinguishing characteristics. Their nature and use are further amplified in the following discussion of the different means of plan implementation.

Financial Powers. In order to perform its functional responsibilities, every government must have power to raise and expend money. Among the major financial powers commonly conferred upon municipalities are the power to raise revenue, the power to borrow, the power to incur indebtedness, the power to make expenditures, the power to collect and distribute funds, and the power to make appropriations. These powers are exercised subject to legislative grants of authority and limitations contained in the constitution and laws of the state and the charter of the corporation.

The ordinary revenues of municipalities include the proceeds from (1) taxes, (2) special assessments, (3) licenses and fees, (4) profits on enterprises, (5) borrowing, (6) trust funds, and (7) bequests. The most important of these sources is that of taxation. By definition, a tax is a compulsory contribution for the support of government. For the collection of taxes, the power of government is needed to compel payment. Unlike the power of eminent domain, no compensation is required to be given to the owner from whom the property is taken by taxation. A tax differs from a special assessment or a fee in that it is collected without reference to any benefit received by the taxpayer.

The power of taxation is an attribute of sovereignty which rests upon force and authority. Except as restricted by constitution, the power to tax is unlimited. Municipal corporations have no inherent power of taxation. Municipal taxes are imposed only under authority delegated by the state legislature.[4] The taxing power is subject to the limitations of due process of law which protects the taxpayer against the use of power in an arbitrary or discriminatory manner. Under the guarantees of due process: (1) Taxes must be levied for a public purpose; (2) the governing body levying the tax must have jurisdiction over the subject matter of the tax; (3) due procedure must be followed in levying and collecting the tax; and (4) there must be no arbitrary discrimination or classification.

The power to borrow money and create indebtedness cannot be exercised unless it is conferred expressly or exists by necessary implication. The power to borrow cannot be implied from the usual grant of power to incur indebtedness for conducting local government in providing for the customary needs and conveniences.[5] The power to borrow, if granted at all, is usually surrounded by a number of constitutional and statutory limitations. Such limitations may be concerned with the amount of the debt incurred either in terms of a fixed sum or an amount based upon a percentage of assessed valuation. In some instances the limitation on borrowing may relate to purpose.

---

[4] *Louisville v. Babb,* 75 F. (2d) 162 (1935).
[5] McQuillin, *op. cit.,* Vol. 16, Sec. 44.05, pp. 13–20.

Commonly, borrowing is prohibited unless approved by vote of the people.

All indebtedness may not be funded—that is, evidenced by bonds or other municipal obligations providing for fixed time of payment and payment of interest. Such other indebtedness is termed "floating indebtedness." The power to incur such indebtedness is conferred by express legislative delegation or from the grant of other express powers which cannot be exercised without the incurring of indebtedness or the expenditure of money.[6] All expenditures of public money and the indebtedness created thereby must be for a public purpose.[7]

The power of appropriation relates to the setting apart a designated sum of money for a particular purpose or purposes. Like other financial powers, the power to make appropriations is commonly defined and limited by constitution and statute. The transfer of money from one municipal fund to another is usually not considered to be an appropriation. In most jurisdictions money may not be paid out of the treasury until appropriated by law, and no debt or liability may be incurred unless an appropriation has been previously made. Appropriations must be made for corporate and public purposes. Appropriations made for a particular purpose cannot be used for a different purpose.

Eminent Domain. The power of eminent domain is an essential governmental power used for the purpose of taking private property needed for a public use. Literally the term signifies paramount ownership. In practice it is a power to acquire by condemnation not only land or easements, but also intangible property such as franchises and contracts where needed to carry on the necessary functions of government. Formerly the "taking of property" was restricted to the physical appropriation of property. Today, however, it is generally held that property is taken if a person is deprived of certain rights to property even though title and possession are not disturbed. Eminent domain is an inherent power of the sovereign state. It is not conferred by the constitution or statute but rather is limited thereby.[8] Under the power of eminent domain, the sovereign state may take any private property within its jurisdiction for public use without the consent of the owner, subject to the condition of payment of just compensation in accordance with the methods prescribed by law. The

[6] *Georges Township v. Union Trust Co.*, 293 P. St. 364, 143 Atl. 10 (1928).
[7] *James v. Seattle*, 22 Wash. 654, 62 Pac. 84 (1900).
[8] *State v. Superior Court*, 77 Wash. 585, 137 Pac. 994 (1914).

power of eminent domain is not inherent in municipal corporations but must be conferred on them by law.

The power of eminent domain is often confused with other powers, particularly the police power and the power of taxation. It is necessary to an understanding of these powers that the distinguishing characteristics be recognized. The police power is essentially regulatory. It may restrict the use of property or even destroy it because it is harmful to the public welfare, but it does not appropriate a property right because it is useful. However, unreasonable restrictions placed upon the use of property or an unreasonable destruction of property under the guise of the police power may be held to constitute a taking of property, and the payment of compensation is required.[9]

The power of taxation differs from the power of eminent domain in that, under the taxing power, a contribution to the support of government is required of all persons similarly situated in proportion to their share as provided by law. Under eminent domain, a certain piece of property of an individual is taken by government because that particular property is needed for a public purpose. Under eminent domain, the person who is required to give up his property must be justly compensated. No compensation is required to be given in the case of property taken under the taxing power.

The Police Power.   The most comprehensive and pervasive of all powers of government is that known as the police power. The word "police" is derived from the Greek word *polis* which means "city." In its original and broadest sense, the term "police power" denotes the inherent power of every sovereignty to govern men and things.[10] As commonly used today, the police power is not conceived to be all governmental power. In its more limited sense, it is the power to establish the social order, to protect the life and health of persons, to secure their existence and comfort, and to safeguard them in the enjoyment of private and social life and the beneficial use of their property.[11] It includes the power of government to regulate the conduct of individuals subject to its jurisdiction in their relations toward each other and the manner in which each shall use his property when regulation becomes necessary in the public interest. The police power embraces regulations designed to promote the public convenience and general prosperity as well as the public health, morals, and safety.

[9] *Milwaukee Electric Railway Company v. Milwaukee*, 209 Wis. 656, 245 N.W. 856 (1932).
[10] *Munn v. Illinois*, 94 U.S. 113, 24 L.Ed. 77 (1877).
[11] *Holmwood v. Wolfe Oil Co.*, 232 Ala. 634, 169 So. 288 (1936).

Although it may be used to suppress that which is offensive, disorderly, or unsanitary, it is not limited to such purposes and may be broadly used to promote the general welfare of the state or the community.

The police power must be clearly distinguished from the administration of criminal law and from police regulations of the police department. Likewise, it should not be confused with the power of eminent domain or the power of taxation. The police power is not primarily concerned with the punishment of offenses against society as is the penal power. As distinguished from eminent domain and taxation, the police power is concerned with regulating the conduct of individuals and groups and their uses of men and things in the interest of the public welfare, but normally does not take their possessions into public ownership. If, however, property is taken under a valid and reasonable exercise of the police power, no compensation need be paid to the owner as in the case of eminent domain unless it is expressly provided for by statute. While these powers are clearly distinguishable in legal theory, no classification is perfect and in their application they frequently overlap and are often used in conjunction with each other.

Although the nature of the police power is easily understood, it is not susceptible of exact definition. The reason is that the power is not something that is rigid and definitely fixed. By its nature it must be flexible and elastic in order to meet new conditions resulting from shifts of population and changes in our economic and social order. The police power is not unlimited. It is subject to the constitutional limitations of due process of law, the equal protection of the laws, and other constitutional restraints upon the arbitrary exercise of powers of government. In the justification of any regulation under the police power, three questions are commonly raised:

1. Is there a public interest to justify the regulation?
2. Does the regulation involve a constitutional right?
3. Is the regulation reasonable?

The scope of municipal legislation and administrative action under the police power encompasses an extremely wide range of subject matter. Among these are such fields of activity as the prevention and suppression of nuisances, prohibiting vice and gambling, regulating the sale of intoxicating liquors, establishing hours of business, regulating the disposal of wastes, controlling land use through comprehensive zoning, regulating businesses, occupations, and trades, safeguarding the purity of food and drugs, protecting against the hazards of fire and casualty, establishing building, health, and safety codes, controlling traffic and transportation, destroying diseased animals or dangerous buildings, prohibiting activities determined to be nuisances, and regulating numerous other phases of our economic and social life.[12] No other power of government is so far-reaching with respect to the relationships between government and the individual's personal and property interests.

Licensing Power. The licensing power, although closely related to and sometimes embraced within the police power, is a separate and distinct power. A license is a permit or privilege to do that which otherwise would be unlawful. A privilege for which a license is required signifies a special right which may be enjoyed only by virtue of the license and one which does not belong to persons in general. In a broad sense, the licensing power includes the issuance of both licenses and permits and the imposing of fees and taxes therefor.[13]

Licenses and permits may be issued for a wide variety of purposes. The primary functions for which they are issued are: " (1) A means of passing in advance upon the legality of a proposed business activity or thing, (2) A mode of permanently registering businesses, activities, things and persons, (3) facilitation of inspection and regulation, and (4) financing the cost of these other functions." [14] Municipal licensing requirements must be for a public purpose. In order to be valid they must be definite and certain, reasonable and uniform in their operation.[15]

License fees may be imposed for purposes of regulation or purposes of taxation or both depending upon the grant of authority from the state legislature. If the license fee is imposed under the police power for purposes of regulation, the amount of the fee must not exceed a reasonable amount to cover the cost of issuing the license and inspecting and regulating the business or activity. A license fee levied for revenue purposes is not so restricted as to amount. When levied for revenue alone, license fees may be sustained under the taxing power. The courts will not uphold the validity of a revenue tax levied under the guise of licensing under the police power.[16] Since the distinction is not always clear in the language of statutes and ordinances,

[12] McQuillin, op. cit., Vol. 6, Sec. 24.01, pp. 438–440.
[13] McQuillin, op. cit., Vol. 9, Sec. 26.01, pp. 8–9.
[14] McQuillin, op. cit., Vol. 9, Sec. 26.02, p. 10.
[15] Tucson v. Stewart, 45 Ariz. 36, 40 P. (2d) 72 (1935).
[16] North Star Line v. Grand Rapids, 259 Mich. 654, 244 N.W. 192 (1932).

the matter must frequently be resolved by judicial interpretation. Even though license fees are for revenue only, they are to be distinguished from ordinary taxes since they are levied for a benefit or privilege to which the person paying the fee would not otherwise be entitled.[17]

Penal Power.   The power of municipal corporations to enforce its laws by penalties is known as the penal power. It is a distinct power of government, although it is often exercised in conjunction with the police power and other powers. The essential characteristic of the penal power is the inflicting of punishment upon individuals for acts against the law. Punishment frequently but not always implies, more or less, disgrace to the one punished. Punishment under the penal power may take a variety of forms or combinations thereof. In some instances, the punishment may be mild, as in the case of a small fine, or it may be more serious through the imposition of a large fine, the destruction of property, forfeiture of certain rights or property, imprisonment, or even capital punishment. Thus, the function of the penal power is to provide sanctions which serve to back up other powers.[18]

In many respects the penal power resembles the police power, the power of taxation, and the power of eminent domain. The power, being regulatory, has characteristics of the police power. Since fines and penalties add revenues to the treasury, it partakes of the nature of taxation. To the extent that property such as gambling devices may be seized under forfeiture provisions, the power is similar to taking by eminent domain. However, the requisites which characterize these several powers are not present. The principal purpose of imposing fines, forfeitures, or restraints on liberty is to exact penalties for wrongful conduct. Normally penalties are imposed only after conviction by a court of law.

As a general rule, municipalities have power to enforce ordinances by penalties only if that power has been expressly conferred by law or authorized by implication.[19] Penalty provisions in ordinances are strictly construed, as is the power of a municipal corporation to im-

---

[17] *Sonora v. Curtin,* 137 Cal. 583, 70 Pac. 674 (1902).
Guntersville v. Wright, 223 Ala. 349, 135 So. 634 (1931).
   For a detailed discussion of the licensing power of cities see, Ernest H. Campbell and Sidney Coleman, *Licensing by Washington Cities* (Seattle: Bureau of Governmental Research and Services, University of Washington, December, 1951), Report No. 117.
[18] William Anderson and Edward W. Weidner, *State and Local Government in the United States* (New York: Henry Holt and Company, Inc., 1951), pp. 96–97.
[19] McQuillin, *op. cit.,* Vol. 5, Sec. 17.03, pp. 349–350.

pose a penalty in the ordinance. Wherever a particular penalty is prescribed, that penalty and no other may be imposed.[20]

IMPLEMENTATION BASED ON DIRECT GOVERNMENTAL ACTION

In their corporate capacities, local governments carry on a great volume of business transactions. Government has become the custodian of a considerable amount of the people's property through the ownership of buildings, land, and various types of facilities. In supplying services, local governments construct, maintain, and operate many kinds of enterprises. By these means many of the major policies of government are carried out. The degree to which direct government action is utilized varies with municipalities to the extent that services and functions have been made public responsibilities as distinguished from private enterprises.

THE ACQUISITION OF PROPERTY

In almost every municipality, government is directly responsible for providing many public buildings and facilities for transacting public business and carrying out public services. Thus, the action taken by the city council in locating, designing, and constructing the city hall, public libraries, civic center, fire stations, parks, playgrounds, or other public structures and facilities in accordance with the comprehensive plan is the essential mode of plan implementation. To the extent that government owns and operates the public utilities, transit system, port facilities, or furnishes specialized services, plan accomplishment through direct governmental action is correspondingly enlarged. In order to provide public facilities and services, a municipality must acquire both land and personal property.[21]

Methods and Practices of Property Acquisition. Municipalities may become the owner of land and other property not only through purchase or condemnation, but also as a result of gift, dedication, or devise. In the United States, the general rule is that land and other property which is acquired out of public revenues can be lawfully acquired only if it is for a public use. There is nothing to prevent the

---

[20] *Alameda County v. Freitas*, 8 Cal. App. (2d) 653, 48 P. (2d) 165 (1935).

[21] The general rule applicable to municipal powers is that municipal corporations may exercise only those powers which are granted in express words, and those that necessarily are fairly implied in, or incident to, the powers expressly granted and those which are essential to the accomplishment of the declared objectives or purposes of the corporation, not merely those which are convenient, but those which are indispensable.

city from accepting and holding land for other than a public purpose providing public tax money is not expended for acquiring and holding the land for such purpose.[22] If a municipality accepts land as a result of gift, dedication, or devise, it may use it only in accordance with the conditions contained in the grant. However, the city could not legally accept property to be used for any purpose inconsistent with the city charter, state law, or provisions of the constitution. In the event land is acquired by a municipality, subject to restrictions in the grant, it may, under certain circumstances, be possible for the city to remove these restrictions through the exercise of the power of eminent domain.[23] However, this power may be exercised only providing the use to be made of the land is for a public purpose.

The phrase "public purpose" is difficult to define. In general it relates to a purpose which is intimately related to, if not identified with, the general welfare of the inhabitants of a politically organized community.[24] The question of public purpose arises most frequently in connection with the exercise of the powers of taxation and eminent domain and when municipalities undertake to provide services which prior thereto had been furnished by private enterprise. Differing views among the courts in the several states have led to varying results according to the jurisdiction. In certain instances these differences of interpretation have been based upon specific wording of state constitutions, but in others upon the common law of the state. Sometimes the term "public purpose" may be given one meaning under the provisions of the federal constitution and a somewhat different meaning under the state constitution. Final determination of the meaning under the federal constitution, of course, rests with the United States Supreme Court. It is only natural that with the growing responsibility of government to provide public services, many activities which were at one time regarded as private in character have now come to be regarded by the courts as being for a public purpose.

Since property does not consist of "things," but rather of the right to the use and enjoyment of things, legal questions are often raised

[22] Flavel Shurtleff, *Carrying Out the City Plan*, The Practical Application of American Law in the Execution of City Plans (New York: Survey Associates, Inc., 1914), pp. 3–4.

[23] As to the right to dispose of property held under use restrictions, see Association of Washington Cities, *Acquisition, Conveyance, Leasing, and Condemnation of Real Property of Cities and Towns*, Information Bulletin No. 135 (Seattle: University of Washington, July 14, 1951).

[24] Ernst B. Schulz, *American City Government* (New York: Stackpole and Heck, Inc., 1949), pp. 77–79.

as to what constitutes a "taking of property." [25] Thus, the courts are frequently called upon to determine whether a city, which, as the result of construction, has flooded land, restricted access to property, or cut off light or air, has taken property which requires the payment of just compensation. The taking of property does not in all instances require a transfer of title. Many states hold that there has been a taking if there has been damage to property which would be actionable if caused by an individual. Courts, however, have been reluctant to accept the view that damages caused by smoke or noise constitute a taking of property which requires compensation. Logically, however, there seems to be no sound distinction between damage from such causes and many other types of damage for which compensation is given. If the court finds there has been a taking, normally the just compensation to which a person is entitled is the market value of the property. Where only a portion of a man's property is taken, the court may consider the effect of such taking to the remainder. In some instances, benefits as well as damages may result from the partial taking. The court is entitled to weigh these benefits and damages in determining the amount of just compensation.

In acquiring land for public improvements, municipal officials have a public responsibility to avoid excessive costs and to distribute costs in an equitable manner. The two principal methods of land acquisition are through purchase and condemnation. The acquisition by purchase as a result of negotiated sale has been sharply limited in most jurisdictions. Where negotiated purchase is authorized, frequently the city is at a disadvantage in buying in the open market because of the likelihood that private owners, knowing that the city needs the land, will hold out for higher prices. Consequently, the system most widely used for land acquisition is condemnation under the power of eminent domain. In order to insure that municipalities are not paying excessive prices for land, enabling legislation has been provided in most states setting up detailed requirements for condemnation procedures.

The principle of eminent domain, under which land is condemned, is based on the postulate that the needs of the community should take priority over the wishes or interests of the individual citizen. The procedural requirements may vary from state to state, but the usual process begins with the preparation of a plan by the city engineer

[25] John Mabry Mathews, *The American Constitutional System* (New York: McGraw-Hill Book Company, Inc., 1940), pp. 454–455.

which, after approval by the appropriate authorities, is submitted to the city council for approval. Following this approval, the procedure usually is to turn the matter over to the city law department which prepares public notices and arranges such hearings as may be required by law. At these hearings there are opportunities for protests and intervention. In some states the hearings are submitted to eminent domain commissions or other statutory authority; in others, the action goes directly to the courts. In general, the same procedure is followed whether the city acquires the property in fee simple or whether it acquires only a right of way over the property, leaving the title in private ownership.

If the costs of acquisition and development of public property are to be distributed in an equitable manner, this should be accomplished through a well-planned capital improvements program based upon a long-range financial plan. Among the objectives of long-term planning for public buildings and facilities should be the acquisition of sites in anticipation of future needs. The timely reservation or acquisition of such sites can often avoid the burden of costly condemnation proceedings which inevitably result from rising real estate values or the removal of structures.

A few cities, notably Milwaukee, have had success with the organization of real estate departments created to purchase and sell land for the city. Guided by the comprehensive plan, such a department may devote its attention to acquisition of land offered by voluntary sale, purchases of tax delinquent land, and the exchange of land deemed undesirable for municipal purposes for other lands considered more desirable. By information gained through its activities, such departments may be helpful in saving money for the city by suggesting minor shifts in proposed site locations which will not upset the objectives of the plan while permitting acquisition in more advantageous terms. By this method it may be possible to reduce considerably the need for use of the power of eminent domain. Experience with such departments has not been extensive, and their legality may be open to question in some states.

Land Acquisition for Public Housing and Urban Redevelopment. The elimination of blighted areas and slums has presented special problems which, in most instances, have been solved by the creation of housing authorities and urban redevelopment corporations. Urban redevelopment may be carried out through the use of private corporations or public agencies. Some municipalities have undertaken redevelopment programs through private corporations which have been delegated the right to condemn and acquire property for redevelopment purposes. Under other redevelopment programs, the property is first acquired by public corporations with public funds and is then sold or leased to private corporations for redevelopment.

Under some redevelopment plans, acquisition of property, replanning of the area, and the construction of replanned structures is carried out by public authority. In other instances, the public authority merely acquires the property and replans the area and then sells the lots to private interests under proper covenants or other controls for the erection of suitable structures. The variations in these plans may be governed to a large extent by the interests of private individuals and the availability of private capital. The main reason for creating redevelopment corporations is to make possible the assembly of land on a proper scale to remove the existing blight and replan it in a way to keep it immune from the blighting influence of adjacent unreconstructed areas. Private corporations, without power of eminent domain, are faced with an almost impossible task of land assembly since one property owner who refuses to convey may defeat the whole project.

Although governmental acquisition is usually necessary to redevelop blighted areas, normally ownership and management of redeveloped properties are not the objectives of public policy. The general practice is to restore the reconstructed property to private ownership under appropriate controls necessary to protect the area from future blight. Slum clearance projects which result in the construction of low-cost public housing may more appropriately remain under public ownership and operation.

Special Problems of Street Rights of Way. The acquisition of property for streets, sidewalks, and parking strips presents certain special problems. Usually the municipality does not acquire the property for streets in fee simple, but rather acquires rights of way or easements. All the functions which streets perform for communities are not readily visible to the eye. Most people realize that streets carry the surface traffic of automobiles, motor buses, trucks, taxicabs, delivery wagons, streetcars, and crowds of pedestrians. It is apparent also that the street provides the location for street lights, hydrants, utility poles, signs, and various types of public installations. The average citizen, however, often is not fully aware of the fact that below the ground, streets provide for water mains, sewers, wire conduits, subways, and many other types of public utilities. Furthermore, streets often provide the main channel through which light and air come to basement shops and dwellings. They also frequently serve as playgrounds for children. Thus, a street has three dimensions: the surface, the subsurface, and the overhead.[26] Consequently, street development becomes one of the most important means by which public policy of planning is carried out through direct governmental action.

Where the city does not own fee simple title to the street, but acquires only a right of way or easement, the abutting property owner usually retains title to one-half of the street with use limited to the city's rights under the dedication of the street area for street purposes. Hence, the abutting property owner may beautify the parking strip with trees and acquire an interest in them that the law will protect against anyone who injures or destroys them without lawful authority. Nevertheless, an abutting property owner plants trees in the street subject to the rights of the public, and he must make certain that they are maintained so as not to obstruct or impair free or full use of the sidewalk or street by the public.[27] Sometimes the taking of only a right of way or easement for streets has been found not to be sound public policy because of difficult legal problems that arise in connection with placing pipes and conduits in the street or in making some other use of the street. If these uses are not consistent with the purpose of the easement, it may be necessary for the city to proceed further by condemnation which would require the public to pay further compensation.

The property or right of way for streets is acquired by one of three methods: (1) dedication, (2) purchase, or (3) condemnation. Land or rights of way are acquired either when new streets are laid out or when old thoroughfares are widened. Dedication is a method which is usually used when streets are laid out in newly opened suburban areas. The municipality which approves a plat may at the time of plat approval require the subdivider of the tract to make adequate reservations for streets. The usual procedure is to require that the land needed for street purposes be dedicated to public use in return for the permission to develop and sell building lots. By this device,

[26] William Bennett Munro, *Municipal Administration* (New York: The Macmillan Company, 1935), p. 260.

[27] Joshua H. Vogel and Ernest H. Campbell, *Planting, Maintenance, and Removal of Trees from Streets* (Seattle: Bureau of Governmental Research and Services, University of Washington, June, 1950), Report No. 111, p. 33.

the city may carry out its street plan through acquisition of adequate rights of way. As a rule, very little street area is ever obtained by dedication in the older and more densely settled parts of the city. Consequently, when land is needed in a downtown section for street widening or for other public purposes, it can usually be obtained only through direct purchase or by condemnation proceedings.

Very often existing streets prove to be inadequate to carry the traffic load, and the city finds it necessary to establish new building lines and acquire additional rights of way. The establishment of building setback lines may not always be construed to be a taking of property for which the payment of compensation is required. As will be indicated subsequently, in some jurisdictions building line setbacks may, under some circumstances, be established under the police power as a restriction upon the erection of structures upon private property in favor of a public use. When the city is ready to widen the street, it buys or condemns the remaining rights and the land lying between the building line and the existing line. Where the building lines are established by the local legislative body under the police power, the lines are protected by withholding the building permits for structures that would be in violation of them. When a building line lies within the area occupied by an existing structure, special problems are presented with respect to removal. When building lines are established under the power of eminent domain, the compensation for easements may be substantially equal to the entire value of the property over which the easements are taken, or it may be nominal, or there may actually be no compensation if the resulting benefits and damages are found to be about equal.

Public Works

In carrying public policies into effect, every large city must perform many activities concerned with the construction, maintenance, and operation of physical facilities. Although the type and character of "public works" varies from city to city, the term commonly includes such physical facilities as streets, bridges, sidewalks, viaducts, public buildings, sewers and sewage disposal systems, refuse collection and disposal systems, comfort stations, drinking fountains, parks and playgrounds, docks, wharves, cemeteries, markets, airports, water supply systems, and other utilities. In order to facilitate the most efficient and convenient use of such facilities, public works responsibilities usually require the performance of a number of related services, including such matters as street lighting, street naming, erection of street signs, house numbering, traffic engineering, planting and care of trees, street cleaning, snow removal, leasing and control of property, and servicing and repair of public equipment. To carry out the public works functions, city departments must be equipped to perform many engineering and business activities, including mapping, surveying, designing of structures, preparation of cost estimates, letting and supervising of contracts, and the actual performance of construction, maintenance, and management operations.[28]

Construction. There are two principal methods commonly employed for constructing public works projects. One method is by "force account" which means that the city performs the construction work by using laborers from the city payroll. The other method is by "contract" whereby a job is performed by a private contractor in accordance with previous agreement between the city and the contractor as to specifications and costs. Where work such as street paving, bridge construction, or building is done under contract, the city prepares the specifications and calls for bids. State laws, charters, and ordinances commonly require that contracts be awarded only after competitive bidding. Before submitting their bids, contractors are usually required to qualify by supplying evidence of their ability to perform the job by showing their experience with such type of work, the adequacy of their machinery, the nature of their organization, qualifications of their personnel, and their financial resources. Before entering upon the performance of the contract, a contractor should be required to furnish a surety or performance bond to guarantee performance in accordance with the terms of the agreement and compliance with industrial insurance codes, safety regulations, and other state or local laws. The purpose of these legal requirements is to protect the public against the hazards of collusive bidding, the rigging of specifications, the playing of favorites, and also to insure that the job will be done at lowest cost. Where work is undertaken by private contract, it is essential that the public works department keep its own inspector on the job to check continuously to determine whether or not the work is being done according to specifications. Since, here again, there is danger of collusion, it is most important that the honesty and integrity of the inspector be carefully determined.

[28] John M. Pfiffner, *Municipal Administration* (New York: The Ronald Press Company, 1940), pp. 435–451.

There is no clear rule as to when work should be done by contract and when by force account. Although some cities maintain equipment and plant facilities to enable the city to do a sizable share of its construction by force account, the trend is toward performance of all major construction by contract. However, on a particular project it may sometimes be found advantageous to perform part of the work by contract and other parts by using the city's own equipment and workmen. The method used may depend upon the size of the project, the number of projects being carried on at that time, and availability of labor and of interested contractors. Obviously, it would not be economical for a city to maintain large and expensive equipment and specialized man power for projects which would be undertaken only occasionally.[29] Some of the larger cities have found it good business to maintain a reasonably well-staffed construction division which is equipped to compete with private contractors in order to keep bids within bounds. Quite often the practice is that the city division will submit bids in competition with the bids of the private contractor.

Maintenance.   If municipalities are to perform their functions satisfactorily, public buildings, public facilities, and public equipment must be kept in a proper state of repair. Maintenance work, like construction work, may be carried out either by force account or by contract. Quite often cities that are faced with difficulties in balancing their budgets may seek to postpone expenditures for maintenance and repair. The results of such action may not be apparent to the public for several years. Many cities have found to their dismay that failure to finance an adequate maintenance program often results in high replacement costs which are greatly in excess of what the cost of normal maintenance would have been. A sound maintenance program is essential to protecting the capital investment which the public has in its buildings, facilities, and equipment.

Some jurisdictions have found that high maintenance costs of highways and other public works may be reduced in many instances by undertaking rather extensive rehabilitation programs. In the case of older streets which were not designed and constructed for modern traffic conditions, maintenance costs may be disproportionately high unless steps are taken to bring them up to modern standards of width, alignment, curvature, and surfacing to accommodate modern high

[29] Arthur W. Bromage, *Municipal Government and Administration* (New York: Appleton-Century-Crofts, Inc., 1950), p. 555.

speed traffic.[30] Cities have sometimes found it to their advantage to establish some kind of central management of the purchase, use, maintenance, and disposal of land and buildings. Although each department under such arrangement exercises care over the particular buildings or facilities which it uses, central control makes it possible for city officials to determine whether the best possible use is being made of the property which it owns. This helps to avoid the situation where one department is seeking to acquire new property for its use, while some other department may have control over property or facilities which it does not need. The placing of maintenance under centralized control results in keeping public property in a more satisfactory state of repair.[31]

Operation. While every city engages in numerous operational functions, the extent of these activities is increased with the number of utilities that are publicly owned and operated. Of cities of over 5000 population, approximately three-fourths own their own water supply and distribution systems, or water distribution systems, and about half operate sewage treatment plants. A substantially smaller percentage own or operate other types of utilities. Approximately 20 percent own electric generation and distribution systems or electric distribution, and a slightly higher percentage own and operate airports. An additional number of cities own airports, but instead of operating them, lease them to private operators or to another governmental agency.[32] The importance of utility operation as a means of implementing the comprehensive plan is the same whether the utility is owned and operated by the public or by a private corporation. In the one instance, however, plan implementation is achieved through direct action of government, whereas under private operation it is achieved through regulation by franchise or as otherwise provided by law.

IMPLEMENTATION BASED ON GOVERNMENTAL REGULATION

Not all elements of the comprehensive plan can be implemented by direct action of government. Some are carried into effect by the

---

[30] John H. Swanberg, "Rehabilitating Old Concrete Pavements to Get a Second Generation of Service," *Public Works*, Vol. 86, No. 5, p. 75, May, 1955.

[31] Marguerite J. Fisher and Donald G. Bishop, *Municipal and Other Local Governments* (Englewood Cliffs, N.J.: Prentice-Hall, Inc., 1950), p. 534.

[32] *The Municipal Year Book, 1954* (Chicago: The International City Managers' Association, 1954), p. 79.

actions of private individuals taken pursuant to regulatory controls established by government to insure conformity with the plan. Among the controls which are of special concern to the planner are those represented by the official map ordinance, the zoning ordinance, subdivision regulations, building and construction codes, architectural controls, health and sanitation codes, licensing of commercial activities, and nuisance abatement. While each of these devices is designed to accomplish a particular purpose, all of them are most effective in plan implementation when they are used to supplement and reinforce each other. If a community lacks authority to establish these controls, or if having the authority fails properly to apply and enforce them, it cannot hope to direct growth of the community in an orderly manner.

For the most part, regulatory controls are carried out under the police power. The principle on which the police power is based is that all individual rights of liberty and property are held subject to such reasonable limitations and regulations as are necessary for the protection of the general welfare. The exercise of the police power must, however, be in harmony with the constitutional guarantees of due process which seek to maintain a proper balance between the necessities of governmental regulation, on the one hand, and the protection of individual and civil rights on the other. Since every exercise of the police power interferes to some extent with individual rights, the constitutional question becomes one of whether the regulation is reasonably necessary to the promotion of public health, public safety, public morals, and the general welfare. A definite boundary between the liberty of the individual protected by due process and the police power of the state is a rather difficult line to draw. The constitutional limitations upon the exercise of the police power are to be found from an examination of the judicial decisions with respect to specific types of regulations and with regard to particular policy objectives.

THE OFFICIAL MAP ORDINANCE

Planners have long been concerned with the problem of how they can control the building of structures in the beds of proposed streets and other sites intended for public use prior to the time that the city is in a position to acquire the land or rights of way. If such controls cannot be established, the cost of future developments may be prohibitive and the best type of land utilization may be defeated. One of the most successful devices for accomplishing this purpose has been the official map ordinance. Under this type of ordinance, projected future streets or other public areas are designated on an "official map" which is recorded. The legal effect of the recording of this map is to prohibit the erection within the boundary lines of the designated areas, of buildings and structures which would have to be removed at the time the street is opened or the area developed.

Nature and Purpose. A number of states have enacted official map and building permit acts which contain detailed legislation enabling the legislative authority of municipalities to adopt official maps establishing the location and widths of streets and the location and extent of sites for certain other proposed public improvements. It is common for such acts to provide that no permit shall be issued for any building or structure in the bed of any street, drainage right of way, or other public area shown on the official map. Some acts include special provisions with respect to reservations located within the areas of plats of proposed subdivisions. The function of the official map is not to compel a dedication of land for streets without payment of compensation, but rather to prevent the owner from building on the areas which the city proposes to acquire at some future date. The primary purpose of the restriction upon use is to keep the municipality from having to pay excessively high acquisition costs for the land or rights of way when the city is in a position to acquire them.[33]

In a great number of jurisdictions, the official map ordinance pertains only to streets. In some others the act also seeks to control building within the mapped areas of sites designated for parks, playgrounds, and certain other public uses. The municipal map act recently adopted by New Jersey enables municipalities to reserve not only the location and width of streets and drainage rights of way but also areas for parks and playgrounds.[34] The reservation of areas for parks and playgrounds in subdivisions is subject to the limitation that the municipality must purchase the land or institute condemnation proceedings for such land within one year after approval of the final plat or within such further time as agreed by the applying party.[35]

[33] Kenneth T. Leque, "Advantages of Official Map," *The Municipality*, Vol. 50, No. 3, p. 49, March, 1955.

[34] Official Map and Building Permit Act (1953) Chap. 434, Laws of 1953 (New Jersey).

[35] See Harry E. Bernstein, "The Impact of the New Official Map on Municipalities," *New Jersey Municipalities*, Vol. XXXII, No. 2, pp. 23–24, February, 1955, and *Legis-*

Otherwise the applying party is not bound to observe the reservation.

Preparation and Adoption. The preparation of the official map is a responsibility that usually devolves upon the engineering department. The map should be prepared after careful engineering surveys have been made, and should show not only the street plan but also the recorded land subdivision plats and the planned and existing public open spaces. During preparation of the map, it is important that the planning agency work closely with the engineering department in order to insure that the official map will be in conformity with the comprehensive plan. It should be submitted to the legislative body for adoption only after it has been carefully checked in every detail. The legislative authority, from time to time, may make additions to, or modifications of, the official map by designating thereon the lines of new streets or street extensions, widenings, narrowings, or vacations. Such action should be preceded by public hearings held after due notice as provided by law. The ordinance should make it clear that the effect of the adoption of the map does not constitute the opening or establishment of a street or the taking or acceptance of any land for street purposes.

The adoption of the official map can be a means of putting into effect controls upon the municipality as well as upon individuals. In order to coördinate the planning of utilities with the street plan, the mapped-streets enabling legislation should provide that after the establishment of the official map, no public water facilities, sewers, or other public utilities or improvements should be constructed in any street, other than existing streets established by law, until such street is placed on the official map.

Legal Effect. In construing the legal effect of official maps and building permit acts, courts of the several states have not been in agreement as to what specific action may be taken under the police power and what action constitutes a taking of property under eminent domain requiring the payment of compensation.[36] In general, it can be said that the recording of a map of a proposed public improvement does not of itself amount to a taking of property. It is also held that merely passing an ordinance directing the purchase or condemnation

---

lation Pertaining to Planning, Official Maps and Mapping, New Jersey State Planning Section, Department of Conservation and Economic Development, January, 1954.

[36] Ernest H. Campbell and Bert A. Balmer, Establishment of Official Maps (Seattle: Bureau of Governmental Research and Services, University of Washington, June 10, 1954), Research Memorandum No. 42.

of a piece of property does not constitute a taking.[37] However, the enactment of an ordinance providing for the opening of a street does constitute a taking of property which entitles the owner to compensation.

It is not so clearly established as to whether the denial of a building permit constitutes a taking when the denial is for the purpose of avoiding high costs of acquisition at some future undetermined date. On this point there is a split of judicial authority. Likewise, there is a split of authority on the question of whether, if buildings are erected on land within the beds of projected streets after the recording of the official map, the city must compensate the owner for their value or pay for the cost of removing them when the street is opened. In Pennsylvania and Connecticut, for example, the court holds that the prohibition of buildings in mapped streets is a valid exercise of the police power and that the city is not required to compensate the owner for the value of buildings erected after the official map is recorded.[38] On the other hand, in New Jersey and Maryland, the courts have taken the position that the restriction on building cannot be sustained as an exercise of the police power, and if buildings are erected, they must be compensated for by the municipality.[39] This does not necessarily mean that such acts have no value, as they do place property owners on notice of projected streets and enable them to develop their property accordingly.

Courts which have upheld the official map as a valid exercise of the police power have tended to limit its application to streets (including within the term, boulevards, parkways, viaducts, etc.), but have not been disposed to extend its legal effect to other purposes such as parks and playgrounds.[40] While this distinction seems difficult to justify, the courts which have upheld the acts apparently feel that they are already on somewhat doubtful ground and hesitate to extend

[37] McQuillin, op. cit., Vol. II, Sec. 32.31, pp. 329–331.
[38] Town of Windsor v. Whitney et al., 95 Conn. 357, 111 Atl. 354 (1920).
Busch et al. v. City of McKeesport, 166 Pa. St. 57, 30 Atl. 1023 (1895).
[39] Grasso v. Board of Adjustment of Millburn Tp. in Essex County et al., Supr. Ct. of N.J., 61 A. (2d) 167 (1948).
Moale v. The Mayor and City Council of Baltimore, 5 Md. 314, 61 Am. Dec. 276 (1854).
It would seem that some of the legal objections raised by the New Jersey courts against the earlier acts may have been overcome by the 1953 Official Map and Building Permit Act which fixes a time limit within which the property may be purchased or condemned.
[40] Campbell and Balmer, op. cit., p. 18.
Miller et ux. v. City of Beaver Falls, 368 Pa. 189, 82 A. (2d) 34 (1951).

the doctrine further. Because of this precarious legal position, many states have hesitated to rely on the police power to support the validity of official map acts. On the other hand, the police power is under constant review by the courts and is continuously being interpreted with respect to new demands and new situations. It is, therefore, not possible to predict with certainty how far the courts may go in the future in permitting municipalities to reserve public areas as an exercise of the police power. One provision which has strengthened the laws where the acts have been upheld has been that of fixing a statutory time limit within which the legislative body must take official action to open the proposed street. Some statutes have fixed a period of five years after which time the building restrictions no longer apply.

A somewhat different situation exists with respect to the application of the official map act to subdivisions for which plats are sought to be recorded. The control which a municipality possesses over the development of subdivisions through the requirements for recording plats places it in a much stronger position with respect to the matter of reserved areas for streets and other uses than if plats were not involved. While courts insist that the compulsory creation of a street must be by eminent domain, they nevertheless hold that the municipality may, as a condition of recording a plat, require a dedication of streets, and under certain conditions, may also require a dedication of areas for playgrounds and open spaces without the payment of compensation.[41] Although such requirements must be supported as a reasonable exercise of the police power, the differentiation seems to be justified in part by the fact that the application for plat recording is a voluntary act on the part of the applicant and also by the fact that the subdivider has an opportunity to recover the cost of the property dedicated through the sale of his property.

Relief of Hardship.   Most official map statutes recognize the possibility of hardship in individual cases if certain persons are denied the right to build in beds of mapped streets pending the decision of the city council to open or not to open the street. Therefore, a common provision in the official map ordinance is to provide that if the property cannot otherwise yield a reasonable return to the owner, a building permit may be granted by a board of adjustment following a

[41] See, however, Opinion of Don Eastvold, Attorney General, State of Washington, December 20, 1955, to Hugh H. Evans ruling that land for parks, playgrounds, and schools must be acquired by eminent domain under statute providing that the plat must make appropriate provision therefor.

public hearing on the matter. If there is no board of adjustment, relief may be granted by the city council. In granting a building permit to relieve hardship, the board of adjustment or the council, as the case may be, should always keep in mind the major purpose of the official map, namely, that of keeping down the cost of future acquisitions, and should, therefore, make a minimum of changes in the map. Although the final decision in hardship cases should be made by the Board of Adjustment, the planning agency can be most helpful by providing information relative to priorities in proposed street developments and the probable degree of hazard to the proposed street project if the permit should be granted.[42] The planning agency may be of assistance also in helping the property owner to meet his needs by working out some alternative plan which will avoid the necessity of issuing a permit to avoid undue hardship. Since the exercise of the police power must meet the test of reasonableness of due process of law, a provision in the official map ordinance for hardship relief would seem to strengthen its validity.

CONTROL OF LAND USE

In addition to the land-use controls provided by the official map ordinance, municipalities when authorized by state enabling laws possess many other important means for regulating the use of private property. Among the most important of these are zoning, subdivision control, and the establishment of building line setbacks.

Zoning. Of the many tools of plan implementation, zoning is perhaps the most extensively used. Courts have long recognized that many callings and occupations and property uses have implications involving matters of public interest and have been willing to uphold the validity of reasonable governmental regulation of them to protect the public health, safety, morals, and general welfare. When the constitutionality of zoning ordinances was first challenged, courts were inclined to uphold them as a type of nuisance control. Prior to 1900, the courts had sustained numerous municipal ordinances restricting objectionable businesses to protect residential areas. Among those which the courts declared to be nuisances in residential districts were laundries, brick manufacturing, machine shops, stone crushers, and slaughterhouses.[43]

[42] For example, erection of a temporary structure which would be removed before the time set for undertaking the street project would present no problem.
[43] Robert Averill Walker, The Planning Function in Urban Government (Chicago: The University of Chicago Press, 1950), pp. 54–57.

Since a nuisance may be only a lawful business in the wrong location, the mere segregation of nuisances does not guide urban development in any positive way. The most important step forward in plan implementation through zoning began with the acceptance of comprehensive zoning as a lawful exercise of the police power. The first case decided by the United States Supreme Court which recognized the planning concept of zoning was *Village of Euclid v. Ambler Realty Company*.[44] Under the doctrine of this decision zoning has thus become accepted as a lawful means of achieving a rational land-use pattern, and courts are no longer required to find legal support for such ordinances on the theory of nuisance control. The control of nuisances is, nevertheless, an important tool of plan effectuation in matters not directly concerned with zoning.[45] Because of its importance and the many special and complicated problems which it presents, the subject of zoning is given special treatment in a separate chapter.[46]

Subdivision Control.   Public control of land subdivision is another very important tool of plan implementation which is also considered in more detail in a subsequent chapter.[47] As in zoning, the basis of subdivision control is primarily that of the police power. Most cities in the United States have experienced at one time or another the harmful effects of scattered and excessive land subdivisions which have resulted in economic loss for the developers and investors, high costs to the municipality in providing services, and unsightly areas where unsold lots have grown up in weeds. Land subdivision regulations are an attempt to guide subdivision developments along orderly lines in order to avoid in so far as possible the perpetuation of these economic losses and ill-planned communities.

Subdivision control is enforced through the power to withhold the privilege of recording plats which do not conform to the standards and requirements established under the law. Where a plat is not publicly recorded, lots within it may not be sold by reference to the plat. Usually the difficulties of selling only by descriptions of metes and bounds constitute an adequate deterrent to the evasion of land subdivision regulations. However, municipalities have sometimes found it desirable to prohibit street paving or laying of water mains

[44] 272 U.S. 365, 47 S.Ct. 114, 71 L.Ed. 303 (1926).
[45] Methods of abatement and control of nuisances are considered in Chap. 5.
[46] See Chap. 8.
[47] See Chap. 9.

or sewers within a street or of the erection of a building on an abutting lot unless the street is shown on a recorded plat.

Subdivision control acts of different jurisdictions vary greatly in the scope and nature of requirements. Most regulations require as a condition of approval of the plat that adequate provision be made for suitable grading and paving of streets and for the installation of street lighting standards, water mains, and storm and sanitary sewers. Regulations in many states require a dedication of proper streets, and, under certain circumstances, also require a dedication of areas for parks for recreational purposes and the setting aside of a prescribed percentage of the land for public use.

In supporting subdivision regulation under the police power, the courts have recognized the public interest in developing the community as a "social, economic, and political unit." [48] However, subdivision control is deficient in that it does not provide an effective means of promoting land development for uses other than those determined by the developer. Good planning may at times dictate that controls be established whereby municipalities may be able to withhold building permits entirely in areas where, in the interest of public welfare, such areas should not be built upon. Consequently, subdivision control must be supplemented by zoning and other regulations in order to give more positive direction and guidance in attaining the most appropriate land use.

Building Line Setbacks. In recent years many communities have found it to be in the public interest to establish building lines along streets and highways for the purpose of defining a reservation adjacent to the thoroughfare within which physical structures may not be placed. The need for such reservations arises from the demands for greater space to dilute exhaust gases, to provide better opportunities for maneuvering traffic, to take care of the need for off-street parking, and to insure greater vision clearance at intersections. [49] Where a building line setback is a greater distance from the center line of the street than is the edge of the street boundary which it parallels, the difference between the two represents a strip of private property which becomes subject to regulation for the purpose of prohibiting permanent structures from being erected thereon. Property which is

---

[48] *Mansfield and Swett v. Town of West Orange*, 120 N.J.L. 145, 198 Atl. 225 (1938).

[49] Joshua H. Vogel and Ernest H. Campbell, *Municipal Regulation of Traffic View Obstructions* (Seattle: Bureau of Governmental Research and Services, University of Washington, February, 1953), Report No. 122, p. 74.

thus impressed with such public use is alienated from the parent property only to the extent that it is made permanently available for some or all of the many uses to which streets are devoted.[50]

Where the necessity arises to establish building line setbacks, the legal question is presented as to whether they can be upheld as a legitimate exercise of the police power.[51] Until recently the prevailing opinion was that such restrictions amounted to the taking of property under the power of eminent domain. In recent years, however, there has been a tendency on the part of the courts to uphold the establishment of building lines under the police power.[52] The essential advantage to the community of establishing building line setbacks under the police power is that the owner is not entitled to compensation and the municipality does not have to comply with the requirements of condemnation proceedings.[53]

The establishment of setbacks by regulation is somewhat analogous in theory to the requirement for dedication of reservations for streets under subdivision control except that the establishment of setbacks is compulsory and not based upon the granting or withholding of a recording privilege. Building setback lines may be established under zoning ordinances by the adoption of the official map or by special ordinance. Aside from the questions of legality and method, there may also arise questions of equity. In cases where building setbacks result in undue hardship due to costly removals or by creating lots of unusual shape or depth, it would seem that the city should proceed by eminent domain or negotiated purchase.

BUILDING AND CONSTRUCTION CODES

Plan implementation is directly concerned with the adoption and enforcement of a number of building and construction codes enacted for the purpose of safeguarding public safety and health through the regulation of building construction, building use and maintenance,

[50] Gordon Whitnall, *Are Building Line Setbacks Valid?* (Los Angeles: Gordon Whitnall and Associates, October 15, 1952), p. 5.

[51] For an analysis of the use and legality of setback building line legislation, see a monograph by Paul L. Leramur, *Setback Building Lines in the United States,* January 16, 1947, published by the Bureau of Public Administration, University of California, Berkeley, California; "The Law of Zoning Ordinances in Pennsylvania," (Notes) *University of Pittsburgh Law Review,* Vol. 16, No. 2, pp. 169–172, Winter, 1955, for a discussion of the "majority rule building line."

[52] *Headly v. Rochester,* 247 App. Div. 562, 288 N.Y. Supp. 277, 5 N.E. (2d) 198 (1936).

[53] *Town of Winsor v. Whitney, supra.*

and through the installation of utilities and the furnishing of certain types of services.[54] One of the primary functions of municipal government is to insure and promote the comfort and security of persons and the safety of property within its boundaries. Among the natural elements which constitute the principal sources of peril are gravity, earthquake, wind, fire, lightning, and flood. In addition to these natural elements, there are also the hazards of disease, panic, and accident due to carelessness or neglect. Through scientific study and experience, municipalities have gained technical knowledge which has made it possible to eliminate or greatly reduce many of these hazards by the adoption and enforcement of building and construction codes. The primary function of such codes is to insure that within the community the design and construction of all structures and the installation of all utilities and fixtures shall be in accordance with established principles and practices in the interest of public safety.[55]

Nature and Purpose.   Public codes appear to be as old as recorded history. In America, the authority of municipalities to regulate construction and maintenance of buildings in the interest of public safety was recognized early in the colonial period. Many of the early regulations were aimed at preventing the collapse of defective buildings. Other interests have been to promote the civilian economy through sound practices of construction because of the influence on mortgage charges, insurance rates, and market values. Building and construction codes prescribe limits on what a private builder may do without endangering himself, his neighbors, or without creating a public nuisance. The modern building and construction codes are predicated upon the principle of public safety through preventive rather than punitive regulations. Their purpose is to set up standards of accepted practices which provide the necessary minimum measures for safety and general welfare through safe, healthy, and livable conditions of housing and other building construction.[56]

Due to the fact that the technical and practical features of con-

---

[54] In some cities building codes include housing requirements for health, sanitation, ventilation, light, etc. In others they are separate from the building code.

For a discussion of the use of housing codes as a means of furthering urban renewal policies, see p. 512.

[55] Alfred L. Miller and Joshua H. Vogel, *A Suggested Basic Building Code for Washington Cities* (Seattle: Bureau of Governmental Research and Services, University of Washington, revised June, 1948), Report No. 57.

[56] George Strehan, *Building Code Philosophy and Principles*—Proceedings of the Forty-Third Annual Meeting of the Conference of Mayors and Other Municipal Officials of the State of New York, Lake Placid, N.Y., June 11–13, 1952, pp, 79–83.

struction are becoming more complex, the hope for a simple building code cannot be realized. Building codes in present use tend to be handbooks of technical data and structural theory that can be followed only by those with the requisite background of technical training and experience. Uniformity of standards in communities of comparable size and where comparable conditions exist is highly desirable. With this objective in mind, several standard building codes are in general use and all or parts of these codes have been adopted by many municipalities, either by specific enactments or through adoption by reference. The three codes which are most extensively used are those prepared by the Building Officials Conference of America, Inc.,[57] the National Board of Fire Underwriters,[58] and the Pacific Coast Building Officials Conference.[59] In addition, there are numerous codes which have been prepared and adopted by municipalities without reference to standards suggested by any of the national associations.

A number of national associations have also worked out standards for plumbing codes,[60] electrical codes,[61] and fire codes.[62] The primary function of all such codes is to protect persons and property from the hazards of ill-advised use of construction materials, faulty types of assembly, and improper workmanship. Construction codes vary with the different cities. Some municipalities have included the regulation of all phases of construction in a single code. Other cities have adopted a number of individual codes, including building codes, plumbing codes, electrical codes, fire codes, and mechanical codes. Related to these, but not directly concerned with standards of construction, are housing codes. Housing codes usually cover room sizes and arrangements, light and ventilation, water and sanitary conditions, and occupancy and maintenance.[63]

Types of Codes. Building codes are generally classified into two types—specification and performance.[64] The specification type of code

[57] *Basic Building Code*, 1950 ed., Building Officials Conference of America, Inc.

[58] *National Building Code*, 1949 ed., National Board of Fire Underwriters.

[59] *Uniform Building Code*, Vols. I, II, and III, 1952 ed., Pacific Coast Building Officials Conference.

[60] *American Standard Plumbing Code*, ASA A40.7–1949, sponsored by the American Public Health Association and the American Society of Mechanical Engineers.

[61] *National Electrical Code*, National Board of Fire Underwriters Pamphlet No. 70 (1951).

[62] *Suggested Fire Prevention Ordinance* (1947), *Fire Prevention Code*, abbreviated ed. (1950), National Board of Fire Underwriters.

[63] Housing environment is more fully considered in Chap. 10 in relation to urban renewal.

[64] Joshua H. Vogel, Alfred L. Miller, and George D. Smith, *What Building Code*

sets forth in detail the minimum standards to be followed by the builder, architect, or engineer. As such, it is frequently a voluminous engineering handbook, filled with innumerable items including detailed specifications for the thickness of walls made of specially listed materials, and for the amount of fireproofing, with the description for specific materials. The performance code, on the other hand, states the conditions to which the building may be subjected, such as wind forces, gravity, weight, fire hazards, earthquake, and "live" and "dead" loads, and generally enumerates forms of construction that have already demonstrated their ability to resist these forces. Inasmuch as the emphasis is upon the requirements to be met rather than the specific type of material or construction to be used, the code is more flexible and adaptable to changing conditions than the specification type of code. New types of materials or new forms of construction developed in the future may qualify when proved satisfactory by unbiased tests.

The selection of a code, to some extent, becomes a matter of preference, based upon local considerations as well as principle. The codes may differ slightly as to the minimum standards to be applied, but in general the minimums given in any of the standard codes can be safely adopted. The code should be carefully worked out so that interests of the manufacturer, the builder, the financial agencies, and the public have adequate protection. Standards must be reasonable and the requirements clearly understandable. It should be the aim of both policy and administration to provide needed protection without penalizing good design, without restricting advances in methods of construction, and without prejudicing the use of new materials.[65] Care should be taken not to freeze the technological processes of any particular period where unnecessary to achieve general objectives.

Effective administration of building and construction codes demands that all forces of the building industry, building officials, and technical and professional groups representing public interests be united in their efforts to see that the codes adopted contain fair and adequate standards and that they are honestly enforced. The usual methods of enforcement require that a permit be obtained before construction can begin. This permit is secured from the authorized

(or Codes) May Be Adopted? (Seattle: Bureau of Governmental Research and Services, University of Washington, March, 1953), Information Bulletin No. 147.

[65] Municipal Administration (Supplement contributed by Associated Institutes of Government of Pennsylvania Universities), Administrative Objectives of Building Regulation and Inspection, January, 1953.

city official, usually on condition that suitable bonds be filed with the city to protect it against any damages which might be recovered from the city on account of injury or damage to persons or property resulting from the issuance of the permit, from anything done pursuant to the permit, from the occupancy or the disturbance of streets, alleys, sidewalks, or from other causes.

In addition to requiring a permit for construction, most codes also require a permit for use or occupancy. This permit is granted upon a determination that the structure is fit for the use intended, and it implies that if the occupant proposes to use it for any other purpose, the municipality must be assured that the structure is suitable for that use, or that alterations conforming to the code are made to render it fit. The machinery for enforcement varies according to the code and the jurisdiction. The primary responsibility for inspecting and determining that provisions of the code have been complied with rests upon the building inspector. Under some ordinances, however, certificates from qualified architects or contractors as to compliance are accepted as evidence of fulfillment of certain requirements under the code. This latter practice does not relieve the municipality of the responsibility of supervision, but does eliminate the necessity of the building inspector's having to supervise a number of inconsequential details, which can be done by the architect, engineer, or builder, and enforced by penalty.

In the administration of building and construction codes, the interests of the city are best served when the building official administering the code gives proper recognition to the convenience of the applicant. The builder should not be treated as one seeking favors. By complying with the provisions of the code, he is accommodating himself to some inconvenience and expense to insure that the interests of the public are protected. Since a good building in the right place is a community asset, the building department should make every reasonable effort to facilitate the processing of applications for building permits. Good building code administration requires that (1) rules and procedures be clearly presented and readily available, (2) plan review and construction inspection be prompt and considerate, (3) forms used be clear and concise, (4) required approvals from other departments be handled within the building department, and (5) common courtesy and convenience be accorded to the persons served.[66]

[66] Ibid.

State Laws and Regulations. It should also be emphasized that regardless of the type of building code a city adopts, each municipality is governed by a number of "hidden building codes" contained in state laws and in rules and regulations of various state departments and agencies.[67] These laws, rules and regulations often have uniform application throughout the state and supersede provisions in municipal codes which may be in conflict with them.[68] Frequently, cities may find it advantageous to supplement their building codes by adopting by reference certain laws, rules, and regulations issued by the State Health Department, the Department of Labor and Industries, and other state agencies which are directly concerned with construction standards.

ARCHITECTURAL CONTROL

Most planners have long recognized that attractiveness of design and outward beauty of private buildings have a definite bearing upon the happiness and comfort of the inhabitants. Architectural design is also a factor in stabilizing property values. Consequently, the erection of a freak type of house in a first-class residential district may have the effect of depreciating surrounding property values and detracting from living enjoyment in much the same way as the existence of a nonconforming use. Up to the present time, public controls over the architectural design of private buildings and structures in the interest of promoting the general welfare have been of little significance. For the most part, the success of programs of city beautification involving private buildings has depended largely upon civic pride developed through education, demonstration, and competition. Nevertheless, in a few cities, architectural control has been utilized with considerable success. It should be noted that the public and judicial attitude toward architectural control is undergoing a change which will undoubtedly have an important bearing upon future public policies designed to implement planning through this device.[69] In the case of subdivision developments, harmony in neighborhood appearance has frequently been achieved through restrictive covenants. The method usually employed to provide architectural control has

[67] *Hidden Building Codes of the State of Washington* (Seattle: Association of Washington Cities, September 26, 1949), Information Bulletin No. 120.

[68] Gilbert R. Barnhard, *A Report on Administrative Procedures for Enforcement of Building Regulations* (Washington, D.C.: Housing and Home Finance Agency, April, 1954), pp. 11–21.

[69] See pp. 421–423 for the promotion of aesthetics under the zoning ordinance.

been to require building plans to be submitted to an architectural jury. Although such control is based upon subdivision regulations, it is essentially private in character.

Ordinance Requirements and Administration. Apart from sub-division regulations, the legal device which is normally employed for architectural control is a special type of building permit ordinance which creates an Architectural Board of Review with authority to pass upon the exterior architectural design of buildings in the districts subject to such control. The ordinance is administered through the office of the building inspector. The principal objective of the architectural control ordinance is to prevent excessive uniformity, dissimilarity, inappropriateness, or poor quality of design in the exterior appearance of buildings erected in or in the immediate vicinity of residential neighborhoods. The ordinance often contains rather detailed standards for measuring these factors.

The Architectural Board of Review is sometimes composed of a group with required experience in architecture, planning, and related fields. In others it may be composed of interested lay citizens chosen from a number of vocations without occupational designations. For example, the 15-member Building Board in Wauwatosa, Wisconsin, in 1952 included an architect, a teacher, a real-estate man, a builder, a real estate loan man, a banker, an insurance man and several manufacturing executives. The chairman was a manufacturer.[70] This Board is made up of three citizens from each ward appointed for one-year terms by the mayor with the approval of the council. Reappointments are relied upon to give continuity to the program. In practice each ward group passes on the plans for that ward. If the ward group rejects the plan, the owner may appeal to the full board. Where subdivisions have committees of their own which study architectural plans, the Wauwatosa Board gives careful consideration to their views. From the evidence which has been accumulated since the ordinance was adopted in 1945, it seems reasonably clear that the act has been an important factor in raising building standards.

In the City of Rye, New York, architectural control is supervised by a Board of Architectural Review consisting of five members who serve without compensation. They are required to be specially qualified by reason of training or experience in architecture, land de-

[70] William B. Knuese, "Building Board Achieves Architectural Control," *The American City*, Vol. LXVII, No. 3, p. 119, March, 1952.

velopment, city planning, real estate, landscape architecture, or some other relevant business or profession or by reason of civic interest and sound judgment to judge the effects of the proposed building upon property values and the development of surrounding areas. At least one member of the Board is required to be a registered architect in the State of New York. The members are appointed by the Mayor with Council approval for a term of three years.[71] The terms are staggered in order to give the program continuity. The objectives of the City of Rye Ordinance are indicated in the statement of purposes contained in Section 1:

Section 1. The Common Council hereby finds that excessive uniformity, dissimilarity, inappropriateness or poor quality of design in the exterior appearance of buildings erected in or in the immediate vicinity of a residential neighborhood adversely affects the desirability of the immediate area and neighboring areas for residential purposes and by so doing impairs the benefits of occupancy of existing residential property in such areas, impairs the stability and value of both improved and unimproved real property in such areas, prevents the most appropriate development of such areas, produces degeneration of residential property in such areas with attendant deterioration of conditions affecting the health, safety and morals of the inhabitants thereof, and destroys a proper relationship between the taxable value of real property in such areas and the cost of municipal services provided therefor. It is the purpose of this local law to prevent these and other harmful effects of such exterior appearance of buildings erected in residential neighborhoods and thus to promote and protect the health, safety, morals and general welfare of the community.[72]

For the most part, architectural control has been limited to one or two family residence zones, although, under some ordinances, permits are required for building in business zones within certain distances of residential districts. The City of Rye Ordinance provides:

Section 4. Every application for a building permit for the construction, reconstruction or alteration of a one or two family dwelling or for any other structure in excess of 2000 cubic feet of cubical contents, proposed for construction within a residence district as identified on the building

[71] Local Law No. 1, 1951. Passed by the local legislative body of the City of Rye in accordance with the provisions of the City Home Rule Law. Became law August 11, 1951.

[72] City of Rye, Local Law No. 1, 1952, amending Section 1 of Local Law No. 1, 1951, adopted November 19, 1952. Passed by the local legislative body of the City of Rye in accordance with the provisions of the City Home Rule Law.

zone map, or for the construction, reconstruction or alteration of any structure in excess of 2000 cubic feet of cubical contents proposed for construction within a business zone as identified on said map which structure is less than 250 feet distant from any such residence district boundary and will be visible from any part of such residence district, shall be referred by the Building Inspector to the Board of Architectural Review within three days of the date of application, provided it conforms in all respects to all other applicable laws and ordinances.[73]

Other municipalities which have adopted mandatory regulations in an effort to control architectural design include: San Diego and Santa Barbara, California; Washington, D.C.; and Garden City, New York.[74] Under the provisions of the Shipstead Act of 1930, the architectural design of buildings in Washington, D.C., facing a principal government building must be approved by the National Commission of Fine Arts. Recently, Garden City, New York, created a five-member board with authority to regulate the exterior design and site layout of all new residential buildings. This board was given power, by the city council, to disapprove applications for residential building permits if the design was either too similar or too different from neighborhood homes. The board was also given authority to require relocation of a proposed building to achieve a more attractive appearance. The city building inspector was made ex officio secretary of the board. The board has authority to disapprove an application for residential building permits only by unanimous vote. Decisions of the board can be appealed by the builder to the city's board of zoning appeals.[75]

Legal and Practical Difficulties. There are many difficulties involved in attempting to regulate architectural design by public controls. Some of these are legal and others are practical. The legality of architectural control has been a matter of some dispute for a number of years. One reason for the doubts as to its validity arises from the fact that it is peculiarly susceptible to the charge that it is based solely upon aesthetic considerations. With few exceptions, the courts have not been willing to uphold regulatory ordinances designed solely

[73] *Ibid.*, Section 4.

[74] Architectural control is common in European countries. Robert D. Sundby, "Architectural Control in Residential Districts," *The Municipality*, Vol. 49, No. 3, p. 55, March, 1954. In view of the more liberal attitude being taken by the courts in upholding public regulations in the interest of promoting aesthetics, it seems reasonable to anticipate that in the near future many more American cities are likely to adopt architectural control ordinances of some form.

[75] *News Bulletin* (Chicago: Public Administration Clearing House, Release No. 5, February 6, 1953).

to preserve the aesthetic beauty of the community. Consequently, decisions upholding legislation concerned with architectural control have usually been based upon the general welfare aspects of the police power and not upon aesthetic considerations alone. However, the language used by the courts in a number of jurisdictions would seem to indicate a trend in the direction of sustaining reasonable architectural control as a valid exercise of the police power.[76] The practical difficulty of establishing valid aesthetic standards has already been noted in a preceding chapter. In addition there is the practical difficulty of obtaining impartial architectural advice or of securing a jury of competent architects who are willing to pass judgment upon the designs of other architects. For these reasons, it appears that, as of the present time, much of the success in controlling architectural design must continue to rest upon education, demonstration, and the power of persuasion.

The Regulation of Billboards and Other Forms of Outdoor Advertising

Most building codes contain certain provisions relative to the structural requirements of billboards, overhanging signs and various forms of outdoor advertising. However, the public interest in controlling outdoor advertising is not always confined to the hazards to public safety resulting from improper construction. Municipalities have frequently found it in the interest of public health, safety, and welfare to enact specific regulations governing their use.

Nature and Purpose of Control. Although outdoor advertising has long been recognized as an important means of telling the advertiser's story, and many attractive and appealing devices have been developed for this purpose, a number of problems have arisen with respect to their use which have required the exercise of public control. In some instances, billboards represent a potential fire hazard because of the accumulation of combustible materials that frequently tends to collect behind such signs. Sometimes, also, signs are found to be structurally dangerous. In recent years, however, the hazard which has appeared to be most serious is the hazard to traffic. With the development of high-speed vehicular traffic, the various types of eye-arresting devices used to reach the public constitute a potential diversion factor for the driver which may occasion accidents.[77] The

[76] For a recent case upholding architectural control, see *State ex rel. Saveland Park Holding Corporation v. Wieland,* 269 Wis. 262, 69 N.W. (2d) 217 (1955).
[77] J. Malcolm Smith, *Regulation and Control of Outdoor Advertising* (Seattle:

direct relationship of billboards to traffic accidents has been a subject of much debate. While the degree of the hazard has not been definitely determined, it seems clear that billboards have been a contributing factor.

More than half of the states having legislation regulating billboards along public highways specifically prohibit commercial advertising upon highway rights of way, and about the same percentage restrict the placing of billboards near road or railroad intersections. Most of the statutes specify that no signs shall obstruct the highway user's "clear view" of the road ahead. Other common regulations include prohibitions against signs (1) that are so brilliant as to dazzle highway users, (2) that have moving, blinking, or flashing parts, (3) that have red lights or reflectors, or (4) that resemble any official marker erected by a governmental agency or display such words as "Stop" or "Danger." [78]

The regulation of billboards and other forms of outdoor advertising on city streets presents more difficult problems than the regulation of such advertising on highways. The extent to which private businesses and various other agencies including religious, charitable, patriotic, and even governmental organizations utilize these media to reach the city public makes the problem of control a troublesome matter. Under these circumstances, public policy can hardly justify the complete elimination of outdoor advertising. Nevertheless, a number of cities have adopted ordinances prohibiting all billboards.

Legal Basis of Regulation.   In general, the regulation of billboards has been premised upon the traditional health, safety, and morals concept of the police power. It has been urged in recent years that the court should sustain the regulation of those things which are offensive to one's "aesthetic sense." Under this view, "aesthetic sense" includes not only signs which are offensive to the eye, but also those which obstruct the natural view of the landscape. The reluctance of the courts to accept this doctrine has been due to the almost insuperable task of establishing aesthetic standards in view of the great diversity of individual tastes.[79]

Although the great weight of authority is that the "aesthetic sense" does not afford a valid basis for regulating billboards, a few jurisdic-

---

Bureau of Governmental Research and Services, University of Washington, September, 1947), Report No. 76, p. 4.

[78] Smith, op. cit., p. 5.

[79] St. Louis Gunning Advertisement Co. v. City of St. Louis, 235 Mo. 99, 137 S.W. 929 (1911).

tions have held to the contrary.[80] The Supreme Court of Massachusetts has taken the position that the regulation of outdoor advertising to preserve landscapes from defacement promotes the public welfare and is a public purpose. The Court observed that: "Even if the rules and regulations of billboards and other advertising devices did not rest upon the safety of public travel and the promotion of the comfort of travelers by intrusion, we think that the preservation of scenic beauty and places of historical interest would be sufficient support for them."

For the most part, however, courts have been willing to recognize aesthetics only as secondary objectives to declared purposes for the promotion of public health, safety, morals, and general welfare.

REGULATION OF BUSINESS ACTIVITIES BY LICENSING

Regulation and control of certain businesses and occupations can be most effectively achieved through licensing. A license for purposes of regulation is a temporary nonassignable privilege granted under the police power by some competent governmental authority, often revokable at the will of the licensor, to do some particular act or to engage in some activity of a continuing nature which could not be done lawfully without such a license.[81]

A license is to be distinguished from a permit. A permit is an authorization by a competent governmental authority of a particular act or activity which is not of a continuing nature. Upon completion of the act or activity, the permit is executed or terminated.[82] A permit authorizes the grantee to do some act not forbidden by law, but not allowable without such authority. Permits are frequently used in administering certain aspects of zoning ordinances and building and construction codes.

Objectives and Legal Limitations. While the licensing power may be exercised to regulate various business activities, such businesses are subject only to reasonable regulations. As a general prop-

---

[80] *General Outdoor Advertising Co. v. Department of Public Works*, 287 Mass. 147, 193 N.E. 799 (1935).

[81] McQuillin, *op. cit.*, Vol. 9, Sec. 26.01, p. 8.

Ernest H. Campbell and Sidney Coleman, *op. cit.*, p. 1.

The issuance of licenses may sometimes be premised upon an exercise of the taxing power for revenue only, and in other cases upon the police power and the taxing power.

[82] McQuillin, *loc. cit.*

Henry C. Black, *Law Dictionary* (St. Paul: West Publishing Company, 1933), p. 1353.

Campbell and Coleman, *loc. cit.*

osition, the power of municipalities to license does not extend to the prohibition of lawful business activities. The courts have, however, long recognized that certain types of business may be fraught with injurious results to public health, safety, and morals, and that municipalities may refuse to grant such businesses a license.[83] For example, cities have been upheld in denying a license for a pool hall where it is established that the owner and operator is not of good moral character. Courts have also upheld the refusal of a license for the operation of a soft drink parlor to an applicant who had theretofore conducted the same place of business in a disorderly fashion detrimental to the welfare of the community. In certain types of business, applications for licenses may be denied on the ground of the adequacy of existing circumstances. For example, an application for a license to furnish transportation service may be denied if it is found that the effect of permitting such additional service might jeopardize the financial stability of existing licensees. The denial of licenses on the ground of the adequacy of existing service is limited to particular types of business with respect to which the establishment of a monopoly, as distinguished from a competitive economy, may be in the public interest.

Licensing ordinances providing for the issuance and revocation of licenses of lawful businesses or activities must prescribe appropriate standards to guide the officials who administer the ordinances. If such standards are not provided, the ordinances may be held unconstitutional as an invalid delegation of legislative power. While lawful businesses in which one has an inherent right to engage may not be prohibited under the licensing power, the courts, nevertheless, recognize that certain kinds of business activity contain elements so inimical to the public interest that they may be prohibited altogether. One of the perplexing problems that many municipalities face in this regard is that of effectively curbing the annoyance to householders caused by the solicitations of peddlers and itinerant vendors. Municipal ordinances that have sought to prohibit peddling completely have generally been held invalid as an abuse of the exercise of the police power.[84]

The "Green River" Ordinance. The principal difficulty in regulating peddlers has been one of drafting a valid ordinance which will

[83] Campbell and Coleman, op. cit., p. 8.
[84] *Good Humor Corporation, et al. v. City of New York, et al.*, 290 N.Y. 312, 49 N.E. (2d) 153 (1943).

protect the householders' desire for privacy, and at the same time preserve freedom for welcome visitors to the homes. Some municipalities have sought to achieve this balance by the adoption of the so-called Green River Ordinance [85] which does not prohibit peddling as such but makes peddling, hawking, and soliciting by uninvited house-to-house canvassing a nuisance punishable by fine and imprisonment.[86] This type of ordinance usually excepts the sale or solicitation of orders for sale of milk, dairy products, vegetables, poultry, eggs, and other farm and garden produce, and leaves open the usual methods of solicitation by radio, periodicals, mail, and local agencies. The constitutionality of this type of ordinance was upheld by the United States Supreme Court in a landmark decision in *Breard v. City of Alexandria* [87] decided June 4, 1951, which affirmed the decision of the Supreme Court of Louisiana sustaining the "Green River Ordinance" of Alexandria, Louisiana.[88] This ordinance was alleged to be unconstitutional on the ground that it violated (1) the due process clause of the Fourteenth Amendment of the Federal Constitution, (2) the federal commerce clause, and (3) the guarantees of the freedom of speech and freedom of the press of the First Amendment made applicable to the states by the Fourteenth Amendment.[89]

With respect to due process of law, the United States Supreme Court stated:

The Constitution's protection of property rights does not make a state or a city impotent to guard its citizens against the annoyances of life because the regulation may restrict the manner of doing a legitimate business. The question of a man's right to carry on with propriety a standard method of selling is presented here in its most appealing form—an assertion by a door-to-door solicitor that the Due Process Clause of the Fourteenth Amendment does not permit a state or its subdivisions to deprive a specialist in door-to-door selling of his means of livelihood. But putting aside the argument that after all it is the commerce, i.e., sales of periodicals, and not the methods, that is petitioner's business, we think that

[85] Originally adopted by Green River, Wyoming.

[86] Ernest H. Campbell and Ben C. Grosscup, *Regulation of Peddlers* (Seattle: Bureau of Governmental Research and Services, University of Washington, July, 1951), Report No. 116, p. 3.

[87] 341 U.S. 622, 95 L.Ed. 1233 (1951).

[88] *City of Alexandria v. Breard*, 217 La. 20, 47 So. (2d) 553 (1950).

[89] It is to be noted that this decision relates only to commercial transactions and does not overrule earlier cases such as *Martin v. Struthers*, 319 U.S. 141, 63 S.Ct. 739, 87 L.Ed. 1119 (1943) upholding the right of solicitors to make house-to-house canvass for noncommercial purposes in disseminating ideas and for religious purposes.

even a legitimate occupation may be restricted or prohibited in the public interest.[90]

HEALTH AND SANITARY CODES

Plan implementation in its broad aspects is concerned with many regulations other than those pertaining strictly to the physical elements of the community. Among some of the most important of these are the health and sanitary codes establishing standards and acceptable methods of handling milk, meats, and various kinds of foods and drinks.[91] Such codes usually provide for inspection of food handlers and of the conditions of the premises on which such foods are prepared, packaged, stored, served, or sold.

Sanitation Requirements. Sanitation requirements in restaurants and drinking places usually establish standards with respect to plans, floors, walls and ceilings, doors and windows, lighting, ventilation, toilet facilities, water supply, lavatory facilities, construction of utensils and equipment, cleaning and bactericidal treatment of utensils, dishwashing machines, disposal of wastes, refrigeration, wholesomeness of food and drink, storage and display of food and drink, cleanliness of employees, and many miscellaneous matters.[92] Milk inspection ordinances usually cover sanitary conditions of the dairy farms, milk plants, and systems of bottling and distribution. They require that diseased cattle must be segregated from the herds, and they set up sanitary standards for premises, utensils, equipment, and personnel similar to restaurant and food handling codes.

Such ordinances usually make it unlawful for any person who is affected with disease in communicable form or who is a carrier of such disease to work at any dairy farm or milk plant or in any capacity which brings him in contact with the production, handling, storage, or transportation of milk, milk products, containers, or equipment. Producers and distributors are forbidden to employ such persons and are required to notify the health officer if they find or suspect that an employee has contracted a communicable disease or is a carrier thereof.

Administration and Enforcement. Milk inspection codes commonly provide that when suspicion arises as to the possibility of in-

---

[90] *Breard v. City of Alexandria, supra.*

[91] Other types of sanitary and health codes relate to waste disposal, smoke control, and general maintenance.

[92] Ernest H. Campbell, *Meat and Restaurant Inspection* (Seattle: Bureau of Governmental Research and Services, University of Washington, January, 1947), Report No. 70.

fection from any person concerned with the handling of milk or milk products, the health officer may require any of the following measures: (1) the immediate exclusion of that person from milk handling, (2) the immediate exclusion of the milk supply concerned from distribution and use, (3) adequate medical and bacteriological examination of the person, of his associates, and of his and their body discharges. These enforcement provisions are backed by penal statutes providing for fines and imprisonment.[93]

Sanitary codes such as those relating to milk, meat, and restaurant inspection are enforced through the granting, withholding, or revoking of permits. These ordinances usually make it unlawful for anyone to operate an establishment or engage in an activity covered by the ordinance unless he possesses a valid permit issued by the health officer. Only persons who comply with the requirements of the ordinance and the rules and regulations issued thereunder are entitled to receive and retain a permit. Such a permit may be suspended by the health officer and revoked after proper hearing. Violators are liable to fines and imprisonment.

In some states considerable confusion exists as to which level of government—the federal, state or local—should undertake the inspection of meat packers, dairies, milk processors, and food distributors. Since the processor commonly supplies restaurants and retailers in a number of communities and since his plant is often located outside the territorial boundaries of all the municipalities which he supplies, there is frequently a great deal of duplication of inspection responsibilities.

PLAN IMPLEMENTATION BY MEANS OF NONCOERCIVE CITIZEN ACTION

As has already been indicated, plan implementation rests primarily on government authority. Nevertheless, there are many aspects of planning which can be effectuated by citizen action without government sanction. However, if the noncoerced efforts of citizens are to have a maximum influence in achieving the overall goals of community development, they must be related to official governmental processes.[94]

[93] Joseph A. Hearst, *Milk Inspection and Milk Standards in King County* (Seattle: Bureau of Governmental Research and Services, University of Washington, October, 1947), Report No. 77.

[94] Gerald Breese and Dorothy E. Whitman, eds., *An Approach to Urban Planning* (Princeton, N.J.: Princeton University Press, 1953), p. 33.

PUBLIC OPINION AND COÖPERATIVE ACTION

Although the chief value of citizen participation is in the stage of plan formulation, there are, nevertheless, many important functions which can be performed by citizen action in carrying the plan into execution. In the final analysis, the force of laws rests upon public opinion. Sound public opinion is developed through an intelligent understanding of public problems. Unless the public is prepared to accept a government program and conform to public controls, it is unlikely that public policies can be successfully enforced. Citizen groups can, therefore, greatly assist in informing the public of the planning objectives and of the procedures and methods to be used for accomplishing them. They can provide organized support for particular programs and can help to disseminate information with respect to the need for, and effect of, proposed courses of action and the dangers to the public interests if particular action is not taken or if controls are not instituted.

One of the areas in which citizen efforts can be most successful is that involving tax levies, bond issues, and appropriations for needed capital improvements. Taxpayers, suspicious of the vested interests of public officials, will often be swayed by the recommendations of respected civic organizations or business or professional groups to which they belong. Planning agencies will usually find it easier to get public support for the planning program if they first enlist the interest and secure the backing of established civic, business, and professional organizations including such groups as service clubs, real estate boards, engineering, architecture, and landscape societies, and labor organizations.[95] Such groups can frequently be helpful not only in promoting public acceptance of plans and enforcement programs, but also in combating pressures for deviation from the long-range capital improvements program and the financial plan.

There are many occasions for making planning effective through voluntary coöperative efforts. A great deal of community improvement can be achieved through private initiative as a result of persuasion, both from public officials and civic organizations. For example, citizens' groups interested in the "city beautiful" may perform valuable community service through appeals to community pride which may result in such activities as establishing cleanup weeks and contests for most attractive homes, gardens, and neighborhoods.

[95] S. E. Sanders and A. J. Rabuck, *New City Patterns* (New York: Reinhold Publishing Corporation, 1946), pp. 48–49.

In the long run, many of the plan objectives are better achieved by the coöperative efforts of citizens who have pride in their own community than can ever be accomplished by compulsory regulations imposed by governmental authority.[96] Many of the most successful programs of neighborhood rehabilitation have been carried out almost entirely by voluntary coöperative citizen action.[97] Also voluntary coöperation has sometimes made possible the development of recreation, transportation, and other facilities for use of the public, but operated by private agencies.

PROGRAMS OF CIVIC EDUCATION

Citizens' groups may be used to carry on broad programs of civic education, including the promotion of desirable planning legislation, taking part in city council meetings when planning is under discussion, and attending hearings held by the city council or any of its committees when planning matters are under consideration. Work of citizens' organizations should be carefully tied in with the use of such public information media as newspapers, radio, and television. When citizen interest is fostered by direct participation, stories on planning have greater appeal from the standpoint of newspaper circulation, listening audience, and general civic interest. The maintenance of public relations with newspaper reporters, feature writers, and program directors is, therefore, a necessary part of plan implementation.

The importance of developing a broad program of public education has been recognized by the American Institute of Planners in its study of the subject of civic education in planning. In its preliminary report [98] a detailed program of civic education was outlined showing, by tests and charts, a rather comprehensive procedure for developing a program of civic education. This report points out that planning education must be continuous, and should be considered in relation to four main groups: public officials, adult citizens, civic organizations, and the schools. In practice, the program of civic education calls for coördinated efforts on the part of the planner with all these groups.

[96] The International City Managers' Association, *Planning for Post War Services* (An Analysis of Problems and Trends with Suggestions for Developing Local Policies) (Chicago: The International City Managers' Association, 1945), p. 19.

[97] See Chap. 10.

[98] *Civic Education in Planning* (American Institute of Planners Subcommittee on Civic Education, October, 1951).

CITY BEAUTIFICATION PROGRAMS

Although the "City Beautiful" is no longer regarded as the central goal of urban planning, city beautification should be considered as an important objective of physical planning. The achievement of this objective requires certain steps to be taken by direct action of government; some by regulatory controls; and still others by coöperative citizen action.

Public Buildings and Facilities

In the planning of public buildings and facilities, each community is in a favorable position to develop structures of pleasing proportions and attractive architecture. Usually this can be done without sacrifice to their functional design or utility. Excellent opportunities for enhancing civic beauty are also presented through the architectural design and site planning of viaducts, grade separations, street lighting facilities, and fire hydrants. Landscape treatment of public open spaces and parking areas, traffic dividing strips, and traffic channelization may add little to the cost of government but a great deal to the attractiveness of the city. City appearance is kept up through neat clean streets and well-cared-for public properties. Civic beauty can also be greatly improved with little cost through a well-coördinated policy relating to the location and appearance of mailboxes, trash receptacles, street signs, signals, and pedestrian islands. Aesthetic values can be greatly enhanced by carefully worked out plans for the location of street lights, the elimination of overhanging business signs, unattractive billboards and sidewalk encroachments, and the placement of utility lines underground.[99]

Television Antennas

A recent development tending to mar the appearance of our communities is the unattractive design and location of television antennas. Many cities have enacted ordinances regulating the height, type of construction, guy wires, and other factors in the interest of safety.[100] Some cities also have ordinances aimed at eliminating radio and television interference. Although some ordinances provide that poles, cables, wires, antennas, conduits, and appurtenances shall be

[99] The problem of underground utility installation has been previously considered.
[100] *Television Ordinances* (Seattle: Association of Washington Cities in coöperation with The Bureau of Governmental Research and Services, University of Washington, February 26, 1953), Information Bulletin No. 154.

constructed in a neat workmanlike manner, little progress has been made in finding a solution to the problem of aesthetics created by the age of television. It is possible that with the development of new types of television equipment this problem may automatically be eliminated.

ORNAMENTAL TREES

A program for improving attractiveness in residential areas, which almost every city can carry out, is through the establishment of a plan for street trees. A carefully worked out plan of tree planting is an asset to any city. It tends to soften the formal aspect of the street and building lines and bring out the natural beauty of the locality. In addition, shade trees have many beneficial results such as the reduction of reflected heat from sidewalks and pavements and the purification of the atmosphere by absorbing carbon dioxide and releasing oxygen.[101]

Unless trees are properly selected and appropriately planted, certain problems may arise. For example, if trees are planted too close to the curb or too near street intersections, they may interfere with proper vision and create hazards to traffic. Likewise, if they are selected without regard to their ultimate size or root structure, they may interfere with overhead utilities or may clog sewers or disturb sidewalks and underground utilities.[102] Certain trees may be objectionable because of their odor or because they are too brittle or drop fruit, nuts, berries, or leaves, which make streets and sidewalks slippery. For these reasons it seems obvious that a program of tree planting should be under some form of public regulation. Some cities have found it of sufficient importance to place the control under a city forester or some city department. Under a system of this kind, tree care can usually be maintained at reasonable cost; and if trees die or are injured, they can often be replaced from municipal nurseries. Where the city does not see fit to plant or maintain ornamental trees, it is possible that the plan can be carried out by public controls, using a permit system.

SCENIC PROTECTIVE AREAS

A few cities have attempted to protect and enhance their natural

[101] *Street Trees for Cities* (Eugene, Ore.: Bureau of Municipal Research and Service, University of Oregon, October, 1947), Planning Bulletin No. 1.
[102] Vogel and Campbell, *Planting, Maintenance, and Removal of Trees from Streets*, op. cit., p. 6.

scenic beauty by the device of establishing scenic protective areas which are designated on a map. For example, the city of Niagara Falls, New York, has prescribed regulations providing that no building may be constructed, reconstructed, or altered in exterior appearance unless and until plans therefor have been approved by the planning board. Approval is likewise required for any sign which is established on or in connection with any building. The standards specified are rather general, leaving wide discretion to the planning board to make certain that the design, appearance, and relation of buildings and signs will enhance rather than impair the attractiveness and pleasantness of the appearance of the environs of Niagara Falls, the gorge of the Niagara River, and adjacent parks.[103]

[103] See Zoning Map and Sections 4 and 4A to 4W of the Niagara Falls Zoning Ordinance, adopted March 5, 1951, Niagara Falls, N.Y.

CHAPTER 7

The Public Improvements Program
and Financial Planning

THE PUBLIC IMPROVEMENTS PROGRAM

Every municipality of any size finds it necessary to expend substantial sums of money each year for the land, buildings, materials, construction, and equipment needed to provide facilities for the protection of the community, and to supply the numerous services demanded by the citizens. Municipal budgets usually distinguish between funds which are to be expended for the physical plant and equipment and those expended for salaries, operations, and debt service. The physical facilities are variously designated as "public improvements," "public works," or "capital improvements." The expenditures for these facilities are usually called "capital expenditures" or "capital outlays."

Since public improvements have a vital influence in determining the degree and direction of community development, and since the cost of such improvements represents a sizable proportion of all municipal expenditures, it is of utmost importance that all public improvement projects be developed as related items in an integrated program. The failure to coördinate properly individual projects may result not only in serious financial dislocations to the municipality, but also may be highly detrimental to its proper physical development.

THE PURPOSES AND OBJECTIVES OF LONG-RANGE PROGRAMMING

Few jurisdictions are so fortunate as to have available at any given time sufficient revenues to supply all demands for new or enlarged public improvements. Consequently, most municipalities are faced with the necessity of making decisions as to the relative priority of specific projects and of establishing a schedule for their commencement and completion. The orderly scheduling of capital improvements is accomplished under the long-range public improvements program.

Nature and Importance of Programming.   In substance, the public improvement program is simply a planned program for providing public capital improvements. In operation, it proceeds on the basis of a priority list of capital items prepared against the background of current and anticipated demands and present and potential financial resources of the community. The public improvements program should be considered as a major tool of planning for guiding public improvements of the community along desirable channels and for insuring that they proceed in an orderly manner.[1] It is not a device to encourage the spending of more public moneys, but rather a means by which an impartial evaluation of needs can be made, and a timetable established for the development of those projects which are authorized or contemplated.

Long-range programming of public improvements is based upon three fundamental considerations. First, the proposed projects must be selected on the basis of community needs. Second, the projects must be developed within the financial resources of the community pursuant to a sound financial plan. Third, the program must be kept flexible through periodic review and revision. The observance of these considerations implies the analysis of many factors within the community as well as an evaluation of the proposed improvements.

Failure to establish a sound long-range public improvements program is highly uneconomic. Nevertheless, many communities have not appreciated the importance of this phase of planning and have continued to resolve priorities on the basis of political pressures. Unfortunately, efforts to develop a sound public improvements program are often defeated because of the influences brought to bear at the city hall to secure a high priority listing of some project favored by

[1] Philip P. Green, "The Capital Budget—How Cities May Efficiently Schedule the Construction of Public Facilities," *Popular Government,* Vol. 19, No. 8, p. 5, April, 1953.

a special interest group. Equally unfortunate is the result which may come from the confusion produced by a variety of pressure groups which may induce the legislative body, the mayor, and even the planning agency to attempt to satisfy all interests by trying to include a little in the current budget for everyone, and thereby deferring many urgently needed projects for future years.

Benefits from Programming. The benefits to be derived from the programming of public works are numerous. In the first place, programming requires the heads of operating departments to plan for the future and to anticipate their needs for capital expenditures over a period of years. Since the program contemplates annual review, each project is examined a number of times before it is authorized in the annual budget. This annual reëxamination helps to guarantee that priority will be given to those projects most essential to the community, and that those which were hastily conceived or ill-considered will be eliminated. It may also minimize the danger of constructing "white elephants" caused by impulsive action influenced by a momentary wave of popular enthusiasm. Moreover, from the political standpoint, the programming procedure may afford the public official a certain degree of protection from pressure groups seeking to secure approval of their pet projects.

Programming offers a better prospect of getting first things first. It establishes a sounder basis for budgetary decisions and helps to insure that current decisions will be related to long-term trends. Programming enlarges the whole picture of needs, and thus makes it possible to make a better evaluation of the requests of each individual department. The listing of long-range projects in a public document also has the advantage of keeping the public better informed as to municipal needs and the plans for meeting them.

From the standpoint of economics, a sound public improvements program may produce substantial savings and point the way to needed budgetary or financial reforms which will have a lasting value in improving overall city management. The public improvements program offers the municipality an opportunity to prorate the cost of a number of improvements over a period of years, thereby tending to establish a more nearly constant tax level.[2] Programming of improvements often makes it possible to achieve economies through the acquisition of land as sites for public buildings and other facilities at a more op-

[2] Charles L. Crangle, "Advantages of Long-Term Capital Budgeting," *The Tennessee Planner*, Vol. X, No. 2, p. 39, October, 1949.

portune time since the future needs can be anticipated in advance of actual budget authorization, and hence the land may frequently be acquired at a lower figure. As a result of long-range programming, engineering plans may be prepared well in advance of construction, thus making more time available for checking and rechecking. Furthermore, through programming, it is possible to facilitate a more even work program, thereby minimizing layoffs, rehiring and training, and contributing to the scheduling of work during slack periods in which there is a labor surplus. Also, a better utilization of equipment may produce substantial savings in capital outlay or rental costs.

In some instances the undertaking of public improvements may be planned to help lessen the burdens of unemployment relief. It is possible that by careful long-range planning of public works projects, large cities may be able to absorb some of the workers who would otherwise be unemployed during seasonal variations or periods of economic depressions. However, there are obvious weaknesses in attempting to time the construction of public works with unemployment cycles. Usually public works projects must be built when they are most needed and cannot wait for periods of widespread unemployment. Furthermore, it is open to serious question whether it is sound public policy to subordinate the satisfaction of public needs to the labor demands of private enterprise. Nevertheless, careful study of the labor market and employment trends and conditions is important in order that communities may plan their long-range public improvements program to take the best advantage of the available labor supply. At the same time they should take into account the possibilities of furthering major welfare objectives.

The Program Period and the Budget.   There are obviously many practical difficulties in long-range planning. Future conditions are never wholly predictable and, therefore, any long-range plan of public improvements must be kept flexible in order not to impose a rigid pattern of development upon a community. The period of time to be included in the program depends upon a number of factors. The period should be long enough to indicate trends, but not so long that estimates for later years are mere guesses. The adoption of too short a period eliminates the advantage to be gained through long-range programming, while too long a term tends to make the programming meaningless because it is too indefinite and uncertain. The National Resources Planning Board suggested that ten years is about the longest period over which an advance program of public works construction can be considered effective.[3] Although there is not complete uniformity as to the number of years to be included in the long-range capital improvements program, six years has generally come to be accepted as a most logical and convenient period for detailed programming.

The improvements which are projected over the six-year period are listed in the capital budget. This budget is to be distinguished from the annual budget. The annual budget is the key to all programs of government. It determines the operational activities and the capital improvements that will be undertaken during a fiscal year. The annual budget establishes the municipality's "standard of living." Consequently the adoption of the budget represents the most important policy decision of the city council.[4] Annual budgets cover too short a period to reflect long-range plans. However, the annual budget, together with the appropriations ordinance, is the means by which specific capital improvements are authorized.[5] The annual budget sets forth the part of the long-range program which is actually approved by the legislative body.

The capital budget shows the public improvements which the municipality contemplates will be needed in the foreseeable future. Thus, the six-year program consists of the annual budget with a five-year advance program. Only the first year of the program is a definite budget recommendation. The five additional years are estimates of the probabilities. Annual revision is an essential feature of programming. This should be a part of the annual budget procedure. Each year the advance program is reappraised and a new sixth year is added. The previous order of projects is revised in the light of new conditions. By this procedure a new six-year program is developed of which the first year becomes a definite budget recommendation. This process is repeated annually.

The period for financial planning should look considerably beyond the six-year period for programming specific projects. Where public improvements are financed by borrowing, the obligations incurred therefor may possibly extend over a period of 20 or 25 years. Thus,

---

[3] National Resources Planning Board, *Long-Range Programming of Municipal Public Works* (Washington, D.C.: U.S. Government Printing Office, June, 1941), p. 4.

[4] *Administrative Manual*, City of San Jose, Calif., loose-leaf, p. 21–1.

[5] A modern approach is through the "performance" or "program" type of budget which helps to connect the itemized budget with the elements of finance, procurement, and personnel administration. See for a discussion of this relationship, Eugene R. Ellis, *Program Budgeting—A Method for Improving Fiscal Management* (Morgantown: Bureau for Government Research, West Virginia University, 1955), Publication No. 14.

the ability of any municipality to meet expenditures for current operations and capital outlays during any future period depends upon the soundness of the long-range financial plan.

Relationship to Financial Planning.   Since one of the fundamental considerations of public improvements programming is that projects must be developed within the financial resources of the community, no program could be realistic which was not developed pursuant to a sound long-range financial plan. Actually financial planning should precede project planning. It should originate with the first planning studies of the community and proceed with all plans and programs which affect the economics of the community, both present and future.

The long-range financial plan is a comprehensive program which takes into account estimates of all municipal expenditures and revenues. It includes estimates of expenditures for public services as well as capital outlays and estimates of all revenues, including not only taxes but also those from grants-in-aid, borrowing, municipal enterprises, and all others.[6] Before any intelligent approach can be made to the programming of capital improvements, a careful analysis should be made of the financial resources of the community, which will indicate what the revenue potential is likely to be in the period covered by the capital improvements program and for such additional period as may be necessary to gauge the ability of the municipality to retire bonds and other long-term indebtedness. Financial studies are concerned with both legal and practical considerations. Many legal limitations on the financial plan will be found in the provisions of the federal and state constitutions, in the state statutes, and in the city charter. On the policy side, the decision to undertake or not to undertake a particular project may often turn upon the political expediency of a proposed method of financing or the timing of a tax levy or bond issue. Effective programming of public improvements can be achieved only in conjunction with a long-range financial plan taking into account all these factors.

Relationship to the Public Services Program.   Likewise, the capital improvements program cannot be successfully carried out without reference to public services and programs. Operating costs of services

[6] "Fiscal Programming" by Walter H. Bucher, Gerald Breese and Dorothy E. Whiteman (eds.), *An Approach to Urban Planning* (Princeton, N.J.: Princeton University Press, 1953), Chap. 6, pp. 92–105. On the need for giving consideration to all financial factors, see Norman W. Wood, "Long-Term Financial Planning," *Municipal Finance*, Vol. XXIX, No. 1, pp. 30–33, August, 1956.

and programs must also be financed out of available revenues. Each municipality must determine what kind of program it desires to provide with respect to fire protection, police protection, health protection, recreation, and every other municipal function. The kind of service provided is, to a considerable degree, governed by the finances available. The extensiveness of a given service program has a bearing upon the capital outlay required to carry on the program. Likewise, the type and location of facilities to be developed has a relationship to operating costs. If, for example, a city provides for capital outlays to establish parks and playgrounds, it becomes necessary to provide funds in its operation budget for personnel to operate and maintain them. Too frequently municipalities have failed to give adequate attention to the effect that capital expenditures have upon the need for increased operating budgets.

The programming of public services presents a somewhat more difficult problem than the programming of capital improvements. Many public services are highly intangible and, consequently, their justification and worth are difficult to evaluate. The International City Managers' Association has suggested several procedural steps as a means of developing a related public services program.[7] Among these it is suggested that each municipality seek (1) to identify the objectives of each department and measure how the need for services in each department can be expected to vary as the city grows and develops, (2) to determine the level of adequacy at which service is to be provided, and (3) to identify the key cost factors and express the service program in terms of them.

It is apparent that no very satisfactory yardstick can be applied in measuring adequacy of service or the accomplishment of objectives. Nevertheless, analysis of the service program in terms of objectives, standards of adequacy, and accomplishments makes it possible to achieve a better relationship of the public services program and the capital improvement program and fit the two more properly into the long-range financial plan.

Programming Procedure

Before the actual preparation of the long-range public improvements program is undertaken, a great deal of basic information should be gathered and analyzed. The public improvements required by a

[7] *Local Planning Administration* (Chicago: The International City Managers' Association, 1948), p. 271.

given community depend upon many factors such as location, climate, economic base, industrial growth, population trends, local practices and attitudes, and many other conditions which have a bearing on current and future demands.

Function of the Planning Agency. Different cities have established different practices for the preparation of the long-range public improvements program. Actual responsibility for the compiling of the capital budget is normally vested in the budget director or other chief financial officer. It is essential, however, that in the process of its preparation and development, the planning agency be given a major role, including authority to review all project proposals in order that it may determine if they conform to the comprehensive plan and in order that it may make recommendations with respect to priorities, special projects, and methods of finance.[8]

In those jurisdictions in which the planning agency is integrated within the administrative structure, the planning director may well play the dominant role in representing the chief administrator in bringing together all the various agencies that will participate in developing the program. This is possible, however, only if there is full and active coöperation among the financial, administrative, and policy making officials who should contribute their experience and judgment to the overall result.[9] The coöperative development of the program with the chief financial officer as well as administrative officials will help to make it possible to ascertain whether particular proposals are financially feasible. Working with department heads in a group will make it necessary for each department head to justify the need for his particular projects in relationship to those of all others. It will also help him to see each proposed project in perspective and make him more realistic in outlining future departmental programs. In the formulation of the public improvement program, the role of the planning agency should be not merely that of a coördinating agency, but it should function also in a positive role by furnishing constructive proposals for achieving a well-balanced program. The long-range public works program involves three principal steps: [10] (1) the financial

[8] Frank Lombardi, "The Planning Agency and Capital Improvement Programs," *Journal of the American Institute of Planners*, Vol. XX, No. 2, p. 101, Spring, 1954.

[9] William Stanley Parker, "Capital Improvement Programs," *Journal of the American Institute of Planners*, Vol. XX, No. 4, p. 192, Fall, 1954.

[10] See National Resources Planning Board, *op. cit.*, p. 3, which lists as other steps in the program consideration by the legislative body and public acceptance.

analysis, (2) the listing of needed public improvements, and (3) the evaluation and determination of priorities.

Financial Analysis. The financial analysis should be prepared by the fiscal officer or the department of the municipality primarily responsible for financial matters. The financial analysis should seek to provide reliable information of the present and future ability of the community to pay for the cost of construction and maintenance of all public improvements. This determination should be based upon (1) estimates of the present financial resources and probable future trends in revenues and expenditures, (2) an appraisal of the various factors influencing the operation of the program, and (3) ascertainment of the legal limitations and prior commitments which restrict the freedom of the municipality to adopt a particular policy. From these considerations the municipality must determine the amount of funds available for the construction of public improvements.

Among the most valuable data to be included in the financial analysis is the historical record of financial statistics which should cover ten years, if possible. Often records for past years are not always comparable, due to various changes in program, system of accounting, or organization. To the extent to which they are comparable, the historical record provides an invaluable guide in indicating future trends. To be meaningful, financial statistics should be illustrated by graphs and tables and be supported by miscellaneous background data explaining the substantive content and methods of presentation, and should reconcile inconsistencies which may have a bearing upon their interpretation. Data to be included in the historical period should be grouped according to classification. Among the classifications should be: (1) revenues by source, (2) operating expenditures by department and by purpose, and (3) capital expenditures by department and purpose.

The study of revenues should not only include a study of existing and possible sources, such as taxes, fees, fines, grants-in-aid, earnings from utilities and their potential productivity, but also should take into account and be related to the rate of population growth and direction of movement, and such matters as economic status, industrial and commercial activity, and other factors that may affect property values and other tax sources. Political trends which may result in state legislation enlarging or restricting the tax base or in providing greater or reduced state aid are a proper part of the analysis.

The analysis of operating expenditures should include both a departmental and functional breakdown. As in the study of revenues, all relevant factors that may affect the demands for expenditures should be taken into account. The historical record of debt service broken down by categories showing the rate at which past debt has been incurred will provide some indication of what policies may have to be devised for the future. Statistics showing the past expenditures for capital outlay and the method of financing them have an important bearing on policy decisions with respect to future projects. Historical record has much less bearing in predicting future demands for capital expenditures than is the case with operating costs. Often the neglect of the physical plant or failure to undertake needed construction may result in the necessity for unusually heavy future expenditures. On the other hand, a municipality which has gone through a period of heavy capital expenditures may be somewhat relieved of such a heavy burden in the years immediately ahead. Nevertheless, statistics on capital expenditures and their analysis are an essential part of the financial analysis.

Listing of Public Improvements.   Since the primary purpose of public improvements programming is to establish a logical order for the development of specific projects, the starting point for the process is the listing of the various projects or improvements needed or desired in the community, together with pertinent explanatory data for each. As previously indicated, it is usually the responsibility of the planning agency to prepare the list in coöperation with the various department heads whose activities are affected.[11] In addition to projects suggested by department heads, the list should include improvements proposed by the mayor, the legislative body, responsible community organizations, and civic-minded groups and individuals. In order better to understand the program, it is desirable that the listing of proposed projects include or be accompanied by a report on progress of construction of projects authorized.[12] It is desirable that the list also show the proposals of autonomous municipal agencies and other governmental units having jurisdiction within the area in order that an effort may be made to coördinate the programs of overlapping jurisdictions to avoid conflicts and duplications. Although this approach requires a great deal of collaboration among a number of agencies, coördinated group action will be valuable in helping to

[11] *Local Planning Administration,* op. cit., p. 275.
[12] Lombardi, *op. cit.,* p. 96. For example, see *Capital Program* (City of Philadelphia, Philadelphia City Planning Commission, 1955–1960, January, 1955), pp. 81–96.

minimize competition among bond issues which voters may be required to approve and in maintaining taxes at an even level.

There is not general agreement as to what items should be included in the list of projects. In general, the term "public improvements" includes "projects of large size, fixed nature or long life, which provide new or additional public facilities or services." [13] It includes such items as public buildings, parks, sewers, waterworks, streets, bridges, tunnels, and all major types of construction. In addition to such fixed items it is frequently desirable to include certain types of large equipment which is expensive and has reasonably long life. Such items as road graders, fire engines, heavy trucks, and similar equipment may involve heavy investments, and, under certain circumstances, may be appropriately listed in the public improvements program. This is particularly true in the smaller cities. In the larger cities expenditures for such items would usually be included in the operations budget. Likewise, it may be desirable to list the initial equipment for new buildings including items such as furniture and fixtures. On the other hand, the list should not include minor equipment items such as typewriters, office supplies, and the usual maintenance materials. Nor is it desirable to include official automobiles, since these are commonly traded in every year or two, and, like minor types of equipment, are more appropriately included as operating equipment. In some instances, it may be desirable to include preconstruction engineering costs in the public improvements program, where such costs are considered to be appropriately a part of the capital cost of the project.

The listing of items for programming purposes cannot be governed by the accounting system which the particular municipality may employ. It may not be desirable to include in the list all items shown by the accounting system as capital expenditures. Furthermore, as has been indicated, it may be desirable to list a number of items of major equipment which may not be carried on the books as capital expenditures.

The National Resources Planning Board suggests the following classification as generally covering those items which are in keeping with the objectives of programming:[14]

1. New construction and major repairs and additions, including the purchase of land.

[13] National Resources Planning Board, op. cit., p. 19.
[14] National Resources Planning Board, op. cit., p. 21.

2. Major equipment, covering, in general, items for which a separate
authorization is called for in the annual budget.

The procedure for listing projects will, of necessity, vary with practices of the various jurisdictions. Some municipalities have found it
advantageous to design special forms to insure that information will
be presented adequately and with a degree of standardization. A number of cities have adopted the practice of carrying on the inventory of
needs as a continuous operation. This has the advantage of always
being up to date and simplifies the problem at the time of program
preparation and annual review.

Evaluation and Determination of Priorities.   After the comprehensive list of projects is compiled, initial review will frequently indicate certain proposals which are obviously impossible or impractical.
The planning agency should eliminate these from consideration and
arrange the remaining proposed projects in order of priority based
upon criteria of need and ability to finance. A written statement of
explanation should be made with respect to all projects eliminated
and should accompany the list. Since, in most jurisdictions, the list
of proposed public improvements will contain many more projects
than can be undertaken, the evaluation of projects for the purpose
of determining priorities becomes most important and frequently
difficult. This stage of the process becomes subject to many pressures.

The relative position of a project in the program must be considered in the interest of the orderly accomplishment of the comprehensive plan and the financial ability of the community. Each project
should be viewed not only in the light of current needs, but also in
the light of long-range trends. For example, a bridge or street widening which appears desirable today might conceivably not be necessary
in two or three years in view of the accomplishment of the overall
street plan or of plans of the state highway department or the county
engineer which might alter the traffic pattern.

To the extent possible, it is desirable to establish certain criteria
as a basis for evaluating proposed projects. Generally speaking, preference should be given to projects that are vital to the protection of
life, health, and safety. Sometimes, special consideration must be
given to emergency situations or to proposals designed to conserve
existing property or resources. Although recognizing the arrangement
as arbitrary, the National Resources Planning Board has suggested

the following criteria for guidance in trying to ascertain the relative importance of projects: [15]

1. Protection of life;
2. Maintenance of the public health;
3. Protection of property;
4. Conservation of resources;
5. Maintenance of physical property;
6. Provision of public services;
7. Replacement of obsolete facilities;
8. Reduction in operating costs;
9. Public convenience and comfort;
10. Recreational value;
11. Economic value;
12. Social, cultural, or aesthetic value;
13. Promotional value through effect on future developments; and
14. Relative value with respect to other services.

In determining priorities, many practical and political factors must be taken into account. One factor is that of weighing the importance of community-wide projects against those benefiting only a small neighborhood or a particular interest group. It is also important to recognize the fact that poorer neighborhoods are frequently short-changed in getting their fair share of public improvements, because they are often unorganized and inarticulate in comparison with wealthier neighborhoods. A carefully worked out long-range public improvements program, coördinated with the comprehensive plan, may help to secure a more equitable distribution of needed projects and, at the same time, be a factor in checking the spread of blight in declining neighborhoods.[16]

While there may be positive factors to support the prior relative position of a particular project, there are also special considerations which may necessitate that certain projects, even though meritorious, should be deferred. The International City Managers' Association states that certain projects may have to be deferred for one or more of the following reasons: [17]

1. Until more satisfactory state legislation can be obtained because of litigation and the delays incident thereto;

[15] National Resources Planning Board, op. cit., p. 27.
[16] Lombardi, op. cit., p. 97.
[17] Local Planning Administration, op. cit., p. 276.

2. On account of pending negotiations with neighboring or overlapping political units;
3. Because preliminary research, surveys, and plans are needed and will require considerable time;
4. Until methods of financing and cost distribution as between benefited property and the city as a whole can be worked up;
5. Because of lack of coöperation on the part of property owners who refuse to dedicate or sell the needed land; or
6. For other reasons.

Even after projects have been arranged in the order of need or urgency, it may be necessary to shift certain ones in order to achieve a balanced program.[18] For example, several large projects may appear to be of high priority, but it may not be feasible to undertake all immediately because of their size and problems of finance. Therefore, it may be necessary to allocate them over several years and advance certain minor projects which are within the realm of feasibility. Discussion, at this stage, with departments and agencies whose programs are affected is most important in order to maintain internal harmony and future coöperation. Final responsibility rests with the legislative body, which may accept or revise any of the budget recommendations in the light of legislative policies. The priorities thus determined should result in a proposed program of public improvements as follows:

1. The first year program which is implemented through the annual budget, contains detailed specifications with at least preliminary engineering and architectural designs.
2. The second through the sixth years' programs, which are still subject to revision, contain descriptions and approximations of costs but with less detail than those for the first year, and
3. Subsequent years' programs contain more generalized descriptions and cost estimates without attempting to establish definite priorities.

As with other aspects of planning, success in programming requires

---

[18] It has been suggested that projects which are finally included are selected on the basis of:
1. Urgent necessity and benefit to the community.
2. Readiness—considering funds on hand or available, plans completed, and land acquired.
3. Proper sequence of construction of related projects.
4. Balancing the program through the inclusion of reasonable proportions of different types of projects and by restriction to the recommended annual total cost.
See Virgil H. Hurless, "Obtaining Improvements Through Balanced Financing," *Municipal Finance*, Vol. XXVI, No. 4, p. 137, May, 1954.

not only coöperation from operating departments and approval by the legislative authority but also general acceptance by the public. The public should be kept informed as the development of the program proceeds. The press, radio, television, and public hearings should be utilized to keep the public advised as to the nature, purpose, and benefits of various proposals. In many instances municipal elections are necessary to authorize bond issues or tax levies for the purpose of financing particular projects. If the public is kept fully informed as the program is developed, there is less likelihood of confusion and misunderstanding when the issue is placed on the ballot.

THE FINANCIAL PLAN

Long-range financial planning is gradually coming to be accepted as an essential part of the process of comprehensive planning. As a rule, the long-range financial plan covers a much longer period of time than that covered by the public improvements program. Very often municipalities must anticipate their financial needs and financial resources as far in advance as 20 or 25 years. This is particularly necessary when a substantial part of the program of public improvements is financed by bonds or other long-term obligations.

POLICY CONSIDERATIONS IN DEVELOPING THE FINANCIAL PLAN

The ability of a community to finance a program of public improvements is governed by its economic base, the legal limitations imposed by constitution, charter, and statute, and by the willingness of the people to pay the costs to meet the needs of the community. Within these limitations, policy considerations are concerned with developing an orderly, coördinated expenditure program for capital improvements in relation to expenditures for operations and maintenance and a well-balanced revenue program to provide for the financing of all projects and programs.

Principal Methods of Financing Improvements. In the financing of public improvements a municipality has a choice of several methods or a combination of methods. The three major choices are: (1) Undertake the improvement and pay for it out of current revenues; (2) accumulate funds in a reserve to supply the improvement at a later date; and (3) borrow money to pay for improvements currently undertaken. The choice of methods involves both practical and ethical considerations. One of the most significant factors in making a choice is that expenditures for public improvements are often irregular and spasmodic and are not usually made until social and economic pressures demand them. Where such a situation exists, financing the capital expenditure out of current revenues may subject the tax rate to violent fluctuations from year to year. This would tend to depress property values and adversely affect the tax base itself. Stabilization of the tax rate is an important consideration to merchants and industry.[19]

To defer the public improvement until reserve funds may be accumulated may, on the other hand, result in heavy social and economic costs resulting from the lack or inadequacy of needed municipal facilities. Furthermore, there are strong pressures against imposing current taxes to provide facilities for use by persons who may not have contributed to their cost, and also there is the danger that funds accumulated may be diverted to other purposes. This method, however, has definite advantages where the city has moneys which are not immediately needed. The creation of reserve funds safeguards the accumulated funds and assures their availability when needed. It also provides additional capital through earnings from investment which may help offset the increases in acquisition or construction costs.[20]

If the public improvement is paid for initially by borrowing, the cost or a part of the cost is shifted to those who may be benefiting from the improvement in future years. The ethical justification commonly urged for financing long-life improvements by borrowing is that those who benefit from the improvements should pay for them.[21] Practical considerations may be concerned with current interest rates, trends in money values, current debt service charges, market for bonds, and many other matters.

Two devices for financing public improvements which have come into recent use deserve study by persons responsible for financial planning. They are the "authority" and the "lease-purchase agreements." The "authority" has come to be used in increasing numbers for the construction and operation of certain types of public works. "An au-

[19] Fred W. Lawrence, "The Capital Improvement Program—A Challenge to a Small City," *Municipal Finance*, Vol. XXVI, No. 4, p. 147, May, 1954.

[20] Carl W. Clepper, "Use of Capital Reserve Funds for New Improvements," *Municipal Finance*, Vol. XXVII, No. 1, pp. 44–48, August, 1954.

[21] T. E. McMillan, Jr., *State Supervision of Municipal Finance*, (Austin: The Institute of Public Affairs, University of Texas, 1953), Public Affairs Series No. 12, p. 66.

thority is a governmental business corporation set up outside of the normal structure of traditional government so that it can give continuity, business efficiency, and elastic management to the operation of a self-supporting or revenue-producing public enterprise." [22] Most authorities are not separate governmental units, but rather are semi-autonomous instrumentalities for performing certain services with which charges are associated. They are frequently used to develop and operate such facilities as ports, toll bridges, housing projects, and certain public utilities. Authorities usually issue revenue bonds which are backed by the revenue from the project and also by the credit of the authority.

The use of "lease-purchase agreements" as a method of paying for public improvements is of quite recent origin.[23] It has been utilized to finance public buildings and other nonrevenue-producing public improvements which are commonly financed by bond issues. The lease-purchase method has been described as follows: [24]

1. A public jurisdiction prepares specifications for a public works facility and makes them available to a private company, either following direct negotiation or some form of bidding procedure;
2. the company then constructs the facility, frequently on land already owned by the jurisdiction and leased to the company for a token fee, and "leases" the facility back to the public body for an annual or monthly "rental";
3. at the end of the lease period the title to the facility is conveyed to the public jurisdiction without any further payments to the company, aggregate "rental" payments having covered the original cost of the facility, together with interest.[25]

Rental payments are made from general tax funds. Under this plan no bonds are issued and delays and expense of holding bond elections are avoided. The plan has been criticized as a "devious method of circumventing restrictions on bond issues which, if obsolete and unworkable, might better be changed by law." [26]

[22] Luther Gulick, " 'Authorities' and How to Use Them," *The Tax Review*, Vol. VIII, No. 11, p. 47, November, 1947.

[23] Lease purchase agreements are sometimes referred to as lease with option to purchase.

[24] Eugene C. Lee, "Use of Lease-Purchase Agreements to Finance Capital Improvements," *Municipal Finance*, Vol. XXIV, No. 2, p. 78, November, 1951.

[25] "Many leases, sometimes called 'carefree' leases, quite often provide that the lessor, after he has constructed the building, is free from all costs of maintenance, repairs, applicable taxes, and insurance, so that the base lease payment is net to the lessor." *Ibid.*

[26] Jeanne-Louise Haviland, "Paying for Public Works," *Tax Policy*, Vol. XX, No. 5–6, p. 11, May–June, 1953.

There appears to be a conflict of authority as to whether such agreements are in effect purchases rather than leases and, therefore, incur a debt within the debt limit.[27] The general rule laid down by the courts holds that such agreements do create a debt within the debt limitation. However, two recent cases arising in California and Michigan hold to the contrary.[28] Where such agreements are held to be purchases in effect, they are also subject to the requirements of law for competitive bidding.

In some states, public authorities have been created to construct public buildings by the sale of revenue bonds. The buildings are then leased by the authority to the municipalities or to other governmental units or agencies. The revenue bonds of the authority are paid off from rental provided by taxes levied by the local government.[29] The opportunities for using this means of financing have not been fully explored. State statutes and court decisions in each jurisdiction will determine the limits within which they may be employed by any municipality. The most important reason for creating authorities is to secure funds for building without violating the constitutional debt limits. Since the administrative board of the authority is commonly made up of state elected officials ex officio, legal questions have been raised as to whether such composition so identifies the authority with the state as to make its obligation simply that of the state. This view was taken by the Supreme Court of Illinois.[30] The main criticism that has been made of appointing a group of private citizens to the board is that the authority is removed one stage from direct democratic control.[31]

[27] *Ibid.*, p. 10. For a discussion of earlier cases, see Attorney General's Opinion, State of Washington, to Josephine Corliss Preston, June 11, 1926.

[28] *Dean v. Kuchel*, 35 Cal. (2d) 444, 218 P. (2d) 521 (1950) and *Walinske v. Detroit-Wayne County Joint Building Authority*, 325 Mich. 562, 39 N.W. (2d) 73 (1949).

[29] Authorities have been created in a number of states including Alabama, Georgia, Illinois, Kentucky, Maine, Michigan, and Pennsylvania to finance buildings and facilities of state agencies or state and local agencies. The State of Washington in 1955 created a State Building Financing Authority for the purpose of financing the construction and rehabilitation of certain public buildings for lease to institutions of higher learning and departments and agencies of the State. Local units of government were not included. See Chap. 12, Laws of Washington, 1955, Extraordinary Session. This act was held unconstitutional in *State of Washington, ex rel. State Building and Finance Authority v. Yelle*, 47 Wn. (2d) 705, 289 P. (2d) 355 (1955).

[30] *People ex rel. Greening v. Green*, 382 Ill. 577, 47 N.E. (2d) 465 (1943) and *Loomis v. Keehn*, 400 Ill. 337, 80 N.E. (2d) 368 (1948).

[31] Gilbert Y. Steiner, *A State Building Authority: Solution to Construction Needs?* Reprint from *Current Economic Comment*, Vol. 17, No. 1, pp. 22–30, February, 1955 (Urbana, Ill.: The Institute of Government, University of Illinois).

Current Revenue Financing Versus Borrowing.   It is not possible to lay down hard and fast rules to determine when public improvements should be financed out of current revenues (pay-as-you-go) and when they should be financed by borrowing. Within the framework of legal authority, the financial policy of a municipality must be developed according to the size of the city and existing local conditions. For example, a project which represents a costly and unusual undertaking in a small city might fall under the category of a regularly recurring improvement in a large city. Thus, the construction of a library or a school building which would occur infrequently in a small city might represent a heavy expenditure, that, for practical purposes, could not be financed except by borrowing money on a long-term basis. In a large city, however, where such construction and replacements occur regularly, it would seem more practical that they be financed from current revenues.[32]

As a general principle, borrowing by any municipality is not justified except where the municipality is faced by extraordinarily large expenditures for long-life improvements or is confronted with immediate need for funds which are not at the time otherwise available. In the latter case, borrowing normally is justified only to provide operating revenues in anticipation of tax or other revenue receipts or to meet some unforeseen emergency or other nonbudgeted expenditure which could not reasonably have been anticipated when the budget was adopted. Borrowing for such purposes should be for short periods of time, and provision should be made for repayment in the next annual budget.

The considerations involving questions of long-term borrowing for financing public works present somewhat different issues. The irregularity with which the demands for public improvements have arisen have led many jurisdictions to adopt a policy that all long-life capital improvements should be financed by borrowing. In recent years, however, a number of cities have moved in the direction of placing all public improvements on a pay-as-you-go basis. This was done in Kalamazoo, Michigan, by raising the tax rate sufficiently to retire its outstanding debt, and thereby making it possible to finance public improvements on a current basis. Milwaukee, Wisconsin, established an amortization fund to retire the debt and in 1936 went on a cash basis for financing capital improvements. Some modification

[32] Ernst B. Schulz, *American City Government, Its Machinery and Processes* (New York: Stackpole and Heck, Inc., 1949), p. 518.

of the policy has been made to accelerate postwar public improve-ments.[33] Other pay-as-you-go plans, with some modifications, have been adopted by Buffalo, Syracuse, Rochester, White Plains, Schenec-tady, and Scarsdale, New York; Cambridge and Belmont, Massachu-setts; San Juan, Texas; Columbus, Canton, and Cleveland Heights, Ohio; Columbus and Macon, Georgia; Baltimore, Maryland; Green-wich, Stamford, and Hartford, Connecticut; Detroit, Grand Rapids, and Fond du Lac, Michigan; Colorado Springs, Colorado; and others.[34]

The supporters of the pay-as-you-go plan point to the elimination of debt service charges and the lowering of tax rates. They maintain that borrowing supplements current revenues only for a short time and that eventually the debt must be paid from current revenues, so that in final analysis, the expenditures are limited by the yield from taxes and revenue sources other than borrowing. If borrowing is gradually eliminated and outstanding debts are amortized, interest charges would no longer be a cost, and the annual volume of con-struction could thereby be increased or the cost of improvements be reduced.

The argument of the pay-as-you-go advocates is not accepted by all financial experts who have seen real advantages in borrowing at the available low interest rates and during a period when the dollar has been experiencing a devaluation trend. Furthermore, the exemption of municipal bonds from federal income taxes has provided munici-palities with a favorable market and has kept down the costs of mar-keting and debt service. It is further urged that the pay-as-you-go policy often tends to defer projects, with consequent social and eco-nomic loss to the community, and that it is inequitable for current taxpayers to pay the entire costs of improvements which will be used over the years by many others who are not currently paying taxes.

For practical purposes, the accumulated capital reserve or capital fund method of financing public works can be considered as closely related to the pay-as-you-go plan and can be supported by most of the same arguments. The difference is that the fund is accumulated out of current revenues for a period of years and then used to finance needed improvements. Although the plan has met with some success, rising costs and pressures of various kinds have caused some localities to divert the funds for other purposes. Where, however, the plan is

[33] Haviland, op. cit., p. 5.
[34] Ibid.

carried out, municipalities have been able to eliminate interest charges and other costs involved in marketing bonds and servicing the debt.[35]

On the basis of experience, it seems likely that in most cities the need will arise for costly public improvements which are unusual and nonrecurring. To attempt to meet this cost out of the current budget would result in serious financial dislocations in the community. In such cases, resort to borrowing presents the only logical course. As a guiding principle, however, every community should apply the pay-as-you-go principle to as much of the public improvement program as possible without bringing about sharp fluctuations in the tax rate from year to year.[36] This can be achieved only by a carefully worked out long-range public improvements program and a sound financial plan. A pay-as-you-go program cannot be put into effect overnight as it would drastically upset the revenue structure. Municipalities can, however, work in that direction, and the eventual goal of a pay-as-you-go system should be part of the financial policy of each community, except perhaps for the very small cities, where the infrequency of large capital expenditures would seem to make the goal impractical.

If the construction and replacement of public improvements are scheduled with reasonable uniformity, the equitable argument for deferring the payment to the future generation which may derive a share of the benefit loses much of its weight. If programming is properly done, the spasmodic presentation of expensive projects in the capital budget can be avoided. The annual outlay for public improvements then becomes rather constant and great variations in the burden placed upon any generation does not occur. Taxpayers of tomorrow are then carrying comparable burdens with the taxpayer of today, as tax rates are kept reasonably stable. The period of financing a particular project need not necessarily be identified with the period of its benefit. Equity is served if burdens upon succeeding generations are comparative, and there is some merit in the argument that those who decide on the improvement should pay for it. Particularly is this valid if the project should prove to be unwise or unsound. Above all, it is important that the financial condition of the municipality be kept on a sound basis. Any policy which would pro-

[35] Haviland, op. cit., p. 6. Cities which have successfully used this method of financing include: Chula Vista, Napa, Palo Alto, Rio Vista, and San Bruno, California; and Eau Claire, Janesville, Kenosha, and Watertown, Wisconsin.
[36] Schulz, op. cit., p. 518.

duce any other result would be unwise, regardless of the considerations of the time which seemed to make it an expedient choice.

A sound financial policy can be developed only by taking into account and giving careful consideration to all matters which relate to financial resources, obligations, and administration. The National Resources Planning Board has suggested the following items as points to be kept in mind by those charged with the responsibility of developing and preparing the public improvements program:[37]

1. The city's obligations must fall clearly within its economic resources for payment;
2. Plans for debt repayment must be soundly formulated;
3. The municipality must possess and use adequate taxing power;
4. The municipality must maintain a sound current account;
5. The city's administration must provide the services, the physical facilities, and the forethought which are essential to meeting and perpetuating a livable community;
6. The city's administration must be conducted with reasonable economy and efficiency; and
7. There must exist a genuine quality of responsibility and integrity in those who administer and control a city's governmental affairs.

Those responsible for preparing and developing the public improvements program must carefully weigh not only the productivity of various sources of revenue but also must consider their impact upon the economy of the community. Where borrowing is to be recommended as a means of financing certain improvements, the various types of securities which may be issued and their probable effect upon the entire revenue structure must be studied.

SOURCES OF LOCAL REVENUE

There are few municipalities in the United States which are not faced with revenue problems represented by such descriptive terms as "financial plight," "financial difficulties," or "inadequate revenues." Increased population, inflation, demand for expanded services, and deferred construction and maintenance of public improvements have placed heavy burdens upon a revenue base which has not kept pace with the factors of rising costs.[38]

The Local Revenue System. The financial powers of municipalities

[37] National Resources Planning Board, op. cit., p. 29.
[38] Jack Isakoff and Gilbert Y. Steiner, *Illinois Municipal Revenue, Staff Memoranda of the Legislative Commission on Municipal Revenue* (University of Illinois: The Institute of Government and Public Affairs, 1953), p. 1.

are much more restricted than are those of either the national government or the states. Municipalities may exercise only those powers granted to them by the state. Many of the most lucrative sources of revenue have been preëmpted for state purposes. In other cases, the limited territorial jurisdiction makes certain types of taxes impractical. Even with respect to the taxes which local governments may impose, most states have numerous statutory or constitutional provisions restricting the extent to which they may be utilized. With respect to the property tax these restrictions may take the form of limitations upon assessed valuations, upon millage rates, or both. Likewise, states often limit both subject matter and rates for income, sales, admissions, business, and other types of taxes. On the other hand, state legislatures frequently impose mandatory financial obligations upon municipalities which must be met from local revenue sources, as for example, requiring the payment of employee retirement pensions, publishing reports, providing for public welfare, or creating certain offices and fixing salaries therefor.

Municipalities derive their revenues primarily from the following sources: (1) the general property tax, (2) miscellaneous sales, gross receipts, and income taxes, (3) licenses, permits, and fees, (4) charges for services and miscellaneous receipts, (5) contributions from enterprises, and (6) aid from other governments. Of the above sources, the general property tax supplies the greatest percentage of municipal revenues. In cities throughout the United States having populations of 25,000 or more, property taxes account for almost two-thirds of the revenue. In recent years the trend has been to rely somewhat less on the property tax and more upon other sources. In part this is due to legal limitations, in part to political pressures, and in part to conscientious efforts to devise a better balanced and more satisfactory revenue system.

Few people will agree upon what specific taxes constitute a well-balanced revenue plan. There are, however, a number of objectives which are generally accepted as basic to a satisfactory revenue system. Among these are:

1. Adequacy—to be satisfactory, the system must produce the needed revenue.
2. Equitableness—each person benefiting from the services of government should pay his fair share of the cost.
3. Flexibility—the system should be one which is readily adaptable to the changing economic conditions in order to maintain stability of yield.

4. *Economy in administration*—the lower the cost of administration, the greater is the productivity for general purposes of government.
5. *Simplicity*—the tax should be one which is easily understood and can be conveniently administered from the point of view of the taxpayer.
6. *Integration with the revenue systems of other governments*—harmony with related systems is essential to a well-balanced revenue system at any level.

The Property Tax.   Generally speaking, taxes are levied upon that which is owned, that which is earned, or that which is spent. Property taxes are based upon ownership. Prior to the depression, the general property tax was relied upon by most municipalities almost exclusively as the source of revenue for general purposes of government. Although still constituting the greatest single source of local revenue, property taxes have failed to keep pace with the fiscal needs of municipal government. The general property tax may apply to both real and personal property. Real property includes not only land but also improvements on the land. Personal property includes tangible personal property such as automobiles, furniture, jewelry, and intangible property such as stocks, bonds, and other securities. More than 80 percent of the property tax is derived from real property.[39]

One of the chief criticisms of the property tax is that it places an inequitable burden upon the owners of real estate. In our present industrialized urban society, the ownership of real property does not represent a fair measure of ability to pay as it did in an agricultural society where a much greater part of the wealth was in the land and buildings from which the income was derived. Today, the ownership of real property has less direct relation to income or ability to pay. Much of the wealth today is in the form of stocks and bonds and other intangibles. Since such property has no fixed *situs*, it can easily be hidden or moved from one jurisdiction to another for purposes of tax avoidance or evasion. Where the tax is high, a premium is placed upon evasion and dishonesty, and wholesale concealment or nondeclaration is common. To a lesser degree, the opportunity for evasion exists with respect to certain other kinds of personal property. In view of the obvious injustices inherent in and the difficulties in fairly administering personal property taxes, the tendency has been to place the tax burden upon those classes of property that cannot be easily hidden, such as land, buildings, machinery, and stocks of

[39] Marguerite J. Fisher and Donald G. Bishop, *Municipal and Other Local Governments* (Englewood Cliffs, N.J.: Prentice-Hall, Inc., 1950), p. 219.

goods.[40] Some states have found it advisable to exempt from the property tax intangibles and certain items of tangible personal property, such as household furnishings, and to attempt to replace the loss of revenue by other taxes, the collection of which can be more equitably enforced.

Not all real property is subject to taxation. Certain exemptions are to be found in the constitutions or laws of all the states, such as property owned by the United States government and other governments, religious, charitable, and educational institutions, veterans' organizations, cemeteries, and certain types of industries. The questions of public policy underlying these exemptions should be frequently reëxamined since oftentimes the tax base becomes seriously narrowed and inequities result from tax relief granted under strong political pressures.

Many of the limitations of the property tax and also some of the inequities in its administration result from matters beyond the control of the municipalities. Most of the state legislatures have seen fit to place limits upon either the assessed valuation, the maximum millage rate, or upon both. The principal argument in favor of tax limitations is that it is necessary to give protection to the property owner as compared to other taxpayers, and that it compels local units of government to achieve a better distribution of the tax burden and to practice economies in government.

Tax limitations do not in themselves produce an equitable tax system. Inequalities are produced in a number of different ways. In many states assessments are made by the locally elected county assessors. The partisan character of such offices has frequently led to political favoritism and discrimination in valuations. Correction of this situation is not within the power of the municipality. Even in those offices in which fairness and honesty exist, the lack of scientific knowledge and technical skills necessary for assessment may produce serious inequities. The failure to place buildings on the assessment rolls or to recognize the difference in costs and values of different types of construction and the difference in rates of depreciation or obsolescence can produce discriminations as serious as those resulting from intentional favoritism.

Financial policy must, therefore, be concerned with something more than the amount of money which can be raised from existing

[40] William Anderson and Edward W. Weidner, *American City Government* (New York: Henry Holt and Company, Inc., 1950), p. 585.

or authorized tax rates applied to assessed valuations. The manner in which a tax is administered may have as much influence in the decision of a business to locate or not locate in a community as the assessed valuations and tax rates. The improvement of the assessment machinery and removal of tax discriminations, to the extent that it is within the power of the municipality to effect them, fall appropriately within the scope of the financial plan.

Whether or not property taxes still carry more than their fair share of the tax burden is a controversial question. The fact is that property tax restrictions, plus increased demands for governmental services, have forced municipalities to seek other sources of revenue. Furthermore, it is entirely possible that as a result of certain constitutional or statutory limitations, municipalities have had to resort to taxes which are more regressive in their effect in that they place disproportionately heavy burdens upon persons with limited incomes.

Aid from Other Governments. The difficulties of solving the local revenue problems on a local basis have tended to cause municipalities to turn more and more to the states for financial aid to finance their operations. This means that in order properly to analyze and evaluate the municipal revenue system, study must be given to the revenue structure of the state and other related taxing jurisdictions. The taxpayer is ordinarily interested in the total tax bill he has to pay, and not just that of a particular unit of government. This makes it important that all tax programs at the various levels of government be coördinated. Certain types of taxes can be better administered and collected by one jurisdiction than by another. It should, therefore, be the aim of a coördinated program to have those taxes administered and collected by the jurisdiction best fitted for the purpose.[41]

Next to property taxes, the largest single item of municipal revenue is that received as aid from other governments. During the depression years, a substantial amount of aid was provided to cities by the federal government.[42] Since that time, this has been considerably reduced in amount, although federal aid is furnished directly or indirectly (through the states) for a number of purposes such as airports, highways, and so forth. In some instances, the federal government makes

[41] Isakoff and Steiner, op. cit., p. 48.
[42] For a discussion of the policy of scheduling public works as a means of economic stabilization see National Resources Committee, Division of Costs and Responsibility for Public Works (Washington, D.C.: U.S. Government Printing Office, 1938).

payments in lieu of taxes on account of federal property located within the jurisdiction which is exempt from taxes.

Most of the aid from other governments comes from the states. This represents on an average approximately 18 percent of the municipal revenues.[43] State programs provide for (1) grants-in-aid, and (2) state-administered locally-shared revenues. Grants-in-aid are funds given for general or specific purposes without reference to the particular method by which the funds were obtained. The state-administered, locally-shared revenues are those which are collected by the state and distributed to the local governmental units in accordance with some formula.

Frequently, grant-in-aid programs require that municipalities match the state grants in some proportion from their own revenue sources. Among the functional areas for which aid is frequently given are public health, highway, welfare, education, and law enforcement. Sometimes the objective of state policy may be that of raising minimum standards of service or administration, or equalizing the financial resources of the wealthy and needy communities. In some cases, the policy may be one of providing financial relief because of the inadequacy of financial resources of local government or on account of conditions resulting from periods of financial distress, such as depressions, disasters, or emergencies.

State-collected locally-shared taxes involve the assignment to some other governmental unit of a fractional part of the receipts the state collects from some particular revenue source. Among the sources of revenue which are frequently shared are gasoline taxes, liquor profits and taxes, and motor vehicle taxes. Usually these revenues are of a character which, by the nature of their source, are more appropriately collected by the state than by local governments. Frequently they are derived from sources which are often preëmpted by the state. In some instances shared taxes are earmarked for particular purposes. While this enables the state to promote general state policies, it has, from the cities' standpoint, the disadvantage of preventing the use of these funds for purposes which the municipality may consider to be of greater relative importance.

As an aid to solving the revenue problem of the municipality, there

[43] United States Department of Commerce, Bureau of the Census, *Compendium of City Government Finances in 1946* (Washington, D.C.: U.S. Government Printing Office, 1948), p. 6. In some states it is much higher. In the State of Washington, for example, the state collects approximately 40 percent of the municipal revenues.

is no significant distinction to be made between one form of aid and the other. The chief advantages claimed for grants-in-aid are that the yield to the municipalities is stabilized and does not rise and fall with the phases of the business cycle. It also is better adapted to providing assistance on the basis of need and maintaining minimum standards of service and administration. Municipalities may, however, feel more secure in their sources of revenue when state statutes provide for the sharing of certain specific revenues collected and administered by the state.

Leagues of municipalities in the various states now maintain vigilant representatives at the legislative sessions to protect or expand their financial interests in the aid received from the state. Many municipalities, however, are aware of the fact that extensive state aid may not be an unmixed blessing. Local autonomy in controlling local affairs is rather basic to our system of representative government. The danger that this autonomy will be curtailed is ever present under a system where local services must be financed from sources not controlled by local government. Financial aid usually is accompanied by conditions, restrictions, and obligations. The extent to which administrative and financial responsibility should go hand in hand is a matter of public policy that needs to be carefully studied.

Some attention has been given to the enactment of enabling legislation which would empower municipal authorities to add supplemental rates to certain state-collected taxes. Under this plan, the state makes the collection and turns the revenue over to the city. However, the responsibility for the levy rests with the city. This plan would seem to be best suited to certain types of income, sales, and gross receipts taxes. There has been little experience thus far to evaluate this plan as a feasible compromise between principle and practicality.

State aid to municipalities must be considered in the light of the very complex systems of federal, state, and local relationships. Functions today cannot be easily compartmentalized. Often one level of government must deal with only a segment of a particular governmental responsibility. It is not always possible to determine that a particular governmental function is one for the state, the county, or the municipalities. In such matters as public health, highways, education, and recreation each jurisdiction must play a part in working out a coördinated program. Thus, it seems logical that an integrated plan for financing such activities may have advantages over one which would seek to identify strictly the responsibility of financial support with the responsibility of service.

The methods of establishing the amounts of state aid as well as the methods of distribution, limitations, and controls governing aid and the formulas for allocating aid vary greatly among the different states. However, the United States Census Bureau has noted that recent state legislation on aid programs has indicated two trends:

1. A trend away from the direct earmarking of specific revenue sources, or shares thereof, for particular functional grants in favor of legislative appropriations payable from "general" or at least multiple-source funds. This tendency has been especially noted regarding schools.
2. A trend toward the increased use of per capita grants for general local government support—as earmarked shares of particular state taxes, percentage shares of general state revenues, or as appropriated sums.[44]

The first state to provide for per capita local grants for general governmental activities was the State of New York. In 1946, New York undertook a complete revision of state fiscal relations and replaced the shared-tax system with one providing for per capita, general-purpose grants to localities.[45] The state budget and the general fund were divided into separate parts, one for state purposes and one for local assistance purposes. Tax stabilization reserve funds were created for the two portions of the general fund. By terms of the statute, the per capita grants replacing the abolished shared revenues are for the support of local government and the reduction of real estate taxes.[46] The New York plan (Moore Plan) is not an equalization plan but is aimed essentially at ending the cyclical difficulties experienced by local government under the shared-tax program and is designed to afford a greater degree of stability through the creation of reserves. The plan did not increase the amount of state aid, but enabled local units of government to count on a fixed amount of state aid without reference to the rise or fall of the state revenues.

In 1951, Ohio amended its statutes to provide for a local government fund from sales tax collections. Allocation to local units of government is made on a formula basis through the County Budget

[44] United States Department of Commerce, Bureau of the Census, *State Aid to Local Governments*, G–SS–No. 28 (Washington, D.C.: U.S. Government Printing Office, December, 1948), p. 5.

[45] David M. Blank, "Reform of State-Local Fiscal Relations in New York—I," *National Tax Journal*, Vol. 3, No. 4, p. 81, December, 1950.

[46] Laws of New York (1946), Chaps. 200, 201, and 301–308.

Commission of each county.[47] The funds thus provided are available for all essential local services, including those provided by home rule charter. A number of other states including California, Massachusetts, and Michigan have provided a certain amount of state aid which is not restricted to specific functions. The majority of states, however, tend to designate the specific purposes for which the aid may be used.

From the standpoint of financial planning, it is important to keep in mind that the municipal long-range financial plan must be coordinated with the financial planning of the state and other local units of government. Service functions which determine the public improvements program are often carried out as part of a joint federal-state-local program. Whether theoretically desirable or not, the fact seems to be that local governments will continue to rely heavily upon the state for financial aid. Municipalities must, therefore, work through their municipal leagues or associations to develop a fiscal policy at the state level as well as the local level which will enable each community to evolve a long-range financial plan in which they can place some reliance.

Political theory in the abstract is basic to sound public policy; yet there are many practical considerations which must, in the final analysis, govern decisions relative to financial aids. A report of the United States Treasury Department has indicated a number of governing factors as follows: [48]

Aids are, however, a product of stubborn economic, social, and fiscal facts, among which may be listed: (1) the developing interdependence of local units, creating general interest in many of what were formerly strictly local functions; (2) the inequalities in financial ability between local districts; (3) the inadequacy of local sources of revenue in view of local responsibilities of government; (4) the superiority of central units in the administration and collection of most taxes; and (5) the unacceptability and probable inadvisability, of wholesale centralization of governmental functions. The aids persist and grow, not so much because of any arguments, as because of certain conditions which make them the best available means to an end.

One other form of aid which needs further study is that of "in lieu" payments. The great amount of property owned by the federal,

[47] *Baldwin's Ohio Code Service* (1951 cumulative issue), Secs. 5546–18 ff. and 5625–19.

[48] United States Treasury Department Committee on Intergovernmental Fiscal Relations Report, *Federal State and Local Government Fiscal Relations*, Senate Doc., No. 69, 78th Cong., 1st Sess. (Washington, D.C.: U.S. Government Printing Office, 1943).

state, and other units of government within the corporate limits of many of our municipalities has resulted in considerable loss of tax revenue. Frequently, the location of these government properties may add substantially to the burdens which local government is called upon to solve such as parking problems, providing street facilities, police and fire protection, and various other services. The federal government has seen fit, under certain circumstances, to make payments in lieu of taxes for the loss which local governments have sustained. State governments have done very little to compensate for tax losses due to state ownership. Such assistance as has been given by either the federal government or the states has not been based upon any carefully worked out policy or principle. With the expansion of government ownership and the acquisition of added facilities by tax-exempt institutions, municipal officials are becoming increasingly interested in developing a satisfactory policy of "in lieu" payments.

Sales, Income, and Miscellaneous Excise Taxes.   For the great number of municipalities, taxes other than the general property tax supply a small percentage of the total revenue. The character and utilization of other taxes vary so greatly that comparisons and generalizations as to their use and productivity are quite meaningless. Within recent years, however, municipalities, faced with the pressure for expanded services and added public improvements and restricted by the limitations on the use of the property taxes, have been seeking other sources of revenue which are productive, publicly acceptable, legally permissible, and which can be equitably and economically administered. The sources to which cities have turned include a wide variety of sales, gross receipts, income, and miscellaneous privilege and other excise taxes. In this area of taxation, municipalities are again confronted with numerous legal restrictions and practical limitations. Many states rely heavily upon taxes of this character and some have seen fit to preëmpt various types of such taxes for state purposes. Certain of these taxes, even though not preëmpted, cannot be practically used by municipalities because of their limited territorial jurisdiction. Other practical difficulties arise because of the competitive problems that are involved where adjoining cities or unincorporated areas do not employ similar taxes. Furthermore, certain communities may be confronted with peculiar industrial, commercial, or economic features that make particular types of taxation not feasible.

The major forms of municipal nonproperty tax sources which have been utilized throughout the United States include taxes on (1) admissions and amusements, (2) alcoholic beverages, (3) cigarettes and tobacco, (4) income, (5) business, (6) motor fuels, (7) motor vehicles, (8) payroll, (9) public utilities, (10) realty transfer, (11) sales and use, (12) tenants and occupiers, (13) transient occupancy (hotel rooms), and (14) other miscellaneous sources.[49] Frequently, such taxes are combined with the licensing of businesses and professions under a granted power to tax and license. Where, however, the licensing power is primarily for the purpose of regulation or permission to locate, the license fees are usually insignificant as a source of revenue.

State legislatures have been reluctant in most states to extend to municipalities broad powers of taxation in the income and excise field, but are more inclined to share such taxes collected by the state to enable local governments to carry on specific functions. Even where adequate legal authority exists, it seems probable that many municipalities have not utilized these taxes because of the difficulties of administration. The administration of the business gross receipts tax presents complex problems and often necessitates the employment of a competent staff for auditing and enforcement. Excises, such as taxes on cigarettes, gasoline, and alcoholic beverages, are less difficult to administer but are more likely to be restricted for state purposes.

The equitableness of the tax burden is another factor to be weighed in the choice of available tax sources. An income tax levied at flat rates (which may otherwise be unconstitutional in some states) is regressive in its impact upon individuals having low incomes. Serious inequities may result also from a business gross receipts tax unless tax rate differentials are utilized to apply to different businesses in accordance with profit margins and competitive situations. Furthermore, there is considerable reluctance to impose taxes upon the same commodities and of the same character as those employed by the federal government and by the states.

The quest for new forms of revenue is met with competition from other levels of government of which the federal government and the states have superior authority. Municipal authorities are thus faced with the necessity of setting a financial policy which must be geared to the policies of other governments as well as to the economics of the community and to political feasibility.

[49] Isakoff and Steiner, op. cit., p. 84. This study provides an interesting comparison of the use of the various forms of taxes and their relative yields.

Licenses, Permits, and Fees. The terms "licenses," "permits," and "fees" are commonly used as catchall phrases to include various and sundry miscellaneous revenue items. Sometimes small tax items, such as dog taxes and bicycle taxes, are included in these classifications. Since licenses may be for purposes of taxation or regulation or both, the use of the term is sometimes ambiguous. Actually, where the purpose of the license fee or permit charge is for regulation, it produces no revenue except when the charge exceeds the cost of regulation. Sometimes, license fees and permit charges under the guise of regulation may, in fact, produce substantial amounts of revenue. This is frequently the case where fees are exacted from corporations or individuals for the right to exercise a business or nonbusiness privilege. Even though license fees and permit charges are levied for regulation and do not serve to defray the costs of general government, they are, nevertheless, a part of the revenue picture to be considered in the financial plan.

The payment of fees extends over a wide variety of privileges which may include the granting of motor vehicle operator's licenses, amusement licenses, parking meter charges, permits for private use of streets, extension of building lines, building permits, installation of equipment, installation of public utilities, erection of poles, animal licenses, filing of plats, and numerous other privileges.

Some of these fees, such as those derived from parking meters, produce a substantial amount of revenue. Parking meters in most jurisdictions are authorized as a means of regulating traffic. They do, nevertheless, in most municipalities produce revenue considerably in excess of the cost of regulation. In fact, in many cities, parking meter revenues are looked upon as one of the most lucrative municipal nonproperty sources of revenue. However, some jurisdictions require that the revenues derived be used for street purposes or traffic regulation. In a few jurisdictions, steps have been taken to increase the revenue from parking meters by selling advertising space on them. Where the authorization of parking meters is for traffic regulation, the legality of this practice may be open to doubt.[50]

Charges for Services. In recent years, many municipalities have sought to increase their revenues by charging for services which were previously financed from general revenues. Illustrative of these services are garbage and refuse collection, sewage disposal, snow removal,

[50] See Attorney General's Opinion, State of Washington, Smith Troy to Ralph G. Swanson, March 23, 1950.

oiling streets, weed cutting, and caring for shrubs and trees in parking strips. In some jurisdictions certain services such as fire protection, cleaning streets, and libraries are financed by special tax levies. However, these are not properly considered as service charges.

Whether the cost of particular services should be supported out of general revenues or paid for by the persons for whom they are directly rendered is a matter of policy on which there is not uniform agreement. The community interest in public health and safety is ample justification for providing for the cost of many services from general funds. The special benefit to the person served is also a valid consideration for making special charges. However, the decisions of most municipalities to impose special charges for particular services has generally resulted from pressures to find new revenue sources rather than from any careful balancing of public versus private benefits.

Municipalities have utilized a variety of methods for imposing special charges for services. In the case of sewerage services, some cities have made flat rate charges. Others have established charges based upon water consumption, the number of plumbing fixtures, sewerage connections, and the type of property served. Municipalities have also employed a variety of methods for imposing service charges for garbage and refuse collection. Some cities make a fixed monthly or annual charge for each family or residence. Usually different rates apply to commercial or industrial establishments. Other cities charge on the basis of the number of cans of refuse or garbage or by the quantity collected, time consumed, or distance from vehicle to container.[51] Charges for services such as street oiling, weed control, and many other specialized services, which are usually rendered at irregular periods and at varying degrees in different localities, can often be equitably allocated on the basis of property frontage.

Persons responsible for developing the long-range financial plan should carefully weigh the public policy questions of relative public and private benefits before deciding to recommend a program of charging for numerous services closely related to public health or safety. From the political point of view, it is usually easier to charge for a new service than for an old established service which residents have long been accustomed to think of as "free." Public officials usually encounter considerable opposition when they start charging for services which have for a long period of time been financed out of

---

[51] J. Maurice Miller, "Service Charges as an Important Revenue Source," *Municipal Finance*, Vol. XXVI, No. 1, p. 54, August, 1953.

general taxes. On the other hand, tax conscious groups are often more sensitive to increased taxes for supplying new services than they are to the imposition of charges for them. Another side of the picture is that pressure groups demanding special services frequently may be discouraged if they recognize that the services they are demanding can be financed only by a special charge.

Contributions from Enterprises and Subsidies.   Another source of revenue, the use of which raises a number of policy considerations, is that of contributions from municipal enterprises. Many municipalities throughout the United States own and operate various types of utilities such as water systems, transportation systems, electric power and light systems, gas plants and facilities, airports, and port facilities. In many instances, the revenues received from these operations exceed the cost of operation, debt service, capital reserve requirements, and other obligations. Where this is the case, municipalities are in a position to use these profits for defraying the cost of general governmental services provided such practice is permitted by law.

A general policy of operating city-owned enterprises with the objective of returning a profit to support general government services is open to criticism. One of the arguments for municipal ownership and operation has been the elimination of the profit feature in order that the residents of the community can be provided with these services at lower cost. Where enterprises are operated at a profit, this objective is not carried out. Furthermore, inequitable burdens may sometimes be placed upon the users of the utility services since the heavier costs tend to fall disproportionately upon persons of low income, thereby violating the principle of ability to pay.

On the other hand, it is not always possible to operate certain enterprises at a profit even though the municipal policy might be to do so. In fact, some municipally owned and operated enterprises have run into financial difficulties which have necessitated financial support from general revenues in order to maintain service. In particular, transit systems in many cities during recent years have faced serious financial difficulties. This is due to many factors, such as high costs of supplying service to marginal service areas, necessity of maintaining schedules during off-peak hours, and the predilection of so many persons to use private automobiles. In some cases rates cannot be raised without serious loss of patronage. Under such circumstances, subsidy from general revenues seems the only alternative if mass transportation service is to be maintained. Aside from considerations of loss of patronage, arguments are sometimes made that subsidies from general revenues are advisable in order to maintain low rates. It is urged that this is equitable not only for the benefit of low income groups who use the transportation services in greater proportion than persons of high income but also to encourage the use of mass transportation as a solution to the serious traffic problems.[52] The establishment of basic policies with respect to these questions is important not only to the operation of the enterprise, but also in working out the long-range financial plan.

MUNICIPAL INDEBTEDNESS

Most municipalities find it necessary, at some time or other, to finance the cost of major public improvements through borrowing money and the issuance of bonds. The power to borrow, like other municipal powers, must be conferred by the state. Although borrowing creates indebtedness, the power to borrow is not the same as the power to incur debts. Debts may be created by any action of the municipality which obligates the municipality to pay moneys, as for example, the employment of personnel or the entering into of contracts for work or equipment. Debts are either funded debts or floating debts. Funded debts are represented by the issuance of bonds or other forms of municipal security. Floating debts are those obligations for which no provision for payment has been made by the issuance of bonds. They may, however, be represented by interest-bearing warrants or some other evidence of indebtedness. Floating debts may become funded through bond issuance. Frequently floating debts occur as a result of poor budgeting and accounting practices.

Indebtedness with which municipalities are primarily concerned in the financing of public improvements is long-term indebtedness which is funded through the issuance of various types of bonds. A bond is a promise of the government to pay a specified sum at a certain time and at a stipulated rate of interest. Indebtedness thus incurred represents a valuable supplement to the revenue powers of municipalities. Borrowed money must, however, be repaid from the various revenue sources available to municipalities. Consequently, money obtained from borrowed sources is revenue obtained in anticipation of income

---

[52] The argument for subsidy would not seem to have the same validity with respect to most other enterprise operations.

to be received in other ways. In the final analysis, therefore, all revenues must be provided eventually out of current income.

Debt Limitations. Since municipalities are creatures of the state, the state has an interest in the financial stability of each municipal corporation. The fact that a number of cities in a given state may have financial difficulties and become unable to pay their debts may affect the credit of other political subdivisions of the state and handicap them in their ability to borrow money. Such a condition becomes a matter of concern to the state as a whole. Furthermore, the state has an overall interest in protecting taxpayers and bond buyers from unsound practices of its political subdivisions. For these reasons, each state has seen fit to establish certain restrictions upon and supervision over municipal debts.

Types of restrictions vary greatly from state to state. They may be concerned with the purpose of borrowing, the amount of indebtedness, provisions for repayment, procedures to be followed in borrowing, and various other aspects of creating and retiring indebtedness. In some instances limitations are imposed by state constitutions and in other instances by statute. Since bonds issued in excess of the legal debt limit are invalid, such restrictions constitute a warning to bond buyers. Commonly, constitutional debt limitations are concerned with the amount of indebtedness. The common provision is to fix the amount of indebtedness which any municipality may incur on a percentage of the assessed value of the property.[53] Statutory restrictions are also frequently concerned with the amount of indebtedness and, in addition, often deal with procedural matters for incurring indebtedness.

Restrictions on debt limitations have not always prevented borrowing and the creation of debt as the provisions were undoubtedly intended to do. In the first place, it is very difficult for anyone, including municipal officials, to determine at a given time what the amount of indebtedness is. For instance, municipalities utilizing various funds for financing different services and programs may accu-

---

[53] The lowest limit is 1½ percent of the assessed value which the State of Washington authorizes city councils to incur without vote of the people. However, this amount can be increased to 5 percent by vote of the electorate and an additional 5 percent can be incurred by popular vote for supplying certain utility services. The highest ratio of debt to assessed values is the 20 percent reported by Missouri. T. E. McMillan, Jr., op. cit., p. 71. Since in most states obligations to be retired from special assessments or utility revenues are not within the general constitutional or statutory debt limits and do not create liens upon the general credit of the municipality, the actual rate of indebtedness may be much higher than that specified by law.

mulate sizable surplus revenues for later use. Other programs may be financed out of borrowing. The question is thus presented as to whether cash reserves and accumulations in various funds shall be counted in offsetting the amount of funded debts. Furthermore, there are many types of obligations that are not usually considered to be within the debt limit. Among these are the amount of floating debts, including current bills, judgments, and short loans in anticipation of taxes. Usually, debts created through the issuance of revenue bonds and special assessment bonds are outside the debt limit.

There is also, under the laws of most states, the opportunity for legal avoidance of debt limits through the creation of special districts or the establishing of authorities to carry out specific functions. Unless the constitution or statute provides for overall debt limits, each jurisdiction which embraces the same property may incur separate indebtedness to the extent permitted by law. In final analysis this defeats the objective of the limitations. Nevertheless, state supervision of municipal debt as it exists at present has helped to preserve the credit of municipalities and has given some protection to taxpayers and bond purchasers.

Debt Policy. No matter what the state does to promote sound and intelligent borrowing practices, each municipality must work out its own policy with respect to municipal indebtedness. Each city is responsible for its own financial plan which must conform to the state law. Whether a city should borrow or attempt to operate on a pay-as-you-go plan has already been discussed. Most states have found it necessary, on the one hand, to steer a somewhat middle course between the extremes of paying for all public improvements out of borrowed money, and, on the other hand, of paying for all of them out of current revenue. As a matter of general policy, cities should borrow as little as possible. In particular, they should avoid borrowing to finance current operations and should seek to avoid borrowing for financing alterations, replacements, and recurrent outlays.

Since the serious consequences of poor debt policies are not usually foreseen by most citizens, professional politicians have sometimes sought to perpetuate themselves in office through advocating a program of putting off the payment of the cost of improvements as long as possible. As a result of such practices, some cities have borrowed so much in the past that 70 to 80 cents out of each dollar of current revenue must be set aside for debt service.[54] Where this occurs, serv-

54 Fisher and Bishop, op. cit., p. 295.

ice must eventually be curtailed; tax rates must be raised; or the community must further postpone the day of reckoning by borrowing more money. Usually where debt service charges exceed 25 or 30 percent of the annual budget, the problems of indebtedness have become serious.

Communities which have high debt usually have high tax rates, and communities which have low indebtedness usually have lower tax rates. These facts alone, however, cannot be taken as a valid basis of measuring either efficiency or sound public policy. While it seems true that a pay-as-you-go plan discourages extravagances, it may also be true in many cases that it will retard needed improvements with consequent social and economic losses to the community which cannot be measured by the tax rate. In arriving at a decision as to whether borrowing is advisable, municipalities should take into account the economic conditions existing at the time and the probable prospects of inflation or deflation during the period that the obligations are to run. While these are matters which cannot be accurately predicted, they should nevertheless be analyzed by experts and reliance should be placed upon their opinions.

In working out a policy on indebtedness, consideration should be given to the matter of interest rates and trends in the market for bonds. During the past several years, there has been considerable fluctuation in the interest rates at which municipal bonds will sell. Interest rates within the past few years have risen to the highest they have been since 1939. The Bond Buyers' Index of June 18, 1953, showed the index of municipal bond yield at 3.02 percent. On September 1, 1939, and October 1, 1939, it was 3.21 and 3.30 percent respectively. After October, 1939, the index on bond yields dropped until it reached a low point of 1.29 percent on February 14, 1946. Among the factors which kept the municipal rates down were the low cost of federal borrowing, the scarcity of municipal bonds, and the high demand for tax-exempt securities because of high federal taxes and the inherent safety of municipal securities.[55] At the present time, the rate for federal borrowing has been permitted to rise, and the volume of municipal bonds is high. Consequently, interest rates of municipal bonds have tended to go up.

The length of time that bonds should run is a matter for policy decision. In the past it has been common for municipal bonds to be

[55] Carl H. Chatters, "Looking Ahead in 1954," *American Municipal News*, Vol. VIII, No. 1, p. 1, January, 1954. Somewhat lower rates have been obtained in 1954 and 1955.

issued for long terms of 30, 40, or 50 years. The present trend is to issue bonds for shorter terms. Generally speaking, the term of the bond should not exceed the life of the improvement. Thus, the type of improvement may have an important bearing upon the term for which the bond is to be issued. The term for bonds issued to pay the cost of paving streets should not exceed 15 or 20 years; for buildings, not more than 20 or 30 years; and for schools, not more than 30 years. Authorities on municipal finance are in general agreement that bonds should be issued for the shortest possible maturity period, and that it would be an exceptional purpose that would justify a term extending beyond 30 years.[56]

Frequently bonds are issued for the purpose of refunding debts. These are commonly known as refunding bonds. Refunding bonds are usually issued: (1) when the city has no money to pay off the bonds when due, or (2) to replace bonds before the due date at lower interest rates. Except in case of emergencies or financial stress, the issuance of refunding bonds simply to prolong the life of the original bonds would appear to be evidence of unsound financial practice or planning. On the other hand, it may be a wise and sound policy to issue refunding bonds prior to the date of redemption where the city finds that its financial position can be improved by selling bonds having lower rates of interest. Bond issues, therefore, commonly contain callable provisions which would permit this practice to be followed. Thus bonds which may be issued for a period of 20 years conceivably could be called at the end of 10 years and the debt refunded with securities bearing lower rates of interest.

The Issuance and Sale of Bonds

The issuance and sale of bonds present many complicated problems and involve many complex procedures. Bonding houses, banks, and other purchasers of bonds must feel secure in the safety of their investment before they will risk their capital. A bond issue of any great size can be sold successfully only through the employment of the service of recognized experts including a nationally-known consulting engineer, a financial adviser, and a bond attorney.

The validity and the security of any bond issue depends upon a number of factors. Among the many requirements are the following: (1) The bond must be issued by a legally existing municipality; (2) the municipality which issues the bond must have authority under

[56] Fisher and Bishop, op. cit., p. 302.

the constitution, statutes, and charter to issue the type of bond which is offered for sale; (3) the purpose for which the bond is issued must be one for which municipalities are authorized to borrow money; and (4) the bonds sought to be issued must be within the constitutional and statutory debt limits on borrowing and taxing powers. All legal procedural requirements such as enactment of proper ordinances or resolutions, signing, advertising, submission of bids, etc., must be fully complied with, and the financial resources must be carefully analyzed in order to indicate the ability of the city to meet its obligations for carrying out the bond contract.[57]

Types and Characteristics of Bonds. Municipalities issue many kinds of bonds. They are usually classified according to certain of their distinguishing features including: (1) methods of transferring ownership and making interest payments, (2) methods of redemption, and (3) security back of the bonds. Since these distinguishing features have a bearing upon the marketability of the bonds, they are matters to be taken into consideration in preparing the financial plan where borrowing is a recommended policy.

With respect to methods of transfer and payment of interest, bonds are of two basic types: (1) coupon bonds, and (2) registered bonds. Coupon bonds are usually made payable to the bearer, and ownership is transferred simply by delivery. Interest is paid to the person who presents the interest-bearing coupon when it falls due. Registered bonds, on the other hand, are recorded in the register of the issuing authority, and interest payments are usualy mailed to the registered owner. Although transfer is less convenient than with coupon bonds, registered bonds give greater protection to the investor against possible loss.

According to their method of redemption, bonds are of two major types: (1) term (sinking fund) bonds, and (2) serial bonds. All term bonds of a given issue mature at the same time. In order to provide for the redemption of term bonds, the municipality creates a sinking fund into which annual payments are made for the purpose of retiring the principal at the date on which the bonds mature. Interest is paid on the total amount of the principal during the life of the bonds. Serial bonds differ in that they are retired on an installment basis. Maturity dates are arranged so that a certain number of bonds are redeemed each year following the date of issue. Under this method

---

[57] Michael Borge, "General Obligation Municipal Bonds—Legal Aspects," *Municipal Finance*, Vol. 25, No. 4, p. 144, May, 1953.

the interest payments decrease each year. Arguments can be made favoring one type of bond over the other. The trend appears to be toward the serial bond plan.[58] The primary reason for this is that the installment feature permits municipalities to meet their obligations without the necessity of setting up a sinking fund with the problems of administration and the dangers of mismanagement.

In recent years many municipalities have found it to their advantage to include a clause in their bonds which permits them to be called prior to maturity. This call feature has particular value during a period of falling interest rates since it permits a municipality to call in an issue before the date of maturity and refund the debt with bonds bearing a lower interest rate. Since the call feature is not always liked by the investor, municipalities may find it necessary to provide for a reasonable premium to be paid to the bondholder when the bond is redeemed prior to maturity.

From the standpoint of their security, most bonds fall into three major classes: (1) general obligation bonds, (2) revenue bonds, and (3) special assessment bonds. The decision as to the type of security to be offered must be based upon many considerations, including the purpose for which the money is to be used, the outstanding indebtedness, legal limitations on borrowing, and the marketability of particular types of bonds.

General Obligation Bonds. General obligation bonds are those secured by an unconditional pledge of the municipality's credit including its taxing powers.[59] General obligation bonds are sometimes made payable initially from certain pledged taxes or revenues. This feature does not, however, release the municipality from its obligation to pay the bonds from other revenues in the event the pledged revenues are insufficient since such bonds are backed by the full faith and credit of the municipality. State statutes frequently require that voters approve before the bonds are issued.

The issuance and sale of general obligation bonds involve a complex legal process which requires the guidance of a competent bond attorney. Investors ordinarily will not buy any bond issue until they are reasonably satisfied that the municipality has legal authority to issue and sell the bonds and to levy the taxes for paying off the issue and that all the procedural steps have been met and that the bonds

[58] Austin F. Macdonald, *American City Government and Administration* (New York: Thomas Y. Crowell Company, 1951), p. 428.
[59] McMillan, *op. cit.*, p. 67.

are in proper form to bind the municipality.[60] While a legal opinion from the bond attorney does not validate the bond issue, it is normally a prerequisite to marketing any large bond issue. Municipalities should consult with the bond attorney before any steps are taken since the preliminary steps are often most important, and, if improperly carried out, may defeat or delay the issue. General obligation bonds which are backed by the full faith and credit of the municipality frequently find a more ready market than other types of bonds and often may be sold at lower interest rates.

Since the amount of general obligation bonds is subject to the debt limits and many other restrictions provided by state constitutions and statutes, many municipalities have turned to other methods of financing public improvements, including the use of revenue bonds.[61]

Revenue Bonds. Revenue bonds are those bonds secured by the income received by a municipality from the earnings of some revenue-producing enterprise rather than by the general credit and revenue sources of the municipality. Revenue bonds are payable solely from the revenue of projects they have made possible and are designed to be self-liquidating obligations. Revenue bonds are extensively used to finance the construction and development of waterworks, gasworks, toll bridges, toll roads, tunnels, parking lots, electric systems, airports, and athletic fields.

Since revenue bonds are not backed by the full faith and credit of the municipality which issues them, they are generally considered to be outside the municipal debt limit. They do, however, carry the tax-exempt status of governmental securities. The use of revenue bonds for financing revenue-producing enterprises often permits the financing of nonrevenue-producing public improvements within the debt limit.

It has been pointed out that revenue bonds often can be redeemed more rapidly than general obligation bonds due to the fact that tolls and charges are paid in cash at the time of use and provide a surer basis for collection than taxes which may sometimes be late. Furthermore, it is often easier to adjust the amount of service charges to income needs than it is to increase tax rates.[62] Most revenue bonds are, therefore, made callable to permit redemption before maturity date if enterprise earnings warrant it.

[60] Borge, op. cit., p. 145.
[61] Haviland, op. cit., p. 5.
[62] Ibid., p. 7.

Revenue bonds, being backed only by self-liquidating projects, usually carry a higher interest rate than general obligation bonds. There are, however, many exceptions. Some municipalities have obtained lower rates by issuing revenue bonds backed by the general credit and taxing powers, although the project is expected to pay off the bond obligations.

Since revenue bond investors ordinarily do not have recourse to general revenue sources, it is essential that adequate provision be included in the bond indenture guaranteeing to the fullest extent possible the proper application of the revenues produced and the continuance of the enterprise as a revenue-producing project until the revenue bonds are paid off.[63] The bond indenture must contain the details with respect to the pledge of revenue, management of the enterprise, and the rights and remedies of the investor. As in the case of general obligation bonds, it is highly important that the municipality obtain the services of a competent bond attorney to guide the municipality in observing all the legal requirements with respect to the issue and sale of revenue bonds. In order to obtain the best price and lowest interest rates, assistance should also be obtained from a nationally known consulting engineer and an expert financial adviser.

Special Assessment Bonds. Special assessment bonds are those secured by the proceeds of a special tax or assessment usually levied against property in a particular area which is specially benefited by an improvement made by the municipality. Improvements which are frequently financed by special assessment bonds include such projects as street paving and widening, sewer projects, sidewalk construction, and water mains. Although improvements financed by special assessment bonds are presumed to benefit one area in particular, the extensive use of this means of financing is often employed where the local government has reached its debt limit. Special assessment bond obligations are usually outside the debt limit,[64] and in some jurisdictions certain special assessments are outside the tax limitations. Another justification for creating special assessment districts is to create an assessment area which may overlap and include portions of several governmental units.

[63] John T. Trimble, "Public Revenue Bonds," *Municipal Finance*, Vol. XXV, No. 4, p. 157, May, 1953.

[64] Although special assessment bonds are usually outside the general debt limitations, state laws commonly establish a limitation upon the amount of such issues based upon the value of the lot, front footage, or some other basis.

Special assessment districts may be organized for many different purposes. There is no consistent pattern with respect to organization, powers granted, or method of financing from state to state or even within a state. The basic purpose is to provide legal machinery for the construction of public works which will be paid for by the property benefited. In theory, benefit to property is the sole justification for special assessments. Sometimes, however, the element of special benefit, as distinguished from general benefit to the community as a whole, is not easy to determine. Although the bond obligations of special assessment districts are intended to be met from the special assessments upon the property within the district, some municipalities have found it necessary to guarantee their payment with the full faith and credit of the city to insure their marketability. This is usually done when the legislative body determines that, as a matter of public policy, the public improvement is desirable in the general interest. Guarantees are often justified to relieve distressed situations or situations where the property presumed to be benefited is of doubtful value, but where the improvement is essential to the health or safety of the city as, for example, the construction of a sewer system in a poor district to relieve a serious health menace resulting from faulty septic tanks.[65]

Financing public improvements through special assessment bonds presents many complicated problems. Initially the determination must be made as to whether there are special benefits for which an assessment may be levied, and, if there are, what area should be included for assessment purposes. These are questions to be resolved by the legislative body. Methods and procedures for making assessments are usually prescribed by statute, and assessments are usually made a lien upon the property like a lien of general taxes. The requirements for issuing and marketing special assessment bonds are much the same as those for other bonds once the assessment procedure has been completed.[66]

Considerations in the Issuance and Marketing of Bonds. The success of any municipality in marketing bonds depends to a large extent upon the care and preparation with which the local officials lay the groundwork for the sale of the issue.[67] Once the decision is made

[65] Eugene K. Sturgis, "The Place of the Special Assessment Proceedings in City Finance," *Western City*, Vol. XXIX, No. 8, p. 54, August, 1953.

[66] H. L. Chapman and Henry J. Crawford, "Special Assessments and Special Assessment Bonds," *Municipal Finance*, Vol. XXV, No. 4, p. 155, May, 1953.

[67] *A Model County and Municipal Bond Law* (New York: National Municipal League, 1953), p. XX.

to finance a public improvement by long-term borrowing, the major concern becomes that of securing the most favorable interest rates and most favorable retirement schedule. Although these matters are governed to some degree by general market conditions, much of the success of favorable marketing depends upon the credit status of the municipality and the technical preparation for the bond issue.

Among the principal factors that directly influence the credit status of the municipality are the ratio of debt to assessed valuations, the per capita indebtedness, the tax structure, the record of tax collections, the long-range public improvements program, and the general record of fiscal operations.[68] There are also many indirect factors which affect the credit status of a municipality. These include such matters as the character and reputation of public officials, the economic base of the community, the record of the community in meeting previous obligations, the quality of government and administrative management as reflected by such features as sound structural organization, sound community planning, and well-enforced zoning and subdivision ordinances.

As an aid to establishing a good credit rating, municipalities may find it advantageous to include investment services such as Dun and Bradstreet, Inc., and Moody's Investors' Service on the mailing list for their annual financial reports. The investment firms that determine the interest rates rely to a considerable extent upon the credit ratings which these service agencies assign to a particular bond issue.

In preparing a bond issue, many legal and practical considerations must be observed. The authorization to issue bonds and many of the legal requirements are specified by general law. The wide variation which exists among the laws of the different states has complicated the problem of marketing to some degree since the national firms that buy most of the large issues must determine their bids according to the laws of each of the separate jurisdictions.[69] Obviously, these firms will not purchase any issue unless they are well assured of the legality of the authorization and that all legal requirements have been met.

Where state legislation permits, municipalities may find that under

[68] Beldon H. Schaffer, *Local Bond Sales and Interest Rates, A Guide to Marketing General Obligation Bonds of Connecticut Towns and Cities* (Storrs, Conn.: Institute of Public Service, University of Connecticut, April, 1954), p. 8.

[69] In order to promote uniform legislation with respect to procedures for bond issues, the National Municipal League prepared, in 1953, a publication entitled "A Model County and Municipal Bond Law," which it recommends for adoption.

certain circumstances bonds may be more readily sold through negotiated sale than by competitive bids. For example, in cases in which
the per capita debt ratio is high and there is no historical operating
record, it may be more feasible to utilize the assistance of the under-
writer to work out the financial plan including the sale of bonds. The
principal reason why municipal authorities hesitate to negotiate the
sale of their bonds is their inability to determine what constitutes a
favorable price. However, situations frequently occur where no bids
are received in conformity with the provisions of the advertisement
of sale, but underwriters may present bids subject to different terms.
Under these conditions the most favorable terms are usually accepted
and thus what purports to be a sale by competitive bid actually becomes one by negotiation.[70]

In addition to the legal considerations, municipalities must take
into account certain practical factors that affect the market and other
financial interests. For one thing, the timing of the sale is important.
The market for bonds, like the market for commodities, is subject to
the laws of supply and demand. Municipal bonds as an investment
are more attractive at certain times than they are at others. This may
be due to the number of municipal bonds being offered for sale at a
given time, to the fact that other types of investments are currently
more or less profitable, or because of the fluctuation of interest rates
in general. By observation and study of market conditions, municipal
officials may, to some degree, be able to time their bond issues to
take advantage of the most favorable market conditions.

Another practical consideration is concerned with the type of bond
to be issued. If certain types of bonds are favored by investors at a
particular time, this factor should be taken into account in deciding
what method of financing should be used. For some improvements
a city may have the choice of general obligation bonds, revenue bonds,
or local improvement district bonds. The effect upon the debt and
revenue structure must be weighed along with the probable interest
rates for each type in arriving at a choice. Likewise, practical considerations may be involved in choosing between a serial type of bond or
a term bond. When borrowing is quite frequent, the use of straight
serial bonds is normally desirable, all other conditions being equal,

[70] Emil C. Jensen and Joshua H. Vogel, *Sewage Collection and Treatment Works in
the State of Washington* (Seattle: Bureau of Governmental Research and Services, University of Washington, February, 1949), Report No. 86, p. 55.

since it results in a progressively downward trend in annual debt service on outstanding indebtedness and thus reduces correspondingly the impact on the budget of the debt service for new bond issues.[71]

Sometimes the insertion of optional call clauses may have a retarding effect upon the market for the bonds. The inclusion of such a feature gives the municipality a degree of flexibility in revising its debt structure. However, if there is no likelihood that some source of revenue will become available to permit the bonds to be called earlier than their date of maturity, or unless there is good prospect of reissuance at lower interest rates, such optional provisions have little value.[72] Nevertheless, the advantage of flexibility to the debt structure and the possibility of saving interest is a very important consideration and, for these reasons, callable provisions are generally desirable unless they seriously depress the market for the bonds.

Because of the many legal technicalities which must be met to validate a bond issue, most investment banking firms will not bid on an issue of any size unless it is supported by a legal opinion of a nationally-recognized bond attorney. The legal opinion advises the municipality that it has the authority to issue the bonds, that the powers have been exercised in a legal manner, that adequate provision has been made for the repayment of principal and interest, and that the bond is in proper form and binding upon the municipality. Prospective buyers will rely upon this opinion and will usually not consider bidding on the bonds unless such an opinion is furnished. The opinion of a local attorney, unless he is also a nationally-recognized bond attorney, will usually not be adequate.

With the issuance of revenue bonds it is also of importance to support the proposed issue with a report of a recognized consulting engineer. The engineer will prepare a preliminary survey on the required facilities of the proposed improvement, together with recommendations as to sites and the cost of the project. He will also prepare detailed plans and specifications, supervise construction, and, in some instances, supervise the initial operations of the facilities.

With respect to public improvements of considerable size, municipalities will usually find it in their interest also to engage the services of a financial adviser. The financial expert can recommend to the city the most acceptable means of financing the particular project and

[71] *A Model County and Municipal Bond Law, op. cit.,* pp. XVIII–XIX.
[72] Lewis Miller, *The Municipal Bond Market,* January, 1954, p. 15.

can supply the bond attorney with essential information to be included in the ordinances. One of his most important services with respect to the marketing of the bonds is the preparation of the prospectus upon which the bond purchasers will base their bids.

CHAPTER 8

Zoning

ZONING AS A MEANS OF PLAN IMPLEMENTATION

Zoning as an instrument of plan implementation is basic to any intelligent systematic planning program. Zoning provides a means of control over private property to protect the community against harmful invasions of buildings and structures and thereby encourages the most appropriate use of land. Although the use of private property has long been recognized as being subject to public regulation, zoning in the United States is a comparatively recent application of the police power to carry out the objectives of planning.[1]

NATURE OF ZONING

Zoning is the division of a community into zones or districts according to present and potential use of properties for the purpose of controlling and directing the use and development of those properties.[2] It is concerned primarily with the use of land and buildings, the height and bulk of buildings, the proportion of a lot which buildings may cover, and the density of population of a given area. It is not concerned particularly with land ownership. As an instrument of plan implementation, zoning deals principally with the use and development of privately owned land and buildings rather than with public land, buildings, and facilities.[3]

[1] Zoning was practiced extensively in European cities before it was recognized in the United States. See E. C. Yokley, Zoning Law and Practice (Charlottesville, Va.: The Michie Co., Law Publishers, 1953), Vol. 1, p. 3.

[2] Devaney v. New Haven Board of Zoning Appeals, 132 Conn. 527, 45 A. (2d) 828 (1946).

[3] See, however, Frances Reed Goodman, "Municipal Corporations—Zoning—Bind-

Purpose and Objectives. The division of the community into zones is necessary in order to provide special regulations for different sections of the community in accordance with the planned development of each particular section. In this respect, zoning regulations differ from building codes, plumbing codes, and other codes regulating property which have uniform application throughout the community. Although zoning regulations vary according to the uses established for each type of zone, regulations within a given zone or the same kind of zones must be uniform. Thus, zoning contemplates different regulations to effectuate different land uses in different zones, but seeks to avoid discrimination in the application of those regulations to the use of property similarly situated within a given zone or in the same kind of zone.

Zoning attempts to group together those uses which are most compatible. Zoning has among its purposes: (1) conserving the value of property, (2) assuring orderly community growth, and (3) safeguarding the general public welfare. It seeks to preserve the planned character of the neighborhood by excluding uses and structures which are prejudicial to the restricted purposes of the area and to achieve the gradual elimination of existing nonconforming uses.[4] At the same time, zoning legislation is designed to protect the owners of nonconforming property from unreasonable hardship occasioned by the compulsory elimination of nonconforming uses.[5] By guiding community growth along orderly lines, zoning helps to minimize the demands for providing school facilities, utilities, streets, policing, fire protection, and other facilities and services in particular areas before the city is prepared to do so.

The objective of zoning legislation is to establish regulations which provide locations for all essential uses of land and buildings and to insure that each use is located in the most appropriate place. While zoning helps to exclude nuisances which would tend to create blight in a particular district, zoning should not be thought of solely as a means of nuisance control.[6] Legitimate business operations which may be undesirable in one location may represent appropriate land

---

ing Effects of Zoning Ordinances on the City," *Baylor Law Review*, Vol. VII, No. 4, pp. 464–465, Fall, 1955, indicating that in some jurisdictions proprietary functions of the city are controlled by the zoning regulations.

[4] Yokley, *op. cit.*, p. 13.

[5] *Goodrich v. Seligman*, 298 Ky. 863, 183 S.W. (2d) 625 (1944).

[6] *Effective Zoning for Your Community* (Trenton: State of New Jersey, Department of Conservation and Economic Development, State Planning Section, 1953).

uses in some other area. The designation of appropriate land for all legitimate uses is the problem and responsibility of zoning.

Conflicts Between Public and Private Interests.   The enactment of zoning regulations has met with much bitter opposition from property owners whose rights to develop their property as they saw fit had been made subject to governmental restrictions. Zoning brings into focus many of the conflicts inherent in preserving individual freedom and in exercising the police power to provide the greatest good for the greatest number of people. The essence of the police power is the promotion of the general welfare by means of restraint and compulsion applied to individuals. Zoning seeks to enlarge the freedom of the greatest number of people in the community by restricting the use of private property in the interest of public benefit. Under this concept, the rights of an individual to complete freedom to use his property as he pleases must give way to the superior authority of the state to impose reasonable controls upon that use in the public interest.

In complying with zoning regulations an individual may sometimes be required to bear certain loss or hardship in order to provide greater advantage for the community as a whole.[7] For example, residential property owners frequently could derive much larger incomes if they were allowed to devote their properties to commercial or industrial purposes. However, courts will not invalidate zoning ordinances because they deprive an individual from gaining the maximum return on his property unless it can be shown that the regulations as applied to him are unreasonable and discriminatory and are not related to the promotion of health, safety, morals, or the general welfare. This does not mean that the matter of financial loss is of no consequence. Although constitutional rights are not measured in terms of money, the effect of heavy financial loss will be given consideration by the courts, particularly where the benefit to the public would be negligible or slight.[8]

Relation to the Comprehensive Plan.   Although zoning may be put into effect independently of community planning, it can be most effective as a constructive means of community development only when it is an integral part of the comprehensive community plan. Zoning is not synonymous with planning. Planning is a much broader term which is concerned not only with the uses of land and build-

[7] Devaney v. New Haven Board of Zoning Appeals, supra.
[8] West Bros. Brick Co. v. City of Alexandria, 169 Va. 271, 192 S.E. 881 (1937).

ings, but also with the development of all the other physical features of the community, such as highways, schools, and recreational areas, the performance of all functional responsibilities, and the maintenance of a sound financial structure. Zoning is not to be considered as a substitute for planning, nor should it represent the ultimate goal of planning. Zoning is rather one of the many tools of planning designed to help carry out the overall plan of land use. The zoning ordinance and the zoning map constitute part of the comprehensive plan. The legislative, administrative, and judicial controls established by the ordinance are among the legal devices which are utilized for executing the land-use part of the plan.

Unfortunately, the functions of planning and zoning are often confused, and zoning in many communities is looked upon as being synonymous with or a substitute for planning rather than as a device of plan implementation. The fact that many more municipalities engage in zoning than engage in planning is evidence that many zoning ordinances are not based upon a comprehensive plan of land use.[9]

Zoning enabling acts commonly contain a statutory directive that the zoning ordinance shall be in accordance with a comprehensive plan. However, courts have tended to construe such provisions to mean only that the zoning ordinance must be geographically comprehensive and that it must be a reasonable exercise of the police power.[10] In view of this situation, it is obvious that zoning may often fail to serve as an effective means of plan implementation. In fact, it may, in some instances, actually thwart good land-use planning. Consequently, many jurisdictions are well advised to review their zoning practices and also to give consideration to the advisability of amending the state enabling legislation to make the validity of the zoning ordinance depend upon accordance with the comprehensive plan of land use.

Comprehensive and Spot Zoning. In order to be effective in achieving the intended purposes of planning and to be legally defensible, the zoning ordinance should be comprehensive in character in that it should be applied to the entire area of the jurisdiction which enacts it. Sporadic or piecemeal zoning is not favored by the courts, nor does it represent good public policy. Courts have pointed

[9] Planning and zoning are usually authorized by separate enabling acts. This may have contributed to the tendency to view each of them as self-contained activities.

[10] For a discussion of the legal aspects of this relationship, see Charles M. Haar, "In Accordance with a Comprehensive Plan," *Harvard Law Review*, Vol. 68, No. 7, 1955, pp. 1154–1175.

out that it is a responsibility of zoning to keep in view the welfare of the inhabitants of the city as a whole.[11] Like any other application of the police power, zoning must not be arbitrary or unreasonable. Courts are inclined to look with disfavor upon any zoning ordinance which lays out a small portion of the city as a residential district or some other kind of district without reference to a plan which takes into account other areas of similar character. Unless zoning is comprehensive in scope, it may place restrictions upon persons and property that result in unjust discrimination. The comprehensiveness of the zoning plan is, therefore, a factor which the courts will take into account in determining whether or not an ordinance is arbitrary and unreasonable and without substantial relation to public health, safety, and the general welfare.[12]

Where a comprehensive zoning plan has been developed, the court will not permit indiscriminate variances to be established within a classified zone if the effect is to create "islands" of more or less restricted use which have no pertinent differentiating factors from the rest of the zone.[13] One lot may not be singled out and be made subject to restrictions which are more or less onerous than those imposed upon the rest of the district. This does not mean that every ordinance which permits small business districts to be scattered in residential sections is invalid per se even though the effect may be to cause such districts to be spotted. The test of whether such uses result in illegal "spot zoning" depends upon whether the different uses are designed for the promotion of public health, safety, morals, or general welfare pursuant to a comprehensive plan or whether they are established for special privilege or to impose special restrictions.[14] Spot zoning commonly occurs from the enactment of amendatory ordinances which seek to classify one or more districts or lots for uses which are prohibited in the zone by the original zoning ordinance. Such enactments are often upheld by the courts if they do not destroy the spirit and intent of the comprehensive zoning plan. Their legality is

[11] Chapman v. City of Troy, 241 Ala. 637, 4 So. (2d) 1 (1941).
Yokley, op. cit., p. 86.
[12] Wilbur v. City of Newton, 302 Mass. 38, 18 N.E. (2d) 365 (1938).
[13] John M. McKee and Moree Levine, "Zoning—The Nonconforming Use and Spot Zoning," The Buffalo Law Review, Vol. 1, No. 3, p. 292, Spring, 1952.
[14] See, for example, Leahy v. Inspector of Buildings, 308 Mass. 128, 31 N.E. (2d) 436 (1946). In Kuehne v. Town Council of Town of East Hartford, 136 Conn. 452, 72 A. (2d) 474 (1950) the court held that proposed spot zoning for retail shops was not related to a comprehensive plan and was not proper.

determined by the facts and circumstances in each particular case.[15]

Sometimes the reclassification of certain areas within a zone is necessary to meet unusual situations or changed conditions.[16] Technically, such alterations should not be considered as spot zoning, but rather as legitimate amendments to the zoning ordinance.[17] Spot zoning results when a small lot or parcel of land is singled out and placed under regulations establishing a use inconsistent with the character of the zone in which it is located, with the effect of conferring special benefits or imposing special burdens upon particular property owners.

Interim Zoning. Frequently, a community which has not been zoned is confronted with the proposed erection of some building or the use of land which threatens the orderly development of the community. Under this circumstance, the community suddenly awakens to the need for zoning control, but finds that it does not have time enough to develop a comprehensive plan to prevent the threatened objectionable use. Some communities have sought to meet the problem by hastily enacting an ordinance declaring the threatened area to be a residential zone and prohibiting business or industry from locating within it. Such stopgap devices do not represent sound public policy and are usually frowned upon by the courts. Nevertheless, interim zoning ordinances have been upheld in some states where it has been clearly apparent that they were temporary emergency measures and preliminary to a *bona fide* attempt to develop a comprehensive plan.

Interim zoning ordinances usually do not designate districts on a map but approach the problem by providing that the class of district in which a particular piece of property is situated is determined in each case by the application of general rules to the existing conditions of the neighborhood. Such interim zoning ordinances, although comprehensive in scope, are open to the objection of being arbitrary and uncertain. They are extremely difficult to administer and usually lead to much litigation making them of doubtful value. They should never be resorted to except in case of emergency.

In many cases, efforts to control land use through stopgap zoning

[15] *State v. Matthews*, 362 Mo. 242, 240 S.W. (2d) 934 (1951).

[16] *Eggebeen v. Sonnenburg*, 239 Wis. 213, 1 N.W. (2d) 84 (1941).

[17] See, however, *Miller v. Town Planning Commission*, 142 Conn. 265, 113 A. (2d) 504 (1955), wherein the court held invalid an effort by amendment to extend a business zone 500 feet into a residence zone. The court held that the amendment was not in accordance with the comprehensive plan for community development.

legislation have been defeated because the ordinances have been held to be arbitrary or have been found inadequate on procedural grounds.[18] On the other hand, a number of courts have been inclined to recognize the validity of such ordinances for preserving the *status quo* pending the adoption of a comprehensive zoning ordinance and have upheld them in a number of well-reasoned decisions.[19] Courts upholding interim zoning have been inclined to look at the overall objectives and consider the ordinance as a precautionary measure designed to prevent persons from taking action which might make it difficult to put into effect a comprehensive permanent zoning ordinance which would establish the most appropriate land use. Since courts in passing upon the validity of interim ordinances are inclined to take into account their temporary character, it would seem that such an ordinance would be strengthened if it contained a time limit fixing the date of its expiration.[20]

Areas Subject to Zoning Control.   The areas which can be zoned within or by any given jurisdiction are not usually specified in the enabling legislation. In general, all privately owned land is subject to zoning control. Zoning may extend to land which is under water to the extent that the municipality may exercise jurisdiction over the area.[21] Thus, the zoning ordinance may be used to restrict or control the type of business or industry which might be conducted from barges or other floating structures anchored in navigable waters off the shores of land zoned for residential use. Although zoning is usually applicable only to land available for buildings, it is well to zone railroad lands and rights of way in order to prevent the erection of nonconforming buildings in the event of a sale of land following a straightening of tracks or change of grade.[22]

Although the basic purpose of zoning is to prevent the inappropriate development of lands, the time at which zoning controls may be legally established over vacant and unimproved land presents ques-

[18] *State ex rel. Gulf Refining Company v. DeFrance, et al.*, 89 Ohio App. 334, 101 N.E. (2d) 782 (1950).

[19] *Miller v. Board of Public Works*, 195 Cal. 477, 234 Pac. 381 (1925). See discussion of this case by way of distinction in *Kline v. City of Harrisburg*, 362 Pa. 438, 68 A. (2d) 182 (1949).

Cahn v. Guion, 27 Ohio App. 141, 160 N.E. 868 (1927).

Fowler v. Obier, 224 Ky. 742, 7 S.W. (2d) 219 (1928).

[20] *Kline v. City of Harrisburg*, 362 Pa. 438, 68 A. (2d) 182 (1949).

[21] Edward M. Bassett, *Zoning, The Laws, Administration, and Court Decisions During the First Twenty Years* (New York: Russell Sage Foundation, 1940), p. 30.

See also *Wynn v. Margate City*, 9 N.J. Misc. 1324, 157 Atl. 565 (1931).

[22] Bassett, *op. cit.*, p. 30.

tions of much legal uncertainty. In a recent case,[23] the Supreme Court
of Michigan held that a township zoning ordinance which placed 33
acres of the plaintiff's property under residential and industrial zones
and prohibited trailer camps was invalid as not having a reasonable
relationship to public health, safety, morals, or general welfare. Evidence on which the decision was based indicated that the land would
not be developed for at least 20 years. The court held that the test
of the validity of the zoning ordinance was not the relationship that
it bears to the future, but rather its relationship to present conditions.
Although the timing of probable development is a factor to be considered in determining the reasonableness of zoning regulations,
courts in general have recognized that zoning is prospective and ordinances which are enacted in reasonable anticipation of expansion
and future growth are a valid exercise of the police power.[24]

Although zoning regulations are adopted primarily to control the
use of privately owned land, the zoning ordinance should be concerned also with the sites for public buildings and facilities. The
zoning map should show the areas designated for streets, public
buildings, and recreational use. To the extent possible, legal steps
should be taken to avoid granting any building permit for construction of a building in a mapped street or other area designated for
public use.[25]

Whether or not a city is bound by its own zoning ordinances depends upon the law of the jurisdiction and the nature of the function
being carried out. For example, the Supreme Court of Georgia has
held that the erection of a fire station was a necessary public use of
land that was not controlled by the city's zoning ordinance.[26] The
court held in effect that the city could not legislate or contract away
its power of eminent domain. From the court's reasoning, it would
seem to follow that land already owned by the city may also be used
for such a public purpose without restriction by the zoning ordinance.
This same ruling appears to be applicable to the use of land within
the city by other units of local government.[27] In some jurisdictions
a distinction is made between "governmental" and "proprietary" functions, the court holding that with respect to proprietary functions,

---

[23] Gust v. Township of Canton, 342 Mich. 436, 70 N.W. (2d) 772 (1955).
[24] See "Zoning—Unimproved Land—Planning Future Development," Minnesota
Law Review, Vol. 40, No. 3, pp. 286–289, February, 1956, which accepts the conclusion but criticizes the court's reasoning.
[25] See discussion of official map ordinance, Chap. 7.
[26] Mayor of Savannah v. Collins, 211 Ga. 191, 84 S.E. (2d) 454 (1954).
[27] See Decatur Park District v. Becker, 368 Ill. 442, 14 N.E. (2d) 490 (1938).

municipalities are bound by their own zoning regulations in the same manner as an individual would be.[28]

Municipalities may be prevented from extending zoning control over public lands because of the superior legal jurisdiction of the state or the federal government. Municipal zoning ordinances cannot control the use of land owned by the federal government or the state. The authority of the federal government to carry out its powers is supreme. Also the state which confers the police power upon the municipality is not subject to municipal regulations. Consequently, where federal or state lands are involved, compliance with the objectives of the municipality's comprehensive land-use plan are to be achieved through negotiation with the appropriate federal or state agencies rather than by zoning. It is nevertheless good zoning practice to extend zoning regulations to federal and state owned lands so that in the event that they are sold to private individuals they will immediately become subject to public control.

Urban Fringe Zoning. Lands which are situated alike should be zoned alike.[29] Since lands situated alike do not always lie within the boundaries of a single political subdivision, adequate legal controls necessary to insure the same treatment seldom exist. Suburban areas which are being developed in the unincorporated fringes surrounding all our major cities are in need of zoning controls as much as the areas within the cities themselves. Uncontrolled growth is resulting in many of these suburbs' being developed in a haphazard and often undesirable manner.

Control over urban fringe area developments can be achieved either by giving the municipality authority to zone beyond its corporate limits or by vesting zoning powers in the county. To date neither method has been very effective. Since zoning by a city beyond its territorial boundaries presents many political and practical difficulties, extraterritorial zoning powers have been rarely granted.[30] Counties and other units of local government primarily concerned with rural problems often do not possess adequate legal powers to zone, or else they show little interest in zoning urbanized areas.

[28] *Taber v. City of Benton Harbor*, 280 Mich. 522, 274 N.W. 324 (1937). For a discussion of this subject, see Frances Reed Goodman, "Municipal Corporations—Zoning—Binding Effects of Zoning Ordinances on the City," *Baylor Law Review*, Vol. VII, No. 4, pp. 464–468, Fall, 1955.

[29] Bassett, *op. cit.*, p. 48.

[30] See pp. 59–62. For a discussion of the subject, see Otis J. Bouwsma, "The Validity of Extraterritorial Municipal Zoning," *Vanderbilt Law Review*, Vol. 8, No. 4, pp. 806–815, June, 1955.

It is often urged that the central city should have some authority to shape the overall metropolitan development. Whether, in order to accomplish this purpose, a city should be granted jurisdiction to zone beyond its boundaries is a matter on which there is a wide difference of opinion. Extraterritorial zoning around cities which are not hemmed in by other incorporated areas is a concept that appears to be gaining some public acceptance.[31] Nevertheless, in actual practice only 40 out of 756 cities with zoning ordinances reporting to the International City Managers' Association indicated powers to zone beyond their city limits.[32] Zoning jurisdiction of those having such power ranged from distances of $\frac{1}{4}$ mile to 5 miles beyond the corporate boundaries. Obviously, describing extraterritorial jurisdiction in this manner is not entirely satisfactory because urban growth does not always occur within these lines.

Authority for cities to zone extraterritorially is usually granted by special act or by general law applicable only to cities of a given class. In North Carolina, for instance, certain cities have been given authority by special act to zone the urban fringe for a distance of 1 mile beyond their corporate limits.[33] Nebraska has conferred extraterritorial zoning powers upon the city of Omaha under an act providing such authority for cities of metropolitan class.[34] The state of Kentucky has empowered the city of Louisville to zone all land lying within 5 miles of the city limits providing zoning authority has not been exercised by Jefferson County.[35]

It is basic legal principle that cities cannot exercise extraterritorial zoning powers unless they are specifically conferred by the legislature or by the state constitution. Nevertheless, in some states such authority has been implied from the language of the planning enabling act and the grant of police power authority. The state of Alabama furnishes an illustration. In that state the municipal planning commission is empowered to make and adopt a master plan for the phys-

[31] *The Municipal Year Book, 1952* (Chicago: The International City Managers' Association, 1952), p. 277.

[32] *Ibid.*

[33] See, for example, North Carolina Laws 1949, c. 540, conferring extraterritorial zoning powers under N.C. Gen. Stat. 1949 (1943 and Supp. 1949), Secs. 160–172 to 160–180 upon the city of Raleigh and also North Carolina Laws 1949, c. 629, conferring similar powers on the city of Chapel Hill.

[34] Law applies to cities with populations of 150,000 or more. Neb. Rev. Stat. (1943), Secs. 14–401 to 14–418. Extraterritorial authority is also given to cities of primary class (population 40,000 to 150,000) under Neb. Rev. Stat. (1943), Secs. 15–901 to 15–903.

[35] Ky. Rev. Stat. (Baldwin, 1942 and Supp. 1950), Secs. 100.031–100.098, 100.980, and 100.990.

ical development of the municipality, including any areas outside its boundaries which, in the commission's judgment, bear relation to the planning of such municipality. The enabling statute declares that the master plan shall be made for the general purpose of guiding and accomplishing a coördinated, adjusted, and harmonious development of the municipality and its environs. It confers upon the municipality such powers as may be necessary to enable it to fulfill its functions, promote municipal planning, and carry out the purposes of the statute. No zoning powers are specifically provided for, but subdivision control is specifically authorized over areas within 5 miles of the corporate limits. On the basis of the objectives set forth in the planning and subdivision enabling acts, the Attorney General of Alabama has ruled that since planning would be of little use without zoning authority, it is to be presumed that extraterritorial zoning authority was intended by the legislature within those areas in which subdivision control is exercised.[36]

While the foregoing examples serve to indicate measures that have been taken in some jurisdictions and may be taken in others to meet the need for fringe area zoning control, the conclusion must be drawn that in the aggregate their constructive effect has been negligible. It seems probable that political and practical objections are likely to continue to restrict the use of extraterritorial zoning by municipalities. On the other hand, there is little encouragement that a solution to the fringe problem will come from county zoning. Although counties more frequently exercise zoning powers in unincorporated urban fringe areas than cities do, county zoning is usually less comprehensive and often not oriented to urban problems.[37]

One of the difficulties of interesting counties in urban zoning has been that the problems and objectives of rural zoning have been somewhat different from those of urban zoning. Rural zoning has been designed primarily to prevent scattered agricultural settlement of rural lands which are suitable only for forestry or recreational uses and to aid in guiding settlement toward more desirable locations.[38]

[36] Quarterly Report of the Attorney General of Alabama, July–September, 1944, p. 34. For a more complete discussion of extraterritorial authority in Alabama, see Robert T. Daland, Municipal Fringe Area Problem in Alabama (Bureau of Public Administration, University of Alabama, 1953).

[37] Actually, only 46 percent of the counties do zoning in the areas not subject to city extraterritorial zoning. The Municipal Year Book, 1954 (Chicago: The International City Managers' Association, 1954), p. 55.

[38] United States Department of Agriculture, Bureau of Agricultural Economics, Rural

The restricting of these rural lands to such uses is aimed at avoiding the necessity of providing schools, relief, all-weather roads, and other services and facilities in such areas at disproportionately high costs. The prevention of scattered settlements in forest and recreation areas also helps to reduce the hazard of forest fires and avoid the problem of protecting crops from damage by game birds and animals from the surrounding forest areas.[39]

While these objectives continue to be of major importance in rural zoning, counties also have a growing responsibility to help guide the development of the urban fringe. Possibly the most practical solution for many communities, until some effective plan of metropolitan government is devised, is to be found in coöperative action between cities and counties. The adoption of uniform regulations by counties and municipalities in the metropolitan region will simplify the problem of administration and enforcement for all units of government and will make it easier for builders and real estate owners to understand and comply with the laws. Under some circumstances, coöperative action in establishing uniform zoning controls may be facilitated by the creation of a joint city-county planning commission. If several units of government in the area have zoning powers, all should be represented on a regional planning commission. Such commissions can aid in the formulation of an overall land-use plan and in securing the adoption of uniform zoning ordinances through parallel action.

LEGAL BASIS OF ZONING

Although zoning was started late in the United States, its legality as an exercise of the police power has now been well established by a long line of decisions of the federal courts and state courts.[40]

Historical Development of the Law. When comprehensive zoning was first considered in the United States, many lawyers believed that it would result in a taking of property which could be done only through the exercise of the powers of eminent domain.[41] Obviously, zoning by this means would be laborious and cumbersome. Since any

---

Zoning and Land-Use Planning (Washington, D.C.: U.S. Government Printing Office), County Planning Series, No. 7, 1940.

[39] *Local Planning Administration* (Chicago: The International City Managers' Association, 1948), p. 219.

[40] For a comprehensive treatment of the development of the law of zoning and planning, including citations and excerpts from cases, see Charles A. Rathkopf and Arden H. Rathkopf, *The Law of Zoning and Planning* (New York: Clark Boardman Company, Ltd., 1956), Vols. 1 and 2.

[41] Bassett, *op. cit.*, pp. 26–27.

restriction on the use of one's property would require a city to pay for the loss to private owners, the cost would have to be paid from public funds or from special assessments levied against the property benefited. The cost of zoning through eminent domain would be prohibitive. Zoning as an exercise of the police power does not require the payment of compensation.

Most of the early cases upholding zoning legislation were based upon the theory that zoning was a form of nuisance control. Some of the first cases which came before the courts involving the power to zone were those concerned with the exclusion of laundries,[42] brick manufacturing,[43] slaughterhouses,[44] livery stables,[45] and other alleged disagreeable businesses from residential districts. The type of zoning control which was upheld in these early cases sought to segregate nuisances or near nuisances from other land uses. The legislation did not attempt to guide urban development in any positive sense as comprehensive zoning seeks to do today.

One of the first important cases which seemed to open up the way to developing the planning theory of zoning was that of *Welch v. Swasey*,[46] which upheld a Boston ordinance limiting the height of buildings. This ordinance, however, was not a comprehensive zoning act. The first comprehensive zoning ordinance was enacted by New York City in 1916. This step marked the beginning of zoning as a tool of plan implementation and the departure from zoning as merely a form of nuisance control.

The planning theory of zoning has come to be recognized in a long line of cases, the most important of which is the case of *Village of Euclid v. the Ambler Realty Co.*[47] This action was brought to enjoin the enforcement of the comprehensive zoning ordinance enacted by the Village of Euclid on the ground that it violated the Fourteenth Amendment of the Constitution of the United States in that it deprived the complainant of his property without due process of law. Thus, a federal question was raised which brought the case within the jurisdiction of the United States Supreme Court. The Supreme Court was called upon to pass upon the question of whether or not zoning, to carry out the objective of comprehensive planning, was a

[42] *Matter of Yick Wo*, 68 Cal. 294, 9 Pac. 141 (1885).

[43] *Hadacheck v. City of Los Angeles*, 239 U.S. 394, 36 S.Ct. 143, 60 L.Ed. 348 (1915).

[44] *Cronin v. People*, 82 N.Y. 318, 37 Am. Rep. 564 (1880).

[45] *Reinman v. City of Little Rock*, 237 U.S. 171, 35 S.Ct. 511, 59 L.Ed. 900 (1915).

[46] 193 Mass. 364, 79 N.E. 745 (1907). Affirmed 214 U.S. 91, 53 L.Ed. 923 (1909).

[47] 272 U.S. 365, 71 L.Ed. 303 (1926).

legitimate exercise of the police power within the limitations of due process of law. In its decision the court departed from the nuisance theory of zoning and upheld the action of the municipality as a legitimate exercise of the police power to achieve the orderly physical development of the community. Specifically, the decision in the Euclid case upheld the authority of the village to zone as residential a strip of land along a railroad that had been acquired by the owner for industrial development.

Prior to the decision of the Euclid case, the planning concept of zoning had been upheld in a number of decisions by state supreme courts.[48] Since, however, zoning legislation presented a federal constitutional question, the legality of zoning laws was left uncertain until the question was passed upon by the court of last resort.

Constitutional Limitations Affecting Zoning. The power to zone under the police power is not without constitutional limitations. No principles of our Federal Constitution are more fundamental or more jealously guarded than those of due process of law and the equal protection of the laws. Essentially, due process of law is designed to give protection to individual liberty and the right of property while the equal protection of the laws clause is designed to prevent unjust discrimination in the carrying out of governmental powers.

These limitations as applied to the police power are not easy to define and can be understood only by reference to numerous court decisions which have sought to strike a balance between the necessity of public regulation in the public interest on the one hand, and the preservation of personal liberty and rights of private property on the other.

Zoning legislation is no different from other applications of the police power in that it must be reasonable and fair and must bear a substantial relationship to the public health, safety, morals, and general welfare.[49] Any zoning ordinance which does not have a substantial relation to these objectives is a palpable invasion of rights protected by the fundamental law and will be held unconstitutional.[50] The validity of each ordinance must be determined according to the circumstances of each case. Zoning legislation which may be upheld as

[48] See Robert A. Walker, *The Planning Function in Urban Government* (Chicago: University of Chicago Press, 1950), pp. 67–77, for a discussion of the important state court decisions rendered between 1920 and 1925 upholding the planning theory of zoning.
[49] *Kinney v. City of Joliet,* 411 Ill. 289, 103 N.E. (2d) 473 (1952).
[50] *Mugler v. Kansas,* 123 U.S. 623, 8 S.Ct. 273, 31 L.Ed. 205 (1887).

constitutional in one instance may be held invalid as being unreasonable as applied to a different situation. For example, legislation which might be construed to be reasonable in a highly congested area might be invalidated by the courts as unreasonable and arbitrary in an area that was not congested.

Enabling Legislation.   The power of municipalities to enact zoning ordinances comes from the state. Unless the power is specifically given to the municipality by the constitution or is conferred by a grant of very broad powers to adopt police power regulations, municipal authority to zone is derived from specific enabling legislation enacted by the state legislature. Most state enabling acts which authorize municipalities to undertake zoning also establish the procedural requirements for putting the zoning plan into effect.

Since the enabling act provides the framework for the policies and procedures set forth in the municipal zoning ordinance, it is important that this statute be carefully drafted. The act should set forth clearly and concisely the grant of authority to the municipality, the general objectives to be achieved, the methods of procedure to be adopted, the rights to be observed, and the remedies to be followed in the matter of administration, enforcement, and appeals.

Local Legislation and Administrative Action.   Within the framework of the enabling act, and subject to the limitations of the Federal Constitution, the state constitution, and the municipal charter, the matter of zoning policy becomes a decision for the municipal legislative body. It is a cardinal rule of construction that the provisions of the zoning ordinance must be consistent with the enabling statute. This is true whether the provisions relate to establishing or changing zone boundaries or descriptions, to administrative procedures, or to any other steps in carrying out the zoning program.

The zoning ordinance should be prepared under the direction of the municipal planning agency in order that it may be based upon the most accurate information available on the current status and probable future development of the municipality. It is most important that the ordinance be drafted by or with the guidance of a competent planning consultant or trained planner. This is necessary not only to insure proper draftsmanship, but also to make certain that the zone classification scheme conforms to the comprehensive plan of land use.

The zoning ordinance should enumerate the various zones to be established and designate the classifications within each major zone.

It should also require that the zone boundaries be designated upon an official zone map of the municipality, and that no building or structure shall be erected, altered, or used for a purpose other than that permitted in the zone as indicated on the official zone map. Since, in general, zoning is prospective rather than retroactive, the policy with respect to nonconforming uses should be set forth in the ordinance.

The zoning ordinance should clearly set forth the specific functions of the agencies responsible for carrying out the zoning policies. For example, the functions of the planning agency in the preparation of the ordinance and amendments should be distinguished from the functions of the board of adjustment in granting variances and other forms of relief. Likewise, the ordinance should carefully spell out the duties of the building inspector in issuing building and occupancy permits and in enforcing the provisions of the zoning law.

ESTABLISHING ZONES AND ZONE REQUIREMENTS

The characteristic feature of zoning control is the division of the community into zones or districts with each classification having its own special regulations. Different regulations for different classes of zones are necessary to establish and preserve the character and function of the different parts of the community. Although zoning is concerned with area and height of buildings and the density of population as well as the use of land and buildings, it is ordinarily not desirable to create separate zones for each of these types of regulations.

Zone Classifications. Zoning ordinances customarily establish three major classes of zones: (1) residential, (2) business or commercial, and (3) industrial or manufacturing. Each major classification may contain several subclassifications of higher or lower uses. Some ordinances also provide for unrestricted zones and other zones for accomplishing specialized objectives. Usually the zoning ordinance names the kinds of uses permitted in the particular zone and prohibits all other uses. Certain uses may be permitted only on appeal or on approval of the health department, the board of adjustment, or some other agency.[51]

The most restricted zone is usually the single-family residence zone.

[51] For a discussion of recent trends in zoning, see Henry Fagin and others, *Zoning Advances in the New Jersey–New York–Connecticut Metropolitan Region* (New York: Regional Plan Association, Inc., May, 1956), Regional Plan Bulletin, No. 86.

The next most restricted zone is the two-family residence zone which normally permits all uses permitted in the single-family residence zone plus two-family residences. Other residence zones usually permit all the uses of the more restricted zones plus the addition of the particular uses permitted in that zone. Business and industrial zones, like residential zones, are subdivided into classifications, some of which have higher or lower restrictions than others. Also, business or commercial zones are sometimes classified according to central business districts or local business districts. Industrial zone classifications usually distinguish between light industrial districts and heavy industrial districts. These classifications are frequently subdivided.

Zoning regulations may establish the authorized uses in zones by an enumeration of the permitted uses or by listing the prohibited uses, or by both. In the more restricted zones it is a better practice to list the permitted uses in order to avoid difficult problems arising from failure to designate particular undesired uses. In the less restricted districts the policy of merely listing the excluded uses may be preferable since such a list will be less extensive than a list of permitted uses. In order to make the ordinance more applicable to changed or newly developed uses,[52] the listing of either permitted or excluded uses should normally be according to types of use with illustrative examples rather than according to specific uses. In recent years a number of jurisdictions have established uses on the basis of performance standards rather than by specific listing, particularly for industrial zones.[53]

Location of Zones and Boundaries. Obviously the arrangement of zones must be determined by the specific needs and existing growth pattern of the community. The most desirable arrangement of zones would seem to be one in which each zone was bordered by the next least restricted or the next most restricted zone. Since this is not always possible, the establishment of zones must be determined according to the plan which seems to be most feasible, taking all factors into account.

Frequently, difficulties arise in establishing suitable boundaries for certain zones. For example, where a street serves as a boundary between a residential zone and a business zone, it is often difficult to justify a different treatment for the properties on opposite sides of the

---

[52] *Local Planning Administration* (Chicago: The International City Managers' Association, 1948), p. 225.
[53] See pp. 385–386.

street. Courts have been inclined to frown upon the establishment of residential zones on a street where the opposite side is built up with stores and zoned for business use.[54] Even where the circumstances seem to justify zoning on one side of the street for residence and the other for business, difficulties are likely to be encountered in preserving the character of the residential district. Eventually certain houses on the street will become dilapidated and pressures to rezone to permit the owners to replace them with stores or markets are unlikely to be successfully resisted.

In order to insure that opposite sides of a street will be located within the same zone, it is usually more desirable to establish the boundary line between two zones in the interior of the block along the rear lot lines rather than dividing the zones by the center of the street. The boundary line should, in so far as possible, be a straight line usually parallel to the street. In some instances a lot, because of a variation in depth from adjoining lots, may fall into two zones. If unusual hardships arise from this situation, it is better to give relief through granting of a variance rather than to make the boundary line follow the rear lines of the lots. Otherwise the fact of ownership may result in discrimination and be injurious to the interests of other owners. In the event two zones divide the frontage on a block, care should be taken to be sure that the boundary lines are established along the side lines and that they do not intersect the lots.

Zoning for Use

Zoning for the purpose of regulating the use of land and buildings has developed much more opposition and presented more difficulties for the courts than has the regulation of height and bulk of buildings and the area of the lot to be occupied by buildings.[55] Courts have gradually come to recognize the legality not only of use districts, but also of the graduation of use districts as long as the distinction can be shown to be justified in the interest of public health, safety, morals, and the general welfare. For example, the courts have upheld the validity of separate regulations for single-family residence districts as distinguished from multiple-family residence districts; for central business districts as distinguished from neighborhood business districts; and for heavy industrial districts as distinguished from light industrial districts.

[54] Bassett, op. cit., p. 82.
[55] Bassett, op. cit., p. 46.

The earliest purpose for use zoning in this country was for fire protection.[56] The modern purpose is to protect social and property values on the theory that interfering uses hinder development. Industry injures a commercial section, and both industry and business are harmful to residential areas. The proper restriction of all three areas, with their graded refinements, guarantees the greatest community land values and incomes as well as the highest social enjoyment. Overzoning for any one of the three major uses may produce the opposite effect.[57]

When a city or county decides to introduce zoning regulations, the use districts are usually considered first. After they have been agreed upon, it is a comparatively simple matter to establish the height and area requirements. The first step in the process is to decide the predominant character of every section of the area to be zoned. If a district is composed entirely of homes, or entirely of office buildings, it can be classified without difficulty, but seldom will such homogeneity be found. In the average American city or county, stores and public garages have forced their way into residential neighborhoods. A block of homes may be flanked by a delicatessen store and a filling station. Such a situation presents a serious problem to the men whose task it is to frame a zoning ordinance. Shall the neighborhood be classified as residential, and other stores and filling stations be excluded, or does the presence of a few businesses suggest that the future development of the section is properly along business lines? The answer is certain to have far-reaching effects upon the district's growth and emphasizes the importance of basing the zoning classifications on a comprehensive land-use plan.

Residence Zones. Residential properties in the average city comprise about 40 percent of the developed area of the municipality and exceed the number and value of all other kinds of properties combined.[58] Zoning ordinances frequently distinguish residential districts by providing different regulations for (1) single-family residence zones, (2) two-family residence zones, (3) four-family residence zones, and (4) multiple-family residence zones. In some of the newer

[56] *City Planning and Zoning in Relation to Fire Prevention and Fire Protection* (Proceedings of the Thirty-Seventh Annual Meeting of the National Fire Protection Association, 1933), Chap. V.

[57] Henry G. Hodges, *City Management* (New York: F. S. Crofts & Co., 1939), p. 261.

[58] *Local Planning Administration, op. cit.*, p. 225.

types of zoning ordinances, zones are established by population density rather than by housing types.[59]

Restrictions in single-family residence zones may vary considerably in different jurisdictions with respect to the required lot area per dwelling, the proportion of the lot that may be covered by the dwelling, and the area required for front, rear, and side yards. Likewise, variations are to be found in the permitted uses of public and semi-public buildings and institutions which are allowed. Usually such uses as schools, churches, libraries, art galleries, fire stations, telephone exchanges, golf courses, and open spaces are permitted. Sometimes permitted uses include gardening and farming.

Two-family and four-family residence zones allow any use permitted in single-family residence zones, and customarily permit additional uses such as private schools, hospitals, clubs, lodges. In some smaller communities rooming and boarding houses are permitted. Although some of the earlier state court decisions held that the separation of single-family residences and multiple-family residences could not be judicially supported as a reasonable exercise of the police power,[60] the contrary view has now become clearly established.[61]

In the multifamily or apartment house zones all uses permitted in other residential zones are usually allowed and, in addition, permitted uses usually include hotels and lodging for transients. Of particular importance in multifamily districts are the requirements of height and area to insure adequate light, air, open space, and parking space. The proper location of apartment house districts is important in carrying out the comprehensive plan. Such districts may legitimately serve as buffers between the business zones and the other classes of residential districts, and thus help to prevent the encroachment of blighting influence on these zones. Other factors may, however, dictate a different location. In fact, some authorities suggest that apartment houses might well be located in any part of the city provided sufficient controls are exercised with respect to requirements of height, area, and surrounding open spaces.[62] With more and more Americans turning to apartment living, it seems unwise to force them into the less desirable neighborhoods. When apartment houses are required to set back greater distances from the street and lot lines (so as not to cut

[59] See p. 397.
[60] R and B Realty Co. v. Jelleme, 2 N.J. Misc. 356, 130 Atl. 365 (1924).
[61] Providence v. Stevens, 47 R.I. 387, 133 Atl. 614 (1926).
Bismark v. Hughes, 53 N.D. 838, 208 N.W. 711 (1926).
[62] Local Planning Administration, op. cit., p. 226.

off the light and air of their neighbors) and to furnish off-street parking facilities for their tenants, most of the objections to them are eliminated. A growing number of cities are permitting them in the more restricted residential districts, with these limitations.[63]

The location of institutions sometimes presents special problems.[64] Schools and churches should, of course, be convenient to the child and adult population and, therefore, are seldom excluded from any residential district.[65] There is often opposition, however, to residential locations for hospitals, especially those institutions that serve special cases such as the mentally ill and the alcoholic. This opposition arises primarily from the depressing effect that such hospitals have upon certain persons living in the area. The basis of other opposition is more tangible. Hospitals create problems in low-density districts because of the large amount of transient parking which may flood the nearby residential streets. In addition, there is some objection to the noise created by emergency vehicles. Consequently, a number of recent zoning ordinances have excluded hospitals from low-density residence districts. In those communities with little or no multiple-family residence zoning, this often means their exclusion from all residence districts.[66]

Ordinances which exclude hospitals from residential districts give little consideration to the special needs of hospitals. Modern medical care needs quiet and pleasant surroundings, preferably with a bit of greenery which is so conducive to recovery from physical and mental illness. Unfortunately these are usually found only in low-density residential areas. Some of the objections which are raised against locating hospitals in residential zones can be met by requiring hospitals to provide extensive yards, landscaping, attractive architectural design, and adequate off-street parking facilities.

One of the most perplexing problems of regulating uses in resi-

[63] E. C. Moore and Maynard W. Weaver, "The General Residence District," *The American City*, Vol. 43, No. 4, p. 129, April, 1948.

[64] See pp. 416–418.

[65] Public schools are sometimes justified by the courts in residential districts because one of the avowed purposes of zoning may be that of facilitating the adequate provision of schools. See *Union Free School District No. 14 of Town of Hempstead v. Village of Hewlett Bay Park*, 279 A.D. 618, 107 N.Y.S. (2d) 858 (1951).

[66] Actually, on strict constitutional grounds, it seems difficult to justify regulations forbidding uses in one type of residential district which are not prohibited in another. If a police power objective is served by excluding a hospital from a single-family district, it is probably served to the same extent by exclusion from a two-family district, and it is difficult to see a valid reason for discriminating between property situated in the two districts. Nevertheless, many cities make a distinction between uses permitted in a higher-level residence district and those permitted in lower-level residence districts.

dential areas is that concerned with incidental home occupations. Zoning ordinances usually provide that the resident family located in a residential district may carry on within the dwelling customary home occupations. This is an equitable principle, but it often gives a great deal of trouble to the zoning administrator.[67]

Business or Commercial Zones. Regulations for business [68] zones vary widely. Some cities have only one type of business district. Others have business districts in the center of town, and neighborhood trading areas in or near the residential districts.[69] The larger cities usually have two types of central business districts, one reserved for retail establishments and the other available for noisier businesses, such as wholesalers and light manufacturing operations.

The most common error in municipal zoning is the designation of too great an area for business purposes. A mistaken belief that all lots on main thoroughfares are potential business sites has resulted in the setting aside of a considerable portion of this frontage for such purposes. The sporadic business development which results from this policy ruins the remaining area for residential use. Overzoning for business may have repercussions that become community-wide in effect. Land speculation, excessive public expenditures for improvements, and rising tax delinquencies on unimproved property are among the conditions that may result from unwise business zoning.[70]

Most of the newer zoning ordinances in cities with populations of 20,000 or more provide for "neighborhood trading areas" or "neighborhood business districts." This type of district is designed to accommodate the small shopping centers (containing drug stores, cleaning establishments, self-service laundries, etc.) which serve a particular residential area. Provision for such districts is desirable, because it helps to relieve some of the congestion from downtown marketing areas and furnishes convenient shopping facilities for the housewife who is short of time or lacks ready transportation. They have the disadvantage of causing a drop in the residential value of the land immediately adjacent to them. Most cities in drawing up a zoning ordinance for the first time will find that such little shopping

---

[67] See p. 414 for a discussion of this problem.

[68] In some jurisdictions they are called commercial zones.

[69] *Local Planning Administration*, op. cit., p. 227.

[70] The American Society of Planning Officials *Newsletter* for May, 1949, contains an article entitled, "Excess Business Zoning Shown by Survey," based on the study of the zoning problem in Seattle made by the Municipal League of Seattle and King County.

"Is Not Your City, Too, Overzoned for Business," *The American City*, Vol. 54, No. 4, p. 64, April, 1939.

centers already exist, and it is quite a simple matter to designate them as neighborhood business districts.[71]

The requirements for business or commercial zones customarily provide that any use that is allowed in the various residential zones is permitted in the business zone.[72] The practice then is to list the permitted commercial uses and indicate the requirements for height, rear yard, side yard, and front yard lines. Some ordinances in establishing lower class commercial zones follow the practice of permitting all uses allowed in Class 1 commercial zones and of listing other permitted activities. Some other ordinances do not list the additional permitted uses, but specify the commercial activities which shall be excluded, thus by implication permitting any commercial use not specifically excluded.

Since business zones are ordinarily not intended to be for business and nothing else, residential uses, if allowed, should be required to comply with yard, height, and use requirements of the residential zone. The most important characteristics of the business zone is the exclusion of industries. Certain light industrial activities may nevertheless be allowed as long as they are in harmony with the character of the business zone. For example, watch repairmen, shoe repair shops, candy stores, tailor shops, and bakery stores are properly located in a commercial zone, although they must engage in certain manufacturing activities in furnishing their products and services. Other light industrial uses which do not constitute a nuisance or produce injurious effects may also be permitted.

The regulations for the central business zone should permit, in proper relationship to one another, retail establishments, hotels, theaters and other entertainment establishments, financial institutions, and wholesale businesses. Regulations for local business districts are usually more restrictive than those for the central business zone.

Industrial or Manufacturing Zones. Industrial zones are the least restricted of all zones.[73] In light industrial zones it is customary to permit any use except trades or industries which are injurious, noxious, offensive, or hazardous by reason of the emission of odors, dust, fumes, smoke, noise, or vibrations.[74] In heavy industry zones there are usually

[71] "Cities Regulate Shopping-Center Districts," *The American City*, Vol. 67, No. 2, p. 155, February, 1952. This article contains a set of guides to be considered in creating neighborhood shopping centers.

[72] It should be noted that some recent ordinances would seem to indicate a trend toward excluding residences from commercial zones.

[73] In some ordinances such zones are called manufacturing zones.

[74] "Twelve Principles of Industrial Zoning," *The American City*, Vol. 67, No. 2, p.

no exclusions as long as the business is for a lawful purpose. Nuisance or dangerous industries may sometimes be permitted only in locations and under conditions as approved by the board of adjustment or the planning agency. Some jurisdictions do, however, exclude residences from both light and heavy industrial zones.

Regulations for industrial districts frequently consist merely of prohibitions against certain industries, which quite possibly could be controlled as nuisances in the absence of a zoning ordinance. In most cities the prohibition of nuisance or seminuisance uses in industrial districts means that they cannot enter the city at all. On the other hand, some ordinances list the types of industries which may be located in each district and any unlisted type would be excluded.[75]

Many modern ordinances do not specify permitted or prohibited uses, but regulate industrial uses through the establishment of standards of performance which must be met by industries in the industrial zones.[76] This type of zoning would bar no industry or use by name. It would admit any use, provided it met the standards of performance set for admission to each zone. Performance standards are usually set in 11 fields: noise and vibration, smoke, odor, dust and dirt, noxious gases, glare and heat, fire hazards, industrial wastes, transportation and traffic, aesthetics, and psychological effects. One writer on the subject states:

> [For each of these, the zoning] performance standard will substitute a quantitative measurement of an effect for the qualitative description of that effect that we have used in the past. It will not use the terms "limited," "substantial," "objectionable," "offensive." Instead, it will measure definite measurements, taken by standardized methods with standardized instruments, to determine whether the effect of a particular use is within predetermined limits and therefore is permissible in a particular zone.[77]

A recent application of this principle is illustrated by the industrial performance standard zoning ordinance recently adopted by the city

---

154, February, 1952. This article presents a set of guides to the proper classification and identification of lands to be zoned as industrial.

[75] Charles W. Barr, "Characteristics of Good Commercial and Industrial Zoning Districts," *The American City*, Vol. 66, No. 7, p. 116, July, 1951.

[76] Edward Heiselberg, "How Anne Arundel County Zones for Industry," *The American City*, Vol. 68, No. 11, p. 98, November, 1953.

[77] Dennis O'Harrow, "Performance Standards in Industrial Zoning," *Planning*, 1951, p. 44.

For a plea for the application of performance standards to residence districts see Frank Horack, "Performance Standards in Residential Districts," *Planning*, 1952, p. 154.

of Columbus, Ohio. This ordinance is designed to reward progressive industries which provide proper enclosures and controls over processes that normally cause noise, odors, dust, smoke, glare and heat, sewage waste, and storage problems. Under this ordinance the traditional heavy and light manufacturing classifications are abolished and a blanket manufacturing classification is established into which industries will be fitted on the basis of their nuisance factors. Uses are classified as being less objectionable and more objectionable. The placement of the more objectionable uses requires the approval of the planning commission. Permits for the less objectionable uses may be granted by the planning director subject to obtaining proper clearance with appropriate administrative officials.[78]

Although most ordinances permit the uses of the more restricted zones in those which are less restricted, a number of cities have adopted the practice of prohibiting residences in industrial districts.[79] This exclusion has often been justified on the theory that factory neighborhoods are not suitable places for men and women to live and rear families. There are also good grounds for excluding residences in order to protect the character of the industrial zone. The subdividing of an area into small lots for residential purposes may result in extremely high acquisition costs when it becomes needed for industrial purposes. When the land is broken up into numerous small holdings, it becomes very difficult, if not impossible, to reassemble it in a large enough tract to vacate the streets and provide the amount of land needed for the industrial purpose. Furthermore, once residences have been built, governmental facilities and services, such as schools, parks, and utilities are needed and are usually supplied. Although no legal rights may exist to be protected from noise, fumes, and smoke from factories, complaints of these annoyances by the residents may have important political consequences.

Certainly a strong case can be made for prohibiting residences in industrial areas for the protection of industry and factory owners who feel, naturally, that if their factories are properly operated and located in an industrial district, they should not be subjected to regulation caused by the harassment of residents who have invaded the district.[80]

---

[78] "Adopts Performance Zoning for Industry," *Public Management*, Vol. XXXVIII, No. 12, p. 276, December, 1956.

[79] *American Land Co. v. City of Keene*, 41 F. (2d) 484 (1930).

[80] For a general discussion of this problem see Seward H. Mott, and Max S. Wehrly, *The Prohibition of Residential Developments in Industrial Districts*, Urban Land Institute Report No. 10 (Washington, D.C.: 1948), 8 pp.

On the other hand, it is often difficult to justify reserving land for exclusive industrial use when it is uncertain that all the land will be needed for that use within the immediate future. Such restrictions may mean that land may be held idle and unproductive for many years. The policy is particularly difficult to justify if there has been an overzoning for industrial use, or if there may be a scarcity of land suitable for residences for factory workers reasonably near their places of employment.

In most jurisdictions zoning ordinances have customarily assigned industrial uses to that land which was currently being used for industry and to other land not considered to be suited for the higher uses of business and residences. Thus, industry has been somewhat a stepchild in the realm of zoning.[81] In recent years there has been developing a tendency to consider industrial activities as an equal among the family of land uses and to protect them against invasions of uses which might be considered detrimental to industrial development. There is little doubt that in some instances in the past, industrial areas have been harmed by the encroachment of residential and business uses. If the protection of industrial zones is to be considered on a parity with that of other use zones, it would seem desirable to exclude uses from such areas which are detrimental to industrial development or to establish requirements which will insure that nonindustrial uses in industrial zones are fitted into a harmonious pattern.

A different approach has been indicated in some planning circles in which there is a growing attitude that, under proper development, many industrial uses are not incompatible with certain residential and commercial uses. This change in attitude comes about in part from recent trends in technological development in factory design and construction which have resulted in improved air conditioning, light, noise deadening techniques, and the installation of devices which prevent or reduce the emission of smoke, fumes, and odors. Furthermore, many industrial plants, as a result of attractive landscaping and site location, have presented attractive appearances which are harmonious with other uses. To the extent that such changed conditions exist, there may be justification for a complete reconsideration of zoning policy.

Airport Zoning. The authority of cities to regulate aviation fields

---

[81] "Zoning for Industry," *Municipal Administration* (Philadelphia: Associated Institutes of Government of Pennsylvania Universities, December, 1952), Supplement, p. 1.

under zoning regulations has been well established by the courts.[82] Because of the nature of their operation, the location of airports may affect rights of neighboring individuals and involve damage to their property. Nevertheless, the development of air transportation has created demands in the public interest for adequate airports and airport facilities.

Although municipalities may regulate airports under a comprehensive zoning ordinance, airport zoning is usually carried out under a special ordinance pursuant to a state airport enabling act. Since, in many instances, it is found necessary to locate airports outside the corporate limits of the municipality, cities under enabling legislation are usually granted extraterritorial powers for this purpose.[83] Unless extraterritorial powers are given there is the danger that small private airports will locate in the urban fringe and adversely affect the land use planning in the surrounding areas. A model airport zoning act which was originally prepared in 1941 jointly by the Civil Aeronautics Administration and the National Institute of Municipal Law Officers and which has been subsequently revised [84] has been the model for enabling legislation in a great number of the states. The model act authorizes all general political subdivisions to adopt zoning ordinances and provides for coöperation between two or more units in applying a joint zoning plan. Under the model zoning enabling act, airport zoning may be integrated with other zoning. In any event, it should conform to the comprehensive plans for the area. The act provides for the usual procedural steps found in most other zoning legislation for the administration and enforcement of the zoning ordinance and adopts the usual provisions with respect to nonconforming uses.

Airport use should be recognized as a commercial or industrial use for purposes of zone classification. Some jurisdictions provide by ordinance that airports are permitted to locate only in business or industrial districts. Others have found it advisable to authorize the location of airports by means of special exception of the planning agency or board of adjustment. This practice would seem to be preferable to a requirement definitely fixing a location in a commercial or industrial district because of the unusual requirements for airport location which, under certain circumstances, may necessitate that an

---

[82] Yokley, *op. cit.*, Vol. 2, Sec. 203, p. 46.

[83] For a discussion of the extent and limits of extraterritoriality, see Chap. 2, pp. 59–62.

[84] *Local Planning Administration, op. cit.*, p. 160.

airport be located within a residential area providing adequate safeguards can be established.

Since the time factor is of such great importance in air transportation, proximity to the center of the city is a matter for careful consideration in weighing the advantages of one location against another. Other factors include the cost of development, the removal of hazards, and the effect upon the surrounding area. Airport location must be determined in relationship to topography, prevailing weather conditions, and access to main thoroughfares and other transportation facilities.[85] Airport zoning to be effective in preventing airplane accidents must be able to control the height of buildings and other structures within the vicinity of the airports.[86]

Closely related to the problems of airport zoning is the regulation of flying itself. The adverse effect upon the enjoyment of living, values of property, and property uses caused by low-flying aircraft have led some cities to attempt to regulate the height at which airplanes must fly over the city on airport take-offs and landings. In a recent decision handed down June 27, 1955, a federal judge in the state of New York ruled that a town did not have the authority to prohibit low-flying planes on airport take-off.[87] In this case, the court granted an injunction against the Village of Cedarhurst, Long Island, which is located near the end of the runway of Idlewild International Airport. The Cedarhurst municipal ordinance made it a misdemeanor to fly over the village at an altitude lower than 1000 feet. The injunction against the village was sought by the major airlines using the airport, the Civil Aeronautics Board, and the Port of New York Authority. The court recognized the paramount interest of Congress to regulate interstate commerce and ruled that Congress had adopted comprehensive air-traffic plans for operation around airports, and therefore municipalities could not establish their own regulations on the subject. The court indicated that the old doctrine that "he who owns the land owns the air above it" is no longer valid. If this concept is upheld by the Supreme Court of the United States, air space must be regarded as part of the public domain.[88]

---

[85] See Chap. 4, pp. 192–196.

[86] For a discussion of factors in site location for heliports, see The Port of New York Authority, *Heliport Location and Design* (New York: 1955).

[87] *Allegheny Airlines et al. v. Incorporated Village of Cedarhurst et al.*, 132 F. Supp. 871 (1955).

[88] "Air Space Declared Part of Public Domain," *Urban Land*, Vol. 14, No. 7, p. 5, July–August, 1955. For a discussion of a related matter, see *Gardner v. County of Allegheny*, 382 Pa. 88, 114 A. (2d) 491 (1955), in which the court held that airline

Flood-Plain Zoning. Flood damage in many populous river valleys has become a matter of serious public concern. In a number of states steps have been taken to meet the problem through the enforcement of "flood-plain zoning" ordinances. Flood-plain zoning is aimed at encouraging a type of land use in areas subject to recurrent floods which will help to minimize the losses when floods occur. Although flood-plain zoning may be carried out in some jurisdictions under the powers granted by general zoning enabling acts, several states including California, Florida, Georgia, South Carolina, and Wisconsin have expressly authorized flood-plain zoning.

Flood-plain zoning may take several forms. In some instances it may require total exclusion of occupancy from the flood plain. In others, sufficient protection may be given by excluding only buildings designed for specific purposes. Under some conditions the problem may be met through the regulation of building construction such as prohibiting basements below the high-water mark.[89]

Added emphasis has recently been given to flood-plain zoning by the Flood Insurance Act of 1956.[90] This Act recognizes the adverse effect of flood damage to interstate commerce, national defense, and the general welfare and establishes a program of federal insurance and reinsurance against risks resulting from floods.[91] Section 12 of the Act provides that no insurance shall be issued under the provisions of the Act on any property declared by a duly constituted state or local zoning authority or other authorized public body to be in violation of state or local flood-zoning laws. It provides further, that after June 30, 1958, no insurance or reinsurance shall be issued under the provisions of the Act in any geographical location unless an appropriate body shall have adopted and shall keep in effect such flood zoning restrictions, if any, as may be deemed necessary by the Administrator of the Housing and Home Finance Agency to reduce, within practical limits, damage from flood in such location.[92]

---

trespass due to low flying over plaintiff's property on landings and take-offs may be enjoined by the state court. Regulations of the Civil Aeronautics Board established minimum floor of navigable air space at 500 feet above ground in rural areas and 1000 feet in congested areas. The regulations did not fix minimum heights for take-offs and landings.

[89] Erling D. Solberg, *Rural Zoning in the United States* (Washington, D.C.: U.S. Government Printing Office, 1952), p. 18.

[90] 70 Stat. 1082, P.L. 1016, 84th Congress, 2d Session.

[91] The Act also provides for loans to assist flood victims.

[92] See also 70 Stat. 1101, 42 U.S.C.A. 1462 (1956 Supp.), which provides financial assistance under urban renewal projects for removal and relocation of dwellings from sites of recurring floods.

OTHER MAJOR APPLICATIONS OF ZONING CONTROL

In addition to controlling land use, the zoning ordinance is designed to achieve a number of other important objectives. Among these are the regulation of the height of buildings and structures, the establishment of area and bulk requirements, and the control of population density.

Height Zoning. Height districts are usually laid out with reference to use districts and area districts, although their boundaries may not always be identical with either. Height regulations are designed primarily to insure an adequate supply of light and air. They have also been utilized, but less successfully, for the purpose of limiting the capacity of buildings to the capacity of the streets. Since, however, much of the street traffic does not originate from the abutting property, and since buildings of the same height used for different purposes do not always generate the same amount of traffic, zoning of height does not offer an entirely satisfactory solution to this problem.

As in the case of use regulations, the validity of ordinances controlling height can be sustained only if reasonably related to the promotion of health, safety, morals, convenience, and the general welfare. The validity of height control as having a reasonable relationship to the police power objectives was recognized quite early by both state courts and by the United States Supreme Court.[93] Among the factors cited as showing a connection between building height regulations and the police power objectives are that tall buildings:

1. Cut off the light and air from their neighbors.
2. Generate increased traffic, as a result of the large number of offices and shops which they contain.
3. Sometimes overload sewerage facilities.
4. Endanger their occupants and their neighbors, because of the difficulties of fighting fires far above the street and of evacuating burning buildings of considerable height.
5. Amplify the noise and confusion of the streets.[94]

In establishing height regulations, it is assumed that in certain areas, as in the central part of the city, there is need for greater density than in outlying areas. The need for people engaged in business to be near each other to carry on their trades, communications,

---

[93] *Welch v. Swasey,* 214 U.S. 91, 53 L.Ed. 923 (1909) affirming *Welch v. Swasey,* 193 Mass. 364, 79 N.E. 745 (1907).
[94] *Ibid.*

financial transactions, and relations with government justify the erection of higher buildings than may be required in other parts of the city. In residential areas, on the other hand, where families rear their children, there is the greatest need for open spaces, air, and sunlight. Other areas have density requirements between these demands.

Three principal methods of limiting the height of buildings are employed. Height limits are sometimes expressed in terms of (1) the number of maximum feet, (2) the number of stories permitted, and (3) multiples of street width. Thus, the buildings in Class H-1 may be restricted to a height of three-fourths of the width of the street on which they face, while in Class H-3 the maximum height may be 2½ times the street width. Zoning ordinances commonly permit buildings in certain districts to exceed the height limits if the upper stories are set back a certain number of feet from the street or lot line.[95] The law may stipulate, for example, that for every foot a building extends above the height limit there must be a setback of one foot. Provisions of this sort, if properly framed, insure a light angle that will permit the lower floors of buildings on the opposite side of the street from a tall structure to receive direct sunlight at least a portion of the day.

The New York City zoning ordinance of 1916 recognized this relation between height and street arrangement with the result that the ordinance has caused a picturesque modification in the architectural design of tall buildings in the metropolis during the past 40 years. The newer buildings no longer resemble packing boxes set on end. Instead their upper stories taper off, providing greater opportunities for ornamentation.[96] The higher the building, the farther it recedes from the street at successive stages and the less its additional volume becomes.

In setting height limitations for neighborhood business districts, the most satisfactory practice has been to fix the height limit by stories or by the number of feet, with appropriate allowances for certain types of buildings, such as theaters, for example, which may have particular needs. In central business zones, the common practice is to establish heights of buildings with respect to the width of the street on which it fronts. Height regulations, if established in industrial zones, are usually limited to three-fourths of the distance to the opposite side of the street but with overall limitations on the

[95] Newman F. Baker, *The Legal Aspects of Zoning* (Chicago: University of Chicago, 1927), p. 67.

[96] Joseph P. Day, "New York City Zoning Law Makes the Skyscraper a Thing of Beauty," *National Municipal Review*, Vol. 19, No. 12, p. 812, December, 1930.

number of stories and the number of feet in height.[97] Regulations of the smaller cities commonly provide that the height of the buildings shall not exceed the width of the street. In the large cities height is usually established with relationship to the width of the street, with maximum limitations on the number of stories or the number of feet in height. Regulations in some cities are established according to the bulk of buildings. Where limitations are on the basis of building mass, the total volume is usually established with reference to the area of the lot and the width of the street.

In single and two-family residence zones it is a common practice to establish height regulations by fixing height limits measured from curb level to peak of the roof as by the number of feet or number of stories (35 feet or 2½ stories). Although the same methods may be used in fixing height limits in multifamily residence zones, other practices which are employed are fixing height limitations with respect to street widths but with overall limits on the number of stories or height in feet. A further method that is sometimes used is that of limiting the total floor area with respect to the area of the lot. Thus, a zoning ordinance may provide that total floor area for an apartment house shall not exceed 275 percent of the area of the lot. Under this type of control, the owner may construct either a low building covering a large proportion of the lot or a tall building covering a small portion of it.

Certain objects such as church spires, radio antennas, water towers, monuments, and chimneys are usually permitted to exceed the height restrictions. It is customary to designate these exceptions in the zoning ordinance.

Area Zoning. Area regulations in zoning ordinances are limitations on the usable building area of land surface. In general, there is more variety in the area regulations of zoning ordinances than in use or height regulations. Area districts are established with reference to use and height districts although not necessarily duplicating them. Several methods have been employed in defining area limitations. In some ordinances several different methods are actually employed. The most usual is the establishment of front, rear, and side yards, courts, and other open space size requirements.

Area regulations may also specify the percentage of total lot area

---

[97] *Local Planning Administration, op. cit.,* p. 230. Because of the variations necessary to meet the needs of specific industries, some cities have found it inadvisable to establish height regulations for industrial zones.

Question: If public welfare is certain, should it
apts & crowded areas be required to have more open
area than more restricted residential areas,

394   Urban Planning and Municipal Public Policy

that may be built upon. Such regulations vary considerably with respect to the character of the particular zone. In the more restricted residential areas the regulations may permit the residence to occupy not more than 25 to 40 percent of the lot. This percentage is increased in the less restricted districts. In the least restricted districts, ordinances sometimes allow as much as 90 percent of its lot area to be covered. Frequently, an additional 10 percent of open space may be allocated on corner lots because of the exposure to two streets.

Area requirements are also concerned with building or setback lines establishing front, rear, and side yards. Essentially there is no difference between the terms "building lines" and "setback lines," but there is some reason to avoid the use of the term "setback line" in establishing yard requirements since some courts have construed it to relate to street widening which, in most jurisdictions, can be accomplished only through eminent domain.[98] Building line requirements are obviously closely related to the percentage of the lot which the building may occupy. Yard requirements are intended to insure adequate light and air, to permit space for tree planting, to prevent fire hazards, and to establish play areas for children.

Front yard building lines vary with the type of district. These normally will range from 30 feet in single-family zones to 20 feet in apartment house zones. Special problems are presented by corner lots since they front on two streets. Ordinances frequently provide that the requirements along the side streets are reduced. If, however, the determination of which street is the front is left to the individual owner, he may face his building in a way which destroys the harmony of the building plan causing injury to his neighbors. For this reason, some cities have found it desirable to provide that the building shall front upon the wider street. Other cities have established front yard maps of the entire city to designate what street shall be considered the front.[99]

Front yard lines require that buildings be set back a certain distance from the street, or from neighboring buildings. The usual method of regulating the front-yard requirement is to calculate the depth, at the time of passage of the ordinance, of more than one-half of the front yards, on either side of the street, between two intersecting streets.

---

[98] Some cities have enacted special ordinances establishing setback lines as an exercise of the police power. See Ordinance No. 888 of the City of Buenadventura, California, adopted February 14, 1955. See also Gordon Whitnall, *Are Building Line Setbacks Valid?* (Los Angeles: Gordon Whitnall and Associates, October 15, 1952).

[99] Bassett, *op. cit.*, p. 60.

This depth determines the line to which new or reconstructed buildings must conform. Adequate front yards afford room for lawns and trees, keep residences farther from the dust, fumes, and noise of the street, and add to the attractiveness and comfort of a residential district. They also afford play space for children and aid in keeping youngsters out of the streets. In addition, by providing a greater distance between buildings on the opposite sides of the street, they tend to reduce fire hazard. The validity of such regulations as a reasonable exercise of the police power has not been seriously questioned since the decision of the Supreme Court of the United States which upheld such requirements in the case of Gorieb v. Fox, et al.[100] Some of the justifications were set forth in the court's opinion:

> The members of the city council, as a basis for the ordinance, set forth in their answer that front yards, (1) afford room for lawns and trees, (2) keep the dwellings farther from the dust, noise, and fumes of the street, (3) add to the attractiveness and comfort of a residential district, (4) create a better home environment, and (5) by securing a greater distance between houses on opposite sides of the street, reduce the fire hazard; [and] that the projection of a building beyond the front line of the adjacent dwelling cuts off light and air from them, and, by interfering with the view of street corners, constitutes a danger in the operation of automobiles. We cannot deny the existence of these grounds—indeed they seem obvious.

Side yards are needed in residential zones to provide access in case of fire, to insure privacy, to give an appropriate setting to the building, and to insure adequate quantities of light and air. Most apartment houses and multiple-dwelling units need side yards since many rooms are lighted solely from the side. They also serve to facilitate deliveries and municipal services.

Side yards are ordinarily not required in business and industrial zones, but they may be highly desirable to provide easy access in case of fire. If they are voluntarily established, they should be required to comply with minimum standards in the ordinance so that the side yards will not become a repository for litter, debris, and trash. When they are required, the ordinances generally regulate the width of side yards by stating the minimum size of the yard in terms of feet of width.

Rear yard requirements in residential districts rest on the same

[100] 274 U.S. 603, 71 L.Ed. 1228 (1927).
See also Eubank v. Richmond, 226 U.S. 137, 57 L.Ed. 156 (1913).

basis as front yards. They should be deep enough to allow for light, air, and vegetation so that a pleasant outlook is obtained. They also provide access and egress to the rear of the buildings. Privacy is provided, and space is made available for accessory buildings. Rear yards are also necessary in business and industrial districts, principally to provide unloading and parking space and a means of entry for fire-fighting and trash-collecting apparatus. Rear yard requirements are usually established in all classes of zones and are expressed as a percentage of the total lot depth or as a minimum number of feet between the rear of the building and the rear lot line. Rear lot requirements should be considered with respect to the width and depth of the lots.

Front and side yard requirements in zoning regulations are sometimes imposed to prevent traffic view obstructions at intersections. By enlarging the angle of vision at the corners, many street accidents may be prevented. Setback lines, to provide corner sight triangles, are frequently established by special ordinances rather than by zoning, although it is common to include corner sight triangle provisions in the zoning regulations.[101]

Provisions in the zoning ordinance establishing minimum widths for courts constitute a further means of securing adequate light, air, and privacy. The width of both outer and inner courts should be established with relationships to the height of the building and the character of the district.

Area regulations are also concerned with space for loading facilities and off-street parking. Some of the newer zoning codes require every hospital, institution, hotel, commercial or industrial building erected after the effective date of the ordinance to provide permanently maintained loading space of sufficient area that no vehicle of any kind, when using the space, will project into any public right of way.[102] Requirements for loading areas should be established on the basis of careful loading zone surveys. The zoning ordinance is only one of the tools for solving the loading problem. Other solutions to the problem are to be found in stringent traffic control of illegal on-street loading

---

[101] Joshua H. Vogel and Ernest H. Campbell, *Municipal Regulation of Traffic View Obstructions* (Seattle: Bureau of Governmental Research and Services, University of Washington, February, 1953), Report No. 122, pp. 8–9. Setback from lot lines of 15'–15', or 20'–10', or 10'–20' produces a sight triangle with two points 90 feet from the intersection point of the center lines of two 60-foot streets and 80 feet from the intersection of two 50-foot streets.

[102] Kenneth Green, "Loading Experience as a Basis for Zoning Requirements," *Traffic Quarterly*, Vol. 7, No. 4, p. 498, October, 1953.

and through encouraging the development of more off-street loading facilities for buildings erected before the enactment of the ordinance. Off-street loading regulations based on major land-use classifications should establish minimum requirements rather than specific site requirements because of the importance of considering specific site needs in relationship to design.[103]

Obviously there must be a close coördination between zoning policy and traffic-control policy. An increasing number of ordinances are including provisions requiring minimum amounts of off-street parking space to be provided for certain classes of buildings or land uses. For residential zones of two and four families these regulations usually require off-street parking space for one car for each dwelling unit. In multifamily residence zones the requirements may require only one parking space for each two-dwelling unit. Requirements for buildings where large numbers of persons assemble should be established on the basis of the probable needs of persons who will be attracted to these buildings.

Population Density Control. Of vital importance to the community is the prevention of excessive overcrowding of the population. Many careful studies have demonstrated that congestion of population breeds problems of health, sanitation, safety, and crime.[104] Courts have held, therefore, that the control of population density to prevent overcrowding has a direct relation to the protection of the public health, public safety, morality, and general welfare, and is a valid exercise of the police power.[105] Since 1920 the authority to control density of population has been granted in most of the new state zoning enabling acts, and some of the older enabling acts have been amended to include authority to control density of population.[106]

Population density is controlled to some extent by the limitation on the height and bulk of buildings. Likewise, yard requirements tend to prevent overcrowding. Population density control may also utilize any one or more of the following different types of methods:

1. Limitations on the number of families per acre.
2. Limitations on the number of persons per acre.

---

[103] *Ibid.*, p. 514.

[104] Harold S. Buttenheim, "Absurd Land-Overcrowding Allowed by Many Zoning Ordinances," *The American City*, Vol. 51, No. 6, p. 81, June, 1936.

[105] *City of Albany v. Anthony*, 2 Misc. 198, 21 N.Y.S. 258 (1940).

[106] Edward M. Bassett, "Regulating Density of Population," *The American City*, Vol. 52, No. 1, p. 57, January, 1937.

3. Limitations on the percentage of a lot which may be occupied by buildings.

4. Minimum requirements as to lot areas on which dwellings may be built.

5. Minimum requirements as to space which must be allocated to each individual occupant of a house.

Where limitations are made by the number of families per acre, it is usually advisable to define the word "family" in the section of the ordinance devoted to definitions.

Because of the enforcement problems inherent in density of population control, most communities have relied upon the more indirect approach of specifying minimum lot sizes and maximum percentages of lots which can be occupied by buildings. These restrictions vary according to the real estate development practices in various cities and also according to the nature of the neighborhood. Although population density control regulations are intended primarily for residential districts, they should be applicable also to commercial or industrial districts, which contain residences.

Frequently, area regulations establishing low population density develop out of a desire to insure large lot areas or open spaces surrounding the buildings. Zoning ordinances may sometimes specify lot sizes as much as 20,000 square feet or two or more acres. Whether or not such regulations are reasonable may depend upon a number of circumstances. For example, zoning regulations specifying unusually large lot sizes may be sustained in areas where fire protection services are not adequate or where there may be special problems of water supply or sewage disposal, but might not be upheld in areas where services and utilities are adequate. Except in the very high-class residential districts, lot requirements are customarily established at about 6000 or 7000 square feet per family in the single-family district, from 2000 or 3000 square feet per family in the two-family district, and from 500 to 1000 square feet per family in the multifamily or apartment house district. In business and industrial districts, the requirements are about the same as those of apartment house districts.

Each city must be prepared to demonstrate a factual relationship between the regulations adopted to limit population density and one of the police power objectives. If the number of families per acre or the percentage of lot which may be built upon has been set very low, or minimum lot size or space per individual has been set very high, the probability is that it has been done in order to preserve a "high-class" residential area as such, rather than to promote the public health, safety, morals, or general welfare. If the courts find that this is the case, the particular provisions may be ruled invalid.[107] The police power cannot be used for merely snobbish purposes. While there are not a great many judicial decisions passing upon the validity of population control ordinances, it appears that the courts will look at the particular facts in each case and the objectives to be served.[108] Depending upon the surrounding circumstances, some judicial decisions have upheld minimum lot sizes for one-family dwelling units of 40,000 square feet,[109] 20,000 square feet,[110] one acre, two acres,[111] three acres,[112] and five acres.[113] Under other circumstances, courts have held the following minimum lot sizes invalid: 5000 square feet for each dwelling unit,[114] and one acre for each dwelling unit.[115] No precise minimum lot size can be indicated for all cities and towns. What is reasonable must be determined in the light of the comprehensive plan and the requirements of each particular area.[116]

Where particular minimum requirements differ for different sections of the city, the question is presented whether there is any legal justification for such differentiation. If standards are adequate for one residential district, a presumption is raised that they should be adequate for other residential districts. If the legality of the ordinance is attacked on this ground, the city must be prepared to overcome this presumption by showing that the differentiation in the requirements is based upon factual differences having a bearing upon the police power objectives.

Minimum House Size Provisions. One of the most recent and

[107] *Dilliard v. North Hills*, 195 Misc. 875, 91 N.Y.S. (2d) 542 (1949). The court ruled that a 2-acre requirement was void as an attempt to protect large estates rather than to further the public health, safety, or morals.

[108] Edward M. Bassett, "One-Family Dwellings and Density of Population Under Zoning." *The American City*, Vol. 56, No. 1, p. 103, January, 1941.

[109] *Simon v. Town of Needham*, 311 Mass. 560, 42 N.E. (2d) 516 (1942).

[110] *Gignoux et al v. Village of Kings Point*, 199 Misc. 485, 99 N.Y.S. (2d) 280 (1950).

[111] *Franmor Realty Corp. v. Village of Old Westbury*, 280 A.D. 945, 116 N.Y.S. (2d) 68 (1952).

[112] *Flora Realty and Investment Co. v. City of Lodue*, 336 Mo. 1025, 246 S.W. (2d) 771 (1952).

[113] *Fischer v. Bedminster*, 21 N.J. Super. 81, 90 A. (2d) 757 (1952).

[114] *Morris et al. v. City of Los Angeles*, 116 Cal. App. 856, 254 P. (2d) 935 (1953).

[115] *State v. Stahlman*, 81 W.Va. 335, 94 S.E. 497 (1917).

[116] Ernest H. Campbell, *Population Density Control* (Seattle: Bureau of Governmental Research and Services, University of Washington, February 11, 1954), Research Memorandum No. 40, p. 10.

controversial uses of zoning has been to establish minimum floor areas for residences. Area requirements in zoning ordinances have, for the most part, been concerned with such matters as limitations upon the minimum lot areas required for homes, the portion of the lot which a building may occupy, the number of families which may be permitted per acre, and other related requirements aimed at securing adequate light and air and preventing overcrowding and congestion. Such controls have been sustained as a legitimate exercise of the police power.

The requirement that a residence must have a minimum floor area of 1000 square feet, 1800 square feet, or some other fixed area presents somewhat different considerations from those restricting the floor area to a certain proportion of the lot. From a realistic point of view, it is very difficult to show that the minimum size of the house tends to lessen congestion, prevent overcrowding, reduce fire hazards or danger of panic, or provide more adequate light, air, or convenience. It is likewise difficult to show that minimum area requirements necessarily promote the public health unless they are related to the number of occupants, the number of rooms, and existing facilities for lighting and ventilation.[117] It is unlikely that many communities at the present time are prepared to regulate the number of persons who may occupy a dwelling or to evict families whose membership has increased beyond the maximum number fixed by law. Because of these factors, the courts have had difficulty in finding a relationship between the regulations establishing minimum floor areas and the police power objectives.[118] Such regulations have sometimes been viewed by the courts as attempts to use the power of government to set aside certain areas exclusively for the higher income families and promote residential segregation by income groups. Courts have consistently ruled that zoning regulations directed against people—especially on the basis of income—are improper in a democratic society and are invalid.[119]

In *Baker v. Somerville* [120] the Supreme Court of Nebraska held that

[117] "The Case of the Minimum House," *Urban Land*, Vol. 11, No. 11, p. 2, December, 1952.

[118] *Flower Hill Building Corporation v. Village of Flower Hill*, 199 Misc. 344, 100 N.Y.S. (2d) 903 (1950). The ordinance involved in this case provided for a minimum of 1800 square feet. See also: "Zoning for Minimum House Size," *The American City*, Vol. 68, No. 1, p. 9, January, 1953.

[119] O'Brien Boldt, "Pennsylvania Court Rules on Snob Zoning," *The American City*, Vol. 65, No. 4, p. 129, April, 1950.

[120] 138 Neb. 466, 293 N.W. 326 (1940).

a requirement that one-story dwellings contain at least 2000 square feet of floor area was intended merely to prevent such dwellings from entering a neighborhood where existing residences were two stories high. Because this purpose had no relation to the police power objectives, the court ruled that the ordinance was invalid.[121] Two cases in the Michigan Supreme Court, *Senefsky v. Huntington Woods*,[122] and *Frischkorn Construction Co. v. Lambert*,[123] also invalidated minimum-size house requirements. The ordinance involved in the Senfsky case provided that in a certain district, each dwelling should have a minimum usable floor area of 1300 square feet. The plaintiff, Senefsky, had applied for a building permit for a dwelling of 980 square feet, which was refused. The court decided in this case that a house of the size the plaintiff proposed to erect would satisfy the requirements of health and well-being and declared the ordinance, as applied to him, unreasonable and invalid. The court did emphasize the fact that the decision was based on the specific facts presented, and the court was not passing directly on the issue of whether requirements of this amount are valid.

Some of the more recent cases have tended to break away from the holdings of these cases and to sustain minimum floor requirements.[124] The leading case supporting this rule is that of *Lionshead Lake Inc. v. Wayne Township*,[125] decided by the Supreme Court of New Jersey. The zoning ordinance of the Township of Wayne provided that one-story dwellings shall have not less than 768 square feet, and that two-story dwellings with garages attached shall have not less than 1000 square feet, and that two-story dwellings without garages attached shall have not less than 1200 square feet of floor space. The Court was unanimous in its opinion upholding the right of a municipality to establish minimum floor area requirements under the police power, but two justices voiced a vigorous dissent based upon the ground that the particular ordinance applied uniformly to the entire township

---

[121] But see *Dundee Realty Co. v. City of Omaha*, 144 Neb. 448, 13 N.W. (2d) 634 (1944) where the same court upheld an ordinance providing for 1000 square feet.

[122] 307 Mich. 728, 12 N.W. (2d) 387 (1943).

[123] 315 Mich. 556, 24 N.W. (2d) 209 (1946).

[124] In *Thompson v. City of Carrollton* (Court of Civil Appeals, Texas) 211 S.W. (2d) 970 (1948), the court decided that the Senefsky Case was not applicable in Texas and sustained an ordinance prescribing a minimum of 900 square feet of floor space. In handing down its decision the court quoted with approval from a dissenting opinion in the Senefsky Case.

[125] 10 N.J. 165, 89 A. (2d) 693 (1952). Appeal to U.S. Supreme Court dismissed for want of a federal question, 344 U.S. 919, 73 S.Ct. 386 (1953).

without being related to the various use districts or lot sizes, and, therefore, was arbitrary and capricious.

Chief Justice Vanderbilt, speaking for the majority of the court, said:

> We may take notice without formal proof that there are minimums in housing below which one may not go without risk of impairing the health of those who dwell therein. One does not need extensive experience in matrimonial causes to become aware of the adverse effect of overcrowding on the well-being of our most important institution, the home. But quite apart from these considerations of public health which cannot be overlooked, minimum floor area standards are justified on the ground that they promote the general welfare of the community. . . . The court in conformance with the constitutional provisions and the statutes hereinbefore cited take a broad view of what constitutes general welfare.

The majority opinion of the court thus recognized that there are minimums in housing below which one may not go without impairing the health of those who dwell therein. The court, however, seemed satisfied to justify its decision upon grounds that the requirements of the ordinance promoted the general welfare of the community, since the size of the dwelling in any community inevitably affects the character of the community and does much to determine whether or not it is a desirable place in which to live.

To the extent that the decision rests upon the promotion of general welfare for conserving the character of the district, the court would seem to have expanded the concept of zoning more widely into the realm of economics.[126] If regulations to preserve the character of the neighborhood fall within the scope of the police power, it is but a short step for the judiciary to uphold many other types of regulations to advance the community as a social, economic, and political unit.[127] Certainly the quality of the house, its design, color, site location, and landscaping are also important factors in preserving neighborhood character. It remains to be seen, however, how far the courts will be willing to go in upholding zoning controls solely for

[126] The Wayne Township minimum-size zoning ordinance and the Lionshead Case have created considerable controversy. See, for example, Herbert H. Smith, "More on Wayne Township and Minimum-Size Zoning," *The American City*, Vol. 66, No. 11, p. 133, November, 1951.

See also Val Nolan, Jr., and Frank E. Horack, Jr., "How Small a House?—Zoning for Minimum Space Requirements," *Harvard Law Review*, Vol. 67, p. 967, April, 1954.

[127] J. Oakley McNight, "Minimum House Size Provisions in Zoning Ordinances," *The New York State Planning News*, Vol. 17, No. 4, p. 3, July, 1953.

the purpose of conserving property values or preserving the character of the neighborhood if not in some way related to public health, safety, or morals.

LEGAL AND PRACTICAL DIFFICULTIES OF APPLYING RESTRICTIVE LAND USE

THE PROBLEM OF NONCONFORMING USES

One of the major obstacles to effective zoning is the nonconforming use. A nonconforming use exists when any land, buildings, and structures do not conform to the use, height, and area requirements of the zoning ordinance.[128] In many cases the actual use of the premises may be conforming, but the building itself does not conform to yard, height, bulk, or lot area requirements.[129] Most zoning ordinances permit a nonconforming use to be continued at least temporarily if such use did not, at the time the zoning ordinance or amendment was enacted, violate any law or any other ordinance of the municipality. The determination of what is to be done eventually with these nonconforming uses poses many delicate problems of public policy. Are they to be permitted to remain and to be treated as exceptions to the new rules? If so, this weakens the zoning ordinance and accepts a situation short of the ideal. Shall the city or county decree that they will no longer be tolerated, and eliminate them or compel their transformation to a conforming use? To require the partial destruction of tall buildings erected in good faith or the removal from residential neighborhoods of legitimate businesses conducted in an orderly manner is to place an intolerable burden upon property owners and can be justified only on major considerations of public policy.[130]

Planning and zoning officials all over the country have become aware of the fact that the handling of nonconforming uses has not been effective. The number of nonconforming uses in most cities, instead of decreasing with the passage of time as expected, has actually increased, due to the excessive number of variances which have been granted by boards of adjustment. On the other hand, it is important to bear in mind that many of the "softening" provisions have been

[128] Bassett, op. cit., p. 14.

[129] Ralph W. Crolly, "How to Get Rid of Nonconforming Uses," *The American City*, Vol. 67, No. 11, p. 107, November, 1952.

[130] An interesting discussion of this problem appears in Dix W. Noel, "Retroactive Zoning and Nuisances," *Columbia Law Review*, Vol. 41, p. 451, 1941.

inserted in the ordinance in order to secure the adoption of the zoning ordinance in the first place and that many an ordinance has been defeated by the opposition of property owners who were afraid of its effect upon their property.

Zoning Ordinance Provisions. Since zoning has been customarily looked upon as a prospective device for stabilizing and protecting property values rather than as a means of correcting mistakes of the past, most zoning ordinances recognize the existence of nonconforming uses and permit those in existence at the time the ordinance went into effect to continue. For a long time the generally accepted view was that nonconforming uses, in existence at the time the zoning ordinance was adopted, which are lawful and not a public nuisance or harmful in any way to the public health, safety, or morals, or the general welfare, could not be prohibited because to give the ordinance retroactive effect would constitute an unreasonable exercise of the police power, and thus be unconstitutional.[131]

As zoning has come to be considered more and more essential to orderly community development, greater attention has been given to the elimination of nonconforming uses. Once the character of a zone has been established, the general zoning policy should be aimed at preventing the extension of nonconforming uses and eliminating existing nonconforming uses in so far as this can be reasonably done without creating undue hardship. Most ordinances place strict limitations upon the extension of nonconforming uses by requiring that the particular use may not be extended or altered and that structural alterations may not be undertaken which would enlarge the nonconforming use.

In the drafting and administration of the zoning ordinance, innumerable problems arise involving both matters of policy and legal technicalities. Many of these center about such questions as the following:

1. What acts constitute an enlargement or extension of a nonconforming use?
2. May the nonconforming use be changed to another nonconforming use?
3. If a nonconforming use is abandoned or discontinued may it later be resumed?
4. May a nonconforming structure be rebuilt after damage or destruction?

[131] McKee and Levine, op. cit., p. 288.

5. How may a nonconforming use be eliminated?

Enlargement, Extension, or Alteration. Zoning policy should seek to provide adequate safeguards to insure that existing nonconforming uses are not enlarged or extended. Although ordinary repairs to a building should be permitted, building permits should not be granted which would authorize structural alterations which do not conform to the requirements of the district in which the building is located or which would unduly extend the life of the nonconforming use. Alterations, such as increasing floor area or substituting permanent brick walls for wooden ones, normally should not be allowed.

The zoning ordinance should contain strict limitations upon the extension of nonconforming uses by either expanding the activities or facilities, or changing their character.[132] Public policy should consistently seek to restrict rather than to increase nonconforming uses. This policy should be applied even though the proposed enlargement of facilities or change of use would be no more detrimental to the character of the district than the existing nonconforming use. Courts have given support to this policy and have held, for example, that proposed additional facilities, such as a pumphouse for an ice company,[133] or fuel oil tanks for a coal dealer to include fuel oil sales in his operations are appropriately denied.[134]

Difficult questions are sometimes presented when permits have been obtained prior to the effective date of the ordinance to erect buildings which, if erected, would be nonconforming structures. Different states have established widely different rules on the rights of individuals to complete such buildings. It would seem to be the best practice to adopt a strict policy against the proposed structure and revoke all such building permits by the passage of the ordinance.[135] Certainly the property owner should not be able to assert any vested rights against the police power of the state by virtue of having obtained a permit. If permits are not revoked, the provisions of the ordinance should require construction to begin (and be completed)

[132] See *Shields v. Spokane School District No. 81*, 31 Wn. (2d) 274, 196 P. (2d) 852 (1948), in which the court held that a proposed enlargement of an elementary school to include use as a trade school was not permitted under the ordinance.

[133] *Everpure Ice Mfg. Co. v. Board of Appeals of Lawrence*, 324 Mass. 433, 86 N.E. (2d) 906 (1949).

[134] *Brandt v. Zoning Board of Adjustment*, 16 N.J. Super. 113, 84 A. (2d) 18 (1951).

[135] It seems fairly clear that in the absence of a statutory provision to the contrary the city may revoke such permits at the time of passage of the ordinance provided no work has commenced. See *Howe Realty Co. v. Nashville*, 176 Tenn. 405, 141 S.W. (2d) 904 (1940); *Caponi v. Walsh*, 228 A.D. 86, 238 N.Y.S. 438 (1930).

within a certain period of time to prevent a flood of applications for permits just prior to passage of the ordinance by owners who do not know whether they will ever utilize them but want them "just in case" it ever becomes profitable to build.

If, however, the construction had been started in good faith and had proceeded to a stage where undue hardship might arise because of materials having been purchased, contracts entered into, and certain work having been performed, it would seem that the case might appropriately be considered for relief by the board of adjustment. Because of the apparent hardship inherent in this situation, most ordinances recognize the issuance of a building permit and the commencing of work prior to the enactment of the ordinance as a showing of good faith and permit completion of the nonconforming use if it is otherwise lawful and would not constitute a nuisance.

The arguments for a strict policy against the enlargement or extension of a nonconforming use apply with equal validity against permitting changes to another nonconforming use. Courts have upheld this policy in the interest of eliminating nonconforming uses even though the proposed change of use would not be more harmful to the community than the original one. Under this principle, for example, an application for a permit to operate a dry cleaning establishment in a residential zone where the premises had been used for a tailor shop which cleaned clothes by hand should be denied on the ground that the continuance of a nonconforming use contemplates the same use and not some other kind of use.[136]

Discontinuance and Abandonment. It is customary to provide in the zoning ordinance that when a nonconforming use is discontinued or abandoned it may not be reinstated.[137] There is a distinction between discontinuance and abandonment. Abandonment of a nonconforming use involves an intent to abandon or relinquish such use, as well as an actual discontinuance.

Because of the difficulty of proving intent, most modern ordinances define "discontinuance" clearly in the ordinance. This is done by providing that discontinuance results from the occurrence of one of the following conditions: (1) vacancy of a building designed or arranged for the nonconforming use for a continuous period of six months to one year; or (2) vacancy of land for a period of 90 days;

[136] *Sverbo v. Board of Adjustment of Jersey City,* 4 N.J. Super. 409, 67 A. (2d) 472 (1949).

[137] "Discontinuance of Non-Conforming Uses," *The American City,* Vol. 58, No. 8, p. 93, August, 1943.

or (3) vacancy of any building other than in (1) for a period of six months, or (4) clear intent on the part of the owner to abandon the nonconforming use. The time limits in each are often changed to meet local preferences or desires. If the time limit is reasonable, the courts will approve this method as a proper use of the police power.[138]

Damage and Destruction. Buildings devoted to nonconforming uses may be damaged or destroyed by fire or by other calamities such as hurricanes, earthquakes, and floods. Most zoning authorities agree that some degree of such damage or destruction may properly be permitted to be repaired or restored. However, opinion differs widely as to the degree. In some cities, New York City for instance, a nonconforming building completely destroyed may be rebuilt.[139] However, the general practice is to allow rebuilding only when the destruction is partial.[140] Most zoning ordinances follow a middle-of-the-road policy and attempt to make the regulations fair and reasonable as applied to the conditions obtaining in the particular city or county.[141]

It is common to provide that if a building has suffered damage to the extent of 50 percent or more of its value, it must be rebuilt in conformity with the regulations of the district in which it is located. In such instance, the assessed value is normally designated as the value to be applied in computing the percentage of destruction.[142] Where permission to rebuild is granted, it is sometimes found advisable to place a limit on the time in which rebuilding must take place.

Compulsory Elimination of Nonconforming Uses. Reliance upon discontinuance, abandonment, or destruction to terminate nonconforming uses leaves the community with much uncertainty as to

[138] *King County v. High et al.*, 36 Wn. (2d) 580, 219 P. (2d) 118 (1950).

[139] The proposed rezoning for New York City will attempt to change this. See Norman Williams, Jr., "Striking Innovations in New York City's Proposed Rezoning," *The American City*, Vol. 66, No. 6, p. 99, June, 1951.

[140] See *D'Agostino v. Jaguar Realty Co.*, 22 N.J. Super. 74, 91 A. (2d) 500 (1952), which involved a rubber manufacturing company which was a nonconforming use in a residential district. The building was almost completely destroyed by fire. The court said the building could not be rebuilt since the zoning ordinance permitted reconstruction of nonconforming uses "in the event of partial destruction thereof." The court held that reference to "partial destruction" indicated an intent to forbid reconstruction in cases such as this.

[141] O. C. Hormell and R. H. Owsley, *Zoning Manual for Maine Towns* (Brunswick, Me.: Bowdoin College, Bureau for Research and Municipal Government, 1940), Research Series No. 11, p. 44.

[142] In *Behrend v. Town of Pe Ell*, 136 Wash. 364, 240 Pac. 12 (1925) the court approved a fire ordinance prohibiting the repair or renewal of buildings in the fire limits when the cost shall exceed 50 percent of the actual value of the buildings.

when, if ever, such uses will be eliminated. Some jurisdictions have sought, therefore, to eliminate nonconforming uses by means of so-called retroactive regulations providing for the outlawing or amortization of the nonconforming use after a specified period of time as provided in the ordinance. Generally speaking, retroactive regulations have not been favored either by the courts or as a matter of general policy. Consequently, until recently, the universal rule has been to permit nonconforming structures to remain, treating them as exceptions,[143] unless they constitute a nuisance.[144]

Some states, by statute, restrict the power of municipalities to enact retroactive zoning ordinances.[145] This reflects the attitude of the legislatures of those states which have concluded that the municipalities should have no power to pass retroactive zoning laws and force the removal of lawful uses of property that do not correspond to the use classification of the district unless they are actually nuisances.

In the early days of zoning, leniency in favor of nonconforming structures was necessary so as not to injure the cause of zoning by adverse court decisions due to lack of an appreciation of the principles involved. Zoning today is on a firm and solid foundation, and the benefits to be derived from its application are greater than initially realized. For this reason, more attention is being given to the use of retroactive regulations to eliminate nonconforming uses in order to make zoning even more effective. However, authorities are still not in agreement as to the wisdom of retroactive zoning regulations.[146] Actually, all zoning laws are to a certain extent retroactive in that their effect may be to depreciate the value of particular lands which were owned by individuals at the time the ordinance was adopted.

In many instances the elimination of nonconforming uses may not require the actual removal of buildings. For example, nonconforming uses may exist where only the land is used and no buildings are involved as in the case of junk yards, dumps, parking lots, used car lots, trailer camps, and other uses where there is no heavy investment or

---

[143] For cases dealing with retroactive ordinances see *People v. Kesbeck*, 281 N.Y. 785, 24 N.E. (2d) 475 (1939); *Bayinsky v. Kesbeck*, 259 A.D. 467, 19 N.Y.S. (2d) 716 (1940).

[144] *Hadacheck v. Sebastian*, 239 U.S. 394, 60 L.Ed. 348 (1915). For comparison with a more recent case, see *State ex rel. Miller v. Cain*, 40 Wn. (2d) 216, 242 P. (2d) 505 (1952), holding that the perpetuation of a nonconforming use is not a vested right.

[145] See, for example, *Maine Statutes* (rev. 1930) Chap. 5, Sec. 142.

[146] Compare Crolly, *op. cit.*, pp. 106–107, and Yokley, *op. cit.*, Vol. 1, pp. 369–372, and also Bassett, *op. cit.*, pp. 112–116.

structure.[147] The outlawing of such uses within a reasonable time does not impose any serious hardship. Undue hardship in cases where structures are involved is mitigated to some extent by the fact that during the period between the time of the adoption of the ordinance and the date fixed for compulsory elimination, the owner has been placed in a favored monopolistic position since other owners have been precluded from similar or competing uses.

Probably the best plan, from the standpoint of overcoming constitutional obstacles to retroactive regulations, is the so-called amortization provision.[148] Under this method immediate removal of all nonconforming uses is not required, but the ordinance prescribes various periods within which different uses must be removed. For example, junk yards, with virtually no investment in real property other than land, may be required to leave within a year. More expensive store buildings or manufacturing establishments may be given as much as 60 or more years from the time of the passage of the ordinance.[149] When properly computed [150] such provisions would enable the owner to minimize any loss from the change-over and to plan ahead for the most advantageous use of his property. They would serve the public interest by forcing removal of the nonconforming use, but would not place such a crushing burden on the user as might be the case if he were required to terminate the use immediately.

The distinction between ordinances restricting future uses of property and those requiring the termination of existing uses is but one of degree, and the constitutionality of the latter depends upon the relative importance to be given to the public gain and to private loss. Due to the relatively limited use of compulsory termination provisions in zoning ordinances, courts have had few occasions to pass upon their legality. However, recent California decisions would seem to indicate the direction of judicial thinking. One of these cases,

[147] Crolly, loc. cit.

[148] See "Amortization of Property Uses Not Conforming to Zoning Regulations," University of Chicago Law Review, Vol. 9, No. 3, p. 477, April, 1942.

[149] In "Compulsory Elimination of Non-Conforming Uses," The American City, Vol. 65, No. 5, p. 149, May, 1950, the author of the note indicates that a reasonable period for the amortization of a billboard might be from one to five years and that the period for a building might be from 20 to 100 years.

[150] They would take into account such factors as the anticipated time when the difference between the cost of changing to a conforming use and the cost of repairing the old building to meet safety requirements would be at a minimum; the amount of fixed investment involved in various businesses and the feasible rate of amortization; the difference in the value of the property when utilized for a conforming and for a nonconforming use, etc.

Livingston Rock and Gravel Co. v. County of Los Angeles,[151] upheld the validity of a provision in the Los Angeles county zoning ordinance requiring the termination of nonconforming uses after a period of years. The other case, *City of Los Angeles v. Gage,*[152] upheld a similar provision in the zoning ordinance of the City of Los Angeles.

Under the zoning ordinance of the County of Los Angeles, existing nonconforming uses were protected as automatic exceptions for a period of 20 years. However, the Los Angeles Regional Planning Commission had authority to revoke such exception under certain specified conditions, including a finding that the use was detrimental to public health or safety or was a nuisance. The specific use involved in the case was a concrete mixing plant which had become nonconforming when the district in which it was located was rezoned from M-3 (unlimited manufacturing) to M-1 (light manufacturing). In a four to three decision, the Supreme Court overruled the lower court which had held that the "automatic exception" procedure was merely a subterfuge for direct termination. The Court found that, under the circumstances of the case, sufficient protection was provided for existing owners and stated:

However, zoning legislation looks to the future in regulating district development and the eventual liquidation of nonconforming uses within a prescribed period commensurate with the investment involved. . . .

Manifestly, care has been taken in such rezoning regulations to refrain from the interference with constitutional guarantees, and in the light of such express language it would be a contradiction in terms to hold that the regulations are nevertheless unconstitutional. Likewise, there can be no constitutional objection to the authorized revocation by the planning commission of an automatic exception where after a public hearing, upon notice, it is found that the nonconforming use is "so exercised as to be detrimental to the public health or safety, or so as to be a nuisance." . . .

It, therefore, follows that the rezoning regulations authorizing the revocation of "automatic exceptions" are constitutionally valid as a whole and come within the prescribed objectives of the police power.[153]

The Los Angeles City Zoning Ordinance, which was construed in the Gage case, contained a number of different provisions for the compulsory termination of nonconforming uses with amortization periods ranging from 20 to 40 years for commercial or industrial buildings in a residence zone and five years for nonconforming signs

---

[151] 43 Cal. (2d) 121, 272 P. (2d) 4 (1954).
[152] 127 Cal. App. 442, 274 P. (2d) 34 (1954).
[153] *Livingston Rock and Gravel Co. v. County of Los Angeles, supra,* pp. 8–9.

and open uses of land, and for nonconforming uses in a residential building in a residence zone. The nonconforming use involved in the Gage case was the use of part of a structure of a two-family residence for a wholesale and retail plumbing supply business. On the basis of the finding of the lower court, it appeared that the plumbing supply business had not caused any substantial harm to the neighborhood and that compulsory removal of the business to another location would put the owner to considerable expense. Nevertheless, the court gave its support to the principle that a particular zone may be cleaned up by compulsory termination of nonconforming uses after a period of amortization and reversed the ruling of the lower court. In its opinion the Court said:

The theory in zoning is that each district is an appropriate area for the location of the uses which the zone plan permits in that area, and that the existence or entrance of other uses will tend to impair the development and stability of the area for the appropriate uses. The public welfare must be considered from the standpoint of the objective of zoning and of all the property within any particular use district. *Rehfeld v. City and County of San Francisco*, 218 Cal. 83, 85, 21 P. (2d) 419. It was not and is not contemplated that preëxisting nonconforming uses are to be perpetual. *State ex rel. Miller v. Cain*, 40 Wn. (2d) 216, 242 P. (2d) 505. The presence of any nonconforming use endangers the benefits to be derived from a comprehensive zoning plan. Having the undoubted power to establish residential districts, the legislative body has the power to make such classification really effective by adopting such reasonable regulations as would be conducive to the welfare, health, and safety of those desiring to live in such districts and enjoy the benefits thereof. There would be no object in creating a residential district unless there were to be secured to those dwelling therein the advantages which are ordinarily considered the benefits of such residence. It would seem to be the logical and reasonable method of approach to place a time limit upon the continuance of existing nonconforming uses, commensurate with the investment involved and based on the nature of the use; and in cases of nonconforming structures, on their character, age, and other relevant factors. . . .

If the amortization period is reasonable, the loss to the owner may be small when compared with the benefit to the public. Nonconforming uses will eventually be eliminated. A legislative body may well conclude that the beneficial effect on the community of the eventual elimination of all nonconforming uses by a reasonable amortization plan more than offsets individual losses.[154]

[154] *City of Los Angeles v. Gage, supra*, pp. 43–44.

OTHER ILLUSTRATIVE MATTERS OF LEGAL AND PRACTICAL DIFFICULTY

Few devices of public control have produced a wider variety of controversial issues than have zoning regulations. Every community has its particular interest groups, each of which has its views as to what specific regulations are in the interest of the general welfare. In developing zoning policy, many of these varying points of view must be reconciled, harmonized, or compromised in order to devise an ordinance which will meet with public acceptance. Furthermore, even after a politically acceptable ordinance has been enacted, many legal and practical difficulties must frequently be overcome if certain of its provisions are to become effective. A brief discussion of some of these will help to indicate the extent and limitations of zoning as a means of furthering certain specific policy considerations.

Racial Segregation. A number of jurisdictions have sought to use the zoning ordinance as a means of creating separate "white" and "colored" residence districts. Although the Supreme Court of the United States has consistently held such legislation unconstitutional, many efforts have, nevertheless, been made to circumvent the court's ruling. The leading case on the subject is *Buchanan v. Warley* [155] decided by the United States Supreme Court in 1917. In this case the defendant, a Negro, had agreed to buy from the plaintiff, who was white, a lot in the city of Louisville, Kentucky. This lot was located in a block where there were eight residences occupied by whites and only two by Negroes. The sale was made on condition that the defendant should have the legal right to live on the property.

The city ordinance, which was invoked, provided that on and after a certain date, Negroes might not move into a block in which a majority of the inhabitants were whites, and conversely, that whites might not move into a block in which the majority of the inhabitants were colored. The ordinance was entitled: "An ordinance to prevent conflict and ill-feeling between the white and colored races in the city of Louisville, and to preserve the public peace and promote the general welfare. . . ." The opinion of the court centered around the concrete questions of the right of occupancy, and the right to purchase and sell property. The court took the view that the ordinance could not stand, inasmuch as it involved a direct violation of due process of law protected by the Fourteenth Amendment to the Constitution of the United States.

Obviously, this decision did not meet with the approval of a num-

[155] 245 U.S. 60, 62 L.Ed. 149 (1917), reversing 165 Ky. 559.

ber of southern cities, some of which have made attempts to circumvent the ruling of the case. In a few jurisdictions, the state courts have upheld such municipal action. The others have accepted the federal ruling without question and have stricken down local legislation aimed at getting around the ruling of the United States Supreme Court. The Louisiana Supreme Court, for example, held in 1925 that an ordinance forbidding the establishment of residences by Negroes in "white communities" and vice versa, without the written consent of a majority of the residents, was "merely a zoning ordinance" within the police power.[156] The United States Supreme Court took the opposite view and reversed the decision on the authority of *Buchanan v. Warley*.[157] Later that same year the Louisiana Court declared another segregation ordinance unconstitutional in accordance with this ruling.[158]

Winston-Salem, North Carolina, in 1930, adopted a comprehensive zoning ordinance which restricted certain sections to Negroes and other districts to whites. The areas assigned to the different races were conceded to be located fairly and apportioned equitably according to the respective percentage of each race as compared with the population of the whole city. However, the North Carolina Supreme Court held, in the case of *Clinard v. Winston-Salem*,[159] that the ordinance was invalid and void. Racial discrimination of this sort does not fall within the scope of the police power, the court declared, and therefore the fact that it is included in a zoning ordinance is of no assistance.[160]

A recent federal court decision on this point is *City of Birmingham v. Monk*.[161] This case originated in Birmingham, Alabama, and involved an attack on the validity of certain provisions in the Birmingham zoning ordinance which attempted to enforce, by zoning, the segregation of Negroes and whites. The ordinance prohibited Negroes in white or A-1 residential districts and prohibited whites in Negro or B-1 residential districts as laid out and defined in the ordinance. The court held that these provisions were unconstitutional and void on the ground that they denied to the plaintiffs the right to occupy,

[156] *Tyler v. Harmon*, 158 La. 439, 104 So. 200 (1925).
[157] *Harmon v. Tyler*, 273 U.S. 668, 71 L.Ed. 831 (1927).
[158] *Land Development Co. of Louisiana v. City of New Orleans*, 164 La. 172, 113 So. 768 (1927).
[159] 217 N.C. 119, 6 S.E. (2d) 867 (1940).
[160] See "Racial Zoning Again," *The American City*, Vol. 65, No. 11, p. 137, November, 1950.
[161] 185 F. (2d) 859 (1950). Rehearing denied January 25, 1951.

enjoy, and dispose of their property solely because of their race and color and, therefore, violated their rights guaranteed by the Fourteenth Amendment.[162]

Home Occupations. During the formative period of comprehensive zoning, it became evident that districts could not be confined to principal uses only. It has always been customary for occupants of homes to carry on gainful employment as something accessory and incidental to the residence use. The doctor, dentist, lawyer, or notary public has from time immemorial used his own home as his office. Similarly, the dressmaker, milliner, and music teacher have worked in their own homes. The earliest zoning ordinances took communities as they existed and did not try to prevent customary practices that met with no objection from the community. Indeed there would have been great opposition to early zoning plans if efforts had been made to prevent these home occupations.[163] The courts have usually upheld these home occupations on the theory that the use of his home by a doctor or a lawyer will not necessarily lower the standards of the residential district. The courts have stressed that the important thing is that there be a community history of acceptance of certain types of home occupations.[164]

Actually, the validity of "custom" as a criterion in determining the acceptability of home occupations is questionable.[165] The casual dressmaking carried on by a housewife may easily be expanded into a business operation, resulting in displaying of signs, remodeling of the home, and attracting numerous customers, thereby creating traffic and parking problems. Professional work, where the home serves as an office, may lead to similar complications. For these reasons, it is important that the zoning ordinance contain specific restrictions upon this type of use. However, the designation of a zone as residential does not mean that every profit-making enterprise should of necessity be excluded. It is not the intent in setting up such a district to limit the land use exclusively to residential purposes, but rather to protect

[162] The Supreme Court of the United States denied *certiorari* on May 28, 1951, 341 U.S. 940, 95 L.Ed. 1367 (1951).

[163] Some modern zoning ordinances do prohibit these occupations in residential districts, and the provisions have been approved by the courts. See (dentist) *Stewart v. Barker*, 182 Misc. 91, 43 N.Y.S. (2d) 560 (1943), and (dressmaker) *Lemp v. Township of Millburn*, 129 N.J.L. 221, 28 A. (2d) 767 (1942).

[164] "Zoning Laws Allow Money-Making at Home—Within Bounds," *The American City*, Vol. 69, No. 1, p. 151, January, 1954.

[165] Ronald Scott, "Effect of 'Custom' in Home Occupations," *ASPO Newsletter* (Chicago: American Society of Planning Officials), Vol, 19, No. 11, p. 101, November, 1953.

the residences from the invasion of harmful uses. The question of whether a particular use should be permitted or excluded should be determined according to whether the use harmonizes with the character of the district or whether it is injurious to it.

Some zoning ordinances contain elaborate and detailed statements regarding accessory uses and buildings, but the needs of the average municipality would seem to require only that the zoning ordinance include a prohibition of businesses,[166] and establish the conditions under which accessory uses are permitted. Most ordinances merely set out rules designed to insure that the occupations do not get out of hand and cause neighborhood deterioration. Some cities have followed the practice of listing certain permissible occupations and requiring all others to obtain permits from the city. Complaints that any occupation constitutes a nuisance furnish the basis for review; and if the complaint appears to be justified, the permit is revoked. The types of regulations most commonly used are as follows:

1. Restrictions on the amount of space in a house that may be devoted to the home occupation;
2. Restrictions on the type of equipment that may be used, with perhaps a limitation on the amount of horsepower of any motor; and
3. Limitations on the number of persons who may be employed in the occupation. Some communities allow only members of the family to help.[167]

There are fundamental guides which should be observed in determining a permissible accessory use:

1. It should really be incidental and not the main use of the property;
2. It should not attain such proportions as to make it primarily a business if it is to be located in a residential zone;
3. Any accessory building must be on the same lot as the main building, and it may be desirable to restrict the accessory building to the rear part of the lot, or set back a certain distance from lot lines; and
4. No accessory use shall be detrimental to the residential character of the neighborhood.[168]

Because of the number of possible accessory uses and the perplexity of social factors involved in them, it is desirable that the matter of

[166] See *King County v. Lunn*, 32 Wn. (2d) 116, 200 P. (2d) 981 (1948), holding that the operation of a restaurant on the premises was not a "home occupation."
[167] "Zoning Laws Allow Money-Making at Home—Within Bounds," *loc. cit.*
[168] Hodges, *op. cit.*, p. 263.

their permissibility be determined by the zoning board of adjustment and not left to the discretion of the building inspector.

Religious, Educational, and Philanthropic Uses. Many difficult questions are presented in regulating the use of property for religious, educational, and philanthropic purposes. Since institutions devoted to such purposes are declared to promote the health, morals, and general welfare of the community, there is difficulty in establishing a legal basis on which to exclude them from the most restricted residential zones. Early zoning ordinances permitted these uses in all districts as a matter of right.[169] This policy was supported on the consideration that churches[170] and schools[171] had a right to locate in districts in the community which were quiet and in which there was an abundance of light and air.

As zoning has come into more extensive use, many people have urged that some measure of zoning control should be established over the location of religious, educational, and philanthropic institutions. It has been found in many instances that even though such institution do promote the health, morals, and general welfare of the community, their location in particular locations in residence districts causes certain disadvantages to the home environment due to the increased congestion of traffic and parking on residential streets and the increased service activities resulting from delivering materials, removing wastes, and providing power and other facilities. Oftentimes these disturbances are comparable to those created by a small business or industry.

Other adverse effects, although somewhat less tangible, must also be recognized. To many persons, the location in their home neighborhood of an orphanage or a school for the mentally deficient or the handicapped has a depressing physiological or psychological influence. Equally disturbing problems are presented by certain philan-

---

[169] "Religious, Educational, and Philanthropic Uses Under Zoning," *Municipal Administration* (Philadelphia: Associated Institutes of Government of Pennsylvania Universities, April, 1952), Supplement, p. 1.

[170] Some authority can be found for the exclusion of churches from residential districts. *Corporation of Presiding Bishop v. Porterville*, 90 Cal. App. (2d) 656, 203 P. (2d) 823 (1949). Appeal dismissed for want of a federal question, 238 U.S. 805, 94 L.Ed. 487 (1949). Rehearing denied 338 U.S. 939, 94 L.Ed. 579 (1950); and *Chico v. First Ave. Baptist Church*, 108 Cal. App. 297, 238 P. (2d) 587 (1951). This is the minority rule. The overwhelming majority rule (other than in California) is to the contrary. See Yokley, *op. cit.*, Vol. 2, Sec. 222, p. 111.

[171] In general, courts have looked with disfavor on excluding schools from residence zones. See *Livingston v. Davis*, 243 Ia. 21, 50 N.W. (2d) 592 (1951); *Langbein v. Board of Zoning Appeals*, 135 Conn. 575, 67 A. (2d) 5 (1949); *Catholic Bishop of Chicago v. Kingery*, 135 Conn. 575, 20 N.E. (2d) 583 (1939).

thropic uses. For example, the proposed establishment of a shelter for animals or an institution to prevent cruelty to animals may be in the interest of the general welfare, but at the same time may be disruptive or injurious to the peace and happiness of residents within the particular district.[172]

Certainly it is desirable that, in so far as possible, both educational and religious institutions should be provided as near as is practical to the residential area. This is in the interest of eliminating traffic congestion and promoting safety and convenience within the community. Nevertheless, there is also a community interest in preserving the privacy and quiet of a particular neighborhood and protecting property values from the invasion of property uses that have a depressing effect.

Many considerations of practical difficulty are encountered in determining what constitutes an educational or religious use. Often a decision must be made as to whether dormitories, playgrounds, and gymnasiums are necessarily educational institutions.[173] Problems frequently become more complicated where educational and religious uses are combined. On the basis of policy, the question may be raised as to whether, if public schools are permitted in a residential district, private educational institutions must also be permitted.

Because of the difficulty of applying restrictive land-use policy to religious, educational, and philanthropic institutions, the most feasible approach to the problem appears to be to provide, in the zoning ordinance, that such institutional uses shall be permitted only when authorized as a "special exception." It is always possible that many inappropriate uses may be sought to be established under the guise of religious,[174] educational, and philanthropic purposes. The requirement of a "special exception" provides an opportunity for hearing in which the board of adjustment or the planning agency [175] can make

---

[172] A dog pound has been construed not to be a philanthropic or eleemosynary use. *Westchester County Society for Prevention of Cruelty to Animals v. Mengel,* 292 N.Y. 121, 54 N.E. (2d) 329 (1944).

[173] A school of equitation devoted to instructing children in horsemanship has been held not to constitute a "private school," since that term is to be construed in the traditional academic sense. *Wadsworth v. Board of Adjustment of Bedminster Tp.,* 11 N.J. Super. 502, 78 A. (2d) 619 (1951). A kindergarten is a school, *Duncan v. Entrekin,* 211 Ga. 311, 85 S.E. (2d) 771 (1955).

[174] See *Sexton v. Bates,* 17 N.J. Super. 246, 85 A. (2d) 833 (1951), in which the Supreme Court of New Jersey held that a ritualarium or *mikvah* to be used for ritualistic bathing did not constitute a church within the meaning of the Newark Zoning Ordinance.

[175] Although it is generally accepted practice for special exceptions to be granted by the board of adjustment, see p. 431, where it is suggested that it may appropriately be a function of the planning agency.

a determination of whether the proposed use is a *bona fide* use and falls in the category claimed.

The use of the special exception procedure also enables the agency approving the permit to ascertain whether or not the proposed use conforms to area and yard requirements and whether the proposed site is one which would not unreasonably congest traffic, endanger public safety, or in some other manner be injurious to the stability of the neighborhood. Obviously, these decisions cannot be arbitrary and must be made within the limits of standards laid down in the zoning ordinance.

Since certain educational, religious, and philanthropic institutions are often concerned primarily with the interests of a single race, creed, or nationality, there are obviously dangers in granting to a public agency authority to disapprove site location where such authority might be used to discriminate against certain racial or religious groups. Certainly such an agency should not be entitled to deny an application on the grounds that the particular institution was not needed in the community. Neither must a decision be made upon the basis of the strength of the opposition or the interest in the neighborhood.[176] Each permit should be granted or denied in the light of what is in the community interest in carrying out the objectives of the zoning ordinance.

Location of Cemeteries. The location of cemeteries has frequently presented problems of considerable difficulty. Certain authorities have suggested that cemeteries should be allowed in residence districts because it is "shocking to the sensibilities of the living to bury their relatives in business or industrial districts." [177] The general rule which has been recognized by most courts is that cemeteries are allowed in residence zones.[178] However, a number of jurisdictions have recognized that under certain circumstances the public welfare demands the regulation of cemeteries,[179] and some courts have sustained ordinance provisions excluding them from residence districts.[180]

---

[176] For practical suggestions for coordinating church planning with the plan for neighborhood development, see Robert C. Hoover and Everett L. Perry, *Church and City Planning* (New York: National Council of the Churches of Christ in the USA, 1955), Survey Guide 2.

[177] Bassett, *op. cit.*, p. 217.

[178] *City of Wichita v. Schwertner*, 130 Kan. 397, 286 Pac. 266 (1930).
Gordon v. Montgomery County, 164 Md. 210, 164 Atl. 676 (1933).
Perry Mt. Park Cemetery Association v. Netzel, 274 Mich. 97, 264 N.W. 303 (1936).

[179] Foster v. Mayor and City of Beverly, 315 Mass. 567, 53 N.E. (2d) 693 (1944).
Moritz v. United Brethren's Church, 269 N.Y. 125, 199 N.E. 29 (1935).

[180] Fairlawns Cemetery Association v. Zoning Commission, 138 Conn. 434, 86 A.

As in the case of religious, educational, and philanthropic institutions, the difficulties of applying restrictive land-use controls to cemeteries arises because of the extent to which their purpose contributes to the promotion of the general welfare. Nevertheless, the depressing effect which cemeteries create in residence districts appears to justify a public policy of encouraging their location in appropriate unincorporated areas or in farming communities. Where, however, cemeteries are permitted to locate within the municipality, it would seem desirable that their site location be approved as a special exception.

Off-Street Parking Provisions. Public policy in zoning must be coördinated with public policy in other aspects of municipal government. One of the most difficult problems that planners are called upon to solve is that of relieving the congestion of traffic. In order to facilitate the movement of traffic, many cities today are finding it desirable to incorporate in the zoning ordinance requirements for off-street parking.[181]

The extent to which off-street parking controls should be included in the zoning ordinance is not a matter of general agreement or uniform application. Some cities have dealt with off-street parking problems by comprehensive zoning ordinances or amendments thereto, and others have dealt with the problem by special ordinances on the subject. Many communities have adopted zoning ordinances which require that specified minimum amounts of off-street parking space,[182] depending on the use and size of the building, be provided when such building is constructed.[183] Such zoning provisions can usually be sustained under the police power because they tend to further the public safety by lessening the dangerous congestion in the streets and to promote the public welfare by accelerating the movement of traffic.[184] In most cases they can be supported as being reasonable since the property owner is ordinarily benefited directly by providing parking facilities.[185]

(2d) 74 (1952). In this case the Supreme Court of Errors of Connecticut held that cemeteries were lawfully excluded from residence districts, and also that a nonconforming use had not been established since no lots had been sold and there had been no burials by the cemetery association.

[181] Yokley, op. cit., Vol. 2, Sec. 208, p. 76.

[182] A city planning commission has no discretion to select a site for a property owner so long as the requirements of the ordinances are met. State v. City of Bellevue, 45 Wn. (2d) 492, 275 P. (2d) 899 (1954).

[183] Charles S. Le Craw, Jr., and Wilbur S. Smith, "Zoning Applied to Parking," Traffic Quarterly, Vol. 1, No. 1, January, 1947.

[184] Roncka v. Fogarty, 152 Neb. 467, 41 N.W. (2d) 745 (1950); McSorley v. Fitzgerald, 359 Pa. 264, 59 A. (2d) 142 (1948).

[185] David R. Levin, "Requirements for Off-Street Parking Facilities in Zoning and

The amount of space to be provided for off-street parking is commonly determined by the number of family units in multiple dwellings, the number of rooms in hotels, and by the number of cubic feet or square feet in buildings used for business.[186] In industrial zones the parking space requirement is usually based on floor area or on the number of employees working in the plant. Off-street parking ordinance provisions are usually applicable both to new builidngs and to altered, expanded, or new uses of existing structures.

The central business district is usually exempted from requirements specified for other areas.[187] If the requirements are applied to the central business district, most of the business in it will constitute nonconforming uses since most existing structures will not have off-street parking facilities. It therefore becomes necessary to accord the usual protection that is given to a nonconforming user under the ordinance. Compulsory elimination of such nonconforming uses would not appear to be feasible. Such a measure, even if feasible, would be of questionable legality. On the practical side, it would appear to be inefficient to try to provide parking space on the small lots which predominate in the already built-up central areas of most cities; and in certain locations, the establishment of off-street parking facilities would actually be undesirable because of traffic congestion which such a facility might cause. Since large street-level areas devoted to off-street parking may also adversely affect pedestrian trade, it is important that parking facilities be developed according to an overall plan.

Closely related to the parking requirements are requirements for off-street truck-loading and unloading space in business and residential areas.[188] Loading space should be provided by specified types of establishments and must not be part of the off-street parking area. In many cases it is practical to make the provisions of the ordinance

Other Local Ordinances," *Highway Research Board* (Washington, D.C.: National Research Council, 1950), Bulletin No. 24, pp. 81–88.

[186] James E. Pate, *Local Government and Administration—Principles and Problems* (New York: American Book Company, 1954), p. 377.

See also "Zoning for Off-Street Parking," *The American City*, Vol. 43, No. 4, p. 106, April, 1948.

City of New Orleans v. Leeco, Inc., 226 La. 335, 76 So. (2d) 387 (1954), in which the court gave approval to off-street parking provisions in the zoning ordinance, which, with respect to theaters, was to be calculated on the basis of one parking space for each eight seats in the theater.

[187] Yokley, *op. cit.*, Vol. 2, Sec. 210, p. 83.

[188] "Commercial Parking in Residential Areas," *The American City*, Vol. 63, No. 9, p. 147, September, 1948.

applicable only to buildings which exceed a minimum specified size, such as a restaurant seating 100 persons or a hospital with beds for 50 patients.

The Promotion of Aesthetics. There can be little doubt that aesthetic considerations have been in the minds of many planners who have helped to provide and develop zoning legislation. For the most part, however, the improved appearance of the community has been a by-product rather than the direct object of zoning policy.[189] Until very recently, courts have consistently taken the view that the exercise of the police power must be justified by social and economic reasons,[190] even though, from time to time, a number of individual judges have urged a more liberal construction of the police power which would recognize as one of its legitimate objectives the promotion of beauty: "Why should not the police power avail, as well to suppress or prevent a nuisance committed by offending the sense of sight, as to suppress or prevent a nuisance committed by offending the sense of hearing or the olfactory nerves?" [191]

Undoubtedly, the reluctance of courts to expand the scope of the police power to rest solely upon aesthetic values stems from a recognition that aesthetic tastes are far from standardized. Conceivably, to permit the legislative body to set standards of beauty might in fact retard progress in the science of building through the insistence upon conventional styles and conventional types of construction. In judicial matters expert evidence can easily be obtained to determine the effect of light, air, quiet, open spaces, and vegetation. However, disagreement among experts on what is best in color, texture, and style would leave the courts with little help in reaching a decision as to what is a reasonable regulation for promoting matters of good taste.[192]

[189] Thomas W. Mackesey, "Aesthetics and Zoning," *The Planners' Journal*, Vol. V, No. 4, pp. 95–98, October–December, 1939.

[190] See, for example, *Welch v. Swasey*, 214 U.S. 91, 29 S.Ct. 567 (Mass., 1909) and *Forbes v. Hubbard*, 348 Ill. 166, 180 N.E. 767 (1932). One of the principal subjects of aesthetic controls has been billboards and other types of outdoor advertising. For a discussion of the aesthetic possibilities of billboard regulation, see *General Outdoor Advertising Co. v. Department of Public Works*, 289 Mass. 149, 193 N.E. 799 (1935). Contrary to decisions upholding regulations limiting maximum heights of buildings, courts have consistently declared invalid provisions of zoning ordinances prescribing minimum heights for structures as having no real connection with police power objectives since they are, in most instances, based primarily on aesthetic considerations. See: *Brown v. Board of Appeals*, 327 Ill. 644, 159 N.E. 255 (1927); *Oppenheimer v. Kraus*, 221 App. Div. 773, 223 N.Y.S. 467, affirmed 246 N.Y. 559, 159 N.E. 651 (1927); *State ex rel. Sale v. Stahlman*, 81 W.Va. 325, 94 S.E. 497 (1917).

[191] *State ex rel. Civello v. New Orleans*, 154 La. 271, 97 So. 440, 444 (1923).

[192] Bassett, *op. cit.*, p. 98.

For these reasons, the arguments that aesthetic values can best be promoted by education and coöperation rather than by legislation have been quite persuasive. Nevertheless, several recent cases have indicated that our courts may now be prepared to broaden the scope of the police power and recognize that the promotion of aesthetic values is, of itself, a legitimate objective of legislative policy.[193]

One of the most significant of the recent cases dealing with the matter of aesthetics is that of Berman v. Parker,[194] decided on November 22, 1954. Although this case was concerned with urban redevelopment rather than zoning, the language used in the opinion would seem to be sufficiently far-reaching to justify drawing the conclusion that the principles announced are applicable to the exercise of the police power as well as to the power of eminent domain. Mr. Justice Douglas, speaking for the Court, emphasized the matter of aesthetic considerations in the following language:

> We do not sit to determine whether a particular housing project is or is not desirable. The concept of the public welfare is broad and inclusive. . . . The values it represents are spiritual as well as physical, aesthetic as well as monetary. It is within the power of the legislature to determine that a community should be beautiful as well as healthy, spacious as well as clean, well balanced as well as carefully patrolled. In the present case the Congress and its authorized agencies have made determinations that take into account a wide variety of values. It is not for us to reappraise them. If those who govern the District of Columbia decide that the Nation's capital should be beautiful as well as sanitary, there is nothing in the Fifth Amendment that stands in the way.

Relying heavily upon the language in the case of Berman v. Parker, the Supreme Court of Wisconsin, on March 8, 1955, decided the case of State ex rel. Saveland Park Holding Corp. v. Wieland,[195] sustaining a zoning ordinance of the Village of Fox Point which required that as a condition of granting a building permit the Building Board of the Village make a finding that the "exterior architectural appeal and the functional plan" of the proposed structure would not be so at variance with the other structures in the neighborhood as to cause "a substantial depreciation of the property values" of the neighborhood. The village of Fox Point is a residential community

[193] For a further discussion of this point and a documentation of the many cases on the subject, see Robert D. Cochran, "Aesthetic Zoning—The Trend of the Law," Western Reserve Law Review, Vol. VII, No. 2, pp. 171–179, March, 1956.
[194] 348 U.S. 26, 75 S.Ct. 98 (1954).
[195] 269 Wis. 262, 69 N.W. (2d) 217 (1955).

consisting mostly of single-family dwellings. Clearly, the objective of the ordinance provision was the protection of property values. On this point the court observed: "Anything that tends to destroy property values of the inhabitants of the village necessarily adversely affects the prosperity, and, therefore, the general welfare of the entire village."

How far the courts in the various states will go in following the reasoning of the Wisconsin court in the Saveland case in sustaining zoning regulations to promote aesthetic values still remains to be seen. It would seem, however, that the trend is definitely toward a more liberal interpretation of the police power in this direction.

ZONING ADMINISTRATION

THE ENFORCEMENT OF THE ZONING ORDINANCE

The effectiveness of zoning is predicated not only on a sound zoning ordinance but also upon sound zoning administration. Zoning laws which are poorly administered may render a good zoning ordinance inert and destroy the public confidence in zoning. Zoning administration must be carefully coördinated with administration of building codes, construction codes, subdivision regulations, and other governmental controls that affect the use and occupancy of land and buildings.

It is desirable that the responsibility of municipal officials and departments be carefully defined. The ordinances should establish fixed and definite procedures in order that (1) there will be no uncertainty among officials as to who has the responsibility for enforcement, and (2) the individual property owner will be able, from a perusal of the ordinance, to discover what procedure he must follow in order to comply with the ordinance.

The Enforcement Officer. The ability and energy of the zoning enforcement officer are major factors in efficient zoning administration. In most cities, this officer is the building inspector. In some smaller cities, where there is no building inspector, enforcement may be handled by the city manager or by some other official. Direct participation of the planning agency in the details of zoning administration and enforcement should be kept at a minimum.

Since many of the property owners who are subjected to regulation by the zoning ordinance will have contact with no public officials other than the enforcement officer, it is important that the enforcement officer understand his duties thoroughly. The major duties of the building inspector as enforcement officer for the zoning ordinance are:

1. To receive applications for, and issue, building permits.
2. To make inspections and issue certificates of occupancy for completed buildings.
3. To issue certificates of occupancy to owners of nonconforming uses.
4. To make periodic inspections for violations of the ordinance.
5. To initiate such court action as may be necessary to prevent violations.
6. To keep adequate records of all activities.[196]

Decisions with respect to applications for special exceptions sometimes called special property uses are not properly the function of the building inspector but rather matters for consideration by the board of adjustment or the planning agency.[197] Applications for special exceptions should be referred to the designated agency as original matters without prior decision by the building inspector. It is, nevertheless, good practice to provide that the applications be filed originally with the building inspector for purposes of record keeping and determining compliance with other ordinances. However, the building inspector should have no discretion with respect to granting special exceptions.[198]

The zoning enforcement officer has a great deal of responsibility in preserving the zoning plan and achieving the purposes of the zoning ordinance. He can destroy the effectiveness of the ordinance by overlooking violations or permitting exceptions to the regulations. The integrity of such officer is, therefore, most essential. Although the building inspector has primary responsibility for administering the zoning law, other municipal officers, departments, and agencies which have authority to issue licenses or permits or impose regulations of other kinds affecting the use of property, should be charged with the responsibility for making certain that all action taken with respect to matters which they administer comply with the provisions of the zoning ordinance. Departments, thus concerned, should not

[196] Phillip P. Green, Zoning in North Carolina, Law and Administration (Chapel Hill: University of North Carolina, 1952), p. 265.
[197] It is common practice to refer special exceptions to the board of adjustment. For reasons indicated later, it is believed that the better practice is to refer them to the planning agency. See p. 431.
[198] Sometimes this referral is designated as an appeal even though the application is automatically referred.

grant any license or permit which would violate the provision of the zoning ordinance and should revoke such license or permit if it should be granted in error. In the usual case, the zoning enforcement officer will make use of two devices, the building permit and the certificate of occupancy.[199]

The Building Permit. The general statutes of most states have for a number of years included the requirement that persons wishing to build upon their land must first apply to the local building inspector for a permit. With this requirement already in the law, it is logical that most cities have utilized the building permit as a major device in the enforcement of the zoning ordinance. It is important, therefore, that where the city has a building code under which the building permits are required, the provisions of the zoning ordinance be correlated with the provisions of that code.[200]

Zoning ordinance provisions commonly provide that no one may erect, add to, or alter a building without a permit from the zoning enforcement officer, and that the applications for such permits shall contain sufficient information concerning the proposed building for that officer to determine whether the proposed structure will comply with the zoning ordinance. Applications for building permits should be accompanied by plans drawn to scale which show the shape and dimensions of the lot, of the buildings, the accessory buildings existing, and the lines within which the proposed building shall be erected or altered. Furthermore, the application should show the existing and intended use of each building or part of the building, the number of families or housekeeping units the building is designed to accommodate, together with such other information as may be necessary for the building inspector to make his determination as to whether the proposed construction complies with the zoning ordinance.

The duties of the building inspector are ministerial rather than discretionary; consequently, he must issue the permit if he finds that the plans conform to the requirements of the zoning ordinance in every particular. If, on the other hand, he finds that they do not, it is his duty to refuse to issue the permit.

The Use and Occupancy Permit. Since zoning policy is concerned with use as well as structure, the zoning ordinance should re-

[199] *Zoning Administration and Enforcement* (Seattle: Association of Washington Cities, University of Washington, February 15, 1954), Information Bulletin No. 164, p. 17.
[200] *Ibid.*, p. 17.

quire that upon completion of construction, the applicant must obtain a certificate of occupancy. This certificate should be applied for at the time application is made for the building permit. After the building is completed, the building inspector should inspect the completed building to determine if it conforms to the requirements of the building code, and should thereupon issue a certificate of occupancy which permits occupancy of the building if the proposed use is authorized under the zoning ordinance. If the proposed use does not conform to the requirements of the ordinance, the certificate should be denied.

The purpose of a certificate of occupancy is to limit the use of the building to those occupancies which are authorized under the use, height, and area requirements of the zoning ordinance as well as those occupancies for which the construction features established by the building code are intended.[201] Requiring an occupancy permit in the case of altered or converted buildings helps to provide a means of preventing change of an authorized use to a nonconforming one. Under certain conditions, a certificate of occupancy may be required for use of vacant land or a change in the use of land.

In order to insure that nonconforming uses will not be extended, the zoning ordinance should require owners or occupants of structures of nonconforming uses to obtain occupancy permits before a specified date. Such permits should sufficiently describe the premises and uses to make it possible to detect future violations. Occupancy permits should be required not only for new buildings but also for all buildings or uses which are nonconforming. The preparation of a map showing the location of all nonconforming uses is most useful in administering and enforcing the ordinance and in developing policies directed toward the eventual elimination of nonconforming uses.

Detection of Violations and Enforcement Procedures.   Among the most important but also the most difficult tasks of zoning administration are the detection of violations and the enforcement of compliance with the provisions of the ordinance. Unless a program of strict enforcement is followed, zoning policy soon becomes ineffectual. Certain types of violations are difficult to detect. In cases where a violation involves structural changes, it can usually be detected when application is made for the building permit or when the building is inspected prior to occupancy. However, many violations do not re-

---

[201] R. C. Colling, et al., *Modern Building Inspection*, The Building Inspector's Handbook (Los Angeles: Building Standards Monthly Publishing Co., 1951), p. 401.

quire structural changes in the building, but result from changes of use or intensifications of use. For example, permitted home occupations in residential districts may easily be intensified or built into commercial or industrial operations. The character of certain business occupations may be substantially changed without the necessity of making structural alterations.

Most municipalities do not have departments or officials assigned primarily to the work of inspecting for the purpose of detecting use violations. To a considerable degree, detection must result from reports by citizens, often neighbors of the violators. These reports are not usually made unless the violation creates a nuisance or some undesirable situation in the neighborhood. Successful enforcement requires that detection must be regarded as the responsibility not only of the building inspector but also of the police department, public health department, fire department, and others charged with regulatory or protective functions. Furthermore, the public should be made conscious of their responsibility in helping to keep city officials informed of violations.

Violations may be dealt with either by equitable relief or by criminal prosecution. Equitable relief is commonly afforded through injunction. It is well established that a municipality in the enforcement of its zoning ordinance may seek an injunction to halt or prevent the violation.[202] Under certain circumstances, injunctive relief against zoning violations is available to a private citizen if the citizen suffers some special damage peculiar to himself.[203]

Under most zoning ordinances, a violation is made a criminal offense, punishable by fine or imprisonment or both. Quite commonly, each day that a violation continues constitutes a separate offense. Although penal provisions are essential to zoning ordinance enforcement, they should normally be looked upon as supplementary to injunctive relief and other remedies.

Penal provisions, although supplementary to injunctive relief, are nevertheless independent methods of enforcement. Therefore, injunctive action may be properly taken even though criminal prosecution may have failed.[204] Nevertheless, criminal action, in many cases, may be found to be more expedient since civil actions often tend to

---

[202] Yokley, op. cit., Vol. 2, Par. 191, p. 3.
[203] Bouchard v. Zetley, 196 Wis. 635, 220 N.W. 209 (1928).
[204] City of New Orleans v. Lafon (Ct. of App. of La.), 61 So. (2d) 270 (1952).

extend over considerable periods of time before coming to trial.[205] The enforcement of zoning ordinances and building code regulations under penal provisions is usually instituted by the building inspector. In criminal cases the presumptions are in favor of the violator, and technical legal defenses authorized in criminal prosecutions are available to him.

As a matter of procedure the building inspector should, upon discovering a violation from requirements of the zoning ordinance, give the property owner and interested parties notice of the violation and fix a time for the violator to meet the requirements. It is important that in the enforcement procedure the violator be given an opportunity for hearing. If after investigation and hearing, compliance is not obtained, the matter should then be referred to the city attorney.

In certain cases where public officials have failed to discharge their duties required by law for the proper administration of the zoning ordinance, compliance may be obtained through a writ of mandamus. Mandamus is a writ issued by the court commanding the performance of a particular act specified therein or directing the restoration of the complainant to rights or privileges of which he has been illegally deprived. The writ may be directed to any private or municipal corporation or to any of its officers or to an executive, administrative, or judicial officer, or to an inferior court. In zoning matters the writ is frequently used to compel the performance of duties of the building inspector or other municipal official who has acted arbitrarily. Mandamus will lie only in compelling the performance of ministerial duties and cannot be used to control discretionary decisions or to direct a public official to act in a certain way. One of the most common uses of the writ is to compel the issuance of a permit which the building inspector has a duty to issue. Its use is primarily in compelling the administrative official to perform his duties under the zoning ordinance rather than to supply him with a means of enforcement as in the use of the injunction.

Procedure for Granting Relief

One of the principal objectives in drafting a zoning ordinance should be that of devising a zoning plan which is effective and at the same time is not arbitrary. Unfortunately, the perfect ordinance has never been and probably never will be written. Human wisdom cannot anticipate all the exceptional cases that will arise in the adminis-

[205] Colling, et al., *op. cit.*, p. 539.

tration of a zoning ordinance.[206] Consequently the application of the strict word of the law may sometimes be the height of injustice. No zoning ordinance standing by itself can provide for the proper adaptation of the spirit of the law to each exceptional case.

The Board of Adjustment or Appeals. Since a strict application of the provisions of the zoning ordinance may on occasions cause undue hardship to certain property owners, legal machinery of some kind in addition to the courts is necessary to grant these property owners relief. Since the building inspector has no discretion in this matter, the zoning ordinance should provide for a board of adjustment, sometimes called a board of appeals. Without such a board, the strict enforcement of the zoning ordinance may result in serious injustice.[207] Although there is no ideal number of members for a board of adjustment, five-member boards, appointed with staggered terms, have been found to be satisfactory.[208]

The board of adjustment or the board of zoning appeals is ordinarily given the following duties and responsibilities:

1. to correct errors or abuses in the administration of the ordinance by the enforcement officer;
2. to consider certain cases where the city council has given it power to grant permits if specified conditions are fulfilled;
3. to grant relief when hardship results from strict application of the terms of the ordinance.[209]

In order for the board of adjustment to render well-considered decisions, it is most important that it fully understand the responsibility of the planning agency and the objectives of the zoning ordinance. Some jurisdictions have provided that one member of the planning commission shall serve as a member of the board of adjustment. The purpose of such a requirement has been to bring to the board of adjustment the point of view of members of the planning commission. It is very doubtful, however, whether the value of this liaison offsets the advantages of decision making by a board completely divorced from the process of plan making.

Some cities have designated the planning commission to serve as

[206] See Robert Kingery, "Practical Problems Confronting Boards of Appeals," *The Municipality,* Vol. 34, No. 6, p. 103, June, 1939.

[207] Charles K. Sumner, "The Board of Adjustment as a Corrective in Zoning Practice," *National Municipal Review,* Vol. 13, No. 4, pp. 203–206, April, 1924.

[208] *Local Planning Administration, op. cit.,* p. 243.

[209] Phillip P. Green, Jr., "The Power of the Zoning Board of Adjustment to Grant Variances from the Zoning Ordinance," *The North Carolina Law Review,* Vol. 29, pp. 245–279, 1951.

the zoning board of appeals. This is generally considered unwise not only because of the time-consuming nature of the work of the board of appeals, but also because the planning commission would, in many cases, be reviewing its own decisions. In principle, the work of the planning commission and that of the board of adjustment should be kept entirely distinct and separate. It is not sound practice to give to the planning commission responsibility for granting variances or hearing appeals from decisions of the building inspector. Imposing such duties upon the planning commission distracts it from its planning function by involving it in administrative and quasi-judicial functions which may divert it from its major responsibility of planning.

Although the functions of the building inspector and the board of adjustment are closely allied, the building inspector should not be a member of the board of adjustment. Some municipalities have found it good practice to designate the building inspector as secretary of the board but not as a member.[210] As secretary of the board, the building inspector is in a position to supply the board with information regarding relevant ordinances which are of importance to the board in making its decisions. The building inspector can also furnish maps and other data which are essential for proper consideration of the application for relief.

Exceptions and Variances. Much of the time and attention of boards of adjustment is occupied with the consideration of applications for exceptions and variances. Exceptions are concerned with the power to grant certain special property uses which the ordinance authorizes under stated conditions. Variances are concerned with power to grant relief from complying with the terms of the ordinance for the purpose of alleviating "unnecessary hardship" or "practical difficulty."[211]

Certain property uses such as electric power substations, telephone exchanges, fire stations, schools, and churches are necessary to the city's welfare, but if improperly designed or located, may spoil the

---

[210] Floyd M. Jennings and Ernest H. Campbell, *The Board of Adjustment* (Seattle: Bureau of Governmental Research and Services, University of Washington, April, 1953), Report No. 124, p. 12.

[211] The difference between an exception and a variance is noted in *Application of Deveraux Foundation*, 351 Pa. 478, 483, 41 A. (2d) 744 (1945); appeal dismissed, 326 U.S. 686, 90 L.Ed. 403 (1945).

See also *Service Realty Corporation v. Planning and Zoning Board of Appeals of Town of Greenwich*, 141 Conn. 632, 109 A. (2d) 256 (1954), which sets forth the distinction between variances and special exceptions with particular emphasis on the powers of zoning boards of appeals in granting them.

appearance and safety of the neighborhood. Most zoning ordinances, therefore, specify the conditions that must be met before such uses can be located in a neighborhood and direct the planning agency or the board of adjustment to authorize a permit for such uses only where those conditions are found to exist. Such conditions must be set forth in the zoning ordinance.[212] Although it is common practice to authorize boards of adjustment to grant special exceptions, in some respects it would seem to be a better practice to place this responsibility on the planning agency. In contrast with variances, special exceptions normally do not involve hardship. There is not the same need for balancing public interests against private injury. The purpose of permitting special property uses by exception is to insure that those conditions will be met which best protect the interests of the community.[213] It is essential, therefore, that applications for special exceptions be approved by the agency which is most familiar with the zoning ordinance and the objectives of the comprehensive plan.

Although the planning agency or board of adjustment usually has original jurisdiction to hear applications for exceptions, it is generally considered good procedure to require all cases to be presented first to the building inspector who refers the matter without decision.[214] By this practice the applicant does not have to decide whether his remedy is that of an exception or a variance, and the standardized procedures for handling all cases will be less easily misunderstood by city officials and the public.

The major function of the board of adjustment, and the one least capable of precise definition, is that concerned with the granting or denial of applications for variances from the ordinance. This function is the major reason for the existence of the board of adjustment. If it were not for the need of a "safety valve" to grant relief in cases of hardship, such a board would probably not have been included in the zoning mechanism.

A variance is a permit which the board may grant in certain situ-

---

[212] Service Realty Corporation v. Planning and Zoning Board of Appeals of Town of Greenwich, 141 Conn. 632, 109 A. (2d) 256. However, the right to attach reasonable conditions to the grant of a variance is not dependent upon express authorization in the zoning ordinance.

[213] The function of granting exceptions is widely misunderstood. "This is largely because of the name. What is meant is not (as might be supposed) the power to make exceptions to the ordinance, but rather the power to permit certain exceptional uses which the ordinance authorizes under stated conditions." Phillip P. Green, Jr., "Zoning in North Carolina," Law and Administration, op. cit., p. 331.

[214] See pp. 424–425.

ations to enable a property owner to make use of his property in some way which is in conflict with the literal provisions of the ordinance. Sometimes a lot is so shaped, or a fine big elm tree is so placed, that the owner would have great difficulty in complying with the yard requirements and yet erect a suitable building. Sometimes contours of the terrain are such as to create hardships in complying with these requirements. In some cases the lot is located in a cluster of nonconforming uses which will prevent the owner from securing any reasonable return for his land if he complies with the ordinance. When, in order to give relief in such cases, the board grants an exemption from the requirements in the zoning ordinance, it is granting a variance.

Decisions on applications for variances should not be aimed at correcting bad zoning legislation. To do so would distort the function of the board of adjustment. Correction of a poor zoning ordinance should be done by amendment rather than through granting of relief by the board of adjustment. Perhaps no other aspects of administration are more fundamental to success in carrying out sound zoning policy than the work of the board of adjustment. If the board is too liberal in its interpretation of applications for relief, it may thwart the realization of the objectives of the zoning ordinance. On the other hand, if it is too rigid in adherence to the literal requirements of the act, it may fail to relieve serious cases of hardship and incur resentment and opposition to the zoning program.[215]

The board should not make its decision according to what it conceives to be the popular sentiment at the time. Consent of property owners does not necessarily make it in the interest of the public health, safety, or general welfare.[216] The function of the board of adjustment in dealing with requests for variances is to apply the discretion of experts to exceptional instances where it appears desirable that the permits not conform strictly to the regulations.

The hearing and deciding of cases of "unnecessary hardship" and "practical difficulty" which arise from the application of the strict letter of the zoning ordinance constitute the major function of the board of adjustment. Boards of adjustment serving in this capacity function as a quasi-judicial body. Since the decisions of the board of

---

[215] For a concise analysis of powers, standards, and limitations on authority, see John W. Reps, "Discretionary Powers of the Board of Zoning Appeals," *Law and Contemporary Problems*, Vol. 20, No. 2, pp. 280–297, Spring, 1955.

[216] See Ronald S. Miller, "Consent Provisions in Modern Zoning Statutes," *The University of Illinois Law Forum*, No. 2, pp. 309–317, Summer, 1954.

adjustment are subject to review by the courts, the meaning of the terms "practical difficulty" and "unnecessary hardship" have been construed in numerous decisions.

Although each case must be determined on its own merits, certain criteria for determining whether practical difficulties and unnecessary hardships exist have generally received judicial approval: Among these are:

1. That, if the property owner complies with the provisions of the ordinance, he can secure no reasonable return from, or make no reasonable use of, his property;
2. That the hardship results from the application of the ordinance to his property;
3. That the hardship of which he complains is suffered merely by his property directly, and not by others;
4. That the hardship is not the result of his own actions;
5. That the hardship is peculiar to the property of the applicant.[217]

Limitations on the Powers of Board of Adjustment. Zoning enabling acts do not make the board of adjustment a court and a legislative body to exercise its discretion over the entire field of zoning.[218] In fact, the powers of the board are rather limited. Before the board of adjustment can grant a variance to the zone requirements, it must find that there is unnecessary hardship and practical difficulty, and then it must find and prescribe an alternative use that is not prejudicial to the purposes and intent of the zoning ordinance. The courts stress the point that the board of adjustment is not a legislative body and, consequently, that which can be equally well accomplished by a change in the ordinance or maps is not within the power of the board.

The ordinance can be changed only by the legislative body and cannot be accomplished by action of the board of adjustment.[219] If, for example, the zoning ordinance has set aside a certain block as a residential district, it is not for the board of adjustment to say that stores have become so numerous that on the ground of unnecessary hardship it will permit another store to be built by the applicant. That amounts to alteration or amendment and is not adjustment. If the

---

[217] Jennings and Campbell, op. cit., p. 8.

[218] A. J. Rabuck, "The Powers of Zoning Boards of Appeals," *The Municipality*, Vol. 32, No. 9, p. 196, September, 1937.

[219] *Civil City of Indianapolis v. Ostram Realty and Construction Co.*, 95 Ind. App. 376 (1932); Charles A. Rathkopf, *The Law of Zoning and Planning*, 2d ed. (New York: Grosby Press, 1949), p. 154.

district has become so much of a business district that it is unsound public policy to prevent a man from building a store, then it is for the planning agency to recommend to the city council that the area be rezoned as a business district. It is not for the board of adjustment to try to accomplish the same result by granting a variance.[220]

The rule is firmly established that the power of boards of adjustment to grant variances must be sparingly exercised.[221] This rule has been emphasized by the Indiana Supreme Court which said:

. We think it manifest from the general purpose underlying any zoning ordinance . . . that the power of the board of zoning appeals to vary the application of the provisions of the ordinance is to be exercised sparingly. The common council is the legislative body of the municipality, and power to enact ordinances is vested in it. It could not delegate the power to pass a general zoning ordinance to the board of zoning appeals, or the power to amend such an ordinance. Such an attempt on the part of the common council to do so would be clearly unconstitutional.[222]

Confusion as to the scope of the power of the board of adjustment to grant variances has frequently arisen because of the lack of definite "boundary lines" in the statutes. The phrase "practical difficulties or unnecessary hardship" in itself furnishes only a vague guidepost as to when a variance may be granted. Because of this, some boards have believed that there were no limits to their power to set aside the provisions of the ordinance in any case where they perceived real or fancied injustice.[223] Some boards have actually taken pride in the fact that they have never denied a variance, not realizing that in so acting they were destroying the effectiveness of the zoning ordinance.

Irreparable harm to the whole concept of zoning can result from a policy of extreme liberality. When a board makes a practice of granting variances too freely, it lays itself open to a charge of discrimination whenever it denies one. It also bares the zoning ordinance to the more serious attack that it is no longer "comprehensive" and

---

[220] See Phillip P. Green, Jr., "The Power of the Zoning Board of Adjustment to Grant Variances from the Zoning Ordinance," *The North Carolina Law Review*, Vol. 29, p. 559, 1951. See also Stuart A. McCorkle, *The Texas City—Its Power to Zone* (Austin: The Institute of Public Affairs, University of Texas, 1955), p. 17, citing *Board of Adjustment of City of San Antonio v. Levinson* (Texas Civ. App. 1951), 244 S.W. (2d) 281.

[221] *Real Properties v. Board of Appeals of Boston*, 319 Mass. 180, 65 N.E. (2d) 199 (1946).

[222] Concurring opinion to *Board of Zoning Appeals v. Marckle*, 215 Ind. 74, 85, 18 N.E. (2d) 764 (1935).

[223] Edward M. Bassett, "A Warning as to Unlawful Zoning," *The American City*, Vol. 42, No. 1, p. 119, January, 1947.

uniform, since so many cases for special treatment have been recognized.[224]

Review of Board Action by the Court. Subject to the provisions of the ordinance, it is within the discretion of the board of adjustment to permit or refuse applications for variance from the requirements of the ordinance. The board's action will not be held to be illegal unless an abuse of discretion is clearly shown. The discretionary power of a board is not subject to review except by a proper court upon a verified petition setting forth that such board action is illegal, in whole or in part, and specifying the grounds of the illegality.[225] The courts have consistently reiterated the principle that the findings of the board, when made in good faith and supported by evidence, are final, subject to review by the courts only for errors of law and to give relief against orders which are arbitrary, oppressive, or which represent an abuse of authority.[226] Additional evidence cannot ordinarily be introduced on appeal from a board of adjustment, nor can the court order the board to reopen the case to receive such evidence.

In addition, the courts will not accept an appeal in the absence of a clear showing that the petitioner has exhausted his remedies before the board. This requires that the board, in order to assure fairness to all parties, exercise the greatest care to make certain that its factual determinations are correct, because they will ordinarily be final. The court will, of course, scrutinize (and correct, if necessary) the board's interpretation of the meaning of the ordinance. The fact that its interpretation of the meaning of the ordinance may be corrected by the courts should not lead to a relaxation by the board of its efforts to find the correct meaning. Many cases will not be appealed to the courts, and those which are appealed may be very expensive. An incorrect ruling in the first instance may cause the expenditure of large sums of money with resulting loss of popular support for the zoning ordinance and its administration. Since appeals to the court may be on the basis of facts established before the board, it is most important that a complete and accurate record be kept of all hearings before the board and of all actions taken by it.

[224] Phillip P. Green, Jr., "Is Zoning by Men Replacing Zoning by Law," *Journal of the American Institute of Planners*, Vol. 21, Nos. 2–3, pp. 82–87, Spring–Summer, 1955.

[225] *Fandel v. Board of Zoning Adjustment of Boston*, 280 Mass. 195, 182 N.E. 343 (1932).

[226] *In Re Pine Hill Cemeteries, Inc.*, 219 N.C. 735, 15 S.E. (2d) 1 (1941); "Improving Board of Appeals Procedure," *The American City*, Vol. 44, No. 2, p. 145, February, 1949. See also *State ex rel. Wenatchee Congregation of Jehovah's Witnesses v. The City of Wenatchee et al.*, 150 Wash. Dec. 355 (June 6, 1957).

CHAPTER 9

Subdivision of Land and Platting

SUBDIVISION CONTROL AS A MEANS OF PLAN IMPLEMENTATION

NATURE AND CHARACTERISTICS OF SUBDIVISION REGULATION

Almost every large city today is paying high costs for its failure to establish adequate public controls over the subdivision of land for residential and other purposes. Subdivision regulations, along with zoning, provide the community with one of its most effective methods for developing an appropriate pattern of land use.

When vacant lands are improved, the municipality has its best and sometimes its only opportunity to obtain the pattern of land development with which it must live in the future. The amount of money which many cities are compelled to spend annually for street widening, redesign, relocation of utility lines, slum clearance, and redevelopment is grim evidence of the cost of the failure to develop vacant property in a proper manner. In spite of this evidence, a number of communities have engaged in costly replanning and redevelopment projects without having put into effect adequate subdivision controls to prevent a repetition of the same process in other areas.

Purposes and Objectives. The community has many interests to be protected through the establishment of a sound public policy for regulating the subdivision of land. When subdivisions take place, the municipality must assume a number of service obligations to the inhabitants of the newly developed area. For example, utility services must be supplied; fire and police protection must be extended; transportation facilities need to be provided; and space and facilities for parks, playgrounds, and public buildings are required. Subdivision regulations are, therefore, concerned with the dedication of land for streets, alleys, parks, playgrounds, public buildings, and planting strips. They are concerned also with setting standards for public improvements, including water supply, sewage disposal, and essential utilities; with establishing requirements for building lines; and with providing adequate protection in matters of block design, lot sizes, and street layout.

The primary objective of subdivision control is to assure that the land subdivided will constitute a permanent asset to the community, and will provide the maximum degree of health, comfort, convenience, and beauty consistent with true economy. The well-planned subdivision offers a number of particular advantages to the buyer of a home or a home site. As a general rule, the home buyer can be assured of (1) adequate streets and other public improvements; (2) the development of well-located neighborhood shopping districts; (3) proximity to schools, parks, and playgrounds; and (4) the reasonable expectancy of stabilized property values. Proper subdivision control also gives protection to the subdivider by insuring equal treatment, discouraging land speculation, and giving protection from a competitor who develops a nearby area without complying with minimum standards.[1]

In the final analysis, the aim of subdivision control should be to achieve a proper balance which helps to assure a sound physical development of the community and, at the same time, provides adequate protection to sellers, buyers, and investors concerned with the economic returns from the subdivision. Over the long run, the building of sound and attractive neighborhoods is one of the best means of stabilizing property values. While government has an interest in this from the standpoint of tax returns and of preventing developments which will result in excessive costs to the community, it also has an obligation to insure that its requirements are reasonable and equitable in the interest of the developer, the investor, and the home owner.

Relationship to Planning.   The design of the subdivision develop-

[1] *A Guide to Subdivision Regulation*, Southern Association of State Planning and Development Agencies, 1953, p. 9. See also Floyd M. Jennings and Ernest H. Campbell, *Regulating Subdivisions—The Control of Plats, Subdivisions, or Dedications* (Seattle: Association of Washington Cities, University of Washington, May 14, 1954), Information Bulletin No. 167, pp. 2–3.

ment fixes upon the community a character for an indefinite period of time. It sets a pattern which involves many relationships affecting traffic congestion, transportation, school locations, and the furnishing of the many services which municipalities are expected to provide. The character of the subdivision also has a very important bearing upon the health and safety of the entire community. Subdivision control is thus an integral part of the planning process. It is one of the important tools of plan implementation. It follows, therefore, that unless the municipality has developed a comprehensive plan, intelligent subdivision control is not possible.

In the furtherance of the overall planning objectives, the subdivision regulations must be coördinated with many other tools of plan implementation. Subdivision control is very closely related to zoning in that both types of regulations are designed to avert community blight and deterioration by requiring physical developments according to legally prescribed standards. Area zoning relates to the type of building and use that may take place on the land. Subdivision control is concerned with the manner in which the land is divided and made ready for building. Zoning and subdivision control are mutually dependent, inasmuch as the layout and design of areas cannot be separated from the character of the use to be made of the land.

Failure to observe the rules of good land use planning may have serious economic consequences for both the public and the land owner. Subdivisions which are poorly located or improperly planned add materially to the costs of providing municipal services. Furthermore, if the subdivision is not properly designed, as for example, if streets are too narrow, lots are too small, or if recreational facilities are inadequate, the properties located therein are likely to deteriorate much more rapidly than if they had been carefully planned. Subdivision regulations must, therefore, be drafted and administered with reference to furthering the objectives of comprehensive planning.

The Need for Improved Subdivision Control.   The subdivision of land is not merely a business venture of the land owner and the developer. It is also a matter which affects the interests of the purchasing home owner, the investor, and the local government of the community. The developer or a real estate operator who initiates the subdivision project for purposes of financial gain is entitled to a legitimate profit from his endeavors. However, the character of the subdivision is a matter of great concern to the purchaser or lessee, the mortgage bank or insurance company which may supply the credit, and to the local government which is called upon to provide utilities and other services.

The last half of the nineteenth century and the early part of the 1900's witnessed a period when land speculation was at its peak. The extensive subdivision and sale of lots fostered by a desire to speculate and accumulate profits placed little or no emphasis upon a constructive land-use policy based upon the interest of the community. Transfers of subdivided properties were made primarily in the interest of the seller, and purchasers often found that unexpected costs above the purchase price had to be made to provide necessary streets, sidewalks, and water or sewer facilities. Furthermore, land which was subdivided frequently proved to be unsuitable as a building site either because it was uneconomically suited for building or because of certain factors which created unhealthful conditions. Not uncommonly the secondary consequences were equally or more serious than the direct additional costs.

In many subdivisions, even today, streets are laid out with little or no thought to safety or topography, and houses are built on narrow and crowded lots, often without adequate utilities. When this occurs, it is only a short time until irate property owners are petitioning the city to relocate or widen streets, to provide drainage, to extend sewer lines, or to replace water mains that have become inadequate with the building of additional homes in the area.[2] The costs of installing or making needed improvements or extending utilities under such conditions are almost always disproportionately high.

Unregulated subdivision of land has been responsible in many communities for the excessive supply of lots which has threatened the economic stability of the community and eventually necessitated slum clearance or urban redevelopment.[3] When platted lots remain unsold, the result is that taxes become delinquent; mortgages are foreclosed; and titles often become confused. Excessive subdividing not only results in depreciated property values and tax delinquency but also greatly increases the per capita costs of police, fire, and health protection and of providing utility and other services to the area. The uncontrolled or improperly planned subdivision of land is also the cause of many serious suburban and fringe area problems. These problems have become particularly acute in the post World War II

[2] Charles E. Aguar, "Subdivision Standards—A Weapon to Halt Uncontrolled Growth," *The American City*, Vol. 68, No. 4, p. 100, April, 1953.

[3] W. Willard Wirtz, Notes, "An Analysis of Subdivision Control Legislation," *Indiana Law Journal*, Vol. 28, No. 4, Summer, 1953, p. 546.

period as residential communities have increased in what were formerly rural areas. The desire for suburban living has resulted in numerous subdivisions in the urban fringe areas, with the consequence that large urban communities have developed just outside the corporate limits of most of our major cities.[4] These unincorporated urban communities, in their social and economic aspects, are actually a part of the core city but, in the great number of instances, are not subject to any political control by the city for purposes of land use planning. Eventually many of them become annexed to the city. If and when this occurs, the city inherits all the problems resulting from unregulated subdivisions. Even though the territory remains permanently outside the corporate limits of the city, the ills of poor planning are nevertheless problems of the whole community, since the causes of disease and the influences of blight, and unfavorable environment are not confined within political boundaries.

The ills resulting from excessive, premature, unwise, and poorly planned subdivisions can be prevented only through adequate area-wide subdivision regulations intelligently administered and strictly enforced. Proper subdivision control will help to assure that land will be developed for the highest possible use, with all the necessary protection against deterioration and obsolescence.[5] In order that the greatest benefits be derived from subdivision regulations, there must be a high degree of coöperation between the municipality and the land owner in working for the common good.[6]

LEGAL BASIS OF SUBDIVISION CONTROL

The legal basis for subdivision regulation rests primarily upon the police power. Some regulations have been sustained by the courts on the concept of a plat-recording privilege. Actually, however, the withholding of the recording privilege until the plat is approved is merely a means of effectuating the police power.[7] The extent of the legal authority to establish subdivision regulations must be drawn from a relatively small number of judicial decisions. Compared to zoning, there has been comparatively little litigation of subdivision regulation.

[4] Marygold Shire Melli, "Subdivision Control in Wisconsin," *Wisconsin Law Review*, No. 3, May, 1953, p. 389.

[5] Housing and Home Finance Agency, Division of Housing Research, *Suggested Land Subdivision Regulations* (Washington, D.C.: U.S. Government Printing Office, February, 1952), p. 1.

[6] State of New York, Department of Commerce, *Control of Land Subdivision* (Albany, N.Y.: 1954), p. 5.

[7] Wirtz, *op. cit.*, p. 557.

None of the subdivision cases appears to be the equivalent of the Euclid case [8] which established the constitutionality of comprehensive zoning.

Most of the legal attacks on the power to control subdivisions have come from persons contending that they have been deprived of their property without due process of law. It has been urged in certain cases, for example, that provisons in subdivision regulations requiring the dedication of land for streets or other public uses constitute an unlawful taking of property without payment of compensation.[9] In general, courts have pointed out that such arguments have failed to distinguish the power of eminent domain from the exercise of the police power.[10]

Provisions in subdivision ordinances requiring that certain land be dedicated for public use are supported upon the ground that the privilege of lot subdivision and the recording of plats can be made subject to reasonable regulations in the public interest. Some cases have held that such subdivision requirements were not an exercise of the power of eminent domain since the subdivider "voluntarily subdivided." However, the only sound basis for upholding subdivision regulations is the exercise of the police power of government to establish reasonable controls for promoting health, safety, morals, convenience, and general welfare.

Enabling Legislation. The authority of municipalities to regulate subdivisions is derived primarily from state enabling statutes. All states, except Vermont, have authorized or adopted some type of subdivision control.[11] An examination of these statutes, however, indicates a wide variation in their provisions. Under some statutes the regulation provided is limited and may apply only to certain areas or municipalities, or to municipalities with certain populations.

State statutes are generally of two types: One type of statute is mandatory in that the state act requires that all plats must be approved by certain governmental agencies before they are recorded. The other type is enabling and permits the municipality or other unit of government to adopt subdivision regulations and provide for the approval

[8] *Village of Euclid v. Ambler Realty Company*, 272 U.S. 365, 71 L.Ed. 303 (1926).
[9] Melli, *op. cit.*, p. 398.
[10] *Allen v. Stockwell*, 210 Mich. 488, 178 N.W. 27 (1920).
Ridgefield Land Co. v. City of Detroit, 241 Mich. 468, 217 N.W. 58 (1928).
Newton v. American Securities Company, 201 Ark. 943, 148 S.W. (2d) 311 (1941).
Ayers v. City Council of Los Angeles, 34 Cal. (2d) 31, 207 P. (2d) 1 (1949).
[11] Melli, *op. cit.*, p. 399.

and recording of plats which have complied with the standards of the municipal ordinance.

A number of the earlier statutes were aimed primarily at street patterns, seeking to require that each new subdivision conform to the layout of the adjacent land. By this means the subdivision regulations were able to prevent street jogs and dead-end streets, but otherwise accomplished little in promoting the general welfare. In many instances, regulations of this type have merely resulted in carrying over into the new areas the defects to be found in the adjacent area. Early statutes commonly established standards only with respect to public streets, thus making it possible for the subdivider to evade the regulations by designating the streets as private. This was possible, even though eventually these streets became public either as a result of use, acceptance by the city, or by some act from which acceptance might be implied, such as the installation of utility facilities. Statutes which have been enacted recently have included more specific requirements pertaining not only to the street pattern but also aimed at much broader objectives of developing the land according to a comprehensive land-use pattern.

State statutes vary considerably as to their scope. In the state of Washington, the enabling statute applies primarily to the division of land into five or more parcels. In California and Nevada the statute limits the application to cases where land is divided into five or more parcels in one calendar year. The Wisconsin law is limited to subdivisions in which five or more lots are sold within a calendar year. The Michigan act applies to division of land into ten or more parcels. Approximately half of the states do not restrict the coverage. In these states it would appear that the statute would apply to the subdivsion of land into two or more lots. Certain states also have placed restrictions upon the application of the statute to lots of a certain size. In Minnesota, for example, the application of the statute is restricted to lots of one acre or less except when a new street is dedicated, in which case, lots up to ten acres in size are included.

Many of the state statutes specify certain technical requirements with respect to such matters as surveying methods, form of the plat, location of minimums, dimensions of lot, width of streets, and details of procedure to be followed for plat approval. Some of the statutes also specify certain safeguards for the subdivider, such as fixing a time limit within which the plat must be approved. If the municipal agency which has the authority for approval does not act within the specified time, approval is automatically given. A number of the statutes also make provision for a right of appeal for the subdivider who may object to the decision of the approving body. Such regulations usually require that the reasons for the rejection be stated in the records of the approving body.

In at least three states, statutes have specifically authorized approving authorities to deny subdividing when a proposed subdivision is not in the public interest. Such statutes have been enacted to make possible direct action to prevent excessive or premature subdivisions or subdivisions in inappropriate areas, and thus help to prevent the likelihood of the development of slum or blighted areas. Whether or not such provisions will be upheld by the courts is a matter yet to be determined.[12]

Local Legislative and Administrative Action. Unless the state statute is self-executing, authority to control the subdivision of land is dependent upon action by the local legislative body. Most of the enabling statutes are permissive in character, permitting the municipality to exercise subdivision control if the community so desires. Within the framework of these statutes, municipalities are free to determine their own policies, fix the requirements, and create the machinery for the administration and enforcement of the regulations.

Most enabling statutes designate the planning agency as the local authority to approve proposed plats. In some states, however, all matters of subdivision control including both policy and administrative matters are made a function of the city council. In certain jurisdictions the power of subdivision control is conferred upon the city council with authority to designate the planning agency or some other municipal agency as the body to grant or withhold plat approval. Whether adopted by the council or the planning agency, the regulations, once adopted, become binding upon the municipality as well as the subdivider until they are changed by formal amendment.

In some instances the language of the enabling statute is ambiguous, since it fails to indicate clearly where authority rests. In the State of Washington, for example, the enabling statute provides that: "If land proposed to be platted, subdivided, or dedicated is situated in a city or town, the proposal shall be submitted for approval to the legislative body of the city or town. If the city or town has a planning commission, the commission may take appropriate action thereon in lieu of the legislative body on behalf of the city or town." [13]

---

[12] Wirtz, *op. cit.*, p. 556.
[13] Revised Code of Washington, 58.16.030. The statute further provides that: "To

Language such as that used in the Washington statute leaves questions of doubt such as whether "appropriate action" contemplates the adoption of regulations by the planning commission or only plat approval, and if it contemplates the adoption of regulations, whether such regulations supplant or supersede those which may have been formerly adopted by ordinance.

The adoption of subdivision regulations is in the nature of a legislative function and logically should be a responsibility of the city council. However, there are no legal restrictions unless provided by the state constitution upon conferring upon a nonlegislative body authority to promulgate rules and regulations in accordance with standards prescribed by state enabling law. Questions of policy are presented if the planning agency is assigned either legislative responsibility or detailed tasks of administration, since this practice is inconsistent with the general concept that the planning agency should exercise only a staff function. This principle would dictate that the adoption of subdivision regulations should be a function of the legislative body.

Nevertheless, there are a number of persuasive arguments for vesting authority in the planning agency both for adopting subdivision regulations and for granting or withholding plat approval. As a general rule, considerably more flexibility is provided where the adoption and administration of regulations and amendments is made the responsibility of the planning agency. The planning agency is normally in a better position than any other department or agency of municipal government to know what the future physical needs of the community will be. The planning agency is also in a better position than any of the other municipal bodies to determine whether proposed subdivision developments conform to the requirements of the comprehensive plan. However, if the municipality has not adopted a comprehensive plan, the planning agency is actually in no better position to prepare the subdivision regulations and administer them than is any other agency. Some jurisdictions, therefore, confer authority upon the planning commission to adopt regulations only if the municipality has developed a comprehensive plan or at least a major street plan. Municipalities which place authority in the plan-

effectuate the policy of this chapter, every legislative or planning authority charged with the duty of passing upon and giving or withholding approval of plats, subdivisions and dedications shall establish reasonable regulations with continuing right of amendment thereof." . . . Revised Code of Washington 58.16.110.

ning commission to adopt subdivision regulations may, nevertheless, find it preferable to provide for penalities and other enforcement provisions by ordinance. Enactment of such provisions by ordinance tends to give greater weight to the force and effect of the regulations.

Most statutes conferring upon the planning agency authority to adopt subdivision regulations assume that the planning agency is headed by a lay board or commission. Students of public administration generally concede that boards or commissions are particularly well suited for quasi-legislative and quasi-judicial functions. The question is properly raised as to whether a planning agency headed by a single director is as well suited to such tasks. Where the planning agency is integrated into the administrative structure under a single head, it may be advisable to provide that regulations prepared, promulgated, and adopted by the planning agency, in order to become effective, shall have the approval of the legislative body or some lay board or commission appointed for this purpose.

It should be clearly recognized that whereas the planning agency may be designated the principal agency to supervise the administration of subdivision regulations, there are a number of other departments and agencies of government that must aid in administration and enforcement if the regulations are to be effective. Many city and county officials and agencies such as the city engineer, county engineer, fire and police departments, health departments, school boards, director of recreation, transit officials, building inspector, county auditor, and others have important responsibilities. Also the coöperation of officials of adjacent cities and towns is often essential to developing a harmonious pattern of subdivision control.[14]

The Use and Nature of the Plat. The information which is necessary for the approving authority to determine whether the proposed subdivision complies with the requirements of the ordinance is contained in the plat. A plat is essentially a map of a piece of land which shows its location, boundaries, area, and details of lot boundaries, proposed streets, utilities, public areas, and all other data necessary to determine compliance with the subdivision regulations. State statutes provide for the recording of plats and selling lots or parcels of land by reference to the recorded plat. Until the plat is recorded, lots within a proposed subdivision may be sold only by metes and bounds description.

[14] State of New York, Department of Commerce, *Control of Land Subdivision op. cit.*, p. 8.

The power of the approving authority of the municipality to grant or withhold the privilege of recording the plat is the basis of the enforcement machinery of subdivision control. Most regulations make it unlawful for any land owner or agency of an owner to sell land or to negotiate a sale by reference to, exhibition of, or by any other use of an unrecorded plat. Penalties are provided against any person who violates the provisions of the regulations. Some regulations go further and provide that transfers by metes and bounds will not avoid the penalties.

If such provisions are the only penalties in the act, there are obviously loopholes for evading the subdivision regulations by selling lots by metes and bounds description, particularly in view of the difficulty of establishing proof that the seller actually made use of the plat in making the sale. Although the advantages of selling land by reference to a plat are sufficiently great to discourage sales by metes and bounds in the great number of cases, the number and likelihood of evasions have led to suggestions for plugging the loopholes by requiring a survey and approved map of each new land parcel described by metes and bounds. Other suggested deterrents to sales by metes and bounds have been to prohibit the paving of streets, the laying of water mains or sewers, or the erection of a building on a lot abutting on it unless the street is shown on a recorded plat.[15] The extent to which some of these proposals may be legally utilized has not been tested in the courts. Aside from the legal considerations, it is obviously not good public policy to prohibit all sales by metes and bounds, since frequently this method is the only satisfactory way of effecting transfers of parts of a lot or of granting easements or some other interest in property.

Protective Covenants. Subdivision regulations are designed to establish minimum requirements and not necessarily those which are most desirable. Consequently, subdividers of certain areas and prospective purchasers may wish to set standards above those required by the subdivision regulations in order to insure a more restricted residential district than would necessarily result from public controls alone. This is commonly done through the use of protective covenants running with the land. Such covenants provide an important supplement to subdivision regulations for controlling the character of the neighborhood and stabilizing land values. They work to the ben-

[15] Local Planning Administration (Chicago: International City Managers' Association, 1948), p. 248.

efit of the subdivider by furthering his land development program and, at the same time, protecting the investment of the purchasers of the lots.

Both subdivision control and zoning are limited by the scope of the police power for promoting the public health, safety, morals, and general welfare. Protective covenants, on the other hand, are agreements between private parties and may establish controls through deed restrictions which government authority might not be able to justify as a valid exercise of the police power. They make it possible for the subdivider and the lot purchaser by express agreement to prescribe standards much higher than those required under minimum standards of the subdivision regulations, and to establish uses more restricted than those required under the zoning ordinance.

Protective covenants may relate to many of the subject areas covered by design standards in the subdivision regulations and the land use requirements of the zoning ordinance such as the size, width, and depth of lots, the granting of easements, the minimum front, side, and rear yards, and the exclusion of certain trades or businesses or structures which may be regarded as incompatible or offensive to the planned residential use.[16] In other cases protective covenants may provide a means of exercising a high degree of supervision over the type, size, quality, and architectural design of dwellings and other buildings which could not legally be done by government authority. Architectural control and other controls for aesthetic purposes are usually carried out through an architectural control committee which is given authority under the protective covenants to review the plans and specifications for the location and exterior design of all buildings, fences, walls, and plantings proposed to be developed within the area covered by the protective covenants. Such a committee is usually named by the developer and should consist of a number of persons who have no financial interest in the development. At least one member should be an architect.

Protective covenants, running with the land, which are binding upon all property owners within the protected area are preferable to piecemeal control by means of covenants inserted in individual deeds at the time of conveyance. It is preferable that protective covenants covering a subdivision be prepared in proper form for recording under the laws of the jurisdiction and be submitted along with the application for approval of the final plat. Although protective covenants are

---

[16] Housing and Home Finance Agency, *op. cit.*, pp. 53–60.

not part of the requirements of the subdivision regulations, their inclusion as part of the supporting data makes them part of the plan and enables the approving authority to take them into account in determining whether the proposed development meets the minimum requirements of the regulations.

Protective covenants are usually made effective for a stipulated time, after which they may be continued in effect for another stipulated period unless a certain percentage of the property owners, as fixed in the original agreement, agrees upon a change. Although it seems probable that protective covenants could be enforced by actions at law or equity without including a provision to that effect in the covenant itself, nevertheless, authorities recommend that a provision be inserted in the agreement making violations subject to equitable or legal action.[17]

Extraterritorial Jurisdiction. Within the past two decades virtually every major city has been faced with difficult problems resulting from uncontrolled suburban developments just outside its boundaries. Some states have recognized the importance of these problems to the cities and have granted cities extraterritorial power to regulate subdivisions for distances of from ½ to 10 miles beyond their corporate limits. Three to 5 miles has been the most usual provision. Five miles is generally considered the distance to be recommended for control except in small cities.[18] While the granting of extraterritorial jurisdiction helps to relieve some of the difficulties, fringe area problems always remain wherever political boundaries exist. In cases where the granting of extraterritorial power would mean that the jurisdiction of two or more cities would overlap, statutes should provide for dividing the jurisdiction at equal distance from the corporate boundaries of each.

In a number of states legislation has been enacted to enable counties to exercise subdivision control in areas outside the corporate limits of municipalities. Where this has been done it is important that the subdivision regulations of the county and municipalities be carefully coördinated. Especially is this true where cities are granted extraterritorial authority which may result in overlapping jurisdiction.

Certain states which do not grant extraterritorial powers sometimes seek to coördinate subdivision requirements in other ways. In the State of Washington, for example, extraterritorial jurisdiction is not

[17] Ibid., p. 56.
[18] Local Planning Administration, op. cit., p. 252.

conferred upon municipalities. However, the Washington statute provides that when land proposed to be platted, subdivided, or dedicated is adjacent to or part of the suburban area of a city or town, notice of the pendency of the application shall be given to the legislative body or planning commission of the city or town before action is taken by the county commissioners or county planning commission. In this manner, the city may be heard before a decision is made by the county and, to that extent, has a voice in influencing the decision.

Areas of Legal Uncertainty in Subdivision Control. Compared to zoning and many other types of governmental regulation, subdivision control has not resulted in a great amount of litigation. The cases which have been decided do, however, establish some very important guidelines in a number of phases of subdivision control. For example, the subdivision ordinance may legally require subdividers, as a condition of plat approval, to install streets, surface drains, cement sidewalks and sanitary sewers,[19] and to dedicate land for street widening along boundary streets.[20] It would appear from language used in some of the decisions that the validity of design requirements to eliminate excessive street grades and dangerous intersections and to provide for the extension of existing major streets through the subdivision would not be open to serious question. Courts have also upheld the validity of extraterritorial control by municipalities.[21] In ruling upon questions involving subdivision control, as in other exercises of the police power, the courts make it clear that they will look to the facts in the particular case to determine if the requirements are reasonable and that they do not deprive the persons affected of the protection of due process of law.

The relatively few judicial precedents have left our municipalities with a great deal of uncertainty as to the extent to which subdivision control can be used to accomplish certain planning objectives. With respect to this area of legal uncertainty, one writer has raised some very pertinent questions as to whether, under present legislation, municipalities can accomplish the following:

Can we prevent excessive or premature subdivision? Can the planning

[19] *Allen v. Stockwell*, 210 Mich. 488, 178 N.W. 27 (1920).
[20] *Ridgefield Land Co. v. City of Detroit*, 241 Mich. 468, 217 N.W. 58 (1928).
Newton v. American Securities Co., 201 Ark. 943, 148 S.W. (2d) 311 (1941).
Ayers v. City Council of City of Los Angeles, 34 Cal. (2d) 31, 207, P. (2d) 1 (1949).
[21] *Prudential Co-Op. Realty Co. v. Youngstown*, 118 Ohio St. 204, 160 N.E. 695 (1928).

agency substitute its concept of sound land planning for that held by the subdivider? Can the planning agency compel subdividers to conform to its general plan for municipal expansion? Can the planning agency require subdividers to dedicate or even reserve lands for parks or other neighborhood facilities? Can the municipality effectively prevent the evasion of subdivision regulations? [22]

Some of these matters are touched upon in the following discussion of subdivision requirements and public policy considerations.

It seems likely that the relatively small number of judicial decisions on subdivision regulation may be due more to the manner in which control is supervised than to the fact that the regulations are perfectly drawn or that they are not firmly enforced. The administration of subdivision regulations involves a considerable degree of negotiation between the subdivider and the approving authority. During this process many controversial points are discussed and resolved, which, under more rigid types of control, would lead to litigation. This does not mean that definable standards do not exist. It indicates rather that there may be a number of different means of meeting minimum requirements which, in turn, offer many opportunities for reaching agreement through negotiation and compromise.

SUBDIVISION REQUIREMENTS AND PUBLIC POLICY CONSIDERATIONS

Public policy in subdivision control must take many community interests into account. Standards must be sufficiently exact to provide definiteness and certainty and yet have a high degree of flexibility in order to permit the adjustment of minimum requirements to satisfy the demands for the type of development which seems to be justified in a given location.

The Development of Public Policy in Subdivision Control

In developing a policy for subdivision control, conflicting objectives must frequently be reconciled. The encouragement of private enterprise and initiative must be balanced against the regulation of land uses. Public benefits derived from expensive installations need to be weighed against excessive costs to the subdivider and purchasers. In certain instances, for example, the insistence upon high minimal

[22] John W. Reps, "Are Our Subdivision Control Laws Adequate," *Journal of the American Institute of Planners*, Vol. XX, No. 3, p. 131, Summer, 1954.

standards may defeat the construction of low cost housing. It has been found that compliance with minimum standards with respect to street grading and the installation of water mains and sanitary sewers often may increase the total home cost as much as 20 percent. Such factors may be decisive as to whether a particular project can be developed for quick sale.

Matters for Public or Private Determination. Public controls over the subdivision of land can be legally supported only to the extent that they are a means of promoting the health, safety, morals, or general welfare. Any unnecessary interference with private enterprise would be inconsistent with the aims and objectives of subdivision regulation, and in the end would defeat its purpose. Consequently, the point at which the discretion of the subdivider must give way to public decision and supervision is a matter of great importance. Such questions as whether a particular piece of land should be subdivided, whether the size and character of the proposed development are proper, or whether, in fact, there is a need or demand for such development are matters in which the community as a whole has considerable interest. However, public interest in these matters does not necessarily mean that the questions should be resolved by public decision.

Generally speaking, it would seem that decisions with respect to the advisability of a particular development or its economic feasibility should be left to private enterprise, subject only to public controls and requirements necessary to protect the public interest. The judgment of public officials on these questions should not be substituted for that of the developer, investor, and purchaser. The public interest can be protected by establishing requirements which provide minimum standards to be met in order to carry out the objectives of the comprehensive plan, and by leaving all other decisions to the developer.

The degree and type of control necessary in some communities may depend in part upon the persons being regulated. Some subdivisions may be undertaken by professional developers, comprised mainly of real estate men and construction contractors, who engage in such activities more or less as a continuous business venture. Other subdivisions may be undertaken by nonprofessional developers who may happen to own some land, in or on the outskirts of the city, and decide to subdivide it because of the increased urbanization of the area and the demand for residential property. Such developers are unlikely to have more than one such subdivision in a lifetime.

It is usually the nonprofessional developer who suffers most from the imposition of subdivision requirements, since the subdivision he proposes to develop is often of small scale and backed by little capital. Certain jurisdictions have attempted to meet this problem in part by defining a subdivision as the division of land into five or more lots of one acre or less or by means of some other language in the law.[23] Although such provisions may offer reasonable concessions to the special needs and hardships of the nonprofessional developer, they may also provide loopholes for the unscrupulous operator who may use them as a means of escaping all controls. Since the relaxation of requirements over small developments may constitute an invitation to evasion, and defeat the objectives of subdivision control, a safe approach would seem to be one which establishes close public control over all subdivisions, with authority to the proper agency to grant modifications or variations from the strict requirements under specified conditions whereby the public interest will be adequately protected.

Excessive and Premature Subdivision. Public policy in land subdivision should have as one of its primary objectives the discouragement of excessive or premature subdivisions. The great number of vacant lots within our cities has been caused primarily by premature and excessive subdivision. The trend over the past three decades to suburban living has not been due to any shortage of land for building purposes within city limits. In fact, a great many of the major cities in the United States contain more vacant lots than can possibly be absorbed for building purposes in a number of generations.[24] It has been estimated by the Chicago Regional Planning Association that in the Chicago region the number of existing subdivided lots in 1928 would in all probability not be absorbed by 1960.[25] In the city of Detroit in 1935 there were enough vacant lots to accommodate a

---

[23] Harold W. Lautner, *Subdivision Regulations, an Analysis of Land Subdivision Control Practices* (Chicago: Public Administration Service, 1941), Special Publication No. 28, pp. 14–16.

[24] A recent survey of 53 central cities indicates that on an overall average about one-third of the total city area was vacant or unused. The greatest vacancy was found to be in the small cities. Cities of 50,000 population or less had vacancy of 47.01 percent, cities with population of 50,000–100,000 had vacancy of 38.80 percent, cities of 100,000–250,000 population had vacancy of 21.85 percent, and cities of a population of over 250,000 average 20.37 percent. See Harland Bartholomew, *Land Uses in American Cities* (Cambridge: Harvard University Press, 1955), p. 73.

[25] *Local Planning Administration, op. cit.*, p. 262.

population of an additional one million people, and in the adjacent suburban areas there were vacant lots sufficient for the needs of almost two million additional.[26]

Much of this vacant land is represented by premature, poorly planned, or improperly located subdivisions. Many of these subdivisions consist of numerous acres of property, some with streets and other improvements, that have become overgrown with weeds. Premature or poorly planned subdivisions represent not only a substantial financial loss to the subdivider, but also added costs to the community as a whole and a loss of tax revenue to the government. Such vacant property is also taken out of any productive use. The consequences of uncontrolled and haphazard subdividing of land are obvious. However, the proper basis for establishing public controls to prevent these consequences is not entirely clear.

An appropriate aim of land subdivision policy would seem to be one of preventing wildcat or irresponsible subdivision. This can be accomplished to some degree by indirect controls which are aimed at making subdividers and investors investigate and consider all aspects of the proposed subdivision rather carefully before embarking upon the undertaking. Indirect controls would include such requirements as making adequate provision for water supply, sewage disposal, installation of utilities, and the dedication of public facilities for open space and recreation.

Many proposals have been suggested for directly controlling the quantity of subdivisions or of fixing the priority for their development.[27] For example, it has been suggested that applications be made to a public agency which would be authorized to consider such applications on the basis of the supply of building sites, the type of location, and the prospective demand for building sites of the price and character proposed. Presumably the public agency would have authority to determine whether or not there was need for such a subdivision. Under this plan, approval by the agency would be necessary before the subdivision could be undertaken. There are, however, serious questions as to whether the exercise of such authority would be upheld by the courts, and if so, whether it would meet with public

[26] A Study of Subdivision Development in the Detroit Metropolitan Area (Lansing: Michigan Planning Commission, 1939), pp. 10–13.

[27] For a detailed case study of the problem including recommendations for public action, see Philip H. Cornick, Problems Created by Premature Subdivision of Urban Lands in Selected Metropolitan Districts (Albany, N.Y.: Division of State Planning, 1938).

acceptance. Since public policy in subdivision control does not seek to substitute the judgment of government officials with respect to what is needed in homes for that of private enterprise, it would seem that, for the present at least, indirect controls are better suited to discouraging excessive and premature subdivisions.

Control to Insure Conformance to the Street Plan. Although subdivision regulations are designed to serve as a tool of planning, difficult questions arise as to how far the planning agency can legally and practically go in compelling subdividers to conform to specific requirements aimed at plan effectuation. For example, two or more subdividers may undertake the development of property in contiguous or neighboring areas. Frequently these property owners have very different ideas about the type and character of the subdivision they propose to develop. Both may submit plans that meet the minimum standards for design, but fail to present a harmonious street plan for the overall area. If the city has not adopted an official map fixing street locations, the approving authority may not be on very solid ground in insisting that each comply with a street plan which the city has not officially adopted.[28] Furthermore, if the city insists upon a particular plan other than one insuring locations for major thorough-fares, much of the element of flexibility is destroyed.[29] From the public standpoint, however, it is certainly important to have feasible street connections between adjacent tracts. Often a harmonious plan can be worked out through negotiation with the subdividers involved.

Control to Insure Proper Site Location. Public policy with respect to land subdivision must be concerned not only with design but also with site location. Frequently subdivisions are laid out in land which is unsuited for home sites or for the other purposes for which the subdivision is established. For example, the land may be unsuitable because of the fact that the area is subject to floods, because it has a very thin layer of soil, with underlying rock, which makes excavation and utility installation difficult and costly, or because it includes slide areas. The location may be undesirable because of its proximity to land zoned for industrial uses or other purposes which are not com-patible with a proposed subdivision. There are many other factors that may also enter into the suitability of particular sites. Where such circumstances are found, unsuspecting purchasers, as well as the sub-divider, may suffer serious economic loss.

[28] See *Lordship Park Association v. Town of Stratford*, 137 Conn. 84, 75 A. (2d) 379 (1950).

[29] Reps, *op. cit.*, pp. 132–133.

Obviously, there are greater difficulties in establishing satisfactory policies for the control of location than in prescribing requirements with respect to design. In many instances, the proposed subdivision may be discouraged as a result of initial conferences with the planning commission or as a result of requirements for the installation of utilities and the grading and surfacing of streets.

In many instances it may be easier to control location through zoning than by requirements in the subdivision ordinance. For this reason, it is important that zoning policy and subdivision policy be closely coördinated. Where, for example, land may be subject to floods or a health hazard, or consists of a type of soil unsuited for residential use or other buildings, it may be properly zoned for uses which would exclude the location of a subdivision.

Normally the subdividing of unsuitable land as well as premature and excessive subdividing will be sufficiently discouraged by the establishment and maintenance of adequate standards. Where, however, it is clear that the character of the proposed subdivision is such as to place an unreasonable financial burden upon the community, there may be justification for directly prohibiting the development from being undertaken. Depending upon the topographical surface and subsurface conditions of the area, it may be desirable to include in the subdivision regulations a prohibition against subdividing any land which the approving authority has found to be unsuitable for subdivision due to flooding, bad drainage, steep slopes, rock formations, or other features likely to be harmful to the health, safety, or general welfare of the future residents unless adequate methods for their protection are formulated by the developer and approved by the city engineer.

Compulsory Dedication of Sites for Public Facilities. Public open spaces and sites for various types of public facilities have come to form a very important part of community living. The proper location and development of schools, neighborhood parks, playgrounds, and many other public facilities are essential to sound land use planning. The best time to provide for these facilities is when raw land is initially developed. It is important, therefore, that subdivision requirements seek to insure that appropriate sites will be reserved for all necessary public facilities and open spaces. In the event that a proposed park, playground, school, or other public facility shown on the comprehensive plan is located in whole or in part in the subdivision, the approving authority should require a reservation or dedication of such area by the subdivider as a condition of recording the plat. Requirements for such reservations or dedications must be reasonable and should rest upon knowledge of public needs determined as the result of sound planning considerations. The requirements must also take into account the economic effect upon the subdivider.

Since the location and character of public sites and open spaces should be planned to fulfill the needs and demands of the neighborhood or entire community, it would obviously not be good practice simply to require a subdivider to dedicate a certain portion of each tract for these purposes. The result of such a policy would be to create a number of areas of improper size forming a crazy-quilt pattern which would not necessarily fit into the overall plan of land-use development. The important consideration in establishing requirements is to insure that public sites and open spaces will be of appropriate size and appropriate location to conform to the comprehensive plan for the entire community.

In many instances it will be found possible to secure the reservation and dedication of public sites by persuasion and without resorting to the force of law.[30] In other instances, the dedication of sites can be secured only by legal compulsion. The theory underlying compulsory dedication is that the developer who receives the financial gain from the enterprise should safeguard the public interest by providing adequate land areas for public facilities for the use and enjoyment of those who acquire the lots. This is necessary to provide for the health, safety, morals, and general welfare, and to help prevent the spread of blight. In most jurisdictions, however, there is considerable doubt as to how far reservation and dedication requirements can be enforced under the police power. It seems quite clear that courts in all jurisdictions would not uphold regulations which compel a subdivider, without compensation, to dedicate a major portion of the subdivision tract for the purpose of providing a park or school site intended to serve the entire community.[31]

The extent to which the police power may be utilized to require compulsory reservation or dedication of sites for public facilities has not been very clearly established by the courts. In a number of some-

[30] Lautner, op. cit., p. 179.

[31] See, however, Western City, September 1953, p. 53. Opinion of C. E. Luckey, District Attorney, Lane County, Oregon, ruling that the planning commission may require, as a prerequisite of plat approval, that a subdivider dedicate land to widen an existing county road abutting the proposed subdivision if it is a reasonable part of the adopted plan for future development of the area on the theory that the subdivider is not required to plat.

what related cases construing the legality of provisions in official map acts, the courts have rather consistently held that land for public facilities can be reserved for public use only through the exercise of the power of eminent domain.[32] However, the benefits which the subdivider receives from the municipality from the privilege of plat recording raises a question as to whether a stronger case is not presented for upholding reasonable requirements for reservations or dedications under subdivision regulations.[33] Some judicial support for the principle of compulsory dedication can be drawn from the case of *In Re Lake Secore Development Co., Inc.*,[34] in which a lower court in the State of New York in 1931 upheld the requirement that suitable park land be dedicated to the municipality. The decision was affirmed by the appellate court without opinion. Another decision that gives some support to the principle is the case of *Zayas v. Puerto Rico Planning Board* [35] decided by the Supreme Court of Puerto Rico in 1948. In this case the court was asked to pass upon the legality of the subdivision regulations of the planning board which required that 5 percent of the area of every proposed subdivision should be reserved and dedicated for recreational purposes. The court held that the planning board might properly require a reservation of land for recreational purposes, but could not legally demand a dedication which would transfer title from the landowner to the public without compensation.

It is by no means certain how far the various state courts will follow the decision of the Puerto Rican Supreme Court in supporting the principle of compulsory reservation of land for park purposes.[36] The distinction between the legality of a reservation and a dedication appears to rest on a very fine line. Actually, there is little difference in the result to the subdivider in compulsory dedication and compulsory reservation unless the reservation is for a limited period of time. The reservation of land for a public use prevents the owner from selling it or using it for any purpose other than that for which it is reserved. Retention of fee simple title under these circumstances has little value.

While the most universal need of reserved areas is for parks and

[32] See Chap. 6.

[33] Reps, *op. cit.*, pp. 133–134.

[34] 141 Misc. 913, 252 N.Y.S. 809 (1931). Affd. 235 A.D. 627, 255 N.Y.S. 853 (1932).

[35] 69 P.R.R. 27 (1948).

[36] See *Miller v. City of Beaver Falls*, 368 Pa. 189, 82 A. (2d) 34 (1951) invalidating a provision in an official map act which established site location of a proposed park in land being subdivided.

open spaces for recreational purposes, there are many other uses for which reservations may be required. In making provision for community needs, the plat approving authority should carefully investigate the needs for other public uses, such as sites for schools, fire stations, churches, community clubs, parking facilities, parkways, and other public and semipublic facilities. Since it would not be reasonable to require the dedication of land for all such purposes in every subdivision, it is important that reservation and dedication requirements have sufficient flexibility so that adaptations may be made to meet the essential public demands without placing undue burdens upon the developer. It is to be emphasized that no requirements should be made which would result in areas being dedicated in a haphazard fashion. It is essential that all reservations or dedications be in conformity with the comprehensive plan for public facilities, and requirements should be designed to effectuate the overall land-use pattern. Requirements must be analyzed with respect to each proposed subdivision and the needs of each neighborhood.

In the case of large subdivisions, a requirement that adequate spaces be reserved or dedicated for public use would ordinarily not bring any great hardship upon the subdivider. In small subdivisions the insistence upon a dedication of an area adequate for all public needs might place a very heavy economic burden upon the land owner. In those cases where the burden falls disproportionately heavily on a particular subdivider, it would seem as a matter of equity that the public policy should be to reimburse the subdivider for the amount which he contributes over and above his fair share.

One plan which deserves considerable study is that which requires, in lieu of a dedication of open space, a substantial fee to be paid into a public fund by each subdivider at the time of filing the plat, to be used to acquire and develop parks and playgrounds or other spaces for neighborhood use. Fees would be graduated according to the acreage or number of lots subdivided. Such a plan if approved by the court might, for example, offer a method of financing a neighborhood recreational area in the vicinity of the subdivision but not necessarily located within or on any part of it or used exclusively by the residents of the subdivision.

GENERAL REQUIREMENTS RELATING TO STANDARDS

The requirements of subdivision regulations relating to standards are concerned with such matters as street widths and grades, street intersections, the size and arrangement of lots and blocks, building lines, the size, type, and location of utility installations, rights of way, easements, and recreational and public areas. Those requirements which relate to the internal arrangement of the subdivision are usually referred to as design standards. Other major requirements are concerned with the construction and installation of improvements. The primary purpose of establishing design standards is to insure that the type of development proposed will suit the land which is subdivided.[37] It is essential that such standards conform to the comprehensive plan and the official map if either or both have been adopted.[38]

Adequacy of Standards. Subdivision control as a general rule has not been opposed by the better class of subdividers who have come to realize that the requirement of adequate minimum standards is an essential part of the planning process.[39] Sometimes, however, certain requirements have been strenuously opposed as being unreasonable as applied to specific situations. For example, it has been urged that although it may be very pleasant to have sidewalks on both sides of the street, in many subdivisions a requirement that they be installed on only one side is sufficient. In the main, the opposition to subdivision regulations has been related to provisions such as those requiring the installation, at the developers expense, of oversized utilities or excessive roadway widths designed to serve property beyond the development, the payment of all unpaid taxes and special assessments prior to recording the plat, and the dedication of land for extra widths for streets or for other public uses without payment of compensation. Subdividers, on occasions, have also complained that the quality standards which have been set are over and above those necessary, thereby precluding the possibility of selling to purchasers in the lower income brackets who comprise two-thirds to three-fourths of the prospective purchasers.[40]

Failure to establish adequate standards can only result in headaches for the city, high maintenance and replacement costs for the property owner, or both. However, the question of what requirements

[37] Southern Association of State Planning and Development Agencies, *A Guide to Subdivision Regulation*, 1953 (distributed by member agencies), p. 13.

[38] William E. Roach, *A Suggested Guide for Land Subdivision Ordinances for New Jersey Municipalities* (State of New Jersey: The State Planning Section, Division of Planning and Development, Department of Conservation and Economic Development, 1953), mimeo, 32 pp., p. 24.

[39] Stanley L. McMichael, *Real Estate Subdivisions* (Englewood Cliffs, N.J.: Prentice-Hall, Inc., 1949), p. 30.

[40] Wirtz, *op. cit.*, p. 569.

and standards are adequate must be determined in different communities according to local conditions. Some municipalities have gone little further than to enforce minimum standards of street size and width. On the other hand, most communities which have been confronted with a great deal of subdivision activity have found it necessary to outline general principles of design and establish minimum standards over most of the physical features including street and block layout, rights of way, minimum pavement widths for public highways, grades and curves for streets and pedestrian ways, intersections of streets and alleys, parking strips, tree planting, street lighting, sidewalks, lot sizes, shapes, and orientation, and many other matters. Where tidelands and shorelands are involved, special principles and requirements need to be established.

In most of the recently enacted subdivision regulations, the developer is required to construct, according to city specifications, the necessary street pavements, curbs, and sidewalks, and install the necessary fire hydrants, water mains, sewer and drainage lines, street lighting, and certain other facilities as a condition of plat approval, or provide a performance bond to insure the construction or installation of those that may not have been completed at the time of the approval of the plat. As has been previously pointed out, depending upon the size of the development and local circumstances, it may be reasonable to require the developer to dedicate not only streets but also areas for parks, playgrounds, and sites for other public facilities and buildings.

Streets and Alleys. Design standards for streets, alleys, and sidewalks should be aimed at facilitating access, insuring freedom of circulation, and promoting safety and convenience. In general, the street pattern of the proposed subdivision should be required to conform to the most advantageous development of the adjoining areas and of the entire neighborhood. The regulations should require that rights of way be provided for all major and local streets, including utility and other street installations. Streets within the subdivision should follow the continuity of appropriate streets and arteries leading to or from the subdivision and, to the extent feasible, should follow contour lines. Street jogs and intersections, other than at right angles, should be avoided as much as possible to help minimize traffic hazards. Local streets should be designed to function properly in providing access to lots.

One of the main considerations in fixing the location of local streets should be to produce building lots of a desirable elevation, size, shape, and orientation, and make possible the best utilization of the lot area for providing adequate light and air and insuring vision clearance at intersections. In the location of major streets and the more important connecting local streets, special attention must be given to the traffic requirements of the entire community. The arrangement of the street pattern in any subdivision is of necessity governed in part by the size of tract which is developed, its topography, and its location with reference to local or neighborhood shopping centers.[41] If the subdivision constitutes a complete neighborhood unit, including its own shopping center, the street pattern should be so designed as to lead traffic toward this area as well as to the major streets and arteries leading to the city center. Minor or local streets should be laid out in such a way that their use for through traffic is discouraged.[42] Street names should be subject to approval of the planning agency and should not duplicate or be such as to be confused with the names of existing streets.

Alleys probably should be required in commercial or industrial zones except where the approving agency is satisfied that adequate space has been otherwise provided for off-street loading and unloading, parking, and other access and service demands of the development. Dead-end alleys should be avoided if possible, but where found necessary, adequate space for turn-around facilities should be assured.[43] Alley intersections should be designed with a view to furthering safe vehicular movement. In residential areas, alleys are not recommended except in the rear of lots fronting on major streets or where some special circumstance exists, as where it is necessary to eliminate garage driveways leading directly into heavy traffic, or where necessary to provide access to houses built on very steep slopes.

Subdivision regulations should be specific in fixing requirements of the minimum width of streets, the length of dead-end streets, the length and radii of cul-de-sacs, and the radii of curves, taking into account the probable flow of traffic and the demands for parking, access to buildings, space for utility lines, and the requirements for light and air.

Requirements for widths, grades, and curvatures of streets and alleys must conform to the city's street plan and official map if either

[41] Local Planning Administration, op. cit., p. 258.
[42] Lautner, op. cit., p. 54.
[43] Housing and Home Finance Agency, op. cit., p. 23.

or both have been adopted. It is the usual practice to include specific standards in the subdivision regulations also. Many cities have found appropriate widths for important streets carrying neighborhood traffic to be 60 feet between property lines with roadway width of 32 to 38 feet. Minor local streets whose primary function is providing access, space for utility lines, and space for light and air may require widths of only 50 feet with 26 feet reserved for roadway.[44] Alleys and service drives normally should have a minimum of 20 feet, with 16 feet of pavement. Varying widths for *cul-de-sacs* will be determined by the length and character of the development.

Allowable street curvature is usually established on the basis of the radius of the curve for the inner street line. A common requirement is 350 feet for a major street, 250 feet for a neighborhood street, and 100 feet for a local minor street. Grade requirements are determined to a large degree by the terrain. In order to insure drainage, a minimum gradient of 0.5 percent is normally required. The maximum grade allowed for major streets is usually from 5 to 7 percent. Minor streets and alleys may be permitted a grade of from 10 to 12 percent. In some cities the topography may be such that steeper grades must be allowed on minor streets.[45]

Sidewalks, Curbs, and Gutters. Design standards for sidewalks, curbs, and gutters are relatively simple and fairly well standardized. Location of sidewalks, gutters, and curbs is governed largely by the street pattern. Quite frequently all three are constructed at the time the street paving is put in. Often they are all covered by the same contract.[46] Curbs and gutters are usually built integral, utilizing a rounded junction to facilitate cleaning. Form and general appearance, as well as economy and serviceability, should be taken into account in fixing the height of the curb. Five-inch curbs are quite common, with 6 inches generally considered as the maximum. A standard provision is that curb radii at intersections shall be established at not less than 20 feet, with the requirement that property lines shall be adjusted accordingly.

Sidewalks in residential areas are normally required to be located in the right of way. The apportionment of width between the roadway and the sidewalk is a matter that must vary with local conditions. For example, snow and heavy rainfall must be considered. Local con-

---

[44] *Local Planning Administration*, op. cit., pp. 258–259.
[45] *Ibid.*, p. 259.
[46] William Bennett Munro, *Municipal Administration* (New York: The Macmillan Company, 1935), pp. 281–283.

ditions also govern the location from the property line. The width of the sidewalk varies with respect to the type of district. Sidewalks serving areas proposed for single dwelling units should be from 4 to 5 feet in width and should be at least 2 feet from the property line. Sidewalks serving proposed apartment houses or row housing should be at least 8 feet wide and located at least 2 feet from the property line. Sidewalks in proposed commercial shopping and retail areas should have widths of 12 feet or more.[47]

Blocks and Lots. Design standards seek to encourage blocks and lots which will provide the most and best building sites for the location. Requirements governing the length, width, and shape of blocks are contained in most subdivision regulations. Since blocks in each subdivision need to be planned to suit the topography and the character of the development, it is desirable that the regulations permit the developer a great deal of flexibility for this purpose. Both the block and lot size bear reasonable relationships to the planned use of the land and should be designed with this in mind. Quite different sized lots may be needed for residential areas from those required for commercial or industrial developments.

In general, the present trend is toward longer blocks.[48] Long blocks make possible lower initial costs of land and improvements used for streets by reducing the number of cross streets and consequently cutting down maintenance costs. The objection to long blocks has been that hydrants and trolley stops, generally located at street intersections, would be rather far from houses in the middle of the block. Long blocks would encourage rapid driving which would increase hazards to pedestrians at the crosswalks.[49] These objections have little weight in the face of good planning. Very short blocks require a greater portion of the land to be devoted to street purposes, but normally do not provide a corresponding gain in furthering the circulation of traffic.

As a general rule, the block should be as long as practical, taking into account the requirements for fire protection, control of traffic, the providing of public and private services, and access to the property. Normally, blocks are not more than 1200 feet long. Maximum lengths found in most regulations vary from 1000 to 1800 feet and minimum

[47] In wholesale and shipping districts, sidewalks of minimum width should be provided since a wide sidewalk in such districts may actually be a nuisance in that heavy merchandise being loaded or unloaded may have to be carried over it. *Ibid.*, p. 282.
[48] Housing and Home Finance Agency, *op. cit.*, p. 24.
[49] Lautner, *op. cit.*, pp. 141–142.

lengths vary from 400 to 500 feet. In very long blocks it may be desirable to require pedestrian crosswalks to provide circulation, or access to schools, playgrounds, shopping centers, transportation, and other facilities. However, some authorities oppose this, and recommend that crosswalks be used only where circulation cannot be provided by arrangement of the street system or by other methods.[50]

Blocks should be wide enough to include two tiers of lots and such alleys and easements as may be required by the regulations. The requirement of sufficient width to permit two tiers prevents the possibility of some houses in the block facing on one street while others face on another with the result that one man's house may face the back yard of a neighbor. The two-tier requirement also reduces the cost per house for utility installations. Since block width is dependent primarily on lot depth, it is usually desirable to specify that each lot shall have a minimum depth, for example, of 100 feet. Regulations should make allowances for variations when required by topography or when otherwise considered by the approving authority to be justified.

The proper design of lots is basic to good subdivision control, since the lot is the unit of the subdivision intended for sale or building purposes. As in the case of block design, it is desirable that the subdivision regulations permit a great deal of flexibility to the developer in establishing the width and depth of lots. Lot sizes and dimensions should be planned to suit best the topography of the tract, the character of the site, and the type of building most appropriate to the development and the community. Even though lot dimensions are required to conform to the zoning ordinance, it is nevertheless desirable to specify, in the subdivision regulations, minimum depth and width or minimum areas. Except where row or group houses are planned for the development, it is usually recommended that the minimum width for residential lots should be at least 60 or 70 feet at the building line.[51] Lots which are too narrow necessitate the construction of narrow houses, with poorly arranged living space, and with narrow side yards, which frequently do not provide adequate light and air. Where properties within the subdivision are reserved for commercial or industrial use, sufficient depth and width should be required to provide adequate off-street loading, unloading, and other service and parking facilities.

[50] Housing and Home Finance Agency, *loc. cit.*
[51] Local Planning Administration, *op. cit.*, p. 260.

In the case of lots for commercial and industrial use, such variations in demands exist that it may be found preferable to avoid platting individual lots in favor of an overall design of the land to be used for such purposes.[52] Where lots are developed for sale as business sites, a width of 50 feet should be satisfactory for most requirements. Efforts should be made to avoid double frontage and reverse frontage lots, except where this is necessary to separate residential properties from traffic arteries, or to overcome certain disadvantages resulting from topography, orientation, or other reason which the approving authority may consider justifiable. In such cases it may be desirable to require a nonaccess planting screen easement running along the line of the lots abutting the condition requiring the reverse fronting.[53] Lot lines, in so far as possible, should be at right angles to the street or along radial lines if the street is curved in order to prevent rectangular buildings from presenting an irregular or sawtooth appearance. Land should be subdivided in a manner so that each lot will have satisfactory access to an existing public street. Corner lots designed for residential use should be required to have extra width sufficient to permit appropriate building setback and orientation with respect to both streets.

Lot depth should be controlled to prevent lots from being excessively deep or excessively shallow. Usually, lots of 100 feet to 125 feet in depth are adequate for both single-family residences and commercial buildings. Where large apartment houses are planned, lots of greater depth may be required. Where excessively deep lots are permitted, there is danger that the rear yard may become cluttered with buildings and other structures which are unsightly or might create health or safety problems unless used for properly planned off-street parking.

If width provisions are established only by reference to the frontage, it is possible that some irregularly shaped lots may be too wide or too narrow farther back from the street. Although minimum area requirements will provide adequate controls in most instances, it may be advisable in some areas to specify average lot widths or a minimum width at the building line. Area requirements of lots for detached single residences should not be less than 6000 square feet and preferably 8500 square feet for ranch-type dwellings.

Public Sites and Open Spaces. Design standards with respect to

[52] Housing and Home Finance Agency, loc. cit.
[53] Ibid., p. 25.

required areas for parks and open spaces are concerned principally with securing areas of appropriate size and at appropriate locations. The amount of land which should be required to be set aside by the developer cannot be specified as an arbitrary percentage, although in some jurisdictions a standard of not less than 10 percent has been used as a guide.[54] Because of the importance of developing parks and recreation facilities as a part of an overall community plan, regulations should contemplate a money adjustment as well as a reservation and dedication of land. If, in order to carry out the comprehensive plan for recreational facilities, it is necessary for a particular subdivider to contribute a larger percentage of land than his fair share, he should be compensated therefor. On the other hand, if a subdivider is relieved of the requirement of reserving his fair share of land, he should contribute to the cost of acquiring land elsewhere.[55]

Other Requirements.   Many municipalities may find it advisable to include in the regulations requirements relating to a number of other miscellaneous matters including the granting of easements, the planting of trees, and street lighting. Easements for utilities should be required to be granted across lots or centered on rear or side lot lines. Such easements should be from 6 to 12 feet wide.[56] If a subdivision is traversed by a watercourse or drainage way, there should be required a storm water easement or drainage right of way conforming substantially to the lines of the watercourse, with such further width or construction as may be deemed adequate.[57] Tree planting requirements, if included in the regulations, should be made subject to a street-tree plan embodied in a municipal tree-planting ordinance. Appropriate standards should be applied to each proposed subdivision in accordance with the application of the ordinance to that portion of the municipality in which the subdivision is located. Street lights should be required to be of appropriate design as determined by the city engineer, and should be located at each intersection and on both sides of the street. Street lighting installations should be located in reference to the dimension of full-grown trees and in accordance with standards prescribed by the city engineer.

Use of Performance Standards.   Cities adopting subdivision reg-

---

[54] State of New York, Department of Commerce, *Control of Land Subdivision, op. cit.*, p. 25.

[55] See p. 455 for a discussion of the requirements for compulsory reservation or dedication.

[56] Housing and Home Finance Agency, *op. cit.*, p. 23.

[57] *Ibid., loc. cit.*

ulations for the first time or engaged in revising their regulations may profit by examining the possible use of "performance" standards for some requirements rather than the traditional "specification" standards. While the specification type of regulation specifies the exact width of roadway or right of way, the performance type of regulation would specify the required number of moving lanes, parking facilities, and pedestrian ways. Likewise, through performance standards, population density might be controlled by fixing overall density requirements such as a maximum of six dwelling units to the acre with a minimum of lot area of 4500 square feet.[58] Such a provision, while permitting a variety of lot sizes and shapes, would make it possible to work out a better design with relation to contours, vegetation, and other physical features.

In some respects the performance type of provision is more detailed than the traditional specification regulation. On the other hand, it may offer more in the way of flexibility. It is urged that, through the application of performance standards, it is possible to take advantage of the future as well as past and present technological developments, and thus give expression to the ever-changing and improving way of life.[59]

REQUIREMENTS FOR CONSTRUCTION AND INSTALLATION OF IMPROVEMENTS

Effective subdivision control involves more than merely establishing standards for the internal arrangement of streets, lots, and blocks in the subdivision. The installation of adequate utilities and appropriate street improvements is also essential to the development of stable and attractive neighborhoods.

The installation of adequate utilities and street improvements in a new subdivision has a direct economic benefit to all purchasers of lots and has a direct bearing on the costs to the municipality of street maintenance and of providing services.[60] On the other hand, it should be borne in mind that requiring overimprovements may possibly retard a development as much as underimprovement.

Communities have come to realize that the costs of these improve-

[58] K. Izumi, "Performance Standards for Residential Zoning and Subdivision Controls," *Journal of the Royal Architectural Institute of Canada*, Vol. 30, No. 12, pp. 347–370, 1953. Recent trends would seem to indicate an upgrading of these standards to four dwellings per acre.

[59] *Ibid.*, p. 347.

[60] Housing and Home Finance Agency, *op. cit.*, p. 28.

ments are legitimate expenses of subdividing to be borne by the sub-divider or developer.[61] In some instances, however, cities have found it to be sound policy to participate in the initial cost of installation or construction to provide improvements of a type or quality above minimum standards in order to save the city in costs of long-term maintenance. It would obviously be unreasonable to require a de-veloper to install unusually large water mains for supplying water to an adjoining area or to pay the cost of heavy-duty pavement on a street running through the subdivision that is designed to serve as a major artery.

Improvements to Be Installed. The kind of utilities and street improvements that should be required to be installed by the sub-divider must, of necessity, vary with the type of community, the character of the development, and many other factors. Improvements which are commonly required as a condition of plat recording include the paving of streets and alleys, the laying of sidewalks, curbs, and gutters; the providing of water and sewer mains and connecting lines; the installation of storm water drainage facilities; the placement of appropriate monuments; and the completion of satisfactory arrange-ments with telephone, light, power, and other service companies for furnishing needed utility services.

For most subdivisions, regulations should require as a condition of plat recording that streets be surfaced to their full width, that all curbs and gutters be installed, and that sidewalks be constructed on both sides of the street. Under certain circumstances exceptions may be justified. Also, subdividers should be required to place monuments at all corners, angle points, points of curves in the streets, and at such intermediate points as deemed necessary by the city engineer.[62] Monu-ments should be of appropriate material, size, and length, and in-stalled subject to the city engineer's approval. Since conditions vary so greatly with different types of developments, requirements for many improvements must be prepared in such a way as to permit considerable latitude to administrative officials in determining whether specific types of facilities and methods of construction com-ply with the general requirements of the regulations. The material,

---

[61] Southern Association of State Planning and Development Agencies, *A Guide to Subdivision Regulation*, 1953 (distributed by member agencies), p. 14. The report points out that "A recent survey made of 95 communities in the New York area reveals that 95 percent of the communities require the subdivider to grade streets; 86 percent require paving; 74 percent require curbs; 85 percent require gutters; 64 percent require water; 61 percent require sewers; and 82 percent require storm water drainage."

[62] Housing and Home Finance Agency, *op. cit.*, p. 27.

size, and placement of monuments should be a matter for official determination in each particular development.

The type of sewer and water facilities required may vary according to the availability of public water and sewer mains and conditions to be fulfilled to meet public health standards of the city, state, or other political unit exercising jurisdiction in the matter. The best location for sewer and storm drains as well as underground utilities may often be governed by topography or some special circumstances. Culverts and bridges, where needed to form an integral part of street grading or storm drainage or access to and between streets or across surface ditches and waterways, should be required improvements, to be constructed according to official approval. The erection of street signs should be subject to approval of the city engineer.

With respect to streets, sidewalks, curbs, and gutters, regulations may be much more specific in establishing minimum standards of width, thickness, construction, and location. Regulations should require the installation of street lights at street intersections on both sides of the street of appropriate design to be approved by the city engineer. The street light installations should be located with reference to the dimensions of full-grown trees. Tree planting standards, where adopted, should be made applicable to all proposed subdivisions in the area appropriately included in the street tree plan.[63]

Subject to minimum standards of materials, design, and construction appropriate to the locality, as established by the city engineer, the subdivider should be required to install a complete water distribution system with connections provided to each lot and with fire hydrants appropriately located. Only under most unusual circumstances should a plat be approved where water must be individually supplied, and only then if the supply system meets the standards of the state and local health authorities.

A complete sanitary sewer system should be installed if a public sewer main is reasonably accessible. Eight hundred feet is a distance sometimes used for purposes of determining the accessibility of the sewer main. In the event a public sewer main is not available within a reasonable distance, septic tanks may be permitted provided they meet the state and local health requirements. Generally speaking, septic tanks should not be used except where the average size of the

[63] Joshua H. Vogel, Ernest H. Campbell, and J. W. Arch Bollong, *Planting, Maintenance, and Removal of Trees from Streets*, Report No. 111, Bureau of Governmental Research and Services, University of Washington, June, 1950.

lot is one acre or more and where soil conditions have been found satisfactory by the city engineer and health officers.

In areas where water is individually supplied or where septic tanks are permitted for sewage disposal, it may be advisable to require covenants to be entered in the recorded plat and incorporated in each deed calling for the installation of individual water systems and individual sewage disposal systems meeting fully the requirements of the city, county, and state agencies having jurisdiction over health and engineering matters. These covenants should further provide that water connections be made to a public water system and sewerage connections be made to a public sewer system if and when public mains are extended sufficiently near to make connections feasible. Plat approval should not be given until certificates are provided from the appropriate administrative officials or agencies certifying that the installations are satisfactory.

In most jurisdictions it may not be found advisable to require the developer to install electric power and telephone utilities. Regulations should require, however, that the developer establish to the satisfaction of the approving authority that satisfactory arrangements have been worked out with public service companies or with municipal agencies making provision for adequate power and telephone service. Proper location of poles or underground lines is a matter falling within the design standards requirements.

The proper location of certain utilities, particularly those requiring poles and overhead wires, may require the dedication of easements. Often it is found more desirable to run the lines for electric light and telephone service along the rear of lots rather than in the front. Where alleys are provided, utility poles can be located in the alley rights of way. Otherwise, provision must be made for their location over or under part of the lot area by the dedication of an easement for this purpose. Usually easements will not be required for water or sewer lines which are laid in the street right of way. Where wire utilities are placed underground, they also may appropriately be placed in the street right of way. The cost of placing wire utilities underground is usually so high that, except in very high-class subdivisions, such a requirement is not justified. Regulations should specify the width of the easement. The dedication of an easement for a particular purpose does not necessarily dedicate it for any other public use.

Frequently, circumstances exist which necessitate that the subdivider acquire certain easements from other property owners in order to comply with the requirements of the subdivision regulation. This situation may present difficult problems if such persons refuse to grant the easements except at exorbitant prices. One solution may be through the use of the city's power of eminent domain. An example of this is to be found in an ordinance of Glendale, California, which requires that all sanitary sewers and drainage within the subdivision be laid out in a manner satisfactory to the city engineer. The ordinance provides, however, that if the city council finds that the subdivider is unable to obtain an easement, required pursuant to the code, at a reasonable price, the council may authorize the acquisition of the easement by eminent domain proceedings under which the subdivider pays the cost of acquisition.[64]

Timing and Financing of Improvement Installations. To the average lot buyer, the subdivision plat, no matter how well prepared, has little meaning until he can see the actual improvements which convert the raw land into lots suitable for habitation.[65] Since all improvements may not be required at the same time, a program should be worked out so that those most essential be given first priority in installation. Certain improvements such as grading, road surfacing, and storm drainage are essential to transforming raw acreage into lots which are suitable for building and for habitation. Other improvements such as water and sewer mains, which may eventually be needed for occupation, are not necessarily needed at the time of building. Where mains and utility lines are to be installed in the streets, however, such installations must be coördinated with other street improvements.

With respect to the timely installation of public improvements, it is important to bear in mind that each particular area should be developed in so far as possible with relationship to the development of adjacent areas. For this reason, when a subdivision is developed in units, it may be advisable to delay certain improvements in particular units until the improvement can be made for the subdivision as a whole. If such delays are permitted, the city should be protected by requiring the posting of performance bonds.

The timely installation of improvements operates to the benefit of the purchaser, the subdivider, and the community. The installation of improvements prior to plat recording is an advantage to the pur-

[64] *Municipal Ordinance Review*, Vol. 9, No. 11, p. 44, November, 1956.
[65] Aguar, *op. cit.*, p. 102.

chaser since the costs of utilities and improvements are all included in the single purchase price of the lot. The inclusion of improvement costs in the price of the lots results also in definite benefits to the subdivider because of the improved saleability of his lots. From the standpoint of the public interest, requiring the installation and construction of utilities and other improvements to be completed before lots are offered for sale places a very definite restraint upon the tendency toward unjustified land speculation resulting in premature or excessive subdivision. Realtors and investors are not likely to show great interest in developing large tracts at high costs unless a reasonable market seems assured. On the other hand, it is important that care be exercised to insure that requirements for improvements are not set so high that they will retard the proper development of the community. By insisting upon the marketing of an improved, usable lot, the subdivision development tends to relate itself more directly to the needs and demands of lots for habitation.

Equitable administration of subdivision regulations requires that a sound policy be adopted with respect to the extent to which required improvements are financed by public or private funds. As has already been pointed out, there are occasions when good community planning dictates that recreational and other public facilities developed in connection with a subdivision should be designed to serve other parts of the community as well.[66] Where this is necessary, it is only fair and reasonable that the community as a whole should provide part of the cost, either by performing part of the work or by reimbursing the developer for part of his expense. The proper allocation of costs should be worked out, if possible, in conferences prior to filing the preliminary plat.[67] Where, on the other hand, because of the small size of the subdivision, or for other reasons, it does not appear advisable to have the subdivider set aside areas within the subdivision for community facilities, a definite policy should be adopted for determining his fair share of the contribution to finance facilities located outside the tract which will be provided at public expense to serve the subdivision inhabitants.[68]

Performance and Maintenance Bonds. There is always the pos-

[66] See "Methods of Financing Street Improvements in New Subdivisions," *Twenty-Third Annual Report of the Regional Plan Association* (New York: Regional Plan Association, December, 1952), p. 14.

[67] *Ibid.*

[68] For a detailed study of practices and policies, see J. Ross McKeever, *Utilities and Facilities for New Residential Development, A Survey of Municipal Policy* (Washington, D.C.: Urban Land Institute, 1955), Technical Bulletin No. 27.

sibility that through inadvertence certain improvements may not be made or may be improperly installed. This places the municipality in the position of either accepting the improvements as installed or of refusing to approve the plat. The first course results in the development of a substandard subdivision and defeats the purpose of subdivision control. The other course may result in considerable loss to the subdivider. This problem may, in some instances, be avoided and the interests of the public protected through the requirement of performance and maintenance bonds.

Sometimes also there are cases in which it may neither be necessary nor even desirable that certain improvements be completed before final approval of the plat. Where this is so, compliance with the regulations may be satisfied by the acceptance by the municipality of adequate performance bonds guaranteeing that the improvements will be completed. The acceptance of performance bonds prior to complete installation will reduce the financial burden upon the developer.

In addition to demanding performance bonds, municipalities may, as a further precaution, find it advisable to require the developer to provide a maintenance bond. This bond should be in effect for a year or for some other stated period and guarantee that the work was satisfactory and that the standards prescribed in the regulations have been fulfilled. In the event that improvements have not been installed in accordance with the terms of the performance and maintenance bonds, the surety will guarantee to the municipality the reasonable costs resulting from defective installations. The purpose of such bonds is to insure that the subdivision developer will meet the requirements of the subdivision regulations with respect to the installation and construction of improvements.[69]

THE ADMINISTRATION OF SUBDIVISION REGULATIONS

ADMINISTRATIVE SUPERVISION

Subdivision regulations, no matter how well drafted, are effective as a tool of land-use control only if well administered and properly enforced. The administration of subdivision regulations necessitates the participation of more governmental agencies than is required in the administration of the zoning ordinance and most other types of

[69] Harvey E. Bernstein, "Use of Performance Bonds and Maintenance Bonds," *New Jersey Municipalities*, Vol. XXX, No. 9, pp. 21–22, December, 1953.

public regulations. Effective subdivision control requires that direct and continuous supervision be maintained from the beginning of the project development until final approval for plat recording. It is important, therefore, that administrative procedures be carefully worked out in order that requirements will be thoroughly understood, that responsibility for supervision will be fixed and definite, and that adequate machinery for coördinating supervisory responsibilities will be established.

Agencies Concerned with Administrative Supervision. Although it appears logical for the planning agency to assume primary responsibility for the administration of the subdivision regulations, a number of other agencies are concerned with specific matters of subdivision control. The details of subdivision plans must be checked by many officials of state and local government to insure compliance with all legal requirements. For example, the plans of the subdivider must be examined by the city engineer and sometimes by the county engineer to determine the feasibility of plans for providing water supply, sewage disposal, drainage facilities, and other improvements which may be required to be installed as a condition of plat approval. The health officials may also be called upon to pass upon the question of whether or not the plans for these improvements meet state and local health standards. Fire and police departments have a responsibility to examine the proposed development to determine if it conforms to requirements for public safety. Such questions as whether streets and utilities are laid out in a manner to facilitate the movement of fire equipment, or provide adequate water supply at proper pressures, are matters to be cleared with the fire department. Likewise, the plan should pass under the scrutiny of the police department for determining whether the proposed design is such as to facilitate the movement of traffic and provide adequate police protection and traffic control.

Subdivision plans should also be reviewed by school authorities and park and recreation officials. The development and stability of a residential neighborhood is very directly related to the availability of schools and recreational facilities. The school board and park and recreation officials should be called into consultation in order to insure that the proposed development fits into the educational and recreational planning of the neighborhood and the community.

The availability and accessibility of transportation and transit facilities are other matters of great importance to be considered in planning the subdivision development. Subdivisions at scattered or isolated locations may throw heavy transportation burdens upon the city or result in inadequate service to residents of the subdivision. The availability of service is a matter to be worked out with transit officials.

In addition to the matter of checking plans with the administrative officials concerned with functional programs, it is also essential that plans be checked with fiscal officers of the city, county, school districts, and other jurisdictions that may exercise taxing authority or budgetary supervision over the area. Where certain costs of proposed improvements are to be borne by the municipality or some other unit of government, it is necessary that financial arrangements be worked out in advance to insure that the proposed capital improvements can be financed within the bonded debt limits of the municipality or of the particular locality against which the cost may be assessed. Under certain circumstances, other officials may be called upon to give clearance on technical matters. For example, the county auditor or clerk and the city attorney may have to pass upon the question of whether legal descriptions comply with requirements established by state and local authority for recording the plat.

Clearance with federal officials under certain circumstances may be of importance. Under the National Housing Act of 1934, the federal government provides mortgage insurance to private lending institutions for loans on privately owned homes built by private builders. Under the provisions of the Housing Act of 1949 and the Housing Act of 1954, certain financial assistance is available to local public agencies for the purpose of slum clearance and urban redevelopment. In the event that provisions of any one of these acts are invoked, it is necessary that subdivision regulations conform to the standards established by the Federal Housing Administration or by the Housing and Home Finance Agency.

Coördinating Role of Planning Agency. The planning agency occupies a dual role in the administration of subdivision regulations. It has the primary responsibility of checking all subdivision proposals to determine their consistency to the comprehensive plan, and that the plans of each particular subdivision are properly related to other development programs, including plans for contiguous areas under existing plats. In addition, the planning agency has the responsibility of coördinating the supervisory activities of all other agencies participating in the administration of the subdivision regulations. In communities in which there is a considerable amount of subdivision activity, the planning agency should designate some member of the staff as subdivision administrator. This has the value of fixing responsible authority within the planning agency as well as providing more opportunity for specialization, thus contributing to efficiency of administration.

One of the principal duties of the administrator should be to coordinate the actions required to be taken by the different officials and agencies. If the subdivider is required to arrange his own contacts and scheduling with every supervisory official, confusion is likely to be the result. Where review and certification by particular officials is necessary, it should be the duty of the administrator to make certain that these are accomplished at the appropriate time. This means that the subdivider should have to deal only with the administrator, who, in turn, would contact all the other officials who are required to pass upon specific parts of the plan. The duties of the administrator would also include the notification to the planning commission and other appropriate persons of any pending hearings on matters on which their approval is required. Thus, at the appropriate time, the administrator would request the city engineer to inspect and approve water and sewer system installations, and the park and recreational authorities to determine if the need for parks and open spaces for recreational facilities has been met. The routing of plats, maps, documents, and other data necessary to enable the appropriate official to review the proposed plans should be handled by the administrator.

Because of the numerous administrative tasks involved in coördinating the supervisory functions of so many agencies, it may be urged that these duties should be given to some other agency. It has been pointed out that the administrative details in supervising subdivision regulations are time-consuming and may tend to divert the planning agency from its continuing function of comprehensive planning. While this is admittedly a danger, the fact that subdivision control is so intimately related to planning would mean that any other agency which undertook to administer the regulations effectively would have to acquire most of the knowledge which is possessed by the planning agency. Therefore, the designation of some other agency would in most cases simply involve a duplication of effort in the planning field.

PROCEDURE FOR SECURING APPROVAL FOR PLAT RECORDING

Effective subdivision control is predicated upon sound administrative procedure for securing approval for plat recording. Procedures which are logical, reasonable, and comprehensible simplify the problems of the subdivider and help to promote better public relations and public acceptance of subdivision control. Procedure for securing approval for plat recording falls into three major stages: (1) preapplication procedure, (2) procedure for conditional approval of the preliminary plat, and (3) procedure for approval of the final plat.[70] Until all procedural requirements have been satisfied, the final plat may not be recorded and lots may not be sold.

Preapplication Procedure. The purpose of the "preapplication procedure" is to afford the subdivider an opportunity to confer with the planning agency and other municipal officials on proposed plans in advance of preparing and filing the preliminary plat and before formal application is made for its approval. These conferences enable the subdivider to inform himself of the nature of the requirements that would need to be met and thereby save himself time and money in preparing his plan of development. The preapplication stage does not require a formal application or the payment of a filing fee.

In preparation for the preapplication conferences, the subdivider should prepare a simple preliminary plan in sketch form for the purpose of securing advice and assistance. The preliminary plan and program of the subdivider should be reviewed by the planning commission to determine how they relate to the comprehensive plan, design standards, and improvement requirements. The results of this review should then be discussed with the subdivider, who should be informed of the changes which would be needed to comply with the regulations. Review should be concerned with such matters as site, suitability, development opportunities, arrangements for financing, and opportunities for marketing as well as design requirements and the requirements and costs of installing public improvements.

In addition to the simple sketch, the subdivider should provide a location map showing the relationship of the proposed subdivision to existing community facilities which would serve it or have an influence on its development. These facilities would include, among others, main traffic arteries, transportation lines, schools, churches, libraries, hospitals, parks and playgrounds, shopping centers, and principal places of employment.[71] Supplementary information should be supplied as necessary to outline or describe the existing conditions

[70] Housing and Home Finance Agency, *op. cit.*, pp. 12–16.
[71] *Ibid.*, pp. 30–31.

of the site and the proposed development including data on existing and proposed protective covenants.

In the event that the subdivider has not made financial arrangements for development, it should be suggested to him that he secure rather firm commitments from mortgage companies and other lending institutions. Likewise, his attention should be called to the importance of thoroughly investigating market demands and other matters influencing the economic feasibility of the proposed project. Under certain circumstances the developer may well be advised to engage the services of a planning specialist who has had experience in working out subdivision plans and problems. In setting up this preapplication procedure, it is not intended to place government in the role of designer. The developer should be free to develop the subdivision according to the style and character of his own design just as long as the plat's improvements comply with minimum standards for protecting the interests of the neighborhood and the community.

As a rule, preapplication conferences are held with staff members, particularly with the subdivision administrator if one has been appointed, rather than with members of the planning commission. Normally, preapplication conferences should not be required, but should be an informal service made available to the subdivider in the interest of saving him time and money and, at the same time, in promoting a better understanding of the planning objectives of the community, thus avoiding misunderstandings at a later stage of the proceedings. During the preapplication conferences, it may be advisable for the developer to consult not only with the planning agency, but also with the city engineer and other officials who will be called upon to pass upon final plans and supervise surveys, construction, and performance for streets, utilities, and other improvements.

The Preliminary Plat.   After understandings have been reached during the preapplication conferences, the subdivider will be required to prepare and submit a preliminary plat, together with such other plans and supplementary data as may be required to show the character of the proposed subdivision development. This preliminary plat will be prepared with as many copies as may be required by the procedure established by the municipality. Normally, it is presented to the planning agency if that agency serves as the approving authority. Under some procedures, it may be found preferable to have the application and accompanying plat filed with the mayor or chief administrative officer, who would then transmit copies to the planning agency, the city engineer, the health officer, building inspector, and others who would be required to make recommendations to the approving authority.

The subdivision regulations usually provide that within a specified number of days (30 days is commonly specified), the approving authority shall arrange for a hearing on the preliminary plat for which notice is to be given to the developer, the owners of property in the adjacent area, and such other persons as may be thought to have an interest in the proposed development. Within the time between the filing of the preliminary plat and the date of the hearing, the proposed plans should be reviewed by the planning agency, the city engineer, and such other city officials as may be concerned with ascertaining compliance with the requirements. After the hearing, the developer may be required to make certain changes which seem desirable as a result of the hearing. After such changes are made, and if the preliminary plat then appears to meet the requirements of the subdivision regulations, conditional approval will be given by the approving authority.[72] The giving of conditional approval does not constitute a final acceptance of the plat.

After conditional approval has been given to the preliminary plat, the usual procedure is for the approving authority to return one copy of the approved plat to the developer and transmit one copy to the city engineer, the health officer, building inspector, and other officials who may be in charge of supervision of street improvements, water and sewer facilities, and building requirements. The subdivider may then make arrangements for the necessary permits for the construction and for the necessary inspection as the work progresses. It is accepted practice to grant conditional approval, subject to a time limit that the final plat must be filed within a period of one year or two years or some other specified time. After the necessary permits are obtained, the subdivider may proceed to stake out the tract and install or construct the improvements which are required to be made. After this work has been done, the subdivider will prepare the final plat, which, with such other data as may be required, will be submitted with his application for approval.

The preliminary plat is intended to provide sufficient data and information to enable the approving agency to give tentative approval or to suggest changes in the proposed development. The preliminary

[72] Some regulations refer to this as tentative approval or preliminary approval.

plat should contain or be accompanied by data sufficient to supply general information with respect to the proposed type of development, the number of lots, the typical lot width and depth, price range, recreational areas, proposed utilities, street improvements, location of transportation lines, shopping centers, schools, churches, hospitals, and all such additional information as is necessary to present a complete picture of both existing facilities and proposed developments. The data for conditional approval should include topographical information showing boundary lines, easements, streets on and adjacent to the tract, utilities on and adjacent to the tract, ground elevation, subsurface conditions on the tract, and such other conditions both on and adjacent to the tract as have a bearing upon the suitability of the proposed development. The data should also show the zoning on and adjacent to the tract and any proposed public improvements on or near the tract such as highways which are being planned by public authorities for the future. The accompanying data should also indicate with what protective covenants the subdivider proposes to regulate land use in the subdivision.[73] In addition to presenting general information about the tract, the preliminary plat should show some rather specific details with respect to names of streets, cross sections and profiles showing widths and grades of streets, location and widths of rights of way, location of utilities, lot lines, lot numbers and block numbers, sites to be reserved or dedicated for parks, playgrounds, or public uses, sites for shopping centers, churches, industry, and other types of uses, and minimum building setback lines. The plat should show the title under which the proposed subdivision is to be recorded, the scale, north arrow, the date, the date of survey, a certification of a registered civil engineer or surveyor, proposed restrictions and dedications, and the signatures of owners of the tract.[74]

The Final Plat. The final plat which is submitted for approval after completion of all improvements required by conditional approval of the approving authority must show all information necessary for recording. The final plat must conform substantially to the preliminary plat as approved. Most regulations, however, permit the subdivider to apply for final approval of only that portion of the approved preliminary plat which he may propose to record and develop at a particular time. Permitting the developer to record parts

[73] Housing and Home Finance Agency, op. cit., p. 32.
[74] Housing and Home Finance Agency, op. cit., pp. 30–33.

of the plat, as those portions of the subdivision are developed and offered for sale, makes it possible for him to reduce the amount of investment and carrying charges. Compliance with the specified time within which the plat must be filed is usually satisfied by the approval and recording of the improved part of the subdivision. The filing of the final plat must be accompanied by certificates from the appropriate administrative officials certifying that those improvements, subject to their supervision, have been constructed or installed according to the standards prescribed in the subdivision regulations and other codes subject to their jurisdiction. In lieu of actual construction and installation, most jurisdictions permit the subdivider to file a bond to guarantee performance within a specified time.

After the final plat and all supporting plans and data, including the required certificates, covenants in the form to be recorded, and performance and maintenance bonds have been provided, the approving authority will give its approval to the final plat if it conforms to the preliminary plat as conditionally approved. The approved final plat is then given to the subdivider who may then record it with the county auditor or recording authority charged with this responsibility. Sales of lots may then be made by the subdivider within that part of the subdivision included in the recorded plat. Although dedication of land for public use may be required, the approval of the plat does not constitute an acceptance by the public. Dedications in the plat are accepted only as a result of action by the municipal legislative body.

Under the suggested land subdivision regulations outlined by the Housing and Home Finance Agency, the final plat should show the following:

a. Primary control points, approved by the City Engineer, or descriptions and "ties" to such control points, to which all dimensions, angles, bearings, and similar data on the plat shall be referred.
b. Tract boundary lines, right-of-way lines of streets, easements and other rights of way, and property lines of residential lots and other sites; with accurate dimensions, bearings or deflection angles, and radii, arcs, and central angles of all curves.
c. Name and right-of-way width of each street or other right of way.
d. Location, dimensions, and purpose of any easements.
e. Number to identify each lot or site.
f Purpose for which sites, other than residential lots, are dedicated or reserved.

g. Minimum building setback line on all lots and other sites.
h. Location and description of monuments.
i. Names of record owners of adjoining unplatted land.
j. Reference to recorded subdivision plats of adjoining platted land by record name, date, and number.
k. Certification by surveyor or engineer certifying to accuracy of survey and plat.
l. Certification of title showing that applicant is the land owner.
m. Statement by owner dedicating streets, rights-of-way, and any sites for public uses.
n. Title, scale, north arrow, and date.[75]

Fees and Costs. It is common practice to require the subdivider to pay certain fees and costs at the time of filing the preliminary plat. A wide variation is to be found in the provisions of the various jurisdictions as to the amount of these fees and costs and in the manner in which they are to be computed. Costs to the subdivider customarily include filing fees, charges for checking data, and expenses incurred in advertising and recording fees.[76] Fees may be established on the basis of a flat sum or on the basis of so much per acre, per square foot, or per lot. If special fees are levied to provide for recreational needs in whole or in part outside the subdivision, it appears reasonable to fix the amount of the fee according to the number of lots in the tract.

Because of the great variation in costs of checking plats, particularly the survey calculations, some jurisdictions have not found it advisable to establish fixed fees for the cost of checking, but have provided that such costs shall be estimated by the engineer and the amount thereof deposited in the appropriate fund by the subdivider. If, during the progress of the work, it appears the cost will exceed the amount deposited, the subdivider may be required to deposit an additional amount to cover the costs. Some jurisdictions are much more specific in fixing the charges to be collected. For example, the subdivision regulations for Kitsap County, Washington, contain the following paragraphs:

The final plat shall be accompanied by a check payable to the County Auditor to the full amount of filing fees, and actual expenses of the County Engineer. The amount of such check will be determined by the County Auditor and by the County Engineer. A certified check of $25.00 payable to the County Auditor shall accompany the first sketch as a

[75] Housing and Home Finance Agency, op. cit., pp. 33–34.
[76] Lautner, op. cit., p. 37.

guarantee of the expenses of the County Engineer. If the Engineer estimates the expenses are to be more than $25.00, a larger check shall be given.

The filing fees are twenty-five cents for each inclosure and $1.00 for each description, dedication and acknowledgment. The County Engineer shall charge $1.50 per hour for time spent in checking over the plat or for looking over the property. Should a survey be necessary to check the plat, $30.00 shall be charged for each day of such survey. The County Agricultural Agent shall charge $1.50 per hour for time spent in classification of the soil of said plat, and the amount of such charge shall be included in the check to the County Auditor for filing fees and engineering expenses. Should property be under the Torrens Act, an additional charge of $1.50 shall be collected for each transfer certificate.

ENFORCEMENT OF THE SUBDIVISION REGULATIONS

If careful and continuous supervision is maintained over platted subdivision projects during the course of their development, the enforcement of compliance with the regulation requirements presents few difficulties. The major problems arise in preventing evasion of the subdivision regulations by subdividers who seek to sell their lots by metes and bounds descriptions or by resorting to other devices to circumvent subdivision control. Unless adequate means are provided to thwart such evasions, comprehensive land-use planning may be defeated.

Methods of Enforcement. The principal means of enforcement of subdivision regulations results from the authority given to municipalities to refuse to grant approval to proposed plats. Approval is prerequisite to recording the plat. Under most subdivision laws, the sale of any lot, by reference to or other use of a subdivision map or plan before such map or plan has been approved and recorded, is also made a criminal offense. The advantages of the seller's being able to transfer property by reference to a recorded plat are great and usually provide sufficient inducement for him to comply with the requirements of the subdivision law. Under certain circumstances, however, the costs of utility installation and other improvements may be so high as to induce a land owner to forego the plat device and to attempt to make sales by metes and bounds description.

In order to forestall such practices, some jurisdictions have imposed penalties of fines and imprisonment for failure to comply with the subdivision regulations. Some have conferred power upon the municipality to enjoin the sale.[77] However, legal as well as policy questions may be raised with respect to provisions which attempt to prohibit the conveyance of lots by metes and bounds description.

Another method which has been suggested for preventing evasion of subdivision control is to require higher fees for recording deeds where the property is sold by metes and bounds than are charged in the case of deeds to property sold by reference to recorded plats. Since it is difficult to justify such a distinction, the validity of such provisions may be open to question. Other possibilities of control are through ordinances under which the city may (1) refuse to accept public streets that are not part of an approved and recorded plat, (2) prohibit municipal officials from the opening, grading, paving, cleaning, or lighting of nonpublic streets, or (3) deny sewer or other utility connections with mains or lines operated by the city unless the lot is on a recorded plat. Some regulations do not permit the granting of building permits on new lots which do not abut on a public street.[78] If such enforcement provisions are adopted, variances should be authorized for property which does not abut on a public street.

Such enforcement provisions are most drastic in their effect and should be carefully studied before they are included in the ordinance. If the public is not fully aware of the existence of such penalties, serious hardship and financial loss may result to persons who have purchased in good faith. The penalties are thus likely to fall on the unwary purchaser rather than upon the subdivider.[79] Furthermore, they may have the effect of discrediting subdivision control and making the citizens unsympathetic with subdivision control objectives. Obviously, conveyance by metes and bounds should not be prohibited altogether since under certain circumstances any other means of conveyance might not be practical, as for example, in the conveyance of a corner strip from a particular lot or in the transfer of some irregularly shaped plot which had always been described by metes and bounds.

In most jurisdictions the enforcement difficulties have arisen, not

[77] Wirtz, op. cit., p. 561.

[78] The law on this means of enforcement is not judicially settled. Such provisions have been held invalid by courts in Illinois in *People ex rel. Schimpff v. Norvell*, 368 Ill. 325, 13 N.E. (2d) 960 (1938) and in Ohio in *State ex rel. Weber v. Vajner*, 92 Ohio App. 233, 108 N.E. (2d) 569 (1952), but sustained in California in *Mitchell v. Morris*, 94 Cal. App. (2d) 446, 210 P. (2d) 857 (1949) and in *Brous v. Smith*, 304 N.Y. 164, 106 N.E. (2d) 503 (1952).

[79] To minimize this danger, it has been suggested that regulations require the seller to notify prospective purchasers of the status of the street providing access to the lot. See Reps, op. cit., p. 134.

because of the inadequacy of penalties, but rather because of the indefiniteness with which those acts are defined that constitute violations. The standard provision in most of the states defines a violation to be one in which a lot is sold by reference to an unapproved plat, with the added provision that a sale by metes and bounds will not avoid the penalty. Where this is the only violation defined, it is often found difficult to prove that the subdivider ever displayed or made use of a plat in making the sale. Furthermore, the violation cannot be construed to occur under circumstances where the subdivider shows the buyer over the subdivision and concludes a sale without ever having prepared a plat.

Replatting of Old Subdivisions.   One of the indirect consequences of premature or excessive subdivision is that developers may find that by the time that a demand has developed for their properties, material changes have been made in the subdivision regulations or the zoning ordinance upgrading the requirements which must be met as a condition of granting a building permit. For example, amendments to the regulations or ordinance may be enacted, raising the minimum lot size for single-family residences or requiring the developer to install certain utilities and make other improvements at his own expense which were not required at the time the plat was approved. When this situation arises, legal and policy questions are presented as to what rights are conferred or should be conferred as a result of plat approval.

From the policy side, a decision needs to be made as to whether a developer who holds title to an undeveloped tract must resubdivide and sell in accordance with the higher standards or whether he shall be permitted to sell in accordance with the regulations which were in effect at the time the plat was approved. Except in cases of unusual hardship, it would appear that the declared public policy to raise standards as represented by the amended acts should not be thwarted by the fact of earlier plat approval.[80]

In the event that the policy decision is in favor of requiring compliance with the currently effective regulations, legal machinery must be devised for insuring compliance. No clear-cut guidelines appear to have been established by the courts. However, several possibilities would seem to be suggested. One device would be simply to deny a

[80] What would constitute unusual hardship would have to be determined by the facts of each particular case. It would seem, for example, that building permits should be granted for a lot below minimum size if held in single ownership or so located that resubdivision is impractical.

building permit to any person who sought to build on a lot of substandard size. However, such a provision might have the effect of
penalizing the unsuspecting purchaser who bought innocently and
in good faith. If this method were employed, certain exceptions would
need to be provided to authorize sales for purposes other than building. Another means might be to require the developer to replat the
land in accordance with the new regulations and secure approval and
record the plat under the provisions of the amended law. While this
procedure may be workable where all or most of the property remains in the hands of the developer, it would not appear to be an
adequate solution if a considerable part or miscellaneous portions of
the platted area had been sold. Another possible approach would be
to provide that deeds to lots in a plat which did not meet the requirements of the currently effective zoning ordinances and platting
regulations could not be recorded. This device would compel the
developer to meet the new requirements before he could dispose of
his holdings. While such a provision would seem to provide a workable means of accomplishing the policy objectives established by the
later ordinance, it should, if used, be surrounded by adequate safeguards to provide relief in hardship cases. Until the legality of such
devices has been reviewed by the courts, the extent of their usefulness
is attended with considerable uncertainty.

Relief of Persons Adversely Affected.   Since subdivision regulations ordinarily provide considerable elasticity for adapting requirements to the special characteristics of the proposed development, the
need for granting relief to persons adversely affected is usually not as
great as in the administration of the zoning ordinance. Subdivision
requirements are based upon minimum standards which are deemed
to be necessary to protect the public interest. If the subdivider meets
these minimum requirements (and other requirements imposed by
law), he may develop his property in any manner he chooses without
control or direction by government authority. Nevertheless, unusual
and exceptional circumstances sometimes arise which justify the
granting of a variance from the standards established.

A departure from applying the minimum standards should be permitted only where it is clear that strict observance would result in
undue hardship and that the granting of the variation or exception
would not nullify the objectives of the comprehensive plan or vitally
affect the spirit of the subdivision regulations.[81] Under no circum-

[81] Housing and Home Finance Agency, *op. cit.*, p. 35.

stances should a departure from the regulations be granted merely for the convenience of the subdivider or as a matter of expediency. In order to justify the granting of a variance, the approving authority should find (1) that there exist special circumstances or conditions affecting the applicant's property, (2) that the variance is necessary for the preservation and enjoyment of a substantial property right of the applicant, and (3) that the granting of the variance would not be materially detrimental to the public welfare or injurious to the adjacent property.

In most jurisdictions the granting of variances from subdivision regulations is made the responsibility of the planning commission. If, however, the regulations are established by ordinance, or if the legislative body is the approving authority, it may be advisable to provide for the granting of variances by the legislative body upon the recommendation of the planning agency. When a variation is requested, it is desirable that the application be made at the time of filing the preliminary plat in order that the matter may be reviewed by the public officials at that time and considered at the public hearing when the proposed plan of development is before the approving authority for conditional approval. Since, however, in some instances the justification for a variance may not be apparent at the time of filing the application for approval of the preliminary plat, provision should be made in the regulations for applying for appropriate relief after conditional approval has been given. If the application for a variance is granted by the approving authority, an order should be issued, to become a part of the conditional approval of the preliminary plat, specifying the nature and extent of the modification.

Subdivision regulations do not ordinarily contain provisions establishing appeal procedure. Most jurisdictions have deemed this unnecessary since the right of appeal to the courts to enjoin the unauthorized acts of public officials and to protect against the invasion of any other constitutional or statutory rights is well established by general law. Furthermore, by the very nature of subdivision control procedure, most of the controversies and disputes which arise are adjusted during the course of the preliminary negotiations and the approval procedure.[82] Unlike the provisions of the zoning ordinance, which are definite and inflexible in character, subdivision regulations are designed to be elastic, permitting the developer to exercise wide

[82] Lautner, op. cit., p. 30.

discretion as long as minimum standards are met. Because of this characteristic of the subdivision regulations, a special Board of Adjustment or Board of Appeals is not considered to be a necessary part of the administrative machinery for subdivision control.[83]

[83] See Chap. 8 for the use of the board of adjustment in zoning matters.

CHAPTER 10

Urban Redevelopment and Urban Renewal

REPLANNING OUR URBAN COMMUNITIES THROUGH REDEVELOPMENT AND RENEWAL

Virtually every major city in the United States is faced with serious problems of dealing with the physical decay which is taking place in many of the older residential, commercial, and industrial areas. The deterioration of certain of the once fine residential districts and the development of slums and blighted areas surrounding the central business district have become characteristic of our urban growth. Elements of deterioration are also present in some open spaces where dead or arrested subdivisions have had their decaying effects, as well as having thwarted plans for carrying out a sound program of land utilization.

The social, economic, and political consequences of slums and deteriorated commercial and industrial areas have focused attention upon the need to combat the causes of decay and to replan and re-build certain sections on a rather large scale. Many communities have made serious efforts to meet this need through both private and public redevelopment efforts. Actually the redevelopment process has been going on continuously in almost every community. As cities have grown, we have witnessed residential areas replace farms, busi-ness districts replace residential areas, and factories and office build-ings replace shops. Generally, these changes have been in response to demands for more intensive land use. Motivation has usually been economic, and social considerations have been incidental or non-existent. For the most part, the redevelopment that has taken place has been sporadic, unorganized, and without reference to any comprehensive plan of community development. As of today, the fight against obsolescence has been a losing battle, as properties have tended to depreciate much more rapidly than they are rehabilitated.

URBAN REDEVELOPMENT AND URBAN RENEWAL AS A PUBLIC RESPONSIBILITY

Although there has been much concern over slums and deterioration for many years, it has only been within the past two decades that the public has become sufficiently aware of the serious consequences of urban blight to demand that governmental action be taken to prevent its spread and to redevelop those areas which are badly deteriorated. States have been slow to grant local governments adequate power to combat the causes of urban decay. As of May 1, 1957, 38 states authorized urban redevelopment or urban renewal.[1] Enabling legislation enacted in Florida and South Carolina was declared unconstitutional, and a Louisiana statute was held to be inadequate for undertaking urban renewal programs.

Urban Redevelopment and Urban Renewal Distinguished. The mechanisms which are currently being employed by cities in the United States to restore badly deteriorated areas to properly planned and economically sound conditions and the actions which are taken to arrest the processes of urban decay are customarily designated by the terms "urban redevelopment" and "urban renewal." A clear distinction between the two terms is not always made. The term "urban renewal" is of more recent origin and includes within its scope the concept of urban redevelopment. Since, however, "urban redevelopment" has, by longer usage, come to have a rather specific meaning, its use is not entirely replaced by the coinage of the broader term of "urban renewal."

In a general sense, "urban redevelopment" is used to describe any replacement of old structures with new ones. Quite frequently urban redevelopment is thought of as synonymous with slum clearance and rehousing. The term, however, is much broader and may involve com-

[1] States which did not have urban redevelopment or urban renewal enabling legislation as of May 1, 1957 are Florida, Idaho, Mississippi, Montana, New Mexico, South Carolina, Texas, Utah, Vermont, and Wyoming. Proposals for enabling legislation were under consideration in New Mexico, Texas, and Vermont. During the 1957 legislative sessions, New Jersey, North Carolina and West Virginia broadened existing urban redevelopment legislation to embrace urban renewal.

plete redevelopment of areas for commerce, industry, express ways, institutional or public recreation, and other purposes without any reference to housing. Likewise, urban redevelopment may be concerned with rehabilitation or development of open spaces as in the case of dead or arrested subdivisions where no slum clearance or demolition of any kind is involved. By common usage and accepted meaning, urban redevelopment has come to be applied more specifically to any organized effort by a public authority directed to the task of reclaiming or restoring any deteriorated area of substantial size which, under existing conditions, cannot be carried out by the individual owners.

The principal steps involved in an urban redevelopment program have beeen outlined in a bulletin of the Urban Land Institute [2] as follows:

1. Selection and delimitation of an area within which deterioration has progressed so far that complete rebuilding is the only practicable remedy.
2. Acquisition, by purchase or condemnation, of title to all land and structures within the area.
3. Relocation of the occupants of the area and the demolition of all substandard structures and any others blocking the proposed new use.
4. Replanning and, if desirable, rezoning the area for its best use consonant with the general plan for the future development of the whole community.
5. Resale of the cleared land to individuals or organizations, private or public, that will undertake to erect new improvements in accordance with the approved pattern.

The concept of "urban renewal" is a more modern and more comprehensive method of combating urban blight than urban redevelopment. Although clearance and redevelopment of nonsalvable areas are contemplated under urban renewal, the renewal concept also is aimed at preventing the spread of blight and rehabilitating salvable areas through measures short of clearance. Measures employed under urban renewal, which in a strict sense are not a part of urban redevelopment, include such steps as the enactment and enforcement of housing, health, and safety standards, the encouragement of building

---

[2] Robert B. Garrabrant, *Redevelopment for Industrial Use* (Washington, D.C.: Urban Land Institute, May, 1955), Technical Bulletin No. 25, p. 3.

See also J. W. Follin, "Urban Renewal and the Rebuilding of American Cities," *Proceedings, American Society of Civil Engineers*, Vol. 81, Paper No. 785, August, 1955, pp. 785-4 to 785-6.

maintenance and repair, and the rehabilitation of buildings which are still structurally sound and have economic value. Urban renewal is thus aimed not only at clearing our urban communities of slums and blighted areas, but also at eliminating the causes of slums and blight.

In his message to Congress of January 25, 1954, transmitting his recommendations now embodied in the Housing Act of 1954,[3] President Eisenhower outlined the main elements of the attack which communities should make on urban decay in order to receive federal assistance. These include:

First. Prevention of the spread of blight into good areas of the community through strict enforcement of housing and neighborhood standards and strict occupancy controls;

Second. Rehabilitation of salvable areas, turning them into sound, healthy neighborhoods by replanning, removing congestion, providing parks and playgrounds, reorganizing streets and traffic, and by facilitating physical rehabilitation of deteriorated structures;

Third. Clearance and redevelopment of nonsalvable slums.[4]

Under the concept of urban renewal, attack upon the problem of slums and blight may be carried out by employing any one or any combination of the elements outlined above. As will be indicated subsequently, the legal powers and mechanics employed in each method are substantially different.

Sometimes the term "conservation" is used to designate a program concerned primarily with maintaining economic and social values of a neighborhood and where desirable to improve those values.[5] Conservation may include measures of code enforcement and some degree of rehabilitation but not redevelopment. Conservation involves neighborhood improvement and not merely the improvement of a single structure. The conservation approach assumes that the neighborhood area is basically sound, whereas urban redevelopment determines the neighborhood or area to be unsound and not worthy of preservation. Conservation programs are to be distinguished from the enforcement

[3] Public Law 560, 83d Congress, approved August 2, 1954, 68 Stat. 622 (1954), 42 U.S.C.A. Par. 1450 et seq. (Supp. 1954).

[4] Housing and Home Finance Agency, *Approaches to Urban Renewal in Several Cities* (Washington, D.C.: U.S. Government Printing Office, 1954), Urban Renewal Bulletin No. 1, p. 1.

[5] William L. Slayton, "Conservation of Existing Housing," *Law and Contemporary Problems*, Vol. XX, No. 3, p. 436, Summer, 1955 (Durham, N.C.: School of Law, Duke University).

of minimum housing and sanitary standards in "deferred clearance areas" which are areas marked for redevelopment, but as to which redevelopment is deferred because of unavailability of funds or for other reasons.

Planning Objectives of Urban Renewal. Decayed or deteriorated areas have, to some extent, come about from poor planning or failure to plan in the past. Urban renewal provides a means for replanning such areas and thereby correcting some of the evils which have resulted from the absence of sound planning practices. It is important, therefore, that every urban renewal program that is undertaken be based upon the comprehensive plan of the community. The primary objectives of urban renewal are the clearance of slums, the removal of blight, and the elimination of their causes. The action necessary to achieve these objectives in each renewal area must vary in accordance with the treatment which is contemplated for that area.

The satisfaction of demands for adequate housing has been one of the principal arguments for undertaking urban renewal projects. Supplying housing needs is certainly of utmost importance, but it should not be regarded as the only justification. Renewal programs for providing adequate commercial and industrial areas may, in sections of some communities, be of equal or even greater priority. Changes brought about by present-day methods of mechanized production and modern practices in marketing, coupled with the fact that few communities have had the foresight to protect industrial and commercial areas from the intrusion of incompatible uses, have led to deterioration to a degree where redevelopment or extensive rehabilitation of certain areas provides the only means of restoring land to suitable commercial or industrial use.[6]

In areas where clearance is required, redevelopment should be based upon the most appropriate land use for the area as established by the comprehensive plan and should not be governed necessarily by the original land use.[7] It goes without saying that every renewal project, whether or not clearance is involved, should take into account the requirements for streets, utilities, parks, playgrounds, schools, and all other facilities which are essential or desirable for a well-planned area.

[6] Garrabrant, op. cit., p. 6. See also Theodore K. Pasma, United States Department of Commerce, *Organized Industrial Districts, A Tool for Community Development* (Washington, D.C.: U.S. Government Printing Office, June, 1954), p. 11.

[7] Conservation and rehabilitation programs do not offer the same possibilities of altering the character of the original land use.

The planning approach under the federal aid program for fighting blight was emphasized by the Advisory Committee on Government Housing Policies and Programs appointed by President Eisenhower in September, 1953.[8] This Committee pointed out the necessity for lifting our sights from piecemeal thrusts at occasional slum pockets to a broad-scale integrated campaign encompassing all phases of urban blight from its earliest symptoms to its last stages of decay.[9] The Committee's report stated:

A piecemeal attack on slums simply will not work—occasional thrusts at slum pockets in one section of a city will only push slums to other sections unless an effective program exists for attacking the entire problem of urban decay. Programs for slum prevention, for rehabilitation of existing houses and neighborhoods, and for demolition of wornout structures and areas must advance along a broad united front to accomplish the renewal of our towns and cities. This approach must be vigorously carried out in the localities themselves, and will require local solutions which vary widely from city to city.

Justification for Governmental Action. Urban renewal is a responsibility of both government and private enterprise. The urban renewal concept is based upon the utilization of the powers of government to achieve goals of social and economic betterment, while at the same time providing an opportunity for private investment, development, and ownership. Because of the many new and difficult problems which are presented in carrying out such programs, it is important that the public interests and responsibilities be carefully delineated and defined.

The costs of urban blight can be measured only in part. Some of the effects upon governmental functions and costs of services are quite easy to determine. Others are very intangible. It can be rather clearly established, for example, that as areas deteriorate, property values tend to decline rapidly, and fire, police, health, and welfare problems rise sharply. While it may be possible to estimate the actual depreciation in property values, no accurate measure can be placed upon the social cost in terms of health and welfare problems arising from unsafe and unsanitary conditions in which people may be forced to live.[10] Viewed

---

[8] President's Advisory Committee on Government Housing Policies and Programs, Recommendations on Government Housing Policies and Programs, 1953.

[9] See for comment, Follin, op. cit., p. 785–3.

[10] See William B. Randall, "St. Paul Cleans Up Its Capitol Approach," in Chamber of Commerce of the United States, Business Action for Better Cities (Washington, D.C.: 1952), pp. 172–175.

from any standpoint, physical deterioration constitutes a direct economic and social waste to the city. The indirect effects are also far reaching. Blighted areas have a deteriorating effect on adjacent areas. Consequently, conditions of urban blight contribute to the suburban movement and often may force persons to live much farther from the city than they ordinarily would live.

Studies of benefits accruing to municipalities from urban redevelopments suggest substantial gains to the city from wiping out tax delinquencies. Reports from the city of Pittsburgh, for example, indicate that urban redevelopment has not only created a handsome city, but also, through increasing property values, has produced more revenue from property and building taxes. During the five-year period from 1948 to 1953 there was a net gain of over 34 million dollars in property and building valuation in the redeveloped area. The effect of this increase has been to lighten somewhat the load on other areas.[11]

At the same time that revenues from taxes are increased, there may be a reduction in the costs of many service operations including policing, rubbish and garbage collection, street cleaning, snow removal, water meter reading, fire protection, and many other types of maintenance, upkeep, and replacement. Furthermore, the raising of social and physical standards in the neighborhood produces real advantages which are reflected in lower rates of crime and juvenile delinquency and in the consequent savings in the operational costs of courts, welfare agencies, health departments, reform schools, prisons, and asylums.[12] It is, of course, very difficult to determine to what extent these social ills, in a given area, are directly attributable to blighted conditions rather than to poverty. Certainly, such matters as the high rate of crime, infant mortality, and spread of disease are greatly accelerated where blighted conditions exist.

In urban renewal programs where redevelopment is required, the tasks involved are ordinarily beyond the resources of private individuals. Even if the private developer has the financial means, he would normally have serious difficulties in acquiring all the land because of the diversity of ownership, the refusal of owners to sell, and the involved tax situation of much of the property. A successful redevelopment program can be carried out only where all the properties subject to redevelopment are assembled under one ownership. Ac-

[11] *News Bulletin* (Chicago: Public Administration Clearing House, August 26, 1953), Release No. 3.
[12] Manhattan Development Committee, *A Realistic Approach to Private Investment in Urban Redevelopment* (New York: The Architectural Forum, 1945), p. 4.

quisition of property for this purpose almost invariably necessitates the use of the power of eminent domain. Governmental authority is also essential to carry out code enforcement and rehabilitation programs which are dependent upon the exercise of the police power. The necessity for the use of these powers emphasizes the public character of such programs.

The concept of urban redevelopment as a public responsibility is based upon the realization that the problems of slums and blighted areas have become too great for any one owner or group of owners to arrest or rectify. The appropriation of public funds for clearing areas for private redevelopment can be justified in part as a penalty that the community must pay for past errors [13] and in part as an investment which will eventually be repaid from the higher tax values created.[14] Urban redevelopment is justified by the fact that a community liability will be removed and that there will be substituted a community asset. This is of vital concern to the city as a whole which benefits from the higher tax base and the lowered costs of functional services.[15]

Considerable impetus was given to programs of urban redevelopment by the enactment of the Housing Act of 1949,[16] under which federal financial assistance became available not only for the development of public housing, but also for a number of types of redevelopment projects. Title I of the Housing Act of 1949 provides assistance for any or all of the following:

1. Redevelopment of residential slums or blighted areas for any local improvement use.
2. Redevelopment of blighted commercial or industrial areas for residential use.
3. Residential redevelopment of predominantly open land with blight, such as that of dead or arrested subdivisions.
4. Residential development of essentially open land needed for sound community growth.

Loans and grants are made available for the first three types of projects, but only loans are available for the fourth type. The urban renewal approach which is now embraced in the Housing Act of 1954 [17]

---

[13] To the extent that capital grants are made for urban redevelopment, the federal government shares with the community the losses anticipated in the undertaking.
[14] Garrabrant, op. cit., p. 4.
[15] A Fight Blight Plan for Binghamton, New York, Broome County Planning Board, General Plan Report No. 5, December, 1953, p. 1.
[16] 63 Stat. 414 (1949), 42 U.S.C.A. Par. 1450 et seq.
[17] 68 Stat. 622 (1954), 42 U.S.C.A. Par. 1450 et seq. (Supp. 1954).

expands the area of the federal interest by providing financial assistance aimed at helping cities to establish public controls to insure that existing areas of high value will remain unblighted and that redeveloped properties will not be subject to a repetition of blight.[18]

Obstacles to Urban Renewal. Although the importance and desirability of urban renewal has been recognized in many communities, progress has been retarded because of the numerous obstacles which must be overcome.[19] The chief obstacles to urban renewal have been concerned with adverse public sentiment, high financial costs, problems of relocating displaced persons, pressures from special interest groups, inability to reach agreement on a plan for redevelopment, and legal difficulties and inequities. Many of these obstacles are interrelated. To many communities they have appeared to be insuperable.

Renewal projects which involve clearance and redevelopment usually cannot be carried out by private initiative alone because they are not economically profitable. Consequently, public subsidies are required to make such projects feasible. Although it can be demonstrated that urban redevelopment produces definite economic advantages to the community, subsidies for the most part must be justified in the social objectives to be achieved. How much the community can or is willing to pay to achieve these social objectives varies with the ills which need to be cured and the temperament of the people of the community.

In every community there are citizens who do not regard urban redevelopment as an appropriate field of governmental action. To these persons, the use of governmental powers for this purpose appears to be some kind of "new-deal socialism" which tends to take away private property and put it under governmental control.[20] As long as this attitude prevails in a given community, there is small

---

[18] Compare the approach being taken in Great Britain under the "New Towns Act of 1946" and the Town Development Act of 1952. For an excellent discussion of these programs, see Lloyd Rodwin, *The British New Towns Policy* (Cambridge: Harvard University Press, 1956).

[19] Ira J. Bach, "Chicago Redevelopment," *Journal of the American Institute of Planners*, Vol. 20, p. 21, Winter, 1954. The problems of urban redevelopment are much more difficult and complex than those involved in developing a new town. Aside from the problem of demolition and relocating families, commerce, and industries, there are complicated planning problems of rerouting old utilities and the integration of new facilities with old ones which are not involved in the planning of undeveloped areas.

[20] See H. Harold Leavey, "Urban Redevelopment in Sacramento," in United States Chamber of Commerce, *Business Action for Better Cities* (Washington: D.C.: 1952), p. 170.

hope for instituting any comprehensive program of urban redevelopment therein.

Even in communities where public sentiment is favorable to urban redevelopment, public action is frequently hampered because of the high acquisition costs of properties within areas marked for redevelopment. In spite of the fact that most properties in clearance areas carry a low valuation for tax purposes, courts have been inclined to uphold excessively high valuations in condemnation proceedings. Quite commonly, properties in such areas prove to be highly productive to owners who, by overcrowding and other practices, manage to realize a high financial return upon their investment. Some courts have permitted these property owners to establish capital values for purposes of sale or condemnation based upon the income derived from the properties. Such capitalized valuations are invariably out of proportion to the actual value of the physical property and tend to discourage public acquisition for purposes of redevelopment.

One of the most serious stumbling blocks has been that of finding a solution to the problem of relocating persons who are displaced by clearance. Frequently, these persons are not eligible for public housing, but at the same time are not able to find private housing within their financial means. In some cases relocation is complicated because of race problems or because the blighted areas contain disproportionately large groups of male population. Provisions of the Federal Housing Act of 1949 require, as a condition of granting financial assistance for slum clearance, that suitable housing must be found for displaced persons within their economic means. Sometimes this requirement can be met only through providing housing subsidies. These requirements have made the problem so difficult of solution that many communities have raised the question of whether the cure is worth the medicine.

Since a great percentage of displaced persons would not be in a position to live in rebuilt areas, urban redevelopment has been criticized as not providing a solution to the housing needs of persons of low income. A report of the Manhattan Development Committee estimates that only about 20 percent of the people now living in Stage I area could afford to live in the proposed redeveloped project.[21] The report points out that, in our present economy, most of the lower-income groups of our population must live in obsolescent second-hand dwellings, and that as structures are reduced by demo-

[21] Manhattan Development Committee, *op. cit.*, pp. 1–2.

liton, the occupants have a decreasing chance of finding accommodations which they can afford.[22] Granting the validity of the statement that a great percentage of our population are doomed to live in obsolescent structures, there is still the necessity for urban redevelopment if second-hand homes are to be provided for generations of the future. Unless something is done to meet the demands for adequate housing as needs arise, buildings which are now obsolescent will, at the present rate of decay, be absolutely unsafe for occupancy within a period of 20 or 25 years.

Urban redevelopment may in some instances be defeated because of the lack of a comprehensive plan or because of failure to agree upon a plan for redevelopment. Sometimes real estate interests will make strong representations for redeveloping properties in the close-in areas for high residential density. The fact that such developments will result in a higher economic return from the land may appeal to practical businessmen. It can also be pointed out that, as a general proposition, the cost of providing services in low-density areas is much higher than it is where the population density is high. Planners who may urge the development of properties for lower densities, in order to improve living conditions and the prevention of future blight, may be charged as being visionary or idealistic and of failing to recognize the best economic use of land of high valuation. In such controversy it is important not to lose sight of the need for promoting those values which constitute the justification for the program of urban redevelopment in the first instance.

The difficulty of surmounting the many obstacles has caused a number of communities to shy away from urban redevelopment and to turn their attention to the somewhat more simplified task of developing outlying vacant areas which do not involve many of the problems attendant upon clearing and rebuilding. It is sometimes urged that the development of vacant properties provides the best solution to the housing of many persons now living in blighted areas. While this solution may aid in meeting the housing problem, it does not fulfill the basic purpose of urban redevelopment as presently conceived, namely, that of removing blighted conditions.[23] A logical program would seem to be one in which a certain portion of vacant

[22] See "Relocating Slums Families," *Architectural Forum*, Vol. 100, p. 35, February, 1954. This article raises the question of whether slum clearance by redevelopment and public housing breeds new slums.

[23] Robert Averill Walker, *The Planning Function in Urban Government* (Chicago: University of Chicago Press, 1950), p. 350.

land is developed concurrently with the clearance of other areas in order that the built-up outlying areas might provide housing for some of the persons displaced by clearance.

Urban renewal projects which do not involve clearance are also faced with many obstacles. As will be indicated subsequently, some of these are more difficult to overcome than those involving redevelopment. For example, it is not clear at the present time how far the police power may be used to compel extensive rehabilitation. Assuming that the courts do uphold its use, there are equitable considerations presented that may constitute barriers on grounds of policy. Public officials may well ponder the public reaction to government's assuming the financial loss involved in redevelopment programs, while placing the entire financial burden on the property owner to remove blighted conditions in areas of rehabilitation. To a lesser degree the same issues can be raised with respect to conservation programs.

Conditions of Blight Necessitating Renewal Programs

The terms "blight" and "blighted areas" have become a part of the vocabulary of planners, realtors, housing officials, and mortgage companies. Although these terms imply certain conditions with respect to buildings and living conditions, they are not subject to precise definition. The term "blight" is usually applied to an area of large size. It is almost never applied to a single building or structure. The term does not refer to any single characteristic or condition or even to any one set of conditions or characteristics that are regularly found in the same combination. Rather it covers a wide range of conditions and characteristics which may be found in various combinations. It is generally agreed that the two basic characteristics of blighted areas are substandardness and either stagnation or deterioration.[24]

Although the terms "blight" and "blighted areas" have become widely used, there are no commonly accepted standards by which their existence can be statistically measured. Nevertheless, the concept of urban renewal assumes that there are minimum standards and requirements for buildings and living conditions and that there is a public responsibility to maintain these standards by preventing or arresting blighting influences and by rehabilitating or rebuilding areas which reach a certain level of substandardness. To carry out this re-

[24] Coleman Woodbury, ed., *Urban Redevelopment: Problems and Practices* (Chicago: University of Chicago Press, 1953), p. 11.

sponsibility it becomes necessary to determine the causes of blight and to establish criteria for determining the existence of substandard conditions.

Causes of Blight.   Blight results from a complexity of interrelated physical, economic, and social forces and conditions. It is associated with such conditions as inadequate light, poor ventilation, insufficient privacy, inadequate yard and play space, excessive noise and dirt, and many other factors which produce unsatisfactory living conditions. Blight in industrial and commercial areas may also be evidenced by other factors such as traffic congestion, noise, dirt, air pollution, sanitary and safety hazards, inadequate transportation facilities, and improper street designs as well as construction and design of buildings. In many instances it is difficult to distinguish whether certain of these factors are causes or effects of blight.

Blight which is indicated by the dilapidated character of buildings may be due either to neglect or to inadequate original construction. If buildings are poorly constructed or improperly designed, their utility is greatly diminished. Buildings may become inadequate for the purpose for which they were originally designed because of neglect. Neglect tends to breed neglect, producing a cancer of creeping blight over a wide area.[25] Neglect may be due to practices of property owners or it may arise from poor municipal planning, inadequate health and safety regulations, or lax code enforcement.

Among the causes attributable to poor planning is the permission of inharmonious residential and nonresidential land uses which may be harmful to both types of use. The failure to make adequate provision for recreational and educational facilities has been a contributing factor to the spread of blight. Another factor has been the development of lots which are too small to permit sufficient open spaces for children to play and which do not provide adequate light and air. The overcrowding of land with buildings and people is a major factor contributing to blight.

It is not always easy to separate the causes of blight and slums due to economic factors from those due to neglect and lack of community pride. In many cases landlords who live from the rental of slum property are unwilling to spend anything for upkeep of the premises. The tenants who live on the premises are either too poor or have no apparent desire to improve the facilities of the landlord or raise their own standard of living. Consequently, buildings are

[25] Broome County Planning Board, op. cit., p. 1.

allowed to sag and to rot because of lack of paint and proper care. Debris and rubbish are permitted to accumulate in the yards creating fire hazards. Stairways and fences which become rickety or broken go without repair. Wild grass and weeds are permitted to grow in the streets and parkways, and vacant lots become unsightly from the dumping of trash. While many of these conditions could be corrected with a little interest and effort on the part of the inhabitants, once the blighting influences have become widespread, organized efforts seem to be required to alter their effects.[26]

Measuring Blight.   A great deal of controversy exists as to what minimum standards and requirements should be. It is commonly recognized that substandardness can be identified in buildings by their design, equipment, structural soundness, and the repair and maintenance. With respect to land subdivisions, certain standards can be applied with respect to the general layout, the size and shape of lots, the density, provision for community facilities, and utility service, recreation, transportation, accessibility to shopping districts, and provision for new and expanding uses. The fact that buildings or districts may be substandard in certain of these respects does not necessarily mean that an area is blighted.[27]

Blight cannot be measured by simply applying a number of the rule-of-thumb indicators. Blight is determined by many economic and social factors. Generally speaking, a blighted area is one which is an economic liability to the municipality. However, it is not a simple matter to determine the measure of economic liability. This, like determining blight itself, involves analysis of many complex factors. Some of these, such as the matter of tax revenues and government expenditures, are measured in dollars and cents. However, there are many intangible factors such as living satisfaction, costs of inconvenience and frustrations, and many incidental effects resulting from congestion, poor location, and undue loss of time and energy which do not appear in any financial balance sheet.

Since, however, decisions have to be made by public officials before any program of urban renewal is undertaken, it becomes essential that some standards be utilized for ascertaining degrees of area de-

---

[26] Where local pride can be stimulated, much may be done to rehabilitate large areas entirely by citizen action. See Back of the Yards Neighborhood Council, *How You Do It*, Chicago, 1953. Back of the Yards Neighborhood Council, *Conservation by "We the People Back of the Yards*," Chicago, 1953.

[27] See: "Nation's Costliest Redevelopment Project, New York Coliseum Gets Legal Green Light," *Architectural Forum*, Vol. 99, p. 123, November, 1953. This article presents the question of whether or not the Coliseum area is really deteriorated or slum.

terioration and blight. More success has been achieved up to the present time in working out standards of measurement with respect to housing than has been achieved in measuring blight in open spaces or in commercial and industrial areas. Considerable attention is currently being given to this problem, and it would seem that it should be possible to develop criteria having validity equal to that for housing surveys.

Experience with the use of various housing survey methods has resulted in developing criteria for the purpose of determining the degree of substandardness. The three prinicipal methods which have been used rather extensively are: the United States Census of Housing, the Real Property Survey, and the American Public Health Association System.[28] A number of other surveys have been developed and employed locally. Although each of these surveys employs its own technique, they all attempt to evaluate a number of factors and conditions relating to types and size of dwellings, housing quality, including water, sanitary facilities, heating and lighting, general maintenance, nature of occupancy, and the surrounding physical environment. Conduct of such surveys and the analysis of their results are highly technical matters.

Even though accepted criteria have been developed for evaluating the degree of substandardness of structures and other evidence of blight, there are many aspects that must be determined subjectively. It is, therefore, advisable to have surveys conducted in so far as possible by persons qualified to make valid subjective judgments where necessary. For example, some cities have found it to be good practice to employ a licensed professional architect with suitable background and experience for evaluating the physical condition of all buildings.[29] Where such qualified persons are used, great reliance may be placed upon their professional judgment in rating each building on its merits and demerits and in providing an overall picture of the area. Often this can be done by external observation. The survey of the interior condition of the buildings need not be conducted by the same personnel.

Surveys of land use and the physical condition of buildings do not, of course, give a complete picture for dealing with the existence of blight. There are many social factors that must also be weighed. A degree of success has been achieved in developing indexes of blight

28 Woodbury, op. cit., p. 17.
29 Broome County Planning Board, op. cit., p. 39.

through an analysis of social costs based upon the study of the number of cases of tuberculosis, juvenile delinquency, public relief, arrests, fire department calls, and other statistics of the area compared to other areas. The environmental factors are of great weight in measuring blight.

At best, it must be said that the measurement of blight is still far from a scientific technique, but nevertheless does furnish public officials who must make important decisions with respect to urban redevelopment with some guides. The recognized inadequacy of surveying techniques emphasizes the point that the results must be used with caution. In the final analysis, the decision to undertake a renewal program is based upon subjective judgment which is supported by such criteria as may be developed through surveys and analyses.

Factors Determining the Character of the Urban Renewal Program. The formulation of an urban renewal plan necessitates a careful study of the various areas in the community for the purpose of determining the extent of blight and the influences which are producing it. It must be recognized that structural deterioration is not the only cause of blight. Among the other factors are economic obsolescence, overcrowding, lack of open spaces, traffic congestion, noise, and air pollution. An understanding of the cause is necessary in order to reach a proper decision as to the appropriate remedy to be applied.[30]

Based upon the type of treatment to be applied, urban renewal areas may be classified as (1) enforcement or conservation areas, (2) rehabilitation areas, and (3) clearance or redevelopment areas. In certain districts, it may be found that although blighting influences are present, the decay may be arrested or materially retarded through a vigorous enforcement of the building code, housing code, zoning ordinances, fire code, health and sanitary codes, and through the abatement of nuisances. Areas in which only such measures are employed are usually designated as enforcement areas or conservation areas.

In other districts it may be found that there is scattered blight in otherwise sound neighborhoods. In order to prolong the usefulness of structures in these districts, it is necessary to check the spread of blight and remove it. This is done through a program of rehabilitation in which no demolition, or demolition in only a few instances, may

[30] Garrabrant, op. cit., p. 4.

be necessary. Such areas are designated as rehabilitation areas. In still other districts, physical dilapidation or economic obsolescence may have advanced so far that the only feasible solution to the problem is clearance and redevelopment. This involves the assembly of land within the area, removing the structures, and rebuilding. These areas fall under the classification of clearance or redevelopment areas.

It is obvious that enforcement or even rehabilitation programs cannot substitute for clearance and rebuilding where areas have reached the stage of deterioration which makes the conservation program impractical. Furthermore, it would be impractical to spend a great deal of money on expensive rehabilitation of an area that is marked for clearance and rebuilding in the very near future. Sometimes, however, the initial cost of land assembly and clearance exceeds the resources available for this purpose in a given community. Under such circumstances, there is no alternative to instituting a program of blight control aimed at checking and stopping the spread of blight. Blight control under these conditions is confined primarily to the rigid enforcement of the low-minimum standards of occupancy, repair, and maintenance embodied in the average housing code ordinance. It may involve a limited renovation of dilapidated and obsolete buildings in order to bring them up to the minimum levels of decency, health, and safety. Such measures are stop-gap devices and do not remove blight or cure its fundamental causes. They do not represent an acceptable program for urban renewal.

The redevelopment of open spaces presents a somewhat special problem. Oftentimes the areas which are in need of redevelopment have been platted and frequently have improved streets and some utilities, but have not been developed because of obsolete planning or because of blighting influences of existing buildings or other factors. Quite commonly, these properties are tax delinquent and frequently the ownership is obscure. Such areas not only represent an economic waste but also may defeat a sound plan of land use. Intelligent replanning of the area is possible only if all the properties involved in such open spaces can be assembled under single ownership. Although demolition is not involved, such areas normally fall within the classification of redevelopment areas.[31]

Even after the need for a particular type of renewal program is determined, many problems remain to be solved before there can be

[31] Some authorities would establish a separate category of "open areas." See Woodbury, op. cit., p. 385.

an actual decision to proceed. Where redevelopment is involved, it is necessary to settle such matters as the timing and priority of projects, the type of properties to be redeveloped, questions of subsidy, type of agency to carry out the redevelopment, methods of finance, means of control over redeveloped properties, and numerous other issues. Ability to finance and public acceptance are practical considerations which, in the final analysis, determine feasibility.

LEGAL MECHANICS OF URBAN RENEWAL

Urban renewal presents each community with a new set of legal problems. Essentially the problems are concerned with the extent to which private property rights must give way to the general welfare. In order for a municipality to sustain its action which may deprive an individual of the use of his property, a public purpose must be established. In the case of urban redevelopment in which slum property is sought to be acquired, the public purpose of urban renewal is the removal of the slums which endanger the public health, safety, or general welfare and also the carrying into effect of a plan to prevent future slums. Under programs of code enforcement which compel owners of property to maintain their property in a safe and healthful condition, the public purpose is also the protection of the public health, safety, morals, and the general welfare.[32]

Legal Authority and Constitutional Limitations. The principal powers upon which municipalities must rely to implement urban renewal programs are the power of eminent domain and the police power. These are supported by other powers, including the powers of taxation and appropriation. As has been previously pointed out, these powers are subject to various limitations imposed by the Federal Constitution and the constitutions of the respective states. Under the power of eminent domain, private property may not be taken except for a public use and upon payment of just compensation. While restrictions upon the use of private property established under the police power do not require the payment of compensation, they must be justified by a public purpose to promote the health, safety, morals, convenience, or the general welfare.

When the low rent housing programs were initiated about 1935, they were challenged in a number of states on the grounds that the expenditure of public funds was illegal as not being made for a public

---

[32] Slayton, op. cit., p. 445.

purpose and also that the power of eminent domain was not being used for a public purpose. By 1940, most of the state courts in which the issues were raised had upheld the validity of the housing legislation. The first decision resolving the issues was the case of *Matter of New York Housing Authority v. Miller, et al.*,[33] which upheld the power of the state to condemn land for the purpose of clearing slums and providing decent, safe, and sanitary housing for persons of low income. The court pointed out that the great social evils of slums could be attacked with any or all of the three powers available to it: taxation, police power, or condemnation. The court declared that the essential purpose of legislation is not to benefit any class, but is rather to protect and safeguard the entire public from the menace of slums. This, being a public benefit, is a public use.

The constitutionality of redevelopment statutes, not limited to slum clearance, has also been challenged in a number of states. The fact that property would be condemned and turned over to private corporations for redevelopment according to a plan approved by the municipal authorities raised further questions as to whether the lands were acquired for a public or a private use. The courts in upholding these acts have generally taken the position that if the public good is enhanced, it does not matter that a private interest may be benefited. *Schenck v. Pittsburgh, et al.*,[34] decided by the Pennsylvania Supreme Court, was the first case to uphold the validity of a redevelopment project which was not designed to provide improved living conditions or better residential area. The court recognized a public purpose in the redesigning and rebuilding of commercial areas which, by reason of the passage of years and enormous changes in traffic conditions and types of building construction, no longer met the economic and social needs of modern city life and progress. The court took into consideration the existing economically and socially undesirable land uses and the fact that there had been a continuous reduction of appraised value of properties for tax purposes in the area.

Today, the courts in approximately three-fourths of the states, plus the District of Columbia, have passed upon the validity and constitutionality of slum clearance and housing programs and have considered and passed upon the validity of slum clearance and urban redevelopment legislation in approximately one-half of the states plus

[33] 270 N.Y. 333, 1 N.E. (2d) 153 (1936).
[34] 364 Pa. 31, 70 A. (2d) 612 (1950).

the District of Columbia.[35] Slum clearance and urban redevelopment legislation have been upheld in 20 states and the District of Columbia.[36] In two states, Florida and Georgia, legislation has been held unconstitutional on basic grounds which may require constitutional amendments to validate such legislation. In Kansas, the court held the legislation invalid on grounds of an arbitrary classification, a defect which may be remedied by legislative action.

One of the most far-reaching decisions on the subject of urban redevelopment is found in the recent case of *Berman v. Parker*,[37] upholding the constitutionality of the District of Columbia Redevelopment Act of 1945, as applied to the taking of the appellant's property. The property which was sought to be taken under the Act was located in an area declared by the public agencies to be blighted and substandard. The appellant's particular piece of property was not a dwelling but a department store, and there was no evidence that it would imperil health or safety or contribute to making a slum or blighted area. Appellant made the claim that his property was being taken for a private rather than a public use inasmuch as it was commercial, not slum housing, and it would be redeveloped for private and not public use.

The court recognized the intent of Congress to redesign the whole area afflicted with slum and blight and observed that a piecemeal approach would be merely a palliative. The court pointed out that under an integrated plan, adequate provision can be made for schools, churches, parks, streets, and shopping centers. The court took a broad view of the scope of public welfare and recognized that aesthetic and spiritual considerations, as well as physical and economic considerations, may furnish a basis for policy decisions.[38]

A somewhat different problem is presented where the police power is used to raise standards and improve living conditions in conservation or rehabilitation areas. Where the power of eminent domain is used, the owner of a building is paid cash for his substandard structure. Where conservation measures are taken under the police

---

[35] Housing and Home Finance Agency, Office of the Administrator, Division of Law, *Summaries of Slum Clearance and Public Housing Decisions*, Second Supplement, January, 1954, Foreword. See also original Summary published October, 1949, and First Supplement, published July, 1951.

[36] The states are: Alabama, Arkansas, California, Connecticut, Illinois, Maine, Maryland, Massachusetts, Michigan, Missouri, New Hampshire, New Jersey, New York, Ohio, Oregon, Pennsylvania, Rhode Island, Tennessee, Virginia, and Wisconsin.

[37] 348 U.S. 26, 75 S.Ct. 98 (1954).

[38] For a quotation from the Opinion in the Berman case, see p. 422.

power, the owner is either compelled to spend money to bring the structure up to standard or to pay the cost of having it demolished. Thus, certain inequities arise favoring the party whose property was acquired under eminent domain. Particularly is this true in view of the tendency of courts to be generous in making awards in condemnation cases.[39] The inequitable treatment of property owners is particularly apparent in rehabilitation areas where strict code enforcement may require rather substantial expenditures involving painting, landscaping, remodeling of interiors, and installing bathrooms, kitchens, heating plants, and other improvements.

The solution to this problem may be to rely more heavily upon the power of eminent domain to carry out conservation and rehabilitation programs. In at least one state, Illinois, legislation authorizing the use of eminent domain to acquire property in conservation areas has been upheld by the state court.[40] In this case the court rested its decision not upon the public purpose of clearing slums, but rather upon the ground that it is a public purpose to acquire property to prevent areas from becoming slums. If the power of eminent domain cannot be used for rehabilitation short of demolition, much of the success of rehabilitation may have to depend upon the voluntary action of property owners.

Aside from the matter of inequities, which has been suggested, there remains the question, as yet unanswered, of how far the courts will support the use of the police power to establish standards in conservation areas higher than the minimum standards provided for the city as a whole. Strict area enforcement is based upon the assumption that higher housing standards can be established for certain areas than are required for others. The aim of area enforcement is to upgrade certain districts by the use of the police power. As of today, however, there has been very little experience with such programs. The Berman case would seem to indicate that the way is open to upholding reasonable legislation of this kind.

State Enabling Legislation.   Since municipalities can exercise only powers expressly conferred by the state and those which are necessarily and fairly implied therefrom, enabling legislation enacted by the state legislature is a prerequisite to inaugurating any urban renewal

---

[39] Slayton, op. cit., p. 448. Courts have sometimes recognized values based upon capitalized income even though the profitableness of the investment may have depended to a considerable extent upon illegal use and occupancy of the premises.

[40] People ex rel. Gutknecht v. City of Chicago, 3 Ill. (2d) 539, 121 N.E. (2d) 791 (1954).

program. The extent of municipal authority is controlled by the provisions of state laws.[41] These state laws vary considerably in scope and detail. In some jurisdictions the laws are restrictive. For example, in Maine, Maryland, and Nebraska, authority is vested in only one city in each state. Legislation of several other states would seem to require amendments in order to permit effective operation.[42]

Legislation differs in the various jurisdictions as to where powers shall be vested. In nine jurisdictions powers are vested solely in cities. In seven jurisdictions the powers are vested in housing authorities or in certain other local agencies. In seven other jurisdictions the powers are vested solely in redevelopment agencies or in some other special public agencies which are not housing authorities.[43] Varying provisions are to be found in other jurisdictions.

It should be apparent that if urban renewal is to be workable, local governments must be granted necessary powers to carry out the program. In addition to conferring upon local governments the necessary power of eminent domain and the police power, legislative enactments should specify procedures to be followed to insure that urban renewal programs will proceed in harmony with the comprehensive plan of the community and in conformity with general requirements of state law. Most enabling statutes include provisions relating to (1) responsibility of public bodies, (2) finding of need, (3) the preparation and adoption of the plan, (4) authorization of urban renewal agencies, (5) authorization of public development agencies, (6) condemnation powers and procedures, (7) financial provisions, (8) supervision of private development corporations, and (9) other miscellaneous matters.

Local Codes and Ordinances. State enabling legislation is not self-executing. Urban renewal programs are put into effect through action taken at the local level. The enactment of local ordinances and the adoption of local codes are necessary to authorize urban renewal projects and to carry policies into operation. Ordinances enacted to implement state redevelopment legislation must be consistent with the state act. They may supplement the state legislation but cannot be broader in scope than the powers granted by the ena-

[41] As of May, 1957, urban redevelopment or urban renewal laws are in effect in 38 states and the District of Columbia. See p. 490.

[42] Opening statement made by Chairman, Joseph Guandolo, Associate General Counsel, Slum Clearance Branch, Housing and Home Finance Agency, at a panel discussion of the annual NAHRO Convention in Philadelphia, on October 13, 1954.

[43] *Ibid.*

bling legislation. Ordinarily, urban redevelopment ordinances should provide for basic surveys, the determination of necessity for redevelopment, the relocation of displaced persons, agencies to carry out the program, powers and duties of the agencies, methods of financing the program, and the public controls to be exercised over the area. Local ordinances may adopt provisions of the state act either by specifically incorporating its provisions or by reference. Local policies may be embodied in the ordinance to the extent that they are consistent with the state act.

Urban renewal programs which do not contemplate clearance and redevelopment are normally carried out through the enactment and enforcement of a system of codes and ordinances designed to assure minimum standards of health, sanitation, and safety. These codes specify the minimum conditions under which dwellings may be lawfully occupied.[44] Such codes are concerned with both housing standards and building standards. Housing codes prescribe the minimum conditions under which buildings or parts of buildings may be lawfully occupied as dwellings or dwelling units. They relate to such matters as minimum space per occupant, basic sanitary equipment and facilities, light and ventilation, structural condition of the building, heating equipment, and the safe and sanitary maintenance of the building structure. Building codes contain requirements designed to assure structural strength, reasonable safety from fire, and proper plumbing and electrical installations. Building codes may also include standards to insure durability of the structure, thus reducing depreciation and the possibility of future blight.

Housing and building standards may be embodied in a single code, or they may be enacted by the adoption of a number of separate codes.[45] Although standards for housing and building must be established in conformity with the requirements of local conditions, there are a number of so-called model ordinances that are generally recognized as embodying standards which may be used as the basis for local codes in most communities. Suggested standards for housing

---

[44] Housing and Home Finance Agency, *How Localities Can Develop a Workable Program for Urban Renewal* (Washington, D.C.: U.S. Government Printing Office, 1955), p. 5.

[45] The Housing and Home Finance Agency has recently completed a comparative analysis of the provisions of housing codes in effect in 56 cities. For a tabulation of the results, see Housing and Home Finance Agency, *Provisions of Housing Codes in Various American Cities* (Washington, D.C.: U.S. Government Printing Office, 1956).

are to be found in "A Proposed Housing Ordinance," [46] prepared by the American Public Health Association and in "Local Development and Enforcement of Housing Codes," [47] published by the Housing and Home Finance Agency.

There are a number of model building and construction codes which may be adopted in whole or in part. Among these are codes prepared by the Building Officials Conference of America, the National Board of Fire Underwriters, the Pacific Coast Building Officials Conference, and the Southern Building Code Congress. Suggested standards for plumbing codes are to be found in the "Report of the Coördinating Committee for a National Plumbing Code," [48] issued jointly by the Housing and Home Finance Agency and the U.S. Department of Commerce, and the "American Standard National Plumbing Code," [49] sponsored by the American Public Health Association and the American Society of Mechanical Engineers. Suggested standards for electrical installations may be found in the "National Electrical Code," [50] prepared by the National Fire Protection Association and approved by the American Standards Association.

Use of Housing Codes. Experience with rehabilitation and conservation programs in a number of cities in recent years suggests that more consideration be given to the adoption of housing codes as a means to enforce minimum standards of health and safety and sanitation in existing dwelling units. The success of Baltimore, Milwaukee, and other cities in raising housing standards under police power regulations focuses attention upon a rather new but important tool of plan implementation.[51] Whereas building and construction codes are designed to insure adequacy in new construction, housing codes are aimed at filling the gap in police power protection by requiring that existing structures also be adequate for housing regardless of when built. In order to accomplish this objective, housing codes generally establish minimum standards with respect to space, facilities,

[46] Available from the Publication Office, American Public Health Association, Inc., 1790 Broadway, New York 19, N.Y.

[47] Available from Superintendent of Documents, U.S. Government Printing Office, Washington, D.C.

[48] Available from Superintendent of Documents, U.S. Government Printing Office, Washington, D.C.

[49] Available from the American Standards Association, Inc., 70 East 45th St., New York 17, N.Y.

[50] Available from the National Board of Fire Underwriters, 85 John St., New York 38, N.Y., or the National Fire Protection Association, 60 Batterymarch St., Boston 10, Mass.

[51] Woodbury, op. cit., pp. 332–353.

and occupancy. Their use is essential in carrying out any comprehensive program of urban renewal.[52] They have value not only in regulating the conditions under which people live but also in appraising the state of the housing supply.

The housing code, like all tools of plan implementation, must be carefully coördinated with other regulatory devices and in harmony with the programs of those agencies which are concerned with the overall objectives. Representatives of a number of cities which have had pioneering experience with housing codes have offered the following tips on the use of such codes for the rehabilitation of deteriorating housing:

1. Adequate financing from neighborhood or community sources for families who cannot obtain regular bank loans should be available in a code enforcement area. A "Fight Blight Fund" financed by banks and public-spirited businessmen and groups in the community can be set up to help out these families.
2. To obtain compliance by hold-out landlords, some communities have set up special housing courts where the magistrate hears nothing but housing cases. It has been found that regular courts which are concerned with crime and major offenses are apt to be too lenient with housing code violators.
3. To encourage private rehabilitation above minimum requirements, a municipality must do its share in upgrading the neighborhood. It must improve schools, parks, streets, lighting, sewers, etc. The residents should be informed about forthcoming city improvements so they will know that increased property and living values will result from their combined efforts.
4. Plans for housing code enforcement must be tied in with the city's general plans for redevelopment and public improvements, so that a neighborhood which may be cleared for a new expressway in several years will not be wastefully rehabilitated.[53]

A question of current importance affecting urban renewal policy is that of how far a municipality may go, for a given area, in establishing housing standards which are higher than those established under the housing code for the city as a whole. Occasions are certain to arise under which lenders and investors will be reluctant or decline to finance home improvements in a renewal area unless the property within the area is upgraded over the minimum standards provided

---

[52] See p. 539, area rehabilitation and p. 543, area enforcement.
[53] See "Action Clinic Offers 'Renewal Checklist,'" *The American City*, Vol. 71, No. 8, p. 136, August, 1956.

under the housing code. One of the suggestions made for meeting the problem is the use of a "zoned housing code" providing variable standards applicable to different districts.[54] If such a plan can be legally sustained, it offers some interesting possibilities for achieving certain urban renewal objectives. The courts have not as yet indicated the legal limitations upon such regulations.

Federal Aids.   Although municipalities and other units of local government derive no enabling authority from federal statutes, they do benefit from loans, grants, and other forms of federal aid. Consequently, local urban renewal legislation must be in harmony with provisions of the federal law, and local administration must be consistent with federal policy if federal grants are obtained. Both the federal statutes and federal administrative policy lay emphasis on the necessity for local initiative and local responsibility in the prevention and removal of blight. There is no compulsion under federal law upon any community to act. Federal statutes do, however, recognize a federal interest in the problem and offer federal assistance to municipal governments which possess the requisite powers to undertake comprehensive urban renewal projects and which submit "workable programs" to accomplish the objectives of the federal act. The kinds of assistance available are as follows:

1. Technical and professional assistance in preparing the workable program and in planning and developing urban renewal programs. This service is rendered without charge.
2. Loans for preliminary work leading to preparation of the urban renewal project. These are available prior to plan approval.
3. Temporary loans to provide working capital for urban renewal projects.
4. Long-term loans when project land is leased rather than sold for redevelopment.
5. Capital grants which may provide as much as two-thirds of the net cost of the project.
6. Special grants for demonstration projects where results will increase knowledge of methods and techniques.
7. Special grants for urban planning assistance to small cities and for metropolitan planning.[55]
8. Special Federal Housing Administration insurance covering new construction and rehabilitation of residential structures.

[54] Joseph Guandolo, "Housing Codes in Urban Renewal," The George Washington Law Review, Vol. 25, No. 1, p. 42, October, 1956.

[55] See Housing and Home Finance Agency, A Guide to Urban Planning Assistance Grants (Washington, D.C.: 1955) for eligibility and application procedures.

Also 40 U.S.C.A. 461 (1954 Supp.).

9. Special F.H.A. mortgage insurance to encourage the construction and rehabilitation by private industry of low-cost housing for displaced families.
10. Loans and grants to provide low-rent public housing for displaced families.[56]

The basic federal statutes which authorize federal assistance to municipalities for slum clearance and urban renewal are the Housing Act of 1949 [57] and the Housing Act of 1954.[58] The Housing Act of 1949 provided the original basis of slum clearance and urban redevelopment. The 1954 Act broadened the scope to embrace the concept of "urban renewal." In the 1949 Act, Congress declared that the general welfare and the health and living standards of the people require "the elimination of substandard and other inadequate housing through the clearance of slums and blighted areas, and the realization, as soon as feasible, of the goal of a decent home and a suitable living environment for every American family, thus contributing to the development and redevelopment of communities and to the advancement of the growth, wealth, and security of the Nation. . . ." The Housing Act of 1954 broadened the scope of slum clearance and redevelopment to provide assistance also in preventing the spread of blight through the rehabilitation and conservation of blighted and deteriorating areas. Projects which were begun under the provisions of the 1949 Act may be completed under those provisons. However, the projects may be broadened to receive assistance for rehabilitation and conservation if they meet the requirements of the 1954 law.

Projects undertaken under the 1954 statute may involve some or all of the following:

1. Acquisition of slum or blighted areas and other real property, and demolition or removal of buildings and improvements thereon in accordance with an urban renewal plan.
2. Installation, construction, or reconstruction (in the urban renewal area) of streets, utilities, parks, playgrounds, and other improvements necessary for carrying out in such area the urban renewal objectives of the act in accordance with the urban renewal plans.
3. The disposition of any property acquired in such urban renewal area (including sale, initial leasing, or retention by the local public agency

---

[56] See 42 U.S.C.A. Par. 1450 et seq. (1954 Supp.). Also Garrabrant, op. cit., p. 22.
[57] 63 Stat. 414 (1949), 42 U.S.C.A. Par. 1450 et seq.
[58] 68 Stat. 622 (1954), 42 U.S.C.A. Par. 1450 et seq. (1954 Supp.).

itself) at its fair value for uses in accordance with the urban renewal plans.

4. Carrying out plans for a program of voluntary repair and rehabilitation of buildings or other improvements in accordance with the urban renewal plan.[59]

After the planning is completed and approval is given by the federal government, the local public agency and the federal government may enter into a temporary loan and capital grant contract. The temporary loan is made for the purchasing of sites, the demolition of buildings, and other site improvement costs, and for carrying out voluntary programs of rehabilitation. The loans are repaid from the proceeds of land disposition, federal capital grants, and local cash grants. The federal capital grant provides two-thirds of the net project cost or loss. The remaining one-third of the deficit is supplied by the municipality in the form of cash and/or noncash contributions such as donations of land, site improvements, and public works.

Before a contract for redevelopment will be approved by the federal government, the local public agency must demonstrate in its application that the project is eligible for financial aid and that the locality is taking positive steps toward the enactment, improvement, and enforcement of codes and regulations pertaining to health, sanitation, and safety for dwellings and that the slum clearance objectives cannot be achieved through the rehabilitation of structures of the area involved. There must be presented to the Administrator a "workable program" which includes an official plan of action for effectively dealing with the problem of urban slums and blight. This plan must show what is proposed to be done for the establishment and preservation of a well-planned community utilizing appropriate private and public resources (1) to eliminate and prevent the development or spread of slums and urban blight, (2) to encourage needed urban rehabilitation, (3) to provide for the redevelopment of blighted, deteriorated, or slum areas, and (4) to undertake other feasible community activities to achieve the objectives of the program.[60]

The major requirements to be fulfilled before a contract for loan or grant or for grant only will be approved, have been stated as follows:

[59] Commission on Intergovernmental Relations, *Twenty-five Federal Grant-in-Aid Programs* (Washington, D.C.: U.S. Government Printing Office, 1955), p. 148.

[60] Housing and Home Finance Agency, *How Localities Can Develop a Workable Program of Urban Renewal* (Washington, D.C.: U.S. Government Printing Office, 1955), p. 2.

1. The existence of a general plan for the development of the locality as a whole.
2. A plan, approved by the governing body of the locality in which the project is situated, for the redevelopment of the project area which [plan] conforms to the general plan for the development of the locality.
3. Findings by the local governing body that the federal assistance is necessary to enable the project area to be redeveloped in accordance with the local approved plan.
4. Maximum opportunity, consistent with the sound needs of the locality, for the redevelopment of the redevelopment areas by private enterprise.
5. A public hearing, prior to the acquisition of the land, after notice of the date, time, place, and purpose of such hearing.
6. A financing plan, supported by commitments with appropriate public bodies and other assurances that the required amount of local grants-in-aid will be provided.
7. A relocation plan, supported by evidence that there is or will be permanent housing at rents or prices within the financial means of the families displaced from the project area equal to the number of and available to such displaced families, and in areas not generally less desirable in regard to public utilities and facilities and reasonably accessible to their place of employment.
8. Evidence that there are no legal impediments as to the undertaking of the project.
9. Evidence of progress with respect to the enactment, improvement, and enforcement of codes and regulations pertaining to health, sanitation, and safety for dwellings.
10. An official workable program, approved by the Housing and Home Finance Agency Administrator, for utilizing appropriate private and public resources in the locality to eliminate and prevent the development or spread of slums and urban blight, to encourage needed urban rehabilitation, and to provide for the development of blighted, deteriorated, or slum areas.[61]

In order to comply with the requirements of a "workable program," the local community must commit itself to the attainment of the following essential objectives:

Codes and Ordinances—The objective is to assure adequate minimum standards of health, sanitation, and safety through a comprehensive system of codes and ordinances which state the minimum conditions under which dwellings may be lawfully occupied. . . .

[61] Commission on Intergovernmental Relations, op. cit., pp. 150–151.

A Comprehensive Community Plan—The objective is the formulation and official recognition of a comprehensive general plan for the community as a whole. . . .

Neighborhood Analyses—The objective is the identification of the extent and intensity of blight and logical patterns of neighborhoods for purposes of developing a basis for planning of healthy neighborhoods of decent homes and suitable living environment. . . .

Administrative Organization—The objective is a firmly established administrative responsibility and capacity for enforcement of codes and ordinances, and for carrying out renewal programs and projects. . . .

Financing—The objective is the development of means for meeting the financial obligation involved in carrying out urban renewal activities. . . .

Housing for Displaced Families—The objective is to facilitate the rehousing, in decent, safe, and sanitary accommodations, of families displaced by governmental action. . . .

Citizen Participation—The objective is community-wide participation on the part of individuals and representative citizens' organizations which will help to provide, both in the community generally and in selected areas, the understanding and support which is necessary to insure success.[62]

URBAN RENEWAL PROCEDURES AND PUBLIC POLICY CONSIDERATIONS

As long as the requirements of state and federal legislation are met, local agencies have complete authority in establishing policies and procedures to carry out programs of urban renewal. Before any projects are authorized, the community should: (1) adopt a general plan for the development of the locality as a whole; (2) undertake community surveys and analyses to determine the conditions of blight and the need for urban renewal; (3) classify areas for urban renewal treatment; (4) select project areas of highest priority; (5) work out plans for citizen participation; and (6) decide upon a feasible means of financing the program. Where redevelopment or extensive rehabilitation is contemplated, the local authorities must reach decisions as to the type of agency to undertake the assembly of land, the methods of acquisition, the relocation of displaced families, the character and design of the redeveloped area, and the nature of the public controls to be exercised after redevelopment. Far-reaching public policy decisions need to be made before urban renewal procedures are adopted and put into operation.

[62] Housing and Home Finance Agency, *How Localities Can Develop a Workable Program for Urban Renewal*, op. cit., pp. 5–11.

DEVELOPMENT OF A WORKABLE URBAN RENEWAL PROGRAM

Before any local community can qualify for federal assistance, it must present to the Housing and Home Finance Agency an acceptable "workable program." Until the program is accepted, no contracts can be executed for loans or capital grants. The principal elements of an acceptable workable program have already been indicated. Essentially, the requirements of a workable program are intended to accomplish the following objectives:

1. To present a complete picture of slum and blight conditions within the locality.
2. To insure the preparation of a comprehensive and coördinated program of public and private activities for the correction of slum and blight conditions.
3. To commit the community to a program aimed at the development of a well-planned community free from slums and blight.

General Planning. One of the fundamental objectives of a workable program for urban renewal as outlined by the Housing and Home Finance Agency is the development of a comprehensive general plan for the community as a whole. The general plan, to be acceptable, should be developed under procedures provided by state and local legislation, and should be supervised and administered by an official local planning agency having adequate resources and authority to insure continuity of planning.[63] To comply with the federal requirements the general plan should provide for the physical development through the following:

1. A *Land Use Plan*—which shows the location and extent of land in the community proposed to be used for residential, commercial, industrial, and public purposes.
2. A *Thoroughfare Plan*—which indicates the system of existing and proposed major thoroughfares and distinguishes between limited access thoroughfares, primary thoroughfares, and secondary thoroughfares.
3. A *Community Facilities Plan*—which shows the location and type of schools, parks, playgrounds, and other significant public facilities, and, where appropriate, indicates buildings required.
4. A *Public Improvements Program*—which identifies those future public improvements necessary to carry out the community development objectives envisioned in other general plan elements, and which recommends priorities for their execution.[64]

[63] *Ibid.*, p. 7.
[64] *Ibid.*, p. 7.

The general plan requirement also obligates the local community to establish the following administrative and regulatory measures to control and guide physical development:

1. A *Zoning Ordinance*—which establishes zoning regulations and zone districts covering the entire community (and surrounding territory where appropriate and authorized by law) to govern the use of the land, the location, height, use, and land coverages of buildings, and which may establish suitable requirements for the provision of off-street parking and off-street loading space.
2. *Subdivision Regulations*—which provide for control of undeveloped land in the community (and immediately surrounding it where appropriate and authorized by law), through review by the local planning agency of proposed subdivision plats to insure conformance to the general plan, adequate lot sizes, appropriate street grades and widths, provision of adequate street and utility improvements, and establishment of proper official records.[65]

Since each urban renewal project for which the local community receives financial assistance under the federal law must conform to the general plan of the community, the urban renewal plan is thus one of the elements of the general plan for community development.[66] The requirement that there must be a general plan as a prerequisite of a workable program is a recognition by the federal government of the principle that good planning is fundamental to any program of community development.

Community Surveys and Analyses. Each community contemplating participation in a federally-aided program must be prepared to make a selection of areas for clearance and redevelopment, rehabilitation, and conservation. In order to insure that each urban renewal project is soundly conceived and planned, basic surveys should be undertaken and the results should be carefully analyzed. Accurate information about the existence, extent, and location of blight is essential to orderly and effective execution of any renewal program. After project areas have been selected, surveys should be made on a structure by structure basis to determine which particular structures fail to meet minimum standards. This entails a study of housing quality, housing occupancy, and environmental conditions. From such

[65] *Ibid.,* p. 7.
[66] Randy H. Hamilton, "The 'New Look' in Slum Clearance and Urban Redevelopment," *League of Iowa Municipalities,* Vol. IX, No. 6, p. 10, August, 1954.

surveys, the type of treatment is determined and preliminary estimates of the cost of improvements can be made.

The Housing and Home Finance Agency suggests that neighborhood surveys and analyses be undertaken by the locality to accomplish the following purposes: [67]

a. The determination, on a city-wide basis, of the extent, intensity, and location of blight and of income, racial, and other characteristics of families directly affected.

b. The identification of the causes of neighborhood deterioration in order to indicate appropriate remedial action. These causes may include some detrimental influences which extend beyond a particular neighborhood, and which must be dealt with on a community basis. Such detrimental influences, for example, might be lack of adequate housing supply for the city as a whole, resulting in overcrowding of existing structures, nearby adverse or nuisance land uses (such as a slaughterhouse or dump) or absence of an adequate air-pollution control program. A common and particularly acute detrimental influence is the lack of adequate housing for minority groups, forcing their concentration in tightly congested central areas.

c. The delineation of residential neighborhoods based upon such considerations as land-use designations of the general plan, already established neighborhood patterns, natural boundaries such as streams and thoroughfares.

The suggested analyses of the Housing and Home Finance Agency recognize the neighborhood concept of community development in the expressed goal for the establishment and preservation of sound healthy neighborhoods and of decent homes and suitable living environment for adequate family life. Under this concept, each residential neighborhood which is reasonably self-contained, should be appraised, not only with respect to housing quality and occupancy, but also with respect to adequacy of school facilities, playgrounds, transportation, community facilities, public services, local shopping facilities, traffic, street arrangement, and all other factors which are a part of the neighborhood picture. Such appraisal will help to identify the blighting influences and point the way to the type and extent of the remedial action that is needed.

Classification of Areas and Project Selection. Upon the basis of

[67] Housing and Home Finance Agency, *op. cit.*, p. 8.

For suggestions as to the development and use of surveys see Housing and Home Finance Agency, *How to Make and Use Local Housing Surveys* (Washington, D.C.: U.S. Government Printing Office, 1954).

community analyses, urban redevelopment areas may be selected and classified according to the treatment required to prevent the spread of blight or to restore the particular area to standards in conformity to the comprehensive plan. In general these areas may be classified as (1) conservation areas in which the spread of blight is sought to be checked through strict code enforcement, (2) rehabilitation areas in which the usefulness of existing structures can be prolonged by strict code enforcement and the removal of existing blight through reconstruction and limited demolition, and (3) clearance and re-development areas in which blight has progressed so far that demo-lition and rebuilding are the only feasible solution. Each area should be clearly defined in terms of size, recognizable boundaries, total supply of housing, and other characteristics. Treatment within these areas is determined by many factors. However, the starting point for the treatment begins with the classification of the area.

Since in most communities all projects embraced within a com-prehensive urban renewal program cannot be undertaken simultane-ously, the matter of project selection is a matter of considerable importance. Particularly is this true in areas in which clearance and re-development are required because of the extremely complicated problems of land acquisition, relocation of occupants, and the resale and rebuilding of the area.

Project selection raises many practical problems involving numer-ous legal, economic, and political considerations. Legal difficulties of land assembly, high acquisition costs, or the magnitude of the project in a particular area may sometimes make it necessary for the local authorities to give first priority to some other area which, in terms of obsolescence or deterioration, has a lower priority rating. Market-ability is likewise a factor that enters into the matter of project se-lection. If it is clearly demonstrated that the proposed development on a particular project will make the resale of the land certain as against the doubtful marketability of another, this factor cannot be ignored.[68] Furthermore, the community's need for the proposed re-developed properties in a given project in relation to the community's need for the proposed development in another must be taken into account. It is also true that in certain communities there may be political pressures so strongly supporting one project against another that a selection on the basis of priorities determined by surveys and analyses has little determining influence.

[68] Garrabrant, op. cit., p. 4.

Whatever may be the practical factors that influence the selection of projects, it is important that the basic objectives of urban redevelopment be kept to the forefront, namely, eliminating blight and its causes and restoring neighborhoods to healthy and suitable living environments. If practical economic or political factors are given too much weight, there is danger that the primary objectives of urban renewal may be submerged or lost.

Citizen Participation. One of the elements of an acceptable "workable program" is that there be active citizen participation in the urban renewal program. The objective outlined by the Housing and Home Finance Agency is "community-wide participation on the part of individuals and representative citizens' organizations which will help to provide, both in the community generally and in selected areas, the understanding and support which is necessary to insure success." [69] This stated objective indicates a recognition of the fact that public action should be based upon public opinion. Success in achieving the objectives of urban renewal depends upon citizen understanding and citizen support. Citizen groups should be made to feel that they are sharing the responsibility with public officials for achieving the objectives of the urban renewal program.

No particular form of organization is to be suggested for developing citizen participation. This will vary with each community. Efforts should be made to enlist the coöperation of various group organizations including business, professional, labor, welfare, religious, educational, and other interests. Special consideration should be given to the participation of minority groups. It is most important that citizen participation should be solicited at the outset of the urban renewal planning activities and continued through to the completion of the project. Citizen participation should be organized in a way to insure that all groups are focusing their attention on a common goal and working toward the same end.

Among the suggested forms of community organization is the citizens' advisory committee. Such a committee is frequently made up of prominent citizens appointed by the mayor. The committee should have wide group representation and the individuals should be selected because of their knowledge of community affairs and their interest in the urban renewal program. Although the responsibility for policy decisions must rest with the public officials, such advisory

[69] Housing and Home Finance Agency, *How Localities Can Develop a Workable Program for Urban Renewal*, op. cit., p. 10.

groups can often render invaluable service in providing consultation and advice on the consequences of alternative courses of action. Neighborhood groups and special study groups may be found to be extremely helpful in obtaining information and providing advice on localized problems and on specialized or technical matters. Special advisory groups may be appointed, for example, to advise on matters of real estate valuations, welfare services, hardship cases, rehousing, finance, architectural design, and numerous other important problems.

Financial Planning. Every community contemplating an urban renewal program must face the fact that it will cost the taxpayers money. Urban renewal projects involve expenditures for both administrative costs and capital items. Although financial assistance may be obtained from the federal government for projects which meet the requirements of a workable program, a very heavy financial load will still have to be carried in many instances by the local community. It is, therefore, important to develop a carefully worked out financial plan for meeting the financial obligations involved in carrying out the urban renewal activities. This requires the setting up of an operational budget projected into the future to the extent necessary to meet the financial obligations of the program contemplated. Some cities include urban renewal projects in their regular capital improvements program.[70]

Any community which qualifies for federal urban renewal financial assistance must contribute its share of the project cost, either in cash or in the form of local grants-in-aid such as public facilities and improvements. A city may thus meet its share by making provision therefor in its operating budget or by scheduling public improvements to be made which may be counted as its share of the contribution. The federal contributions may account for as much as two-thirds of the net project cost.

Although renewal programs will certainly involve expenditures of local revenues, experience has shown that over the years many of these costs are recoverable through increased tax revenues. Particularly is this true under programs where clearance and redevelopment projects are involved.[71] It is also true that, in many instances, a stepped-up program of code enforcement to improve the quality of

---

[70] *Ibid.*, pp. 9–10.

[71] Some of the major problems of financing redevelopment projects are considered in a subsequent section.

housing and community facilities will upgrade neighborhoods and, as a result, enhance the tax base and operate to offset some of the costs through increased tax revenues.

Processing Applications for Federal Aid. It is important that municipalities desiring financial aid from the federal government for urban renewal prepare their applications with care and in strict conformity with the regulations of the Housing and Home Finance Agency. Any locality can obtain assistance in developing its workable program from the appropriate Housing and Home Finance Agency Regional Office. The Agency issues a number of publications which may be secured to supplement the assistance rendered by the Regional Offices.

The application for initial certification of a workable program should be submitted to the appropriate Regional Office of the Housing and Home Finance Agency. This application should be supplemented with the necessary codes and ordinances, appropriate maps, resolutions, descriptions of organizations and activities, and such other data as may be required. Narrative statements concerning the various elements, together with a list of all the exhibits and supplementary material, are required to be submitted in triplicate.[72] Only one copy of the exhibits and supplements need be submitted. After the material submitted has been accepted by the Regional Office, it will be forwarded to Washington, D.C., for approval by the Administrator. Upon approval, the Administrator certifies the fact, both to the locality and to the various constituent organizations within the Housing and Home Finance Agency which administer the several federal programs from which the community desires assistance. The certification will remain in effect for 12 months and constitutes authorization for the constituent organizations to proceed.

While the approval of a workable program is a prerequisite to eligibility for federal assistance under the Housing Act of 1954, it does not, of itself, qualify the municipality for any of the aids, nor does approval of the workable program constitute approval of proposals in the program or delineation and treatment of specific areas. Before federal aid may be obtained, the local community must also meet the particular requirements specified in the federal statute and the regulations of the Housing and Home Finance Agency. When

---

[72] For details of the material to be submitted with the workable program, see Housing and Home Finance Agency, *How Localities Can Develop a Workable Program for Urban Renewal*, op. cit., pp. 5–11.

all requirements are fulfilled, a contract for loan or grant or for grant only may be executed between the local community and the federal government.

ADMINISTRATION OF THE URBAN RENEWAL PROGRAM

The administration of the urban renewal program presents many new and difficult problems for the municipality. Every city that has undertaken a redevelopment project has become aware of the complexity of the operation which requires the application of the knowledge and skills of many specialists, the coördination of numerous governmental activities, and the coöperation of various public and private agencies. The administrative problems are magnified under the broader programs of urban renewal which add responsibilities of code enforcement and rehabilitation to those of clearance and redevelopment. While these problems are difficult, they are not insurmountable. A sound plan of administrative organization and procedure will aid materially in developing sound administrative policies and in securing the coördination of activities necessary to the success of the program.

The Local Public Agency.   State enabling statutes usually specify the type of public agency which cities may employ to carry out urban redevelopment projects. Under some statutes the public agency is the city itself; under others it is the public housing authority; and under others it is a separate redevelopment authority. The present trend appears to be away from using the public housing authority as the urban redevelopment agency. This seems to be justified because the objectives of urban redevelopment are much broader in scope than slum clearance and rehousing.

The pattern of administrative organization for urban renewal is not settled. There are sharply opposing views represented by students of public administration and organized groups interested in urban renewal as to whether urban redevelopment and urban renewal powers should be vested in a separate authority or in the existing municipal structure. It is possible, of course, to place redevelopment responsibilities under a separate agency and carry out other urban renewal functions by established municipal departments. It would seem to be preferable, however, for all urban renewal responsibilities to be centered in a single agency.

The case for the separate authority to carry out the urban redevelopment and urban renewal program seems to be based principally upon the following arguments:

1. The new and specialized character of the program makes it important that administration be placed under a new and specialized agency fully cognizant and sympathetic with the objectives of urban renewal.
2. Existing municipal departments and agencies, to date, have shown little interest or initiative in undertaking such programs.
3. If urban renewal is to be accomplished efficiently and effectively, the administrative agency must have independent powers which are free from political control and political pressures.
4. Existing city departments have their city-wide functions to administer and should not be disturbed or expected to absorb the heavy responsibilities of urban renewal to be carried out within specific areas of the city.
5. Since urban renewal operations overlap the functions of so many municipal departments, coördination can be achieved better by a separate agency with powers which are independent of the municipality.

A number of responsible organizations including the National Association of Real Estate Boards, the National Association of Home Builders, and the Urban Land Institute have urged the establishment of a separate agency created for the specific purpose of urban redevelopment or urban renewal.[73]

If a separate agency is created, it of necessity must have many of the powers of a municipal corporation. However, it would not be subject to the same political controls and would not be directly responsible to the voters. The urban renewal authority would need to be granted the power of eminent domain, the power to levy taxes and special assessments, the power to borrow money and to issue bonds and other securities, the power to enforce building, housing, and construction codes, and such other powers as are necessary to perform the responsibilities entailed in the program. Normally, the only check the city would have over the authority would be to the extent that the mayor participates in the appointment of the members of the authority board.

Students of public administration who oppose the creation of a separate authority for urban renewal argue that:

[73] See Slayton, op. cit., p. 459.
See also Garrabrant, op. cit., p. 20.

1. The establishment of an independent agency would produce difficult problems of coördination because the functions of the authority would duplicate many of those performed by the municipality.
2. All functions of government should be subject to responsible and responsive democratic controls in order that the public policy-making authority can be held within reasonable limits.
3. Too many independent or semi-independent governmental agencies complicate the governmental organization to a point where the average citizen loses interest because of his inability to understand it.
4. Coördination of municipal functions can be more readily achieved through an agency integrated in the municipal structure than by an agency with autonomous or semiautonomous status.[74]

These are persuasive arguments which, in view of the growing multiplicity of local units of government, should be given considerable weight.

In the event that the urban renewal program is administered by the municipality rather than by an independent agency, there must be a centering of authority and responsibility for directing action. All plans require some kind of coördinating device. If the city elects to use one of its established departments for carrying out the program, coördination should be worked out through the appointment of a coördinator responsible to the mayor. If the city has a city manager, the coördinator should be an assistant to the manager. Many cities may find it more satisfactory to create a new department with authority to perform the functions of certain other departments within the project area. Where this is done, it is highly important that the delineation of the responsibilities of each department be clearly defined.

A plan which is now being put into effect in Baltimore, Maryland, is worthy of special study. This plan, which is based upon recommendations contained in the *Report of the Urban Renewal Study Board to Mayor Thomas D'Alesandro, Jr.,*[75] establishes an agency to be known as the Renewal and Housing Agency. Under its jurisdiction are incorporated the programs and powers of the Redevelopment Commission, the housing bureau of the Health Department, and some of the programs and powers of the Department of Plan-

[74] Slayton, *op. cit.*, pp. 459–460.
[75] This plan, published in September, 1956, was prepared under the direction of a number of nationally recognized planning authorities. Professor William L. C. Wheaton, Director of the Institute for Urban Studies, University of Pennsylvania, was chairman of the study board.

ning and the Department of Public Welfare. The Housing Authority of Baltimore City will be placed under the jurisdiction of this agency.

Under the study board's proposal, the Renewal and Housing Agency is to be responsible for preparing detailed neighborhood plans in urban renewal areas in conformity with standards established by the comprehensive general plan developed by the planning department.[76] It is proposed that the agency will administer the neighborhood organization services of the planning department, and the community organization services of the Department of Public Welfare. It will also carry out the program of land clearance and redevelopment and assume responsibility for housing code enforcement, which now is the responsibility of the Health Department.

No matter what type of local public agency is created, it is essential to the success of the urban renewal program that it function in close coöperation with the planning agency. Urban renewal is not an independent function, but is a tool of planning. This concept must be recognized and accepted by the urban renewal agency if the broad objectives of urban renewal legislation are to be achieved. Questions have sometimes been raised as to whether the creation of an independent redevelopment authority does not seriously complicate the problem of urban planning because of the lead which it may take in formulating redevelopment programs.[77] This danger does not seem to be so great today in view of the provisions of the National Housing Acts which require, as a condition of federal aid, that the urban redevelopment and urban renewal plans be based upon a comprehensive plan of community development. However, the responsibilities which an urban renewal program places upon a community make it necessary that many planning agencies do a great deal more planning than they have in the past, and that the scope of their planning interests be correspondingly enlarged.

Acquisition and Assembly of Land. Urban redevelopment projects can be successfully carried out only if all the real property which is to be cleared or which requires extensive rehabilitation is assembled under a single ownership. The most important function of the urban redevelopment agency is the acquisition and assembly of the land

[76] The study proposes that the City Planning Commission and the Department of Planning be made an integral part of the Mayor's administrative organization; that a system of capital budgeting be established; and that an assistant to the Mayor be appointed to observe and evaluate the development of activities on a city-wide basis. For a brief summary of the proposal, see ASPO *Newsletter*, Vol. 23, No. 1, p. 4, January, 1957.

[77] Walker, *op. cit.*, p. 353.

within the project area. Under normal circumstances, the redevelopment agency will be able to acquire a large percentage of the properties through negotiated purchase. Purchases should be preceded by appraisals which should not be binding upon the redevelopment agency, but should be used as a guide and for purposes of public record. Where owners hold out for speculative profits, and negotiated purchase is not possible, the redevelopment agency must resort to the use of the power of eminent domain. Condemnation proceedings may often be necessary to clear clouded titles.

After extensive studies of the assemblage of substantial plots, the City of New York reached the conclusion that it is virtually impossible to assemble a site more sizable than two acres without resorting to condemnation proceedings.[78] In order to determine the probable costs of acquisition, the City of New York contracts with private realtors to make acquisition appraisals. The estimates of probable cost take into account many factors affecting the value of the properties to be acquired, including (1) present use and condition of the improvements on the site, (2) the general character of the neighborhood, (3) transportation facilities, (4) educational, cultural, and religious facilities, (5) rentals, and (6) values of property within the site as evidenced by recent sales and condemnation proceedings. Experience indicates that certain properties may be acquired through purchase or option at an amount somewhat below the appraised valuation, but this is frequently offset by high awards given under condemnation actions.

The cost of land acquisition has an important bearing upon the decision as to the type of urban renewal project, if any, to be undertaken. The determination of the value of property presents extremely difficult problems. Whether appraisal should be made upon the basis of tax assessments, investment less depreciation, income capitalization, market value, or some complex formula is not a matter of general agreement. Property owners frequently refuse to sell except at prices which represent the owners' speculative hopes or which reflect values based upon present uses inimical to the social welfare. Even in condemnation proceedings, courts are inclined to allow speculative values in making their awards. For these reasons, some

[78] The City of New York, *Washington Square Southeast, Slum Clearance Plan Under Title I of the Housing Act of 1949* (Report to Mayor Impellitteri and the Board of Estimate by the Committee on Slum Clearance), August, 1953, p. 57. This is the fourteenth of a series of reports on slum clearance projects undertaken with federal assistance under the Housing Act of 1949.

authorities have recommended that properties be allowed to deteriorate until the price is sufficiently low to enable them to be acquired at a price at which they can be economically converted to socially desirable uses.[79] A more logical policy would seem to be to exert every effort to convince the courts that speculative values should be disallowed and prices should be established which represent the true value for a socially desirable type of development.

Financing the Redevelopment Program. Blight and blighted conditions can be eradicated only at very high costs. Usually, property with buildings to be demolished must be acquired at its current market value, which makes redevelopment a much more costly enterprise than the development of relatively inexpensive vacant land. Therefore, under highly competitive conditions, clearance projects cannot be expected to be self-liquidating, and in most cases could not be carried out without the aid of government subsidy. Funds for this purpose must be derived from general sources of local revenue and grants-in-aid from the federal government or the state.

Nonsubsidy revenues must usually be obtained from the sale of revenue bonds issued by the city or the redevelopment authority.[80] Revenue bonds are redeemed from income derived from the sale of properties to be redeveloped or the sale or lease of redeveloped properties. Since income from bonds of the redevelopment agency is exempt from federal income taxation, they normally command a low interest rate in the market. Some redevelopment plans, in order to attract private capital and keep down bond interest rates, have provided for tax exemptions, tax abatement, or tax freezing of redeveloped properties. Such expedients are to be regarded as dangerous and unsound public policy and should not be resorted to unless absolutely necessary. The resale price to be placed upon properties to be sold for redevelopment or the lease value to be placed upon redeveloped properties where redevelopment is carried out by a public agency will, in the final analysis, be set by the market.[81] However, the redevelopment agency should establish an upset price based upon an appraisal of the properties under current market conditions. The City of New York bases its resale appraisal upon an analysis of the value

[79] *Local Planning Administration* (Chicago: International City Managers' Association, 1948), p. 217.

[80] Where areas are redeveloped for purposes such as parks or public facilities, it may be necessary to authorize the issuance of general obligation bonds.

[81] Chamber of Commerce of the United States, *Business Action for Better Cities* (Washington, D.C.: 1952), p. 184.

of the property in the condition acquired, less the costs of obtaining possession and of clearance. For the Washington Square Southeast project, for example, the reuse value appraisal of the land as if cleared was $12.47 per square foot or $543,193 per acre.[82] Since the New York redevelopment plan contemplates the sale of the land assembled with existing improvements, a discount is applied to the appraised value to compensate the purchaser for the attendant cost of obtaining possession from the occupants of the buildings and for the cost of demolition. The estimated resale value in its existing condition was approximately $9.47 per square foot.

Actual sale or lease should be through competitive bidding with authority in the redevelopment agency to reject certain bids or offers. The agency should be authorized to hold the property for a period of time if circumstances should seem to indicate that other groups might be interested in bidding later, or if it appears that the market may be more favorable in the near future. However, lengthy delays in putting the property to productive use cannot be justified even if it should necessitate a reasonable writedown of the price.

Because of the large capital investment and the low rate of return on certain types of redeveloped properties, speculative builders may not be interested in purchasing and redeveloping. Where very large areas are rebuilt, it is probable that redevelopment can be undertaken only by institutional investors or by the government. Insurance companies, trust companies, and savings banks whose policies are geared to operate on a low rate of return may be interested not only in supplying mortgage money, but also in direct management, including aid in site selection and planning as well as building.

Although urban redevelopment projects are almost certain to result in an immediate financial loss to the public, over the years the amount of government subsidy may be recovered as a result of increased taxes and decreased costs of rendering police, fire, and other services. Experience in many cities has shown this to be true.[83] Where properties are developed for public use, as for public parks or public buildings,

[82] City of New York, *Washington Square Southeast*, op. cit., p. 59. The reuse value varies considerably with the particular district. The appraised valuation for the Harlem project was $3.50 per square foot or $152,460 per acre with a discount which would make the resale value of its existing condition approximately $2.18 per square foot. See Reports for Harlem and other projects published by the City of New York.

[83] "Urban Redevelopment Program Nets Financial Gain for Pittsburgh," *News Bulletin* (Chicago: Public Administration Clearing House, August 26, 1953), Release No. 3.

acquisition and development costs simply become costs of capital improvements.

Relocation of Displaced Persons.   Although urban renewal is not strictly a housing program, the rehousing of persons displaced by clearance, rehabilitation, code enforcement, and other urban renewal activities is a matter of great public concern. The public responsibility for relocation is recognized by most state enabling statutes as well as by the National Housing Act. One of the objectives of a "workable program" as stated by the Housing and Home Finance Agency is to "facilitate the rehousing, in decent, safe and sanitary accommodations, of families displaced by governmental action." [84] In order to meet the requirements of the Federal Act, the locality seeking federal aid must make analyses to show the extent to which new construction is needed to eliminate housing shortages and must present acceptable plans for facilitating such construction and for rehabilitating existing structures. Particular attention is required to be given to the problem of rehousing displaced minority group families. The Federal Act contemplates that for displaced families, suitable housing will be found within their financial means.

Even if there were no legislation on the subject and if no legal rights were threatened, it would seem unthinkable as a matter of public policy that the eviction of residents would be permitted if they have no place to go. However, the extent to which the public can and should assume responsibility for relocation must vary with the needs in each community. In each locality it should be made clear that the first and principal responsibility for relocation rests with the individual family, and that each family must exert initiative and do all that it can to find a home. Families should be assured, on the other hand, that every effort will be made to help them. Resistance to relocation by site tenants can sometimes be so great as to threaten the success of the urban renewal project. In New York in 1945, site tenants organized to protest the relocation necessitated by the slum clearance project for the site of Stuyvesant Town. Because of the bitter opposition, and in order to prevent the postponement of the project, the Metropolitan Life Insurance Company, which was the private housing developer, spent some $200,000 to help tenants find homes, although this was not required by law. [85]

[84] Housing and Home Finance Agency, *How Localities Can Develop a Workable Program for Urban Renewal, op. cit.*, p. 10.
[85] Woodbury, *op. cit.*, p. 414.

The importance of a sound relocation and rehousing policy is emphasized by the experience of some of our large cities which have discovered that slum clearance via redevelopment breeds new slums. In the City of New York, between January 1, 1946, and March 31, 1953, 45,810 families and 17,820 individuals totaling approximately 170,000 persons were required to move because of slum clearance. Of these, 37 percent were nonwhite and Puerto Rican. A study of what happened to these displaced persons indicated that about 29 percent wound up in public housing, but officials were not certain what had happened to the other 71 percent.

The relocation survey seemed to indicate that during this period there was an extremely heavy influx of Negroes and Puerto Ricans to the west side of Central Park, taking up housing under conditions which seem to be turning this once fine residential area into a rapidly growing slum area.[86] Legal and illegal conversion of brownstone flats to accommodate more families in less space is rapidly producing, in this district, the conditions of crowding and deterioration which is characteristic of the slum areas which were brought under redevelopment. Such results make clear the necessity for conducting broad programs of slum and blight prevention in conjunction with clearance and redevelopment.

Ideally, relocation should be worked out so that families may be able to move from one site to another in accordance with well-defined development schedules in order to cause a minimum of inconvenience and a maximum of opportunity for better living. Public assistance can be rendered by such methods as establishing a file of vacant dwellings. This can be accomplished by means of house-to-house canvass, contacts with real estate offices and rental agencies, public appeals, and through enlisting the coöperation of family welfare agencies and civic organizations.

The matter of providing financial assistance for relocation presents some rather controversial problems. Subsidies may sometimes be found necessary to insure that relocated persons are placed in living quarters that meet the municipality's minimum standards. One of the greatest difficulties faced by displaced persons is that of providing funds to cover moving expenses and the advance payment on the first month's rent. In cases where site occupants are on relief, coöperation may be given by welfare and relief agencies. A U.S.H.A. Bulletin on relocation of site occupants suggests that financial as-

---

[86] "Relocating Slum Families," *op. cit.*, p. 35.

sistance should never be provided for this purpose unless it is clearly demonstrated that the family is unable to move without such assistance.[87] However, there appears to be considerable evidence of a growing acceptance of public responsibility to provide funds to assist persons displaced by governmental action.

It has sometimes been urged that persons displaced under urban renewal programs should be given first priority for any housing which may be built in a redeveloped area. While a good case can be made for establishing such a policy, carrying it out would present a number of practical difficulties. Original parcels of property, after assembly, lose their identity, making reacquisition of specific pieces impossible. Where rebuilt properties call for lower density residence, reacquisition rights would have to be established on the basis of priorities, as all former residents could not be accommodated. Furthermore, if reacquisition rights were given, it is highly probable that many of the displaced persons would not desire to return, or if so, would not be able to live in the rebuilt housing because of financial or other reasons. In view of these and other difficulties, it does not appear to be feasible to attempt to establish any relocation rights for displaced tenants.

Most communities that engage in any extensive programs of urban renewal may find it advisable to set up a permanent relocation service to assist persons displaced by public renewal projects to find suitable housing which they can afford. Considerable help in solving the relocation problem may be given by the creation of an advisory committee made up of representatives of various social agencies, departments of municpal government, the churches, the schools, and civic organizations. Such a device tends to assure the coöperation of these various agencies and community groups and provides a means of interpreting the program to the community.

A sound public relations policy is basic to the success of relocation. The manner in which relocation problems are handled may sell or defeat the renewal program. The confusion which is produced by relocation emphasizes the need for careful planning in advance of taking any action. Such plans must take into account human relations as well as the physical layout. Relocation brings into sharp focus the realities of producing changes in a community which alters radically many relationships of families, institutions, businesses, and other

[87] United States Housing Authority, *Relocation of Site Occupants*, Bulletin No. 10, June 30, 1938, revised April 3, 1941.

neighborhood ties and which may have serious political consequences for certain public officials.

Character and Design of Redeveloped Areas.   In few instances do planners have the opportunity to influence the character and design of a community as they do through urban redevelopment. By means of public controls for this purpose, municipalities should not only seek to eliminate the evils of faulty planning of the past, but also to insure, through the character of the new land use and the design of buildings and facilities, that everything humanly possible will have been done to avoid the recurrence of blight in that area. Urban redevelopment is a costly process. Serious miscalculations in planning the land use and design of the rebuilt area may defeat the long-range objectives and produce blighting conditions which may become permanent. For the most part blight can be traced to deficiences in basic design of street pattern, traffic pattern, lot pattern, and land-use relationship pattern. These deficiences must be eliminated through redesign if the return of blight is to be prevented.[88]

Planning the character of land use and design of the redeveloped areas must take into full account the trends of community growth. Current trends in means of transportation, industrial decentralization, community shopping center location, and the emphasis on neighborhood units are the product of many influences which need to be analyzed. Studies should also be made to determine the degree to which decentralizing trends in a particular community result from blighted conditions. The aim must be to bring the blighted areas once more into full productivity, not just for housing, but for the highest and best use to which they are adapted.

The possible use of nuclear weapons presents an entirely new set of problems to city planners. The American Institute of Planners has pointed out the weakness of our planning from this standpoint and the importance of planning to reduce the nation's vulnerability.[89] The Institute points out that it is a prime responsibility of the science of city planning, working with other technologies concerned with urban development and national defense, to plan a type of community which will provide the "optimum combination of immunity to damage from air-borne weapons and efficiency and economy in producing the goods, services, and amenities of modern living."

[88] Paul Van T. Hedden, "Redevelopment," *Georgia, Local Government Journal,* Vol. 4, No. 2, p. 13, February, 1954.

[89] "Defense Considerations in City Planning," *Bulletin of the Atomic Scientists,* Vol. IX, No. 7, September, 1953.

Urban redevelopment offers opportunities for control of architectural design in the interest of community aesthetics. Whether or not this should be a matter to be determined by public authority or by private builders is highly controversial. The officials of most redevelopment agencies are conscious of the importance of aesthetic values and have sought to avoid structures that are aesthetically monotonous and institutional in appearance or which are too high. Both public authorities and private architects have been paying a great deal of attention to the outward appearance of entire projects to make them pleasing to the eye.[90] Not only is attention being given to size, shape, and grouping of structures, but also to construction material and colors. The layout and separation of buildings by lawns, playgrounds, and sidewalks is also a factor of considerable importance in aesthetic considerations.

Control of Ownership, Operation, and Use After Redevelopment. Most redevelopment statutes contemplate that land assembled for clearance will be turned back to private enterprise for redevelopment and operation. This transfer can be made either through direct sale or through leasehold arrangements. Private capital will become interested in acquiring and redeveloping properties only if the venture offers a fair economic return.

Since the financial feasibility depends in part upon the marketability of the cleared land, the public has an interest in promoting a type of development which will attract private capital. Although this is a practical aspect of urban redevelopment to which considerable weight attaches, the primary considerations from the public standpoint must be to insure a type of land use which is in harmony with the comprehensive plan and which will not be subject to the recurrence of blight. In order to accomplish this, it is necessary that adequate public controls be established over the design, type of building, and the ownership, operation, and use of the redeveloped properties. This can be done through zoning, licensing, building codes, and other police power regulations, and by means of covenants running with the land.

The fact that the land sold is assembled under public ownership makes it possible to make effective use of covenants running with the land. Covenants which run with the land are promises which bind the property owner and user.[91] They can be utilized to a high degree for

---

[90] New York City Housing Authority, 19th Annual Report, 1952, pp. 15–19.

[91] The City of New York, which has carried out demolition, and the relocation of

requiring something to be done affirmatively such as making an annual contribution to a common fund. They can also be used negatively in requiring an owner to refrain from making certain otherwise lawful uses of his property such as erecting a particular type of structure.[92] Covenants may be used for many purposes, including, for example, the control of purchase and lease agreements, special uses of the premises, alteration of structures, maintenance and repair of buildings, and many details of operation.[93] They can be used to compel private companies to grant equal privileges to racial minorities in the rental or use of properties.[94]

Through the use of covenants, it is possible to establish special requirements and higher standards than might be possible under zoning and building regulations alone. However, there are many legal limitations, as well as legal formalities, involved in creating valid covenants. These should be carefully checked by competent legal authority before placing reliance upon their binding effect. Also, the remedies for enforcement of covenants through an action of damages for breach of contract do not always provide an adequate public remedy. Thus, while covenants serve a valuable purpose, they should be relied upon as a supplement to control under the police power and not as a substitute for it.

Under certain circumstances, it may be found desirable for the public agency to retain title to land until after it is redeveloped. Whether this is possible will be governed by provisions of the enabling legislation. Some statutes require the land to be sold to a redevelopment corporation, individual, or partnership to build in conformity with the general plan and do not permit the redevelopment agency to erect buildings or utilize the property except temporarily.[95] However, a strong argument can be made for putting the property to use

tenants as well as redevelopment by contract with private redevelopers, has entered into lengthy agreements to insure that public policy will be given effect. See for illustration, *Agreement Between the City of New York and the East River Housing Corporation,* May 22, 1952, re the redevelopment of the Corlears Hook Area. See also agreements with Columbus Circle Apartments, Inc., dated January 15, 1953, and Triborough Bridge and Tunnel Authority, dated January 15, 1953.

[92] Woodbury, *op. cit.,* p. 247.

[93] Pasma, *op. cit.,* pp. 37–38.

[94] See *Dorsey v. Stuyvesant Town Corporation,* 299 N.Y. 512, 87 N.E. (2d) 541 (1949), *certiorari* denied 339 U.S. 981 (1950), in which the court held that in the absence of a controlling covenant, a private redevelopment corporation could select its tenants and that discrimination on the basis of race or color did not violate equal protection clauses of State or Federal Constitutions.

[95] Chamber of Commerce of the United States, *Business Action for Better Cities, op. cit.,* p. 184.

after clearance and redevelopment under long-term lease rather than by outright sale. By exercising permanent ownership over the property, the public may be able to control its use more effectively, and in the event that it should again be affected with blight, the land would not have to be reacquired to eliminate it.

As a general proposition, outright sale should be favored over the leasehold arrangement. In the first place, it offers the prospect of greater immediate economic return and enlists the support of private enterprise and the possibilities of more extensive development. From the public relations standpoint, it avoids the danger of having the program defeated on the charge that redevelopment is simply a form of socialism which is intended to take away private property and put it under the control of the government.

Area Rehabilitation. One of the main elements of the urban renewal legislation, embodied in the Housing Act of 1954, is the "rehabilitation of salvable areas, turning them into sound, healthy neighborhoods by replanning, removing congestion, providing parks and playgrounds, reorganizing streets and traffic, and by facilitating physical rehabilitation of deteriorated structures." [96] Although the scope of the activities embraced within the concept of area rehabilitation is not yet clearly defined, the aim of the program is to make the area more desirable, (1) by encouraging the maintenance and improvement of structures, (2) by the installation of needed community facilities, (3) by the removal of adverse uses, and (4) by the replanning of the area to the extent possible within the basic design. While the demolition of certain unsound structures may be embraced within the idea of rehabilitation, clearance is not a major part of the program.

The basic difference between rehabilitation areas and redevelopment areas is the extent to which clearance is required and the extent to which major changes must be made in the basic physical pattern of the area.[97] In carrying out the rehabilitation program, the community builds primarily around the existing pattern. In general, the rehabilitation program will take the form of modernization and remodeling. It may include the installation of new heating plants, improved lighting, bathrooms, kitchens, and other facilities. It may also correct inadequate maintenance through painting exteriors, putting

[96] Message of the President transmitting recommendations for the Housing Act of 1954 (Public Law 560, 83d Congress, approved August 2, 1954).
[97] Woodbury, op. cit., p. 318.

on new siding, and making structural repairs. The major objective of these activities is to upgrade the properties in the area and extend their life for a period of years.

The decision as to whether a particular area is worthy of rehabilitation, or whether it is so far deteriorated that the only satisfactory solution is clearance and redevelopment, is an important one and one that is usually difficult to make. Before making this decision in doubtful cases, municipal authorities should attempt to anticipate the most appropriate use of the properties over the next 25 or 30 years and give consideration to the relative desirability of the character of the existing use as against other uses more in harmony with sound land-use planning.[98] Questions of financial and political feasibility may also have to be weighed in the balance.

In many respects the problems of rehabilitation are more difficult to solve than are those of clearance and redevelopment. While the use of the power of eminent domain is clearly established for the assembly of land for clearance, its application to rehabilitation is not so clear. Although the provisions of the Housing Act of 1954 would seem to contemplate public acquisition for purposes of rehabilitation, Chicago appears to be the only city which has legislation authorizing such action.[99] The Illinois enabling statute empowers the conservation board to acquire, by purchase or condemnation, improved or unimproved property which is necessary or appropriate for the implementation of a conservation plan in a conservation area.[100]

Even though the courts uphold the general principle of public acquisition for rehabilitation, difficult policy decisons must be made and administrative obstacles overcome. If the rehabilitation required is drastic, there will undoubtedly be heavy costs which would have to be written down on the resale of rehabilitated properties. Under some circumstances these costs might be almost as much as the cost of new construction. If so, the question is raised as to whether rehabilitation is the appropriate remedy. If the decision is made in favor of public acquisition and rehabilitation, further policy questions are raised such as: (1) Should the rehabilitation be performed by a public agency or by private enterprise? and (2) Should the original owner

[98] Woodbury, op. cit., pp. 330–331.
[99] Slayton, op. cit., p. 452.
[100] The Urban Community Conservation Act of 1953, Ill. Rev. Stat. C 67½, §91.8–91.16 (1954). See People ex rel. Gutknecht v. City of Chicago, 3 Ill. (2d) 539, 545, 121 N.E. (2d) 791 (1954), which upheld this statute.

be given certain rights to repurchase the rehabilitated property at the writedown price?

With respect to the first question, many of the considerations which are applicable to making such a decision under redevelopment programs are applicable to rehabilitation. However, rehabilitation normally does not contemplate the dispossession of the original owner, but rather the making of his property more desirable for living or use. If this distinction is preserved, there is not the justification for resale to private enterprise for purposes of rehabilitation. It would seem to be more feasible for the public agency to carry out the rehabilitation under private contract while ownership remains in the public.

Assuming the workability of such a plan, rehabilitation might, nevertheless, result in forcing an owner to give up his property. Even though original owners were given first priority to repurchase, many might be unable to do so because of lack of financial ability. Thus, the program might be open to attack on the grounds that it is discriminatory because it compels those persons of low economic status to dispose of their property, but makes it possible for those who are better off to retain theirs.

Although some rehabilitation can be accomplished through strict code enforcement, this alone is usually not adequate. One possible supplement to usual code enforcement is through the use of the police power to establish higher minimum standards for housing construction and use than are required throughout the municipality generally. This necessitates setting up variable standards in the housing code and zoning ordinance. These variable standards would be applied according to the designated type of renewal area. In a rehabilitation area they would be aimed at compelling the owner to recondition his property and make such alterations and installations as would be required to meet the standards set for the area. This might be carried to the extent of ordering specific repairs and improvements to be made at the expense of the owner.

While such a plan is flexible and avoids high public acquisition costs, there is the possibility that the courts might declare such standards to be arbitrary and a taking of private property without just compensation. As has previously been indicated, there is also a question of equity involved in using the police power to compel persons to upgrade their property. Under urban redevelopment projects, the persons whose property is taken under eminent domain are paid a fair price, sometimes an inflated price, for their property. The loss in redevelopment is paid by the public for the social gains achieved. If compulsory rehabilitation is required under the police power, the cost is paid solely by the property owner. This discrimination is an aspect of compulsory rehabilitation which is always likely to develop strong opposition even though held to be within the legitimate exercise of the police power.

Ideally, the best solution to the problem of rehabilitation is through voluntary action. This method does not involve the legal questions of property rights nor the difficult policy decisions that must be made under compulsory methods. Voluntary rehabilitation is essentially an administrative matter based upon the power of persuasion. It is possible for the municipality to do much to encourage rehabilitation through such means as supplying technicians to advise on the character of needed improvements, type of architecture, and in matters of finance. The Housing Act of 1954 recognizes and gives encouragement to voluntary methods by providing favorable terms for rehabilitation financing.[101] There are, however, obvious weaknesses in reliance upon voluntary rehabilitation. Nothing can be done to compel a recalcitrant property owner to coöperate. This factor can defeat the whole program unless some supplementary means of compulsion can be worked out beyond that embodied in the regular code enforcement procedures.

The demonstrated success of voluntary rehabilitation, nevertheless, warrants careful study of its possibilities. Many communities have accomplished a great deal with little and varying degrees of government support.[102] One of the outstanding examples of this type of program is that carried out in Chicago by The Back of the Yards Conservation Committee, the Hyde Park-Kenwood Community Conference, and numerous other community organizations.[103] Literally thousands of volunteers made detailed studies and worked tirelessly

[101] Section 220 of the Housing Act of 1954 adds a new tool for urban renewal by authorizing F.H.A. to insure mortgages in an approved urban renewal area for new construction and the financing of structures to be rehabilitated, 68 Stat. 596, 12 U.S.C.A. 1715 K (1955 Supp.). See also Housing and Home Finance Agency, Replacing Blight with Good Homes, F.H.A.'s Section 220 Mortgage Insurance for Urban Renewal (Washington, D.C.: U.S. Government Printing Office, October, 1955).

[102] Housing and Home Finance Agency, Approaches to Urban Renewal in Several Cities (Washington, D.C.: U.S. Government Printing Office, 1954), Urban Renewal Bulletin No. 1.

[103] These efforts were the basis for the All-America Cities Award given to Chicago in 1954 by the National Municipal League and Look magazine. See Look, February 8, 1955, pp. 73–74.

in rehabilitating blighted neighborhoods. Funds were contributed by businessmen. Numerous publications were issued explaining the program and methods of operation.[104] To help out on the program, the city named a redevelopment coördinator. The success of programs such as this depends to a great extent upon the enthusiasm in the community. These elements are seldom spontaneous but can be developed by intelligent and capable leaders.

Area Enforcement. In those districts where blight has not spread sufficiently far to warrant programs of clearance or rehabilitation, the life and usefulness of structures can frequently be prolonged through an intensive program of area enforcement. The tools of area enforcement are those which are in effect in almost every city. They include the building code, housing code, electrical code, plumbing code, sanitation code, zoning ordinance, subdivision regulations, and ordinances for abatement of nuisances.

The purpose of the enforcement program is to prevent or slow down the spread of blight and thereby preserve the character of the district and the capital investment in the structures within the area. Except to a limited degree, code enforcement does not result in the improvement or modernization of structures. It is designed to arrest and control the blighting influences, but does not remove or cure their fundamental causes. Enforcement programs must not be looked upon as a substitute for redevelopment or major rehabilitation. Strict enforcement will guarantee minimum standards provided by the codes and thus insure better living conditions, but it does not convert bad housing into good, correct the faulty design of the area, or alter the pattern of land use. Nevertheless, area enforcement has a very important place in the renewal program.[105]

Area enforcement differs from the usual referral or complaint type of code enforcement in that all pertinent regulatory police power measures are concentrated on one or more designated conservation areas. Under such a program, a vigorous effort is made to bring all these regulations to bear in a way that will slow down, stop, or postpone the spread of blight. Usually this is accomplished through a house-to-house inspection, together with such other investigations

[104] See, for example, *Operation Destiny* (Chicago: Back of the Yards Conservation Committee, 1954); *How You Do It, op. cit.; Conservation by "We the People Back of the Yards," op. cit.*

[105] Compare with the use of the zoned housing code and other methods of raising housing standards and environmental quality for a given area above those applicable to the city as a whole. Guandolo, *op. cit.*, pp. 42–48. See also p. 513.

as appear to be necessary.[106] Area enforcement does not eliminate the need for complaint referral enforcement which is an important supplementary means of detecting violations. Another supplement is "permit enforcement" which is a routine part of the administration of the building code, zoning ordinance, and certain other local regulations.

Most cities which have undertaken successful area enforcement programs have found it advantageous to concentrate all pertinent area enforcement responsibilities under an area enforcement officer in the renewal agency rather than to function through the regular department heads.[107] Actual inspections may be carried out by a team of inspectors made up from personnel assigned from the regular operating departments. The advantage of using a team made up of persons qualified to inspect for all purposes is that the entire inspection can be made at one time. This results in less inconvenience to the residents and insures better coördination of results of the surveys. In order that necessary enforcement steps will be taken to correct substandard conditions, the coöperation and support of all municipal departments is essential. This coöperation is best assured where the urban renewal agency is integrated in the administrative structure and made responsible to the mayor or to the city manager if the city has a manager form of government.

Code enforcement, which is ordinarily the only tool of urban renewal in conservation areas, and the major tool in rehabilitation areas, frequently has an important place also in clearance areas. After an area has been marked for clearance and redevelopment, a considerable time may elapse before the project can actually be carried out. In the meantime, it is important that all structures and facilities be made as safe and healthful as can practically be done through a reasonable enforcement of regulatory measures. While it may not be feasible to conduct the intensive area inspections that would be undertaken in the conservation area, much can be accomplished through a less intensive program which will remove the worst accumulations of dirt and filth and compel those repairs which are necessary to insure the safety of the inhabitants and the public. It is important, however, that such steps are not accepted as a substitute for necessary

---

[106] For a practical application of these methods see, A Fight-Blight Plan for Binghamton, New York, op. cit., pp. 29–38.

[107] Woodbury, op. cit., pp. 328, 332–370.

rehabilitation or clearance and should not be undertaken for the purpose of delaying such action.

The Follow-Up Program. Cities considering the inauguration of urban renewal programs should clearly recognize both the values and the limitations of each type of area treatment. Every building eventually outlives its usefulness even though it has been adequately maintained to comply with minimum code standards. Strict code enforcement, as well as rehabilitation measures, serve to lengthen the period of usefulness. Beyond a certain time, however, it becomes uneconomic to prolong this life. When this time is reached, demolition is the only solution if the area is to yield a fair economic return and provide a livable environment.

Vigorous code enforcement in badly deteriorated districts tends to become very expensive since each year more stringent policing is required to insure minimum livable standards. These costs may, in the long run, exceed the costs of major rehabilitation or even clearance and redevelopment, particularly when the substantial increase in tax values of improved and redeveloped properties is taken into account. Just when the classification of an area should be changed from that of conservation to rehabilitation, or from rehabilitation to clearance and redevelopment, involves important policy decisions which must be made periodically. If they are made intelligently, they should be based upon careful studies of all the relevant social and economic factors which should govern such a decision. The follow-up program should be carried on as a continuous survey as part of the general planning program.

Part IV

THE FUTURE OF PLANNING

CHAPTER 11

Guidelines to Planning Progress

THE EXPANDING SCOPE AND CHANGING DEMANDS

Throughout the United States, urban communities are turning more and more to planning for guidance in developing positive programs for community improvement. The demonstrated success of planning in providing solutions to practical problems of municipal government has overcome most of the earlier suspicion that planning was either a kind of socialistic experiment, foreign to our American system, or a frill of local government devised by impractical ivory-tower dreamers. Although planning has come to wear the cloak of respectability in the family of municipal functions, it has not as yet realized its full potential as a force in formulating public policy and in coördinating functional programs.

The scope of planning seems certain to expand in the future at a rate even greater than it has over the past 30 years. This conclusion is reached not only from the fact that planning has now come to be universally recognized as an essential function of local government, but also because local government is being called upon to assume an ever-increasing role in promoting the public welfare.

The principal tasks of the planner are likely to continue to develop much along the lines which are now established in many of our progressive cities, but the subject matter which falls within the scope of his interest will become much broader. Furthermore, many planning practices which now have general acceptance will become outmoded with the progress in science, new technological developments, and the changing attitude of people as reflected in the policies of government. In some instances these changes will necessitate an entirely new approach to planning problems.

NEED FOR NEW PLANNING CONCEPTS AND TECHNIQUES

In order to meet the future demands upon government, planners must continuously be testing generally accepted principles, examining new concepts, and seeking for new tools. It is entirely possible that many planning principles which are considered sound today may not meet the needs of our communities and our society in the future. As new developments take place in science and industry, new demands are imposed upon government. Our concept of the responsibility of government today is vastly different from what it was 50 years ago. What we may consider to be the legitimate functions of government in the future may be greatly different from our ideas at the present time.

Planners must constantly be looking at planning concepts and planning techniques in the light of current trends and technological and social changes. For example, zoning policy today is, in general, based upon the accepted classification of land uses into three major classifications: residential, business, and industrial. It is generally assumed that a mixture of these uses is detrimental to economic interests and the social welfare. However, as progress is made in industrial operations, it is possible that objectional factors such as noise, smoke, dirt, ugliness, and heavy traffic will be eliminated to a high degree. If so, the value of locating certain industrial plants in close proximity to residences may greatly outweigh the value of separation which requires much time spent in travel to and from work, results in corresponding loss of time for personal interests, and adds to the congestion of traffic. Also, as the character of our cities changes, we may find that multiple and single-family uses are entirely compatible, even in first-class residential districts, and that there is no longer need to assign apartment houses to the fringes of the business district. Actually, some of these ideas are already well into the trial stages.

Planners have devised many important and effective tools for the purpose of plan implementation. Zoning, subdivision control, and other forms of regulation have been most effective in guiding the physical development of the community. However, these regulations are essentially negative in character. It is entirely possible that in the future more positive types of control may be found necessary to insure the proper development of the type of community that the future citizens will desire. Urban redevelopment, although long recognized as an important tool of plan implementation, is still in its infancy. Even where the policy objectives are clear, urban redevelopment may fail of accomplishment because, as yet, we have not satisfactorily worked out the techniques for the relocation of displaced families, the measurement of blight, methods of financing the projects, or the proper delineation of the responsibilities of public and private agencies.

The attitude of the courts as well as the attitude of the people in general is constantly changing with respect to what matters are appropriate subjects of governmental control as distinguished from private control. Illustrative of this are recent decisions of the courts which seem to indicate a willingness to uphold reasonable aesthetic controls as a proper exercise of the police power. If aesthetic control becomes a major objective of public policy, new tools may have to be devised to implement it. Thus, as new perspectives modify public policies, so do modified policies require new tools for policy implementation or the refinement or improvement of old techniques for that purpose.

NEED FOR IMPROVED PERSONNEL AND INCREASED BUDGETS

Planning progress in the future is also dependent upon the availability of trained planning personnel and the amount of appropriations that local units of government are willing to devote to the planning function. Personnel and budget are closely related inasmuch as professionally trained planners become interested in planning in a community only if funds are available to enable them to perform a creditable planning job. On the other hand, municipalities are unlikely to appropriate funds for planning work in the absence of available trained personnel. At the present time, the widespread growth of planning interest in urban communities has outstripped the availability of competent planners. A number of institutions of higher learning have in recent years recognized the importance of professional training for planning and have established graduate curriculums to prepare graduate students for planning work. In most communities, budgets for planning are still too small. Gradually, however, municipalities are beginning to recognize that each dollar spent for planning may save many dollars, both in capital outlays and in operational budgets.

Only a small proportion of city planning agencies have adequate technical assistance. In some jurisdictions the lack of planning staff results from the fact that municipal officials have conceived the role of planning to be primarily that of preparing a zoning ordinance. In some other jurisdictions, technical planning staffs are unbalanced in that they consist only of persons trained in engineering, drafting, or architectural design, but do not include persons trained in statistical analysis or the social sciences. In many jurisdictions planning staffs are inadequate because personnel are unable to give adequate attention to overall planning since their time is so completely absorbed in administrative duties with respect to zoning regulations and approval of subdivision plats. Comprehensive planning will not be possible until well-balanced staffs and adequate budgets are provided and planning responsibilities are carefully defined.

THE NEED FOR SOCIAL SCIENCE RESEARCH

Up to the present time, planning has been influenced more by the point of view of the architect and engineer than by the analyses of the sociologist, the economist, and the political scientist. This is not to say that the engineering and architectural aspects are not important. The point is that the physical design and development have too frequently been worked out without adequate attention to the influences of environment and the other forces that motivate people's actions and desires. Perhaps this comes about from the fact that we have achieved more success in the design and construction of streets, bridges, and public buildings than we have in determining the values that individuals place upon convenience, comfort, aesthetics, light, air, open spaces, and numerous other factors that contribute to our living enjoyment. However, until these values are ascertained, we cannot be certain that we have an adequate background for intelligent comprehensive planning.

RESEARCH NEEDED TO INTERPRET ENVIRONMENTAL INFLUENCES

Conditions in urban society are constantly changing. New inventions, scientific achievements, new technology, and changes in legal rights and relationships are constantly influencing our cultural and social system and our pattern of living. As of today, there is no conclusive evidence as to the influence upon our cultural habits of such developments as television, suburban living, or the refusal of courts to enforce racial covenants in deed restrictions. While we know that a great many persons prefer to drive their private cars to work, we do not know how much they are willing to pay for this privilege. We also know that many persons place considerable value upon suburban living where there is greater open space and the possibility of green lawns, shrubs, and trees; but we are not certain how far they are willing to drive and what inconveniences they are willing to accept in getting to their work in order to enjoy these more pleasant surroundings. Neither do we have data which indicate the influence of living in rented homes as distinguished from those which are individually owned, or the influence of living in public housing as against living in private housing, or living in racially segregated neighborhoods as distinguished from mixed neighborhoods.

Intelligent planning for the future must be based upon extensive research in many areas in the social science field. This research should be comparative in its nature. With the experience which many cities have had with zoning, subdivision control, and other means of plan implementation, planners should, through a program of research, be in a position to determine the results accomplished in planned communities as distinguished from unplanned communities. It would be of inestimable value to each community to have more reliable information regarding the influence of congestion, crowding, and blight upon such matters as rates of crime, juvenile delinquency, and the disruption of family life. Accurate information about such matters would materially aid the policy makers in arriving at decisions concerning such problems as street design, providing mass transportation, developing neighborhood shopping centers, developing programs of slum clearance, urban redevelopment, public health programs, and recreational facilities and programs.

A great deal more information needs to be gathered as to the effect and influence of traffic, dust, noise, and obnoxious odors upon living enjoyment. Also more knowledge is needed with respect to the influence of working environment and the relationship of working environment to residential environment. Likewise, planners need to know more about the environmental influences of geography and topography. For instance, it would be helpful to the planner to know the extent to which hillsides, rivers, and hilltops influence residential characteristics and density of population, and whether such factors tend to isolate residents according to social classes. The planner would also find it helpful to have more information about the effect of legislation establishing minimum wages and minimum standards of housing. Reliable conclusions as to the effect of such legislation upon health, industry, economic well-being, happiness, crime rates, public welfare, and costs of services would provide valuable data from which informed decisions could be made with respect to alternative courses of action.

RESEARCH NEEDED TO ESTABLISH VALUES

In the past, planners have often been accused of being visionary or dreamers. It has been urged that planning must be based upon practical considerations and must be concerned with practical problems. While this is true, there is nevertheless danger in becoming complacent and accepting findings of the past as guidelines for the future. The planner cannot take for granted that the considerations which have governed policy decisions in the past will necessarily be valid in the future. Our urban society is dynamic, and the planner must be ever seeking to discover what are the factors and the influences that are motivating the activities of individuals. It is possible that much of the motivation comes from social values and intangible influences rather than from the influences of physical environment. Planning progress for the future should seek to discover what these values are and take them into account. Research for this purpose is certainly not visionary or divorced from practical considerations.

Planners of the future must give careful study to current trends in all types of developments and activities with a view to determining the future conditions which they produce. A study of current trends should give some indication, for instance, of the kinds of housing, types of recreation, modes of transportation, and working conditions that will be demanded in the future. Such studies should also provide information as to the preferences of people to shop in the central business district as distinguished from shopping in neighborhood shopping centers.

If planning has as its objective the development of a better community in which to live, knowledge of our social structure is as important to comprehensive planning as are design and site location. This does not imply any change in the concept of planning. Planning today is already recognized as comprehensive in character. Greater emphasis on research in the social science field is needed primarily for the purpose of discovering what are the factors and influences in life on which individuals place the most value. For example, it would be of material benefit to the planner to know the extent to which pleasant living conditions, as distinguished from narrow economic advantages, motivate man's actions or to what degree cultural values are factors in living enjoyment. Unfortunately, the social scientist thus far has not been able to define clearly what these relative values are. This remains a problem for future solution.

Need for Organizing Research

The planning agency can never hope to conduct all the research needed for supplying basic data in the social sciences. As in other areas of research, planning agencies must rely primarily upon outside organizations. One of the tasks of the planner must be to encourage competent outside research and to utilize the knowledge which is developed. Even though the planner to a large extent relies upon outside agencies to gather research data, the analysis, synthesis, and interpretation remain as his most important planning responsibilities. Upon the accuracy of this interpretation depends the value of the planner's advice to policy makers as to the probable consequences of alternative courses of action, including the benefits or detriments to various groups and the costs which may be imposed upon the community.

ORGANIZATIONAL IMPROVEMENTS FOR BETTER PLANNING ADMINISTRATION

Adequate legal authority and sound structural organization are basic to sound planning administration. Planning legislation should be drafted with the aim of creating a scheme of organization and establishing administrative procedures which will enable the planning agency to work most effectively with operating departments and policy making officials.

Need to Reëxamine Enabling Legislation and Basic Ordinances

Planning experience during the past 25 years has produced many new concepts with respect to function, organization, and plan implementation. These ideas are reflected in improved planning practices only when incorporated in the legal framework of planning. It is, therefore, important that state enabling statutes and basic local ordinances be reëxamined frequently, and amended when necessary to include meritorious changes in planning powers, and administrators in the future will need to give much more attention than they have in the past to keeping legislative enactments in harmony with sound current planning concepts.

NEED FOR A MORE INTEGRATED STRUCTURE

Because of the origin of planning programs as civic activities outside the governmental structure, it is natural that planning has tended to be developed under semiautonomous agencies headed by lay boards or commissions. As a consequence, the planning function carried out under the direction of the independent commission has come to be regarded throughout the United States as the accepted plan of organization. During the period when planning was gaining acceptance, this structure perhaps had certain advantages. In the first place, it provided an acceptable method of transition from planning as a civic activity to a recognized function of local government. Moreover, the establishment of planning activities under a lay board or commission helped to enlist public interest in planning and to increase the likelihood of acceptance of proposals of the planning agencies. Another value of the independent planning commission has been that planning has been encouraged in certain communities which otherwise would have gone without planning because of lack of enthusiasm or actual hostility of the elected officials.

In the present stage of planning, other considerations should be taken into account. Public officials throughout the country have become more and more planning-minded, thinking in terms of the economic and social advantages which sound planning will bring. With this acceptance by public officials, there is little likelihood that the planning agency will not be used, and consequently there is less justification for the semiautonomous commission.

Today, students of public administration in general are committed to the values of an integrated structure. Any structural organization which utilizes independent boards and commissions tends to violate this principle. The formulation and execution of public policy requires a high degree of coördination and fixed administrative responsibility under the executive authority. Questions which involve major policy decisions must be resolved by weighing many complicated social, economic, and political considerations. This makes it necessary for policy making officials to rely upon capable staff agencies for guidance and recommendations. Complete harmony seems more likely to be achieved if the staff agency is directed by persons in whom the policy making officials have confidence and over whom they have some direction and control. Although in many communities very satisfactory and harmonious relationships are established between the independent planning agency and the politically responsible officials, some communities may find that planning effectiveness will be enhanced by a greater integration of the planning agency in the administrative structure.

DEVELOPING MORE SATISFACTORY AREAS FOR PLANNING ADMINISTRATION

Satisfactory structural organization, capable personnel, and efficient administration are basic to good planning. Nevertheless, even where these requisites are met, planning may fail to achieve its objectives because the planning process is confined by political boundaries to geographical areas unsuited to fulfilling the needs of comprehensive planning for the entire community. Developments on the fringe areas of a municipality may cause blight and create problems as serious as if the area were included within the corporate limits of the city. Yet in spite of the fact that this is almost a universal problem, most communities have made little headway in finding a solution to it.

INADEQUACY OF ORGANIZATION FOR REGIONAL PLANNING

Many attempts have been made in the past, and some are being made at present, to develop regional plans to help to avoid the unfortunate consequences of uncontrolled urban growth. For the most part, these plans have depended upon voluntary coöperation for their implementation. In some instances they have met with considerable success, but in many cases plans have remained unexecuted because of lack of coöperation on the part of certain of the units of government whose action has been necessary to make them effective. In other instances, good faith and a desire to coöperate have been defeated because of legal obstacles or limited financial resources.

Although community planning has often failed because of unsatisfactory areas for planning administration, planners have not as a rule devoted much attention to finding a solution to the problem. For the most part, they have tended to accept the fact of political boundaries and have sought to work out their plans within those boundaries without trying to develop a better organizational scheme for the entire urban community. Planners in the future must assume a more active role in promoting a type of metropolitan organization that will make possible both the development and implementation of plans on an area-wide basis.

PROGRESS TO BE ACHIEVED THROUGH AREA SOLUTIONS

A great deal of study and thought still needs to be given to the type of organization that is best suited to providing essential controls for achieving the objectives of planning throughout the metropolitan area and still leave to each local unit of government within that area sufficient autonomy to carry out those responsibilities which can be properly administered on a local basis. As there are advantages in unified control, so are there values in preserving local identification and local autonomy. Local pride and economic interests are often tied to local self-government. Arbitrarily to force smaller communities into an amalgamated community to which they are opposed would be fraught with inherent dangers.

Success in implementing plans throughout the metropolitan areas seems likely to be achieved only when it can be demonstrated to the inhabitants of the whole area that public policies developed and effectuated on an area-wide basis contribute in the overall balance to their social and economic well-being. With the continuing trend toward suburban living, it is apparent that planning progress in our growing urban communities will be determined in a large measure by how successfully the problems of areas are solved.

DIRECTION OF THE EXPANDING SCOPE

Although planners in the future will continue to concentrate their time and attention on the physical pattern, greater efforts will be directed toward relating the physical plan to the major functional operations of government. Unfortunately, planning has often been thought of as something separate and apart from the service and program functions. Too frequently, the planner has tended to regard his responsibility as one of developing a plan for the physical community according to certain generally accepted planning principles but without making serious inquiry into the overall social, economic, and political objectives that government should seek to attain.

Today it is becoming recognized that physical planning cannot be separated from the planning of services and programs. The physical plan represents sound planning practice only to the extent that it serves to further sound public policies as represented by all the major functions which government performs. Unless this approach is taken, the plan is not truly comprehensive.

Planning in the future must also be concerned to a greater degree than in the past with matters of governmental organization. The effectiveness of planning is influenced by the type and organization of the planning agency, the placement of the agency in the administrative structure, the manner in which working relationships are established between the agency and operational departments, the maintenance of proper relationship between municipalities and other units of government, and the success in creating satisfactory geographical areas for providing functional services in metropolitan areas. In many instances corrective legislation is needed to establish satisfactory relations. Progress along these lines will necessitate greater use of the services of the political scientist and the lawyer.

If planning is to realize its full potential as a force in policy making and program coördination, the scope of the planner's interest must be as broad as government itself. Only when planning is approached from this overall point of view can the planning agency fulfill its primary function as a staff arm to the politically responsible elective officials.

Index